Gay Press, Gay Power
The Growth of LGBT
Community Newspapers in America

Edited by Tracy Baim

Foreword by John D'Emilio

With contributions by
Tracy Baim, C. Todd White, Margaret Rubick
Marie J. Kuda, Sarah Toce, Owen Keehnen
Jorjet Harper, Lou Chibbaro Jr., Chuck Colbert
Yasmin Nair, St. Sukie de la Croix

Senior Editors
William B. Kelley and Jorjet Harper

Design by
Kirk Williamson

Prairie Avenue Productions and
Windy City Media Group
Chicago • 2012

Images and photos used in this book provided courtesy of the following:
Tracy Baim
Windy City Times/Outlines newspaper archives
Marie J. Kuda Archives
Rich Wilson
Leather Archives & Museum, www.leatherarchives.org
Chuck Renslow
Gay, Lesbian, Bisexual, Transgender Historical Society (San Francisco)
Kay Lahusen
Abe Peck
Jonathan Ned Katz
C. Todd White
The Homosexual Information Center
Chicago History Museum
Todd Evans and Rivendell Media
Susan Fleischmann
Cliff O'Neill
Toni Armstrong Jr.
William B. Kelley
Jorjet Harper

First Edition, November 2012

Prairie Avenue Productions and Windy City Media Group
Tracy Baim
1900 South Prairie Avenue
Chicago, Illinois, USA 60616-1321
editor@windycitymediagroup.com

This book is available in both black-and-white and color editions.
It will also be available in e-book form soon.

ISBN-10: 1-4800-8052-7
ISBN-13: 978-1-4800-8052-2

To Joy and Steve,
who raised me to love the smell of
newspaper ink in the morning

Table of Contents

Part Three: Longtime papers

Part Four: Advertising the News

Part Five: The Ongoing Role of Ever-Changing Media

Appendix

Acknowledgments

Gay Press, Gay Power began as a book proposal I presented to the newly formed National Gay Media Association, started in 2011 by Todd Evans of Rivendell Media. I thank Todd and the NGMA members for their support and contributions to this project, which quickly grew to become something much larger than I originally planned, delving into the history of both gay and non-gay media's advertising, editorial content, business management and community impact.

I also thank Marie J. Kuda and William B. Kelley for their pioneering work in Chicago gay journalism, and their inspiration. Thank you also to Kay Lahusen for advice and input on this book. There were also dozens of reporters, editors and other colleagues who helped me over the years, especially Nan Schaffer, who allowed me to follow my dreams across many tall hurdles.

Thank you also, to all the writers in these pages, especially those who told their personal stories of working in the gay press. Thank you to Sarah Toce and Owen Keehnen for interviewing journalism pioneers; to Kuda, Margaret Rubick, John D'Emilio and C. Todd White for sharing their insightful historical expertise in their essays; and to the other writers who contributed essays, including Chuck Colbert, St. Sukie de la Croix and Yasmin Nair. Many shared their media images from their newspapers, plus Kuda, Todd Evans, Alex Flanagan, Rivendell Media, Rich Wilson, Abe Peck, the Homosexual Information Center and the Gay, Lesbian, Bisexual, Transgender Historical Society of California.

Editors William B. Kelley and Jorjet Harper, along with designer Kirk Williamson, helped immeasurably in bringing this book together in its final form. Thomas Horn of the *Bay Area Reporter* provided additional assistance to complete the book's index, which was done by Harper.

And finally, to my partner, Jean Albright, thank you for never complaining about the candle's burning at both ends.

—Tracy Baim

Foreword
The Leading Edge of Change:
The LGBT Press in the 1970s

By John D'Emilio

Many things changed in the 1970s. LGBT organizations multiplied faster than anyone could count. In larger cities, police raids of gay and lesbian bars became much less common. Annual Pride marches brought thousands—sometimes tens of thousands—of queer folks out into the open together. Many people stopped leading double lives and came out to their friends and family. And, for the first time, thriving print media appeared, produced by and for the community.

There were powerful reasons for this explosion of a community-based LGBT press. Mainstream journalism had been one of the bastions of homophobia. In the 1950s, when a newpaper like the *Chicago Tribune* reported on things gay, it typically used terms such as "degenerates," "misfits," "nests of perverts" and "moral depravity." The press wrote about the danger that queers posed for national security, or it covered police raids of gay and lesbian bars. In the 1960s, big-city newspapers occasionally departed from this mold. Enterprising journalists might do a special series alerting residents to a growing homosexual world in their midst. "Twilight World That's Tormented," a *Chicago Daily News* headline announced in 1966.

Homophile organizations in the 1950s and 1960s attempted to provide alternative perspectives through publications such as the *Mattachine Review*, *The Ladder* and *ONE*. But these were magazines obtained almost entirely through subscription.

In 1967, *The Advocate* began to publish, first as an organizational newsletter devoted to events in Los Angeles, but soon shifting to a newspaper format and attempting to have a national reach. Just two years later, its circulation was in the tens of thousands.

In the wake of the Stonewall uprising in New York City and the militant movement that sprang from it, a queer press proliferated in the 1970s. *Come Out!* in New York; the *Detroit Gay Liberator*; the *Lesbian Tide* in Los Angeles; *Gay Community News* in Boston; the *Blade* in Washington, D.C.; the *Bay Area Reporter* and the *Bay Times* in San Francisco; *Ain't I a Woman?* and *ACCESSline* in Iowa; *Out Front* in Denver; the *Gay Crusader*, *Lavender Woman* and *GayLife* in Chicago; the *Philadelphia Gay News*; and the *Seattle Gay News* were just some of the papers in this decade. All were labors of love and sacrifice. Initially, they depended on volunteer labor and on contributions to stay afloat. Because of this, some papers came and went in just a few years. Advertising revenue was not readily available in the early 1970s. There were few LGBT businesses except for bars, and many bars were cautious about publicly identifying themselves because of fears of police harassment.

Two Chicago newspapers can give some feel for the content and value of this new press. *Lavender Woman* ran from 1971 to 1976 and was explicitly lesbian in its focus. *The Chicago Gay Crusader* (1973–76) was largely male in its orientation.

Both newspapers were filled with notices about upcoming meetings and events as well as reports on meetings and events already held. Gatherings of Chicago-area law students, teachers and medical students, lesbian softball games and music concerts, meetings of gay and lesbian Catholics and Presbyterians, and Metropolitan Community Church services were all announced regularly. The press played a vital role in giving these new efforts visibility and making it possible for their potential constituencies to coalesce into something organizationally solid.

Organizations with a specifically activist orientation also got their space. *Lavender Woman* reported on the work of Chicago's Black Gay Liberation, which had a speakers' bureau. Chicago Lesbian Liberation had a range of activities, including a monthly health night on the South Side. The *Gay Crusader* kept readers up to date on the Chicago Gay Alliance, which staffed a community center, as well as on organizations such as the Chicago Transvestite Association. Readers learned about demonstrations, for example, one against the nationally syndicated columnist Ann Landers, whose negative statements about gays and lesbians provoked pickets chanting "Ann Landers, we won't take your slanders!" Most of all, perhaps, Pride Month activities received a lot of attention. They were previewed in the months before, as a way of recruiting participants, and described in great detail afterward.

Gender differences emerged in these papers. Because there were fewer lesbian bars and other businesses, *Lavender Woman* faced much greater challenges in developing advertising revenue. As early as its third issue, its publishing collective announced that it was having a hard time. In terms of content, it carried much more first-person writing, in which women addressed issues of coming out, the impact of sexism on their lives, and broader debates within the lesbian/feminist movement. Consciousness-raising and political philosophy were a central aspect of its mission.

By contrast, the *Gay Crusader* devoted more space to what might be considered hard news. It frequently reported on local incidents, like police raids and harassment, hostile articles in the mainstream press, and demonstrations by local activists. It also developed a much more extensive advertising base, largely from gay bars and the gay-friendly disco clubs that were opening in the '70s. Whereas *Lavender Woman* made some effort to report on events and organizations on the South Side, with its high concentration of African-Americans, the *Gay Crusader* was much more focused on the emergent gay community on the city's North Side.

When I look back at these papers at a distance of more than a generation, I find myself thinking, How would an LGBT movement have grown without them? A good argument can be made that these community-based newspapers played a decisive role in building LGBT organizations and communities and in fostering political mobilization.

With a hostile mainstream media, and before the technological revolution that has brought us the Internet, this infant press provided the information and reported the news that was nowhere else to be found. How else would someone have learned about the many new organizations that were forming, or the frequent demonstrations that were held? Where else would one encounter the new rhetoric of pride and militancy that these liberationist movements were articulating? What other resources were there to encourage individuals to come out? The community press was, really, the only resource other than word of mouth for letting people know that a new world, a new outlook, and a new community were in formation.

Introduction

Gay Press, Gay Power investigates the synergies between the U.S. gay-rights movement and the print publications that covered this community. These publications were the voice of the community, intertwined for better or worse with the battle for equality. They were also the frontline activists and historians documenting the community for future generations.

But first, some definitions. What is a gay newspaper? Is it a newspaper that loves same-gendered newspapers? Is it printed on copy paper, newsprint or glossy magazine stock? Is it daily, weekly, monthly or bimonthly? Or is it not in print form at all, like music "albums" that only exist in digital format to be downloaded?

This book is focused primarily on weekly or biweekly U.S. regional LGBTQI newspapers (lesbian, gay, bisexual, transgender, questioning and intersex, or "gay," for simplicity's sake), those print publications using the traditional newsprint format. But it also summarizes the history of gay media, including the rich diversity of magazines, digests and 'zines, both local and national. Since most of these publications are also available on the Internet, their reach is, of course, no longer circumscribed by the physical boundaries of city, state or country. But for those papers based in cities, their focus is still primarily regional.

Most gay publications changed during their lifespans. Some that are weekly newspapers now were once monthly or bimonthly newsletters. Some that are now national glossy magazines were once regional newsletters or newspapers. Some weeklies are now published every other week. Quite a few publications have even changed their names over time. When printing and publishing technologies were more expensive, mimeograph was sometimes the only way to get the gay news out—so we wouldn't call them "newspapers" by today's standard, but they fulfilled that role.

In light of these factors, I have chosen to use a wider definition of newspaper than might be the typical dictionary definition. It's important to take into account what was in the pages of the publication, not just what it was printed on. For sure, today there are thousands of gay websites, some of them focused on gay men, others on lesbians, transgender issues, families, sports, culture, leather, bears, and beyond, but this book is not about the World Wide Web; it is primarily about the web press, and those papers printed in that traditional printing format.

There are currently more than 100 weekly, biweekly or monthly regional gay publications in the U.S., some of them founded more than 40 years ago, some less than a decade ago. *Gay Press, Gay Power* explores a few papers that have survived several decades and a few that have evolved from previous newspaper companies. The book is divided into five parts.

Part 1 covers early mainstream and gay media history, and the publications that laid the groundwork for what would later be a flourishing gay movement, as well as the groundwork for more substantial, commercial gay newspapers. The line between activists and journalists was most permeable during the pre-1969 era of gay media.

Part 2 provides insights from key journalists among the thousands who documented the gay movement, some of whom began writing on gay subjects in the 1950s. We selected journalists who have worked around the country; a number of them are still working in gay media today. Of course, there were many other frontline journalists who contributed to the fledgling gay press movement as well. Some have even written books about their experiences—and I hope that more of them will eventually tell their stories.

Part 3 features chapters on gay periodicals in a few key U.S. cities and states. They are representative of the frequent struggles of all gay regional media. From sometimes-chaotic and tormented beginnings, to struggling through the AIDS crisis and other difficult times, to developing the ability to survive in a changing economic and media climate—these challenges are mirrored in the histories of almost all gay media, no matter the town. These crucial elements help to frame a perspective for the discussion of gay newspapers and their role in the movement. Since these pieces are primarily written from the perspective of the publications' owners and staff, they present firsthand—rather than objective or academic—accounts of their media histories.

Part 4 takes a look at how some gay media have joined forces over the years to strengthen their businesses, and how advertising and marketing have played a critical role in the growth of gay newspapers. There has always been a tug of war between the business and editorial sides of the publishing business, and this section offers a detailed look at the debates that have flared up around the push for advertising in gay media.

And finally, Part 5 assesses the role of gay media for historical research, current events and the future. Since the mainstream media are now covering gay issues more than ever, and more openly gay reporters are working in the mainstream—including the newly open Don Lemon and Anderson Cooper and always-open Rachel Maddow—does the gay press still serve a need? Given the changing economy, and the changing way in which people are consuming media, is there even a future role for newspapers at all?

Gay Press, Gay Power addresses these issues and much more, exploring the vital contributions of community media in the fast-changing media landscape.

—Tracy Baim

PART ONE:

Early History

"There is much to be said in favour of modern journalism. By giving us the opinions of the uneducated, it keeps us in touch with the ignorance of the community."

— Oscar Wilde

1

All the News That's Not Fit to Print

By Tracy Baim

While this is a book about gay newspaper history, let's first take a look down mainstream-media memory lane.

There is a reason a gay press was needed. When the media of the previous two centuries were not wholly ignoring everything about homosexuals and the growing gay-rights movement, they were doing far worse: moralizing, demonizing, criminalizing, medicalizing, "repairing," proselytizing, polarizing, ostracizing and often just pitying those poor, sad, pathetic "avowed" homosexuals.

The worst stories compared gays to pedophiles, murderers, rapists and more. We were called "perverts," "inverts," "abnormal," "deviants" and "a menace." Thus, while much of the pre-1980 American press did just simply miss the story about an important segment of society, there are some important exceptions—mostly bad ones.

Why does it matter what the media say and do? Because media in the U.S. exert a powerful influence in our society. They can lead by example or they can play to the status quo. They can justify junk science or they can question authority. Especially in the pre-Internet and pre–cable-television days, the "mass media" were influential in deciding what was news, who was important enough to interview and just what side to take on the social-justice issues of the day. If you look back far enough, to the days before radio, television and cinema, print media were all-pervasive in influencing the hearts and minds of the public.

This chapter focuses on a few key mainstream-media examples—the good and the bad—as representative of most media during the past 100-plus years. There are countless other cases, but the ones here show a range of how the media covered homosexuality. While I have included a lot of different media, I have especially focused on *The New York Times* as the national "newspaper of record" over time. The back of this book also includes an extensive bibliography of related books on gays in the media.

The Wilde Days and Oscar Wilde

During the late 1800s, much of the newspaper coverage that related to homosexuals or people who were "different" dealt with gender nonconformity and responses to women and men who dared cross the sacrosanct hard line of "gender-appropriate" dress and behavior. This included performers, women who fought as men in the Civil War and everyday citizens who flouted conventions (and bans on cross-dressing). Periodically these would lead to arrest, or discovery when someone was treated for a medical illness, or even posthumous revelation during an autopsy, and then mainstream newspapers would cover the "scandal."

For example, in the late 1800s the San Francisco press focused on cross-dressing, covering several high-profile cases of women dressed as men, as documented in *News and Sexuality: Media Portraits of Diversity*, edited by Laura Castañeda and Shannon Campbell.

In the late 1880s, gay writer Oscar Wilde provided American media with an opportunity to cover the love that dare not speak its name—through euphemisms. His court trials in England were covered in the States, as were his speaking tours here.

The New York Times on January 10, 1882, covered a lecture by Wilde. The subhead stated: "Talking in a sepulchral voice to wondering men and women—an opportunity to laugh that was readily seized—Mr. Wilde's views on poetry and criticism." The lecture was matter-of-fact, but it was his delivery that was treated as an oddity.

Wilde gave an estimated 200 lectures in the U.S. during the 1880s. The *Chicago Daily Tribune* covered this and other visits and news about the British writer. The *Tribune* ran *The New York Times* story on January 12, 1882, and one from *The Courier-Journal* of Louisville on January 25. The *Courier* story was about the historic meeting in Camden, New Jersey, between Wilde, 27, and writer Walt Whitman, 62.

Here is how the elaborate prose of the *Courier* began: "At last. It is done. They have met—O. Wilde, the Flower of the Utter, and W. Whitman, the Boomer of the Boundless."

The *Tribune* and other papers reported on Wilde's 1884 lectures in the U.S. as he discussed his opinions about America, including how noisy it is and how far apart everything seems to be.

Wilde's legal troubles in England were news in the U.S. *The New York Times* on May 2, 1895, ran a portion of his eloquent defense speech in court. He called the love between men "the noblest form of affection." But the *Times* editorialized in its writing about the trial, even in an April 8, 1895, headline, "Oscar Wilde's Disgrace; A Mother, Wife, and Two Children Must Share His Shame."

On April 3, the *Times* reported details of the court case. Wilde was pithy in court. When asked about the immorality of articles in *The Chameleon* periodical, which he said he was not associated with, Wilde added, "They were worse; they were badly written." About his essay "Philosophy of the Young," Wilde said, "I rarely write what I believe is true." Wilde also said he did not believe that any book could affect the conduct of the reader, the *Times* reported.

Wilde's death on November 30, 1900, was reported around the world. *The New York Times* of December 1, 1900, said in part:

"It was in 1895 that the great scandal broke which ruined Wilde. It came about through an action brought by the Marquis of Queensberry, whose motive was the protection of his son, Lord Alfred Douglas, over whom Wilde had exercised an evil influence. The evidence at Wilde's trial shocked the civilized world and covered him with disgrace which it was not possible for him to outlive. He was sentenced to prison for a term of years. ... From a pet of society he had become the most despised of social outcasts." The *Times* editorialized about Wilde's "evil" influence, a clear message to anyone who did not follow social norms.

Wilde died at the dawn of the new century, but it would take most of that century for homosexuals to see less subjective coverage from the *Times* and other mainstream newspapers and magazines (and from the new media of radio, TV and film).

Women's Suffrage and the 'Lesbian Problem'

The fight for the right of women to vote ran parallel to the continued repression of women's sexuality. Naturally, this sometimes evolved into a debate about homosexuality.

The *Chicago Daily Tribune* noted on December 7, 1890, that some people feared that a woman's involvement in public life would lead her to "degenerate into a sexless, undefinable creature too dreadful to contemplate." This was not unlike the way the media covered the modern feminist movement that started in the 1960s.

After women won the right to vote in 1920, you can see the signs that a mainstream society was pushing back against the role of women even as they started to achieve some equality, albeit very, very slowly.

Harper's Magazine carried several articles on this topic in the 1920s. John Macy wrote a challenge to feminists in November 1926, "Equality of Woman With Man: A Myth." He called some prominent feminists "vinegar-faced shrews." He quoted from Dr. H.W. Frink's *Morbid Fears and Compulsions*: "A certain proportion of at least the most militant suffragists are neurotics who in some instances are compensating for masochistic trends, in others, are more or less successfully sublimating sadistic and homosexual ones (which usually are unconscious)." Frink followed this with a statement that he hoped it would not cast mud on women's suffrage, because he was in favor of it, and that the neurotics are the pioneers in most reforms. Macy did include this in his excerpt from Frink in *Harper's*.

Edna Yost's essay in *Harper's* of July 1927 focused on "The Case for the Co-Educated Woman." She argued in favor of coeducation because it was more likely to lead women to marrying men, because, she warned, women-only schools were influencing women away from men:

"There is no conscious effort being made at our women's colleges to close the minds of their students to marriage, yet this is exactly what is happening. For they take a girl at eighteen and, during those years when she is emotionally ready to fall in love, when it is easier for her to accept young men for what they are than it will ever be again, she is being consciously molded and led into good habits, one of which is to be happy and satisfied for four years without the real companionship of men. ...

"[One] of two things is likely to happen: The development of her emotional nature may halt while her intellectual development leaps ahead; or she may find in other girls the substitute which forms an outlet for her emotions. ... [Today] we are facing the disconcerting truth that intense homosexual friendships of an undesirable nature form a problem that is admittedly disturbing some of our best women's colleges and unadmittedly disturbing the others; and that though some girls come out of this relationship and adjust themselves successfully to life, others do not. Instead, they find happiness or devastation, as the case may be, in the continuance of their homosexual interests only. ...

"Dr. Katharine B. Davis, whose intelligent, open-minded studies of the sex life of women stamps her as an authority whose opinion on this subject must carry weight, says that 'there is no question but that the problem of homosexuality in women's colleges is an important one—one that should be studied further,' and that 'the segregation of young women during the years when she is emotionally ready to fall in love is quite possibly a factor tending toward actual homosexual experiences.'"

A few months later, in March 1928, *Harper's* published "Why They Failed to Marry," an essay by that very expert, Katharine Bement Davis (a social reformer and women's suffrage advocate). She blamed increased college education as a factor in women's avoidance of marriage. She also warned of the societal dangers if "inferior stocks" reproduced. She argued that it would be better for society to have more educated women who also were breeders.

A fascinating study was reported in that article: a survey of 1,200 unmarried female college graduates who were at least five years out of college. Among those surveyed, 813 graduated from women's colleges and 335 from coed; 48 did work at both types of schools; and five did not answer. There were 29 answers as to why they were not married, everything from "Never met the right man" to "Fear of child bearing." "Homo-sexual relations" was marked by 17 of the women, or 1.6 percent of the total.

Davis wrote: "Last winter the presentation of the play, 'The Captive,' and the discussion which followed, focused the attention of the public upon the problem of homosexuality which before that time had never been made a topic of conversation in polite society. Many adults, particularly women, claimed they did not know such a condition existed. In answer to the question as to why she had failed to marry, 17 women replied that it was due to their relations with other women; but in another section of the questionnaire dealing with 'intense emotional relations with other girls or women,' 22 women stated that this relationship had been one influence in causing them to remain single, while 41 others stated that it was possibly a factor."

The details went on, and the writer concluded that in some cases mothers (or bad fathers) or strong-older-women role models are to blame for how women are attracted to other women.

The Legacy of Magnus Hirschfeld

German physician and sexologist Magnus Hirschfeld (1868–1935) had influence well beyond the borders of his home country. His 1892 visit to the U.S., which included partaking in the World's Columbian Exhibition in Chicago, was covered in newspapers across the country. His subsequent troubles with authorities and his eventual death were also covered in America.

Early U.S. homosexual rights activists, including Henry Gerber in Chicago and Harry Hay in Los Angeles, were influenced by the work of Hirschfeld and the organization he founded, the Scientific Humanitarian Committee (in German, Wissenschaftlich-humanitäres Komitee). The group's focus was on homosexuals, and it sought to repeal Paragraph 175, a German law passed in 1871 that criminalized homosexuality. The group held international conferences on sexual reform in the 1920s and early 1930s. Hirschfeld also founded the Institute for Sexual Research (Institut für Sexualwissenschaft), but it was targeted in an early censorship action by the Nazis on May 6, 1933. Many of his books were burned.

The New York Times reported on the institute raid on May 7, 1933, with the headline "Nazi Students Raid Institute on Sex; Seize Half a Ton of Scientific Material at Dr. Hirschfeld's Berlin Establishment." The *Times* reported that about 80 students rushed through the building. The "un-German" materials were slated for burning, and the names of men who corresponded with Hirschfeld were reportedly going to be used to "root out the Hirschfeld establishment."

The institute may have been targeted to keep it quiet about the ongoing homosexual scandal involving Ernst Röhm, who had been appointed chief of staff of the SA (the Nazi Storm Battalion) by Adolf Hitler. Röhm was executed in 1934 as part of the Night of the Long Knives. Hirschfeld had actually argued against the left-wing press' tactic of politicizing homosexuality by connecting it with fascism.

At the time of the 1933 raid, Hirschfeld was on a worldwide speaking tour, and he never returned to his home country. He died of a heart attack on his 67th birthday. The *Times* obituary of May 17, 1935, mentioned his accomplishments in the field of sexuality studies but did not mention his own homosexuality, or the names of his surviving partners, Tao Li and Karl Giese. The *Times* policy of not listing the partner (or partners) of prominent gays and lesbians who died would not change for many decades, and it is still inconsistent today.

Sexuality on Trial

The gay publication *ONE*, women's pinup magazines, and men's physique periodicals were subjected to censorship by the Post Office Department and local and national criminal-justice authorities. Courts finally started to move in favor of freedom of the press in the 1950s and into the 1970s. (See Chapter 3 for details on the *ONE* court case.)

Lesbian Margaret Anderson started *The Little Review* in Chicago in 1914. Over time, she ran it with lovers Harriet Dean and (later) Jane Heap. It was among the most influential literary and art magazines of its time. It featured many queer writers, including dancer and poet Mark Turbyfill, Hart Crane, Djuna Barnes and Amy Lowell. She also was the first to publish Ernest Hemingway.

Anderson even published her own defense of homosexuality in *The Little Review* as a response to a Chicago lecture on February 4, 1915, by Edith Ellis, the openly lesbian wife of sex researcher Havelock Ellis. Edith's "Sexuality and Eugenics" lecture is believed to be the first in the U.S. to call for homosexual equality. But Anderson wanted more. St. Sukie de la Croix in his book *Chicago Whispers* calls her response, "Mrs. Ellis' Failure," published in the March 1915 *Little Review*, "the first printed, and certainly the most militant, defense of homosexuality ever published in America." Anderson noted that people are "tortured and crucified every day *for their love*—because it is not expressed according to conventional morality," but that Ellis failed to push hard enough for change.

De la Croix also reports that Emma Goldman was excited by Anderson. She wrote to her lover Ben Reitman, noting "the stirrings as a result of my friendship with Margaret—expressive of my previous theoretic interest in sex variation."

In 1916, Anderson's partner Jane Heap was named co-editor, and the two women lived openly as a couple in Chicago.

The Little Review fought a court battle over the sexually explicit James Joyce novel *Ulysses*. The publication serialized the book from 1918 to 1920, before Sylvia Beach, also a lesbian, published it in book form in Paris in 1922. *The Little Review* was prosecuted for obscenity based on the section about masturbation. As a result of the court battle, the work was banned in the U.S. In 1933, another court ruled in favor of the work, so it was finally allowed to be published in this country.

While *Ulysses* was not a gay-themed book, the frank treatment of sexuality was the threat, and similar arguments were later made against portrayals of homosexuality in literature, theater, film and television.

After fights with censors from the U.S. post office because she had published *Ulysses*, Anderson stepped away from the magazine, and Heap took it in different directions.

On May 25, 1930, *The New York Times* ran a review of Margaret Anderson's history of *The Little Review* and her own life, called *My Thirty Years' War*. The *Times* review ended by saying that *The Little Review* had left "the old gods shattered, the old conventions powerless." The media were not always bad on gay issues, but in this case they were not pointing to any gay angles, either—errors by omission.

In 1928, a London court found Radclyffe Hall's lesbian novel *The Well of Loneliness* indecent, and the trial was covered in *The New York Times* and other U.S. media. All copies of the book were ordered destroyed. The *Times* reported that the attorney general called the book "more subtle, demoralizing, corrosive and corruptive than anything ever written. … The book seeks to glorify vice or to produce a plea of toleration of people who practice it. It is propaganda."

After a lengthy legal fight in the U.S., the novel was allowed to be published here. A court in New York ruled in April 1929 that the work was not objectionable. *The New York Times* reported April 20: "The book in question deals with a delicate social problem, which, in itself, cannot be said to be in violation of the law unless it is written in such a manner as to make it obscene … and tends to deprave all corrupt minds open to immoral influences."

Another interesting publication during the early 20th century was *The Quill* in Greenwich Village, New York. Arthur Moss and Harold Hersey founded it in 1917, and it covered the very bohemian nature of that neighborhood. Moss and his then-future wife Florence Gilliam moved to Paris and started *Gargoyle* magazine, which like *The Quill* attracted the edgy new artists of the day, many of them gay, including Hart Crane. Moss later started *The Boulevardier* with Erskine Gwynne and published Noël Coward, among others.

There is a fascinating collection of 1921 editions of the Greenwich Village *Quill* published by the University of Michigan Library. A July 1921 essay by Robert Edwards is particularly interesting, noting the hypocrisy of those who would legislate against the behavior of others: "There are well defined medical categories to include every type of person who has the inverted passion for suppressing in others the recreative instincts the zealot perversely denys [*sic*] himself. And I might add this interference with others is most hideously unChristian." There are lots of coded references to Sappho and flouting of the conventions against dancing, plus reports on theatrical culture and some very campy essays.

Fire!! Breaks Out

Fire!! was a literary magazine of the 1920s Harlem Renaissance in New York. *Fire!!* was the "first black magazine that was both independent and essentially literary," according to authors Abby Arthur Johnson and Ronald Maberry Johnson, writing in their book *Propaganda and Aesthetics: The Literary Politics of African-American Magazines in the Twentieth Century. Fire!!*'s editor was Wallace Thurman. The Johnsons said that Thurman signed some copies of *Fire!!* "Flamingly, Wallace Thurman."

Fire!! was criticized even from within the African-American community for its depictions of homosexuality, bisexuality and interracial relationships. It published just one edition, in 1926, and its headquarters burned to the ground. But it nevertheless had an impact on the publishing world.

Several gay writers were published in its pages, including Thurman, Langston Hughes, Countee Cullen and Bruce Nugent. Cullen had been married to Nina Yolande Du Bois, daughter of the great W.E.B. Du Bois, but they were divorced after he told her he was attracted to men. Thurman also married a woman but she, like Du Bois, ended her marriage because her husband liked men.

In 1946, Nugent published the short story "Smoke, Lilies and Jade," believed to be among the first stories by an African-American to openly discuss homosexuality. The first part of that story was included in that 1926 issue of *Fire!!,* under the pseudonym Richard Bruce. The Johnsons noted that the story "detailed the amours of bisexual black artist Alex, known to his male lover Adrian (alias Beauty) as Duce." It was pretty racy stuff. "No other black literary magazine had previously included an explicit portrayal of a homosexual affair," the Johnsons wrote.

Alain Locke reviewed *Fire!!* in *Survey* magazine in 1927, and he said it was an obvious artistic cousin to *The Little Review* and *The Quill. The Afro-American* newspaper ran the headline "Writer Brands Fire as Effeminate Tommyrot" over an article by Rean Graves, as reported by the Johnsons in their book. Thurman defended *Fire!!* in an essay for *The New Republic* in August 1927.

All the World's a Stage

The presence of gays in the theater has long been a subject of debate in the media, even up through today, with the large number of gay plays and actors on Broadway.

Time magazine reported on stage "Noncensorship" in its issue of February 21, 1927. "Broadway has lately blazed with headlines: 'Sex Plays Raided,' 'Police Rout Vice Show,' etc. etc. What actually occurred was more polite. By arrangement with the managements, detectives called in police limousines for the actors, actresses, producers and authors of *The Captive, Sex* and *The Virgin Man.* ... The evident lack of heart in the police procedure against *The Captive, Sex* and *The Virgin Man,* was doubtless due to the fact that the public censor is also a public servant requiring votes to hold office. Nevertheless, pending the hearings on these three plays, the management of a 'homosexual comedy drama' called *The Drag,* after being barred in Bayonne, N. J., last week disbanded its cast of 62 players, not daring to enter New York City."

In May 1932, *Harper's Magazine*'s Elmer Rice, the Pulitzer Prize–winning playwright, wrote about "Sex in the Modern Theater." Rice said the church has always seen the theater as a "formidable rival." In focusing on sex and the theater, Rice said he would "discount the fulminations of the clergy, which have deafened and blinded so many presumably reasonable persons."

Following are excerpts from Rice's lengthy essay: "There are, in addition, certain other topics, such as masturbation, venereal disease, and commercialized prostitution, and certain relationships such as miscegenation, incest, and homosexuality which are, or have been until very recently, regarded as subjects wholly unfit for discussion or presentation upon the stage, irrespective of the manner of treatment. Ibsen's 'Ghosts,' Brieux's 'Damaged Goods,' and Shaw's 'Mrs. Warren's Profession' are outstanding examples of plays which, although now more or less generally performed, were almost universally condemned when they were first presented because they dealt with subjects which were deemed unfit for public discussion however familiar they may have been to the individual theater-goer. ...

"Quite recently the theater has begun to pay attention to the problem of homosexuality, a subject which, especially in Anglo-Saxon countries, is still rigorously tabu. When one considers the relatively large number of homosexual individuals who are engaged in one branch or another of the theatrical profession, it is not surprising that in the theater itself, a tendency appeared to throw emphasis upon this subject, as soon as the ever-changing *mores* made its introduction at all possible. Nevertheless, in spite of the fact that the last twenty years have seen the production of a great number of novels and poems dealing more or less openly with the subject and the accumulation of a mountain of scientific and pseudo-scientific treatises upon it, almost no one in the theater has made an attempt to treat the subject in other than its sensational or scandalous aspects. Bourdet's 'La Prisonnière' ('The Captive'), which created such a furor a few years ago (and the presentation of which in New York resulted in the enactment of a law making the dramatic treatment of homosexuality 'obscene' per se), is nothing more than the conventional French formula play, except that the wife's lover happens to be a woman instead of a man."

Broadway Brevities and Society Gossip, a New York tabloid believed to be the first national weekly gossip publication, warned about the growing number of "queers" in the city. In a 1933 front-page report, it said "hordes of third sexers have descended upon Broadway and Times Square," according to the book *News and Sexuality*.

Walt Whitman Laid Bare

In May 1929, Walt Whitman was the target of an essay in *Harper's*, "Alias Walt Whitman," by Harvey O'Higgins: "He was neither sensual, nor rough and rugged, nor truly healthy, nor lusty, nor even very masculine. He was what is nowadays called a Narcissan, in love with himself, introverted; and so wrapped up in his own ego that he got no free delivery of energy except in his exhibitionism. Hence his constitutional laziness. He was arrested in his sexual development very near the homosexual level, as several of his poems show; and like many another case of arrested development he was always 'a man's man.' He speaks of the 'fiercely loved land of his birth' in one of his anonymous blurbs, and in another he assumes 'to himself all the attributes of his country'; but when the Civil War broke out on April 12, 1861, he disappeared for eighteen months from the sight of his biographers ... .

"The sexuality in his poems is a compensation, in phantasy, for his lack of potency in experience. Much of this sexual expression is dangerously near the homosexual level—which is to be expected where the sexual impulse is anchored by a mother-fixation and unable to achieve a heterosexual goal."

Impressionable Youth

One of the earliest published reports of an attempted suicide by a possibly gay youth is recorded in *Harper's* June 1933 edition. The essay, "On Playing God," is by Lillian Symes, and in it she discusses situations where "God-players" judge the lives of others. She also notes a fascinating twist relevant today, about those self-loathing people who are more likely to judge others. Today, we might call them closeted homosexuals who are hypocrites in lobbying against gay rights. She writes:

"Sometime during the past year a hitherto normal and happy fourteen-year-old boy tried to shoot himself in the heart with his father's pistol and missed that vital organ by a fraction of an inch. For a month after this affair his dismayed parents could elicit no explanation from a silent and moody convalescent. Then suddenly, at some significant words of understanding sympathy from an outsider, the dam of repression broke and the whole story came out.

"The boy ... had come in contact with a young high-school teacher who had aroused in him a genuine passion for poetry. … He was, in short, going through one of those very common cases of the adolescent 'crush' from which many thousands of youngsters have graduated into perfectly normal hetero-sexuality. But his experience aroused in the breast of a very knowing friend of the family the irresistible impulse to enlighten the child about the 'real' nature of his attachment. An impressive and highly clinical study of homosexuality, illustrated by case stories of adolescent school life, was mailed to the boy with a note to the effect that a perusal of the book would open his eyes to certain truths about himself. In his horror and shame at what he read the boy had attempted suicide.

"The reaction of this particular child was probably an extreme one. … It is obvious that the inveterate God-player is not entirely normal; that he is a person whose own adjustment to life in general, and probably to sex in particular, is a faulty one; that he is afflicted with a sort of psychic itch. It is my theory that he is particularly common among those fairly numerous individuals in modern society who are divided against themselves, whose emotional impulses are neither definitely hetero- or homo-sexual and who, being unable to find satisfaction in either type of relationship, use up their frustrated energies and assuage their own dissatisfaction in manipulating other lives, in creating among others some of their own confusions. …

"Somehow he must assuage his own inner turmoil and division and the easiest way to do this is to reproduce it in others. In his efforts to do so he is quite capable of wrecking the immediate world about him. …"

A Stein Is a Stein Is a Stein

The boldly gender-norm–defying Gertrude Stein and Alice B. Toklas also provided headlines during their travels across the U.S. Stein was another case of a "celebrity" creating a stir for her unique way of being, allowing the media to allude to, but rarely express explicitly, just what her uniqueness was.

This funny headline appeared in *The New York Times* of October 25, 1934: "Gertrude Stein Arrives and Baffles Reporters by Making Herself Clear." It described her outfit, including "mannish shirt." It also said she wore "a gay hat."

With the successful 1933 publication of Stein's *Autobiography of Alice B. Toklas*, the expatriate couple returned to the U.S. in 1934 "to be lionized on a national book tour. Stein made quite a stir when she hit Chicago that year," according to Marie J. Kuda, writing in *Out and Proud in Chicago*. Stein had been away from America for 31 years. "She lectured at the Arts Club, rode around in a police car, and stayed at the Drake Hotel during the premiere of her opera at the Auditorium Theatre. *Four Saints in Three Acts*, with libretto by Stein and music by homosexual composer Virgil Thomson, opened in November 1934 with an all-'Negro' cast and cellophane scenery."

The *Chicago Daily Tribune* reviewed the *Four Saints* production on March 3, 1934. It said the work had "fine music but lacks meaning."

Vice, Medicine and the Social Scene

In the early 20th century, cities began a strong crackdown on vice districts. A 1911 Chicago Vice Commission report looked at the "social evil" within the borders of the city, including "sex perversion."

The media often excitedly assisted in the police crackdown on homosexuals. Henry Gerber had started what is believed to be the first homosexual-rights group in the U.S.—in 1924 in Chicago. He also published two issues of a newsletter, *Friendship and Freedom*, before he was subjected to censorship and arrest. (More in the next chapter.)

Time magazine reported on September 23, 1935, about the manufacture of testosterone: "True to his promise of a month ago that he would soon be able to manufacture the hormone secreted by the testes which accounts for masculinity, Dr. Leopold Ruzicka, Swiss chemist, last week announced that his assistants in his Zurich laboratory had just cabled him word of their success. Testosterone is the name of the new hormone. ... Natural testosterone, long anticipated, was discovered in human testicles only last June by Dr. E. Laqueur of Amsterdam. ... German and Swiss chemical laboratories are already prepared, said Dr. Ruzicka last week, to manufacture from sheep's wool all the testosterone the world needs to cure homosexuals, revitalize old men."

The mainstream media reported on crimes involving "perverts," while a few media, including the African-American publications *Jet* and *The Chicago Defender*, dared to cover the social life of homosexuals, as expressed through the popular Halloween drag balls.

In an essay for Brett Beemyn's *Creating a Place for Ourselves: Lesbian, Gay, and Bisexual Community Histories*, Allen Drexel writes about race, class and male homosexuality on Chicago's South Side from 1936 to 1960. The following is from his essay "Before Paris Burned": "The first Finnie's Ball, staged in 1935 by a black gay street hustler and gambler named Alfred Finnie, was held in the basement of a tavern on the corner of 38th Street and Michigan Avenue. ... Until 1943— the year that Finnie was killed in a gambling brawl—the ball was held up to five times annually at a number of different venues. ... [N]ews accounts of Finnie's Balls typically drew attention to the most 'extravagant' aspects of the events. *Ebony*'s story on the 1953 ball, for example, reported that 'More than 1,500 spectators milled around outside Chicago's Pershing Ballroom to get a glimpse of the bejeweled impersonators who arrived in limousines, taxis, Fords, and even by streetcar.' ... In the *Chicago Defender*'s extensive coverage of the 1955 ball, for example, John Earl Lewis, the honorary 'Mayor of Bronzeville,' was depicted on stage flanked by 'the finery bedecked winners' of that year's extravaganza."

Coverage of racial and gender diversity within the homosexual community was rare in the mainstream media, which mainly focused on white men in their reports on the topic.

The Kinsey Report

Dr. Alfred Kinsey's sexuality research provided the mainstream media an excuse to cover homosexuality (because of the high rates of alternate sexuality Kinsey found), but most reporters did not stray far from the negative coverage of the past. Kinsey's book on men, *Sexual Behavior in the Human Male*, was published in 1948, and *Sexual Behavior in the Human Female* came out in 1953.

The New York Times reported on Kinsey's efforts, including an article of June 5, 1948, when Kinsey defended his book against critics. At a lecture, Kinsey told members of the American Psychopathological Association that the behavior they called abnormal is "part and parcel of our inheritance as mammals and is natural and normal biologically."

Harper's Magazine had a very fun cover when the women's report came out, featuring Kinsey as a miniature man next to a large woman made up of the faces of many types of women. *Harper's* Editor Anne G. Freedgood wrote a detailed and very factual report for the magazine's September 1953 issue. It included the following:

"The Kinsey findings on homosexuality indicate that the main factors leading to it are: (1) the human being's basic sexual capacity to respond to any sufficient stimulus; (2) the chance that leads a person to his or her first sexual experience with a person of the same sex; (3) the effects of that experience, pleasant or unpleasant; and (4) the powerful conditioning effects of the social code. Thus a man or woman who has had a homosexual experience, Dr. Kinsey suggests, may find himself rejected by persons of the opposite sex and be driven into exclusively homosexual activity. Contrariwise, the social pressure against premarital intercourse with a person of the opposite sex may drive an individual, especially a woman, against whom the pressure is apt to be more strongly applied, into homosexuality. Carried to its farther conclusions, all this seems to indicate that, if the homosexual taboo were removed, our society might follow the pattern of ancient Athens or Shakespearean England in which bi-sexuality was an accepted form, and the society remained sound and productive."

Lesbian and Gay Media Advocates, in its book *Take Back! The Gay Person's Guide to Media Action,* said the male Kinsey Report "paved the way for the first truly positive discussion of homosexuality in the mainstream media. In 1949, an exchange of views on male homosexuality developed quite spontaneously in the letters pages of the *Saturday Review of Literature.* These letters, including one by a self-identified gay man, are ... unprecedented."

When Kinsey died in 1956, at age 62, he was remembered for the impact he had on society and the scientific community. *Time* magazine reported September 3: "Thus 'The Kinsey Report' became at once a radio comedian's joke and a hard-worked (and in many phases perhaps valuable) scientific contribution. It was also a fascinating moral symptom of its age."

The Lavender Scare: The 'Perverts' Are Coming

The government's crackdown on homosexuals within its ranks was at its height soon after World War II. Newspapers across the country eagerly reported on developments over the course of several years. While most non-gay Americans who are old enough remember the era for Senator Joseph McCarthy's anti-Communist witch hunts, homosexuals were just as much in the crosshairs of McCarthy and some other members of Congress, the military and the White House.

Newsweek reported on the military's anti-gay campaigns on June 9, 1947, confirming that three to four thousand people were discharged for being homosexual. The magazine tackled the subject of gays two years later in an article, "Queer People," on October 10, 1949. It told readers that some believe homosexuals to be benign, but then "the mangled form of some victim focuses public attention on the degenerate's work." *Newsweek* was saying homosexuals are a danger to society by killing people in "dastardly and horrifying" crimes.

The McCarthy era swept up thousands of gays in its dust storm. Following is an outline of a few of the media reports during the peak years of the naming and firing of gays who worked for the federal government.

• "Sex Perverts Invade D.C., House Told," *The Washington Post*, July 20, 1948.

• "Male Pervert Arrests Rise In District," *The Washington Post*, November 7, 1948. U.S. Attorney Morris Fay said homosexuals were a problem in D.C.

• "Assert Truman 'Gag' Is Hiding Moral Laxities," *Chicago Daily Tribune*, March 26, 1950. The paper told of President Harry Truman's preventing the FBI from reporting on federal employees to the Senate committee investigating communism and homosexuality. The *Tribune* compared Truman's move to that of Kaiser Wilhelm II when he was plagued by rumors of a homosexual infiltration of his ranks from 1906 to 1909. A few weeks later, Truman created a commission to study a change in the law, but he wanted to avoid violating "the rights of American citizens," as reported in the January 24, 1951, *Tribune* article, "Truman Sets Up Board to Alter Security Laws." This was seen as a slap-down of Congress' own efforts.

• "Congress Hears 5000 Perverts Infest Capital," *Los Angeles Times*, March 29, 1950.

• "Perverts Called Government Peril," *The New York Times*, April 17, 1950. "Perhaps as dangerous as the actual communists are the sexual perverts who have infiltrated our Government in recent years," said Republican Party National Chairman Guy George Gabrielson.

• "Report Asks Firm Action on Perverts," *The Washington Post*, December 16, 1950: "A Senate subcommittee yesterday recommended new and more drastic penalties against sex perverts here, and a more 'realistic' effort to remove such persons from Federal jobs. ... The Senators concluded that sex perverts are not suitable for Government positions; that they are poor security risks and 'prime targets' for espionage agents ... ." The Senate was mad that even though 91 gays lost their government jobs, they were allowed to resign for "personal reasons," and therefore some of them were able to get other government jobs.

• "Object Lesson," in *Time* magazine's issue of December 25, 1950, presented the depressing story of one gay man who killed himself: "Colonel Alfred Redl was a master of his craft. While still in his 30s he rose to the General Staff and became chief of counter-intelligence for Austro-Hungary. ... But talented Alfred Redl had one terrible weakness: he was a homosexual. Russian agents contrived a trap and caught him one day; then they threatened to expose him unless he turned traitor. Redl turned, for eleven years served Russia as a master spy-within-a-spy. The extent of his treason was discovered after war broke out in 1914: Russia knew the Austro-Hungarian and German war plans. Two fellow officers visited Alfred Redl one night, left him a loaded pistol. Alfred Redl took the hint, stood before a mirror and fired a bullet through his brain."

Time did not question the status quo—that the abhorrence of homosexuality was what made gays more subject to blackmail.

Time went on to report that Senator Clyde Hoey, "with three other Democratic Senators and three Republicans, had been quietly looking into a sordid matter: the problem of homosexuals in the Government. ... Senator Hoey's investigators ... found a record of homosexuality or other sexual perversions among workers in 36 of 53 branches of Government, as well as in the armed forces. Between Jan. 1, 1947 and last April, [a total of] 4,954 cases had come to light among some three and a half million people in Government service. Most were in the armed services, which are far larger than civilian Government departments and traditionally aggressive at searching out perverts.

"There were 574 cases involving civilian Government employees and 69 are still under investigation; in all the other cases the accused had either quit, been cleared or fired. The investigators found the greatest batch of civilian cases—143—in the State Department."

• "54 Acheson Aids [*sic*] Found Perverts And Are Ousted," *Chicago Daily Tribune*, April 26, 1951.

• "126 Perverts Discharged [since Jan. 1, 1951]," *The New York Times*, March 26, 1952.

• Columnist Max Lerner at the *New York Post* was one of the few voices of reason, and he did a series, "Panic on the Potomac," that questioned the legitimacy of the government's ban on gays.

• *The Saturday Evening Post* magazine risked McCarthy's ire on July 29, 1950. The *Chicago Daily Tribune* reported August 9 that McCarthy "rebuked" the *Post* and newspaper columnists Joseph and Stewart Alsop on the Senate floor: "McCarthy said the Alsops in the article condemned the campaign against sex perverts in the government. McCarthy said the article was sarcastic about the people of the Midwest because they object to 'perverts and traitors in our government.'" The *Post*'s Alsop column had called the efforts to purge gays "vulgar" and "nauseating."

• After President Dwight Eisenhower was elected in 1952, he appeared to take a more eager approach than Truman to rooting out alleged subversives, "perverts" and others in government. The *Chicago Daily Tribune* reported on his 1954 State of the Union speech in its March 2 edition. Eisenhower told Congress and the country that 2,200 government workers had been let go under a new security program he implemented in April 1953. Of those, 190 were called "sex perverts."

Eisenhower did give a speech on May 31, 1954, about the divisions within the U.S. caused by anti-Communist hunts—he called for "less prejudice and passion." Nevertheless, the pressure to fire subversives continued. On January 4, 1955, the *Los Angeles Times* headlined: "8008 Dropped as Risks to Security Under Eisenhower." Sex perversion was listed for 655 of the persons dropped as government employees.

Raids and Arrests

Bar raids and arrests of gay men in police entrapment incidents were covered by newspapers in cities large and small. Sometimes just the bartender was arrested, as in the arrest of the Windup tavern staff member in a raid reported in the *Chicago Daily Tribune*. On January 17, 1949, the *Tribune* reported that 15 men and nine women were arrested in a "war on degenerates." The article noted that, in the previous week, police had arrested 93 men in the gay Windup lounge, which the *Tribune* called "a hangout for perverts." Police Captain Thomas Harrison told the paper he thought Chicago had at least 18,000 men whom he called "sexually maladjusted ... , all potentially dangerous." Harrison told the paper that many homosexuals maintained luxurious apartments where they entertained young, unsuspecting "recruits" with food, music, liquor and obscene literature. Harrison even claimed that Chicago's gays were part of a national group run by a man named "Brown" living in or near Miami.

The November 22, 1949, issue of the *Tribune* reported on the formation of a special Cook County commission to "study the problem of sexually deviated persons" whom it linked to "atrocious murder" and "shocking crimes" against boys and girls.

One of the most notorious Chicago bar raids was in 1964 on Louie's Fun Lounge (commonly known as Louie Gage's), at 2340 North Mannheim Road in Leyden Township. There were 109 people, including six women, arrested in the raid, conducted by officers under Cook County Sheriff Richard B. Ogilvie (later, governor of Illinois).

The *Chicago Tribune* on April 24, 1964, printed the names and occupations of those arrested, including Louis Gauger, the bar's owner. The *Tribune* reported April 28 that Gauger was an "avowed friend of Tony Accardo, crime syndicate figure."

The *Tribune* did a story April 27 specifically about the teachers and school officials who were arrested, "Boards to Get Vice Raid Data on 8 Teachers," and it again listed their names and where they taught. The next day, the *Tribune* reported that at least two of them had quit.

The *Tribune*'s account read in part: "Lt. James Donnelly said that many of the men carried powder puffs and lipsticks, and that some wore wigs. The lounge has catered to sex deviates from all over the nation, Donnelly added, and has been raided many times in the last 15 years by police of the state's attorney's office and the sheriff's department."

This was a final straw for some gays, and Mattachine Midwest, an independent organization that borrowed from the name of the once-national gay Mattachine Society, was formed out of the anger generated by this raid and other police harassment.

That same year, the Lincoln Baths, at 1812 North Clark Street in Chicago, was raided. One of the raids was documented in the June 14, 1964, issue of the *Chicago Tribune* in an article titled "33 Men Seized Thru Vice Raid on Bathhouse." Two years later, on March 6, 1966, the *Tribune* reported that another 32 men were arrested there. The 1964 article listed the professions of those arrested, but only one name. The 1966 article listed all the men's names and their ages, addresses and occupations. The article said an undercover detective witnessed lewd acts being performed in the steam room. It also said the business was controlled by members of the crime syndicate.

Here are excerpts from the 1964 raid article: "Thirty-three men, including a County physician, two teachers, and two attorneys, were arrested early yesterday in a vice raid on the Lincoln Baths ... . [A detective] saw four men performing indecent acts in a steam room. [Lieutenant Thomas] Kernan said the bathhouse has been a national meeting place for perverts. ... He said files of the bathhouse confiscated in the raid listed various meeting places for perverts throughout the United States."

Sergeant James Reilley of the Police Department's prostitution unit was in charge of the 1966 raid, and he said the patrons of the bathhouse were "required to show identification and to sign a register," the *Tribune* reported. The police also said the bathhouse was controlled by the Mafia, including Michael "The Fireplug" Glitta and Lawrence "The Hood" Buonaguidi.

Some men arrested in these raids lost their jobs or their families, or both. And some were said to have committed suicide.

Time magazine looked at laws across the country in an August 5, 1955, article, "Sin & Criminality." It was a report on the annual meeting of the American Law Institute, at which the institute voted on a Model Penal Code:

"By a heavy majority, the lawyers agreed that adultery should not be a statutory crime. Sodomy proved more controversial. In the end, the model code provided criminal penalties for homosexual behavior 'involving force, adult corruption of minors and public offense.' But a broader provision caused a sharper argument. This clause held that 'a person who engages in an act of deviate sexual intercourse' commits a crime."

Judge John J. Parker, 69, of the 4th U.S. Circuit Court of Appeals, "opposed the argument that private homosexuality should not be enjoined by the law merely because the law, pragmatically, cannot stop it," *Time* reported.

But Learned Hand, 83, retired chief judge of the 2nd U.S. Circuit Court of Appeals, disagreed. *Time* reported him as saying: "Criminal law which is not enforced practically is much worse than if it was not on the books at all ... I think it [sodomy] is a matter of morals, a matter very largely of taste, and it is not a matter that people should be put in prison about."

The group voted 35–24 to recommend that sodomy and adultery "be removed from the list of crimes against the peace and dignity of the state," *Time* reported.

One of the most pernicious attacks on homosexuals occurred in 1955 in Boise, Idaho. All the city's institutions—business leaders, the *Idaho Statesman* newspaper, schools, public officials and police—were involved. Journalist John Gerassi explored the moral panic in detail in *The Boys of Boise: Furor, Vice, and Folly in an American City*. Officials believed there was a wealthy gay man, "The Queen," who was leading a group of homosexuals trying to take over the city and state. Arrests began on October 31, and the *Statesman* reported the scandal on November 2. The panic was in high gear, as officials believed there was a child molestation ring involving more than a hundred people.

Time reported on this "homosexual underground" that "preyed on hundreds of teen-age boys" on December 12, 1955. A man who had investigated gays in the infamous State Department gay purges was hired to do the same in Boise, and he tallied a list of 500 suspects in the city of about 35,000 residents. But there was backlash from the far-reaching investigation, and Boise was eventually embarrassed by the national attention. The really rich gays had never been arrested, and people started to realize that gays really were involved at every level of society. So the officials slowly backed off their efforts—but not before several men were arrested, and some served years in jail. Charges included the "infamous crime against nature."

Miami, Florida, experienced its own gay panic in the mid-1950s. Len Evans has since compiled a "Gay Chronicles, Florida" website highlighting incidents in the state. He writes: "1953: In the wake of a number of highly sensationalized cases of child molestation and murder, public hysteria was directed at the homosexual community by an orchestrated campaign of Miami area newspapers, politicians and police."

The Miami Herald was very much a part of the panic problem. A July 28, 1954, editorial attacked police for creating a "Powder Puff Lane" but also warned against comparing homosexuals to rapists and child molesters.

On August 3, the *Herald* reported that a William Simpson was killed by two men; their defense was that he made a pass at them. Evans writes: "The murder is used to further stir up public hysteria against homosexuals." An August 11 editorial, "Clean This Place Up," stated: "This shoulder-shrugging by police is the cause of Miami's reputation as a comfortable haven for homosexuals."

On August 15, Dade County Sheriff Thomas J. Kelly ordered raids on 11 bars. Fifty-three people were arrested, and 19 were booked. A September 2 *Herald* editorial headline read: "Soft Police Policy Towards Perverts Results Only In Evil." On October 26, Miami passed a law making it illegal to sell alcohol to a homosexual, for bars to employ a homosexual, and for them to allow two or more homosexuals to congregate on the premises, according to Evans.

Making matters worse, Florida state Senator Charley Johns formed the Johns Committee to go after Communists and homosexuals. In 1958 it focused especially on educators. Sixteen staff and faculty members at the state university in Gainesville lost their jobs in 1958. The Johns Committee continued into the 1960s.

The mainstream media did not simply report on police and official harassment of homosexuals—they helped to fuel the fire.

More than four decades later, in the 2000s, Miami started to aggressively court the gay market for tourism dollars. A 2012 booklet from the Greater Miami Convention & Visitors Bureau was titled "Pride Celebrated Daily." It is a far cry from the purges of teachers and the raids on bars.

Christine Jorgensen Makes History

The first highly covered person to have a sex change was Christine Jorgensen, and her case sparked a worldwide media frenzy. Born George William Jorgensen Jr. in 1926, Christine, a former Army private, went public with her desire to have surgery and bring her physical body into line with what she believed herself to be.

The New York *Daily News* front page of December 1, 1952, was "Ex-GI Becomes Blonde Beauty." Jorgensen had gone to Denmark for the surgery. She was not the first to undergo a sex change, but she was the first to also have hormone therapy. *The New York Times* reported February 13, 1953, that "Miss Jorgensen Returns." As reported in *Christine Jorgensen: A Personal Autobiography* (first published in 1967, it was reissued in 2000 with an introduction by Susan Stryker), in the 18 months after her story came out, "more than half a million words about Christine Jorgensen rolled off the world's presses."

In 1959, Jorgensen tried to obtain a marriage license with her fiancé, Howard J. Knox. *The New York Times* reported April 4 that because her driver's license still said she was male, the city clerk rejected their application. Knox lost his job once news of the engagement reached his employer.

Inspired by the new dialogue about Jorgensen, *Time* magazine ran an article on December 15, 1952, about various medical terms for gender: "Such words as 'hermaphroditism' and 'pseudohermaphroditism' have been mostly textbook talk in the U.S. until last week." The article gave definitions of those terms, and then homosexuality: "Because of emotional disturbances, usually in childhood, physiologically normal males may develop the social attitudes of females, and vice versa. Homosexuality is not inherited and has little (usually nothing) to do with hormone balance. But many homosexuals refuse to admit this, and they reject the psychiatric treatment which offers them some chance of a normal social life. Many of them wear the clothes of the opposite sex, and pester endocrinologists for hormone injections to make them more, not less abnormal. A few homosexual men have tried to persuade U.S. surgeons to operate on them to change them into pseudowomen. Most surgeons will have nothing to do with what they consider a crime against nature and the laws of the 48 states."

Jorgensen was on *The Dick Cavett Show* in 1968 but reportedly walked off when he inquired about her sex life. She lived to 62 years of age, and her death in 1989 was covered by major media outlets.

2 Steps Forward, 3 Steps Back

By the 1960s, the mainstream media made a few attempts to actually cover more of the homophile movement through print, radio and television shows. There was still bad news for the gays, as police and psychiatrists were usually given the upper (or only) hand.

Harper's did a special issue on "The American Female" in October 1962. One essay, by the University of Chicago psychoanalyst Dr. Bruno Bettelheim, looked at issues of relationships between men and women and suggested the modern complications may lead to homosexuality for both partners.

"With both sex and household work often less than satisfying, it is not surprising that so many modern marriages turn sour, and that the phenomenon of homosexuality looms as importantly as it does today. ...

"The results are often men who want women, but don't know what to do with them when they get them; and women who get men, but who are disappointed in them and in themselves when they live together. Mutually disappointed, it is natural that each sex seek out its own company; for only then can they really be themselves on a truly equal basis, freed of anxiety, disappointment, or inferiority feeling. Who has not observed the tendency of the sexes to segregate themselves in certain married circles? However, when relations between the sexes are so plagued, then a kind of homosexuality may also become rampant. And indeed, psychiatrists have recently been noting an alarming rise in both female and male homosexuality.

"However, if I can trust my experience, female homosexuality is not increasing so much as the number of women who are unwilling to pretend they enjoy having a role forced on them that frustrates their aspirations; and so they seek the company of a partner who can share them. Sometimes two such women find it convenient to live together, and slowly, as in a good marriage, the partners blend their lives.

"In some cases—but much less often than is sometimes assumed—this leads to a desire for sexual relations. But unlike most male homosexuals, such women can often switch their affections to the other sex if they can find a male who really wants and needs to 'look outward with them' (and I would add inward) in the same direction. (This, of course, does not hold true for a hard core of female homosexuals."

The next year, in March 1963, *Harper's* ran a piece by William J. Helmer on "New York's 'Middle-class' HOMOSEXUALS." Helmer wrote that "homosexuality is a condition which takes so many forms that the word is of little use in describing any single group of people. And many homosexuals insulate themselves from hostile heterosexual society, taking refuge in a separate homosexual community which possesses its own customs, social structure, ethics, argot, organizations and even business establishments."

Helmer did his homework: He spent several months speaking to self-segregating gays. Therefore, he told readers that his story was about the "homosexual bourgeoisie—people who are community-oriented, provincial, critical of undesirables. They are themselves frequently disdained by other homosexuals, some of whom are less preoccupied with their deviancy and participate freely in both gay and 'straight' society."

Despite his use of the word "deviant" and other judgmental terms (saying that one "type" of homosexual is a child molester), Helmer briefly mentioned lesbians and discussed "drag" parties and balls and "genuine transvestitism." It was a sociologist's-eye view of New York's gay world, and important for its day.

Media even in San Francisco, which was becoming more and more gay, struggled with how to cover the community. A pivotal event helped move the media more in favor of the homosexual community—police harassment of an innocuous San Francisco gay gathering hosted by religious leaders on New Year's Eve in 1964.

The Council on Religion and the Homosexual held a costume party benefit at California Hall. When the ministers told the San Francisco Police Department, police attempted to force the hall's owners to cancel it. At the event, some of the ministers and ticket takers were arrested, creating a brief riot, according to John D'Emilio in his book *Sexual Politics, Sexual Communities: The Making of a Homosexual Minority in the United States, 1940–1970*.

While the national Mattachine Society had disbanded by 1961 after many internal battles, some individual chapters remained—or similarly named groups started up later. Frank Kameny and Jack Nichols founded the Mattachine Society of Washington. They were aggressive and forward-thinking, taking the D.C. organization to far riskier heights than most Mattachine Society people had proposed. The Mattachine Society of New York, which had been a chapter of the national Mattachine Society before becoming independent, could not contain the energy of a young gay man intent on changing the world. Randy Wicker left New York Mattachine to form his own one-man Homosexual League of New York, and he used it to get into the mainstream media with his push for equality.

The New York Times, the standard bearer of mainstream media in the U.S., had no clue how to cover the growth in out gay people in its own hometown, much less across the country.

"Growth of Overt Homosexuality in City Provokes Wide Concern" ran on the front page of the December 17, 1963, issue of the *Times*. Reporter Robert Doty used Wicker as a resource, and Wicker's efforts were repaid with a slanted story that discussed bar raids and a seedy, threatening homosexual underground. As Edward Alwood writes in his book *Straight News: Gays, Lesbians, and the News Media*, "the story became a lesson in how the supposed objectivity of the media is often selective in what it includes and what it ignores." The focus was on the criminal and psychiatric "experts."

The *Times* story included these choice words: "The city's most sensitive open secret—the presence of what is probably the greatest homosexual population in the world and its increasing openness—has become the subject of growing concern of psychiatrists, religious leaders and the police." The paper said homosexuals tend to be promiscuous and seek pickups, but it discussed the treatment of homosexuals, religious opposition, gay nightlife, gay publications and groups, and much more. It was important to have a cover story in the *Times*, but Wicker felt betrayed after he helped the reporter with sources.

The 1964 arrest of President Lyndon Johnson's adviser Walter Jenkins, for alleged lewd behavior in a YMCA men's room, gave the media another excuse to cover the exotic homosexual world.

'Notes on "Camp"'

Susan Sontag's essay "Notes on 'Camp,'" published in the political and literary quarterly *Partisan Review* in 1964, was an important essay that garnered attention across the media world. It helped Sontag's career, but it also played into the dialogue (and stereotypes) about homosexuality.

Sontag wrote, in part: "The peculiar relation between Camp taste and homosexuality has to be explained. While it's not true that Camp taste *is* homosexual taste, there is no doubt a peculiar affinity and overlap. Not all liberals are Jews, but Jews have shown a peculiar affinity for liberal and reformist causes. So, not all homosexuals have Camp taste. But homosexuals, by and large, constitute the vanguard—and the most articulate audience—of Camp. (The analogy is not frivolously chosen. Jews and homosexuals are the outstanding creative minorities in contemporary urban culture. Creative, that is, in the truest sense: they are creators of sensibilities. The two pioneering forces of modern sensibility are Jewish moral seriousness and homosexual aestheticism and irony.) ...

"Homosexuals have pinned their integration into society on promoting the aesthetic sense. Camp is a solvent of morality. It neutralizes moral indignation, sponsors playfulness. ... Nevertheless, even though homosexuals have been its vanguard, Camp taste is much more than homosexual taste. Obviously, its metaphor of life as theater is peculiarly suited as a justification and projection of a certain aspect of the situation of homosexuals."

Late in life, Sontag and photographer Annie Leibovitz were partners, though their relationship was mostly ignored in the mainstream media—even after Sontag died in 2004.

Getting a 'Life'

It was not a cover story, but it should have been. On June 26, 1964, *Life* magazine did a major story about "Homosexuality in America." It was mainly about white men, but it was still groundbreaking. Its publication date and place were ironic, given the end-of-June 1969 Stonewall rebellion in New York just five years later and its annual commemoration on that date since.

Looking at the issue, it's fun to observe sexist portrayals in the advertising, from the Goodyear Tire ad "When there's no man around" (to change your tire) to a very sexually naughty Rath Wieners ad, "All wieners look alike on the outside, but bite into this one."

The subhead on the *Life* story was: "A secret world grows open and bolder. Society is forced to look at it—and try to understand it." There were several photos with the piece. The main one was captioned: "A San Francisco bar run for and by homosexuals is crowded with patrons who wear leather jackets, make a show of masculinity and scorn effeminate members of their world. Mural shows men in leather." Other photos were from Los Angeles and New York City. They showed an anti-gay bar owner with a now-famous sign, "Fagots [*sic*] - Stay Out."

Two men showed their faces and used their names, Hal Call of the Mattachine Society in San Francisco and Don Slater of *ONE* magazine. Other people nationwide were interviewed as well, including gays in Chicago and Washington, D.C.

While the *Life* stories (there was a second article on medical and scientific issues) were sensational and mostly negative in their portrayal, the simple act of inclusion in such an important national magazine helped bring visibility to the burgeoning gay movement.

The introduction to the articles stated: "Homosexuality shears across the spectrum of American life ... homosexuals are discarding their furtive ways and openly admitting, even flaunting, their deviation."

Paul Welch wrote the main article for the magazine. He started with examples of homosexual life in Greenwich Village, in Chicago's Bughouse Square, and on Hollywood's Selma Avenue. Welch said that while homosexuality is everywhere, it is "most evident in New York, Chicago, Los Angeles, San Francisco, New Orleans and Miami." Welch called San Francisco the "gay capital," with more than 30 gay bars. He described various types of gay bars, including S&M bars for those into sadism and masochism. Yes, in *Life* magazine, in 1964.

Welch gave many examples of gay men, including those who pair off in a "marriage," "sometimes lasting for years."

The Mattachine Society was discussed in the article, including the separate Mattachines in other cities. ONE, Inc., and its magazine, *ONE*, were also mentioned.

Welch pointed out that homosexuals everywhere "fear arrest—and the public exposure that may go with it." He went into detail about the Los Angeles Police Department's relentless pursuit of gays, and he gave an example of one such attempt at entrapment of a gay man.

The article also pointed to the 1957 British Wolfenden Report, which recommended that Britain change its laws so that homosexual behavior between consenting adults would "no longer be a criminal offense." It noted that many of that report's recommendations were adopted by the American Law Institute when it wrote a model penal code (see *Time*'s May 20, 1955, article, noted above) and that in 1961, Illinois "based a redraft of its penal code on the American Law Institute's paper."

Welch recounted an attempt in Florida to ban gays from state employment and noted the same type of effort starting in the early 1950s by the federal government.

The second article in that same issue of *Life* was titled "Scientists search for the answers to a touchy and puzzling question: Why?" and was written by Ernest Havemann. It was full of stereotypes and bad medical research, but it did quote some people from the pro-gay spectrum. It was mostly negative, including citations to those who blamed mothers for their gay sons. Dr. Evelyn Hooker, one of the few open-minded psychologists in those days, was mentioned only briefly.

In that second article, again mostly about men, Havemann dismissed lesbians: "There are also women homosexuals, of course, but the number is much smaller."

Life rarely covered gay issues over the years. But on December 31, 1971, a year before the magazine stopped publishing weekly, it ran the 12-page essay "Homosexuals in Revolt." The essay began: "It was the most shocking and, to most Americans, the most surprising liberation movement yet. Under the slogan 'Out of the closets and into the streets,' thousands of homosexuals, male and female, were proudly confessing what they had long hidden. They were, moreover, moving into direct confrontation with conventional society. Their battle was far from won. But in 1971 militant homosexuals showed they were prepared to fight it … . And while most will admit that 'straight' society's attitudes have caused them unhappiness, they respond to the charge that all homosexuals are guilt-ridden and miserable with the defiant rallying cry 'Gay is Good!'"

Airwaves: TV and Radio News Find the Gays

Television and radio networks have licenses granted by the government's Federal Communications Commission. This means they are under pressure not experienced by publishers of newspapers and magazines, which may explain why the networks were even more reticent about covering homosexual topics in the pre-Stonewall era. They considered themselves "family"-friendly, and they were worried about losing their licenses.

The 1950 formation of the gay Mattachine Society in Los Angeles provided media in that town with some basis for stories about the community during that decade. On April 25, 1954, *Confidential File* on KTTV, hosted by Paul Coates, had a story about the men and women of Mattachine. On the other side of the country, the Mattachine Society's New York chapter President Tony Segura wore a hood on a TV interview for WABD on March 10, 1958. WBAI, a "progressive" and listener-supported FM station in New York, carried a panel of alleged experts on homosexuality in July 1962. They were all non-gays discussing mental illness. *The Columbia Reader on Lesbian and Gay Men in Media, Society, and Politics* reported that Randy Wicker "marched into the station the next day and demanded equal time." Wicker and seven other gay men were given their own 90-minute segment later that month.

The *Times* reported on October 18, 1963, that Wicker, as part of the Homosexual League of New York, addressed a crowd of 350 students on the topic of acceptance of homosexuals, an event sponsored by the WBAI club, which supported WBAI-FM.

In 2012, Wicker was inducted into the National Lesbian & Gay Journalists Association's LGBT Journalists Hall of Fame. In giving Wicker the award, the group said it is believed that on January 31, 1964, "Wicker was the first openly gay person on East Coast television through his appearance on *The Les Crane Show*."

A groundbreaking TV show aired in 1967, the first nationwide network program on gay issues. *The Homosexuals*, an episode of *CBS Reports* on March 7, was anchored by Mike Wallace. It had taken three years for the show to be completed. Two gay men were pictured on-screen, Jack Nichols (using the name Warren Adkins) and Lars Larson, but another man was shown hidden behind a plant. Forty million people saw the horrible stereotypes of homosexuality once again played out in the media.

Previous television shows had aired in local markets, including *The Rejected* on public TV's KQED in San Francisco in 1961. But the CBS program was the first major network show. Wallace said this in his commentary: "The average homosexual, if there be such, is promiscuous. He is not interested or capable of a lasting relationship like that of a heterosexual marriage. His sex life, his love life, consists of a series of one-chance encounters at the clubs and bars he inhabits. And even on the streets of the city—the pickup, the one-night stand, these are characteristics of the homosexual relationship."

Gay author Gore Vidal was also on the episode, debating homosexuality with English professor Albert Goldman. Vidal said: "The United States is living out some mad Protestant 19th-century dream of human behavior … . I think the so-called breaking of the moral fiber of this country is one of the healthiest things that's begun to happen."

Wallace concluded: "The dilemma of the homosexual: told by the medical profession he is sick; by the law that he's a criminal; shunned by employers; rejected by heterosexual society. Incapable of a fulfilling relationship with a woman, or for that matter with a man. At the center of his life he remains anonymous. A displaced person. An outsider."

Lesbians, bisexuals and the transgender must have been even further outside the norm, since they were ignored totally in the program. Some pro-gay materials were edited out of the final version. Even though it was tamed, no advertisers purchased spots on the episode.

In the 1990s, Wallace said he regretted participating in the show, since he did have gay friends when he made it.

Time Lambasted

Time magazine's January 21, 1966, essay titled "The Homosexual in America" was simply horrible.

The essay began: "It used to be 'the abominable crime not to be mentioned.'" It went on to reinforce almost every stereotype about homosexuals (mainly males).

"Beset by inner conflicts, the homosexual is unsure of his position in society, ambivalent about his attitudes and identity—but he gains a certain amount of security through the fact that society is equally ambivalent about him. A vast majority of people retain a deep loathing toward him, but there is a growing mixture of tolerance, empathy or apathy. Society is torn between condemnation and compassion, fear and curiosity, between attempts to turn the problem into a joke and the knowledge that it is anything but funny, between the deviate's plea to be treated just like everybody else and the knowledge that he simply is not like everybody else."

The "homosexual mafia" ("Homintern") influence in the theater, art, design, music and film professions was discussed. Even if some had great talent, *Time* quoted a psychiatrist who thinks most were "failed artists, and their special creative gift a myth."

Time continued: "Today in the U.S., there are 'mixed' bars where all homosexuals, male and female, are persona grata; 'cuff-linky' bars that cater to the college and junior-executive type; 'swish' bars for the effeminates and 'hair fairies' with their careful coiffures; 'TV' bars, which cater not to television fans but to transvestites; 'leather' bars for the tough-guy types with their fondness for chains and belts; San Francisco's new 'Topless Boys' discotheques, featuring bare-chested entertainers. San Francisco and Los Angeles are rivals for the distinction of being the capital of the gay world; the nod probably goes to San Francisco. ...

"The once widespread view that homosexuality is caused by heredity, or by some derangement of hormones, has been generally discarded. The consensus is that it is caused psychically, through a disabling fear of the opposite sex. The origins of this fear lie in the homosexual's parents. The mother—either domineering and contemptuous of the father, or feeling rejected by him—makes her son a substitute for her husband, with a close-binding, overprotective relationship. Thus, she unconsciously demasculinizes him. If at the same time the father is weakly submissive to his wife or aloof and unconsciously competitive with his son, he reinforces the process. ...

"Fear of the opposite sex is also believed to be the cause of Lesbianism, which is far less visible but, according to many experts, no less widespread than male homosexuality—and far more readily tolerated. Both forms are essentially a case of arrested development, a failure of learning, a refusal to accept the full responsibilities of life. This is nowhere more apparent than in the pathetic pseudo marriages in which many homosexuals act out conventional roles—wearing wedding rings, calling themselves 'he' and 'she.'"

While Freud did not believe homosexuality was curable, *Time* noted that many of his successors "are more optimistic. Philadelphia's Dr. Samuel Hadden reported last year that he had achieved twelve conversions out of 32 male homosexuals in group therapy."

Time reported on recent gay organizations and protests, as well as a push against sodomy laws.

The community was outraged at the *Time* piece. Kay Tobin Lahusen wrote a scathing rebuke in the February 1966 edition of *The Ladder*, the publication of the lesbian Daughters of Bilitis group. She reported on a lecture by Isadore Rubin, presented on February 25 to the gay Janus Society in Philadelphia, as a response to the *Time* piece. Rubin, editor of *Sexology* magazine, pointed out the essay's one-sided look at the research on homosexuality. Since the mainstream media were not going to cover all sides of the issue, it was up to *The Ladder* to confront the bias of *Time*. (Lahusen's article is reprinted in *The Columbia Reader on Lesbian and Gay Men in Media, Society, and Politics*.)

Harper's did no better in running an essay by the psychiatrist Dr. Samuel B. Hadden in March 1967, "A Way Out for Homosexuals." He wrote that "homosexuals are deeply troubled people" and he wanted to treat their condition "as a handicapping disorder. And I further believe that society has a right to expect those afflicted to seek treatment, just as we expect the cooperation of the TB patient and his family." It goes on with more dreadful "expert" advice.

Harper's published one letter for and one against the piece in May 1967. Mattachine Society of New York President Dick Leitsch said it was "one of the more reprehensible articles I have ever seen published in *Harper's*." (Harper Lee, author of *To Kill a Mockingbird* and rumored to be a lesbian, also wrote to *Harper's* for that edition, but it was about a different column.)

Also in 1967, the *Los Angeles Times* had a rare neutral item about gays, "Homosexuality to Be Topic," on January 15. It noted that an ACLU forum was being held and speakers included Don Slater, editor of the gay *Tangents* magazine.

Fighting Back

The first efforts to fight against this media homophobia were mainly letters to the editor protesting biased stories in mainstream media (this happened even as early as the 1920s, but more steadily in the 1950s and 1960s). *The New York Times, Life, Time, Newsweek* and others viewed the community through a heterosexist lens, and the gays tried to break through that one-dimensional view.

Public protests by gays began in the 1960s. The first documented picket in the U.S. was organized by Randy Wicker and Craig Rodwell (the latter founded the country's first gay bookstore, the Oscar Wilde Memorial Bookshop, in New York in 1967). On September 9, 1964, a group of 10 people protested in front of the U.S. Army's Whitehall Street Induction Center in Manhattan. There was no mainstream media coverage.

In April 1965, a handful of gays and lesbians from the Mattachine Society of Washington protested outside the White House for the first time. Jack Nichols, Frank Kameny, Barbara Gittings and Kay Tobin Lahusen were among the few brave souls to make history that day. Their protest was in response to rumors that Cuban leader Fidel Castro had sent gays to work camps. The mainstream papers ignored the protest; the only paper to cover it was the *Washington Afro-American*. When protesters returned to the White House on May 29, 1965, there were nine men and three women protesters— and several media. *The New York Times* ran a United Press International wire service story May 30, "Homosexuals Stage Protest in Capital." It is not known why more media covered the second protest.

There were subsequent pickets outside the Civil Service Commission, the Pentagon, and the United Nations in New York, as well as an annual rally in front of Independence Hall in Philadelphia, held every July 4 from 1965 to 1969.

David Sanford wrote "Boxed In" for *The New Republic* magazine on May 21, 1966. It addressed the issues of gays in the military, including the protests by the National Capital Area Civil Liberties Union against the ban.

Ongoing protests against the American Psychiatric Association's classification of homosexuality as an illness were mounted at APA annual conferences starting in the late 1960s. Gittings, Lahusen, Kameny and Nichols were among the activists who confronted the APA. They also took on media who used so-called experts from the APA when writing about gays, and they helped fight from the inside at the annual conventions. They were joined by John E. Fryer, "Dr. H. Anonymous," on a pivotal 1972 panel at the APA's convention. Homosexuality was removed from the *Diagnostic and Statistical Manual of Mental Disorders* the next year. The change was covered nationally by both gay and straight media.

These protests were not uniformly supported even in the homosexual community. Some people did not want to stir the waters and considered public protests as too aggressive.

Perhaps influenced by these very public displays of gays, *The Washington Post* ran a series starting January 31, 1966. "Those Others: A Report on Homosexuality" by Jean M. White did include the voices of some gay people. The *Chicago Sun-Times* was among the newspapers that ran parts of the series.

The start of the series updated readers on the status of the debate about homosexuals: medical, scientific, social, legal and more. Once again, the main focus was on men "because female homosexuality poses less of a social problem." White reviewed the organizations serving gays and said they disown "flaming faggots" who swish along the street. She wrote that most homosexuals "try to pass in the 'straight' hetero-sexual world."

While the *Post* was more positive than most media, the general coverage of homosexuals was still negative.

In New York City, the *Times* also covered the pushback against police harassment and crimes targeting gays. An April 2, 1966, *Times* story, "Garelik Urges Public to Report Trappings of Homosexuals," was about the Police Department's response to charges that officers were entrapping gay men—which was a crime.

On March 3, 1966, the *Times* reported on a "Nationwide Ring Preying on Prominent Deviates." Men pretending to be police were victimizing homosexuals, including some prominent ones. As the *Times* noted: "So brazen is the operation that in one instance gang members, posing as New York City detectives, walked into the Pentagon and walked out with a high officer in the armed services. The man, whom they shook down for several thousand dollars, committed suicide the night before he was scheduled to testify before a New York County grand jury." The man was Rear Admiral William C. Church, a cousin of U.S. Senator Frank Church. The *Times* said more than a thousand victims paid millions of dollars rather than risk arrest and exposure.

In a July 11, 2012, look back at the crime ring, "The Chickens and the Bulls," Slate.com noted that the ring was nationwide:

"In the year following the Western Union arrest, the NYPD and the FBI, working in parallel (and sometimes at odds), would uncover and break a massive gay extortion ring whose viciousness and criminal flair was without precedent. Impersonating corrupt vice-squad detectives, members of this ring, known in police parlance as bulls, had used young, often underage men known as chickens to successfully blackmail closeted pillars of the establishment, among them a navy admiral, two generals, a U.S. congressman, a prominent surgeon, an Ivy League professor, a prep school headmaster, and several well-known actors, singers, and television personalities. The ring had operated for almost a decade, had victimized thousands, and had taken in at least $2 million. When he announced in 1966 that the ring had been broken up, Manhattan DA Frank Hogan said the victims had all been shaken down 'on the threat that their homosexual proclivities would be exposed unless they paid for silence.'

"Though now almost forgotten, the case of 'the Chickens and the Bulls' as the NYPD called it (or 'Operation Homex,' to the FBI), still stands as the most far-flung, most organized, and most brazen example of homosexual extortion in the nation's history. And while the Stonewall riot in June 1969 is considered by many to be the pivotal moment in gay civil rights, this case represents an important crux too, marking the first time that the law enforcement establishment actually worked on behalf of victimized gay men, instead of locking them up or shrugging."

Midwestern Values

Chicago's Mattachine Midwest was getting itself into the news in the mid-1960s—and it was monitoring anti-gay (and pro-gay) media representations in its *Mattachine Midwest Newsletter*.

The newsletter is a treasure trove of facts about police harassment, media coverage and community news. The group hosted a conference in November 1965, which prompted the respected journalist Irv Kupcinet to do a program, "The Homosexual Movement in America," on his televised *Kup's Show.* Other media also covered the conference.

The next summer, perhaps the first large series on Chicago's gay community ran, but it was not a positive picture of the community. Award-winning reporter Lois Wille's *Chicago Daily News* four-part series, "Chicago's Twilight World," started on June 20, 1966. She wrote: "Big cities act like lodestars, drawing homosexuals who can't hide their deviancy in small towns." It was only about white male homosexuals.

Author and historian John D'Emilio wrote the following for *Windy City Times* on July 9, 2008, about that 1966 series:

"In the series, a judge described homosexuals as 'sick people.' James O'Grady, the police lieutenant in charge of the anti-prostitution detail (who was to become police chief briefly in 1978), talked about 'fag bars' and 'queers.' The doctor who directed the municipal court's psychiatric unit referred to homosexuality as 'socially distasteful.' The reporter described gay men as 'disturbed' and as 'deviates.'

"The headlines and section headers that the *Daily News* employed were just as bad: 'Twilight World That's Tormented'; 'Cops Keep Watch on Deviate Hangouts'; 'Homosexuality a Sickness? '"No" Say the Deviates'; 'His Bizarre Double Life.'

"But our contemporary eyes are not the best ones for judging how these articles were viewed at the time. In the context of 1966, they represented progress, a journalistic opening wedge of sorts. Why? Because tormented and deviate and disturbed and affliction were not the only points of view expressed in the series. I wouldn't go as far as to say the articles displayed balance—if by balance we mean equal weight to anti-gay and pro-gay sentiments. But it is definitely true that the reporter, Lois Wille (who had already won a Pulitzer Prize for a 1963 series on refusal to provide contraceptive services to poor women), allowed dissenting opinions to be heard. She found ways to insinuate that there was more than one viewpoint about homosexuality. She thus gave legitimacy to a debate about homosexuality where, before, there was nothing but a negative consensus. ...

"Wille held public policy up for criticism, too. A major topic in the series was police behavior. She wrote at length about the crackdown against gay bars, the raids and the closings, and the mass arrests. But Lieutenant O'Grady's defense of police activity did not go unchallenged. Wille interviewed Pearl Hart, whom she described as a lawyer with 52 years of practice in civil liberties law. Hart called police conduct unethical and said the raids and arrests were a waste of time and taxpayers' money. 'It just doesn't make sense to go after homosexuals,' she told Wille."

Wille, reached in 2012, said "I cringe at the words" used in those early reports about the gay community.

After a summer of more police raids and more naming of names in the newspapers, as well as a refusal by some papers to take ads for their organization, members of Chicago's Mattachine Midwest had reached their boiling point. In September and October 1966, there were gay protests outside the *Chicago Daily News* and the *Chicago Sun-Times.*

The New York Times continued to cover gays. On January 23, 1966, "Homosexual Drama and Its Disguises" was published. It was about the cultural influence of gays. The daughter of the paper's founder was not amused. Iphigene Sulzberger wanted homosexuals off the front pages of her family-friendly paper. The edict was taken very seriously and it negatively influenced the paper's coverage of the community for many years.

Just a few months before the Stonewall rebellion, *The New York Times* published an essay by a gay man, "Why Can't 'We' Live Happily Ever After, Too?" It was written by Donn Teal, using the name Ronald Forsythe, and ran on February 23, 1969. It was on the front page of the culture section. He said he was tired of all the negative images of gay people in the media, from murders to suicides.

The paper asked him for another column on the cast album for *The Boys in the Band*, and that ran on June 1, 1969, under Teal's real name. In it he said self-hate was no longer the style of the homosexuals.

A few weeks later, during a summer of many bar raids, Teal was proved very right.

Game Changer: Stonewall

The rebellion against police harassment of people who were going to gay bars came to a boil in late June 1969, inside and outside the Stonewall bar in New York City. The reports were buried deep in the pages of *The New York Times* and other media, and even the liberal *Village Voice* used derogatory gay language ("the forces of faggotry")—and then refused to run an advertisement with the word "gay" in it. On June 30, the *Times* reported on the second night of outrage, "Police Again Rout 'Village' Youths, Outbreak by 400 Follows a Near-Riot Over Raid."

But gays across the country were finding their news from other sources—*The Advocate* and the growing number of gay periodicals and groups. The number of gay papers dramatically increased after Stonewall. (See Chapter 2.)

The protests against media bias took more frequently to the streets in the post-1969 era. The Stonewall rebellion in New York that year rode the wave of 1960s civil-rights and feminist protests and carried with it the burgeoning gay activist community.

The Gay Liberation Front in New York was an in-your-face activist group that took on the media, police and any other institution that got in its way. The group soon split in two, with the Gay Activists Alliance taking a more structured approach to seeking equality.

Morris Kight led in forming a GLF group in Los Angeles. Kight joined with several members of the Homosexual Information Center in a November 5, 1969, *Los Angeles Times* picket. The *Times* published a story about it the next day, "Homosexual Unit Pickets The Times." Activists were upset that the paper would not carry ads for HIC. The Times-Mirror Company issued a statement saying it had a right to refuse ads that do not "meet the standards of acceptability."

The *Chicago Sun-Times* ran two stories in its December 1969 *Midwest Magazine*. One was titled "The Homosexuals: A Newly Visible Minority," and the other was an interview with three anonymous gay men, "Three Speak Out on Harassment, Parents, Analysts and Girls."

Time Revisits Homosexuals in America

Time addressed homosexuality again, this time in a cover story on October 31, 1969—after the Stonewall rebellion. The cover-story kicker words were "The Homosexual in America," the same as the title of the magazine's 1966 article. The main photo was from the same photographer who illustrated the *Life* series five years earlier—and appears even to be from that same set of photos. As if the writer were Margaret Mead on a trip to Samoa in the early 20th century, *Time* wrote about homosexuality at a clear distance. The article was titled "The Homosexual: Newly Visible, Newly Understood."

"Though they still seem fairly bizarre to most Americans," the article said, "homosexuals have never been so visible ... . [Male] and female inverts have been organizing to claim civil rights for themselves as an aggrieved minority." The article listed gay organizations and recent court cases and protests, including the Stonewall uprising. It even defined "fag hags."

Time also made note of then-recent gay theatrical plotlines, including those of Mart Crowley's *The Boys in the Band* and films such as *Staircase*, *Midnight Cowboy* and *Satyricon* and the lesbian films *The Fox*, *Thérèse and Isabelle* and *The Killing of Sister George*. *Time* even wondered if there were a "homosexual conspiracy afoot to dominate the arts and other fields." Despite this, *Time* warned that most straights "still regard the invert with a mixture of revulsion and apprehension, to which some authorities have given the special diagnostic name of homosexual panic."

Time then went on to categorize the "homosexual types." One of them was the blatant homosexual, "the eunuch-like caricature of femininity that most people associate with homosexuality." His lesbian counterpart "is the 'butch,' the girl who is aggressively masculine to the point of trying to look like a man." The next was "the secret lifer," hidden from most of society, passing as straight. Other categories: The desperate, the adjusted, the bisexual and the situational-experimental. The piece went into detail about the popular and professional views of homosexuality.

The lives of four people were profiled in a sidebar to the *Time* piece: one gay man, one lesbian, one bisexual, and one person who claimed to be a former homosexual. All four used pseudonyms.

Perhaps most important in the *Time* special section was a sidebar featuring eight people, with their faces and names, discussing homosexuality. Some were anti-gay psychologists, but it also included two "admitted homosexuals" as part of a panel discussion in New York City. *Time* put the symposium together. Included were Wardell Pomeroy, who was a co-author of the Kinsey reports on men and women; anti-gay Dr. Charles Socarides; the Reverend Robert Weeks, an Episcopal priest who allowed gay groups to meet at his church; Mattachine Society of New York Executive Director Dick Leitsch; Mattachine Society of Washington President Franklin Kameny; sociologist John Gagnon; anthropologist Robin Fox; and sociologist Lionel Tiger. (All of them were white men.)

Socarides at one point called for gay rights but also labeled homosexuality an emotional illness, "which can be treated, that these people can be helped."

Kameny responded: "With that, you will surely destroy us."

GLF in New York was outraged at the coverage and organized a protest on November 12, 1969, at the Time-Life Building. Daughters of Bilitis members joined the few dozen from GLF.

Feminist Backlash

Feminists were also fighting back against media bias in this era, and many of those feminists were also lesbians. Their efforts resulted in better coverage of women and inclusion of lesbians in at least some of the mainstream stories of the gay community. *Ms.* magazine, founded in 1971 (first as an insert in *New York* magazine, later as a stand-alone, in 1972), was certainly a response to the lack of adequate coverage of women in the mainstream, but mainstream changes were still necessary.

In her memoir *Tales of the Lavender Menace*, Karla Jay writes about actions she participated in, including one she organized March 18, 1970, against *The Ladies' Home Journal* for its stereotypical portrayals of women (demonstrators were also angry with representations in all "women's magazines").

About 200 activists from several groups (including Media Women, New York Radical Feminists, NOW and Redstockings) held a successful 11-hour sit-in and were later paid $10,000 to produce a supplement for the *Journal*. They later distributed those funds to women's causes. In her memoir, Karla Jay said she believes the *Ladies' Home Journal* sit-in was "the most successful one-day action taken by the Women's Liberation Movement." A short time after their protest, on March 23, 1970, 46 women at *Newsweek* filed a sexual-discrimination lawsuit against that magazine. (Lynn Povich documents the *Newsweek* battle in her 2012 book *The Good Girls Revolt: How the Women of Newsweek Sued Their Bosses and Changed the Workplace.*)

The nine-page *Ladies' Home Journal* supplement ran in the August 1970 issue. The first page was a letter from Editor and Publisher John Mack Carter. In it, he briefed readers about what happened earlier that year. "You may find this New Feminism section enlightening, or baffling, or infuriating," he wrote. "It is an unusual section produced in an unusual manner." It was done by a collective and no one used a byline. Articles addressed work, education, having babies, unvalued women's work at home, marriage problems, women's beauty issues, women and sex (mostly straight, but a mention of lesbians), starting a consciousness-raising group, and women's resources and publications across the country (including *off our backs* newspaper).

Contrary to the (still) prevailing attitude that the women's movement did not care about women who did housework or about those juggling work and home life, the liberationists introduced their section by clearly showing their alliance with issues all women face. Their push for day care centers at work was especially strong. They asked the magazine to hire nonwhite women in proportion to their numbers in society. They sought to have a base minimum wage.

This was truly a Stonewall-like moment for the women's liberation movement, one fought for in the offices of a traditional woman's magazine.

McCall's women's magazine ran an article, "What Makes a Homosexual?" (as if some cause was known) in 1971, and it was picked up for the *Reader's Digest* in September of that year. (In 2000, lesbian performer Rosie O'Donnell became editorial director at *McCall's*, and the next year it was renamed *Rosie*. The magazine folded in 2002, and there was a lawsuit between O'Donnell and the publisher; it was eventually dismissed by a judge.)

On December 18, 1970, *The New York Times* ran "The Lesbian Issue and Women's Lib," with this choice lead: "The Lesbian issue, which has been hidden away like a demented child ever since the women's liberation movement came into being in 1966, was brought out of the closet yesterday." The news of the day involved women's movement leaders and activists who were standing by the homosexual movement. They were responding to a *Time* magazine article of December 14 that said *Sexual Politics* author Kate Millett (who had been good enough to be the magazine's cover girl a few months before, on August 31) "discredited herself as a spokeswoman for her cause" by coming out as a bisexual.

Millett read a statement prepared by Daughters of Bilitis, the National Organization for Women, Radical Lesbians and Columbia Women's Liberation. Among those standing with Millett were Gloria Steinem, DOB's Ruth Simpson, Florence Kennedy, author Susan Brownmiller, and NOW members Ivy Bottini, Dolores Alexander and Ti-Grace Atkinson, according to the *Times*. Kennedy, the only African-American leader there, called for a "girlcott" of *Time* magazine advertisers. U.S. Representative-elect Bella Abzug sent a letter of support.

The same *New York Times* writer, Judy Klemesrud, wrote a lengthy article about the DOB on March 28, 1971. The feature was an important piece to have in the *Times*, but it contained phrases like "mannish-looking women" and lots of descriptions of what people were wearing and whether they were pretty. The news hook was the opening of a lesbian center in the lower Village neighborhood. But the reporter quoted "experts" about lesbianism, including one psychiatrist who said such women were "very troubled individuals."

Women's movement leader Betty Friedan was quoted in the DOB piece as speaking about that press conference the previous December, which she called a "terrible mistake. … I don't think we should have a sexual red herring diverting us." The *Times* quoted one anonymous leader as saying "lesbians actually prey on lonely and confused women who are new to the movement."

At the end of the piece, the reporter changed to a first-person analysis of the women she met. She admitted that the kissing she saw disgusted her at first but then said she did not believe the women should face discrimination.

But at least the lesbians had a voice in the New York media—at *The Village Voice*, where longtime columnist Jill Johnston came out in a July 2, 1970, column.

Harping on Homophobia

A year after Stonewall, *Harper's Magazine* ran a particularly egregious cover essay in September 1970, "Homo/Hetero: The Struggle for Sexual Identity," by Joseph Epstein, a Chicago-born writer and later a Northwestern University faculty member. In it he said the worst thing his four sons could be would be homosexual. He also said if he had the power to, "I would wish homosexuality off the face of the earth." The Gay Activists Alliance in New York occupied the magazine's offices for a day in protest on October 27, 1970. One of the organizers, Peter Fisher, emphasized to the staff: "There's been a revolution!"

The essay did note some of the accomplishments of homosexuals, in the old vein of stereotyping some as very cultured. If the piece had run in the 1950s, it might even have been welcomed for some of its thoughtful insights, despite some negative opinions:

"[In] discrete but significant instances, as everyone knows, homosexuals have been responsible for some of the most magnificent works we have—it has seemed of recent years not merely commonplace but dominant. *Camp*, a Susan Sontag production, was in its origin wholly a homosexual phenomenon. Leslie Fiedler, in *Love and Death in the American Novel*, has instructed us that the great American novelists form one long daisy chain of failed queers while the principal preoccupation of our national literature has been a disguised (but obsessive) homosexuality. As recently as five years ago, Philip Roth wrote an attack on Edward Albee the main argument of which was that homosexual writers ought to stop concealing their true subject—homosexuality—in elaborate and guileful metaphors, and deal with it openly and directly. … In the middle and latter part of the Sixties, the novels and plays of James Baldwin, a writer of major talent, began to mix the themes of blackness and homosexuality till it became somewhat unclear which of the two was really the chief source of Baldwin's eloquent rage."

Epstein called attention to then-recent comments about "the new homosexuality" by Tom Burke in the December 1969 *Esquire* magazine. "The new homosexual of the Seventies [is] an unfettered, guiltless male child of the new morality in a Zapata moustache and an outlaw hat, who couldn't care less for Establishment approval, would as soon sleep with boys as girls … ."

Epstein inflicted his own bias against the gays, believing them cursed. He wrote: "One can tolerate homosexuality, a small enough price to be asked to pay for someone else's pain, but accepting it, really accepting it, is another thing altogether. I find I can accept it least of all when I look at my children. There is much my four sons can do in their lives that might cause me anguish, that might outrage me, that might make me ashamed of them and of myself as their father. But nothing they could ever do would make me sadder than if any of them were to become homosexual. For then I should know them condemned to a state of permanent niggerdom among men, their lives, whatever adjustment they might make to their condition, to be lived out as part of the pain of the earth."

The November 1970 letters section of *Harper's* was filled with responses to the essay from across the country. One was from a member of Boston's Gay Liberation Front. Epstein was allowed a response to his critics, and his supporters. (Epstein declined comment for this book.)

The *Harper's* homophobia had an unexpected positive consequence. Famed writer Merle Miller, a former *Harper's* editor, came out because of the protests. He submitted a historically important essay that ran in *The New York Times Magazine* of January 17, 1971, "What It Means To Be a Homosexual." (It was later published in a book, with additional material. It was re-issued in 2012.) Decades later this essay is cited as a groundbreaking first-person look at homosexuality that was published in the nation's most important daily newspaper.

Miller explored the ways gays are treated, even in polite circles. One pull quote says it all: "A 'fag' is a homosexual gentleman who has just left the room." Miller talked about the damage of his own closet. He served on the board of the ACLU, which stood silent when gays were fired from government jobs in the 1950s. "And the most silent of all was a closet queen who was a member of the board of directors, myself." The article was about his childhood and young adulthood, trying to find his way in a heterosexual world. It was a wonderful, important essay in a major national newspaper. And it ended on a positive note: "… I would not choose to be anyone else … ."

Thousands of people wrote in to the *Times* in response to Miller's brave essay.

Gays in New York protested a lot in the early 1970s—because there was a lot to protest against.

Arthur Bell of the Gay Activists Alliance wrote for the new gay activist press, but also for *The Village Voice*, covering protests he helped stage. Bell was fine with balancing activism and journalism. He was arrested at an April 1972 hundreds-strong protest at the New York *Daily News* for its editorializing against gays.

On July 26, 1971, *The New York Times* ran a feature, "Christopher Street: From Farm to Gay Center," two years post-Stonewall. It was a partial census of the businesses and landmarks on the street, with a map and interviews of straight and gay people. The article started with news about a protest of the "exploitation by the syndicate" (Mafia) of bars for gays. "Their chief targets were Christopher's End ... and the club's proprietor, Michael Umbers, whom the Gay Activists Alliance calls 'a front man for the syndicate.'" There was a large photo of Umbers confronting protesters. The group also asked the city to turn the infamous Women's House of Detention into a community center.

Taking on Cronkite and Royko

On December 11, 1973, the Gay Raiders, represented by Harry Langhorne and Mark Segal (two years before he launched *Philadelphia Gay News*, in January 1976), famously protested inadequate gay coverage on the *CBS Evening News with Walter Cronkite*. Douglas Brinkley's book *Cronkite* details the incident: The duo "interrupted a Cronkite broadcast, causing the screen to go black for a few seconds. ... Segal leapt in front of the camera carrying a yellow sign that read, 'Gays Protest CBS Prejudice.' More than sixty million Americans were watching. ...

"But both Segal and Langhorne were charged with second-degree criminal trespassing ... . Segal had previously raided *The Tonight Show*, the *Today* show, and *The Mike Douglas Show*. At Segal's trial on April 23, 1974, Cronkite, who had accepted a subpoena, took his place on the witness stand. ... When the court recessed ... Segal felt a tap on his back—it was Cronkite, holding a fresh pad of yellow-lined paper, ready to take notes with a sharp pencil.

"'Why,' Cronkite asked the activist with genuine curiosity, 'did you do that?'"

After Segal rattled off a list of complaints, Cronkite seemed impressed. Brinkley wrote: "Cronkite asked to meet privately with him to better understand how CBS might cover gay pride events. ... Before long, Cronkite ran gay-rights segments on the CBS News broadcast with almost drumbeat regularity. ... Not only did Cronkite speak out about gay rights, but he also became a reliable friend to the LGBTQ community."

On May 6, 1974, Cronkite did a major segment on gay rights, according to author Edward Alwood in his book *Straight News: Gays, Lesbians, and the News Media*.

Other early media activism efforts included the monitoring of anti-gay coverage in *The New York Times*, *Time* magazine, *Newsweek*, the *Chicago Tribune*, and other print media, plus radio, television and film. Gay pioneers often were interviewed in the shadows on TV shows, while a few brave souls showed their faces and used their real names.

A homophobic slip by the *Los Angeles Times* on April 27, 1975, resulted in a *Times* reporter fighting from the inside to make changes. It was an innocuous Cecil Smith review of the new cop TV show, "Barney Miller: A Cop Who Copes with Funny Folks." Smith pointed to the "thieves and con men and hookers and flashers and gunsels, the faggots and fauna ... ."

In his book *Straight News*, Alwood recounts what happened next. Entertainment reporter Gregg Kilday wrote a six-page letter to his editors at the *Times*, speaking about being a homosexual himself and his own frustration with how slowly the *Times* was changing. While some editors were sympathetic, Alwood said others suggested Kilday "butt out"—or they ignored him.

Also in 1975, same-sex marriage percolated up from Colorado to national prominence in *The New York Times*, which covered marriages allowed by the county clerk's office in Boulder. In its April 27 edition, the *Times* reported on the controversial move and looked at the legal issues surrounding the marriage battle—two decades before the issue would gain traction in the mainstream. The *Times* recapped previous marriage attempts, including "the most important" in Minnesota in 1971, "when two men attempting to get a marriage license were turned down by the state's highest court." Early in 1975 a Phoenix gay male couple had gotten a license that was soon revoked.

Anita Bryant: Save Our Homophobes

The anti-gay crusades of Anita Bryant, an orange-juice spokeswoman and former beauty queen, caused uproar in the gay community and gay media and resulted in increased coverage of gay issues. Her 1977 "Save Our Children" campaign overturned the gay-rights law in Dade County, Florida (it had just passed earlier that year). The media also covered other anti-gay legislative efforts across the country—and the campaigns of an openly gay man, Harvey Milk, to be elected a San Francisco supervisor. He was not the first openly gay person to be elected, but he was the highest-profile.

The New York Times reported on June 8, 1977: "Miami Vote Increases Activism on Homosexual Rights." Gays protested Bryant appearances across the country, and parts of the community called for a boycott of Florida orange juice because Bryant was the industry's spokeswoman. (The gay community was split on whether to boycott, in part based on her right to free speech, a sentiment that was echoed in 2012 when the community debated the best response to the unbridled homophobia of the Chick-fil-A restaurant chain's leadership.)

Anita Bryant successfully framed herself as the victim in the eyes of many mainstream reporters. *Time* magazine wrote "The Gaycott Turns Ugly: Homosexual militants are tormenting foe Anita Bryant," on November 21, 1977: "She has received death threats—and been socked in the face with a banana cream pie. When she showed up in Manhattan to tape an appearance for the *Today* show, NBC was so worried for her safety that guards spirited her out of the building after the performance. She called off a press conference at the nearby Hilton Hotel because of warnings that hostile demonstrators would be in the streets. Appearing in St. Petersburg, Fla., last week, she had to change hotels for security reasons. The victim is Singer Anita Bryant, 37 ... ."

Media Monitoring

While many activists and grassroots groups picketed, wrote about and sent letters against media bias, a more formal effort began in the 1970s to monitor media bias.

The Gay Media Project in Philadelphia operated for a few years in the 1970s. It started as a response to homophobic coverage at the *Philadelphia Inquirer*. The Gay Media Task Force started in Los Angeles.

Gay Media Action formed in Boston in the 1970s, and the Lesbian and Gay Media Advocates started after the 100,000-strong 1979 March on Washington for Lesbian and Gay Rights. Activists were upset that the march received so little mainstream media coverage, especially in LGMA's hometown of Boston. They started meeting with mainstream media representatives to seek a change. In 1982 Lesbian and Gay Media Advocates published *Talk Back! The Gay Person's Guide to Media Action.* The handbook discussed the history of media activism and then provided extensive practical advice.

LGMA said its efforts in Boston had been successful. In *Take Back!*, LGMA said one of the earliest attempts at gay media activism took place in Los Angeles in 1952, when "in a three-page letter, the media was invited to attend the trial of Dale Jennings, an original Mattachine member who had been arrested on a soliciting charge. Of course, no media representatives attended, but at least a step had been made in trying to get fair coverage of a gay man's life."

The National Gay Task Force, formed in New York in 1973, made media monitoring a critical part of its work. Founders included Dr. Howard Brown, Barbara Gittings, Frank Kameny, Dr. Bruce Voeller and the Reverend Robert Carter. The group's name eventually changed to the National Gay and Lesbian Task Force.

The New York Times reported on October 27, 1973, that officials at NBC "acknowledged that the network had at times dealt unfairly with homosexuals in its programs, and they agreed to maintain a continuing liaison with homosexual organizations for advice in future treatment of homosexual topics." The agreement was between NBC and four representatives from the Task Force. The meeting had been planned before Mark Segal disrupted the *Today* show a few days prior to its being held. Segal's protest was in response to a homophobic episode of *Sanford and Son.*

Ronald Gold worked on media issues for the Task Force in the 1970s. He helped review a pending episode of ABC's *Marcus Welby, M.D.* that linked pedophilia with homosexuality. "The Outrage" episode aired October 8, 1974. While some sensational elements had been changed, it was not enough to satisfy activists.

Loretta Lotman, as part of Gay Media Action in Boston, had organized what became the first nationwide protest campaign against a network show. Gold focused on advertisers, according to *Straight News* author Edward Alwood, while Lotman worked the grassroots. Seven sponsors pulled out, including Colgate-Palmolive, Lipton, Breck and Gillette. *The New York Times* reported on the controversy September 28: "2 Stations Reject 'Welby' Episode." Eventually, 17 affiliates also pulled the show, the first time a major TV network experienced such a loss, according to Alwood.

The Task Force's Voeller told the *Times* the *Welby* episode would "have a chilling effect on legislation which would protect gays from discrimination in employment and housing."

Take Back! reports: "Members of the gay community met with representatives of the major networks, the Writers and Directors Guilds, and the Association of Motion Picture and Television Producers. The National Gay Task Force and others organized the Gay Media Task Force in Hollywood and, after much struggle, all three networks began consulting with this group about scripts involving gay men and lesbians."

The mere fact of some success against ABC doesn't mean the networks changed much. NBC aired a *Police Woman* episode November 8, 1974, about lesbian killers. Lesbian Feminist Liberation protested at NBC in New York.

Lotman's short time working on media matters included a stint at the Task Force, and in 1975 she was the first openly gay person to address the National Association of Television Program Executives. By 1976, more-positive gay characters started to appear on TV shows. Alwood said most protests were effective in getting a change in script or in the time at which the show would be aired.

The *ABC News Closeup* series aired "Homosexuals" in December 1979, the first network show on gays since the 1967 CBS report. It was full of stereotypes but did include gay voices. It aired December 18, with no sponsors willing to risk being associated with the program—and with several affiliates refusing to carry the show.

Take Back! also reported on a 1980 CBS documentary about San Francisco's gay male community, *Gay Power, Gay Politics.* The distortions and stereotypes were so awful that many called CBS to complain. But San Francisco journalist Randy Alfred went further. He documented all 44 problems with the show in a 20-page complaint to the National News Council. "The Council found that CBS had indeed been unfair in numerous respects," according to *Take Back!*

Forward, March

The image of Air Force Technical Sergeant Leonard Matlovich on the cover of *Time* magazine was perhaps one of the most important and iconic magazine covers for the 1970s gay movement. The September 8, 1975, headline, "I Am A Homosexual," foreshadowed Ellen DeGeneres' coming out on *Time*'s cover 22 years later, on April 14, 1997, stating "Yep, I'm Gay."

Matlovich was fighting to stay in the U.S. military, and his story was picked up across the country, including extensive coverage in the gay media. The gay community held fundraisers to help with his living expenses while he waged his battle.

Time reported of Matlovich in 1975: "Addressing a Gay Pride Week rally in New York in June, he broke down and cried. Says he: 'I found myself, little nobody me, standing up in front of tens of thousands of gay people. And just two years ago I thought I was the only gay in the world. It was a mixture of joy and sadness. It was just great pride to be an American, to know I'm oppressed but able to stand up there and say so. They were very beautiful people out there.'"

Another story about gays in that issue of *Time* looked at "Gays on the March," starting with the story of 300 homosexuals taking a cruise together. "Since homosexuals began to organize for political action six years ago, they have achieved a substantial number of victories," *Time* told its readers. There were some classic clichés, such as "Publicly, at least, lesbianism is far less flamboyant than male homosexuality, with less promiscuity and more stable relationships," but it was certainly more inclusive of diverse opinions than previous *Time* articles on gays.

Chicago Media Open Up

There were at least three 1970s series in Chicago papers that attempted to bring readers up-to-date on homosexuality. The first was in *Chicago Today* in June 1972, by Barbara Ettorre. The series started in the women's section, though it was about men and women. It included people of color as well. "Homosexuals cry out for acceptance" was the headline on the June 25 first article. It opened with brief profiles of three people, using their real names. Ettorre noted that homosexuals are misunderstood and mistrusted, but they are "fighting back." Separate stories focused on the issues facing gay men and lesbians. The series provided an excellent view of the complex issues and people involved in the movement.

Ettorre, who is not gay, spoke about the series 40 years later for this book. She said she did not recall if she initiated it or if it was assigned to her. *Chicago Today* was an afternoon paper owned by the larger and more conservative *Chicago Tribune*. She was not aware of gay colleagues at *Today*, except for Bruce Vilanch, who was very out. (Ettorre went with Vilanch to one of Bette Midler's early shows in Chicago.) And it was a few years before her own sister came out to her. "I had a couple of gay friends in Chicago, so it was not as if I was uncomfortable," she said. "I was naïve and didn't know much about [gays], but I did not have active antipathy." Ettorre said the reporters were doing so much writing back then that it was "move on and forget," so she had not thought much about the series until she reviewed it for our interview.

"Even as I read it, it is so florid, and concentrated on the 'secret shame', etc. We were really very unevolved back then," she said. "I'm glad that I wrote it. I did get a couple of nasty calls, calling me cunt, bitch, etc., that were upsetting. I had to report it to the editor."

Chicago Sun-Times writer and editor John Teets was part of a mid-1970s series on gays, and he later came out as a gay man himself. The weeklong series was in the summer of 1977. The writing team was Roy Larson, the religion editor, a former Methodist minister; Pat Anstett, a general-assignment reporter who came to the *Sun-Times* when her Detroit home paper went on a long strike; and Teets, who had just been appointed to the editorial page. Local gays and lesbians featured in the series included attorney Renee Hanover and activist William B. Kelley.

Teets said in a 2012 interview that he thinks the series was Anstett's idea. "I remember that we wanted to let readers know that lesbians and gay men were, as somebody put it, about as diverse as people who, say, drink coffee: every station, every profession, every problem and joy that you'd find in the straight world; but that they largely navigated that world in the face of immense discrimination," Teets said. "We wrote about gay clergy, homeless kids, social workers, lawyers, businesspeople, rights activists—only some of them 'out' and willing to be named or photographed. ...

"One was a fairly long profile of Renee, which was nifty because we could tell her own story, as well as anecdotes about some of her clients' travails and victories in a legal system that was demonstrably loaded against lesbians and gays. She relished the battle and was a fantastic guide through lesbian Chicago nightlife. The other was an almost Hunter Thompson–esque profile of Chuck Renslow, highlighting his business empire by way of a Saturday-night tour with him, place to place, from the Gold Coast and Machine Shop to the Man's Country baths and the disco at Center Stage, with peripheral glimpses of the White Party at his home in the Swedish Engineers Society mansion. Those were both great fun to report, and almost as much fun to write."

Teets was dating a woman when he wrote the series. "My reverse gaydar must have been on high beam. On one of my nights with Renslow, on the way out of Man's Country, he had the desk guy (possibly Gary Chichester) give me a membership card, offhandedly saying I might use it someday. I did, later that year, driving home late from a birthday dinner the girlfriend had made for me. I met Robert [his partner Robert Rymer] that night, and the rest is history.

"In retrospect, I'm glad I was not 'publicly' gay just for the ammunition it would have given such low-lifes as Joe Scheidler, the anti-abortion zealot. There were others, but he stands out in vile relief. He ran a recorded phone hotline that advocated all sorts of nagging activism by right-to-lifers, including pleas to call media types like me, complete with office and home numbers. Somehow he found out I was adopted, and made that a supposed self-hating argument about my support for women's rights to choose. The calls were disgusting and disheartening. I can't begin to think of what he would have done with the information that I'm queer, too."

Teets certainly walked a fine line as both an activist in the growing movement and an editorial writer. He even marched in a Chicago anti–Anita Bryant protest in 1977. "It was in those years that I latched onto the [National Gay Task Force] and the nascent gay-rights campaign in Springfield—the Illinois Gay [Rights] Task Force—as human-rights causes every bit as valid as the fights against apartheid or for equality for women. Reporting those issues, I had the great good fortune to meet Bill Kelley and Renee C. Hanover and was inspired by their persistence and courage, not to mention the rightness of their cause," Teets said.

He came out at the paper in 1978. "Sometime in 1979 or 1980, Randy Curwen of the *Tribune*'s features department called me on the QT—the rivalry and often enmity between our papers was huge—and asked me to meet with a group of gay *Tribune* staffers (as I recall, they were all men) to discuss coming out in the workplace. We met in Randy's apartment, with maybe a dozen *Trib* staffers present. They seemed completely cowed by their management and feared losing their jobs if they were at all out at work."

Teets left the *Sun-Times* when Rupert Murdoch took over in 1984, and he eventually worked for seven years in the *Tribune* "bureaucracy," as he calls it.

In September 1979, Lynn Sweet and Abe Peck addressed the topic again for the *Sun-Times*, with an in-depth series featuring photos of gays and lesbians, captioned "Gay in Chicago: A diverse minority is 'coming out'—and coming of age." It also included people of color and was an excellent overview of the city's growing gay and lesbian movement. The writers even did an undercover investigation of housing bias against gays, showing discrimination they experienced firsthand. The series was a far cry from the story published in the *Sun-Times*' Sunday supplement *Midwest Magazine* 10 years earlier, on December 14, 1969, when some of the same old medical definitions, and treatments, were discussed.

Peck, who had come to the mainstream media after working at *The Seed* underground newspaper, said in a 2012 interview that he does not remember if he and Sweet sought the assignment or if it was handed to them. He said the stories were framed from the straight perspective, given their audience. "Lynn and I didn't advocate in the story, but we were gay-friendly in our own politics," said Peck, who also pointed out that one of his sons, born two years after the series ran, is now an out gay man. "My son never even had to come out; he's very postmodern that way."

Peck noted that one piece he wrote never made it into print. It was an interview with a street hustler, about that subculture. Its nonpublication may have been because it would have stereotyped the gay community in a damaging way. Peck said it would be as if an article on prostitution were to be included in a story on "straight" Chicago. Peck recalled no pushback on the series from management or the community, except that he said some activists called it "mild."

The alternative weekly *Chicago Reader* newspaper did a special feature on gays on November 2, 1972, "'Sexual Orientation' at City Hall," looking at bias faced by gays across the city, including arrests for cross-dressing, and the push for a city gay-rights law. It was the first of several *Reader* cover stories on gays over the years.

(In the early 1980s, the *Tribune* once again looked in-depth at the gay and lesbian community, this time for its City Trib section. The main story, "Dollars, votes promote gay power" by Barbara Mahany, ran March 4, 1983. On an interesting side note, the City Trib was edited by long-time *Tribune* staffer Steve Pratt, who was my stepfather and who was very accepting of my coming out to him just a couple of years earlier, while I was in college. When I graduated in 1984, I started work at *GayLife* newspaper and briefly freelanced for the *Tribune*, writing innocuous stories such as safety tips for space heaters and about recreational sports leagues.)

Also in the Windy City, famed columnist Mike Royko upset the gays in two *Chicago Daily News* columns. On March 22, 1974, he did a satirical column about the "Banana Lib Movement," called "Going Bananas Over Liberation." It was about the right to love monkeys. The Chicago Gay Alliance picketed the paper March 28, but Royko refused to apologize and wrote a second column the same day, "There'll Be No Apology."

The Chicago Gay Crusader reported on the angry response to Royko. It said the column "recast every objective of the gay movement in man-monkey terms, perhaps to indicate how ridiculous Royko feels the movement is." Activist William B. Kelley called for gay people across the country to send a banana or banana peel to Royko's office. (During his 1994 arrest for drunk driving, Royko called the police "fag" and "queer," among other epithets.)

Chicago gays also protested against nationally syndicated advice columnist Ann Landers, who had called gays "sick." Landers, whose real name was Eppie Lederer, later became far more supportive of gays and lesbians. The *Gay Crusader* covered Landers' evolving views on the issue in its January 1974 issue, next to the cover story "20,000,000 GAY PEOPLE CURED!" about the changed designation from the American Psychiatric Association.

Thou Shalt Not Be 'Gay'

The New York Times took a tiny step forward by covering a gay cruise line in 1975, but Publisher Arthur Sulzberger was so upset he banned the word "gay," a policy that would not change until his son, Arthur Jr., took over in the 1980s. Executive Editor Abe Rosenthal was reportedly so homophobic that some reporters left the company, according to author Edward Alwood.

One of the last gay-related mainstream articles of the 1970s was a *Time* magazine cover story, "How Gay Is Gay? Homosexuality in America," on April 23, 1979. The article started with a description of gays in the streets of New Town (the Lakeview neighborhood) in Chicago, combating homophobia through street patrols organized by *GayLife* newspaper: "Homosexual men and women are coming out of the closet as never before to live openly. They are colonizing areas of big cities as their own turf, operating bars and even founding churches in conservative small towns, and setting up a nationwide network of organizations to offer counseling and companionship to those gays—still the vast majority—who continue to conceal their sexual orientation." The article also discussed gay political clout, legal and legislative battles, and the different issues facing gays across the U.S. It noted: "Lesbians often feel themselves to be the most persecuted minority of all." While the article still had some tired stereotypes, it was light-years ahead of *Time's* 1960s coverage of the community.

By the end of the 1970s, gay organizations and gay media were at a high point, culminating in the October 14, 1979, National March on Washington for Lesbian and Gay Rights. An estimated 100,000 people participated in an event that was mostly ignored by the mainstream media. But they couldn't keep a good story down—gay media made sure people across the country had the information.

The movement was out of the closets and getting stronger every year. The strength would be needed to face an opponent more deadly than anything anyone could have anticipated—an opponent allowed to grow and become deadlier because it was fed by homophobia. Had officials spoken up, had there been more trust in government and science, perhaps AIDS would not have killed millions. But it did, and the gay community fought the right wing, fought the government and fought for our lives.

Palimony, Sports and the Closet

By 1981, Billie Jean King was near the end of her illustrious, history-making tennis career. She may have felt a huge amount of pressure in her winning the highly publicized "Battle of the Sexes" match against Bobby Riggs in 1973, but the court battle she faced against her secretary, Marilyn Bennett, brought an extreme amount of unwanted attention to a woman who just wanted to make a difference for women in sports.

This forced outing made King the first openly lesbian mainstream athlete.

The story was made initially worse by King when she denied the affair, then called it a "mistake." The *Los Angeles Times* reported on April 29, 1981, "Hairdresser Sues, Claiming Billie Jean King Was Her Lover." King issued a statement calling the claim "untrue and unfounded." A short time later, King's husband Larry was by her side when she faced the media. The *Chicago Tribune* headline of May 2 was "Billie Jean admits gay affair in 'palimony.'" The article reported on a news conference she held with Larry and noted that the couple kissed for cameras.

The New York Times editorialized on May 3: "Women's professional tennis survived Renee Richards and, despite much fretting, it will no doubt survive the 'image crisis' that welled up around Billie Jean King … ."

Martina Navratilova, King's rival on the courts, also came out as a lesbian in 1981. Both women felt their sponsorship deals had been hurt by their openness.

When Renee Richards won the right to play in the U.S. Open in 1977, the mainstream media had to learn tough lessons on how to better cover the transgender community. Richards had played as a man in the tournament much earlier in her career.

Football player Dave Kopay's coming out in 1975 also was covered in the mainstream media, but he was not as well-known as the tennis stars.

Sports Illustrated covered a short-lived CBS sports fiction show, *Ball Four*, in 1976. It was among the first TV series to have a gay character, this one a rookie baseball player.

The *Los Angeles Times* addressed the serious issue of anti-gay crime in an article on March 6, 1981, "Cities Face a Growing Problem: Vicious Attacks on Homosexuals," by Bill Curry. "The rise in physical attacks here and nationally is seen by gay rights leaders as the product of increased verbal attacks on homosexuals by political and religious leaders as well as the result of a resurgence of white hate groups," the article noted.

The next week, on March 15, the *Times* ran another in-depth piece on the gay and lesbian community, by Austin Scott, "L.A. Homosexuals Create Own Brand of Political Activism." It focused on the clout of gays in the upcoming city elections. Democrats and Republicans, and both men and women, were interviewed.

The New York Times wrote about "Tapping the Homosexual Market" on May 2, 1982, specifically looking at the new wave of gay-themed movies coming out of Hollywood: *Partners*, *Making Love*, *Personal Best*, *Deathtrap* and *Victor/Victoria*.

AIDS Bursts Open the Closets

AIDS forced news media to address the crisis both inside and outside the newsroom. Several prominent journalists died of the disease, and although early reporting was often filled with homophobia, the media covered AIDS in better ways by the 1990s, even if most papers rarely covered it at all.

The *New York Native* had the first news story, on May 18, 1981, about what would later become known as AIDS. The *Los Angeles Times*, the *San Francisco Chronicle* and *The New York Times* all soon covered the early reports from the U.S. Centers for Disease Control during the summer of 1981.

The *Los Angeles Times* headline of June 5 was "Outbreaks of Pneumonia Among Gay Males Studied." *The New York Times* headline of July 3 was "Rare Cancer Seen in 41 Homosexuals." Both a pneumonia and a cancer were striking down gay men, and the news began to come with more urgency from the CDC.

Interestingly, the June 5, 1981, issue of Chicago's *GayLife* newspaper featured several articles on gay health, with a special focus on sexually transmitted diseases. Managing Editor Mike Bergeron wrote in a commentary: "While some may feel that the responsibility for sexually transmitted diseases lies in the hands of the health department, we must all realize that it is our responsibility to be aware of and prevent these diseases in our community." There were articles on anal warts, herpes, hepatitis, syphilis, crabs, scabies, drug use and alcoholism. One article reviewed a lesbian health book.

A few weeks later, the July 10 *GayLife* ominously reported on a local clinic's response to gay cancer reports nationally.

The mainstream media mostly did a bad job in the early years of the epidemic, with some exceptions. The *Times* was protested over its inadequate coverage of a disease that had struck New York especially hard.

Newsweek ran a cover story on April 18, 1983, "EPIDEMIC," about AIDS. But such articles focused a lot on heterosexuals and AIDS (*Time* cover of August 12, 1985: "AIDS: The Growing Threat, What's Being Done"; *Time* cover of February 16, 1987: "The Big Chill: How Heterosexuals Are Coping with AIDS"; and *Life* of July 1985: "Now No One is Safe from AIDS") despite the statistics in the U.S. The story of a straight youth with AIDS, Ryan White, broke hearts across America, and provided the media with a safer way to tell the story of the devastation of AIDS (*People* cover, August 3, 1987).

Newsweek did look at "Gay America" in an August 8, 1983, cover story subtitled "Sex, Politics and the Impact of AIDS." The cover featured two white men hugging and looking defiant.

Mother Jones ran a provocative cover in November 1987, "25,000 Died, While President Reagan Turned His Back."

The right wing, of course, took advantage of AIDS to fundraise and to preach more homophobia. The cover caption on Jerry Falwell's *Moral Majority Report* of July 1983 was "Homosexual Diseases Threaten American Families."

Some in the gay press also were slow to respond, because officials knew very little about the disease, and the gay community was afraid of a backlash against its newfound freedoms. *The Advocate*'s coverage lagged, but it eventually ran a cover story on March 18, 1982, "Is the Urban Gay Male Lifestyle Hazardous to Your Health?" *The Advocate* had openly HIV-positive basketball star Magic Johnson on its cover of April 21, 1992.

The important news around AIDS eventually also led to the appearance of magazines such as *POZ*, *Arts & Understanding* and *Positively Aware*, which focused exclusively on HIV and AIDS, covering every aspect of the disease in a way the mainstream and gay media could not.

AIDS forced a lot of people to reassess their lives as well. That meant more people were coming out of the closets, fighting in the streets and getting covered in the media.

The biggest pivot point for the media on AIDS came in 1985, when Rock Hudson died and the mainstream community was forced to see a face of AIDS that it knew. Elizabeth Taylor also then boldly took up the cause of AIDS, helping bring others into the fundraising. *Vanity Fair* ran a piece about Taylor's work, "Liz's AIDS Odyssey," in November 1992. The piece ended with this: "The world's most famous movie star is now the world's most famous AIDS activist. And once again she is center stage. 'In Amsterdam, people from ACT UP were demonstrating outside the building where we held my press conferences. As I walked past them one day they yelled. "Act up, Liz. Act up." And I thought, Well, you've got the right girl. Worry not. I will.'"

The 1980s: ACT UP, Fight Back

The push against corporate and media homophobia and AIDS phobia led to the formation of the Gay & Lesbian Alliance Against Defamation in New York in 1985 (at first known as the Gay and Lesbian Anti-Defamation League). GLAAD has been the longest-lasting and most effective gay media monitoring organization.

New Yorkers, like gays across the country, had had enough of homophobic media. Their first AIDS protest was on December 1, 1985, against the *New York Post*, which had been using scare tactics in coverage of the epidemic. GLAAD later pressured *The New York Times* to change from using "homosexual" to using "gay." GLAAD quickly grew to become a national organization that today has huge influence in the media and Hollywood (though some say it has lost sight of its mission by focusing so much on celebrities).

Gay journalists and writers across the country were part of GLAAD's early years, including co-founders Vito Russo, Gregory Kolovakos, Darryl Yates Rist, Jewelle Gomez, Allen Barnett and later Michelangelo Signorile (who "outed" celebrities and politicians in articles for *OutWeek* magazine).

The group's Announcing Equality campaign helped push more than 1,000 newspapers to include same-gender wedding announcements.

Russo was also part of ACT UP, fighting for research and funding—and corporate responsibility. Burroughs Wellcome was among the group's targets for its high price of the first anti-AIDS drug, AZT. After thousands took to the streets, and Wall Street, the drug firm finally gave in and sold AZT at a lower price.

The Illinois Gay and Lesbian Task Force, through such means as letter-writing campaigns by Al Wardell and Paul Varnell, also pushed hard against media bias. In cities across the country, gays were making their voices heard loud and clear in the mainstream media.

In the 1990s, *The New York Times*, which used to be seen as an enemy of LGBTs, finally began covering a wide range of LGBT issues, and from a progressive position. *The Advocate* ran a Michelangelo Signorile cover story about the *Times* on May 5, 1992, "Out at *The New York Times*: Gays, Lesbians, AIDS, and Homophobia Inside America's Newspaper of Record," calling attention to the changes being forced on the old homophobic leadership by new *Times* publisher Arthur Ochs Sulzberger Jr. (His father, Arthur Ochs Sulzberger Sr., died in 2012.) In a January 1992 meeting with the editorial staff in the newsroom, Sulzberger Jr. told the staff that "diversity" would be a priority at the paper going forward. He even used the phrase "sexual orientation," which shocked those gays, lesbians and allies on staff.

The new rules contrasted with past coverage in dramatic ways. New York was an epicenter of the AIDS epidemic, and New York media monitor Stephen Miller told Signorile that the *Times* coverage in the early years of the epidemic was "just criminal."

Why did all of this matter for the gay movement? Because the *Times* had such an impact on how other media covered gays. And gay reporters were also coming out at other news media across the country. As more and more journalists were out to their colleagues, they were able to confront homophobia in the newsroom before it leaked into the stories and newscasts.

This also meant that some LGBT media adjusted to how they covered the community, expanding and adapting to make sure to stay relevant in a world where at least some mainstream newspapers were covering LGBT issues.

The Gay Beat

In Chicago, the *Sun-Times* and *Tribune* briefly had straight reporters covering the gay and AIDS beats in the late 1980s: Tom Brune and Jean Latz Griffin, respectively. A lesbian, Terry Wilson, eventually took over the beat part-time from Griffin, and open lesbian journalist/author Achy Obejas also wrote for the *Tribune* for a few years, but today the papers do not have special reporters assigned solely to this beat.

For this book, I interviewed both Brune and Griffin about their "gay/AIDS" beats for the *Sun-Times* and *Tribune*. They came to their assignments by different routes, but both earned respect from the Chicago gay community for their fair treatment of gay and AIDS issues.

Brune came to the *Sun-Times* after eight years with the investigative journal *Chicago Reporter*, which focuses on race and poverty issues. Brune started at the *Sun-Times* during the days of Rupert Murdoch's ownership, in the mid-1980s. He said there was a revolving door of editors, including one particularly homophobic one from Australia. "He had a real problem with gays; he did offensive things, probably even stories offensive to gays and lesbians," Brune said.

After a new editor came on board, Brune said it appeared the paper was trying to build bridges with communities that had been offended. Howard Wolinsky was covering a lot of AIDS news for the *Sun-Times*, but the paper wanted someone to cover the disease more in-depth. "The *sub rosa* issue was they wanted to show they weren't a bigoted or homophobic paper. I quickly surmised that you really can't do a good job covering what's going on with AIDS unless you get to know the gay community better. So I expanded the beat for more lesbian and gay issues."

Brune spent about two years with the focus on AIDS and gay stories. Wolinsky stayed doing the AIDS beat, but Brune moved on, periodically coming back to the beat for special assignments. "I think there was a fair amount of mainstreaming by that point," he said, adding that he was thankful to the community leaders who were "willing to meet with me, talk with me, to get an understanding of what was going on with the AIDS crisis and the gay and lesbian community. I've even said, in Chicago's gay community there was a model with helping reporters get the stories, that really changed the coverage. It was just a smart awareness of the importance of getting it right in the mainstream media."

Jean Latz Griffin started covering gay and AIDS issues for the *Tribune* in 1986, but officially as a beat in 1987. Her motivation for requesting the assignment was very personal. A colleague and friend at the *Tribune*, award-winning reporter Mark Zambrano, was living with AIDS. He died at age 27 on March 21, 1987.

"We worked together on a number of things," Griffin said. "Being with him in the last months of his life, I had my eyes opened to a lot of things. I was really touched by it and very sad he was gone. I was public-health reporter at the time. AIDS was one of the biggest stories out there. At that point, if you were covering AIDS you had to understand what was going on in the gay community. The gay community was a fascinating thing on its own to me."

Griffin said the death of Zambrano, a rising star, hit *Tribune* staffers hard—and opened a lot of eyes to the disease.

"I went to Managing Editor Dick Ciccone, and I told him I wanted to cover the gay community and stuff on AIDS," she said. "There were others working on AIDS on a national level, but I was more a local AIDS reporter at the time. Dick was a really nice guy and a good managing editor; he reached into a drawer and pulled out a stack of letters from the gay and lesbian community complaining about the *Tribune*'s coverage. He said 'start with this—figure out what we should be doing, contact these people, go ahead and cover it.' Not everybody at the *Tribune* was thrilled."

Griffin reached out to those letter writers, including Paul Varnell, Al Wardell, Tim Drake and artist Gabor, as well as Joanne Trapani. I remember one meeting with Griffin at my office, where she genuinely seemed interested in learning about all the levels of gay and AIDS activism in the city.

She started her work prior to Zambrano's death but officially took on the gay and AIDS beat in 1987 after he died. She said it took around 50 or 60 percent of her time, because she had other editorial obligations. Her work lasted several years, until the early 1990s.

Many activists credit the work of Griffin with helping the Chicago community pass the city's gay-rights bill. She said she also wrote some of the early coverage of gay men who were raising children, and she wrote about the death of AIDS activist and political cartoonist Danny Sotomayor in 1992. But she also refused to do some stories, including ones she thought were too sensational. One editor insisted she "out" openly gay reporter Randy Shilts because he thought Shilts had AIDS and therefore should not be covering the epidemic. Griffin refused, though she did call to ask Shilts if he had AIDS. He said he did not—at the time, he was HIV-positive but did not have AIDS. Griffin said Shilts later told her that he was not sure what he would have said if she had asked whether he had HIV.

Achy Obejas was a *Tribune* freelancer from 1991 to 1996 and then full-time from 1996 to 2003; then she went part-time for a brief period.

"I was the first openly gay person hired by the *Tribune*," she wrote by email. "I was not the first gay person at the *Trib* or the first openly gay person at the *Trib*, but the first person who got hired who the *Trib* knew was unequivocally queer. The truth is that most folks were absolute gems. I had great editors for the most part, and my colleagues were smart and good people. They weren't unaware of my queerness, and it wasn't a topic avoided, but it wasn't the point of any conversation but one that I can think of, with a top editor, after some gigantic queer issue had broken and he wanted an opinion."

Obejas said the *Tribune* is "a vast white bastion of privilege—and I have far more troubling stories on issues of race and class—but sexuality wasn't that big a deal in my experience. Of course, I was out and no one had to adjust to any changes, but most people who thought they were closeted were, amusingly, understood to be gay by most of the newsroom anyway."

I'm Not Coming Out

Activist journalist Michelangelo Signorile was not the first to out people as closeted gays, but he certainly took it to a whole new level in the brief years of *OutWeek*, which started in 1989.

Josef Bush, writing as Angelo d'Arcangelo, wrote a very campy book, *The Homosexual Handbook*, published in 1968. It was a hilarious look behind the curtain of homosexuality, for the edification of gays and non-gays alike. Some of the people he named were clearly meant as a joke, but others he was dead serious about, both those still living and those long gone. Among those listed: Leonard Bernstein, Ned Rorem, Gore Vidal, Gary Cooper, Montgomery Clift, Joel Grey, J. Edgar Hoover, Tab Hunter, Roddy McDowell, Cole Porter and even Zeus.

Signorile took his work a little more seriously, and he created a years-long debate about the ethics of outing. The debate was within and outside the gay community, and it allowed the media to cover closeted gays simply by covering the outing craze. Signorile's biggest outing was that of Malcolm Forbes, after Forbes died, in the March 18, 1990, issue of *OutWeek*.

I'm Coming Out

The National Lesbian & Gay Journalists Association, founded in 1990 by Leroy "Roy" Aarons, has worked internally within mainstream media to profoundly change the way most media cover the gay community.

The American Society of Newspaper Editors asked Aarons to coordinate a 1989 survey of gay and lesbian journalists. The results showed that most of the 250 who responded were closeted and were concerned about the way their newspapers covered gay issues. Aarons presented the results at the 1990 ASNE convention and came out in the process. A few months later, Aarons joined with several reporters to form NLGJA.

While NLGJA is no longer at the same strength it once was, during its peak years in the 1990s it helped shepherd in change at newsrooms across the country. Those changes affected a generation of reporters and editors, and they helped to produce effects that are still felt today.

There had been a few brave openly gay journalists at mainstream and non-gay alternative publications prior to NLGJA's founding in 1990.

An early media pioneer was Carl Griffin Jr. Edward Alwood writes in his book *Straight News* that Griffin, an African-American, joined the *Minneapolis Tribune* in 1972, and he "may have been the first openly gay journalist at a mainstream newspaper."

NLGJA said Gail Shister "is widely regarded as the first 'out' reporter in mainstream news media in the United States" when it inducted her into its LGBT Journalists Hall of Fame in 2008. But she began her work in 1974 at the *Buffalo Evening News*, two years after Carl Griffin assumed his post. Shister still broke ground as the first female sportswriter at three mainstream newspapers.

Two other groundbreaking out reporters were Randy Shilts at KQED in San Francisco and Jill Johnston at *The Village Voice*. Shilts had also worked at *The Advocate* before he became the first openly gay person hired by a major metropolitan daily paper to cover the gay beat, for the *San Francisco Chronicle* in 1981. (Johnston died September 18, 2010, and was inducted posthumously into the NLGJA's hall of fame in 2012. Shilts, who died February 17, 1994, was inducted in 2005.)

The same year Shilts was hired in San Francisco, Christine Madsen was fired in Boston after seven years with *The Christian Science Monitor*. The editor asked Madsen about her sexuality, and Madsen was honest—and then she was fired. She filed a lawsuit. *The New York Times* reported August 22, 1985, on Madsen's case: "The Massachusetts Supreme Court today upheld the constitutional right of *The Christian Science Monitor* to dismiss a lesbian employee who refused to participate in a church-ordered 'healing.'" Madsen eventually settled in 1989, but her high-profile firing had sent a chill through the journalist community.

A few brave journalists with AIDS used their diagnosis as an opportunity to educate the public. The best-known was Tom Cassidy of CNN, who did magazine and television reports on his battle until he died in June 1991. Alwood also tells of journalist Robert O'Boyle, who wrote about his battle with AIDS in *The Seattle Times*, and *New York Times* editor Jeffrey Schmalz's coverage of the AIDS crisis and gay community after his own diagnosis in 1990. O'Boyle died in 1992, and Schmalz died in 1993. KGO-TV journalist Paul Wynne in San Francisco reported boldly on his own AIDS diagnosis, even taping some episodes from his hospital bed. The shows aired from January through July 1990, the month he died.

Two lesbians also made big news in coming out in their mainstream jobs. In 1992, *The Detroit News'* Washington Editor Deb Price started the first mainstream column on gay issues. She later became the first syndicated openly gay columnist in the mainstream media. *Essence* magazine's Senior Editor Linda Villarosa came out in a May 1991 article co-written with her mother. A gay reporter, Juan Palomo, came out at *The Houston Post* in 1991. He was fired and then rehired.

A pioneering African-American journalist, Thomas Morgan III, made history when he was elected president of the National Association of Black Journalists in 1989. Morgan started his career in 1972 at *The Miami Herald* and later was a reporter and editor for *The New York Times*. He broke new ground for LGBT journalists of color and was inducted into the NLGJA's LGBT Journalists Hall of Fame in 2005 (he died in 2007).

Early in his career Shilts worked at *The Advocate*, and there were other journalists who had their roots in gay media, later becoming mainstream reporters, successful authors or both. Whereas in the past working for a gay paper might have been a strike against reporters (and some often used pseudonyms), by the 1990s it was often considered a bonus. Writers who were out and successful included Audre Lorde, Rita Mae Brown, Frank Robinson, Adrienne Rich, Robin Morgan, Ray Mungo, Allen Young, Vito Russo, Kay Tobin Lahusen, Sarah Schulman, Barbara Grier, Jack Nichols, Jack Fritscher, Barbara Smith, Jewelle Gomez, Karla Jay, Martha Shelley, Jeanne Córdova, Allen Young, Victoria Brownworth, Maida Tilchen, Terri Jewel, Doug Ireland, Donald Suggs, Jim Provenzano, Maria Maggenti, Mark Zubro, Michelangelo Signorile, Jon-Henri Damski, Paul Varnell, Felice Picano, Mubarak Dahir, Sarah Pettit, Gabriel Rotello, Sean Strub, Masha Gessen, Albert Williams, Andy Humm, Michael Bronski, Yvonne Zipter, Rex Wockner, Jorjet Harper, Toni Armstrong Jr., Gregg Shapiro, Jennifer Vanasco, St. Sukie de la Croix and more.

Mark Schoofs was managing editor of the *Windy City Times* and later went on to win a Pulitzer Prize. Achy Obejas also wrote for the *Windy City Times* and later shared in a Pulitzer Prize. Cartoonists who started in the gay niche but made a name in the mainstream include Alison Bechdel and Howard Cruse. Andrew Sullivan came out big-time at *The New Republic* and is now with *Newsweek*'s *The Daily Beast* website. Armistead Maupin and Lindsey Van Gelder wrote for the mainstream media as openly gay writers. Van Gelder wrote an article in March 1982 for the *Columbia Journalism Review* about the straight-press coverage of gay issues.

Ann Northrop helped push for gay coverage when she worked for ABC's *Good Morning America* in 1981 and when she later worked with *CBS Morning News*. Joe Lovett did the same at CBS in the 1970s, according to Alwood in *Straight News*.

There are prominent transgender writers, such as Janet Mock, and openly gay editors and reporters at mainstream media across the country. And while Hank Plante and Garrett Glaser were among the first openly gay reporters in television, there are now openly gay anchors on the major TV and radio networks: Rachel Maddow, Anderson Cooper, Don Lemon, Thomas Roberts, Stephanie Miller, Steve Kmetko and more.

LZ Granderson, an openly gay African-American, has managed to be very out and proud as both a print and television sports journalist. He has created a terrific niche in covering both sports and gay issues. Jonathan Capehart is also an openly gay African-American. He is a an editorial board member and writer for *The Washington Post* and a frequent guest on television news shows.

The list does go on, and today it would be impossible to track all the openly LGBT writers in the mainstream. But how about openly LGBT people in the boardrooms and ownership of corporate mainstream media? That is a rare bird, indeed. On September 23, 2012, one of the highest-ranking owners of media in the U.S. came out in an interview with *The New York Times*. It was a double-punch as he is also a former owner of the Pittsburgh Pirates Major League Baseball team. Kevin McClatchy, chairman of the board of the McClatchy Company, the third-largest newspaper company in the U.S. (it has 30 daily newspapers in 15 states, including *The Miami Herald*), came out in an interview with Frank Bruni, who in May 2011 became the first openly gay op-ed columnist for the *Times*. (Interestingly, McClatchy did not come out in one of his company's own papers.)

McClatchy told Bruni: "I'm sure people will criticize me because I came out later, and I should have come out while I was in baseball and in the thick of it. … I could find excuses for why not to do this article until I'm blue in the face. I've got a birthday coming up where I'm turning old [he turns 50 in January 2013]. I've spent 30 years—or whatever the number is specifically—not talking about my personal life, lying about my personal life. … There's no way I want to go into the rest of my existence and ever have to hide my personal life again."

Welcome to the Future

The difference starting in the 1990s is there for the historians to document. In the 1960s, 1970s and 1980s, there were protests and pickets outside of newspapers for their biased coverage of gays. They printed names of people arrested in gay-bar raids, causing lost jobs and even suicides. They mostly missed important stories such as the 1979 and 1987 marches on Washington. Now, it is very common to see LGBTs on the covers of major newspapers and magazines, for reasons that range all the way from being celebrities to being in gay marriages.

In fact, 1993 seemed to be the "year of the lesbian" for magazines and newspapers. *Vanity Fair* ran a cover photo of Cindy Crawford fake-shaving k.d. lang in August, while *Newsweek* carried a cover photo of a white lesbian couple for its "Lesbians" story of June 21. Melissa Etheridge came out in January of that year, which led to a series of articles in the mainstream, gay and lesbian media. Also that year, *Married With Children* actress Amanda Bearse became the first prime-time television star to come out as a lesbian.

Entertainment Weekly featured a large number of queer photos for its September 8, 1995, cover story titled "The Gay '90s: Entertainment Comes Out of the Closet." In the first decade of the 2000s, gay-related magazine covers were still not ubiquitous, but they were more common than before. For example, *Time* had a cover feature on "The Battle Over Gay Teens" in its issue of October 10, 2005.

Some of the national media did focus on serious questions facing gays, such as the October 1998 murder of gay student Matthew Shepard. "The War Over Gays" on the October 26 cover of *Time* looked at Shepard's murder, featuring his photo, inset against the photo of "the deer fence where he was left to die." *The Advocate*'s cover of November 24 was even starker: "The Ultimate Ex-Gay, Matthew Shepard 1976–1998," under a photo of the posthumous hero of the gay movement.

The increased coverage means that sometimes the media explore more than just the surface of the community and go into nuances. For example, on October 31, 2008, *Time* wrote about "The Gay Mafia That's Redefining Liberal Politics." It was an analysis of a new group of gay donors who were trying to shape elections.

A 2012 report from the Opportunity Agenda "suggests that support for LGBTs among African-Americans and Latinos is on the rise, especially in media serving both communities," the organization said. "Public Opinion and Discourse on the Intersection of LGBT Issues and Race," a study of public attitudes toward LGBTs and of Latino and African-American niche media's coverage of LGBT issues, reported that pro-LGBT voices far outweigh anti-LGBT voices. It "suggests that historically marginalized communities are pulled between support for LGBT equality and [a] traditional sense of morality and religiosity. Still, experts concluded that media outlets serving Latino and African-American communities are supportive of LGBT people," according to the Opportunity Agenda, which was launched in 2006 "with the mission of building the national will to expand opportunity in America."

The non-gay press certainly has come a long way, with Fox News the outlier, not the norm. *Rolling Stone* of June 9, 2009, did a cover story on Adam Lambert when the *American Idol* runner-up officially came out. *Newsweek* ran a January 18, 2010, cover story with two female cake-top figurines bookending the type: "The Conservative Case for Gay Marriage," written by Republican lawyer Theodore Olson, who continues to fight against the Proposition 8 gay marriage ban in California. *Black Enterprise* featured a cover story on "Black & Gay in Corporate America" in July 2011. *The Crisis*, the magazine of the National Association for the Advancement of Colored People, featured Obama with rainbow stripes for its summer 2012 issue.

But even though *Newsweek* may give Obama a "gay" rainbow cover for supporting same-sex marriage (May 21, 2012), or the *Times* may do a cover story on gay male couples raising children (August 10, 2012), and *People* ("Ellen and Portia's Wedding!" September 1, 2008) and *Entertainment Weekly* ("The New Art of Coming Out in Hollywood," June 20, 2012) will report on gay and lesbian celebrity coming-out stories, weddings and breakups, there is still enough to cover on a daily basis to keep gay newspapers and websites busy 24 hours a day.

The role of gay media continues not just because the gay press can give gay stories more space, and more perspective. It continues because there are still so many cases where the mainstream media are simply parachuting into a story and therefore providing an incomplete and thus inaccurate picture for their readers. In a glaring example in 2012, *The New York Times* coverage of the posthumous coming-out of astronaut Sally Ride was embarrassing in its tone-deaf reading of this historical moment. The same happens in many other stories, of the living and the deceased—it again occurred when Ron Palillo (Horshack on the *Welcome Back, Kotter* TV sitcom of the 1970s) died in 2012. He was survived by his partner of 41 years, and while this time *The New York Times* did mention his partner, other mainstream media did not.

By incompletely reporting on our lives and our deaths, the mainstream media continue to sustain the vacuum, one that is at least partially filled by gay media.

OSCAR WILDE PLAINTIFF

Cynicisms on Literature and Manners in an English Court.

MARQUIS OF QUEENSBERRY'S LIBEL

The Writer Rarely Writes What He Believes Is True and Thinks that Self-Realization Is the End of Life.

LONDON, April 3.—The Central Criminal Court, Old Bailey, was packed with people long before the hour of opening, 10:30 A. M. to-day. The attraction was the trial of the action of Oscar Wilde against the Marquis of Queensberry for libel. Justice Collins took his seat on the bench promptly.

The trial of Oscar Wilde as covered in *The New York Times*, April 4, 1895.

WHY THEY FAILED TO MARRY

BY KATHARINE BEMENT DAVIS

"I WISH I knew," writes a forty-six-year-old woman journalist in reply to a question as to her reasons for not marrying. "If there could be such a thing, I should say I was 'marked' for spinsterhood. I think marriage is always best where possible, but, although eight fine men have proposed, not one of them appealed." One of a family of twelve children, brought up by a mother "who taught us to face things and conquer them," this woman is now teaching a motherless thirteen-year-old nephew "the things he should have learned years ago." "He cries and resents it, but I tell him it is like winds and waves, grain growing, ocean currents, radio—just life's interesting fact."

A sane woman from her paper and, reading it, one also wonders why.

From the time, more than sixty years ago, when college doors were thrown open to women, the opinion has been rather widely prevalent that a college education is detrimental to a woman's matrimonial chances. Answers from a relatively large group of unmarried college women may tell us what part, if any, in their own failure to marry they believe was played by their academic training.

Geneticists are pointing out the danger to the race of inferior stocks as go on reproducing their kind in increasing proportions while the birthrate of the better stocks is declining. The various schools of eugenics may not yet know, and certainly do not yet agree, as to the how and what of the transmission by human beings to their offspring of various characteristics, physical and mental. But the layman going to agricultural fairs and flower shows does not need to be convinced that there is something in heredity, and that it is a good thing to pass on goodness and beauty. Heredity must be at least as important to humans as it is to plants and animals.

On the other hand, psychiatrists and students of child behavior are stressing increasingly the importance of environment, particularly to the young child. His whole future life, his happiness or misery, his success or failure hinge, they tell us, on the surroundings of the first few years. Some go so far as to maintain that his behavior patterns are irrevocably fixed in the pre-school period.

Be that as it may, again the layman believes in the importance of environment. Far be it from me to maintain that the college woman invariably comes from the better, more desirable stock. So far as I know, no study has been made which would give us data for such an opinion. Observation and acquaintance with many college women for many years lead me to believe, however, that on the whole the families from which they come are of the better type, representing better than the average health and intelligence. Great economic efficiency resulting in wealth, and the type of intellect that produces genius, are not necessary ingredients in the type of families which it is socially desirable to reproduce.

From the point of view of eugenics I shall maintain until it is otherwise proven that it would be a good thing for the race if a higher per cent of our college women were to marry and produce children. In the matter of ability to furnish

THESE TWO IMAGES: *Harper's Magazine* **of March 3, 1928, looked at why women don't marry—including some interesting lesbian statistics.**

WHY THEY FAILED TO MARRY   463

TABLE I
REASONS FOR FAILURE TO MARRY

REASONS	NUMBER	PER CENT
1. Never met the right man	305	28.3
2. In love with man she could not marry	97	9.0
3. Was never in love with any man	89	8.2
4. "No one ever asked me"	55	5.1
5. Engagement broken—never loved another	54	5.1
6. Lack of opportunity to meet men	52	4.8
7. Childhood conditioning	36	3.3
8. Fiancé died—never loved another	33	3.1
9. Financial (family) obligations of woman	31	2.8
10. Too shy—not attractive to men	22	2.0
11. Desire for a career	22	2.0
12. "Never loved men who asked and men I loved never asked"	21	1.9
13. Was never asked—never wanted to be asked	19	1.7
14. Engaged now. Never in love before	19	1.7
15. Financial (family) obligations of man	18	1.6
16. Homo-sexual relations prevented	17	1.6
17. Ill health of woman	17	1.6
18. No desire to marry—marriage never appealed	16	1.6
19. Too particular, critical or cautious	14	1.2
20. Parental objections to particular man	13	1.2
21. Could not love men who asked	12	1.1
22. Sex relations distasteful	9	.8
23. Desire for freedom	8	.7
24. Mother's advice against marriage in general	7	.6
25. Sex intercourse with man who could not marry prevented marriage with anyone else	4	.4
26. Ill health of fiancé	3	.3
27. Fear of child bearing	3	.2
28. Special cases—several reasons	33	3.1
29. Reasons given each by a single individual	49	4.6
TOTAL	1077	99.5

Why were they too particular, critical, or cautious? Was this the result of "childhood conditioning" or of their college training? Did caution "run in the family," as one woman says spinsters do in hers?

One of this group feels it is just chance that keeps the right man out of her way. She, in common with a good many others, will marry if he comes.

"Was never asked—never wanted to be asked," say nineteen. Perhaps the second phrase explains the first, but *why* didn't they want to be asked? That would obviously get us nearer to the real reason of failure to marry.

Eighteen women say they have no desire to marry. "Marriage never appealed." *Why* doesn't it appeal?

The fifty-five who were never asked do not give us any clue as to what in their judgment was the deterring cause of this backwardness on the part of their men friends. In brief, we could go over the entire list of reasons with why? why? why? Nothing short of careful individual study could get behind the alleged causes, so obviously we must go on from here unsatisfied, awaiting further exhaustive personality studies which one day undoubtedly will be made of normal as we now have them of abnormal women.

Next on the list to the 305 who never met the right man is a group of ninety-seven women who fell in love with men they could not marry. Some of them were on the active list at the time of reporting. All but one of them tell why. "He is already married," 20 cases. "He does not reciprocate," 24 cases. "He died," 10 cases. "He married another," 7 cases. Differences in race and religion, 3 cases. Unexplained "circumstances separated," 4 cases. "Differences in personality and social status," and "He was not a college man" (the women felt it would make for unhappiness), two cases each. "He was unable to marry," unexplained; and, "He was found to be sexually promiscuous," 3 cases each. Eight reasons are given by

NAZI STUDENTS RAID INSTITUTE ON SEX

Seize Half a Ton of Scientific Material at Dr. Hirschfeld's Berlin Establishment.

Wireless to THE NEW YORK TIMES.

BERLIN, May 6.—The Crusade of the German studenthoods against the "Un-German Spirit" in print and picture got under way in all the German university centres today. In Berlin it opened with a formal attack on Dr. Magnus Hirschfeld's "Institute for Sexual Science," which has long been a place of interest for some tourists as well as a centre for scientific research.

The signal for today's raid was a shrill trumpet blast, whereupon about eighty students rushed the premises, forcing an entry through the doors and windows. Dr. Hirschfeld was not there to receive them since he is still being held in protective custody.

In less than an hour the studenthood raiders had gathered about half a ton of books, pamphlets, photographs, charts and lantern slides, which they hauled away to the headquarters of the students' social centre, where the material will be sorted by medical experts and the scientific part reserved for legitimate use.

The "Un-German" part will be consigned to the Nazi fires that are to light up the university campus Wednesday.

The archives of the institute contained extensive correspondence with professional men in all parts of Europe and the United States. This correspondence, the students said, would be treated as confidential and would be destroyed later, since they are determined to root out the Hirschfeld establishment.

LEFT: The raid on Dr. Magnus Hirschfeld's Institute for Sexual Science, covered in *The New York Times*, May 7, 1933.

BELOW: *The Little Review* fought a court battle over the sexually explicit James Joyce novel *Ulysses*. The publication serialized the book from 1918 to 1920, before Sylvia Beach, also a lesbian, published it in book form in Paris in 1922. *The Little Review* was prosecuted for obscenity based on the section about masturbation.

Courtesy of the M. Kuda Archives

THE LITTLE REVIEW

VOL. VI.   AUGUST, 1919   No. 4

CONTENTS

Subscription price, payable in advance, in the United States and Territories, $2.50 per year; Canada, $2.75; Foreign, $3.00. Published monthly, and copyrighted, 1919, by Margaret C. Anderson.

Manuscripts must be submitted at author's risk, with return postage. Entered as second class matter March 16, 1917, at the Post Office at New York, N. Y., under the act of March 3, 1879.

MARGARET C. ANDERSON, Publisher

24 West Sixteenth Street, New York, N. Y.

Foreign Office: 43 Belsize Park, Gardens, London N. W. 3.

THE LITTLE REVIEW
A MAGAZINE OF THE ARTS
MAKING NO COMPROMISE WITH THE PUBLIC TASTE

"ULYSSES"
by
JAMES JOYCE

PUBLISHERS LOSE APPEAL.

British Court Upholds Seizure of Radclyffe Hall's Novel.

Wireless to THE NEW YORK TIMES.

LONDON, Dec. 14.—Jonathan Cape, Ltd., the publishers of Miss Radclyffe Hall's novel, "The Well of Loneliness," lost their appeal today against the decision that all copies of the book must be seized and destroyed by the police.

Sitting in the crowded court room was Rudyard Kipling, who was apparently prepared to testify for the government in favor of the book's suppression. Previously George Bernard Shaw, H. W. Wells, but not Mr. Kipling, had strongly disapproved of the censorship of the book. Forty literary witnesses were in the court at the previous hearing prepared to defend Miss Hall's much discussed novel.

Mainstream newspapers covered the obscenity trial of Radclyffe Hall's *The Well of Loneliness*. This is from the December 15, 1928, issue of *The New York Times*.

The only edition of *Fire!!*, which came out in 1926 and featured many new African-American gay voices.
Courtesy of Rich Wilson

Expatriate Declines to Be Abstruse in Explaining Why Most of Her Writings Are—Does Not Wish to Influence Others, Saying, 'It Is Enough if You Influence Yourself.'

Gertrude Stein returned to America yesterday after thirty-one years, a square-shouldered woman of 60 with a constant chuckle in her throat and a rollick in her gait.

Dressed in rough tweeds and wearing the enigmatic countenance that has marked her literary adventures for the last score of years, she sat in the lounge of the French liner Champlain for more than an hour, crossing swords with a dozen baffled reporters.

Her feet were in thick woolly stockings, and round-toed, flat-heeled oxfords. A brownish tweed suit covered a cerise vest of voluminous proportions and a mannish shirt of cream and black stripes. The hat was a Stein hat, a hat as persistent as the repetitions which are a feature of her abstruse writings.

Peaked in front above her candid brown eyes, it roamed backward tightly about the close-cropped head to a fold at the rear; a gay hat which gave her the appearance of having just sprung from Robin Hood's forest to enunciate another word pattern of her own literature—literature which she said must await the reverence of our grandchildren's children.

Secretary Enjoys Repartee.

No one enjoyed that interview more than Miss Stein, unless it might have been Miss Alice B. Toklas, her secretary and companion, who sat, dark and small, on the periphery of the attentive circle. Miss Toklas gazed raptly at Miss Stein carrying on with parry and riposte, chuckling mellowly at the discomfiture of her questioners.

Miss Stein surprised interviewers by speaking a language every one could understand. She said she left America thirty-one years ago after being "born and raised a Republican in Pennsylvania." During those years abroad a veritable hurricane waged about her, and she was ridiculed, scorned, attacked and fêted for her writings.

During the interview she spoke no such sentence as "It makes it well fish," or "Remain to narrate to prepare two saints for saints" (from "Four Saints in Three Acts"), nor

Associated Press Photo.
Gertrude Stein.

cause "you don't miss anything you do not have. If you are busy in New York you do not miss Chicago."

Gertrude Stein garnered media attention during her U.S. trips, including this *New York Times* story of October 25, 1934.

DR. KINSEY DEFENDS STATEMENTS IN BOOK

Dr. Alfred C. Kinsey replied yesterday to critics, chiefly psychiatrists and sociologists, who have attacked his book, "Sexual Behavior in the Human Male."

The attacks were made principally because he described as "normal" and "natural" practices they maintain are abnormal and the result of individual emotional disturbances.

This was the first public answer made by the Indiana University professor to charges brought by social scientists against parts of the book that has aroused such controversial discussion. He addressed 200 members and guests at the opening session of the thirty-eighth annual meeting of the American Psychopathological Association at the Commodore Hotel.

He asserted that most of the sexual behavior called abnormal in our particular culture is "part and parcel of our inheritance as mammals and is natural and normal biologically."

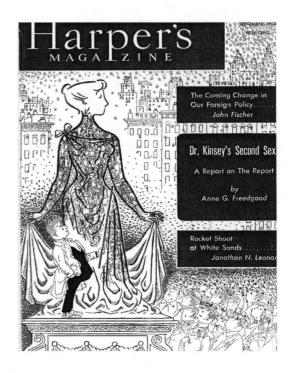

The publications of Dr. Alfred Kinsey's men's and women's sexuality books created a media stir across the country. Here is coverage in *The New York Times* of June 5, 1948 (for his men's book), and in *Harper's Magazine* of September 1953.

MEDICINE

Queer People

The sex pervert, whether a homosexual, an exhibitionist, or even a dangerous sadist, is too often regarded merely as a "queer" person who never hurts anyone but himself. Then the mangled form of some victim focuses public attention on the degenerate's work. And newspaper headlines flare for days over accounts and feature articles packed with sensational details of the most dastardly and horrifying of crimes.

For the past sixteen years Dr. J. Paul de River, New Orleans-born criminal psychiatrist, has studied every type of sex pervert from the apparently harmless to the most vicious. To the Sex Offense Bureau of the Los Angeles Police Department, of which he is head, comes every person accused of a sex crime by the Los Angeles police.

With hundreds of case histories at his disposal, Dr. de River has written a factual, scientific book, "The Sexual Criminal,"* published this week. For doctors, lawyers, teachers, and criminologists, the volume, including 43 actual case histories with pictures and clinical observations, clarifies and elaborates on the meager treatises on sex abnormalities by Kraft-Ebbing, Havelock Ellis, and others. To the general reader, it reveals frank facts on one of the least-discussed aspects of psychiatric investigation.

Hurt and Be Hurt: Lots of very queer people indeed turn up in Dr. de River's pages. There is the sadist (named from the French Marquis de Sade, con-

*THE SEXUAL CRIMINAL. By J. Paul de River, M.D. Charles C. Thomas. 304 pages. $5.50.

"Queer People" was the headline on this outrageous *Newsweek* story of October 10, 1949.

PERVERTS CALLED GOVERNMENT PERIL

Gabrielson, G.O.P. Chief, Says They Are as Dangerous as Reds—Truman's Trip Hit

Special to THE NEW YORK TIMES

WASHINGTON, April 18—Guy George Gabrielson, Republican National Chairman, asserted today that "sexual perverts who have infiltrated our Government in recent years" were "perhaps as dangerous as the actual Communists."

He elevated what he called the "homosexual angle" to the national political level in his first news letter of 1950, addressed to about 7,000 party workers, under the heading: "This Is the News from Washington."

Giving National Committee support to the campaign of Senator Joseph R. McCarthy, Republican of Wisconsin, against the State Department, but without mentioning him by name, Mr. Gabrielson said:

"As Americans, it is difficult for us to believe that a National Administration would go to such length to cover up and protect subversives, traitors, working against their country in high Governmental places. But it is happening. If there is but one more (Alger) Hiss or (Judith) Coplon still in a key spot, he should be ferreted out. It's no red herring."

The New York Times,
April 19, 1950.

The U.S. government was on a witch hunt against sexual "perverts," Communists and others in the late 1940s and 1950s. These headlines indicate how the media played a role in feeding the frenzy.

State Dept. Reports It Fired 126 Sex Perverts in 14 Months

By the Associated Press

The State Department has fired 126 homosexuals since January 1, 1951, and is determined to remove any others from the department, it was disclosed yesterday.

Similar efforts to eliminate homosexuals should be made by all Federal agencies, said Chairman John J. Rooney (D-N. Y.).

"This has been extensively advertised as a problem which is

The Washington Post,
March 26, 1952.

Congress Hears 5000 Perverts Infest Capital

WASHINGTON, March 28 (U.P)—The head of the Washington vice squad told Congress today there are about 5000 homosexuals in the capital and three out of four of them work for the government.

tary of State John' O. Peurifoy, who told the subcommittee that 91 sex perverts have been forced to resign from the State Department.

Special precautions have been ordered by the Senators to safeguard police vice files. They

Los Angeles Times,
March 29, 1950.

Los Angeles Times,
January 4, 1955.

Sex Perverts Invade D. C., House Told

Rep. Grant Offers Bill for Merger Of Metropolitan And Park Police

The Nation's Capital has become "the haven of sexual perverts and criminals" who are "converging upon Washington in ever-increasing numbers."

That was the indictment of the District made yesterday on the floor of the House by Representative George McInvale Grant (D., Ala.).

The Washington Post,
July 30, 1948.

8008 Dropped as Risks to Security Under Eisenhower

2096 Linked to Subversive Data in New Report

WASHINGTON, Jan. 3 (P)—The Eisenhower administration reported today that the number of persons it has dropped from the Federal payroll and classed as security risks has reached 8008, of whom 2096 had subversive data in their files.

Miami officials—and the media—went after "perverts" in that city in the 1950s. This collage of headlines was published in the gay ONE magazine of October 1954.

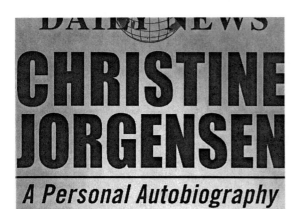

A Personal Autobiography

In 1952, She Was a Scandal

············

When George Jorgensen decided to change his name—and body—the nation wasn't quite ready.
—Newsday

BRONX 'BOY' IS NOW A GIRL

Danish Treatments Change Sex of Former Army Clerk

COPENHAGEN, Denmark, Dec. 1 (AP)—Christine Jorgensen, a 26-year-old blonde American girl—who until recently was a man—said from her hospital bed tonight that she was happy, although scared to be facing the world as a female.

Born the son of a carpenter who lives at 2849 Dudley Avenue, the Bronx, New York, and named George Jr., the youth once served as a clerk in the United States Army.

Danish specialists at the state hospital here brought about the sex conversion; which took two years, involving hormone treatments and surgery.

During the long conversion period Christine studied color photography. She intends to return to the United States some day—with a United States woman's passport—to continue her career.

Dr. Christian Hamburger, Danish hormone expert who directed the operation, said the treatment was about complete and Christine would be released from the hospital soon.

Christine Jorgensen made headlines around the world after her sex-change announcement. This article is from _The New York Times_ of December 2, 1952. Also pictured is the cover of her reissued autobiography.

WILLIAM J. HELMER

New York's "Middle-class" HOMOSEXUALS

A report on a quietly embattled—and barely known—community which has evolved its own precarious conventions and style of life.

AS MIGHT be expected, the common view of homosexuality we find in recent novels, plays, and films is often very limited. Even the more "understanding" studies of the problem seem to consider homosexuals as a definable group—distinct from heterosexuals—whose chief concern in life is to satisfy their sexual desires while shamefully concealing them from friends and associates.

In fact, homosexuality is a condition which takes so many forms that the word is of little use in describing any single group of people. And many homosexuals insulate themselves from hostile heterosexual society, taking refuge in a separate homosexual community which possesses its own customs, social structure, ethics, argot, organizations, and even business establishments. To the extent that police or anonymity permit, every large city in America contains a homosexual community. It has no physical dimensions, and it certainly does not include everyone who would legally, psychiatrically, or otherwise qualify as a homosexual. But for some it offers a virtually complete personal world where one can pursue a busy and varied "gay" life, socially as well as sexually, independent of "straight" society.

Like most heterosexuals I was barely aware of the gay community in New York when I first came to work in the city. A friend who knew it well offered to introduce me to his friends, with the understanding that I would try to write an objective study of their way of life. I spent several months talking chiefly to homosexuals who participate in gay life more or less exclusively, sometimes to the extent of working in a so-called "gay trade" (such as hairdressing) or in an office where other employees are homosexual. This article thus concerns itself with what might be called the homosexual bourgeoisie—people who are community-oriented, provincial, critical of undesirables. They are themselves frequently disdained by other homosexuals, some of whom participate freely in both gay and "straight" society. Still other homosexuals live more private and self-sufficient lives and have little or nothing at all to do with gay society.

But the homosexuals who confine themselves to their own "middle-class" community seem to me the appropriate group from which to gain some insight into the social aspects of homosexuality. Because they are much concerned with their own position in the community, they draw many distinctions among themselves which are too subtle to be reflected in police records or psychiatric studies of the isolated individual. In introducing some of the habits and styles of their life, I must however emphasize that the varieties of actual behavior among homosexuals are endless and I have undoubtedly oversimplified them here. Furthermore, the homosexuals who described themselves and their friends to me could be expected to generalize in defensive and self-interested ways—even unintentionally—when talking to a "square" reporter.

New York probably has the country's largest homosexual community if only because of its size, but few reliable statistics are available. The late Dr. Robert Lindner, drawing selectively on the statistics of several psychologists, psychiatrists, and sexual researchers (including Kinsey), arrived at an estimate of 4 to 6 per cent of "the total male population over age sixteen" who are homo-

LEFT: _Harper's Magazine_, March 1963.

BELOW: _The New York Times_, December 17, 1963.

Growth of Overt Homosexuality In City Provokes Wide Concern

By ROBERT C. DOTY

The problem of homosexuality in New York became the focus yesterday of increased attention by the State Liquor Authority and the Police Department.

The liquor authority announced the revocation of the liquor licenses of two more homosexual haunts that had been repeatedly raided by the police. The places were the Fawn, at 795 Washington Street near Jane Street and the

and restaurants that cater to the homosexual trade. Commenting yesterday on the situation, Police Commissioner Michael J. Murphy said:

"Homosexuality is another one of the many problems confronting law enforcement in this city. However, the underlying factors in homosexuality are not criminal but rather medical and sociological in nature.

"The police jurisdiction in

The June 26, 1964, issue of *Life* magazine included a major story about "Homosexuality in America."

TV: *C.B.S. Reports* on Homosexuals

Growing Social Problem Soberly Considered

By GEORGE GENT

"C.B.S. REPORTS" finally unveiled its long-awaited study on homosexuals last night It was not the program originally planned more than two and a half years ago, which was said to stress the more sensational aspects of the gay life. It was more a sober, intelligent discussion of a growing social problem that only recently has reached the public forum.

To be sure, nothing really new was disclosed. There were interviews with various types of homosexuals—those who had come to terms with their sexual proclivity and those who had not. There were some fuzzy shots of homosexual bars and poolrooms, and a rather heartrending sequence about a 19-year-old soldier being arrested for the first time, for committing a lewd act in public.

By and large the program concentrated on the social, medical, sexual, legal and moral dimensions of the problem. Psychiatrists believe that the first three years of a child's life are crucial in determining his sexual orientation. The paramount importance of the mother and father in the homosexual's life was adverted to time and again on the program. Homosexuals, who are under cruel pressures from a condemning society—most Americans want to keep homosexual acts illegal—are crusading to legalize homosexual acts between consenting adult males.

Federal Judge James Braxton Craven of Charlotte, N. C., questioned whether any public purpose was served by imprisoning homosexuals. In some states they can be sentenced to terms twice as long as those served by second-degree murderers, six times as long as the terms for abortionists and twice as long as those for armed robbers.

The persons interviewed included a young college teacher, a representative of the homosexual Mattachine Society, a compulsive homosexual who had been arrested three times and was undergoing

Judge Doubts Fairness of Jailing Offenders

therapy, and a married psychology professor with two children, who said his wife knew that he was a homosexual and that his marriage would probably end as a result of it. There was an interesting debate on the role of the homosexual in the arts, between Dr. Albert Goldman of Columbia and Gore Vidal, the novelist.

Visually the program was disappointing. The faces of most participants were screened, and the discussions could just as well have been done on radio. It also might have been better to give the minority viewpoint that homosexuals are just as normal as anyone else a chance to speak for itself.

Otherwise, the program was a good example of how a difficult subject can be treated with fairness and dignity without sacrificing reportorial depth. Mike Wallace did a solid job on the interviews. "The Homosexuals" was produced for "C.B.S. Reports" by Harry Morgan.

A groundbreaking TV show aired in 1967, the first nationwide network program on gay issues. "The Homosexuals", an episode of *CBS Reports* on March 7, was anchored by Mike Wallace. The show was covered in mainstream print media, including this *New York Times* piece on March 8, 1967.

Time's controversial January 21, 1966, article on "The Homosexual in America."

HOMOSEXUALS WATCHING OLD MOVIES IN SAN FRANCISCO GAY BAR

A post-Stonewall cover story on gays in the October 31, 1969, issue of *Time* was an improvement on earlier coverage, but still full of stereotypes.

HOMOSEXUALS STAGE PROTEST IN CAPITAL

WASHINGTON, May 29 (UPI)—Nine men and three women picketed the White House today to protest what they called Government discrimination against homosexuals

The demonstration was organized by the Mattachine Society of Washington, which said it was acting on behalf of "the nation's second largest minority"—15 million homosexuals.

The pickets said they were protesting the treatment of homosexuals in the military services, particularly the fact they are given less than honorable discharges; refusal of the Government to hire homosexuals, and the fact that Government officials have ignored their requests to discuss the situation.

The local Mattachine group had hoped for a higher number of pickets, but a contingent from New York failed to appear.

The Washington society has 60 members. The New York chapter lists 400 members.

A spokesman said that two of the women who picketed were married. He said the society accepted members without regard to race, religion, sex or "sexual orientation."

LEFT: In April 1965, a handful of gays and lesbians from the Mattachine Society of Washington protested outside the White House for the first time. When protesters returned to the White House on May 29, 1965, there were nine men and three women protesters—and several media. *The New York Times* ran a United Press International wire service story May 30, "Homosexuals Stage Protest in Capital."

BELOW: *The Village Voice* coverage of the Stonewall rebellion, July 3, 1969.

In early 1965, *The Washington Post* ran a series on "homosexuals."

POLICE AGAIN ROUT 'VILLAGE' YOUTHS

Outbreak by 400 Follows a Near-Riot Over Raid

Heavy police reinforcements cleared the Sheridan Square area of Greenwich Village again yesterday morning when large crowds of young men, angered by a police raid on an inn frequented by homosexuals, swept through the area.

Tactical Patrol Force units assigned to the East Village poured into the area about 2:15 A.M. after units from the Charles Street station house were unable to control a crowd of about 400 youths, some of whom were throwing bottles and lighting small fires.

Their arms linked, a row of helmeted policemen stretching across the width of the street made several sweeps up and down Christopher Street between the Avenue of the Americas and Seventh Avenue South.

The crowd retreated before them, but many groups fled into the numerous small side streets and re-formed behind the police line. The police were not withdrawn until 4 A.M.

The New York Times coverage of Stonewall, June 30, 1969.

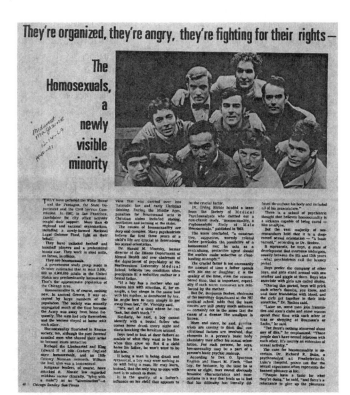

Chicago-based *Midwest Magazine*'s coverage of gays, December 14, 1969.
Courtesy of the M. Kuda Archives

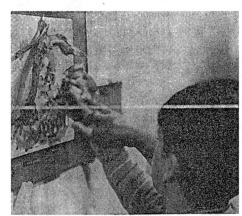

Thomas Basile touches raised Styrofoam collage, with classmate's hand on his

The Lesbian Issue and Women's Lib

By JUDY KLEMESRUD

The Lesbian issue, which has been hidden away like a demented child ever since the women's liberation movement came into being in 1966, was brought out of the closet yesterday.

Nine leaders of the movement held a press conference at the Washington Square Methodist Church, 133 West Fourth Street, to express their "solidarity with the struggle of homosexuals to attain their liberation in a sexist society."

The conference was prompted by an article in the Behavior section of the December 14 issue of Time magazine, which said that Kate Millett, author of

sence of that role is that a woman is defined in terms of her relationship to men. A woman is called a Lesbian when she functions autonomously. Women's autonomy is what women's liberation is all about."

Standing behind Miss Millett as she spoke were about 50 women supporters, who frequently interrupted her statement with cheers. Other leaders in the group were Gloria Steinem, the journalist; Ruth Simpson, president of the New York chapter of Daughters of Bilitis; Florynce Kennedy, a lawyer; Sally Kempton and Susan Brownmiller, journalists and members of New York Radical Feminists; and Ivy Bottini, Do-

gether as Women, Regardless of Sexual Preference," and "Is the Statue of Liberty a Lesbian, Too?"

During the question period, Miss Alexander said she thought the movement had taken an overly long time to deal with the Lesbian issue because many women in the movement were afraid to confront it.

'Such an Explosive Issue'

"It's such an explosive issue," she said. "It can intimidate women. Many women would be reduced to tears if you called them Lesbians."

She added that the movement represented women who were "heterosexuals,

Lesbian issues covered in *The New York Times*, December 18, 1970.

Homosexual Unit Pickets The Times

About 15 persons representing the Homosexual Information Center of West Hollywood picketed The Times Wednesday noon to protest against the newspaper's refusal to print advertisements for the center.

The peaceful demonstration in downtown Los Angeles was marked by distribution of leaflets asking passersby not to buy the newspaper and not to patronize its advertisers "until the Times decides that 'homosexual' is not a dirty word.

"Some 200,000 homosexuals live, work, own or rent houses and apartments and buy products and services in the Los Angeles area and many of them subscribe to The Times," the leaflet said. "We believe The Times has no right to ignore them."

Los Angeles Times coverage of a picket at its offices, November 6, 1969.

Feminists took over the offices of *The Ladies' Home Journal* in 1970, and a few months later they were given a one-time special section to write about their issues.

A S recently as a year ago, most members of the New York chapter of the Daughters of Bilitis, the country's oldest and largest lesbian organization, knew each other only by first names, which were usually false. Meetings, in a small, stuffy, sublet room on West 38th Street, were uninspiring and poorly attended. Younger, more radical lesbians referred to D.O.B., as it is called, as "the N.A.A.C.P. of lesbian groups," and to its members as "Aunt Tabbies."

Today, although they are still in the "Establishment" lesbian group, many Daughters of Bilitis are on the verge of emerging from the closet. A growing minority are using their real names (first *and* last), marching in protest demonstrations, testifying at hearings on discrimination against homosexuals, appearing on television talk shows and lecturing on college campuses.

This new turn of events so angered 31 D.O.B.

court two weeks later, but about 50 members from various homophile organizations did, to protest the summons D.O.B. had received.

In December, nine leaders of the women's liberation movement held a press conference in the Washington Square Methodist Church in Greenwich Village at which they issued a statement supporting their homosexual sisters. Several women publicly identified themselves as lesbians, and urged their sisters to do so, too.

"People must speak up as lesbians," said Barbara Love, a comely blonde. "I am a lesbian. We've got to come out of the closet and fight, because we're not going to get anywhere if we don't."

But perhaps the most significant event for the Daughters of Bilitis occurred on Jan. 3, when members opened the first exclusively lesbian center in New York, one of two in the country (the other is in Los Angeles). The center, at 141

drew laughter when she said: "I dig lesbians. Some of them are my best friends."

The loft was jampacked with women, most of them wearing pants. One man who straggled in was asked to leave, and did. There were teenagers with frizzy Janis Joplin hair; gray-haired grandmotherly types toting shopping bags; black women with Afros; mannish-looking women wearing caps and heavy boots, and a few extremely beautiful women who looked as though they had spent at least an hour applying make-up. Some of the lesbian couples held hands as they sat on wooden folding chairs, listening to the speakers. Everybody seemed to laugh a lot.

R UTH SIMPSON, a petite 44-year-old public relations woman with a big voice and a pixyish quality reminiscent of Claudette Colbert, called the meeting to order by stomping on a black wooden platform at the front of the meeting hall.

The Disciples Of Sappho, Updated

By JUDY KLEMESRUD

members that they recently bolted from the mother organization to form a conservative

Prince Street, in a block of shabby buildings in the lower Village, is a cavernous second-floor

She was wearing a camel-colored pants suit and a cameo necklace given to her for Christmas by

The lesbian Daughters of Bilitis group was featured in *The New York Times*, March 28, 1971.

This post-Stonewall *Harper's Magazine* essay by Joseph Epstein sparked outrage in the gay community. It appeared in the September 1970 issue.

What It Means To Be a Homosexual

By MERLE MILLER

Author Merle Miller came out as a result of the *Harper's* piece and wrote this essay about his sexuality in *The New York Times Magazine* of January 17, 1971. It was later published as a book.

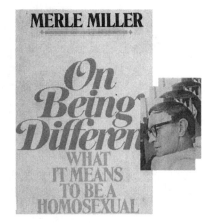

This *Village Voice* edition of September 3, 1970, featured articles on both the gay and women's movements.

A homophobic slip by the *Los Angeles Times* on April 27, 1975, resulted in a *Times* reporter's fighting from the inside to make changes. It was an otherwise innocuous Cecil Smith review of a new cop TV show, headlined "Barney Miller: A Cop Who Copes with Funny Folks." Smith pointed to the "thieves and con men and hookers and flashers and gunsels, the faggots and fauna … ."

Miami Vote Increases Activism on Homosexual Rights

By B. DRUMMOND AYRES Jr.
Special to The New York Times

MIAMI, June 8—Though Miami area residents voted overwhelmingly yesterday to revoke broad legal protection for homosexuals, the argument over their status in society resumed full force today, not only in Miami but also in other parts of the country.

plans to continue the struggle here and elsewhere.

Local homosexual leaders threatened to take their cause to court and prepared to send representatives to New York this weekend for a major conference on homosexual rights at the headquarters of the National Gay Task Force, one of the country's largest homosexual organiza-

Human Rights, the main Miami homosexual group. "We may go to court. We got beaten badly in the battle here, but the war is just beginning. We're coming out of Miami with national unity and momentum."

Exultant leaders of Miami's anti-homosexual forces offered advice and assistance to similar groups elsewhere and an-

Anita Bryant's anti-gay efforts in Florida made news across the U.S. Here is coverage in *The New York Times* of June 9, 1977.

Lesbian and Gay Media Advocates, launched in 1979 in Boston, was among the earliest media-monitoring groups. It published a book, *Talk Back!*, in 1982 to provide tips for other gays. The back cover featured this group of LGMA members, from left: Bill Mulkern, Sasha Alyson (whose Alyson Books published the book), Marcie Hershman, Ed Sams, David Peterson, Diane Green and Raymond Hopkins.

N.B.C. Acts After Complaints By Homosexual Organizations

By LES BROWN

Officials of the National Broadcasting Company yesterday acknowledged that the network had at times dealt unfairly with homosexuals in its programs, and they agreed to maintain a continuing liaison with homosexual organizations for advice in future treatment of homosexual topics.

The agreement was forged after meetings at N.B.C. yesterday afternoon between four representatives of the National Gay Task Force and network executives involved in programing and program standards.

'Today' Show Disrupted

The meeting had been arranged before the disruption of the "Today" show Friday morning by Mark Siegel, who later identified himself as a member of the Gay Raiders, a Phila-

for "instant humor" on all the networks, and it brought to a head the frustrations of organizations trying to negotiate with broadcast companies for more respectful treatment of homosexuals.

The National Gay Task Force and the Gay Activists Alliance have in effect been seeking status as a minority group, much like blacks, Jews, Roman Catholics, Chicanos and others who have been able to persuade the networks not to exploit the myths and stereotypes that have oppressed them. The N.B.C. agreement has been taken as a victory by the homosexual groups.

No National Protest

Nationwide demonstrations appear not to have taken place, at least not on the scale en-

Gay media-monitoring efforts were covered by *The New York Times* of October 27, 1973.

A controversial 1974 episode of the *Marcus Welby, M.D.*, medical drama aired on ABC-TV despite protests, as covered in this *New York Times* article of September 28, 1974.

3 STATIONS REJECT 'WELBY' EPISODE

Homosexual-Rights Groups Fought Molestation Story

By LES BROWN

A forthcoming episode of the television series "Marcus Welby, M.D." that deals with the sexual molestation of a 14-year-old boy by one of his teachers has been rejected for broadcast by three ABC-TV stations, largely as a result of a coordinated national campaign by homosexual-rights groups.

Four regular advertisers have also withdrawn for that episode. They are Bayer Aspirin, Listerine, Gallo Wine and Ralston Purina.

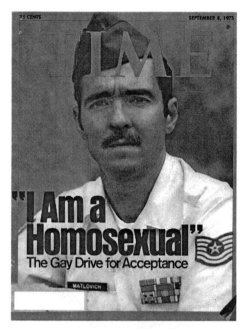

One of the most iconic gay magazine covers of all time was on this September 8, 1975, issue of *Time* magazine, featuring Air Force Technical Sergeant Leonard Matlovich, who was fighting the military's gay ban.

***Chicago Today*, owned by the *Chicago Tribune* at that point, covered gays in this June 1972 series.**
Courtesy of the M. Kuda Archives

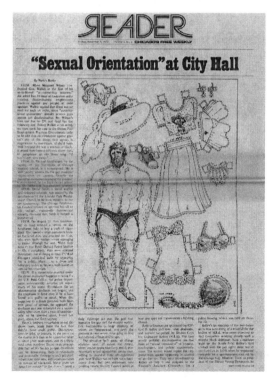

The alternative *Chicago Reader* newspaper's gay cover story of November 2, 1973.
Courtesy of the M. Kuda Archives

LEFT: In September 1979, the *Chicago Sun-Times* ran a series on the gay community.
Courtesy of the M. Kuda Archives

ABOVE: The *Chicago Tribune*'s City Trib section of March 4, 1983, ran a feature on gays.
Courtesy of the M. Kuda Archives

The Chicago Gay Crusader of March–April 1974 covered gays who were protesting an anti-gay column by *Chicago Daily News* writer Mike Royko.
Courtesy of the M. Kuda Archives

The Chicago Gay Crusader in January 1974 covered the changing views of advice columnist Ann Landers, right below a headline noting that the American Psychiatric Association's board had voted to remove homosexuality from its list of mental disorders
Courtesy of the M. Kuda Archives

Cities Face a Growing Problem: Vicious Attacks on Homosexuals

By BILL CURRY, *Times Staff Writer*

PORTLAND, Ore.—The attack came out of the night's shadows. Walking on Irving Street here, the 34-year-old man heard his assailant yell, "Hey, faggot!" and then felt a punch that broke his nose.

Ten minutes of terror followed. The attacker was joined by a second man, and together they pummeled their victim bloody, dislocating his shoulder, fracturing a facial bone and all the while punctuating their attack with sexual epithets: "Queer!" "Faggot!" "You enjoy this, don't you?"

"They could tell I was gay," the man recalled later, showing the

Nov. 5, Richard L. Davidson, a 46-year-old known as a "chicken hawk" for his preferences for younger males, was beaten to death in his apartment with a heavy blunt object and his apartment ransacked. Two weeks later a suspect was arrested on a forgery charge involving the use of credit cards stolen during an earlier attack on another homosexual man.

And Davidson's was not the first such killing in Portland. On March 28, 1979, James Roland Chavez, 26, was fatally beaten by two teen-age brothers who allegedly bragged in a bar about "beating up a queer."

a folded knife. He was attacked on a busy street at the crossroads of the Portland gay area by a band of teen-agers who had assaulted three homosexuals moments before.

"One guy was asked if he was homosexual," said Portland Police Lt. Dan Noelle, in describing another assault, "and he said, 'No, I'm a Christian,' and they smacked him with a two-by-four. Once you're asked or told you're a homosexual, it doesn't seem to matter what the reaction is.

"It doesn't seem to dawn on (straight) people's minds that this could happen to them," said Mike Sandmeyer, 25, of the Portland

"The church and government," Burrows charged, "are validating people's (presumed) right to perpetrate violence."

"It's people who have heard totally bad things about gay people." said Larry Whitson, 31, who helped found the Safe Streets Alliance last year to combat street violence against homosexuals. "Now they're getting permission from society to view people who are different as appropriate victims."

In Portland, religious groups have "stood witness" outside the Embers, urging homosexuals to repent. A recent unsuccessful City Council candidate campaigned with flyers

ty's Laurelhurst Park.

Whitson said he and two friends were in the park one night when a group of three youths with clubs and boards confronted them and for 10 minutes threatened them and taunted them. "We're out killing queers and cleaning up the park," one said to the group. "If we catch you alone, you'll be dead."

Eight to 10 assaults eventually occurred in the park, including one on a young homosexual that was so brutal it left him with brain damage and in speech therapy. Police deployed casually dressed undercover officers to "swish through the park," as one officer described it.

outside of the bar to help someone or we're calling the police."

'Shock to Your System'

"This is more than physical damage." 18-year-old Michael Cortez said through clenched teeth, his broken jaw wired shut. "It's emotional damage and financial damage. It's a shock to your system." A one-punch attack on him outside a gay bar on Feb. 14 left him unable to work for two weeks, costing him $400 in pay and thus his apartment.

Cortez remembers that as he lay on the sidewalk bleeding, his assailant said, "Look at the queer."

In one attack described to the

The *Los Angeles Times* covered anti-gay attacks, March 6, 1981.

L.A. Homosexuals Create Own Brand of Political Activism

Gays, Lesbians Succeed in Building Unusual Network of Election Clout

By AUSTIN SCOTT, *Times Staff Writer*

In the very short history of America's gay and lesbian politics, there has never been a political force quite like the one mixed on flexing its muscles in the upcoming Los Angeles city election.

There have been other success stories. San Francisco has had two openly gay supervisors. Its mayor, as well as the mayor of Washington, D.C., might not have been elected without well-organized homosexual support. Elaine Noble, a Boston lesbian, spent four years in the Massachusetts Legislature, thanks to her community's strong support.

But in Los Angeles, politically active gays and lesbians, supported by their heterosexual friends, have succeeded in building a network of political clout that is based on converting money and influence into political power, rather than electing gays to political office.

"No serious politician in his right mind is going to ignore the gay vote in this town—the gay vote and gay money," said Larry Kaplan, who is helping direct the campaign for Michael Woo, a City Council candidate in the 13th District, which has a large gay population.

Success in L.A.

Not even in San Francisco or New York city have power building attempts succeeded as they have in Los Angeles. Examples of how the clout is affecting the April 14 primary election include:

—Early in February, more than 25 of 51 invited candidates for city and county offices paraded before three interview committees of the predominantly homosexual Stonewall Democratic Club, seeking the endorsement, which can help bring in campaign contributions, precinct workers, more endorsements, and votes.

is destined to ride in this annual Gay Pride parade.

"They didn't tell me they were queens," he later told a reporter. ". . . I said no because I felt I ought to be taken as a queer mayor."

—The Municipal Elections Committee of Los Angeles (MECLA), a gay and lesbian political action committee that has no parallel in the country, expects to raise $100,000 at its annual fund-raising dinner-dance next Friday.

Much of the money will be contributed to local, state and national officeholders who are willing to support gay and lesbian concerns. Candidates from Bradley on down seek contributions from MECLA in the same way they seek endorsements from the Stonewall club.

Four years ago, MECLA pumped $5,000 into Jim

port last month from Stonewall, which instead endorsed Bradley.

The predominantly gay Log Cabin Republican Club has four to five dozen members and makes endorsements. But its recommendations are less influential than others because not many Republicans are deeply involved in the politics of the strongly Democratic city.

And, the GOP does not seem to offer gays the same warm welcome as do the Democrats. "There is resistance within the Republican party," said Chuck LaMoy, president of Log Cabin. "It's a matter of being admitted that's all."

It is not necessarily easy for gay and lesbian activists to agree on an endorsement. In an emotional meeting

The most heavily homosexual precincts were more heavily registered to vote than the citywide average and turned out a higher percentage of voters.

last month, members of Stonewall gathered in an old Hollywood home just off Sunset Boulevard to debate for half an hour over whom they should support in the 13th Council District.

The district stretches in a broad band across some of the most heavily homosexual areas of Hollywood, Silverlake, Echo Park and Highland Park. Councilwoman Bloverson, who represents the area, is counted as one of their longest and most steadfast supporters.

Stephen Schulte, one of the leaders of Los Angeles' traditionally diverse gay community.

The *Los Angeles Times* on gay activism in its city, March 15, 1981.

Billie Jean admits gay affair in 'palimony'

From Tribune Wire Services

LOS ANGELES—Tennis star Billie Jean King admitted Friday that she had a homosexual affair with a woman several years ago, but she called it "a mistake" and asked her fans to show her compassion and understanding.

Mrs. King, 37, who was joined by her husband Larry and her attorney Dennis

Tennis legend Billie Jean King faced the media in 1981 and initially denied allegations of a same-sex affair. This is from the *Chicago Tribune* of May 2, 1981.

Outbreaks of Pneumonia Among Gay Males Studied

By HARRY NELSON, *Times Medical Writer*

Researchers are investigating mysterious outbreaks of pneumonia that have occurred among male homosexuals in Los Angeles and several other cities across the nation.

A report to be issued today by the Centers for Disease Control in Atlanta describes the first five cases, which were all homosexual men in their 20s or 30s stricken by pneumonia caused by a parasite that usually affects only cancer patients.

Another half dozen cases are under investigation in San Francisco, along with an undetermined number in New York, Toronto and Florida, The Times has learned.

According to Dr. Wayne Shandera, a CDC epidemiologist working in Los Angeles, researchers cannot explain why all cases so far have been male homosexuals. One patient died from the pneumonia.

"The best we can say is that somehow the pneumonia appears to be related to gay life style," Shandera said.

Nearly all of the pneumonia normally occurring in the United States is caused by bacteria or viruses, but the outbreak among the gay males has been due to neither bacteria nor virus but rather to a protozoan parasite named *Pneumocystic carenii.*

This organism is a common cause of death in cancer patients and transplant patients whose ability to fight infection has been compromised by anti-cancer drugs or drugs aimed at preventing rejection of a transplanted organ.

According to experts, perhaps half of all adults carry *P. carenii* in their

Please see GAYS, Page 25

This *Los Angeles Times* story of June 5, 1981, was among the first to cover what later became known as AIDS.

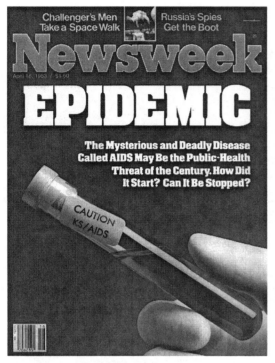

Newsweek cover story on AIDS,
April 18, 1983.

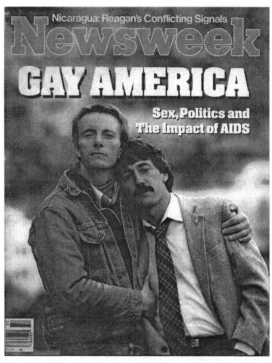

Newsweek cover story on gays and AIDS,
August 8, 1983.

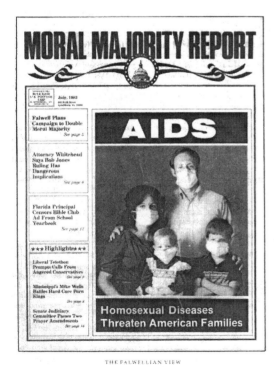

Anti-gay *Moral Majority Report* on AIDS,
July 1983.

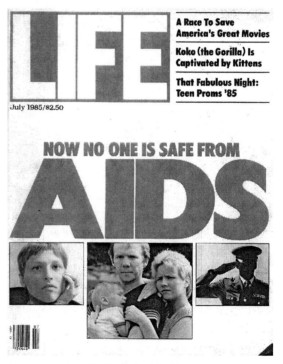

Life cover on AIDS, July 1985.

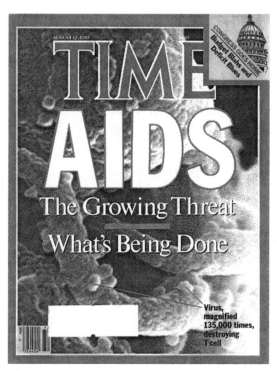

Time on AIDS, August 12, 1985.

Mother Jones AIDS coverage,
November 1987.

People magazine coverage of Ryan White's
battle with AIDS, August 3, 1987.

Time AIDS coverage, February 16, 1987.

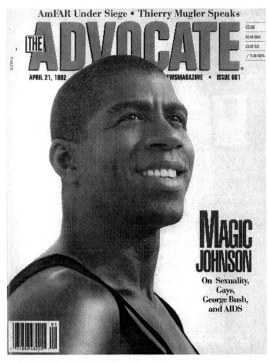

Magic Johnson interview in *The Advocate,*
April 21, 1992.

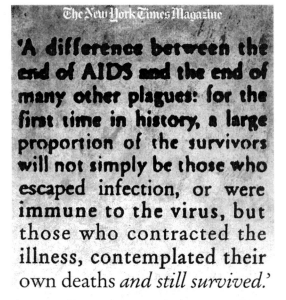

The New York Times Magazine AIDS feature,
November 10, 1996.

Time's April 23, 1979, cover on "How Gay Is
Gay?"

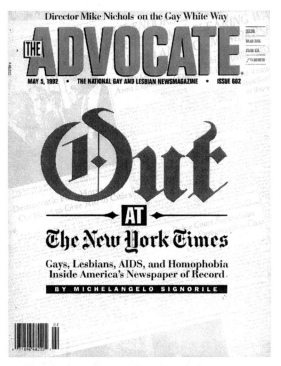

The issue of gays at *The New York Times* was
covered by Michelangelo Signorile in this
May 5, 1992, *Advocate* cover story.

Newsweek looked at lesbians, June 21, 1993.

Vanity Fair attracted a lot of attention for this eye-catching August 1993 cover with Cindy Crawford and k.d. lang.

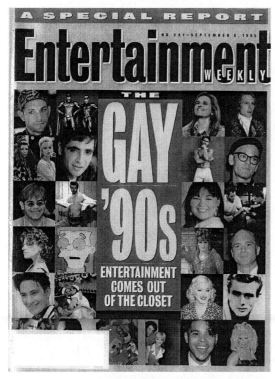

Entertainment Weekly's Gay '90s cover, September 8, 1995.

Time's Ellen DeGeneres "Yep, I'm Gay" cover, April 14, 1997.

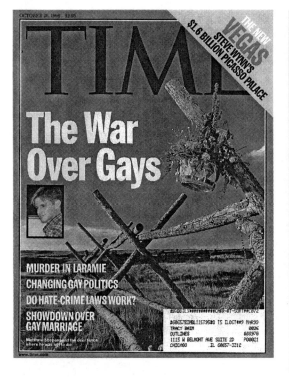

Matthew Shepard's murder was covered in the mainstream and gay media. Here is the *Time* cover of October 26, 1998, and *The Advocate*'s of November 24, 1998.

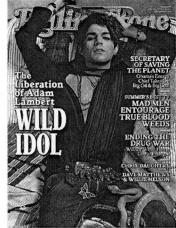

Time covered gay teens, October 10, 2005.

People magazine reported entertainer Ellen DeGeneres and actress Portia de Rossi's wedding, September 1, 2008.

Pop star Adam Lambert on the cover of *Rolling Stone*, June 9, 2009.

Newsweek on gay marriage, January 18, 2010.

Gay bunnies in *The New York Times Magazine,* April 4, 2010.

Black Enterprise on being black and gay in corporate America, July 2011.

Newsweek on Obama's switch on gay marriage, May 21, 2012.

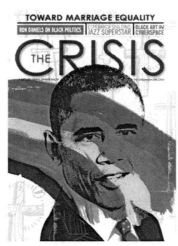

The NAACP's magazine *The Crisis* on Obama and the gays, summer 2012.

Entertainment Weekly's June 29, 2012, cover on gays in Hollywood.

2

Gay News: In the Beginning

By Tracy Baim

There are a lot of "begats" in the world of gay periodicals. An American serviceman saw homosexual publications in Germany during World War I. These inspired him to start his own gay group and newsletter in Chicago, and that man later was a motivator for the founder of the Mattachine Society, which in turn inspired people to create publications springing from the group.

There is not a direct line of descent for the nearly 100 years of U.S. gay journals, newsletters, newspapers, magazines and other forms of media. Rather, their history has taken a twisted, variegated path made up of a motley assortment of activists, writers, editors, photographers, poets, historians, fiction writers and many more who contributed to the patchwork quilt that is our publishing past.

The explosion of gay periodicals in the second half of the 20th century was due partly to the parallel growth of an out gay movement (once called homosexual or homophile), but due as well to the changes in American society—and almost as important, the changes in access to offset printing and, later, low-cost desktop computer technology.

The publishing of newsletters or newspapers naturally flowed from other forms of publishing, and many of the early gay journals reinforced the connection to fiction and poetry by publishing such works in their pages.

A few writers from those early gay print days later blossomed into some of our community's most important fiction and nonfiction authors. The same is true of early gay press journalists who later had distinguished careers in the mainstream media.

This chapter provides an overview of gay periodical history, with an emphasis on newspapers, but some of the long-term gay newspapers are profiled in depth in full chapters later in this book.

The Gay Press: Filling the Void

Chapter 1 listed the good and mostly bad of mainstream media coverage to show just how much of a dearth there was of gay and pro-gay voices in the U.S. prior to 1969, and even prior to 1980.

So what did the gays do? They created their own community, their own press and their own social and entertainment networks. Some didn't have enough money to make it for long. Others thrived and created safe spaces for future generations.

Early publications inclusive of homosexuals may not have called themselves "gay" or even "newspapers"—as in the case of *The Little Review*, run by lesbians, and *Fire!!,* in part run by gay men—but they were kindred spirits, and certainly planted the seeds of change. Many early periodicals were small-format journals, before larger tabloid-format publications started in the 1960s.

OutHistory.org's Jonathan Katz recently found documents that suggest there may have been a publication created by a group of people who gathered in the late 1800s. In newly uncovered papers from Earl Lind, someone involved with a rumored group of "androgynes" in New York in the 1890s, there was reportedly a resort called Paresis Hall, where a group was formed called Cercle Hermaphroditos "for defense against the world's bitter persecution." Little is known about the supposed group, but sections of a lost memoir of Lind suggest it did publish some support materials.

Before more-identifiably gay publications began to appear, some existed that were at least inclusive of a "gay" voice.

The German Connection

Der Eigene (The Exceptional) was the first long-lasting gay journal in the world, according to *Homosexuality and Male Bonding in Pre-Nazi Germany: The Youth Movement, the Gay Movement, and Male Bonding Before Hitler's Rise*, edited by Harry Oosterhuis with translations by Hubert Kennedy. The book features transcripts from *Der Eigene,* which started in 1896.

An article by Manfred Herzer in the *Encyclopedia of Homosexuality* agrees that *Der Eigene* was the first long-lasting gay periodical but mentions another would-be journal that preceded it and one that came just after it, each of them expiring after a single issue: Karl Heinrich Ulrichs' *Uranus* (Leipzig, 1870) and Marc-André Raffalovich's *Annales de L'Unisexualité* (Lyon, 1897).

Meanwhile, famed sexologist Magnus Hirschfeld founded his Scientific Humanitarian Committee in Berlin in 1897. "From this group in 1899 came *Jahrbuch für sexuelle Zwischenstufen*, the first scholarly journal for the study of concerns of interest to homosexuals," as www.glbtq.com recounts. The annual publication lasted until 1923. "Other German publications proliferated throughout the early decades of the twentieth century; among them was one directed toward lesbians, *[Die] Freundin*. Two French journals also appeared quite early: *Akademos*, which was published monthly during 1909 by Count Adelswärd Fersen [*i.e.,* Baron Jacques d'Adelswärd-Fersen], and *Inversions*, which appeared briefly in 1925 before being suppressed by the police."

Der Eigene helped advise and defend gay people, and it even ran personal ads to help gay men meet one another. *Der Eigene* was published from 1896 to 1931 by Adolf Brand in Berlin. In addition to Brand, contributors included Benedict Friedlaender, Hanns Heinz Ewers, Erich Mühsam, Kurt Hiller, Ernst Burchard, John Henry Mackay, Theodor Lessing, Klaus Mann and Thomas Mann, as well as artists Wilhelm von Gloeden, Fidus, and Sascha Schneider, according to Wikipedia. The journal may have had around 1,500 subscribers

Brand was the leader of the Gemeinschaft der Eigenen (Community of the Exceptional), Germany's second gay group. As Oosterhuis notes in his book, "The attitudes of Brand and his followers ... differed substantially from those of Hirschfeld and his supporters ... ."

Brand was an anarchist and the early editions of *Der Eigene* reflected this. It was published "in different forms and with changing frequencies," Oosterhuis reports, adding that in 1898 it changed "from an anarchist into a literary and artistic homosexual journal." Because of a lack of money, the publication stopped for three years, resuming in 1903 as "a journal for male culture, art, and literature," as quoted by Kennedy. Brand also served two months in prison on immorality charges that year for distributing "lascivious writings." Brand published several other journals, often with sexual portraits of young men.

During the homosexual scandal of 1907 that involved officials under Kaiser Wilhelm II, Brand inserted himself into the debate by publishing a pamphlet about the hypocrisy of the chancellor, Prince Bernhard von Bülow, who then sued Brand for libel and won. One might say Brand was among the earliest advocates of "outing" anti-gay politicians who were themselves gay. Brand was sentenced to 18 months in prison. After many years, and after World War I, Brand and Hirschfeld briefly mended fences and worked more together, according to the Oosterhuis book. The niceties ended when Brand published a book that attacked Hirschfeld's work.

Like Hirschfeld, Brand did not escape the rise of Hitler and his Nazi machine. Materials needed to produce publications were seized in 1933 and given to Ernst Röhm. Brand was destitute and sent a letter saying the movement was over. The website glbtq.com reports that on November 29, 1933, Brand wrote to the Sexological Society in London, complaining: "I have been plundered of everything. I have nothing left to sell and am financially ruined. I no longer know from what I and mine can continue to live. For my whole life's work is now destroyed. And most of my followers don't have even the courage to write me a letter, not to mention support my work with any kind of payment. My loss through the confiscations and the prohibition comes to around 10,000 Mark [more than half a million in today's dollars]."

Brand had married a woman (Elise Behrendt, who accepted his homosexuality) after serving in the German army in World War I. The couple died in early 1945 in an Allied bombing raid.

As glbtq.com notes: "Hitler's regime likewise suppressed the publications of the German gay and lesbian movement and destroyed much of Hirschfeld's research; nevertheless, other European groups dedicated to understanding homosexuality and to increasing tolerance for gay men and lesbians arose, and they frequently published newsletters and other periodicals. The journal *Der Kreis* (*The Circle*) began publishing in 1932 in Zurich, and, after World War II, *Vriendschap* (*Friendship*) and *Lesbos* were established in Holland."

Der Kreis, the Swiss periodical, was another important journal outside the U.S., and it ran from 1932 to 1967 (appearing under other names in its early years). It was the only gay periodical that published during the Nazi era. *The Ideal Gay Man: The Story of Der Kreis*, by Hubert Kennedy, "traces the origins of *Der Kreis* from its first lesbian-edited, hectographed pages in 1932 to its transformation into a male-oriented monthly under the editorship of actor Karl Meier."

Hirschfeld was far better-known than Brand in the U.S. He gave lectures here, including one in 1931 at Chicago's bohemian Dill Pickle Club, according to Chad Heap in *Slumming: Sexual and Racial Encounters in American Nightlife, 1885–1940.*

Persecuted by the Nazis, Hirschfeld died in exile in 1935. His life's work was ignored by *The New York Times*. As reported in *The New York Times on Gay and Lesbian Issues*, a 2011 book by Susan Burgess: "Following the custom of the time, his May 17 *Times* obituary did not name his partner, cite the groundbreaking work he performed related to same-sex sexuality, or acknowledge that his Jewish heritage was only a partial explanation for the mistreatment he received from the Nazis." (See more about Hirschfeld in Chapter 1.)

Henry Gerber: The History Maker

While Germany boasted of early homosexual publications, the first known explicitly gay publication in the U.S. was *Friendship and Freedom*, published by Chicago's Society for Human Rights. (The publication's name was the same as the one used for Adolf Brand's periodical, *Freundschaft und Freiheit*. The society's name was a translation of Bund für Menschenrecht, the name of the 1920s group organized by the German publisher, author and campaigner Friedrich Radszuweit.)

The Chicago publication appears prominently in a photo of a collection of early, mostly German, homosexual-emancipation periodicals. But no copies of *Friendship and Freedom* are known to exist today.

Gerber, who had served in the American occupation of Germany after World War I, was inspired in his work by Hirschfeld.

Gerber's own battles are documented by Jonathan Ned Katz in *Gay American History: Lesbians and Gay Men in the U.S.A.: A Documentary History*, and more recently in St. Sukie de la Croix's *Chicago Whispers: A History of LGBT Chicago Before Stonewall.*

The 1924 Illinois charter of the Society for Human Rights said the organization existed to "promote and to protect the interests of people who by reasons of mental and physical abnormalities are abused and hindered in the legal pursuit of happiness which is guaranteed them by the Declaration of Independence, and to combat the public prejudices against them by dissemination of facts according to modern science among intellectuals of mature age. The Society stands only for law and order; it is in harmony with any and all general laws insofar as they protect the rights of others, and does in no manner recommend any acts in violation of present laws nor advocate any matter inimical to the public welfare."

Seven men put their names on the founding document, including Gerber, who was a postal worker. Gerber wrote about his experience more than 30 years later, for *ONE* magazine in 1962:

"Just 37 years ago, in 1925, a few of my friends and myself were dragged off to jail in Chicago causing our own efforts to ameliorate the plight of homosexuals to come to an early end.

"From 1920 to 1923, I had served with the Army of Occupation in Germany after World War I. ... I had subscribed to German homophile magazines and made several trips to Berlin. ... I had always bitterly felt the injustice with which my own American society accused the homosexual of 'immoral acts.' I hated this society which allowed the majority, frequently corrupt itself, to persecute those who deviated from the established norms in sexual matters.

"I realized at once that homosexuals themselves needed nearly as much attention as the laws pertaining to their acts. How could one go about such a difficult task [that of homosexual emancipation]? The prospect of going to jail did not bother me. I had a vague idea that I wanted to help solve the problem. I had not yet read the opinion of Clarence Darrow that 'no other offence has ever been visited with such severe penalties as seeking to help the oppressed.' All my friends to whom I spoke about my plans advised against my doing anything so rash and futile. I thought to myself that if I succeeded I might become known to history as deliverer of the downtrodden, even as Lincoln. But I am not sure my thoughts were entirely upon fame. If I succeeded in freeing the homosexual, I too would benefit.

"What was needed was a Society, I concluded. My boss, whom I had pleased by translating a work of philosophy from the German, helped me write a Declaration of Purpose for our new Society for Human Rights, the same name used by the homosexuals of Germany for their work. The first difficulty was in rounding up enough members and contributors so the work could go forward. The average homosexual, I found, was ignorant concerning himself. Others were fearful. Still others were frantic or depraved. Some were blasé."

Gerber told his new colleagues they would do a publication, *Friendship and Freedom*: "I then set about putting out the first issue of *Friendship and Freedom* and worked hard on the second issue. It soon became apparent that my friends were illiterate and penniless. I had to both write and finance. Two issues, alas, were all we could publish. The most difficult task was to get men of good reputation to back up the Society. I needed noted medical authorities to endorse us. But they usually refused to endanger their reputations."

A Chicago police detective and a newspaper reporter came to Gerber's home. The police took his typewriter, his commission as a notary public, all the literature of the society and his personal diaries as well as his bookkeeping accounts.

Other members were arrested as well, and the following headline appeared in the *Chicago American* of July 13, 1925, "Girl Reveals Strange Sex Cult Run by Dad." This article was uncovered by St. Sukie de la Croix in research for his book *Chicago Whispers*.

De la Croix found a review of Gerber's newsletter in *Paris Gay 1925*, a 1981 French book co-written by Gilles Barbedette and Michel Carassou. It includes the review by Clarens in *L'Amitié* from 1925. The review said in part that *Friendship and Freedom* "is a moral, homosexual American newsletter." The reviewer said its backers wished above all "to lead the way towards modifying the unjust law which oppresses them."

While its members were all eventually cleared of charges, the group folded. Gerber later wrote about homosexuality and his experiences, including articles in mainstream media such as *The Modern Thinker* and a literary magazine called *Chanticleer*, both in the 1930s.

Gerber also published an 8½-by-5½-inch mimeographed newsletter, *Contacts*, just for his friends, from 1930 to 1939. He died in 1972.

Vice Versa: **Lesbian History**

Another early publication, this one serving lesbians, was called *Vice Versa*, with the subtitle "America's Gayest Magazine." It was a typed newsletter produced in 1947–48 by a woman, Edith Eyde, who used the pseudonym Lisa Ben (an anagram of the word "lesbian"). She was a secretarial assistant at RKO Studios in Los Angeles, and *Vice Versa* is believed to be the first lesbian-specific publication in the U.S. *Vice Versa* ran nine issues, and they were all given out for free. Ben made just 10 copies of each one because of limited resources. After initially sending some through the mails, she stopped doing so for fear of running afoul of obscenity laws.

Ben stopped the newsletter after a job transfer. As noted on OutHistory.org, "Though short-lived, *Vice Versa* established itself as a forerunner for gay American publications, providing a more wide-ranging audience with upbeat short stories, editorials, book reviews, and a letter column to entertain and inspire readers to perpetuate the existence of gay editorials and preserve the pleasure of their lifestyle. … Despite being clandestinely circulated in a small community and spread by word of mouth, *Vice Versa* set literary precedent for *The Ladder*, the next lesbian magazine released nationally," by the Daughters of Bilitis, the first national lesbian organization.

Rodger Streitmatter, in his book *Unspeakable: The Rise of the Gay and Lesbian Press in America*, said *Vice Versa* "contained no bylines, no photographs, no advertisements, no masthead ... yet it set the agenda that has defined lesbian and gay journalism for 50 years."

Eric Marcus interviewed Ben for his book *Making History: The Struggle for Lesbian and Gay Equal Rights*. "I put in five copies at a time with carbon paper, and typed it through twice and ended up with ten copies of *Vice Versa*," she said. "That's all I could manage. There were no duplicating machines in those days and, of course, I couldn't go to a printer."

In one essay in *Vice Versa*, from September 1947, Ben wrote: "Perhaps even *Vice Versa* might be the forerunner of better magazines dedicated to the third sex, which in some future time might take their rightful place on the newsstands beside other publications, to be available openly and without restriction to those who wish to read them."

Ben told Marcus that she "never thought of it as being bold at the time. I was just sort of fantasizing." But what started out as a way for Lisa Ben to meet other lesbians did in fact become an important forerunner to future gay media.

The 1950s, Breaking Away

In the 1950s, three important gay and lesbian publications began, each of them lasting longer than the previous short-term periodicals: *ONE*, *Mattachine Review* and *The Ladder*. (There is much more detail on these three publications in the next chapters in this book.)

The Mattachine Society was founded in 1950. Mattachine was inspired by Henry Gerber's work in Chicago. A Californian named Harry Hay learned of Gerber's earlier society from the lover of a former member. According to historian John Poling: "The notion of a gay political organization appealed to Hay, who was struggling with the discrimination and danger of being a gay man. With the help of four friends, Hay built on Gerber's idea of an organized society. The Mattachine Society, as Hay dubbed it, began in Los Angeles in 1951. Hay took the name Mattachine from Société Mattachine, said to be a secret medieval fraternity of unmarried townsmen whose masked appearance gave them the freedom to speak the truth."

In 1952, some people attending a Mattachine discussion group suggested launching a publication. A short time later they formed ONE, Inc. (which later offered classes and engaged in other activities beyond publishing *ONE*). The first issue of *ONE* magazine was published in January 1953, produced by W. Dorr Legg, Martin Block, Dale Jennings, Don Slater and William Lambert (another name for Legg). Started in Los Angeles, *ONE* soon had a national following. By November 1953, its subhead was "The Homosexual Magazine." The Los Angeles postmaster called *ONE* "obscene" in October

1954, and it took four years for *ONE* to win its case, which ended in the U.S. Supreme Court. (See www.OutHistory.org for a more detailed history of ONE, Inc.)

ONE was not the only gay publication to fight postal censors, but it did win its important case. In other cities, local police and postal authorities sometimes monitored or raided newspaper and magazine offices.

ONE was primarily male, but women were involved. After some internal battles common in the gay movement, the publication folded in 1967. ONE, Inc., also put out other journals over the years, including the *ONE Institute Quarterly of Homophile Studies*.

In 1972, there was a short-lived attempt to revive *ONE* magazine, edited by Richard Conger and Jim Kepner, and published by ONE, Inc. There were four issues published. See www.tyleralpern.com/one.html for more details.

Members of the Mattachine Society's San Francisco chapter wanted their own publication, the *Mattachine Review*, and it served an important role documenting the gay movement from its founding in 1955 through 1967. It was a networking tool for Mattachine members and nonmembers, providing information on gay culture, history and events. It was more assimilationist than *ONE*. Harold "Hal" Call was the man who started the *Review*, and he was also a businessman—he owned a press that printed the *Review* and other homophile publications. Call was a leader who used his own name and face in local media in the 1950s when interviewed about the homosexual movement. He also started a bar rag, *Town Talk*, which ran briefly in the 1960s through 1966.

Some of the Mattachine Society chapters had their own publications. In Chicago, two Mattachine affiliates came and went. But eventually, in 1965, a stronger, completely independent group was formed, Mattachine Midwest. For two decades it ran the *Mattachine Midwest Newsletter*, which provided important links for the local and national community. The monthly publication covered police raids, meetings, social events, legal issues and much more.

John Poling did a study of Mattachine Midwest and its effect on Chicago's gay community. The group started in part as a response to police harassment of gays and gay bars. There was one especially horrendous 1964 raid on a bar called the Fun Lounge that was the straw that broke the camel's back, as some activists said.

Issues of the *Mattachine Midwest Newsletter* provide details about the group's progress and work. The organization was very focused on getting its publication out to gay bars and gay-friendly bookstores. One time, the police used the newsletters as evidence against a bar owner for keeping a "disorderly house." The early circulation had already approached 2,000, and by 1970 it was around 8,000 copies.

Daughters of Bilitis, founded in San Francisco in 1955 by Phyllis Lyon and Del Martin, was groundbreaking in many ways. It eventually had chapters across the country, and its national publication, *The Ladder*, was a critical part of the growing lesbian movement. *The Ladder* started in October 1956, edited by Lyon, and ran monthly through 1970 and then every other month through 1972. *The Ladder* name was related to an image on the publication's first cover: a line drawing of women moving toward a ladder that ascended into the clouds.

Like the other early alternative newsletters, initially it was typed on a typewriter, mimeographed, stapled and sent through the mails to subscribers. It was distributed in a "brown paper bag." Even gay publications into the 1990s sent their magazines through the mail in envelopes, not free-standing, so as not to out subscribers. In later years, copies of *The Ladder* were sold on newsstands.

An early *Ladder* supporter was playwright Lorraine Hansberry, known for *A Raisin in the Sun*. She wrote letters to *The Ladder* and donated money.

"The *Ladder* self-consciously attempted to reach out to lesbians away from the large cities and avoided an overtly political stance, concentrating instead on poetry, fiction, history, and biography," states www.glbtq.com. "One of its most valuable features was a column by Barbara Grier entitled 'Lesbiana' that contained succinct summaries of current lesbian literature."

Streitmatter's *Unspeakable* book notes that by the end of the 1950s, the total circulation of *ONE*, *Mattachine Review* and *The Ladder* was 7,000, with 5,000 of the total belonging to *ONE*, about 1,000 to the *Review* and 700 to *The Ladder*. Those numbers would grow slightly in the 1960s, but not much beyond that base. Of course, those publications also had a very high pass-along rate, so their impact went far beyond their print runs.

Kepner's Views

Before he died in 1997, Jim Kepner, one of the most important pioneers of early gay journalism, was able to set down his own reflections on those years. His book, *Rough News, Daring Views: 1950s' Pioneer Gay Press Journalism*, came out the year after he died, from the Haworth Press. The book has an introduction by Kepner, a foreword by Wayne Dynes and a preface by Mark Thompson. The rest of the book is Kepner's own words from his 1950s journalism.

Kepner reports on a 1945 publication, *Equinox Errant*, "ostensibly the newsletter of the New York chapter of the U.S. Rocket Society ... . The publication was [Frank] McCourt's covert way of keeping in touch with homosexual servicemen he'd met." Kepner said that, in the 1940s, Henry Gerber, McCourt and Monwell Boyfrank "had written many letters to U.S. periodicals protesting the treatment of homosexuals, and several of these saw print."

Kepner notes that he actually wanted to start a publication well before *ONE* started, which would have been called *The Gay Fan*. He spoke to various friends and roommates as he moved around the country between 1943 and 1951. "I prepared a few pages and sounded out friends (most were horrified). Betty [Perdue] took me to my first Mattachine discussion group in December 1952 ... . That was a month after Martin Block, Dale Jennings, and Bill Lambert had begun planning what in January 1953 became America's first openly sold magazine by and for homosexuals."

He became a key contributor and co-editor of *ONE* from early on and until he had a falling-out with the staff in 1961. His first article was for the April 1954 issue of *ONE*. He went on to write thousands of articles for *ONE* and other gay and non-gay publications over the years.

Kepner called attention to several early journalism pioneers he felt were overlooked, including Roland Howard of Denver, Barbara Grier (writing as Gene Damon) and Stella Rush.

The reprinting of Kepner's writings from that era is an invaluable contribution to the history of the gay movement and gay journalism. There are thousands of nuggets of information that can start the trail for those interested in finding out more about how the community was covered in the mainstream media and alternative journals, how the police and politicians vilified gays and how the movement truly became much more of a community in the critical decade of the 1950s. The collection of Kepner's writings makes it very clear how important the gay media were in helping shine a light on homophobia and providing a guide to gays who wanted to respond.

Kepner also started *Pursuit & Symposium* in the 1960s as a more high-minded gay magazine, along the lines of *The New Yorker*. According to C. Todd White in his book *Pre-Gay L.A.: A Social History of the Movement for Homosexual Rights*, Kepner mortgaged his house to get money to start the magazine—and when it failed after just two issues in 1966, he lost his home.

Erotica

In addition to the more serious gay publications *ONE*, *Mattachine Review* and *The Ladder*, the 1950s also saw the rise of beefcake magazines. Those may not have been called gay, but their readership was significantly male. *Physique Pictorial* magazine by Bob Mizer was first published in 1951, and Michael Bronski, in *A Queer History of the United States*, said it was "the first physique magazine aimed at the male homosexual interested in appreciating, rather than becoming ... the idealized male form."

Many other male erotic publications were soon to come onto the U.S. scene. These included *Tomorrow's Man, Adonis, Grecian Guild Quarterly* and *Vim*. Meanwhile, Knud Rame, known as Kim Kent, was a Danish publisher, according to Robert Aldrich and Garry Wotherspoon (*Who's Who in Contemporary Gay and Lesbian History: From World War II to the Present Day*). Rame met Helmer Fogedgaard, founder of *Vennen* (*The Friend*), the first Scandinavian gay magazine. Rame, as Kent, started *Eos* magazine in 1958, and in 1963 he published Samuel Steward (writing as Phil Andros) for the first time for Danish readers. In 1962, Rame also started *Amigo* as a German and English title. *Amigo* is cited in *Homosexuality: A Selective Bibliography of Over 3,000 Items*, a 1971 compilation by William Parker. These references show that while *Amigo* was more of a pornographic magazine, both it and *Eos* did deal with political and social issues facing homosexuals. Here is one *Amigo* headline from 1963: "The Homosexual as Novelist," by Martyn Goff, then a bookseller and now a decorated and well-regarded British man of letters. Both *Eos* and *Amigo* stopped in 1975.

There were more than 100 male physique titles in English-speaking countries between 1950 and 1970, according to Thomas Waugh in *Hard to Imagine: Gay Male Eroticism in Photography and Film From Their Beginnings to Stonewall*.

In Chicago, gay entrepreneur and photographer Chuck Renslow opened Kris Studio to take photos for sale and for use in magazines. His three "physique" magazines were *Triumph* (1958), *Mars* (1963–68) and *The Rawhide Male* (1969). Renslow's photos and the drawings by Etienne (Renslow's lover Dom Orejudos) were used in most of Renslow's early men's magazines. When challenged in court on the ground that his magazines were "obscene," Renslow had the benefit of an earlier legal decision in a case brought to the Supreme Court by ONE, Inc., for *ONE* magazine. (For more on this topic, see the book I wrote with Owen Keehnen, *Leatherman: The Legend of Chuck Renslow*.)

Many later gay magazines incorporated full nudity, and some even included much conventional editorial content to inform their readers. These latter included *Drum* in the 1960s and *Blue Boy* in the 1970s.

Alternative Press

The 1960s were proving to be a huge transition period for all forms of media, including those serving the LGBT communities. There were two primary reasons for this: First, the 1960s in general saw a major shift in power, as civil-rights movements and baby boomers started to create their own forms of communication. Second, access to cheaper printing processes meant that more people could afford to start their own newspapers.

Papers that are "alternative" to the prevailing mainstream newspapers of the day go back hundreds of years. Blacks created their own alternatives to racist white-owned papers, and many ethnic groups created their own thriving newspaper culture, often in their native languages.

In response to the heightening Vietnam War, and also because of the availability of lower-cost printing options, the "underground" press started in full force in the 1960s. In cities and towns across the U.S., hundreds if not thousands of newsletters and newspapers cropped up, including *The Seed* in Chicago, *The Rag* in Austin, the *Sun* in Ann Arbor, *The San Francisco Oracle, The Paper* in East Lansing and many more.

In his 1985 book *Uncovering the Sixties: The Life and Times of the Underground Press*, Abe Peck said that in 1965 the *Los Angeles Free Press* "became the first underground paper to publish on a sustained basis. ... By 1967, twenty or so black-and-white or four-color tabloids were being produced in the United States via cheap offset-press technology and a labor pool of former students."

Another book that does an excellent job of including the roles of gay men in the underground press movement is 2011's *Smoking Typewriters: The Sixties Underground Press and the Rise of Alternative Media in America*, by John McMillian.

Peck reported that by 1969, "the highwater mark of protest," at least 500 papers were published in the U.S. and abroad, with hundreds more in high schools. Peck said that by 1973 most of the urgency and energy were gone, and those underground papers that did survive transitioned to become more "alternative" (instead of being called underground) and commercial.

Many of the underground papers came into being and went out of business quickly. Some had influence well beyond their own ZIP codes. And some of the movement's media pioneers went on to careers as writers and journalists in the mainstream. While much of this new 1960s underground press was straight-white-male–dominated, Peck and McMillian documented the gay and lesbian influence in the underground.

The papers sometimes did include gay topics, if nothing else to thumb their collective noses at a "straight" mainstream they despised. But the papers were also hotbeds of internal strife—men against women, straight against gay, left against further left—and by the end of the 1960s, those that did last were not nearly as radical as at their beginnings.

In the late 1960s, Peck worked for *The Seed*, an underground paper later named the *Chicago Seed*. He said in a 2012 interview for this book that people associated with the paper, both on staff and freelancers, started to come out as gay, and it was not a big deal. One 1970 issue of the *Chicago Seed* (Volume 5, No. 2) included special supplements on both Native American and gay issues. The Chicago "Gay Liberation Movement" was credited with pulling the gay supplement together, and it included articles by Michelle (Michal) Brody and Martha Shelley as well as Carl Wittman's "A Gay Manifesto." Staffers were also involved with the underground abortion group Jane. Peck said lesbians were part of both the *Seed* and Jane.

Peck said *Rat*, a New York–based underground paper, is an example of the battles between the sexes. Feminists, many of them lesbian, took over *Rat* in 1970 to make it more inclusive of women's concerns. In his book, Peck detailed the takeover of *Rat* and its subsequent downfall. Robin Morgan's legendary "Goodbye to All That" essay ran in the first women's issue of *Rat*, and it was a laying-down of the gauntlet—women would no longer be second-class to a movement "dominated by the same white men," as Peck noted.

This shot heard round the feminist world helped to birth a new generation of feminist journalists, and they started more and more feminist and lesbian-feminist newspapers across the U.S. *Rat* changed its name to *Women's LibeRATion*.

One of the prominent journalists of the day was Marshall Bloom. Most people believed Bloom was a "gay celibate," according to Peck. He was harassed for his sexuality by an adversary in the underground press movement's Liberation News Service. Bloom committed suicide in 1969. Bloom's LNS colleague Ray Mungo is a gay man who went on to write many books, including *Famous Long Ago: My Life and Hard Times with Liberation News Service*.

Among other gay writers tracked in his book, Peck noted that Arthur Bell, who wrote 179 stories for *The Village Voice* (including coverage of the Stonewall rebellion) in addition to a regular column, died in 1984 of diabetes. Bell was an early member of New York's Gay Liberation Front and a founder of the breakoff group Gay Activists Alliance. Bell wrote a book about his early gay activism and journalism, *Dancing the Gay Lib Blues: A Year in the Homosexual Liberation Movement*, published in 1971. It is a terrific in-the-moment view of what it was like to be both organizing actions against police and media bias and also covering them for the gay and underground press.

Rita Mae Brown, who was part of *Rat* and *The Furies* newspaper, went on to be among the best-known lesbian authors of her generation. She told Peck: "I miss those papers. I miss the energy, the concern, the lively (and sometimes sleazy) debate. I do not miss the arrogance, the lack of credible research (money, again) and cutting copy according to ideology instead of sticking to the facts."

Gay journalist Jim Fouratt, who was part of the Communications Company and *Come Out!* newspaper, told Peck he thinks drugs destroyed much of the underground press: "They were romanticized, and made people into monsters." He now focuses his work on the music industry. Another gay writer from the underground press movement, Allen Young, later worked in gay and then mainstream media. (Young has an essay later in this book.)

Bisexual journalist and author Robin Morgan, who was part of *Rat* and *Ms.* magazine, continues to fight the feminist fight, mostly through her words—fiction, nonfiction, poetry, plays and more. She told Peck: "I look at a lot of people whose lives were destroyed or damaged. ... But there was an idealism before it soured that was remarkable, that was markedly different than the old Left."

McMillian's book reports on Michael Kindman, the founding editor of *The Paper*, which began in 1965 in East Lansing, Michigan. Kindman was gay and very involved in the underground press movement, but unfortunately he gave in to the temptation of LSD and other drugs. McMillian said Kindman "immersed himself in the gay counterculture" of the early 1980s, but he died of AIDS complications in 1991.

While some gays and lesbians were part of this underground press movement, the papers themselves were still pretty "straight." Perhaps the biggest value the underground and alternative press had for the gay movement was as a training ground for future gay, lesbian and feminist newspaper pioneers.

Really Edgy

Fuck You, A Magazine of the Arts, ran from 1962 to 1965. Produced by Fug band member Ed Sanders, it was as in-your-face as the title suggests. While not only for the gay community, it was very liberationist, including its views about sexuality. Sanders wrote about his publication in the 2012 book *Fug You: An Informal History of the Peace Eye Bookstore, the Fuck You Press, the Fugs, and Counterculture in the Lower East Side*. The following are excerpts from a press release for the book launch:

"In February of 1962 I was sitting in Stanley's Bar at 12th and B with some friends from the *Catholic Worker*. We'd just seen Jonas Mekas' movie *Guns of the Trees*, and I announced I was going to publish a poetry journal called *Fuck You, A Magazine of the Arts*. There was a certain tone of skepticism among my rather inebriated friends, but the next day I began typing stencils, and had an issue out within a week. I bought a small mimeograph machine, and installed it in my pad on East 11th, hand-cranking and collating 500 copies, which I gave away free wherever I wandered.

"*Fuck You* was part of what they called the Mimeograph Revolution, and my vision was to reach out to the 'Best Minds' of my generation with a message of Gandhian pacifism, great sharing, social change, the expansion of personal freedom (including the legalization of marijuana), and the then-stirring messages of sexual liberation.

"I published ... a total of thirteen issues. In addition, I formed a mimeograph press which issued a flood of broadsides and manifestoes during those years, including [William] Burroughs' *Roosevelt After Inauguration* ... ."

As with other underground papers, some of *Fuck You*'s contributors were out gay people. In a 2012 news release for the opening of a retrospective of the poetry 'zine, it was called "fearless, sexually provocative and experimental." Contributors included Sanders, Tuli Kupferberg (also of the Fugs), Carol Bergé, Andy Warhol, Lenore Kandel, Joel Oppenheimer, Peter Orlovsky, Allen Ginsberg, Frank O'Hara, Leroi Jones, William Burroughs and many others.

1960s: New Beginnings

Parallel to the growth of straight underground media, there were new publications sprouting up to serve the gay community in the 1960s. The surviving 1950s media continued to have reach nationally, but more media started. The *Mattachine Midwest Newsletter* had most of the 1960s to itself serving Chicago. *Eastern Mattachine Magazine* served East Coast homosexuals. Denver's *Mattachine Newsletter* served gays in that city. *Fifth Freedom* was a 1970–81 digest-size publication produced by the Mattachine Society of the Niagara Frontier in Buffalo, New York. Other cities also started their own regional publications to further serve the needs of the rising gay underground.

Frank Kameny and Jack Nichols started the Mattachine Society of Washington (D.C.) in 1961. It was an independent group and founded first the *Gazette* in May 1963 and later *The Homosexual Citizen* as mimeographed newsletters issued by the group. Lilli Vincenz (originally as Lily Hansen) was editor of *THC*, which started in 1966 and lasted 18 issues. It was called "the movement's first fully militant civil rights publication" by co-founder Nichols, writing for www.GayToday.com. Vincenz later helped produce *The Insider: Newsletter of the Mattachine Society of Washington* from February 1969 to January 1970.

WorldCat lists the *Eastern Mattachine Magazine* as beginning in March 1965 as a continuation of the *New York Mattachine Newsletter* or the *MSNY Newsletter* and as being issued with Mattachine Society of Washington's *Gazette*. Beginning with June 1965, the *Eastern Mattachine Magazine* was listed as being published by both the Mattachine Society of New York and the Mattachine Society of Washington.

Once D.C. ended its relationship with New York over differences of timing and process, the D.C. Mattachine started *The Homosexual Citizen*. *THC* was co-produced with the new Mattachine Society of Florida group run by Richard Inman. WorldCat lists *The Homosexual Citizen* as having been published by the Mattachine Society of Washington and the Mattachine Society of Florida from February 1966 to May 1967, with Lily Hansen (Vincenz's pseudonym) as editor. (WorldCat shows the Mattachine Society of New York to have continued issuing a newsletter until 1970.)

Nichols interviewed Vincenz for GayToday.com about her early gay work and her co-founding of what later became known as the *Washington Blade* newspaper:

"The Mattachine Society of Washington was dedicated, as you know, to civil liberties and social change and was decidedly NOT a membership organization for satisfying members' needs," Nichols quoted her as saying. "Frank Kameny reminded us that it should be sufficient that we were involved in the noble fight for the homophile cause! But many of us thought of the gay community and its needs. I developed the Community Services Committee, dedicated to serve both the gay and straight communities.

"We felt the need for a newspaper for gay people; our Mattachine internal organ, *The Insider* (which I wrote), and *The Homosexual Citizen*, were not adequate for communicating with the larger gay community on the basic level of people needing people. So, the *Gay Blade* was born, named by a man named Frank—not THE Frank Kameny, who thought little of our efforts, of course—and we published a one-page mimeographed sheet in fall of 1969. Nancy Tucker was the first editor ... ."

THC ended after Vincenz left over a dispute about an astrology column she wanted to run—and Frank Kameny, with a Ph.D. in astronomy, was opposed. Vincenz was the one who pulled the paper together, so when she left, it just folded. She did later work on the organization's *The Insider* publication.

Nichols and his partner Lige Clarke used the same name—"The Homosexual Citizen"—for their later column in the straight *SCREW* sex magazine in 1968. The couple also started the *GAY* newspaper, and Vincenz wrote a column in that publication.

There were many splits in gay organizations and publications over the years. There was a bitter two-year lawsuit between ONE, Inc., and Don Slater and others, which ended in dismissal in 1967 and in a permanent division of the groups. Slater, Billy Glover and Tony Reyes had moved ONE Institute's materials for "protection," and for four months there were actually two *ONE* publications. After the lawsuit, ONE, Inc., kept the rights to produce *ONE* magazine, and Slater's group kept the archives that had been taken. The new group founded in 1965 was called The Tangent Group. The group incorporated three years later as the Homosexual Information Center and continued doing business under the Tangent name. Jim Schneider joined the group at that time. From 1965 to 1973, HIC published the gay publication *Tangents*. Don Slater was the founding editor. *Tangents* was a glossy, stapled digest that included news, views, poetry, book reviews, fiction and more.

While *Tangents* never had a large circulation, it carried important discussions that resonate today on politics, the military, legal issues, the police, cultural reviews and scientific studies. (See www. facebook.com/TangentGroup.)

Billy Glover, in a 2012 interview, said the *ONE* journal was his entry point to the gay movement. He wrote for it, helped distribute it, volunteered in the library and more. Slater wanted Glover on the board of ONE, Inc., but W. Dorr Legg was against the move, and the bitter battle ensued, as documented in Vern L. Bullough's *Before Stonewall: Activists for Gay and Lesbian Rights in Historical Context* and C. Todd White's *Pre-Gay L.A.: A Social History of the Movement for Homosexual Rights.*

"I thought then and from the start that a magazine reached more people than the groups could on their own," Glover said. "Publications reach people who would not otherwise be reached, and that's why a publication is important."

Vector was the official publication of the San Francisco–based Society for Individual Rights. The publication was founded in 1964; SIR started the same year. *Vector* appears to have run through at least the summer of 1976. While it was started in San Francisco, it covered topics of national significance. SIR, like ONE, Inc., did far more than publish a journal. Its legal committee produced the *S.I.R. Pocket Lawyer*, a handy guide for those harassed or arrested by police. SIR took a more liberationist approach to gay rights, as compared to the more assimilationist approach of earlier homophile groups. SIR was very focused on building community through events, sports, trips, classes and more. It even opened what is believed to be the first gay center in the U.S., at 83 Sixth Street, San Francisco, in 1966.

Vector provided important news for its readers about health, court cases, politics, protests and events. It also covered the SIR endorsement of political candidates. The publication became more polished over time, with a glossy, stapled, traditional magazine-size format. Its early subtitle was *Responsible Action by Responsible People in Responsible Ways.* Later it was *A Voice for the Homophile Community* and later still *A Voice for the Homosexual Community.* By 1973 it was *A Voice for the Gay Community,* by 1974 *Celebrating the Gay Experience,* and by 1975 it was *The Gay Experience.* The final change was to *The Gay Magazine of the Society for Individual Rights* in 1976.

On March 28, 1969, three months before Stonewall in New York, *Vector*'s editor, Leo Laurence, called for the "Homosexual revolution of 1969." He was urging gays to join with the Black Panthers and other radicals, and for this SIR expelled him.

According to Wikipedia, Laurence then co-founded the Committee for Homosexual Freedom, with Gale Whittington, a man fired from States Steamship Company for being openly gay, after his photo appeared in the *Berkeley Barb* next to the headline "HOMOS, DON'T HIDE IT!" by Leo Laurence. Around the same time, CHF member Carl Wittman began writing "Refugees from Amerika: A Gay Manifesto," first published in the *San Francisco Gay Free Press* and later in other gay publications (and the *Chicago Seed*).

Another California paper, *Vanguard* magazine, shared a name with a historically important gay liberation youth group, Vanguard, in San Francisco. The Vanguard organization published a newsletter and eventually was sponsored by Glide Methodist Church. Vanguard picketed Compton's Cafeteria in the summer of 1966 because a member had been refused service. The *Vanguard* magazine lasted about a dozen years.

Different Drummers

The gay Janus Society of Philadelphia, which ran from 1962 to 1969, published *Drum* magazine starting in 1964. This was one of the most successful gay publications of the era, reaching 10,000 in circulation. The monthly, sometimes subtitled *Sex in Perspective,* included a lot of sexual images but also covered the gay news and culture of the day. Its title was inspired by the Thoreau quote, "If a man does not keep pace with his companions, perhaps it is because he hears the beat of a different drummer." In some ways, getting people to buy a pornographic magazine that also had news helped keep a wider array of gay men informed about the politics and protests.

Drum, which was a glossy, stapled and digest-size magazine, is credited with printing the first full frontal of a male nude (other than statues or paintings) in an American magazine, in December 1965. In 1967, *Drum* Editor Clark Polak was indicted by a federal grand jury on multiple counts of distributing obscene material; he avoided punishment by agreeing to stop publishing. The last issue came out in 1969. Polak also had a run-in with his printer, who was making money by printing extras and selling them on the side.

There were hundreds of short-lived publications started in the 1960s. Among them are ones with few surviving copies and those that have been well-archived at gay and lesbian or mainstream libraries, archives or museums. Here are a few of note; more information is available from Brad Confer on Tyler Alpern's website, www.tyleralpern.com, www.OutHistory.org and www.glbtq.com.

— *After Dark* was a monthly arts-and-culture magazine started in 1968 and published into the 1980s with sometimes-stunning photography. It was never billed as a gay magazine, but it was very homoerotic and barely "in the closet." As a New York–based magazine, it had its finger on the pulse of gay male culture in that city and spanned the gay liberation, disco and AIDS eras.

— The California Association of Private Societies, founded in 1967, published its own *CAPS Newsletter*. ONE, Inc.'s Jim Kepner was among the editors.

— Dick Publishing in New York City published *Dick: The Paper With Balls* in the late 1960s, and it included the artwork of Etienne.

— *The League for Civil Education News* (later *Citizens News*), a biweekly newspaper published in San Francisco, was mentioned in a March 1963 *Harper's Magazine* article on "New York's Middle-class HOMOSEXUALS," along with other periodicals. *The LCE News* started in 1961. The league was founded by Guy Strait and José Sarria. Another important 1960s publication was also produced by Guy Strait, *Cruise News & World Report*. He closed both in 1967 after being sued by the magazine *U.S. News & World Report* for trademark infringement. The two papers merged into *The Maverick Press*, later *Maverick*, but it was short-lived, publishing perhaps just two issues in 1967.

— The Phoenix Society for Individual Freedom in Kansas City, Missouri, published *The Phoenix: Midwest Homophile Voice* from 1966 to 1972. In July 1966 the group published "A Mother's Viewpoint on Homosexuality."

— *Queen's Quarterly* (not to be confused with the non-gay, Canada-based *Queen's Quarterly* founded in 1893) was subtitled *The Magazine for Gay Guys Who Have No Hangups*. OutHistory.org said it "was one of the first national gay magazines." The first issue was published in 1970, according to WorldCat, by George Desantis in New York City. But soon the magazine had changed to *QQ: For Gay Guys*. By November 1971 it became *QQ Magazine: For Gay Guys Who Have No Hangups*. It ceased publication in 1980.

— The Southern California Council on Religion and the Homophile published *CONCERN* in the mid-1960s. Kepner also edited this publication, which was produced in Los Angeles. W. Dorr Legg, also of ONE, Inc., co-chaired the council.

— *Transvestia* is a 1961 magazine found in the archives of the Gay, Lesbian, Bisexual, Transgender Historical Society.

— *The Voice* of Los Angeles came out in the late 1960s with men's news, events, entertainment and photos.

The Advocate

The Advocate, which in 2012 is marking its 45th anniversary, is perhaps the longest continuously operating gay publication in history. *The Advocate* started in September 1967 as a regional newspaper,

The Los Angeles Advocate, and eventually became a nationwide glossy, four-color magazine by the 1990s. By the time of Stonewall, *The Advocate* had already produced 22 issues.

However, it is no longer available as a stand-alone subscription publication and is not sold on newsstands—and, after years as a biweekly, it is now subscription-only and packaged with its sister publication, *Out* magazine (which is published 10 times a year).

Like many gay media in the 1960s and 1970s, *The Advocate* was started by activists. The Los Angeles group PRIDE: Personal Rights in Defense and Education produced *PRIDE Newsletter,* inspired by a police raid on a gay bar, the Black Cat Tavern.

Dick Michaels (the pseudonym of Richard Mitch) and Bill Rand (pseudonym of Bill Rau) became part of *PRIDE Newsletter.* The duo joined with Aristide Laurent and artist Sam Winston and "transformed the newsletter into a newspaper titled *The Los Angeles Advocate,*" according to Wikipedia. "The first issue bore a cover date of September 1967. By early 1968, PRIDE was struggling to stay viable and Mitch and Rau paid the group one dollar for ownership of the paper in February of that year. In 1969 the newspaper was renamed *The Advocate* and distributed nationally. By 1974, Mitch and Rau were printing 40,000 copies for each issue."

The first few issues of *The Advocate* were printed "courtesy of" ABC-TV in Los Angeles—Rand worked in the mailroom and used the offset printing press there to make the copies. Connecting the dots to previous gay publications, Jim Kepner wrote for the first issue of *The Advocate* and for the next 25 years he contributed articles. By spring of 1970 it was a biweekly.

For *The Advocate*'s September 2012 anniversary issue, the "editors and reporters dug through the archives getting a closer look at the past," according to the magazine. "The staff immersed itself in a time of radical politics and sexual revolution, in a legacy that began well before many of the publication's current staff members were born, making the brand's predecessors all the more real to them now and the urgency of their mission all the more tangible."

Banker David Goodstein bought *The Advocate* from Mitch and Rau in 1974 for $300,000, and he also put in more money to boost the publication. It soon became a national brand. After Goodstein died in 1985, the magazine changed from a tabloid newspaper format to a standard magazine size. By 1992, the sex ads that were an insert became a stand-alone magazine, *Advocate Classifieds.*

The Advocate's owners, Liberation Publications, Inc. (later known as LPI Media), purchased *Out* magazine (launched in 1992) in early 2000. LPI Media, Inc., also owned Alyson Publications and acquired *HIV Plus* magazine, aimed at people with HIV, as well as Out.com.

Syndicated gay media reporter Rex Wockner wrote at the time: "The two largest gay magazines in North America will soon be united under one publishing company. Liberation Publications Inc., publishers of *The Advocate*, announced this week they have bought Out Publishing Inc., which produces *Out* magazine. ... According to the Liberation Publications press release, *Out*, a monthly, has a circulation of 115,000; the biweekly *Advocate* has a circulation of 88,000."

The Advocate, *Out*, Alyson Publications and the Specialty Publications (male porn magazines) were purchased by PlanetOut/Gay.com in November 2005, reportedly for more than $31 million. (PlanetOut and Gay.com had merged in 2001.) After a disastrous few years they were sold for reportedly between $4.7 million and $6 million to Here! Media/Regent in 2008. *The Advocate* as a stand-alone biweekly magazine did not survive past 2010; it is now monthly and "packaged" in *Out* magazine. The changes continued in 2012, as Regent outsourced creation of content for *Out*. Grand Editorial, a new company started by former *Out* editor Aaron Hicklin, now oversees editorial content.

Former *Advocate* Editor-in-Chief Judy Wieder wrote a scathing indictment of the new company on November 4, 2009, on The Huffington Post. In it, she looked back at the historic coverage *The Advocate* provided for the community. Wieder pointed out that *The Advocate* relied heavily on paid subscribers for its base of revenue, while *Out* magazine was a cash cow because of its advertising. This dependence on paid subscribers was mainly the domain of national gay media.

"The hard sell is, was, and always would have been *The Advocate*," Wieder said about the push and pull between *Out* and *The Advocate*. "With its harsh features and photos that no advertiser wanted to be anywhere near, the magazine depended on dedicated readers that renewed their costly ($40+) subscriptions year after year. For them to do this, the content had to be astonishing. It was unimaginably difficult for a small staff to keep it up every two weeks, but somehow it happened. You canNOT do a magazine like *The Advocate* for advertisers. They're not thrilled about newsmagazines. They're not fun. Go count the ad pages in *Time* or *Newsweek*. If those magazines depended on ads to survive, they wouldn't. It's their large circulation, their readership combined with their website visitors that carry the brands forward. We do it for the users, the readers. They will pay for it (online or print) if you make it absolutely essential and as exclusive as possible. And I refuse to get into another deadening debate about print media vs. online. It's distracting and sends us flying wildly past the point. The point is content: Information and really great stories! If that's NOT there, no one else will be either. What's the compelling new story?"

While a few regional gay media toyed with charging a cover price in the 1970s and later years, the vast majority of regional gay newspapers started post-Stonewall were given away free at delivery locations. Early gay journals such as *The Ladder, ONE* and *Mattachine Review* relied on membership dues and sometimes subscribers, but when regional gay newspapers sprang up they started to mimic mainstream alternative papers and went for mass free distribution versus more-limited paid subscriptions.

While this book is focused mainly on newspapers serving particular cities rather than on national magazines, *The Advocate* began its life locally in Los Angeles and was an important part of the growing gay media movement of the late 1960s and early 1970s. A few other magazines are also included in this chapter for similar reasons.

Straight for Gay

A mini-battle for the early gay reader and gay dollars took place between two sex-oriented straight publications after they began producing gay newspapers.

First, *SCREW* owner Al Goldstein hired Jack Nichols and his partner Lige Clarke to write the "Homosexual Citizen" column when the magazine launched in November 1968; the column ran until 1973. That gay column helped the straight world see the gay movement through a gay lens and was uncompromising in its presentation of gay sexuality. Headlines written by Goldstein included "Old Boys: They Just Blow Away," "Fruits on Parade," and "Walt Whitman Was a Faggot—What Could Be Verse?"

Post-Stonewall, Goldstein and *SCREW* partnered with Nichols and Clarke for a stand-alone gay publication, *GAY*, in New York. Kay Tobin Lahusen, who worked for the Oscar Wilde Memorial Bookshop in New York, had approached Nichols and Clarke, saying she felt it was time for a gay newspaper. Nichols and Clarke went to Goldstein and his business partner Jim Buckley with the idea, and the four of them formed Four Swords, Inc., to publish *GAY*. Lahusen was the paper's first news editor.

GAY started in a biweekly newspaper format on November 15, 1969, and was the first weekly gay publication in America, from April 20, 1970, until September 28 of that year, when it went back to biweekly. According to the book *Jack Nichols, Gay Pioneer*, by J. Louis Campbell III, Nichols returned later to *SCREW*, writing the "Homosexual Anarchist" column from 1988 to 1999. He also wrote for *The Weekly News*, a gay paper in Miami, during that era.

GAY featured both male and female nudes along with serious editorial copy. At first the nudes were just inside, but soon they graced the cover of the paper—Nichols backed off on that a bit, after advertising complaints.

An editorial in the first edition said the paper "believes that there is only one world and that labels and categories such as homosexual and heterosexual will some day pass away leaving human beings who, like this publication, will be liked and appreciated not because of sexual orientation, but because they are themselves interesting."

GAY was criticized for its attacks on community outliers who, it claimed, gave the movement a bad name. It attacked transvestites and transsexuals in a June 1970 article, saying they were bad for the homosexual movement.

In the *Jack Nichols, Gay Pioneer* book, Campbell writes that a "sampling of the 900 news reports and the 1,200 lifestyle articles in *GAY* illustrates Nichols' editorial commitment to the coexistence of the three movement perspectives [homophile, liberationist and identity] and *GAY*'s priceless value today as a time capsule of the post-Stonewall movement's ferment."

In 1972, while working on *GAY*, Nichols and Clarke wrote *I Have More Fun With You Than Anybody*, and Lahusen wrote *The Gay Crusaders* (listed as co-writer was Randy Wicker). By 1973, Clarke grew antsy and he and Nichols asked Goldstein to put more money into the successful publication so they could have a larger staff. Goldstein refused and the couple left. Campbell said the July 1973 edition was the last one edited by Clarke and Nichols. Goldstein kept the paper going for about a year after they left, turning it more into a gay porn magazine, as *SCREW* was for straights. The experiment failed.

At its peak, more people purchased *GAY* than *The Advocate* in the early 1970s, around 25,000.

Goldstein and Buckley were probably motivated to start *GAY* because their *SCREW* competitor, *Kiss*, was producing *Gay Power*, which had started soon after Stonewall, in August 1969. *Kiss* was part of the East Village Other, or EVO, publishing empire (1965–72), which produced *The East Village Other* underground "comix" publication in New York City plus *Kiss*, *Aquarian Agent* and *Gay Power*.

Gay Power was billed as "New York's first homosexual newspaper." It was an 11¼-by-17¼-inch large-format newsprint publication produced by Joel Fabrikant of EVO. Its statement of purpose said it was for "the straight, uptight politicians, bourgeois, and naive and maybe a pioneer here and there and yes, for you power freaks who adore exciting in the good of any cause, add to the list that of 'GAY POWER.'" The paper included news and sexual photos, as well as fiction and illustrations.

EVO as a company went through problems similar to those of other underground presses, including alleged financial mismanagement, burnout and the obvious changes in the movement itself. On January 11, 2012, The Local East Village website quoted *The East Village Other*'s co-founding editor, the late Allen Katzman, as having written that the paper "shook the foundations of the existing print and visual media. After seven years, it went just as it came—in a hail of livingness. In true American phantasmagoria, it was a legend in its own time. Initiated by poets, painters, artists, seers, perverts and prophets, it shared its pages with the likes of Buckminster Fuller, Timothy Leary, Robert Crumb, Ishmael Reed, Allen Ginsberg, Lenny Bruce, The Beatles, Bob Dylan, Baba Ram Das, Jerry Rubin and Abbie Hoffman—the conspiracy of the 1960s."

As *EVO* went, so did its sister publications, including *Gay Power*. John Heys was editor in its first year, and John Lauritsen, of the competing *Come Out!* newspaper, notes that *Gay Power* writers included "J.Z. Eglinton (Walter Breen), Marion Z. Bradley, Allen Ginsberg, Gregory Corso, Taylor Mead, and Charles Ludlam. After a year, around the end of 1970, Heys was replaced as editor, and the paper became nothing more than sex-industry sleaze."

Come Out! and the Issue of 'Straight' Ownership

The Gay Liberation Front–produced *Come Out!* newspaper started on November 14, 1969. While *GAY* and *Gay Power* were being produced by straight businessmen, *Come Out!* was by a gay collective.

John Lauritsen, writing for Pagan Press Books about *Come Out!,* said the "guiding light of this first issue was Roslyn Bramms," who had been managing editor of *SCREW*. "With patience and enthusiasm she taught us what we needed to know, including news gathering, copy preparation, legal matters, and production."

Contributors to the first issue included John Lawritz (the pseudonym of Lauritsen), Marty Stephan, Martha Shelley (Martha Altman), Leo Martello, Lois Hart, Earl Galvin, Kay Tobin (Lahusen), Marty Robinson, Mike Brown and Jim Owles.

But all was not well in the big city. As Lauritsen writes: "At the next meeting of the Gay Liberation Front (GLF) following publication of this issue, members of the 'June 28 cell' announced that they had taken over *Come Out!*—allegedly in order to rescue it. *Come Out!* staff were strongly opposed to the move, but we were caught off guard. Marty Robinson called the act outright theft, and was so furious that he had to be physically restrained by his friends. Unfortunately, at this point GLF had no structure, and voting was prohibited (everything had to be by 'consensus'), so we were unable to thwart the expropriators. This unpleasant episode was one of the most important reasons that Marty Robinson, Jim Owles and Arthur Evans later split from GLF, in order to found the more orderly Gay Activists Alliance (GAA). At any rate, new people took over *Come Out!,* and I and most of the original staff members were out in the cold."

In that first issue, one anonymous writer took on the issue of straight-owned gay newspapers. The writer attacked the East Village Other company and Joel Fabrikant in particular. The essay, "Joel Fabricant [*sic*] Perverts Gay Power," started out: "It has been the sad plight of the homosexual in our society to be the victim of the money-hungry opportunist: the mafia bar owner, the blackmailer, the sticky fingered rough trade. A recent and deplorable perverting of the gay movement for profits can be found in the biweekly 'Gay Power,' third issue on the newsstands now." The article noted that sales of the second issue of *Gay Power* had declined, so that Fabrikant turned on gay people in the third issue, attacking some of them by name, accusing some of "being homosexuals. Sadists, pimps, alcoholics, prostitutes, drag queens, pornographic authors, drug addicts, and other illegal practices too numerous to name," according to the essay writer.

In a response, issue No. 8 of *Gay Power* carried a bylined essay about the subject of gay papers owned by straight businesses, "Gay Power in Pay Power," written by Dr. Leo Luis Martello, a former chairman of the GLF. He wrote in part:

"Certain gay militants have set themselves up as moral guardians: They have attacked both *Gay Power* newspaper as 'exploitative' and *Gay* newspaper as 'establishment.' They have 'suggested' in strong terms that all writers connected with the former resign without offering anything in return. The 'good of the cause' (their cause) requires sacrificial victims, and further, the victim's consent. Some of the most vociferous opponents to both newspapers are also the same ones who stole another gay community publication [*ComeOut!*] … . This same group tried to pass a 'censure' ruling on *Gay Power*. 'Censure' of course is just one step from 'censor.' … Disguised as altruism, sugarcoated as 'higher consciousness,' masked as morality, denigrated as 'capitalistic' and 'exploitative' these homosexual humbugs hope to hide their power lust. Instead of concentrating their energies on producing a better product they vent their spleen on all competitors. … Blithely they refer to all homosexuals who don't think their way as 'enemies.' …

"*Gay Power* and *Gay*, whatever their faults and limitations, are professionally produced publications that pay their writers and their staff. Unlike another publication, they aren't parasites hoping to get everything for nothing. For those who dislike either their typography or their content they have one sure method of showing their disapproval: Don't buy these newspapers. … *Gay Power* and *Gay* are in a position to reach thousands of gays. They present features and news coverage, plus distribution, that an amateur publication cannot. True GAY POWER IS IN PAY POWER: Paid writers, artists, photographers, staff, distributors. … GAY POWER … means earning and paying one's own way … PAY POWER … the best way to fight Establishment oppression."

Come Out! lasted a reported nine issues.

More New York, New York

The Gay Activists Alliance split from GLF, and early members of GAA included Kay Lahusen, Marty Robinson, Jim Owles, Arthur Bell, Arthur Evans, Vito Russo, Sylvia Rivera and Jim Coles.

The GAA published the *Gay Activist* tabloid. Tyler Alpern, on his website www.tyleralpern.com, describes several editions of this publication, which appears to have run from 1971 to around 1980. It usually was just a few pages and was packed with GAA news and other movement news and views. In the February 1973 issue, it referred to a sister publication, *Lesbian Activist*, which was also produced by GAA. Alpern's website notes that a president's letter by Bruce Voeller stated: "With this issue of the *Newsletter*, GAA is embarking upon a new journey. We want to reach out to the Gay Community here in New York and across the country through our newsletter. ... The press-run of 20,000 for this issue of the GAY ACTIVIST and LESBIAN ACTIVIST will make our newsletter the largest in the country."

In the March 1977 issue an article reported the FBI's spying on GAA, as confirmed in documents the organization received through a Freedom of Information Act request. The cover of the paper stated in big type, "FBI ADMITS SPYING ON GAA." According to OutHistory.org, the paper also included a sidebar about J. Edgar Hoover's own sexuality, referred to "a striking example of a pig fairy in a high place actively working as an enemy of his own kind, and in return being accepted and much appreciated by the heterosexist establishment."

There were other New York gay publications of that era, including *Gay Scene*, started about 1970, a large-format 11-by-17-inch newsprint publication that ran at least until 1975. While it had a lot of event information, it also carried obituaries, news, photos and cultural coverage. It eventually became known outside New York City, taking on *National Homophile Monthly* as its subtitle, according to Tyler Alpern on his website. Volume 2, No. 2, had an interview with Mae West.

Gay Flames was another important early 1970s gay publication in New York. Allen Young (profiled later in this book) was among the founders of *Gay Flames*, which was produced by the 17th Street Collective. Only a few issues were produced, but the pamphlets provide an important historical look into that era of the movement.

Gay Times was a short-lived socialist gay newspaper founded by Stonewall activist John O'Brien, who was investigated by the FBI, according to Streitmatter in *Unspeakable*. (There was also a *Gaytimes* published in Van Nuys, California, in the early-to-mid-1970s, and it later moved to New York. It included male nudes and also cultural coverage. The *Gaytimes National Edition* continued until at least 1981.)

Coming a few years after the radical post-Stonewall gay newspapers, *Gaysweek* was a more "mainstream" gay and lesbian weekly for New York. Alan Bell started *Gaysweek* in 1977 and ran more than 100 issues before the weekly folded in 1979. Bell made history as one of the very few African-American publishers in gay media. "We never missed an issue in that 103 run," Bell said in 2012. "We began with a press run of 5,000 and were printing 20,000 and 25,000 at our peak. In fact, we produced an extra the week of the Everard bathhouse tragedy. Plus we had some pretty notable bylines." Those included Martin Duberman, Harvey Fierstein, Perry Brass, Felice Picano, Edmund White and Eric Bentley. (Bell is the subject of Chapter 15.)

There were also various Fire Island gay newspapers over the last few decades, covering that heavily gay resort community of New York, including *Fire Island* and *The Fire Islander* in the 1970s.

Drag was a quarterly magazine billed as "America's No. 1 Magazine about the transvestites!" with a subtitle *A Magazine About the Transvestite*. It was published starting in the early 1970s.

Gotham, billed as a "ledger of the gay community," lasted a brief time in mid-1970s New York City.

Many essays from early-1970s gay publications and activists were collected into the first anthology of gay liberationists, *Out of the Closets: Voices of Gay Liberation*, edited by Karla Jay and Allen Young. It was reissued in 1992 with a foreword by John D'Emilio. The radical thoughts of the angry new generation of queers were apparent even in the titles of the essays, including: "Out of the Closets, Into the Streets" by Young; "Gay Is Good" by Martha Shelley; "Rapping With a Street Transvestite Revolutionary," an interview with Marcia Johnson; "A Gay Manifesto" by Carl Wittman (which had run in several gay papers when it came out, but was first published in the *San Francisco Gay Free Press*); and "Why We Want, What We Believe," by Third World Gay Revolution.

San Francisco and *Gay Sunshine*

Gay Sunshine was an important newspaper started in August 1970 in San Francisco by the Gay Sunshine Collective, who were "loosely affiliated with the Gay Liberation Front," according to the 1991 book *Gay Roots: Twenty Years of Gay Sunshine*, edited by Winston Leyland. Its legacy has been made more permanent through the publication of much of its content in *Gay Roots* by Leyland, who founded Gay Sunshine Press later in the 1970s.

Leyland was part of the original collective that produced *Gay Sunshine*. He said it was "filled with much local and national news of demonstrations and other gay lib activities." It also printed Black Panther Huey Newton's manifesto on gays.

GLF imploded, and Leyland resurrected and renamed the newspaper in the spring of 1971. At this point Leyland took over running many of the paper's operations. In 1973, he changed its name to *Gay Sunshine Journal*. At first it continued as a tabloid "but became much more in-depth—on number of pages per issue as well as intellectually." It was more of a literary/political quarterly.

The publication ran interviews with some of the most important gay-male cultural pioneers, including Allen Ginsberg, William Burroughs, Jean Genet, Christopher Isherwood, Gore Vidal, Tennessee Williams and John Rechy.

Gay Sunshine Journal was artistically done with news, photos, illustrations, articles, comics, poetry and more. It was subtitled *A Newspaper of Gay Liberation* and later *A Journal of Gay Liberation*. In 1974, the summer issue was produced jointly with *Fag Rag* of Boston. The 10th-anniversary issue in 1980 was an overview of the accomplishments of the publication's first 10 years, with letters of support from a *Who's Who* of movement political and cultural leaders. The last newspaper format of *Gay Sunshine* was in 1981. Its last appearance in book form was in 1982.

San Francisco Gay Free Press, edited by Charles Thorp, was also an important, short-lived, early post-Stonewall paper on the West Coast. It started in December 1970 and was quite radical, calling for violence as a means to fight for gay rights. It also had a male-to-female transgender writer, Angela Douglas, as a regular contributor.

The Boston Gay Party

Gay Community News, founded in 1973 and based in Boston, was housed in the same location as another radical paper, *Fag Rag*, when a fire gutted the building in 1982. Several gay groups and Glad Day Bookshop also operated from the building.

As *The Guide* magazine reported in a November 2007 article, "Pilgrims' Progress: Boston's Gay History," by Jim D'Entremont: "In 1971, Boston-based gay writers—including Charley Shively, John Mitzel, and Larry Martin—created the liberationist Fag Rag Collective. The left-leaning, nationally distributed *Gay Community News* began its 17-year career in 1973 at Boston's Unitarian, gay-friendly Charles Street Meeting House."

GCN was a groundbreaking local paper that went national, but because of its left-wing politics it alienated a lot of advertisers and had to rely on donations to survive. Still, it had a 26-year career, from 1973 to 1999. (Maida Tilchen writes more about *GCN* later in Chapter 16.)

Fag Rag also had a lengthy run, from 1971 to 1987, which was rare for a publication run by a collective. The 16-page first issue, in June 1971, was subtitled *Gay Male Newspaper*; it featured a line drawing of the *American Gothic* painting by Grant Wood, but with a man standing next to the male in the iconic image. Articles inside included "Doctor, Doctor! Fags vs. Shrinks"; photos from a May 12, 1971, protest against a hospital doing electroshock aversion "therapy" on gays; poetry; and an article titled "Cuba Sí? Gayness & the Cuban Revolution." The third issue had an article about the death of FBI Director J. Edgar Hoover titled "Hoover Goes Underground," mentioning the rumors about his homosexuality. Issue No. 9, in the summer of 1974, was a combined issue with *Gay Sunshine*, 48 pages of poetry, fiction, cartoons, news, interviews and much more.

Lavender Vision was another short-lived 1970s Boston-based gay publication. Tyler Alpern's website contains these notes: "Only two issues were published of this rare and historical gay liberation newspaper. With splendid, vintage cover artwork. ... *Lavender Vision* (April 1971) published by the Lavender Vision / Media Collective at 2 Brookline Street, Cambridge, Massachusetts. A large folded newspaper containing 12 pages including front and rear covers. Published for both the lesbian and gay male communities, there are double 'front' covers (on one side, for gay men; on the rear side, for gay women)." The second issue was in May 1971.

1970s Regional Gay Publications

The *Detroit Gay Liberator* (originally the *Detroit Liberator*) was making waves and was connected to the growing network of U.S. gay papers. Published monthly by the Gay Liberation Front of Detroit, it ran from April 1970 into 1971 and then, as the *Gay Liberator,* continued into the spring of 1976. Some of the writers started to self-syndicate their writing, offering it up to papers in other cities as a way to connect the movement.

The first known newspaper-format gay publications in Chicago were in the early 1970s, including *Killer Dyke, Chicago Gay Pride*, and *The Paper*. The first known lesbian publication was the short-lived *Killer Dyke* (1971), produced by Northeastern Illinois University students and based on the design of the underground *Seed* newspaper. Killer Dykes and Freakin' Fag Revolutionaries put out three issues with government funding available for "any group that could put together a paper," as Margaret "Skeeter" Wilson remembers, and then for two more years produced mimeographed copies. The international bibliographic tool WorldCat lists issues for only a nine-month period, from September 1971 to July 1972. The paper itself stated that it was published by the Feminist Lesbian Intergalactic Party, or Flippies for short (likely a takeoff of the name of the late-1960s Yippies counterculture group).

In 1971, Frank M. Robinson started the city's first tabloid-size gay newspaper, *Chicago Gay Pride*, under the imprint of the Gay Pride Week Committee. Its name was later used for the newsletter of the Chicago Gay Alliance, which appeared in a smaller format from February 1972 through June 1973.

But Robinson did not stop there. In the summer of 1972 he started *The Paper*, to cover entertainment and gay culture. It was a slick tabloid written for both men and women. Only two issues of *The Paper* were published. (See more on Robinson later in this book.)

Also in Chicago, Michael Bergeron, at age 21, and his partner, activist William B. Kelley, started *The Chicago Gay Crusader*, which ran from May 1973 through April 1976. The impact of the *Gay Crusader* is immeasurable: It was a serious newspaper covering the community during critical years. Every issue of the *Crusader* was packed with news, interviews, features, entertainment, photos and more. It's also clear that the pre-AIDS years were not without tragedy, as most issues reported on deaths and other losses, whether by fire, car accident, violence, suicides or natural causes.

Chicago's *GayLife* newspaper started in June 1975 and ran for almost 11 years, through January 1986. Grant Ford was the publisher in its early years, but he eventually sold it to Chuck Renslow. Once the *Gay Crusader* folded, *GayLife* became the main newspaper in the community.

A long-standing Chicago gay magazine, *Gay Chicago*, started in 1976 and unfortunately closed shop in 2011. Ralph Paul Gernhardt started *Gay News*, soon renamed *Gay Chicago News*, in 1976 as a free-circulation newspaper covering both news and entertainment. In 1977, he and co-publisher Dan Di Leo transformed it into *Gay Chicago Magazine* together. Di Leo had worked for the newspaper as typesetter and news editor, bringing from his prior mainstream journalism career a serious professional sense to Gernhardt's publication. They clicked as business partners and remained so until Di Leo's 1989 death from AIDS at 51. Gernhardt died of lung cancer in 2006 at age 72.

Gernhardt's first gay business enterprise was a telephone information line in 1976, which easily led to the newspaper and then the magazine. Gernhardt and Di Leo also tried their hand in several regional gay media enterprises, including *Midwest Times*, *Gay Milwaukee, Gay Detroit* and *Gay Ohio*. "The early years were rough, to say the least," Gernhardt wrote after the passing of Di Leo, "but even with the added success of our product, the last few years have been much more painful. As opportunistic illnesses began to affect his body, Dan fought them off one by one, succeeding, according to authorities, beyond their expectations. Yes, Dan, living with AIDS, was a fighter."

Gernhardt's son inherited the magazine, but after a brief conversion to newspaper format in the summer of 2011, *Gay Chicago* folded.

NewsWest was a newspaper based in California in the mid-1970s. In its July 29, 1977, issue, which was called Issue 1, it changed to the name *Out!* Managing Editor Robert Wray explained in a letter to readers: "If you were a reader of *NewsWest*, you are doubtless curious about the name change. ... *NewsWest* started over two years ago, in an effort to bring news, informed comment and lively entertainment to gay publishing in southern California. We plan to continue that tradition." *Out!* had a professional news format, but it does not appear to have lasted much longer.

Christopher Street magazine started in 1976 and was edited by Charles Ortleb (who later founded the *New York Native*). While it was based in New York, it had a national influence. It was a news, features and literary glossy magazine for gay men, and it ran groundbreaking interviews with cultural leaders. Its goal was to be a gay *New Yorker*, and it did feature original fiction. It ceased publication in December 1995.

Mom ... Guess What!, a twice-monthly tabloid based in Sacramento, California, folded in 2010. *Mom ... Guess What!* started as a monthly newspaper in 1978. Publisher Linda D. Birner and Editor David C. Weinerth based the format of the publication on the daily *Sacramento Bee* and named the publication after a popular coming-out catch phrase of the day. After several office locations, including one on S Street that was vandalized shortly after the AIDS crisis began, *MGW* came to rest at 1701 L Street, where it remained for many years.

By 1972, *Our Own Voices: A Directory of Lesbian and Gay Periodicals* listed 150 publications serving the gay communities across the U.S., according to Streitmatter.

Based in Toronto, Canada, *The Body Politic* played an important role in the North American gay movement. It was founded in late 1971, with its first issue dated November/December. The publication faced much official harassment and censorship over the years. For example, on December 30, 1977, the paper was raided by an anti-pornography squad, and 12 crates of material were taken. As reported on www.uwo.ca's website history of the paper, "January 5 [1978] Criminal charges are laid against *The Body Politic* and three officers of Pink Triangle Press, the publisher of *The Body Politic*. The charges are 'possession of obscene material for distribution' (section 159 of the Criminal Code) and 'use of the mails for purpose of transmitting indecent, immoral or scurrilous materials' (Section 164)." It took years for the materials to be returned. Pink Triangle Press launched its *Xtra!* subsidiary in 1984 and closed *The Body Politic* in 1987—its last issue was in February. (See later in this chapter for *Xtra!* publication details.)

Long-Lasting

This book features articles on some of the long-lasting gay regional newspapers in Part 3, including the *Washington Blade* (started in 1969), *Bay Area Reporter* (started in 1971), and *Philadelphia Gay News* (started in 1976). The emphasis in that part of the book is mainly on weekly and biweekly city LGBT newspapers, some of them pre-1980, but there are a few other publications started in that era that are still available today.

The Empty Closet of Rochester, New York, started in 1971. It is a tabloid produced 11 times per year by the Gay Alliance of the Genesee Valley. The complete archives are online at www.lib.rochester.edu/index.cfm?PAGE=4769.

CommUNITY is a tabloid gay newspaper in Albany, New York, published 10 times a year and founded in 1972.

Seattle Gay News has been serving that city (and the Puget Sound area) since 1973. WorldCat says Volume 1, No. 1, was dated June 1974 for the Gay Community Center's *News*, which transformed into *Seattle Gay News* as of December 1975. It is a tabloid weekly covering all aspects of the LGBT community. It is the third-oldest weekly tabloid gay paper in the country. Editor George Bakan was not the founder but has been associated with *SGN* almost since its start.

Pittsburgh's Out, a monthly newspaper, started in 1973. Its website (outonline.com) gives this history of the company: "The publication that became *Out* originated in March 1973 as a single-page newsletter produced by the year-old 'gay liberation' organization Gay Alternatives Pittsburgh; as the newsletter's page count increased, its name changed to *Pittsburgh Gay News* and a tabloid newspaper format was adopted. In February 1977, *PGN* released the first issue of *Gay Life*, a handbill-sized glossy that was revamped in November 1979 to become a magazine titled *Out*. *Out* has been published in its current tabloid newspaper format since August 1980. Out Publishing Co. Inc.'s current publishers Tony Molnar-Strejček and Ed Molnar-Strejček purchased the company in November 1994."

Unfortunately, as this book was going to press in September 2012, the paper announced it was closing the print edition of *Pittsburgh's Out*. Out Online Inc. President Tony Molnar-Strejček wrote: "We have decided to temporarily discontinue the print version of *Pittsburgh's Out* and focus on our wildly popular online site, www.outonline.com. ... The newspaper has published in one form or another since 1973 and is one of the oldest LGBTQ publications (local, regional and national) in the country! ... After a month or so, we may consider the start of a newly refreshed *Pittsburgh's Out* publication, but only with adding outside capital and donations from individuals or companies. We have heard from many of our customers and readers that have major concerns about Pittsburgh's LGBTQ community no longer having a voice and we have seen the 'Support Pittsburgh's Out' and 'Save Pittsburgh's Out' Facebook and website pages. ...Our decision was based on revenue and the loss of [our] building lease."

Metroline of Hartford, Connecticut, is a magazine founded as *MCC News* in 1972. Its predecessor was *The Griffin*, which ran from 1969 to 1972. In February 2012, *Metroline* changed from twice-monthly to monthly. It bills itself as "New England's Oldest GLBT Publication."

Out Front, a semimonthly newspaper founded in 1976, is the Rocky Mountain West's largest and oldest LGBT news organization and network. Founder Phil Price outlined his mission in the first issue: "to bring Colorado a long-awaited, much-needed, quality journal of the gay community. *Out Front* will cater to the needs and desires of gays in the area and will feature articles, thought-provoking editorial, the latest news and exciting photography." Price died in 1993. Jay Klein and Greg Montoya took over until 2012, when Colorado native Jerry Cunningham and his partner, JC McDonald, acquired *Out Front* and its parent company, Q Publishing.

Out Front said it has "evolved from a monthly newspaper for Denver's gay community into a 24/7 media network reporting on issues for a worldwide audience." It has reported on police brutality, the HIV/AIDS epidemic, breaking news around the fight for marriage equality and more. The print edition is delivered every first and third Wednesday of the month. The paper has said *Out Front*'s "life blood is OutFrontOnline.com," with "up-to-the-minute coverage, coupled with a robust social media program."

Bay Times, possibly the first newspaper in San Francisco to be jointly published by both gay men and lesbians, launched in 1978. Co-founder and journalist Roland Schembari (1943–2011) emphasized news and special-interest pages for both men and women. Schembari, along with friend Bill Hartman, relaunched the project in 1979 as *Coming Up*, a monthly calendar focusing on cultural and political events in the LGBTQ community. *Coming Up* quickly expanded in size and began to publish every two weeks. In 1981, Kim Corsaro became the publisher, overseeing further growth. In 1988, the paper changed its name to the *San Francisco Bay Times*. Corsaro remained at the helm until 2011. Now, *Bay Times* is co-published and co-edited by two business and life partners, Dr. Betty Sullivan and Jennifer Viegas, who hope to fulfill Schembari's original vision. They are also working to expand *Bay Times* coverage throughout the San Francisco Bay Area and into other media formats. For example, *Bay Times Live*, a news and arts show recorded in the heart of San Francisco's Castro District, began in December 2011. *Bay Times* is published biweekly.

QVegas is a monthly magazine from Las Vegas, started in 1978. *QVegas* has served southern Nevada since its inception first as *Vegas Gay Times* and later as the *Nevada Gay Times*, *Bohemian Bugle* and the *Las Vegas Bugle*.

Gay Life of Baltimore, Maryland, is a monthly tabloid started in 1979. It is a publication of the Gay, Lesbian, Bisexual, and Transgender Community Center of Baltimore and Central Maryland and has distribution throughout the Mid-Atlantic region. It states: "As a social enterprise of the community center, revenues generated by *Gay Life* support the Center and, in turn, its many community-driven services and programs. We began publishing *Gay Life* in September of 1977, just six months after the inception of the Center."

Michigan's *Metra* magazine began publishing in 1979 and is a twice-monthly bar and entertainment guide.

RFD is a long-running gay magazine for those living the rural life. It bills itself as the "oldest reader-written gay quarterly" and first appeared in the autumn of 1974.

Lesbian Publications

Lesbians had *Vice Versa* and *The Ladder* in pre-Stonewall America, and some lesbians were part of *ONE*, *Mattachine Review*, *The Homosexual Citizen* and other periodicals. But as *The Ladder*'s reach waned in the early 1970s, a new generation of lesbians and lesbian-feminists wanted something much bolder, as well as wider choices in their media.

Fed-up feminists took over the underground *Rat* paper in New York in 1970. Parallel to this, feminists were creating publications such as *Ms.* magazine, founded in 1971 (first as an insert in *New York* magazine and then a stand-alone in 1972). But feminism was sometimes not enough, and with a growing access to the means of printing and distribution, dozens if not hundreds of lesbian and lesbian-feminist media cropped up in the 1970s. Most did not survive into the 1980s, but the groundwork was laid. Many of these journalism pioneers then joined the mainstream as reporters, editors and authors, using the skills they had learned in the lesbian underground.

Lesbian Connection and *Lesbian News* are the longest-lasting lesbian publications in the U.S.

Lesbian News, started in 1974, is a Los Angeles–based monthly magazine with some national distribution. WorldCat lists its first edition in 1975. *LN* states: "The *Lesbian News* is the vehicle for the experience of women's art, music, literature, films and history. ... We are, not only, a magazine published for and about lesbians, but also by lesbians. ... The editorial vision of *Lesbian News* has always been to inform, entertain and be of service to women who love women of all ages, economic class and color. We hope women from all walks of life will not only find something of themselves in the *LN*, but also be accepting of those with differing opinions."

Lesbian Connection, founded in 1974, is a free forum of news and ideas for, by and about lesbians. While based in Michigan, *LC* has built a truly worldwide audience for its unique brand of content—

and its nonprofit publisher, now known as Elsie Publishing Institute, is one of a very few 1970s collectives that have survived into the new millennium.

LC states: "On the pages of this bimonthly magazine you'll find all sorts of info for lesbians—places to live and travel; lesbian land and retirement communities; festivals and conferences; lesbian-run B&Bs; books, music and films; lesbian lawyers and realtors; and two comic strips: 'Dykes to Watch Out For' and 'Bitter Girl.' Readers suggest topics for discussion, and recent ones have included lesbian weddings, coming out at work, and first celebrity crushes. *LC* also has a worldwide network of more than 1,000 'contact dykes'—women who've agreed to be listed so they can provide information about their areas to traveling lesbians or new women in town. In addition, *LC* prints reviews, articles, and letters dealing with whatever issues its readers are talking about, from *The Real L Word* to health issues, relationships or politics. The goal of this grassroots lesbian forum is to quite simply connect the lesbian community worldwide." The website is www.LConline.org.

The Lesbian Tide, which was started by Jeanne Córdova (see Chapter 12), ran from 1971 to 1980 and was the first publicly distributed lesbian publication in Los Angeles. It was a very important pioneering lesbian publication for women in LA but also for those nationally who contributed to it and were able to read a copy.

In August 1971, members of the Women's Caucus of the Chicago Gay Alliance pooled money to publish the first issue of *The Feminist Voice*. One page, devoted to the Women's Caucus, was called "The Lavender Woman." By November, *Lavender Woman* broke off as its own publication and had a national impact. It ran 26 issues at irregular intervals, through July 1976.

Eventually the Chicago Lesbian Liberation group split from *Lavender Woman*. It published its own newsletter in 1973–74, since *LW* was published irregularly. When *LW* pulled the one-page Chicago Lesbian Liberation space in *LW* over a controversial cartoon, CLL countered with publication of two issues of *The Original Lavender Woman* in September and October 1974. Some members of the Chicago Women's Chapter of the New American Movement produced *Blazing Star*, a newspaper, in 1975. It changed formats a few times and continued through January 1980, when it became an insert in *GayLife* newspaper. Eventually, it disappeared, and *GayLife* began an insert called *Sister Spirit* in 1984. In the 1980s, Chicago-based *HOT WIRE: A Journal of Women's Music and Culture* continued the lesbian publication trend, but it was a national journal, not a Chicago lesbian newspaper. Started by Toni Armstrong Jr., Yvonne Zipter, Michele Gautreaux and Ann Morris, *HOT WIRE* had a ten-year run, folding in 1994.

Karla Jay and Rita Mae Brown were two of the most important lesbians in that new media world of the 1970s. Jay tells her story in an essay later in this book, as well as in her autobiography, *Tales of the Lavender Menace: A Memoir of Liberation*. Brown wrote about her life, including those early 1970s journalism days, in *Rita Will: Memoir of a Literary Rabble-Rouser*.

Brown was among those who took over the underground *Rat* paper and remade it into a women's liberation publication. In the summer of 1971 she co-founded the short-lived Furies Collective in D.C. with Charlotte Bunch. Joan Biren, Ginny Berson and others were part of the group, which produced *The Furies* paper starting in January 1972. The paper "shocked the conservative wing of the women's movement. I don't think they believed lesbians could be literate and they never expected us to stick together as a group," Brown wrote.

In his book *Unspeakable*, Rodger Streitmatter writes: "*The Furies* turned Lesbian America upside down. When the members of the collective sent the 3,000 copies of their newspaper to friends in cities across the country, their words and concepts spread like wildfire, exposing thousands of women to an evolving ideology unlike anything they had ever heard before."

As with any tight-knit, politically intense group, and many of the 1970s women's collectives, the group quickly struggled, and members started to be ousted, including Brown. The collective was gone by 1972, but the paper ran through mid-1973 and had national distribution.

off our backs was an important feminist publication started as a tabloid on February 27, 1970. It later changed to a monthly, then a bimonthly magazine, and finally a quarterly, running through 2008. It was a serious newspaper that was inclusive of lesbians, but not exclusive of more general women's issues. The publication covered a wide range of women's issues nationally and around the world. It even inspired (likely much to its dismay) an erotic (some said pornographic) lesbian magazine, Susie Bright's *On Our Backs*, started in 1984. The latter magazine stopped in 1994 but then returned in 1998 after the publishers of *Girlfriends* magazine, H.A.F. Publishing, purchased it and continued the title. *off our backs* archives are online at www.offourbacks.org.

Girlfriends was a national publication. Both *On Our Backs* and *Girlfriends* folded in 2006, after *Velvetpark* magazine purchased the titles. *Velvetpark* launched in 2002 as a national magazine. It even won a trademark for its full name: *Velvetpark, Dyke Culture in Bloom*. The hard times facing other national lesbian publications soon hit *Velvetpark*, but it has survived as an online-only company.

Deneuve, a lesbian magazine inspired by the actress Catherine Deneuve's name, launched in 1990. It had to be renamed in 1995 after Catherine fought against her name being used this way. The newly reminted *Curve* has continued to publish 10 issues a year, surviving the economic downturn by selling in 2010 to Avalon Media, which publishes *BOUND*, an international magazine, and *LOTL (Lesbians on the Loose)* in Australia.

Jane & Jane was a short-lived lesbian national glossy magazine launched in 2006. Two other slick publications for lesbians are *GO Magazine*, founded in 2002 in New York, which does also cover national issues, and *L Style G Style*, a co-gender bimonthly magazine coming out of Texas (they are struggling to remain in print form). Another popular regional magazine, *SHE*, is for women in South Florida. Started in 1999, it is published monthly. *Girl STIR Magazine* (also called *GIRL Magazine*), launched in 2005, is published 10 times a year in Fort Lauderdale, Florida.

Popular lesbian websites of the current era include Autostraddle, AfterEllen (owned by Logo television, along with the AfterElton site), CherryGRRL, Seattle Lesbian, The L Stop, and the websites for individual lesbian publications and general LGBT media.

There have been other influential feminist and lesbian-inclusive publications over the years. Two important ones were *Sinister Wisdom* and *Conditions*.

Sinister Wisdom's website says it is "a multicultural lesbian literary & art journal that publishes three issues each year. Publishing since 1976, *Sinister Wisdom* works to create a multicultural, multi-class lesbian space. *Sinister Wisdom* seeks to open, consider and advance the exploration of lesbian community issues. *Sinister Wisdom* recognizes the power of language to reflect our diverse experiences and to enhance our ability to develop critical judgment as lesbians evaluating our community and our world." It has played an important role in lesbian-feminist arts and culture. Harriet Ellenberger and Catherine Nicholson were the founding editors, and editors over the years have included Michelle Cliff, Adrienne Rich and Elana Dykewomon. Writers have included Andrea Dworkin, Audre Lorde, Gloria Anzaldúa, Julia Penelope, Paula Gunn Allen and Pat Parker.

Conditions: A Feminist Magazine of Writing by Women With an Emphasis on Writing by Lesbians (yes, that was the title) was published in Brooklyn from 1976 to 1990. It focused a lot on writings by lesbians of color and working-class lesbians. As Julie Enszer wrote in the online Lambda Literary Review on August 19, 2012, four feminist writers—Rima Shore, Irena Klepfisz, Elly Bulkin and Jan Clausen—started *Conditions* in Brooklyn in 1976. They were a collective and published one issue a year. *Conditions 5* in November 1979 was an especially important edition and sold more than 10,000 copies. It was edited by Barbara Smith and Lorraine Bethel and was called the first widely distributed work by black feminists in the U.S. The project inspired Smith to create the groundbreaking *Home Girls: A Black Feminist Anthology*, by Kitchen Table: Women of Color Press in 1983. Among the *Conditions* contributors over the years were Adrienne Rich, Amber Hollibaugh, Audre Lorde, Becky Birtha, Bonnie Zimmerman, Cherríe Moraga, Cheryl Clarke, Dorothy Allison, Gloria Anzaldúa, Jewelle Gomez, Joan Larkin, Joan Nestle, Minnie Bruce Pratt, Mab Segrest and Sapphire.

Many of these publications were part of the Women in Print movement, which included women interested in both book and periodical publishing. Trysh Travis wrote about this in "The Women in Print Movement: History and Implications," published in *Book History*, Volume 11, in 2008. The movement was "a group of late-twentieth-century 'book women' whose labor in the realm of print production was intimately connected to their analysis of how gender and power shaped 'the little world of the book.' A product of Second Wave feminism, the Women in Print Movement was an attempt by a group of allied practitioners to create an alternative communications circuit—a woman-centered network of readers and writers, editors, printers, publishers, distributors, and retailers."

Minnie Bruce Pratt wrote about being inspired by the Women in Print movement in a blog about her book *The Sound of One Fork*: "Members of our collective learned all aspects of book production, from editing to page design and layout to burning text into the metal plates required by our old printing press, from the actual printing to hand-collating, stapling, and trimming the magazines with huge clumsy equipment that we borrowed from Lollipop Power, a feminist children's press in nearby Carrboro [North Carolina]."

The website displaced.blogs.com/kore interviewed Lisa Bowden of Arizona-based Kore Press about this movement:

"The Women in Print Movement emerged to pursue justice and equality for women by putting women's writings into print. This contemporary movement developed in the late '60s and was focused by lesbian and feminist print activism. Carol Seajay, who has 20 years experience in publishing and running a feminist bookstore, talked about how 'little of what we needed to know was available … experiences of domestic violence, sexual harassment, pay inequity, racial discrimination, lesbian relationships, and so on … . When we did get coverage in mainstream publications, our ideas were distorted and trivialized, and it became increasingly clear that if we wanted feminist ideas in print we would have to do it ourselves. Freedom of the press, we learned early on, belonged to those who owned printing presses.'

"Women established their own typesetting shops, binderies, wholesale distribution, and bookstores to put literature into women's hands. The development of the movement was a part of that drive for women's independence and radical social change for women—and men—concerned about women's writings, women's rights and politics. Most importantly, it promoted alternatives against the gatekeepers of public discourse by generating cultural product that was also a tool for organization."

Carol Seajay and her long-running *Feminist Bookstore News* periodical were critical components of the 1970s–90s U.S. feminist network (it folded in 2000 after more than 20 years in business). The publication connected the once-thriving feminist bookstore community. Those bookstores, along with the also once-popular gay and lesbian bookstores, were a vital venue for sales of gay and lesbian newspapers, journals and magazines.

Chicago was a strong part of the Women in Print movement, with presses and groups such as the Chicago Women's Graphics Collective, started in 1970 to create posters for the women's movement. It produced thousands of posters during its 13 years.

Here is a summary of just a few of the other lesbian publications that started (and mostly ended) in the 1970s—sometimes the end date is not known. Many of these titles are available in archives across the U.S., including especially those at the Northwestern University Library (www.library.northwestern.edu), the New York Public Library (www.nypl.org) and the Sophia Smith Collection of the Five Colleges Archives & Manuscripts Collections (asteria.fivecolleges.edu). The 1993 book *Lesbian Sources: A Bibliography of Periodical Articles 1970–1990*, by Linda Garber, also provides a fascinating time capsule of lesbian publications, and it lists some articles within those pages; especially important are the more niche feminist and lesbian journals that are noted.

— *Ain't I a Woman?* (based on the Sojourner Truth speech), produced by a collective in Iowa City from the Women's Liberation Front in 1970–74. The newspaper also published the poetry anthology *Because Mourning Sickness Is a Staple in My Country.*

— *Albatross,* which had various subtitles including *A Radical Lesbian Feminist Magazine, The Lesbian-Feminist Sarcasm-Satire Magazine, The Lesbian Feminist Satire Magazine* and *A Publication of the Mid-East Jersey Radical Feminists,* ran from 1974 or 1975 to 1980.

— *Amazon: A Midwest Journal for Women,* by the Amazon Collective in Milwaukee, started in 1971 or 1972 and ran until 1984.

— *Amazon Quarterly, A Lesbian-Feminist Arts Journal,* from West Somerville, Massachusetts, published 1972–75.

— *Atalanta* (formerly *ALFA Newsletter,* 1973–76) of the Atlanta Lesbian Feminist Alliance in Atlanta, 1977–86.

— *Azalea: A Magazine by Third World Lesbians,* 1977–83, a quarterly published for black and Latina lesbians by the New York–based Salsa Soul Sisters Collective, Third World Wimmin Inc. Among the contributors were Audre Lorde, Sapphire and Michelle Cliff. (In the early 1980s the collective also published *Salsa Soul Sisters/Third World Women's Gay-zette.*) Salsa Soul Sisters, believed to be the oldest black lesbian group in the U.S., has its roots in the Black Lesbian Caucus of New York's Gay Activists Alliance.

— *Cries From Cassandra,* from the Amazon Nation in Chicago, 1973.

— *Dyke,* a quarterly from New York, 1975–78.

— *A Feminary,* from Chapel Hill, North Carolina. WorldCat gives numerous titles for this publication at various times—including *Feminary, A Feminary, Feminist Newsletter, Female Liberation of Chapel Hill Newsletter, Female Liberation Newsletter of Durham–Chapel Hill* and *Research Triangle Women's Liberation Newsletter.* The dates for these various iterations range from 1969 to 1985. Google Books shows that at least by 1985 it was called *Feminary* with the subtitle (or maybe part of the title) *Lesbian Feminist Magazine.*

— *Focus: A Journal for Lesbians* (earlier subtitled *A Journal for Gay Women*), from Boston and Cambridge, Massachusetts, 1970–83, started by the Boston Daughters of Bilitis.

— *Heresies: A Feminist Publication on Art and Politics,* by New York's Heresies Collective, which came out from 1977 to at least 1993 (many of the issues are online at heresiesfilmproject.org, including the last one, a focus on Latinas).

— *The Leaping Lesbian,* from Ann Arbor, Michigan, 1977–81. This covered everything from literature to dyke softball.

— *The Lesbian Feminist,* a 1973–79 New York publication.

— *Quest: A Feminist Quarterly,* a 1974–84 journal published in Washington, D.C.

— *Sisters: By and for Lesbians,* sometimes also subtitled *A Magazine by and for Gay Women,* from the San Francisco chapter of the Daughters of Bilitis, 1970–75.

— *So's Your Old Lady,* based in Minneapolis, 1973–79.

The 1980s also saw the birth of more lesbian media, including:

— *Aché: A Publication for Black Lesbians,* also subtitled *The Bay Area's Journal for Black Lesbians, A Journal for Black Lesbians* and *A Journal for Lesbians of African Descent,* from California, 1989–93.

— *Common Lives, Lesbian Lives,* a lesbian quarterly from Iowa City, started in 1981.

— *Golden Threads,* a contact publication for lesbians, produced four times a year. It was founded in 1985 in Quincy, Massachusetts, by Christine Burton, who died in 2000.

— *Hag Rag* from the Intergalactic Lesbian Feminist Press, Milwaukee, 1986–93.

— *I Know You Know: Lesbian Views and News,* a national glossy lesbian magazine published in Indianapolis, 1984–85.

— *Lesbian Ethics,* from Venice, California, started in 1984.

— *Maize: A Lesbian Country Magazine,* which started publishing in 1983. Its home base changed over the years. The website is still active but the last issues it lists are from 2009.

There have also been dozens of lesbian periodicals in Canada, among them *Dyke* of Montreal, in 1977; *Diversity, the Lesbian Rag* of Vancouver, British Columbia (1988–91); *Siren* of Toronto by the wonderfully named No More Sex Please! Press (1996–2004); and the also-wonderfully named *Nomorepotlucks* of Montreal, a more recent publication begun in 2009 that appears in online and print-on-demand formats. Mexico has also seen a few lesbian publications, including *LeSVOZ: Revista de Cultura Lésbica Feminista, Para Todas las Mujeres,* started in 1994 as *Himen* and still publishing. The London-based *Spare Rib*, 1972–93, was also an influential feminist publication, with some U.S. distribution.

There has not recently been as vital, or volatile, a print media community for lesbians as in the 1970s and 1980s. Many reasons exist for this, but as the popularity of collectives and nonprofit models subsided, for-profit businesses producing media filled the void. There was also more inclusion of lesbians on television and in mainstream magazines and newspapers. More gay publications became stronger in their co-gender coverage, especially after the AIDS crisis began and the community came together more than before. But probably the most critical change has been the growth of online options for lesbians and lesbian-feminists to gather, controlling the means of information dissemination just as their foremothers did in the Women in Print movement—this time the message just happens to be traveling not via ink but through the Internet.

The *New York Native*

The *New York Native* was a biweekly publication in the right place at the right time to be a pioneer on AIDS coverage. That was both its strength and its ultimate downfall. It was a regional newspaper that had national circulation.

The publication was started in December 1980 by Charles Ortleb, its editor and publisher. Just five months later, the *Native* became the first paper to report on the disease that later became known as AIDS. It scooped *The New York Times* and all other media outlets.

The *Native*'s medical writer, Dr. Lawrence Mass, used his reporting skills to track down details about a "gay cancer" striking gay men in New York. The U.S. Centers for Disease Control told him it was not true and the first headline was "Disease Rumors Largely Unfounded" on May 18, 1981. But the next month, on June 5, the CDC published details on the disease, and the *Los Angeles Times* (June 5) and *The New York Times* (July 3) then picked up on the looming crisis.

Ortleb was among the more aggressive gay newspaper publishers in informing his readers about AIDS, often with sensational, huge headlines. He was the first to print Larry Kramer's now-famous 1983 essay, "1,112 and Counting." The cover story was a call to arms for the gay community to wake up to the crisis: "If this article doesn't rouse you to anger, fury, rage and action, gay men may have no future on this Earth," Kramer wrote.

Ortleb was increasingly seen as a conspiracy theorist, printing almost every piece of speculation put forth about HIV and AIDS. He soon began to lose readers and advertisers, and the paper closed in 1997. But in those intervening years, the *Native* proved one of the most critical voices in combating ignorance, homophobia and AIDS phobia. Its influence went far beyond New York City.

OutWeek

OutWeek was another sensational New York–based publication with national influence, but it had a much briefer life span than the *Native*. It was so influential, and is so well-remembered, that it is hard to believe it lasted only from 1989 to 1991.

OutWeek was a weekly, on newsprint with a glossy four-color cover, the size of a traditional magazine. It was a hybrid in many ways: It was both local to New York and national in coverage; it was for men and women; it was both newspaper and magazine.

Kendall Morrison and Gabriel Rotello were the founders, but they were both activists. To raise money for the magazine, Morrison sold shares in his lucrative phone-sex company to three men, which proved the magazine's undoing, because the new business partners did not want to subsidize *OutWeek*.

The first issue was on June 26, 1989, during Pride Week in New York. *OutWeek* covered priest sexual abuse, AIDS from many angles, safer sex and a wide range of groundbreaking news and culture stories. It is perhaps most remembered as the home base of Michelangelo Signorile—where he started his "outing" of celebrities and politicians. He did not just go after hypocrites in power. He also went after closeted actors, gossip columnists and other cultural power brokers, and he outed Malcolm Forbes posthumously.

Perhaps because it was so controversial, and even though it sold as many as 40,000 copies at its peak, *OutWeek* did not attract enough advertisers to cover its costs. Morrison used thousands of dollars from his phone-sex company to cover the losses each week. The other owners of the phone-sex company shut the magazine down while Morrison was in the hospital (he was HIV-positive)—it closed in July 1991 after 105 issues. Morrison told an interviewer for *NYQ* newspaper in March 1992 that he felt duped by his business partners, admitting he would sign documents when he had no idea what they were for.

While mainstream advertisers were starting to target gays through print media, *OutWeek* was just too controversial to touch. Interestingly, some of the *OutWeek* team, including Editor Sarah Pettit, went on to work for Michael Goff's *Out* magazine, a national glossy more palatable to advertisers. Pettit later was arts editor at *Newsweek*; she died of cancer in 2003.

Other *OutWeek* staff continued in journalism and other forms of media, both gay and mainstream. Rotello became the first openly gay columnist at a major newspaper, *Newsday*, and wrote the book *Sexual Ecology*. Signorile has a syndicated show on SiriusXM Satellite Radio's OutQ channel and is an editor for The Huffington Post's "Gay Voices" section.

Andrew Miller, news editor of *OutWeek*, wrote an essay in 2012 after CNN anchor Anderson Cooper came out as a gay man.

"Unlike Anderson Cooper, I didn't want to wait until I had a contract with the largest cable network in the United States—and millions and millions of dollars in the bank as a result—before I came out," Miller wrote. "My career in journalism, born of a desire to write about the AIDS crisis, began at Boston's *Gay Community News* in 1988; back then, gay newspapers were the only places one could read about AIDS."

Miller said that after *OutWeek* folded, his career was hurt because he was an openly gay journalist. "By contrast, Cooper's career success has been in part due to his talent for managing his image to his own best advantage. ... Cooper claims that he did not announce he is gay previously because doing so would have endangered his life, as he often reports from countries hostile to gay men. But unless he's planning on staying studio-bound from now on, this makes no sense. Nor is this about his privacy: His being gay was journalism's worst-kept secret. He has even discussed privately how common knowledge of his homosexuality endangered him while reporting abroad."

Miller added: "Those who now see Cooper as a risk-taking role model for aspiring gay and lesbian journalists should also consider the hundreds of journalists in the LGBT press, and those in the mainstream press who came out long ago, who paid the career consequences of being out gay men and women."

1980s–90s Gay Media

The 1980s saw a huge growth in gay and lesbian city newspapers. More also were launched in the 1990s, as print still was king in the decade that saw only the early impact of the Internet.

What follows is a summary of highlights, but hundreds of publications were available in the U.S. starting in the 1980s and 1990s, and there are numerous resources to delve deeper into this information. In the back of this book is a list of current regional gay newspapers and their start dates, plus a bibliography for more information about gay media. There are also lists on Wikipedia and from various archives around the country, plus books that have appeared over the decades listing LGBT media. So this is just an overview of some of the LGBT media from the 1980s and 1990s, a few of which are still publishing today.

The Advocate and *Out* magazine are certainly among the best-known glossy national magazines. But others came and went, and some, such as *Instinct*, are still publishing. *Instinct* is a glossy men's magazine founded in 1997. It has published 10 issues a year but in 2012 said it would be switching to six issues a year in 2013.

Names from the past include a prestigious Minneapolis-based literary quarterly, *The James White Review*, founded in 1983; another literary periodical from Minneapolis, *The Evergreen Chronicles,* started in 1985; and *Out/Look*, a short-lived (1988–92) magazine from San Francisco that contributed important stories to the LGBT dialogue. Others that have folded were such 1990s and 2000s publications as *Genre* (which was founded in 1991, was sold in 2003 to Window Media and published its last issue in 2008), *10 Percent, XY Magazine, YGA* (*Young Gay America*, from Halifax, Nova Scotia), *Hero, BLK* and *Venus* (an African-American lesbian-run magazine which changed to a straight magazine when founder Charlene Cothran went "straight"; the magazine is now known as *Victory* and its website promotes it as a "Christian Lifestyles Magazine").

Niche publications for segments of the community have also been issued, including *Compete*, a monthly gay sports magazine started in 2007; *Adelante Magazine: The GLBT Latino Magazine*, a monthly founded in 1998 in Los Angeles; *Passport*, for gay travelers; *Drummer*, which ran from 1975 to 1989 (see *Gay San Francisco: Eyewitness Drummer*, by Jack Fritscher, founding San Francisco editor of *Drummer*); *A Bear's Life* and others for bears; bisexual and transgender publications and websites; and much more. *Echelon* is a now-online-only bimonthly digital magazine for the LGBT business community. There's even a bimonthly *Gay Parent* magazine (with a website and an annual print edition for New York, New Jersey and Connecticut).

Trikone Magazine said it "offers a supportive, empowering and non-judgmental environment where LGBTQ South Asians and their allies can meet, make connections, and proudly promote awareness and acceptance of their sexual identity." *Trikone* (at that time named *Trikon*) was launched on January 1, 1986, as a small quarterly handout of four pages. It became a full-sized magazine in 1996 and added color in 2008. By email, the magazine's editor, who goes by the name Ali, said: "With the advent of LGBTQ and their issues into the mainstream media, access to resources through multiple channels, appearance of electronic readers, and the global recession in sight, *Trikone Magazine* transformed into a half-yearly publication, for the two major seasons—Summer and Winter … in both print and electronic format."

Here are a few key regional gay newspapers and magazines to remember, but also see later in this book for individual profiles of a few significant long-lasting gay and lesbian regional newspapers (*Bay Windows, Between The Lines, Dallas Voice, Frontiers* and *Windy City Times*):

— *ACCESSline* in Iowa, a monthly launched in 1986. It calls itself "The Heartland's LGBT+ Newspaper." The publication was founded by the nonprofit A Concerned Community for Education, Safer-sex and Support (ACCESS) and is now published by Breur Media Corporation.

— *Ambush*, a biweekly New Orleans–based tabloid founded in 1982. *Ambush* is billed as the oldest of the Gulf South market's LGBT publications, with distribution in its home state of Louisiana as well as Mississippi, Alabama, Georgia, Tennessee and Florida.

— *Black/Out*, a late-1980s publication of the National Coalition of Black Lesbians and Gays.

— *Blade California*, a monthly magazine serving Orange County and Long Beach, California. It started in 1992 (as *Orange County Blade*) and is still publishing.

— *The BottomLine*, a biweekly based in Palm Springs, California, launched in 1980, closed 2012.

— *Chicago Free Press*, a weekly newspaper started in 1999. It folded in 2010.

— *The Community Letter*, formerly known as *The Letter*, a monthly newspaper founded in 1990. It is based in Louisville, Kentucky, and is distributed in Kentucky, Indiana, Ohio, Tennessee, Illinois and Missouri.

— *David Atlanta*, started in 1998. It continues to cover the Atlanta community with weekly bar and entertainment coverage. The digest's owners say it has existed in the Atlanta market in various forms since 1967.

— *Desert Daily Guide* of Palm Springs, California, a weekly, publishing since 1995.

— *Diversity* of Idaho, a monthly tabloid started in 1992. It folded in 2011. It was one of the few gay tabloids published by a nonprofit, in this case The Community Center, the state's LGBT-and-allied community center. The organization's Amy Stinnett says it is still operating in a limited capacity as a community center.

— *Echo Magazine* of Phoenix, Arizona, a biweekly magazine, launched in 1989 and still publishing.

— *Erie Gay News* of Erie, Pennsylvania, launched in 1992 and still in business as a monthly newspaper.

— *Gay People's Chronicle* of Ohio, a Cleveland-based biweekly newspaper launched in 1985. According to the *Chronicle*, it was founded in February 1985 by Charles Callender, a Case Western Reserve University anthropology professor. It started as a monthly in Cleveland but now has distribution throughout Ohio and in neighboring states.

— *The Gayly Oklahoman*, founded in Oklahoma City in 1983. It folded in 2006 and was relaunched as a monthly tabloid a few years later.

— *The Guide*, a radical regional magazine on the East Coast of the U.S. that had a nationwide readership because of its strong coverage of entertainment, travel and community news. It was founded by bar owner Gary Dotterman in 1981 as a Boston bar guide. The Reverend Edward Hougen purchased it in 1983 and changed it considerably. "Farewell to a 'Venerable' Radical Gay Magazine," an article online at www.williamapercy.com, states: "Over the next nearly thirty years, THE GUIDE involved itself in every major gay issue, always taking a provocative and progressive stand." But then Hougen sold to Pink Triangle Press of Canada in 2006; much of the editorial focus that had defined *The Guide*'s strong brand name was stopped, and key editorial staffers were let go. The final print issue, from the new base in Montreal, was in August 2010. It is now online-only as guidemag.com, with a focus on gay travel.

— *Hotspots Magazine* of Central and South Florida, a weekly bar guide published since 1985.

— *Houston Voice*, a weekly newspaper serving that Texas city, starting in 1974 when Henry McClurg founded what he called the *Montrose Star*. After *Houston Voice* (part of Window Media by that point) folded in 2009, a new *Montrose Star* and later a *Houston Progressive Voice* were founded— in 2012, they were in litigation (the *Star* was suing the other entity for using the *Houston Voice* name). The *Montrose Star* is a biweekly tabloid launched in 2010, while the *Houston Progressive Voice* is an online media company.

— *In Touch: The Magazine for a Different Point of View*, a 1970s-era high-quality glossy magazine from Hollywood, California.

— *Just Out* of Portland, a twice-monthly tabloid newspaper serving that Oregon city from 1983. It was relaunched in June 2012 and now has a monthly-magazine format.

— *Lavender*, a biweekly magazine published in Minneapolis, founded in 1995.

— *The Leather Journal,* a monthly tabloid started in 1987 and still publishing today, based in California.

— *Letters from CAMP Rehoboth,* a magazine from Rehoboth Beach, Delaware, published 15 times per year and founded in 1991. It is a program of CAMP Rehoboth Inc., a nonprofit community-service organization that "seeks to create a more positive environment of cooperation and understanding among all people."

— *The Liberty Press*, a monthly magazine published in Wichita, Kansas, since 1994.

— *Magnus: A Journal of Collective Faggotry* (later subtitled *A Socialist Journal of Gay Liberation*), by San Francisco's Magnus Collective. Apparently they did just two annual issues, 1976– 77, and the journal was called a "superior gay left publication" on Tyler Alpern's website.

— *MetroSource* of New York, founded in 1990. It is published six times a year in magazine format. It launched a Los Angeles edition in 2004 and also produces a national edition, all from MetroSource Publishing.

— *Metro Weekly,* launched in 1994 in Washington D.C. It is a weekly glossy magazine. Atypical of magazine-format regional publications, which are often more bar- and entertainment-focused, *Metro Weekly* has established itself as a strong news publication as well, winning awards for its reporting and opinion writing from the National Lesbian and Gay Journalists Association and the Gay and Lesbian Alliance Against Defamation.

— *Next Magazine*, a glossy bar and entertainment weekly, published in New York City. It was founded in 1991 and also has distribution in neighboring cities and states. (Its main rival, *HX Magazine*, folded in 2009.)

— *Nightspots*, Chicago's oldest LGBT bar-and-entertainment glossy magazine still appearing, published biweekly by *Windy City Times*. It started life as *Nightlines* weekly in 1990.

— *Odyssey Magazine Hawaii*, a Honolulu monthly that was launched in 1991. There are other *Odyssey* magazines in Los Angeles and New York.

— *Options*, a Providence, Rhode Island, monthly magazine founded in 1982. Its website states: "The entire Options family—a group of dedicated volunteers and one underpaid, part time staff person—is proud to have produced close to 30 years of issues that have not only chronicled, but in many cases led, advances in understanding and rights for LGBT people in Rhode Island."

— *Out In Jersey*, a bimonthly magazine founded in 1996 and based in Trenton.

— *Out Post*, a biweekly glossy magazine founded in 1990. It refers to itself as "Detroit's gay guide," and its offices are in Ann Arbor, Michigan.

— *Outlines*, which started in 1987 as a breakaway from Chicago's *Windy City Times*. It then purchased *WCT* in 2000 and merged back into that paper. In the 1990s, *Outlines* also launched *Nightlines* (now *Nightspots*), *BLACKlines, En La Vida, Clout! Business Report* and *Out! Resource Guide*, but those eventually folded. *Out!* is still published online.

— *Outlines*, a biweekly digest serving Cleveland since 1997.

— *Outlook Columbus* (formerly *Outlook Weekly*), a monthly magazine based in Columbus, Ohio, and founded in 1996.

— *OutSmart* of Houston, a monthly magazine launched in 1994. It says its distribution includes Houston and surrounding areas, including Galveston, Beaumont and College Station, and select sites in Austin, Brownsville, Corpus Christi, Dallas, El Paso and San Antonio.

— *Outword*, a twice-monthly newspaper based in Sacramento, California, and founded in 1995.

— *PM Entertainment*, a monthly 'zine based on Long Island and in New Jersey, founded in 1992.

— *Prairie Flame*, a monthly tabloid newspaper in Springfield, Illinois, that folded in 2008 after almost 12 years in business.

— *QNotes* of Charlotte, North Carolina, which also covers South Carolina. It appears biweekly in a tabloid format with distribution across the state and was founded in 1986. In 2012, it coordinated coverage of the Democratic National Convention in Charlotte, syndicating content to print and online LGBT publications. "Our partnership with these outstanding LGBT news media offers community members across the country an inside look at this year's Democratic National Convention, where delegates are expected for the first time in history to add support for marriage equality to a leading political party's platform," said Matt Comer, *QNotes* editor.

— *Quest*, a monthly magazine serving Milwaukee that was founded in 1993.

— *She Magazine*, a monthly magazine founded in 1999 for Florida's women's communities.

— *Southern Voice*, an Atlanta-based newspaper founded in 1988 that was one of the victims of the closing of Window Media in 2009. See more details on its legacy in Chapter 30.

— *Watermark* of Orlando, Florida, a biweekly tabloid established in 1994 and covering Central Florida.

— *The Weekly News* of Miami, which was known as *TWN* and folded in 2006 after almost 29 years in business.

— *Wire Magazine*, a Miami Beach weekly magazine serving South Florida, launched in 1985.

— *The Word* in Indianapolis, a monthly tabloid founded in 1989 (though in some places it is listed as starting in 1991). It distributes in Indiana, Ohio, Kentucky, Illinois and Michigan. (*OUTlines* newspaper of Indianapolis, founded in 1991, appears to have closed in 2004.)

This list is certainly not exhaustive and does not include some national glossy magazines or many of the bar/club guides that come and go in cities across the country. Some publications may have been founded in one year and first published in the following year. And because they often were sold or changed hands, sometimes there is confusion about their own histories—discrepancies in dates recorded on websites vs. printed materials, or information logged by national media representation firms. We sent a survey to the publications still in business to try to clarify any information, but not all papers responded.

Numerous serious journals also focus on LGBT issues.

The best-known is *The Harvard Gay & Lesbian Review*. Among the others are the *International Journal of Transgenderism*, the *Journal of Bisexuality*, the *Journal of Gay & Lesbian Issues in Education*, the *Journal of Homosexuality* and *Law and Sexuality*.

The Harvard Gay & Lesbian Review, founded by Dr. Richard Schneider Jr., is an esteemed magazine known now as *The Gay & Lesbian Review Worldwide*. It gives this history for its readers:

"With the publication of the first issue in the winter of 1994, *The Harvard Gay & Lesbian Review* rushed into a huge vacuum in gay and lesbian literary culture—a void that stretched all the way from *The Atlantic* and *The New Republic* to *The New York Review of Books*. Nowhere in Gaydom was there a journal for the literate non-specialist, offering the best writing and thinking our culture had to offer, covering a wide range of topics, handsomely produced, and always a pleasure to read.

"This was the kind of publication *The G&LR* set out to become—all based on the hunch that there was a critical mass of curious, intelligent lesbians and gay men out there capable of supporting such a journal. The fact that we're now in our eighteenth year and still going strong attests to the existence of such a readership, one that wants to be challenged by the play of ideas and to explore our issues insightfully and in depth. Of course, to appeal to this community, this journal would have to be keenly edited and smartly produced.

"Having assembled this readership, *The G&LR* has become something of a lingua franca for the thinking GLBT community nationwide. 'It's our intellectual journal,' remarked Larry Kramer in *The New York Times*. *The G&LR* has become the place where the big debates about gay and lesbian culture and politics are often played out."

The bimonthly magazine, which publishes more than 10,000 copies per issue, is produced by a nonprofit educational organization, and most of its staff are volunteers.

AIDS Media

Several publications have launched over the years to cover just AIDS—not just for gay men, but for anyone living with HIV or AIDS, as well as their allies.

Sean Strub launched *POZ* magazine in April/May 1994 as a national glossy magazine. It has been providing a national voice to AIDS issues ever since.

Chicago-based Test Positive Aware Network is one of the country's oldest organizations for people with HIV/AIDS. It launched *Positively Aware* in 1989 locally and soon made it into a national magazine, with several related publications, including the annual *HIV Drug Guide*.

Arts & Understanding, launched in 1991, covers AIDS from a cultural perspective, often featuring major celebrities on its cover.

HIV Plus is part of the Here! Media company, obtained as part of its purchase of *The Advocate* and *Out* magazines.

The 2000s

A few dozen new U.S. regional gay print publications were launched in the 2000s, and quite a few closings occurred, in part thanks to the bankruptcy of Window Media, which took with it the *Washington Blade* (the employees eventually were able to reopen it), *Southern Voice* (other publications were born from its ashes, including *GA Voice*) and other gay media. In Chicago, *Gay Chicago* and *Chicago Free Press* closed—*Gay Chicago* had been among the oldest gay publications and *Free Press* among the newest. *Windy City Times* was relaunched in 2000 in a merger with *Outlines* newspaper. It had closed for a few weeks and then reopened.

The back of this book has a list of other new gay print media launched starting in 2000, including the *BOI* biweekly digest in Chicago (2000) and *GRAB Magazine* biweekly (2009), also in Chicago. The *Montrose Star* biweekly tabloid newspaper started in 2010 in Houston, and the monthly 'zine *My Scene City* began in Minneapolis in 2007. *ION Arizona Magazine* is a monthly glossy begun in 2001.

Our Lives, a bimonthly magazine serving Madison, Wisconsin, started in 2007. The publication was launched by Patrick Farabaugh. As the magazine states online: "Since arriving in Wisconsin in 2005 he's founded the Madison Gay Hockey Association, *Our Lives Magazine* and co-founded the Out Professional and Executive Network (OPEN). In 2010 Governor [Jim] Doyle named him an LGBTQ Living Hero to our state."

Out & About, a monthly tabloid for Nashville (and all of Tennessee), opened in 2002. A monthly for Utah, *Q Salt Lake*, started in 2004, and *Rage* monthly magazine launched in San Diego in 2007. That city also got *San Diego LGBT Weekly*, a weekly tabloid, in 2010, and the biweekly *Gay San Diego* tabloid also started that year.

South Florida Gay News, a weekly tabloid from Fort Lauderdale (serving Miami-Dade, Broward and Palm Beach counties), started in 2010. Farther south, in Key West, *The Gay Rag* monthly guide launched in 2006. *The Rainbow Times* opened in 2006 and is a Boston-based monthly tabloid serving New England. *Wisconsin Gazette*, a biweekly tabloid, was founded in 2009 and is based in Milwaukee.

Vital VOICE is a monthly magazine. Here is a brief history of that St. Louis publication: "Vital VOICE Omni Media got its start following the sudden shuttering of the venerable *Lesbian and Gay News Telegraph* (founded in 1981) in January 2000. Recognizing the importance of continuity in our community, St. Louis Network, LLC's Pam Schneider approached *News Telegraph* co-founder and editor Jim Thomas about coming on board a new media venture and in June 2000 *Vital VOICE* newspaper was launched at Pridefest. Over the next nine years Schneider raised the bar for LGBT journalism in St. Louis with the help of long-time editor, Nancy Larson." In 2009 Schneider sold the *Vital VOICE* brand to Darin "DSly" Slyman, who relaunched it as a lifestyle magazine in January 2010.

Flawless is a semiannual magazine founded in 2008 in San Diego, at first in print but now online-only.

A few publications founded in the 2000s did not make it, including *OMG!* in Tampa, *Montrose Gem* in Houston, *Inside OUT* in the Hudson Valley of New York and *Stereotyped* in Asheville, North Carolina.

Numerous Canadian gay publications exist, including *GayCalgary Magazine*, a monthly glossy launched in 2003. Also, Pink Triangle Press has issued several similarly named publications plus others: the biweekly newspapers *Xtra!* in Toronto (founded 1994), Vancouver (1993) and Ottawa (1993); *Fab* glossy magazine biweekly, founded in 1994; and various community directories, pride guides, and *The Guide* gay travel website. *Der Gay Krant* is a long-running Dutch gay publication founded in January 1980. It is now known as *GK Magazine*. *Têtu* from Paris is another long-running gay publication.

Millivres Prowler Group (known as MPG) has operated in Europe since 1974. Its website states that it does both media and retail sales, and its "media brands" include *Gay Times* (now known as *GT*), *DIVA* and the former *Pink Paper,* which went online-only as www.pinkpaper.com in 2009. In September 2012, the website was shut down and the company issued this statement September 18:

"After 25 years of bringing news to the UK LGBT community, it is with sadness we announce today that it is no longer practical to continue to update *Pink Paper*'s daily website. … *Pink Paper* was launched in print format as a weekly lesbian and gay newspaper in 1987. Distributed free at scene venues, it quickly became a community mainstay, reporting major national stories such as the campaigns against Section 28 and for civil partnership as well as local news. It also carried interviews, arts reviews, comic strips, listings, job adverts and personals.

"Over the years it was to go through many different incarnations, including a brief period as a paid-for newsstand magazine.

"In 2005 Millivres Prowler Ltd acquired *Pink Paper* after it had gone out of print and re-launched it as a fortnightly newspaper. As the publication's financial backbone of recruitment, housing and display advertising slumped due to the recession, *Pink Paper* suspended its fortnightly print and distribution schedule on 25 June 2009, turning its entire content over to the website at PinkPaper.com."

An interesting and enduring publication outside the U.S. is *Exit* of Johannesburg, South Africa. Gavin Hayward of *Exit* notes: "*Exit* started out as the newsletter of GASA, the Gay Association of South Africa, in the very early '80s. It used to be picked up as a roneo-ed [mimeographed] sheet in the gay venues of Hillbrow and in Cape Town. This then became *Link/Skakel*, a tabloid-type newspaper, which in 1985 changed its name to *Exit* and became a commercial venture independent of GASA which was published every two months. I bought *Exit* in '95 and turned it into a regular monthly publication. We published the 200th issue a few years ago."

The predominant form of new media companies in the 2000s has certainly been online, with blogs, websites and digital-format content for the LGBT community now taking wing through thousands of voices across the Internet.

Straight for Gay and Gay for Straight

An interesting development in the 2000s has also been the partnering of a gay publication, *Gay City News* in New York (profiled later in this book), with a non-gay newspaper company, Community Media (which was sold in 2012). The project is helmed by gay people but primarily owned by a non-gay corporate partner, in an alignment similar to that which existed 40 years ago with *GAY* in New York.

Troy Masters, co-founder and associate publisher of *Gay City News*, pointed to the long tradition of gay papers partnering with straight publications in New York City.

"It's also worth noting that this arrangement is not at all unique," Masters said. "*New York Blade* [which has since folded] was introduced to New York as a partnership that was more than 50 percent straight-owned by Wilbur Ross, the husband of New York state's then-lieutenant governor who served for Republican Governor George Pataki. There's a long history of straight money in just about every gay project in this town. And along the way during my 25 years in gay publishing, I have had straight financial backers at some level or other.

"It's no longer the issue it once was. As we enter the fabric of society, it is less and less a concern—to some perhaps more and more of a concern. But at the end of the day, all that is truly important is the authentic voice of the paper and an effective understanding of the market, and that is entirely a function of me and Paul Schindler, who is editor-in-chief and co-founder of *GCN*."

In that same category, though perhaps even more unusual, is the launch by a daily non-gay newspaper, the *Desert Sun* in Palm Springs, California, of a bimonthly magazine for the gay community, run by the *Sun* company staff. The *Desert Sun* is owned by Gannett, which also owns *USA Today*, so this is perhaps the first time a non-gay major newspaper chain has launched a gay publication. The bimonthly is called *Desert Outlook*. Openly gay journalist Hank Plante is a columnist for the *Sun*, and he wrote a piece in the *Outlook* launch issue in the spring of 2012.

The *San Diego LGBT Weekly* newsmagazine bills itself as "America's First Cable News Affiliated LGBT Media Company." The publisher is longtime Democratic gay activist Stampp Corbin. The publication's cable affiliation stems from its use of CNN Wire content. In the past, a few gay papers have used The Associated Press wire-service copy, something that other publishers criticized. CNN, seeing a new market, started pushing gay papers in 2011 to use its content.

Going Places

This summary of the gay media landscape shows just how volatile the publications of the LGBT movement intrinsically have been—apart from any other issues that affect them from the outside, such as economic downturns and the growing power of the Internet.

By the 1980s as many as 700 publications may have served the U.S. community, many of them organization newsletters or bar guides, but also among them a significant number of newspapers and magazines (more than 200, according to Rivendell Media). Their frequency and quality varied, but they all tried to find a role to play in the growing gay movement.

Why did some papers succeed while others failed? How did some last four decades and some barely four issues? There are a lot of answers to these questions, and perhaps each paper had its own reason for closing. I have compiled a few of the many reasons for failures, as lessons learned from the past.

— The most obvious reason is lack of money, so I won't go into that too much. Suffice it to say that most of the publications in this chapter started out on a wing and a prayer, with too little capital to survive the natural early needs of starting a publication.

— Many of these publications were started by activists who learned how to do a newspaper, journal or magazine "on the job" and between their paying jobs for other companies. They usually burned out rather quickly.

— Many early publications were produced by gay organizations, so they were at the mercy of those groups if the groups folded, but at least they benefited from the groups' revenues (including membership dues).

— Collectives launched many publications, and collectives rarely last for significant periods of time. The nature of collective process, voting, and other features means that there is high turnover and a very high likelihood of closing down.

— Changes in politics were a reality for many early papers, which meant that people came and went quickly as the papers changed their missions.

— The lack of advertising revenue affected those papers that did want to accept advertising to help pay the bills. It was not until the 1990s that mainstream businesses really jumped on the LGBT media bandwagon. Certainly some did earlier, but the true escalation in national ad revenue began in the 1990s.

— A lack of subscriber or paid-circulation numbers also affected those publications that relied on readers to help cover their costs. Even the most successful local and national gay media never came close to the subscriber numbers of mainstream media competitors.

— Competition within markets started to be a big issue during the 1970s and 1980s, as gay papers—especially in larger communities—encountered more competition from an ever-growing list of newspaper founders. Some cities saw a dozen gay papers and bar guides at one point, which meant that some ultimately were forced to fold because of economic reality in those markets.

— Loss of the founders of some papers (including losses to AIDS) meant that the inheritors of their vision had different motivations, and perhaps did not have the same passion to work through difficult cycles and keep the publications afloat.

— The advent of a more business-focused ownership of gay papers also meant they may not have stuck through the tough times as much as activists might have done. That's not to say there was not money to be made by some gay-media owners, but the profits were cyclical and rarely a huge windfall. Even many of the glossy magazines, with their expensive full-page ads, have not figured out a way to survive financially, at least without having to be sold to new owners.

— Substance abuse is a problem that has plagued owners of many gay publications over the years (which is no different from other businesses, gay or straight). But this has led to the closing or forced sale of some gay publications.

— And finally: the personalities attracted to working in, or owning, gay media—the passionate people, the activists, the journalists, the rich and poor people of all races, colors and genders, of many religions (and no religion), of the left, middle and right politically, all trying to work together. It has been no easy task trying to make sure the melting pot does not come to a boil.

Of course, these are just a few reasons papers have failed; in some cases, there were multiple factors leading to their demise.

On the other hand, given the odds against gay media, why have there been success stories? Examples of these regional newspaper success stories are described later in this book, but even those papers in most cases have gone through some ownership transition.

Mark Segal of the *Philadelphia Gay News* is a very rare example of a publisher from the 1970s lasting until 2012. While Segal is motivated as a businessman, he is at his core an activist, which means that he saw his company through some very lean times, motivated not just by money but by a sense of community.

Because print publishing is such an unpredictable business, with competition from the Internet and now even the mainstream media looking for gay dollars, it is going to take innovative thinkers, combined with experienced businesspeople and journalists, to make sure an LGBT publishing voice continues in the coming years. My opinion is that a passion for the community, not just business acumen, is required in order to sustain a media company.

Der Eigene from 1899, 1919 and 1924.

A copy of *Friendship and Freedom*, published by Chicago's Society for Human Rights, appears prominently in this photo of a collection of early, mostly German, homosexual emancipation periodicals, verifying both the existence of the American periodical and suggesting the authenticity of Gerber's account.
Courtesy of Jonathan Ned Katz

THIS STATEMENT MUST BE FILED IN DUPLICATE.

STATE OF ILLINOIS, } ss.
Cook   County. }

To LOUIS L. EMMERSON, Secretary of State.

We, the undersigned   Rev. John T. Graves,

                              Henry Gerber,

                              Al Meininger

citizens of the United States, propose to form a corporation under an Act of the General Assembly of the State of Illinois, entitled, "An Act concerning Corporations," approved April 18, 1872, and all acts amendatory thereof; and for the purpose of such organizations we hereby state as follows, to-wit :

1. The name of such corporation is

      Society for Human Rights, Chicago, Illinois,

            (Incorporated not for Profit)

2. The object for which it is formed is to promote and to protect the interests of people who by reason of mental and physical abnormalties are abused and hindered in the legal pursuit of happiness which is guaranteed them by the Declaration of Independence, and to combat the public prejudices against them by dissemination of facts according to modern science among intellectuals of mature age. The Society stands only for law and order; it is in harmony with any and all general laws insofar as they protect the rights of others, and does in no manner recommend any acts in violation of present laws nor advocate any matter inimical to the public welfare.------

3. The management of the aforesaid Society shall be vested in a board of
   seven Directors.

4. The following persons are hereby selected as the Directors to control and manage said corporation for the first year of its corporate existence, viz:

NAME	ADDRESS		
---	NUMBER	STREET	CITY	STATE
Rev. John T. Graves, President	1151	Milton Ave.	Chicago, Illinois
Al Meininger, Vice-President	1044	North Franklin St.,	Chicago, Ill
Henry Gerber, Secretary	1710	Crilly Court,	Chicago, Illinois
Ellsworth Booher, Treasurer	1151	Milton Avenue,	Chicago, Illinois.
Fred Panaburn, Trustee	1838	East 101st St.	Cleveland, Ohio.
John Sather, Trustee	5855	University Ave.,	Chicago, Illinois
Henry Teacutter, Trustee	1710	Crilly Court,	Chicago, Illinois

5. The location is in the city of Chicago in the county of Cook

in the State of Illinois, and the post office address of its business office is at No. 1710

    Crilly Court Street in the said city of Chicago

SIGNED.

      Rev. John T. Graves

      Al Meininger

      Henry Gerber

The 1924 incorporation papers of the Society for Human Rights.
Courtesy of Jonathan Ned Katz and the Chicago History Museum

60 years ago—America's first gay rights group
Chicago was home to Henry Gerber's Society for Human Rights

By GREGORY SPRAGUE

Sixty years ago, on Dec. 10, 1924, the very first American gay rights organization was incorporated in Illinois under the name of the Society for Human Rights. Henry Gerber, a Chicago postal worker and ex-serviceman, founded SHR in order to help "ameliorate the plight of homosexuals" in America.

But Gerber's organization was short-lived. In the summer of 1925, the Chicago police arrested Gerber and the other officers of the SHR, essentially destroying the infant gay rights society.

Henry Gerber was born in Bavaria, Germany, on June 29, 1892 (76 years almost to the day before the Stonewall riots that gave birth to today's gay liberation movement). Recent research by Chris Hagen of Atlanta indicates that Gerber's name at birth was Joseph Henry Dittmar; he changed his name to Henry Gerber once he immigrated to the United States. Gerber arrived at New York's Ellis Island in October 1913, one year prior to the start of World War I. With several members of his family, Gerber moved to Chicago, which had a large German population. He worked briefly for Mont-

gomery Ward's. But when the U.S. entered World War I against Germany, Gerber, being German, was "offered internment" as an alien, and received, he said, three free meals a day.

After the war, Gerber served with the U.S. Army of Occupation in Germany from 1920 to 1923. While in Germany, he came in contact with the extensive German homosexual emancipation movement. Gerber not only subscribed to German homophile magazines but corresponded with the oldest homosexual rights organization in Europe—the Scientific Humanitarian Committee, founded by Magnus Hirschfield. The Berlin-based SHC served as the model for Gerber's SHR.

After returning from Germany, Gerber left the Army and moved back to Chicago, where he was hired by the U.S. Post Office. Even in 1924, Chicago had a significant gay subculture—much of it located around the Near North neighborhood of "Towertown." Though he was aware of Chicago's gay subculture, Gerber does not appear to have participated in it on a regular basis. Yet he did feel a need to establish an organization to protect the rights of

all homosexuals in America. But he had difficulty finding others to join him in the cause. Gerber's few gay friends advised him against "doing anything so rash and futile" as starting a homosexual rights organization. Thus there was little support for Gerber's cause from the Chicago gay community.

Finally, Gerber recruited about 10 members for his organization; but they were not the upstanding and influential persons whom he had hoped to attract to SHR. His executive board consisted of poor, mostly illiterate gay men.

Gerber described the members of his executive board thus: "John, a preacher who earned his room and board by preaching brotherly love to small groups of Negroes; Al, an indigent laundry queen; and Ralph, whose job with the railroad was in jeopardy when his nature became known. These were the national officers for the Society for Human Rights, Inc. I realized this start was dead wrong . . . ."

Despite the very small membership, Gerber had high hopes for his newly formed organization.

See GERBER, page 6

Gregory Sprague wrote about Henry Gerber in *GayLife* newspaper, December 6, 1984.

ABOVE: Lisa Ben, publisher of *Vice Versa*, the first known lesbian publication in the U.S.

TOP RIGHT: Table of contents for the first issue of *Vice Versa*, June 1947. The table also appears to be the actual cover of the publication.
Courtesy of the Gay, Lesbian, Bisexual, Transgender Historical Society in San Francisco

BOTTOM RIGHT: Table of contents for the October 1947 issue of *Vice Versa*, which used *America's Gayest Magazine* as its subtitle.
Courtesy of the Gay, Lesbian, Bisexual, Transgender Historical Society in San Francisco

VICE VERSA

June, 1947   Volume I, Number 1

TABLE OF CONTENTS

VICE VERSA

America's Gayest Magazine

October, 1947   Volume I, Number 5

TABLE OF CONTENTS

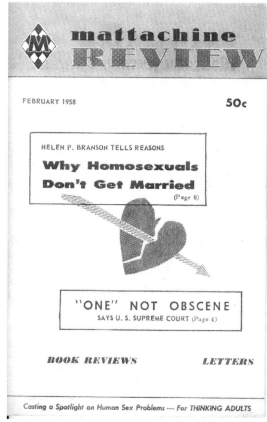

ABOVE: *ONE* **magazine's August 1953 edition.**
Courtesy of C. Todd White

RIGHT: *Mattachine Review*, **February 1958.**
Courtesy of Rich Wilson

The Ladder's **June 1966 edition.**
Courtesy of Rich Wilson

Jim Kepner's *Rough News, Daring Views* **book, published in 1997 by Routledge.**

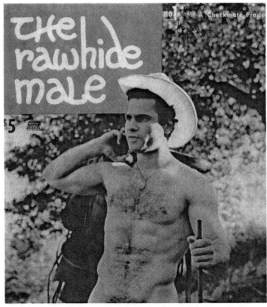

Various men's physique magazines of the 1950s and 1960s attracted a large homosexual following.
Courtesy of the Leather Archives & Museum

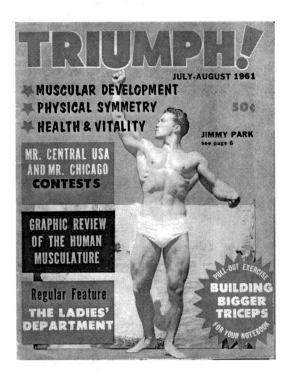

Transvestia **was a 1961 magazine.**

**ABOVE AND BELOW: The Chicago *Seed*
underground paper featured a section on gay
rights post-Stonewall.**
Courtesy of Abe Peck

**LEFT: The underground *Rat* paper in New York was taken over by
women in 1970. They turned it into *Women's LibeRATion*.**

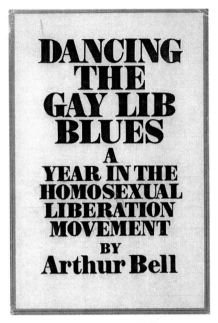

Gay activist and journalist Arthur Bell wrote *Dancing the Gay Lib Blues* in 1971 for Simon & Schuster.

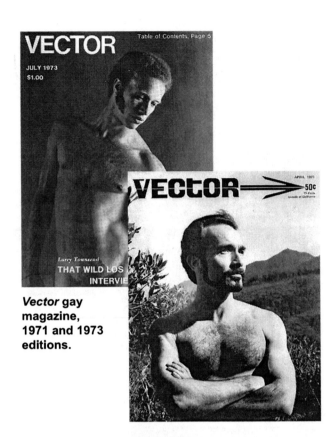

Vector gay magazine, 1971 and 1973 editions.

The gay publication *Tangents*, October 1965.

Drum gay magazine, 1965 and 1967 editions.

FRISCO FROLICS by NOVA CAEN

WELCOME READERS: I want to thank all of you literary types out there for answering the request in the FREEP for contributions to my column. Not a single item, tidbit, or word flowed into my basket! This is a blatant outrage! It's not enough that I risk my reputation by writing a column for this alleged paper, but I have to draw a non-committed readership! What do you assholes out there think I write this for — money? I write it because all you pot farmers need to freak out on the truth every once in a while — and you'll get nothing but the truth here . . . in my own way, of course.

MAIDEN VOYAGE: In this, my first column, I must move to squelch the vicious rumor circulated by the FREEP, rumored to be a newspaper, that I was busted last month. Not true! And a pox on the writer and this sleazy tabloid for indulging in character assassination. I'd better not learn who this undercover word-freak who calls himself "Lordzilla" is, or his ass will be grass, and I'll be the nark. That was the sorriest excuse for a column I've ever seen outside of the establishment press. Twenty paces, "Lordzilla," and you choose the weapons!

PLUGSVILLE: Far-out ideas deserve far-out praise. Mine goes to the innovators at KRENT, a San Francisco based porn outfit, for originating a "Smut of the Month Club." According to a spokesman, a charter membership will bring a new and different erotic photo-publication monthly, and guarantee a 10% discount on all purchases from the company, which handles magazines, photos, films, sex aids, etc. All you porn collectors write to KRENT, P.O. Box 636, San Francisco, Ca 94101.

CIRCUS MAXIMUS: I thank Chicago for the revival of this most brutal of spectacles, being relieved in the courtroom of Julius Caesar Hoffman. Only this time we witnessed the lion being fed to the "Christians." Think about it — Bobby Seale was kidnapped by Federal Pigs to stand trial on a "conspiracy" rap, a new law being roadtested, and shaky at best. Mr. Seale was denied the lawyer of his choice, denied the right to act as

— to page 14

The San Francisco Free Press, November 15–30, 1969.

QUEEN'S QUARTERLY

The Magazine For Gay Guys Who Have No Hangups | FALL 1969

$2.00
ACME

Queen's Quarterly and *QQ,* 1969 and early 1970s editions

The Los Angeles Advocate, October 1968.
Courtesy of Rich Wilson

The Advocate reports about what became known as AIDS, March 18, 1982.

The October 24, 1966, *PRIDE* publication in Los Angeles, which later became *The Los Angeles Advocate* and later still *The Advocate*.
Courtesy of Rich Wilson

The Advocate's Barbara Jordan cover, March 5, 1996.

The Advocate's Bill Clinton cover, June 25, 1996.

In September 2012, *The Advocate* celebrated its
45th anniversary with this special issue.

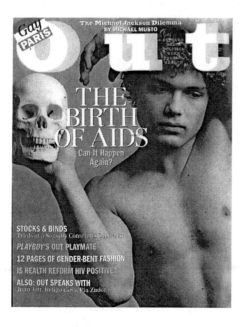

LEFT: *Out* magazine AIDS cover, April 1994.

RIGHT: *Out* Gay Games issue, June 1994.

New York's *GAY* newspaper,
February 16, 1970.

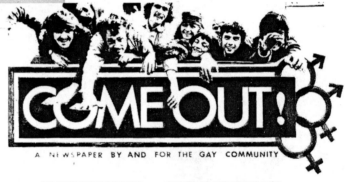

Come Out! first edition,
November 14, 1969.

COME OUT FOR FREEDOM! COME OUT NOW! POWER TO THE PEOPLE! GAY POWER TO GAY PEOPLE! COME OUT OF THE CLOSET BEFORE THE DOOR IS NAILED SHUT!

COME-OUT, A NEWSPAPER FOR THE HOMO-SEXUAL COMMUNITY, dedicates itself to the joy, the humor, and the dignity of the homosexual male and female. COME-OUT has COME OUT to fight for the freedom of the homosexual: to give voice to the rapidly growing militancy within our community; to provide a public forum for the discussion and clarification of methods and actions necessary to end our oppression. COME-OUT has 'COME OUT' indeed for "life, liberty and the pursuit of happiness."

Make no mistake about our oppression: It is real, it is visible, it is demonstrable. IN NEW YORK A HOMO-SEXUAL IS LEGITIMATE AS AN INDIVIDUAL BUT ILLEGITIMATE AS A PARTICIPANT IN A HOMO-SEXUAL ACT. Hell, every homosexual and lesbian in this country survives solely by sufferance, not by law or even that cold state of grace known as tolerance. Our humanity is questioned, our choice of housing is circumscribed, our employment is tenuous. OUR FRIENDLY NEIGHBORHOOD TAVERN IS A MAFIOSO-ON-THE-JOB TRAINING SCHOOL FOR DUM-DUM HOODS. It is just such grievances as these which have sparked the revolutionary movements of history.

COME-OUT salutes militant oppressed groups, offers aid, but realizes that very often other oppressed people are also our own oppressors. THROUGH MUTU-AL RESPECT, ACTION, AND EDUCATION COME-OUT HOPES TO UNIFY BOTH THE HOMOSEXUAL

COMMUNITY AND OTHER OPPRESSED GROUPS INTO A COHESIVE BODY OF PEOPLE WHO DO NOT FIND THE ENEMY IN EACH OTHER.

COME-OUT will hasten the day when it becomes not only passe, but actual political suicide to speak of further repression of the homosexual. WE ARE COMING OUT IN COMMUNITY, A COMMUNITY THAT NUM-BERS IN THE MILLIONS. We shall aggressively promote the use of the very real and potent economic power of Gay people throughout this land in order to further the interests of the homosexual community. We shall convince society at large of the reality of homosexual political power by the active use thereof.

We will not be gay bourgeoisie, searching for the sterile "American dream" of the ivy-covered cottage and the good corporation job, but neither will we tolerate the exclusion of homosexuals from any area of American life.

Because our oppression is based on sex and the sex roles which oppress us from infancy, we must explore these roles and their meanings. We must recognize and make others recognize that BEING HOMOSEXUAL SAYS ONLY ONE THING: EMOTIONALLY YOU PREFER YOUR OWN SEX. IT SAYS NOTHING ABOUT YOUR WORTH, YOUR VALUE AS A HUMAN BEING. Does society make a place for us . . as a man? A woman? A homosexual or lesbian? How does the family structure affect us? What is sex, and what does it mean? What is love? As homosexuals, we are in a unique position to examine these questions from a fresh point of view. You'd better believe we are going to do so – that we are going to transform the society at large through the open realization of our own consciousness.

STEP & FETCHIT FEMALE
MARCHI & PROCACCINO
VILLAGE VOICE GOES DOWN

Gay Power newspaper, 1969.

Gay Activist newspaper, March 1977.

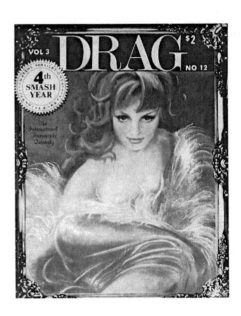

Drag magazine, 1972 and 1973 editions.

Gay Sunshine, spring 1974.

Gay Community News, May 6, 1978.

Fag Rag of Boston, June 1971.

The Gay Liberator of Detroit.

LEFT: *Out!* of Los Angeles, July 29, 1977.

RIGHT: *Gaysweek*, December 12, 1977.

Logo and 1976 first-edition cover of Christopher Street magazine.

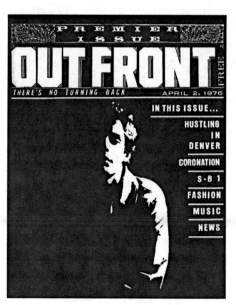

LEFT: The first issue of *Out Front*, a long-running Denver gay publication founded on April 2, 1976, and still publishing today.

RIGHT: The September 6–19, 2012, cover of *Bay Times* of San Francisco, founded in 1978.

Lesbian Connection, October 1978.

The Lesbian Tide, May–June 1977.

LEFT: A *Lesbian News* 2012 edition. *LN* was founded in 1974.

RIGHT: A series of *off our backs* issues.

LEFT: *Curve* magazine, October 2012.

ABOVE: *Amazon Quarterly*, fall 1972.

Ms. magazine marked 40 years in 2012. It stated: "Forty years after Ms. thrilled feminists with its inaugural cover declaring 'Wonder Woman for President,' the magazine once again features the iconic superhero. For its anniversary issue, the *Ms.* cover shows Wonder Woman on the streets of Washington, D.C., with women marching to stop the attacks on their rights and carrying signs bearing the slogan: 'Vote as if your life depends on it.'"

RIGHT: *HOT WIRE*, January 1991.

BELOW: *New York Native*,
January 6, 1996.

OutWeek editions 69 and 102.

BLK, December 1993.

ACCESSline from Iowa, March 2012.

Instinct magazine, the 2000s.

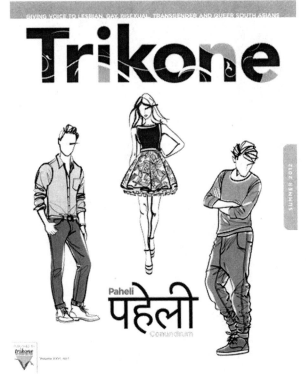

Trikone, summer 2012.

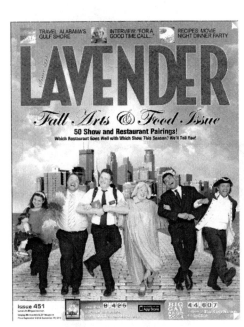

Lavender magazine of Minnesota, September 2012.

QNotes of North Carolina, September 2012.

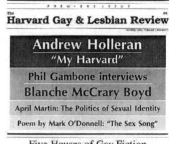

The 1994 first edition of *The Harvard Gay & Lesbian Review (above)*, and the September–October 2012 edition of *The Gay & Lesbian Review Worldwide* (left).

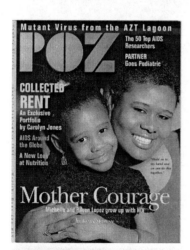

POZ magazine, August–September 1996.

Positively Aware, November 1990.

Positively Aware, summer 2012.

Arts & Understanding magazine,
November 2001.

**First issue of South Africa's *Exit* in 1985
(above), and a 2012 edition (below).**

Wisconsin Gazette, September 6, 2012.

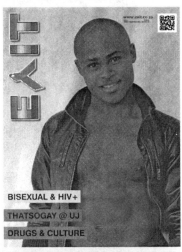

Our Lives magazine of
Madison, Wisconsin,
September–October 2012.

Florida Agenda, September 12, 2012.

Gay San Diego, September 7, 2012.

Montrose Star of Houston, Texas,
September 12, 2012.

Outword Magazine, September 13, 2012.

San Diego LGBT Weekly, September 13, 2012.

South Florida Gay News,
September 13, 2012.

Watermark of Florida, September 13, 2012.

Wire Magazine of Florida,
September 13, 2012.

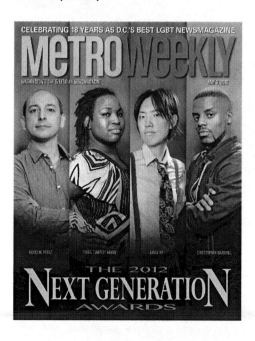

Metro Weekly of Washington, D.C.
Covers of its first issue in 1994
(above) and 18th anniversary issue
in 2012 (below).

Why marriage matters to us all

Pride Foundation is 'all in' for marriage and looks at the big picture

by Kris Hermanns
Special to the SGN

Verdict in on DADT repeal

Study says ending of anti-Gay policy has had positive effect

by Shaun Knittel
SGN Associate Editor

Axis of Evil, Part II

Who's who in the fight to repeal marriage equality

by Mike Andrew
SGN Staff Writer

Rainbow road

Should Seattle follow West Hollywood's lead and install a Pride crosswalk?

by James Whitely
SGN Staff Writer

Seattle Gay News, September 7, 2012.

Baltimore OUTloud, August 10, 2012.

Ambush of New Orleans, August 14, 2012.

Gay People's Chronicle of Ohio, August 24, 2012.

3

Drama, Power and Politics:
ONE Magazine, *Mattachine Review* and *The Ladder* in the Era of Homophile Activism

By C. Todd White, Ph.D.

On the day I write these words, I learn that another great pioneer of LGBT publishing has died.

I like to think that somewhere in gay heaven, Barbara Grier is being welcomed to a grand, ethereal brunch with the other few but great pioneer gay and lesbian journalists who arrived before her. Don Slater, longtime editor of *ONE* magazine, hefts a glass in toast to a life well lived. Jim Kepner sits with Cheshire grin, nodding a silent welcome to the party, and Mattachine founder Dale Jennings in a stout blue jumpsuit grunts a muffled hello. Hal Call is there, in a pensive corner all his own. Gregarious Barbara Gittings laughs behind her owl-wise glasses as she serves up cloud cake on gilded plates. Helen Sandoz receives a slice and passes it to Del Martin, seated beside an empty chair reserved for her spouse, Phyllis Lyon, and then on down the line it goes to the amazed newcomer.

Lesbian and gay activists of today owe a lot to the remarkable editors and writers who created gay and lesbian journalism in the days when there was no *Advocate*, no Internet, no blog. Every branch of today's hyper-prolific LGBT publishing industry can trace its origins back to the three core publications that emerged in the affluent port cities of California in the 1950s: *ONE*, *Mattachine Review* and *The Ladder*. There were other publications before this (including Henry Gerber's *Friendship and Freedom* in the 1920s and Lisa Ben's *Vice Versa*, started in 1947), but these three created the biggest spark for those that would follow.

While the purpose of this essay is to relate the importance of these publications to what I call the pre-gay era, also known as the homophile movement, it will relate the story of these magazines by presenting the core people who edited and published them, especially Grier and Gittings, editors of *The Ladder*; Don Slater, indefatigable editor of *ONE* magazine; and Hal Call, the man who moved Mattachine from Los Angeles to San Francisco in 1954 and launched the *Mattachine Review*.

None of these magazines survived the transition into post-Stonewall lesbian and gay activism (*The Ladder* lasted until 1972). This makes the surviving copies of these magazines not only fascinating time capsules of the homophile era but also, because of the timing and circumstances of their demise, markers of the end of one age and the beginning of another. In considering the contrasts and distinctions between the homophile and gay eras, we can better perceive and explore the philosophical and political differences that mark a categorical shift in the purposes and practices of gay and lesbian activism.

ONE Magazine

The first of the three sister publications of the homophile era was a small-format magazine called *ONE*. The idea for the magazine was first discussed in late fall of 1952 by a few renegade members of the Mattachine Society, a clandestine organization of homosexuals that had proliferated in central Los Angeles since its establishment in 1950, in coordination with a few outsiders to the movement who wanted to become involved but found Mattachine discussion groups no more titillating than a "stitch and bitch" club (White, 2009, p. 31). Dale Jennings, one of Mattachine's five original founders, had become disgruntled with Mattachine's covert and cowardly ways, and he and a cadre of others, such as fellow "Mattaccino" Bill Lambert (later and more famously known as W. Dorr Legg) and local bookstore owner Martin Block, teamed up with recent University of Southern California graduate Don Slater and his partner, Tony Reyes, to launch *ONE* in January 1953.

Ultimately, the trajectory for *ONE*'s creation began with a well-publicized court case from the summer of 1952 where Jennings stood accused of lewd conduct. Through the assistance of his fellow Mattachine activists, he fought the charge and prevailed after the arresting officer was caught in a lie and the jury became deadlocked. Though hardly sensational by today's standard, the case gained notoriety for being the "first time in California history that an admitted homosexual was acquitted on a vag-lewd charge [vagrancy–lewd conduct]," as the Mattachine proudly announced in a flier titled "Victory" (Cutler, 1956, p. 25). Publicly "outed" and greatly humiliated by the trial, Jennings now had nothing to lose. So he led his cohort to create a magazine that would give voice to Los Angeles homosexuals.

In January 1953, the first issue of *ONE* was published and distributed through the bohemian bars and neighborhoods near downtown Los Angeles. Through the magazine's success, its publishers founded ONE, Inc., the first national, legally sanctioned organization dedicated to the promulgation of information on homosexuality and the furtherance of homosexual rights, later that autumn. Named after a quote from Thomas Carlyle, "A mystic bond of brotherhood makes all men one," the magazine and the organization behind it sought to educate and unify homosexuals. From the start, they included women and ethnic minorities (though the voices of the white males unquestionably dominated *ONE*'s pages). Still, *ONE* was a hit, and this little magazine and the ragtag organization behind it made a dramatic impression, first on Los Angeles and later on the nation—and even overseas.

Jennings soon became editor-in-chief and ringleader for the magazine, and his fiery personality and daring voice set a tone for *ONE* that endured until its demise 12 years later. His primary colleague was Don Slater, a fellow USC graduate who shared Jennings' political philosophies and passion for history, literature and philosophy. Though Jennings was compelled to leave the organization early in 1954 (in part for being a Communist and in part for his domineering personality), Slater contributed to and edited the magazine until ONE, Inc., divided in 1965 after an acrimonious power struggle between him and Legg.

ONE never proclaimed itself to be the first known homophile publication. The magazine's editors, Slater in particular, sought to continue a nascent but noble tradition called homosexual journalism. In a 1956 address to the Mattachine Society in San Francisco, Slater tipped his pressman's hat toward the pre-Hitler publications in Germany. He lauded the work of Henry Gerber in Chicago, who had been jailed with three companions in 1925 for their effort to start a homophile organization and publication in the tradition of those German predecessors. Slater also praised the enduring success of *Der Kreis* and *Die Insel* in Europe, as well as the nine notorious issues of *Vice Versa: America's Gayest Magazine*, composed by "Lisa Ben" (Edith Eyde) in 1947 and 1948 and distributed to a small group of selected friends in Los Angeles.

Combined, Slater reported, the Mattachine Foundation and Knights of the Clock (a multiracial men's group in the Silver Lake area of Los Angeles) had distributed some 20,000 copies of reports and updates prior to *ONE*'s founding. Through these earlier publications, "hundreds of homosexual writers have achieved publication who certainly could not have done so otherwise," as Slater put it (Cutler, 1956, p. 4).

ONE, however, had a style and temperament all its own. Its purpose was to challenge "conventional norms" and to do so in a not-so-compromising way, "without being guided by any orthodox literary theory and practice" (Cutler, 1956, p. 6). The magazine was reflective, probing deep into the psyche of the homophile and thereby encouraging homosexuals everywhere to "revolt against the public taste and the guardians of that taste." It was didactic as well, educating gays and straights alike on the history and character of the homophile.

In all of this, *ONE* was wildly successful and served as linchpin for the entire movement, being read by thousands of men and women each month. Hundreds across the nation received *ONE* in their mailboxes on a regular basis and could watch the movement grow from the safety of their own homes. Letters poured into *ONE*'s office from appreciative subscribers, many expressing gratitude to the magazine for making them feel less isolated and afraid. Some made pilgrimages to ONE, Inc.'s cramped downtown quarters, where they were welcomed and put to work on behalf of the movement. Some returned home to seed local organizations in their own communities. The little magazine from Echo Park (the magazine had first been published in that Los Angeles neighborhood by Jennings' sister) soon became a lifeline to homosexuals across the country who began to realize that they were part of a rapidly growing political force, demanding to be heard and influencing change in the public attitudes and laws that had so long repressed them.

The complicating force in all of this, however, was the Comstock Act, which dated to 1873 and prohibited the publication, sale, distribution or possession of prurient material. Slater was well-acquainted with the Comstock law because two issues of *ONE* had been detained under post office scrutiny. The first was the August 1953 issue, which brandished the topic of homosexual marriage and was released by postal authorities after 13 days of official scrutiny. The second was the October 1954 issue, which was determined by officials to contain lewd and lascivious content. Los Angeles Postmaster Otto Olesen's assessment of the content as "obscene, lewd, lascivious and filthy" was first upheld by the U.S. District Court and then, in February 1957, by the 9th U.S. Circuit Court of Appeals. Slater and attorney Eric Julber filed a further appeal soon after.

Ultimately, in January 1958, the U.S. Supreme Court reversed the ban, and the Comstock policies, already weakened through similar cases, came to an end. The Supreme Court ruling was precedent-setting, and after a century, thanks to this and a few other landmark rulings, Comstock had at last been defanged.

Mattachine Review

The *Mattachine Review* was effectively born in November 1953, during the infamous Mattachine convention in Los Angeles where the founders and leaders of the Mattachine Foundation, including Dale Jennings and Harry Hay, were cast out of the organization, new bylaws were adopted, and a new organization called the Mattachine Society was formed.

One of the key figures in this coup was Hal Call, a San Francisco activist who was elected to head the Publication Committee for the new society. Call was a Midwesterner with newspaper experience who had become enchanted with San Francisco during a visit in the 1930s. A seasoned journalist, Call held to two primary ambitions for the *Review*. The first was to educate the populace in general about "the realities of homosexuality and the fact that it wasn't going to destroy society." The second purpose was to raise the "self-esteem" of homosexuals, "helping [them] to fit in—at least on the surface" (Sears, 2006, p. 305).

Call wanted the *Review* to be differentiated from *ONE* in order to better compete against it. His magazine would have a more serious tone—none of the "giddy" attitude fostered by Jennings. The *Review* would aspire to reach a larger audience and not "appeal to the purely 'gay' element." Though neither Jennings nor Slater believed such a thing possible (and frequently said so in writing), Call perceived that *ONE*'s ambition was to establish and foster a distinct "homosexual society." Call felt that such a goal was absurd and might actually backfire and irreparably harm the homophile movement. Instead, he sought articles that would "advance our cause on the fronts of research, law, religion community service, [and] personal adjustment" (Sears, 2006, pp. 297–305).

While he often exchanged bowshots with *ONE*'s editors (Jennings in particular), the truth is that Call, Jennings and Slater had very similar goals for their magazines. While most of Mattachine's founders agreed with Hay that homosexuals did compose a distinct cultural minority, *ONE*'s editorial staff shared many of the new Mattachine Society's philosophies and goals. In fact, much like the original Mattachine, ONE, Inc., was divided from the start between those who fought the idea of a "gay" cultural minority (especially Slater and those who were most dedicated to *ONE* magazine) and those who wanted to establish a homosexual institution dedicated to research and the advancement of what they perceived to be an emergent cultural force. (Most notably in this latter camp were journalist Jim Kepner and *ONE*'s longtime office manager William Lambert, aka W. Dorr Legg.) In turn, Jim Kepner was uncharacteristically critical of the *Review* for assimilationism and "image-polishing"—a criticism now often lobbed at the entire homophile movement by more contemporary LGBT scholars and activists.

Call predicted that the *Review* would have 3,000 subscribers soon after its (anticipated) 1954 launch (Sears, 2006, pp. 296–97). However, by the spring of 1957 there were only 550 subscribers, yielding a gross income of $4,000 (Sears, 2006, p. 355). Call resigned from his job as an insurance agent in 1957 in order to work full time for the printing company that he had founded in 1954, Pan-Graphic Press.

Pan-Graphic printed and published the *Review* (and, subsequently, *The Ladder*)—which, for many in the organization, seemed precariously close to a conflict of interest. Call desired to sell and produce enough commercial printing to make a living, but his earnings soon plummeted to one-third of his former salary (Sears, 2006, p. 363). He anticipated that publication and distribution of the *Review* would eventually provide him a livable income. He persuaded the board of Mattachine to pay Pan-Graphic for its services, which would in turn pay him.

This situation proved to be problematic throughout Mattachine's history, and it continually mitigated Call's position of leadership within the organization. The *Review* managed to earn $5,000 in 1957, but the Society's directors expressed dismay upon learning that less than a third of this had ever entered into the organization's coffers. Call was accused of profiteering from the *Review*, which he denied, stating that Pan-Graphic Press had never charged for his labor (Sears, 2006, pp. 366–67).

Though many acknowledged that Call had sacrificed greatly for the welfare of Mattachine and the *Review*, the situation with Pan-Graphic would fester for the rest of the magazine's run, with many believing that Call was not being upfront with his earnings. Ultimately, as Sears (2006) tells us, the flagrant conflict of interest between Call's ownership of Pan-Graphic Press and his chairing of Mattachine's Publication Committee undermined Call's stature and authority and would cause the demise of the Mattachine Society (p. 300). Eventually, independent Mattachine groups formed in other cities, and some of them launched their own publications that survived the demise of the *Review*.

The Ladder

Two years after the launch of *ONE*, in the fall of 1955, four lesbian couples in San Francisco gathered to form a secret society for resident lesbians. Like their Los Angeles–based precursor, the newborn Daughters of Bilitis began as a clandestine organization to provide fellowship for homophiles. From the start, however, the DOB was exclusively for women (except for a few honorary SOBs— Sons of Bilitis—designated as long-term male allies of the lesbian association).

The DOB's stated mission and purpose were arguably more politically minded than ONE's, and the actuality of publishing a newsletter came a full year after the organization's founding. In 1956, after much internal wrangling, the DOB decided to participate more actively in the ongoing struggle for homophile rights. It embraced a pedagogical mission statement with the charge of educating the public at large on the history and condition of homophiles, lesbians in particular, while advocating and fighting for homosexual rights in general (Gallo, 2006, pp. 11–13).

Soon after, the DOB released the first edition of its newsletter, *The Ladder* (Gallo, 2006, p. 18). Twelve mimeographed pages made up the premiere issue, with a sketch on the cover portraying two women standing at the base of a ladder that stretched far above them to penetrate a cloudy sky. This image, contributed by Assistant Editor Brian O'Brien (a woman), inspired the magazine's title, and the ladder of ascension persisted as a salient theme throughout the magazine's 16-year run.

As with *ONE* and the *Review*, DOB's *Ladder* provided a beacon of hope for hundreds of lesbian homophiles across the nation. Many wrote back with criticism, gratitude or praise. In 1957, a woman wrote from New Jersey to say that she read each issue from cover to cover as soon as it arrived, and she wished there were a DOB chapter in her neighborhood that she could join. According to historian Marcia Gallo, "The letters they received made the work seem worthwhile. For the individual woman who somehow found a copy, *The Ladder* was a means of sharing otherwise private thoughts and feelings, connecting across miles, and breaking through isolation and fear" (2006, pp. 40–41). While urban DOB chapters proliferated under its aegis, those residing outside the core urban centers could also tap into the energy of the movement and participate should they desire.

Future *Ladder* editor Barbara Gittings made a pilgrimage from her Philadelphia home to ONE's Los Angeles office in 1956. This is where she first heard of the DOB (White, 2009, p. 5). Phyllis Lyon was editor of *The Ladder* at the time of Gittings' visit, and the Los Angeles correspondent was Stella Rush. Helen Sandoz was the associate editor. Rush, as "Sten Russell," became *The Ladder*'s official Los Angeles correspondent in the spring of 1957. Sandoz moved to Los Angeles later that year to begin a loving partnership with Rush that would outlive the organizations that brought them together (White, 2009, pp. 80–81).

Rush and Sandoz organized a Los Angeles chapter of the DOB in 1958, and Gittings launched a chapter in New York that same year. Gittings became editor of *The Ladder* in 1963, and this vantage point helped her to become one of the premier lesbian activists in the nation. In the summer of 1970, she helped to establish the Task Force on Gay Liberation within the Social Responsibilities Round Table of the American Library Association. Indefatigable until her death in February 2007, Gittings remained one of the most influential lesbians to bridge the transition between the homophile age and the second wave of the movement, the era of lesbian and gay activism.

Impact

ONE was arguably the most widely circulated of the three homophile periodicals. From the 500 copies printed in 1953, *ONE*'s readership peaked at 5,000 a year later and stabilized thereafter. Kepner reports that this was five times the readership of *Mattachine Review* and 10 times *The Ladder*'s (Kepner, 1998, p. 11), but his figures are probably way off. Gallo reports that after Call printed and delivered each month's run of *The Ladder* to the DOB, copies were distributed throughout San Francisco and shipped to activists in Chicago and Los Angeles, and to Gittings, who facilitated distribution through New York and Philadelphia. Bookstores in Detroit, Portland, Cleveland and Dallas carried *The Ladder* as well, and, alongside *ONE* and the *Review*, it no doubt percolated into other metropolitan areas such as Denver and Kansas City.

ONE's accomplishments, however, set it apart on many levels. By the close of 1954, it had 1,650 subscribers. This is a particularly significant accomplishment when you consider that at this time, "you could be arrested for possessing such a publication, tame as it was" (Kepner, 1998, p. 12). *ONE*'s 12-year run launched the careers of many prominent writers and journalists of both the homophile and later LGBT movements. Among the most notable is Jim Kepner, whose first article appeared in the April 1954 issue, soon after the ousting of Dale Jennings. Kepner was attracted to *ONE* for its feisty, non-assimilationist attitude (Kepner, 1998, p. 6). It was a perfect fit. Over the course of decades, he wrote countless articles pertaining to "Gay news, about who we are, why we are so, what we want and how we might achieve it ... often giving first expression to important ideas now taken for granted" (Kepner, 1998, p. 5).

Under the editorships of Kepner and Don Slater, *ONE* ignited the writing careers of Barbara Grier and Stella Rush, who later contributed to *The Ladder*. Later, in the 1960s, Slater introduced Joseph Hansen to the world. Hansen became famous in the 1970s for his David Brandstetter mystery series featuring a homosexual private detective who resided and worked in Los Angeles County.

The Ladder was a force all its own. As it, too, began to saturate the homophile spirit of the nation, it "showcased 'normal' lesbians to the world at a time when no such images existed" (Gallo, 2006, p. 97). It introduced photo covers of real lesbians, a dramatic breakthrough. *The Ladder* arrived each month like an old friend for a visit, "a vehicle for the individual lesbian to elevate herself, out of the depths of self-hatred and social strictures" (Gallo, 2006, p. 18). It was never intended to be overtly political (Stone, 2012), and this comfortable, accessible style proved a great success. In 1957 and 1958, hundreds of letters were delivered to the DOB's office "written by women living in big cities as well as small towns" from across the country and even around the world (Gallo, 2006, p. 18). "*The Ladder* was a means of sharing otherwise private thoughts and feelings, connecting across miles, and breaking through isolation and fear. ... Finally there was something more than sorrowful stories about elite misfits, paperback novels with tragic endings, psychological treatises about depravity and illness" (Gallo, 2006, p. 41).

Failure

Some of the best queer drama may be found in the histories of these magazines and the corporations behind them. All three publications suffered significant setbacks, as philosophical differences and personality clashes split their organizations. Mattachine, as mentioned, split apart when Jennings and Hay were cast out for being Communists, and Hal Call moved the new Mattachine Society to San Francisco in a so-called act of salvation, protecting the group from its more radical element, its founders. And even the new Society was prone to infighting and tensions that ultimately caused its fission and demise.

Relations between ONE, Inc., and the DOB had a total meltdown in 1961, during ONE's Midwinter Institute in Los Angeles, when several of ONE's directors proposed to draft a Homosexual Bill of Rights. Martin and the other DOB leaders found the idea absurd. DOB President Jaye Bell threatened to withdraw the DOB from the meeting entirely unless the idea were abandoned. Furious, Bill Lambert wrote the DOB off as "assimilationists" who threatened to sever their ties to the greater movement. Stella Rush continued to write for *ONE* for a short while after the Bill of Rights fiasco, but she formally resigned in the summer of 1961 in protest of an editorial, presumably written by Lambert, that seemed to advocate lesbianism as a form of population control (White, 2009, pp. 102–03).

From the start, the primary mission and purpose of ONE, Inc., was to educate and engage the public on issues pertaining to homosexuals and homophiles. At first, it did this exclusively through publishing *ONE*. However, over the 13 years of the organization's existence, the corporation became increasingly factionalized between those who envisioned it as an educational institution and those who remained unfailingly committed to the primacy of the magazine (see White, 2009).

Tensions culminated in the spring of 1965, when ONE, Inc., forever divided. On Easter morning of that year, Slater and a faction of ONE's directors and volunteers loyal to the magazine removed all of ONE, Inc.'s belongings from the downtown office, including the magazine's distribution list, and took everything to a warehouse in Cahuenga Pass, across from Universal Studios. After a frustrating and prolonged two-year court battle, Legg remained in charge of ONE, Inc.'s name, publication and educational facilities, and Slater retained his precious archives and the magazine's distribution list. (Legg, perhaps anticipating such an act, had his own copy of the list.) Since Legg had won the right to retain and use the name "ONE," Slater's faction was compelled to change the name of its publication, which became *Tangents*. In 1967, this faction incorporated as the Homosexual Information Center, doing business as The Tangent Group, which still exists today.

Legg's half of ONE, Inc., continued to distribute *ONE* magazine for a few months after the schism, but soon all of ONE, Inc.'s resources and facilities went to furthering the growth and development of ONE Institute of Homophile Studies, which was ONE's educational division—and to pursuing Slater in court. ONE, Inc., which never formally sought nonprofit tax status, was merged into its nonprofit doppelgänger, the Institute for the Study of Human Resources, after Legg died in 1994. As the nonsurviving entity, ONE, Inc., ceased to exist at that time, and ISHR retained the rights to all of ONE's assets. These have since been ceded to The Williams Institute, at the School of Law of the University of California at Los Angeles.

Both ONE and DOB had been divided from the start between those who wanted the organization to function as a forum for social gathering and those who desired it to be openly dedicated to social action and reform. The DOB fractured in 1970, when Barbara Grier and DOB President Rita Laporte hijacked the magazine's mailing list and moved *The Ladder*'s entire operations to Laporte's home near Reno, Nevada. The old guard, including Gittings, Rush, Sandoz, Martin, and Lyon, called this a theft, just as Legg and his faction had called Slater's action a heist. Similarly, just as Slater perceived ONE, Inc., to have lost sight of its original goals and purposes to the detriment of the magazine, Grier claimed "she took *The Ladder* from the DOB in order to save it" (Gallo, 2006, p. 161).

Grier had reasons to be so attached to the magazine. After becoming editor in 1968, she doubled the page count and recruited many new subscribers. Under her leadership, *The Ladder* became a bit more political and newsy in tone. This approach ultimately failed, however, and *The Ladder* ceased publication in 1972. Grier again appropriated the magazine's mailing list, which she used to start Naiad Press in 1973. Despite Naiad's controversial birth, it grew to become a powerful force in lesbian book publishing (Stone, 2012).

Increasingly through the 1960s, fighting within the homophile organizations mirrored the tensions and frustrations between them. As Kepner put it, "While DOB, ONE, and Mattachine often worked amicably together, Mattachine chided ONE's assertiveness and DOB leaders were often outraged by ONE" (Kepner, 1998, p. 6). Kepner criticized the *Review* for its "accommodationist" style just as the East Coast homophiles lodged the same complaint against ONE. The homophile movement in the mid-1960s seems to have become a fest of finger-pointing, with plenty of blame to go around and everyone attributing the movement's seeming stasis to the wiles and guiles of others.

Each of the three homophile magazines proved to be forces by which their respective organizations were eventually tethered and bound. When internal rivalries fractured the institutions, the splits were often along the lines of who wanted to promote a more intimate and local social gathering place and those whose primary allegiance was to mobilizing the national movement through diligent publication of the magazines. When the magazines faltered and foundered, to a large degree they took their organizations with them. Newly formed institutions resulting from these separations would be hard-pressed to match the status or successes of their progenitors, but the seeds sown during the first phase of homophile activism, the golden era of these magazines, were spread across a land well-tilled and fertile.

Though the demise of these magazines can be attributed to infighting, the root cause of their expiration is that the movement itself began heading in a different direction. As the sexual revolution of the 1960s progressed, the three publications waned in content, frequency and relevance. The turmoil that rocked the organizations in the mid-1960s reflected a tectonic shift toward a new gay sensibility: Integration began to look an awful lot like assimilation. Some old-guard homophiles appeared stodgy and dated, their bickering evoking no more than a bunch of dinosaurs in a spit fest, to paraphrase Harry Hay.

Washington, D.C.-based activist Jack Nichols lamented the split between West Coast "accommodationists" and East Coast "Gay" activists, but I argue that what Nichols perceived was more of a generational split than it was geographic. Nichols and his cohort were dismayed by the cowardice and timidity of their forebears, repeatedly branding them as accommodationists or assimilationists. Few homophile activists were able to bridge this widening gap between the "homophile" and "gay" eras, though writers Martin, Lyon and Hay became sagacious as they aged in the hills of San Francisco. Grier continued to publish and accumulate an impressive archive, now curated by the San Francisco Public Library. Gittings' and her partner Kay Lahusen's papers and photographs reside in the New York Public Library's Archives Division.

The great publications of the homophile movement—*ONE*, the *Mattachine Review* and *The Ladder*—were as constant as Jupiter, Mars and Venus in the minds and imaginings of a people living in fear, branded as criminals and psychopaths by their neighbors, their priests, and their laws. Even today, those fortunate enough to be able to browse the pages of these flagship publications will find humor and history, inspiration, drama, and amusement. In time, these people, the lives they lived and the stories they have left us will continue to inspire thousands of students, activists and the curious every year.

Both Gittings on the East Coast and Jim Kepner on the West remained active and important voices in the movement until their deaths, Kepner's in 1997 and Gittings' in 2007. It stands as testament to their meritorious accomplishments that few other first-wave homophile activists have been so greatly and widely mourned.

The fundamental philosophies that guided homophile activism have not left us. Those who prefer to integrate into society rather than segregate into the gay urban enclaves will find comfort and camaraderie in their works. Indeed, as homosexuals across America are increasingly integrating into their communities, the voices of these activists are again being discovered as classic works of American literature. A new generation of students seems to be walking away from the labels for which their parents' generation had fought. As they seek alternative philosophies and probe into a history that began at least two decades before Stonewall, they too will find warm welcome at the party, hosted by a few dozen driven and eccentric personalities dishing warm cake along with spirited conversation. The homophile tradition will continue, and the movement will continually revitalize itself and grow.

And it will be grand.

References

Cutler, Marvin (editor). 1956. *Homosexuals Today: A Handbook of Organizations & Publications*. Los Angeles, Calif.: ONE, Incorporated. (Cutler is a pseudonym for William Lambert, aka W. Dorr Legg.)

Gallo, Marcia. 2006. *Different Daughters: A History of the Daughters of Bilitis and the Rise of the Lesbian Rights Movement*. New York, N.Y.: Carroll & Graf Publishers.

Kepner, Jim. 1998. *Rough News, Daring Views: 1950s' Pioneer Gay Press Journalism*. New York, N.Y.: Harrington Park Press.

Sears, James T. 2006. *Behind the Mask of the Mattachine: The Hal Call Chronicles and the Early Movement for Homosexual Emancipation*. New York, N.Y.: Harrington Park Press.

Stone, Martha E. 2012. "Barbara Grier, Activist and Founder of Naiad Press (In Memoriam)." *The Gay and Lesbian Review Worldwide* 19(2), p. 7.

White, C. Todd. 2009. *Pre-Gay L.A.: A Social History of the Movement for Homosexual Rights*. Urbana, Ill.: University of Illinois Press.

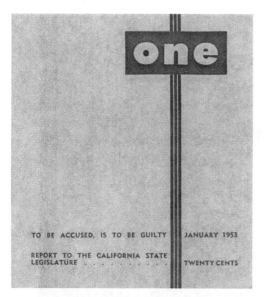

The first issue of *ONE*, January 1953.
All images on this page courtesy of the Homosexual Information Center

ONE, October 1954.

ONE, February 1958.

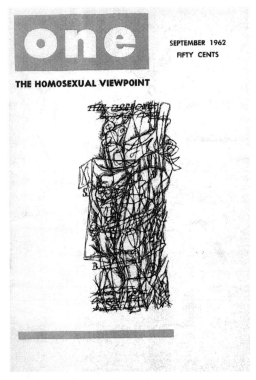

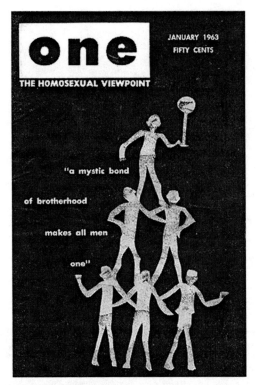

ONE, September 1962.
Images this page courtey of the
Homosexual Information Center

ONE, January 1963.

ONE, June 1963.

Mattachine Review, January 1955.
Courtesy of the Homosexual Information Center

Mattachine Review, August 1956.
Courtesy of the Homosexual Information Center

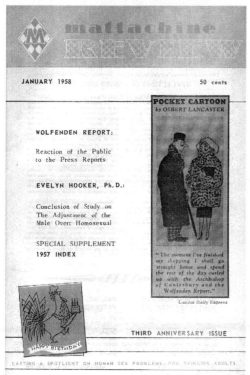

Mattachine Review, January 1958.
Courtesy of the Homosexual Information Center

An advertisement for *The Ladder*, early 1970s.

4

Ascending *The Ladder*

By Margaret Rubick

In gay liberation history, Barbara Gittings and Kay Tobin Lahusen are two names to remember. Together they worked to bring about change through more than 40 years of activism. They helped battle the stigma of mental illness in the *Diagnostic and Statistical Manual*, the handbook of the American Psychiatric Association; they protested, marched, strategized, demonstrated and paved the way for the next generation of activists. They risked being visible. They educated with words and photographs—Lahusen was the first openly lesbian photojournalist; Gittings, a public face in a time when many remained hidden.

The two met at a picnic in 1961. The vehicle that brought them together was a fledgling newsletter called *The Ladder*. Gittings was already active in an organization for lesbian women, and Lahusen was in search of a way to meet them. Through a psychiatrist in New York City, Lahusen obtained a copy of an early edition of *The Ladder* and joined the West Coast–based organization that published it. Together, Gittings and Lahusen then participated in building *The Ladder* and increasing membership in its parent organization before moving on to bolder activism and other media. The two were the first to organize lesbians on the East Coast.

Background

One of the main vehicles for disseminating information post–World War II was the printed word. In an era before computers were developed for general use and when television was in its adolescence, newspapers and magazines informed the public and gave voice to the growing cohorts that were willing to say out loud they were homosexual. The word "gay" would follow in widespread use; in the 1950s, the word "homosexual" itself was bold.

Men and women worked independently and sometimes together on various homophile publications: *ONE* magazine, the *Mattachine Review*, *The Ladder* and, later, *GAY* newspaper. Television interviews, films and books would follow. The Mattachine Society began in Los Angeles in 1950 and began publishing its paper soon after (more details on this in Chapter 3). The organization quickly expanded to San Francisco, New York and elsewhere.

On the West Coast, two brave women in San Francisco, Del Martin and Phyllis Lyon, accepted an invitation from a friend, Rose Bamberger, to start a secret society for lesbians. The response was an enthusiastic yes in September 1955, and the first meeting of eight co-founders was held on October 19 of that year.

Initially a venue for women to meet in each other's homes and avoid police raids, the Daughters of Bilitis, pronounced *Bil-EE-tis*, grew to be a force in giving voice to a silent minority. The name Bilitis came from a fictional character invented by French poet Pierre Louÿs. The name was deliberately obscure; early members avoided saying *Bil-EYE-tis* to keep it from sounding like a disease.[1] According to Marcia Gallo, author of a well-received history of the organization, "Each of DOB's stated goals—self-knowledge and self-acceptance; public education; involvement in research; and lobbying to change the laws criminalizing homosexuality—mirrored the objectives of the two other homophile groups, [the Mattachine Society and ONE, Inc.]"[2]

When Barbara Gittings found DOB in 1956, through New York and Los Angeles Mattachine connections, she was thrilled to come upon a group of like-minded women. The fledgling group was historically groundbreaking, and it was a lifeline for Gittings—she had found some of her people. That same year, the DOB began publishing a lesbian journal called *The Ladder*. "The magazine's aim was to educate both the lesbian and the general public; the name was chosen to suggest the idea of the lesbian individual as well as the lesbian minority achieving higher status in society."[3]

Two years later, after Gittings had met with Lyon and Martin, the San Francisco leaders of the Daughters of Bilitis invited Gittings to start an East Coast chapter. She readily agreed. The DOB chapter on the East Coast started small—six or eight women gathered at first. Over time, Gittings and Lahusen "built up a mailing list of nearly 300."[4] Gittings also produced the chapter newsletter, which was separate from *The Ladder*; it was used to announce local events and to build community and membership. "Gittings did much of the work herself, including stenciling and mimeographing after hours at her office, then typing and stuffing envelopes to ensure absolute security for those on the mailing list."[5]

Did she worry about being caught? Her response was that she *was* caught once.[6] Her manager was a woman who had served in the military and was sympathetic to same-sex attraction. She let Gittings know that she was aware of gay people and told her to be more careful. Gittings was not fired.

Extending *The Ladder*

Gittings was the East Coast DOB chapter president for three years, and it wasn't much later, in 1962, that Gittings became the "corresponding secretary" of *The Ladder*. Initially, women authors did not use their own names. Barbara Grier, under the pen name Gene Damon, wrote book reviews, often five or six per issue. "Lisa Ben" was an anagram disguise for one writer (and Ben had started the first lesbian publication, *Vice Versa*, years before); others adopted their own pseudonyms. They mostly wrote poetry, articles and short stories. That would soon change.

Gittings was asked to be interim editor of *The Ladder* in 1963, when her title changed from "corresponding secretary" to "corresponding secretary and editor." She was editor for three years, and, during that time, she and Lahusen built the subscriber base while making stylistic and philosophic changes. Lahusen photographed Gittings at a chalkboard planning future issues. Visible on the board are sections for December 1964 through May 1965. Some of the topics can be read in the photo, which demonstrates the increase in nonfiction reporting:

"Report on Les Crane ... Report on Becker ...
Married Lesbian - Fiction – Masquerade Part II – Lesbiana – Renée Vivien"[7]

At the suggestion of her partner, Gittings added the subtitle "A Lesbian Review" to *The Ladder*. Although not everyone in the DOB was in favor of having these words on the cover, this subtitle slowly grew in size until in 1966 it was the same height as the title, then appeared in dark typeface as THE LADDER | A LESBIAN REVIEW. The subtitle would remain until September 1968.

Lahusen designed new covers, changing from line drawings to photographs, and "bird-dogged"[8] contributing writers. Her name was added to the credits in March 1966, "Assistant to the editor; art director—Kay Tobin." (Lahusen used the pen name Tobin because it was easier, she said, to pronounce and remember. Later, she used Lahusen so that she would not appear closeted.)

As photographs started replacing drawings on the cover, the content began to change as well. An

Indonesian woman, Ger van Braam, had obtained a copy of *The Ladder* from Holland, a clear sign that distribution was expanding. As Vern Bullough eloquently wrote: "*The Ladder*, for many women of the era, was a lifeline that reminded them that they were not alone, not crazy, and that there was nothing wrong with them. Its circulation grew to be worldwide."[9]

From Indonesia, van Braam wrote a letter to the editor and included a photograph of herself. The letter was printed in its entirety in the June 1964 issue, expressing feelings from abroad. Van Braam's initial letter reflects a larger truth about invisibility and loneliness. "I just learned myself that I am not the only one in the world with my deviation, that there are others just like me!" Like so many of her countrywomen, she had married, but after three months she "revolted against my captivity and broke free." Her family disowned her for the disgrace of divorce. Her relief and gratitude for finding community are moving: "It is so very much in our isolation [*sic*] I would thank all your writers who give us something valuable from their own richness of feeling and understanding. If you could but know what any enlightenment means to us … ."[10]

The Backdrop

Prior to 1973, homosexuality was defined by the American Psychiatric Association as mental illness. The sickness label affected the emotions and lives of many who internalized feelings of inferiority and hid from a society that told them they were socially unacceptable. Gittings knew that "the overriding problem was invisibility. How do you organize people that you can't see?"[11] "One important motivating principle for the whole movement was overcoming invisibility … ."[12]

It was one of the marked differences between the gay civil-rights movement and the African-American civil-rights movement. In the documentary film *Before Stonewall*, Gittings points out that skin color identified a recognizable minority, while lesbians were hidden even from each other. Even the word "gay" was not said in public—"Oh, the word 'gay' was not in such widespread use at all. It was still a code word, a kind of covert word among ourselves."[13]

Ger van Braam presented an opportunity to become more visible. Gittings and Lahusen began to send her literature, beginning a campaign called "Books for Ger." Van Braam was delighted. She allayed their fears about interference from customs officials in Indonesia: "No, I've nothing to fear of our customs in Indonesia for I know that our people are so ignorant they wouldn't even know what those books will be about, if they would think anything at all."[14] It speaks to the isolation that she must have felt and that now ended with help from Gittings and Lahusen. "I just finished reading your letter for the *n*th time and I am still marveling at your ingenuity … it's a way of thinking beyond our mentality."[15] When she was asked if her photograph could be used on the cover of *The Ladder*, she agreed. Van Braam "was the first woman to be portrayed full-face on the cover of *The Ladder*."[16] So it was a vehicle for reaching out, connecting in much more than a superficial way; allowing a woman to come out of isolation and for her American sisters to see her and help her.

Following the van Braam issue, Lahusen's portraits and photographs would grace many covers—in September 1964, "September Sea"; in October, "October Evening, Beacon Hill"; and the readers approved. One subscriber's comment in the December *Ladder* read: "The October LADDER is a love, a small masterpiece … . Every month you move forward by leaps and bounds."[17]

Van Braam's photo encouraged other women to pose full-face; they were previously shown in profile or in sunglasses. The January 1966 portrait of Lilli Vincenz is a headshot, showing her smiling. The photo and interview of Ernestine Eckstein in June 1966 went one step further. She was an African-American lesbian who talked about race as well as sexual orientation. Although her portrait was a profile shot and she chose to use only her first name, she drew parallels with the African-American civil-rights movement and suggested that more needed to be done to change society, rather than the homosexual.[18]

Unlike so many lesbians of her time, Gittings herself went public; starting in the 1960s, she was willing to be photographed, and she was one of the few women who were willing to identify themselves by their real names. She did not think that anyone would piece together her movement persona and her work life, and it appears that she was right.

"Each month she would load copies of the new issue into her new VW and deliver to select bookstores in New York and Philadelphia where *The Ladder* was placed with other cause magazines."[19]

Under Gittings' direction, *The Ladder* continued to publish more nonfiction. In an August 1, 1964, editorial, Gittings openly criticized the Committee on Public Health of the New York Academy of Medicine for its negative views. It was, as she said, "a medical group which myopically sees homosexuality only as a disease." She went on to point out that "[t]he shoddy work behind this report is a discredit to a professional group in a scientific field."[20]

More discussion about research followed. The East Coast Homophile Organizations, comprising the DOB and three other homophile groups in New York, Philadelphia and Washington, met in conference in 1964. *The Ladder* covered the conference in the January 1965 issue and again in the February–March issue, with a debate between activists Frank Kameny and Kurt Konietzko, the former advocating action and the latter education.

The debate had been brewing for a while. One of the principles of the DOB had been educating the public, and many members were still in favor of a quiet, steady approach. Gittings and Lahusen were leaning toward action, and they supported Kameny's point of view.[21] Again, in the February–March issue, Lahusen, writing as Kay Tobin, reported on the picketing of a lecture given on December 2, 1964, "Homosexuality, a Disease." Four picketers asked for rebuttal time and were given it; the challenger pointed out that "research on homosexuality is skimpy and has been conducted almost entirely with unhappy, ill-adjusted homosexuals who were patients undergoing therapy."[22]

Although "picketing was against DOB's philosophy," both Gittings and Lahusen supported it. They "put this debate in *The Ladder*" and called it "Picketing: The Pros and Cons."[23] The two participated in the earliest gay pickets in Washington, D.C. One of the picket signs Gittings carried is now in the Smithsonian Institution—it reads SEXUAL PREFERENCE IS IRRELEVANT TO FEDERAL EMPLOYMENT. The July 1965 issue featured an article without a byline, titled "Homosexuals Picket in Nation's Capital."[24]

The articles in *The Ladder* grew in length and focused more on the ongoing battle for gay rights. Kameny was given a great deal of space, but others, such as Washington activist Jack Nichols and Fritz A. Fluckiger, Ph.D., a pro-gay psychologist, also were featured, and the men and women worked together to combat medical condemnation of same-sex orientation.

Frank Kameny

Lahusen does not remember exactly where she and Gittings met Dr. Franklin E. Kameny. It was at some conference in 1963 or 1964; it might have been a conference of the East Coast Homophile Organizations. Lahusen heard Kameny speak, went and found Gittings, and said, "You have to hear this guy."[25] They were impressed with Kameny's view that the time for trying to primarily educate straights about gay and lesbian concerns was past. Taking his lead from the black civil-rights movement, he put forward a vision and various methods of demanding equal rights for gay citizens.

Kameny's demands began with his own request for equal treatment. Kameny was a gay white male who completed his doctorate in astronomy in the mid-1950s at Harvard and then worked in an Army Map Service job for the federal government. He was fired in 1957 because of his homosexuality. After a lengthy appeal process, he learned that the Supreme Court would not hear his case. He then applied his prodigious intelligence to fighting back on several fronts.

He led in organizing the first gay group dedicated exclusively to gay and lesbian political rights, the Mattachine Society of Washington (other groups had other goals in their mission). Through this organization he challenged the federal government when it dismissed homosexuals both from civil-service employment and military service. "He persuaded gays and lesbians to move beyond the strategies of 1950s gay self-help groups and to adopt the political strategies of the [black] civil-rights movement."[26]

Kameny became the strategist for gay civil rights and, soon afterward, for a scientific challenge to the American Psychiatric Association's position that homosexuality was a mental illness. Gittings credited Kameny with having "articulated a complete, coherent philosophy for the gay movement,"[27] and she did much to spread the word. *The Ladder* published Kameny's 6½-page article in the May 1965 issue. In it, he argued that homosexuality as a sickness is a definition not substantiated by any known research and that homosexuals "are the true authorities on homosexuality." He declared that militancy was necessary to fight the label, "the question of homosexuality as a sickness. This is one of the most important issues—probably THE most important single issue—facing our movement today."[28] He went on to say, "We ARE right; those who oppose us are both factually and morally wrong. We are the true authorities on homosexuality, whether we are accepted as such or not."[29]

Kameny's article drew a rebuttal from Florence Jaffy, research director of the DOB, writing under the surname Conrad. In the August 1965 issue, Conrad's article covered seven pages, and it was a strong rejection of Kameny's approach. Conrad did not think it would help the cause to reject research findings and spoke for the conservative West Coast directors.

Conrad advocated education rather than taking a position: "The homophile movement is not like a new brand of toothpaste which may be 'sold' to the public by superficial promotion techniques."[30] She said that taking a stand on whether homosexuality is a sickness is "ineffective, to say the least ... the question of whether or not they are or should be considered 'sick' is not a question capable of being decided by vote ... ."[31] This statement ironically foreshadowed the historic 1973 vote of the APA that reversed the sickness designation.

Again, *The Ladder* published a long response in October 1965, "EMPHASIS on research has had its day, by Dr. Franklin E. Kameny." It was a lengthy article, demonstrating the change from the poetry-filled journals of 1962. Kameny stated, "Anything, even toothpaste, can be sold thus ... ."[32] And he offered a statement for the entire movement: "The homosexual's problems are political and social—not in essence psychological. They are problems of discrimination and prejudice, of law and custom."[33]

When *Time* magazine published an essay, "The Homosexual in America," which referred to homosexuality as "a pernicious sickness," Lahusen responded with "A Rebuke for TIME's Pernicious Prejudice," followed by "Letters TIME didn't print," criticizing the lack of objectivity, superficial reasoning, and "crippling methodological flaws."[34]

Another significant article titled "RESEARCH Through a Glass, Darkly," was published just before Gittings ended her tenure as editor. It was part of a series of articles by Dr. Fluckiger, rebutting the conclusions in Irving Bieber's book *Homosexuality: A Psychoanalytic Study*. Fluckiger exposed the lack of scientific method and the fact that the researcher appeared to be so in love with his hypothesis as to be blind to the data.[35]

Certain psychiatrists had based their careers on treating homosexuals, using various modalities: shock treatment, psychoanalysis, and aversion therapy. Two of the most vituperative proponents of the pathology of homosexuality were Irving Bieber and Charles Socarides. Both of them were psychiatrists, and both were psychoanalysts. It was Bieber who promoted the idea of environmentally caused homosexuality in men, purportedly resulting from a domineering mother and a distant father. Socarides was even more adamant that heterosexuality and homosexuality were learned behaviors, that homosexuality was the untoward consequence of "wrong" upbringing and that same-sex attraction was a serious psychological disturbance.

The third installment of Fluckiger's response pointed out that "the heterosexual's place in society is not usually determined by what he does in the privacy of his bedroom... ."[36] Fluckiger also underscored the cooperative nature of the work he did with Gittings; he ended the article with a thank-you:

"I wish to express my deep appreciation to Miss Barbara Gittings, editor of THE LADDER, for her substantial contribution to this paper. She has subjected it to several critical readings, made numerous suggestions for editorial changes, and has been of inestimable value to me."[37]

From *Ladder* to Stage

Gittings and Lahusen parted ways with *The Ladder* in 1966. The typing and printing were being done in California, with Gittings providing the content, layout and headlines. She was fired, ostensibly because she was late with her pieces but also because the pair had a more activist stance than the DOB in California. They believed in picketing and joining with men; the California cohort was more interested in cautiously advancing the gay cause and promoting feminism over purely gay rights. The issue of August 1966, Volume 10, No. 11, was the last one listing Gittings as editor and Lahusen ("Tobin") as art director.

Gittings and Lahusen didn't break stride. They continued in other media. Gittings "had a real flair for public speaking."[38] She gave her first speech to a straight audience in 1967,[39] appeared on *The David Susskind Show* and, over time, "addressed over 500 audiences."[40] Personable and likable, she inspired trust.

Her attitude was evident in her personal life and in her work. Her tone was positive and upbeat.[41] When she was fired as editor of *The Ladder*, she said "mea culpa"[42] to being late with some editions and then turned her attention to where she felt she could do the most good. She had already picketed and published articles.[43] Thereafter, she went on to join Kameny as assistant personal counsel in test cases challenging the government's ban on civil service employment, military service and security clearances for gay citizens.[44]

Lahusen said, while Kameny was still alive, "Yes, he is brilliant ... . He was able to challenge the government and the psychiatrists on scientific grounds. And so he provided that kind of ammunition against the psychiatrists, the hard specifics."[45] With Gittings' help, Kameny challenged the APA's contention of mental illness.

Educating the Educated

Gittings was 20 years old when the first *Diagnostic and Statistical Manual of Mental Disorders*, the voice of the APA, was published in 1952. She was a bibliophile all her life. It was natural for her to join the American Library Association's Task Force on Gay Liberation in its infancy. Being a librarian was not a requirement for membership.[46] She became coordinator of this group, later called simply the Gay Task Force of the American Library Association, which had been started by Israel David Fishman, a gay activist in New York. It was at ALA's annual meeting that she ran a "Hug a Homosexual"[47] booth in 1971, where librarians were invited to kiss and hug members of the same sex. The stunt was daring for its time and achieved publicity for the group in the library press.

Lahusen is somewhat self-deprecating in referring to her contribution to the gay movement, saying more than once, "I'm a chronicler." Yet her partner credited her with clear thinking: "Kay was a big help because she's got a very clear mind and some very definite ideas about the world."[48] Also, in 1970 she "helped found Gay Activists Alliance, which really perfected the 'zap,' a bold confrontation tactic, usually quite unexpected by the recipient."[49] Lahusen also originated Gay Women's Alternative, a discussion forum and mixer for gay women in New York City, starting in 1973. She brought in guest speakers, including playwright Tennessee Williams.

Lahusen also helped to design and assemble exhibits at three American Psychiatric Association conventions. The first was in 1972, "Gay, Proud and Healthy: The Homosexual Community Speaks." In the huge APA exhibit hall of health-care professionals, the gay booth was the only place where the word "LOVE" appeared. It caught the attention of psychiatrists, who engaged in conversations with Gittings, while Lahusen photographed the encounters.

"One psychiatrist looked at these pictures of loving couples and said, 'Does this really work for you people?' The psychiatrists were mostly dumbfounded, and their stereotypical views were really shattered in a way," Lahusen said.[50] Once the APA voted to change the *DSM* designation of homosexuality as mental illness, other gay exhibits would follow to continue the education of psychiatrists: "Homophobia: Time for Cure," and, in 1978, "Gay Love: Good Medicine."[51] These exhibits were full of positive photos of gay people.

It was Lahusen who noticed that the panel planned for the 1972 APA convention had two gays and two psychiatrists but no gay psychiatrist. She urged Gittings to try to change this. With the blessing of the organizer of the event, Gittings got on the phone, wrote letters, and finally found just one gay psychiatrist who agreed to be on the panel, but with provisos. So, Gittings and Lahusen were the instigators of the appearance of John Fryer, M.D., as "Dr. H. Anonymous on the panel." Nonetheless, he insisted he would appear only if he could be in disguise. He wore a full-face Nixon mask, a wig, and a tuxedo three sizes too large, and he used a voice-distortion microphone.

Kameny was opposed to having anyone appear in a mask. Lahusen reports: "Frank said, 'This goes against everything we've been fighting for.' So we [Lahusen and Gittings] had a terrific argument with Frank. People thought we were just rubber stamps for Frank, but that wasn't true—because we were all so strong-minded. It was a big struggle, but we prevailed, and we got Dr. H. Anonymous on the panel."[52] Dr. H. Anonymous' talk attracted an overflow crowd of his fellow psychiatrists. It would be years before the speaker identified himself as John Fryer, M.D.

Gittings read excerpts from letters from other gay psychiatrists who felt they couldn't appear. Lahusen, as usual, took photographs of the panel, one of which promptly appeared in *GAY* newspaper (its title used all capitals, and its frequency varied over its lifetime). In 1972, the same year as the panel, Lahusen published a book called *The Gay Crusaders*. The publisher preferred to have a man's name on the cover of the book (the book had been sold to the publisher as having a gay man and a gay woman as authors), so Randy Wicker lent his name, but Lahusen, with Gittings' help, wrote the book. Like Gittings, Lahusen was positive in her outlook. In a December 23, 1970, letter to Craig Rodwell, who was a friend and owner of Manhattan's Oscar Wilde Memorial Bookshop, Lahusen wrote, "We want our book to be the most positive statement possible about the men and women who have been gay crusaders."[53]

Another event in 1972 was the final edition of *The Ladder*, which had gone through several changes since Gittings and Lahusen left the DOB. (The controversy over its demise is detailed in Marcia Gallo's *Different Daughters*.) Another magazine lasted longer: *The Lesbian Tide* produced its first issue in Los Angeles in August 1971 and was in circulation until 1980.

Gays and Lesbians Together

Gittings and Lahusen were not separatists. From the first meeting with the Mattachine Society in LA, Gittings felt a kinship with gay males fighting for equality for gay people. Early meetings of the East Coast chapter of DOB met in Mattachine's tiny office in New York City. Gittings and Lahusen were both in favor of having *The Ladder* be a magazine of interest to both gay men and women, unlike some lesbian feminists who emphasized women-only concerns. Ultimately they were to lose that battle; *The Ladder* dropped the words "A Lesbian Review" from its title in 1968 and became more feminist in its writing. However, Lahusen went on to work on *GAY* newspaper, and Gittings participated in documentaries. In a meeting about feminism vs. gay rights, Gittings said, "If gay men and women don't get together and fight the gay cause, nobody else is going to do it for us."[54]

Gittings had dubbed herself the Fairy Godmother of a handful of mostly young gay psychiatrists who trusted her enough to come out to her in the early 1970s. They held get-togethers offsite from the formal APA meetings and called themselves the GayPA. When Lahusen suggested trying to find a gay psychiatrist for the June 1972 APA panel, Gittings had a ready list of names to call.

Lahusen's photograph of Dr. H. Anonymous on that panel made the front cover of *GAY* newspaper. Under the photograph was the headline, "Shrinks Asked to Join Gay Liberation ... American Psychiatric Ass'n Told: We'll Fight Those Who Oppose Us." Another photograph on the same front page shows Gittings in front of the exhibit booth that proclaimed in large letters "GAY, PROUD AND HEALTHY," which was more publicity proclaiming the normalcy of same-sex relationships.

The panel with the masked psychiatrist at the 1972 Dallas meeting made a huge impression. Meetings took place within the APA over the next year and a half. Gittings, Lahusen and Kameny pressed their case for change in various ways and settings, even while they were occupied with other aspects of the gay movement. Lahusen photographed a group of gay activists who had confronted a psychiatrist. She especially likes that photo. The gay group carried signs saying, "We Are the Experts on Homosexuality."

Inevitably, more activists, psychiatrists and others joined in the controversy. Ron Gold, director of communications for the newly minted National Gay Task Force (now the National Gay and Lesbian Task Force), delivered a provocative talk titled, "Stop! You're Making Me Sick!"[55] Finally, in December 1973, the board of trustees of the APA passed two resolutions, removing homosexuality as illness from the *DSM*.[56] News releases went out, and the press took notice far and wide. *The Chicago Gay Crusader* headline was 20,000,000 GAY PEOPLE CURED!

Conclusion

Over time, leaders such as Gittings and Lahusen significantly affected the self-view of gays and lesbians and provided an alternate image to the outside world, one of healthy and happy individuals and couples. They contributed greatly to the value of *The Ladder.* More magazines and books about lesbians followed. After *The Lesbian Tide* and numerous 1970s and 1980s publications came *Curve*, in 1990; it is still in publication, with a website for online readers. Although Gittings said in 1974, "Most of the material was on male homosexuals,"[57] time and effort have rectified the disparity somewhat. Gittings appeared in several documentaries, and she inspired others.

In 1996, a young Salt Lake City high-school student challenged her school board's decision to shut down all non-academic clubs rather than allow the gay-straight alliance to meet. Kelli Petersen won her fight. The documentary film *Out of the Past* tells her story and more. In 1997 Kelli shook hands with Gittings, who, with Lahusen, rode in an open car as co–grand marshals, along with U.S. Representative Barney Frank (D-Massachusetts), in the Pride Day parade in New York City.[58] GLSEN (the Gay, Lesbian and Straight Education Network) published a teachers guide based on the film. So education continues, hand in hand with activism.

In 2009, Gittings' photograph (taken by Kay Tobin Lahusen, of course) hung on the wall of the GLSEN office in New York City. There is a gay television documentary series called *In the Life* airing since 1992 (closed in 2012). Several states now allow same-sex marriage. The battle is not over, but there is great progress, Lahusen said. Gittings died on February 18, 2007, and Lahusen continues their work, granting interviews with the next generation of journalists and gay authors who are trying to learn from the past.

NOTES

[1] Gallo, 3
[2] Gallo, 13
[3] Tobin, 51
[4] Tobin, 212
[5] *Ibid.*
[6] Katz, 430
[7] http://digitalgallery.nypl.org/nypldigital/dgkeysearchdetail. cfm?trg=1&strucID= 1079390&imageID=1605643&total=52&num=0&word=La dder&s=1&notword=&d=&c=&f=&k=0&lWord=1078769& lField=10&sScope=Source&sLevel=1&sLabel=Barbara%25 20Gittings%2520and%2520Kay%2520Tobin%2520Lahuse n%2520gay%2520history%2520papers%2520and%2520ph otographs&sort=&imgs=20&pos=3&e=w#, accessed March 13, 2012
[8] Phone conversation with Kay Lahusen, March 2012
[9] Bullough, 180
[10] *The Ladder*, June 1964, 11
[11] *Out of the Past*, video with live footage from archives
[12] Katz, 430
[13] Jonathan Ned Katz Papers, Box 84, draft of interview with Gittings labeled "Jonathan Katz/Barbara Gittings" on onionskin paper, page 24
[14] *The Ladder*, December 1964
[15] *Ibid.*
[16] Gallo, 94
[17] *Op. cit.*
[18] *The Ladder*, June 1966
[19] Tobin, 215
[20] *The Ladder*, August 1, 1964, 4-5
[21] *The Ladder*, February-March 1965
[22] *The Ladder*, February-March, 1965, 18
[23] Marcus, 107
[24] *The Ladder*, July 1965
[25] Conversation with Kay Lahusen, April 19, 2009
[26] Bullough, 209
[27] Katz, 427
[28] *The Ladder*, May 1965, 7-8
[29] *The Ladder*, May 1965, 14
[30] *The Ladder*, August 1965, 18
[31] *Ibid.*, 17
[32] *The Ladder*, October 1965, 23
[33] *Ibid.*
[34] *The Ladder*, April 1966, 20
[35] *The Ladder*, September 1966, 22-26
[36] *Ibid.*, 24
[37] *Ibid.*, 26
[38] Phone conversation with Kay Lahusen, April 19, 2009
[39] Marcus, 179
[40] Barbara Gittings biography, October 2004, provided by Kay Lahusen
[41] Israel David Fishman Papers, Box 3, N.Y. Public Library Archives
[42] Bullough, 246
[43] See Fluckiger
[44] Tobin, 214
[45] Phone conversation with Kay Lahusen, April 19, 2009
[46] Bullough, Vern, ed.. Tobin article on Barbara Gittings, p. 247
[47] Marcus, 160
[48] Marcus, 96
[49] Phone conversation with Kay Lahusen, April 19, 2009
[50] *Ibid.*
[51] Barbara Gittings biography, October 2004, provided by Kay Lahusen
[52] Phone conversation with Kay Lahusen, April 19, 2009
[53] Letter from Kay Tobin to Craig Rodwell, Craig Rodwell Papers, Box 1, N.Y. Public Library Archives, Professional and Political Correspondence, 1963–1970
[54] Gallo, 169
[55] Bayer, 125
[56] Marcus, 179
[57] Katz, 421
[58] *Out of the Past* film

REFERENCES

Psychiatric News, March 16, 2007, Volume 42, No. 6, page 12, © 2007 American Psychiatric Association

Bayer, Ronald. 1987; 1981. *Homosexuality and American Psychiatry: The Politics of Diagnosis*. Princeton Paperbacks. Princeton, N.J.: Princeton University Press.

Bullough, Vern L. 2002. *Before Stonewall: Activists for Gay and Lesbian Rights in Historical Context*. Haworth Gay & Lesbian Studies. New York: Harrington Park Press.

Drescher, Jack, and Joseph P. Merlino. 2007. *American Psychiatry and Homosexuality: An Oral History*. New York: Harrington Park Press.

DSM: Diagnostic and Statistical Manual of Mental Disorders. 1952. Washington, D.C.: American Psychiatric Association.

DSM-II: Diagnostic and Statistical Manual of Mental Disorders. 1968. Washington, D.C.: American Psychiatric Association.

Fausto-Sterling, Anne. 2000. *Sexing the Body: Gender Politics and the Construction of Sexuality*. 1st ed. New York, N.Y.: Basic Books.

Freud, Sigmund, and James Strachey. 1975; 1962. *Three Essays on the Theory of Sexuality*. Harper Colophon Books; CN 5008. [*Drei Abhandlungen zur Sexualtheorie*.]. New York: Basic Books.

Gallo, Marcia M. 2006. *Different Daughters: A History of the Daughters of Bilitis and the Rise of the Lesbian Rights Movement*. 1st Carroll & Graf ed. New York: Carroll & Graf Publishers.

Katz, Jonathan. 1992. *Gay American History : Lesbians and Gay Men in the U.S.A.: A Documentary History*. Rev. ed. New York, N.Y.: Meridian.

Marcus, Eric. 2002. *Making Gay History: The Half-Century Fight for Lesbian and Gay Equal Rights*. 1st ed. New York: Perennial.

Spiegel, Alix. 2002. *81 Words. This American Life* radio disk; 204. Chicago: Produced by Chicago Public Radio; distributed by Public Radio International.

Tobin, Kay, and Randy Wicker. 1975. *The Gay Crusaders*. New York: Arno Press.

ARCHIVES

Lesbian Herstory Archives
Brooklyn, N.Y.
       Barbara Gittings File
       The Ladder, 1962–1966
New York Public Library
New York, N.Y.
       Israel David Fishman Papers, Box 3
       GAY newspaper, 1972–1974
       Barbara Gittings and Kay Tobin Lahusen
          gay history papers and
          photographs;
          LGBT periodicals, Box 66
       Jonathan Ned Katz Papers, Box 84
       Craig Rodwell Papers, Series 1,
          Boxes 1, 2 and 5
       Randy Wicker Papers, Silverstein letter,
          February 1973
www.kamenypapers.org/correspondence

PRIMARY SOURCES

Frank Kameny, gay activist
       Phone conversation, December 23, 2010
Kay Tobin Lahusen, lesbian activist, author,
  photojournalist
       Phone conversation, March 24, 2009
       Phone conversation, March 30, 2009
       Phone conversation, April 4, 2009
       Phone conversation, April 16, 2009
       Phone conversation, April 19, 2009
       Phone conversations, March 2012
Cynthia L. Martin, trainer and educator
       LGBT Workshop

The Ladder's first issue in 1956.
Courtesy of Rich Wilson

The Ladder, September 1965.
Courtesy of Rich Wilson

Barbara Gittings, American Library Association Gay Book Awards, Chicago, 1972.
Photo by Kay Tobin Lahusen

Group portrait of ALA Task Force on Gay Liberation holding gay books, showing Phyllis Lyon and Del Martin (top, third and second from right), and Barbara Gittings (bottom, second from right). At the American Library Association annual meeting, Chicago, 1972.
Photo by Kay Tobin Lahusen

Barbara Gittings with display cover of Kay Tobin's *The Gay Crusaders*, annual American Library Association meeting, Chicago, 1972.
Photo by Kay Tobin Lahusen

In 2001, these four lesbian publishing pioneers were together in San Francisco. The event was at the Harvey Milk Branch of the San Francisco Public Library. Back row: Kay Tobin Lahusen and Barbara Gittings. Front: Phyllis Lyon and Del Martin. The event celebrated Gittings' work with the American Library Association.
Photo by Jim Mitulski

Barbara Gittings (right) with women's music pioneer and *HOT WIRE* Publisher Toni Armstrong Jr. at a screening of the movie *Out of the Past* in Chicago, circa 2000.
Photo by Tracy Baim

5

Queer Print in Chicago, 1965–1985:
A Personal History

By Marie J. Kuda

"Print is our medium," proclaimed academic Beth Hodges in 1976 as keynote speaker at the third of five annual Lesbian Writers' Conferences held in Chicago. Hodges, who had edited the "Lesbian Feminist Writing and Publishing" issue of *Margins: A Review of Little Magazines and Small Press Books* (1975) and the *Sinister Wisdom* "Special Issue: Lesbian Writing and Publishing" (1976), noted her amazement that women from the isolated wheat fields of western Kansas were echoing their counterparts in Atlanta, Boston, North Carolina and a thousand miles away in New York City. She realized women all over the country were saying the same things in their articles, journals, books and letters.

Hodges was addressing the rising tide of publishing that would label the 1970s as the "Lesbian Decade." But her words were equally germane to the role of newsprint in the building of a community among gays and lesbians across the U.S.: Print was the medium that would tie us all together in common cause; speaking to each other through the medium of print was a political act.

Chicago's contribution to that cause began early in the 20th century. Henry Gerber's Society for Human Rights, incorporated in Illinois in 1924, is generally conceded to be the earliest gay-rights organization in the U.S. [Katz 1976: 385 *et seq.*] Gerber had served with the post–World War I U.S. Army of Occupation in Weimar Germany and was conversant with that country's homosexual-liberation movement, especially the Bund für Menschenrecht as well as Adolf Brand's periodical *Freundschaft und Freiheit*. He gave the same names (in translation) to his ill-founded and short-lived organization and its publication. Police confiscated the remaining copies of the two issues of his mimeographed *Friendship and Freedom* (about 100 copies of each were published in 1925) when Gerber was arrested and his "strange sex cult exposed." [Kepner: 8]

Gerber's publication was labeled "obscene" by local postal authorities; this bugaboo would be a tactic used to intimidate gay and lesbian publishing far beyond the 1950s, when ONE, Inc., challenged it all the way to the Supreme Court. Gerber hired a lawyer familiar with Chicago-style justice; the criminal charges were dismissed, and the postal authorities never pursued federal charges of "sending obscene material through the mails," though Gerber lost his own job with the post office. No copies of the magazine are known to have survived, though a photograph exists of the cover of one issue in a collage from a Magnus Hirschfeld collection.

Chicago as a 'Gay' Publishing Town

Chicago has always been a town for printers, writers and publishers. Local publisher Ralph Seymour Fletcher brought out an early homosexual-themed novel (*Bertram Cope's Year,* 1919) by Henry Blake Fuller, who also wrote perhaps the earliest American gay play (*At Saint Judas's,* published in 1896 by The Century Co. in New York). Fuller had been the first Chicago writer to challenge the Eastern literary establishment with the success of his 1890s novels. Fletcher also published a posthumous volume of praise (1929) for Fuller that included tributes by other gay writers of the day—including novelists Carl Van Vechten, Thornton Wilder and Arthur Meeker as well as poet Mark Turbyfill.

In 1902, Herbert S. Stone and Co. published the "lesbian relevant" memoir of a young woman, *The Story of Mary MacLane.* [Foster: 244-247, 260–261] Onetime Chicagoan and Harlem Renaissance figure Nella Larsen's novel *Passing* (1929) had a local setting and is perhaps the first novel to portray same-sex love between African-American women. In 1930, Chicago's Eyncourt Press published *The Stone Wall* by Mary Casal, an autobiographical lesbian confessional that would lend its name to the iconic New York City bar of the 1960s.

By the 1970s, Chicago could boast no fewer than four lesbian book publishers and a dozen or more gay and lesbian periodicals.

1900–1950: The Closet Years

In the early years of the last century, Chicago had seven major mainstream dailies and a few weeklies. Prominent gays were featured in the social columns of the day—the comings and goings of Robert Allerton, scion of the banking and cattle family, were regularly detailed in the society columns, as he was deemed the city's most eligible bachelor. He never "married" and in later years legally adopted his male lover.

Novelist Henry Blake Fuller commanded equal space as one of the town's foremost intellectuals. But he was also a contributor to several local and national periodicals, writing literary criticism, reviews and satirical columns; with reformer and Nobel laureate Jane Addams, he inveighed against America's imperialist warmongering in Cuba and the Philippines. He was factotum for Harriet Monroe's **Poetry: A Magazine of Verse**, which survives to this day. Poet and ballet premier danseur Mark Turbyfill was an early columnist on dance for several venues, including **The Chicagoan** (1926–1935), the Windy City's Jazz Age answer to *The New Yorker* magazine. Turbyfill was also a contributor to *The Little Review* and to *Poetry* magazine, where he was the first to have an entire issue devoted solely to his work.

The earliest germane "newspaper" of note in Chicago may have been the unnamed one reflected in a 1910 Chicago Vice Commission report that made note of cult literature that circulated for gay cognoscenti, "much of which is uncomprehensible [*sic*] to one who cannot read between the lines." [Vice: 296; Sprague: 28]

Margaret Anderson created **The Little Review** (1914–1929), flagship magazine of the Chicago Renaissance. She and her partner Jane Heap published the early work of many gay and lesbian writers. Anderson reported on and criticized the shortfall of a Chicago speech (1915) in defense of homosexuality by Edith Lees Ellis, the lesbian wife of sexologist Havelock Ellis. [Katz 1982: 359–366] Later issues of *The Little Review* were confiscated and Anderson was tried and convicted on charges of obscenity for the serialization of James Joyce's *Ulysses,* originally published in Paris by lesbian bookseller Sylvia Beach.

The "alternative press," as we call it today, was well in evidence in those early years also. Chicago had "sporting house" papers to keep customers informed of various demimonde doings, and the country's first horse-racing-handicap paper was started here in 1905. After graduating from Harvard in 1894, classmates Herbert Stone and Ingalls Kimball returned to Chicago (where Stone had grown up), bringing with them their Mauve Decade periodical, *The Chap-Book*. Their magazine aped Aubrey Beardsley illustrations and introduced literary topics for the Chicago aesthete. [Shand-Tucci: 78, 86]

In the absence of "homophile" organizations in the 1910s and '20s, college students and other young people found connections to underground dances, bars and entertainment through their campus newspapers. [Heap: 66–69]

Post–World War II

In the 1950s, newly formed Chicago chapters were receiving publications from nascent West Coast "homophile" organizations: the Mattachine Society, the Daughters of Bilitis, and ONE, Inc. The only early local publications that may have passed for "gay" magazines were Kris Studios' contribution to the male beefcake market. Chuck Renslow, later an entrepreneur in a variety of gay businesses, started three "physique" magazines: *Triumph* (1958), *Mars* (1963–1968) and *The Rawhide Male* (1969). When challenged in court on the ground that his magazines were "obscene," Renslow had the benefit of an earlier legal decision in a case brought to the Supreme Court by ONE, Inc. [Renslow: 56–61]

The West Coast organization's magazine ***ONE: The Homosexual Viewpoint*** had been confiscated by the post office, and ONE sued the postmaster, relying on a 1957 Supreme Court decision that reset the standards for judging obscenity. [Kepner: 217 *et seq.*] ONE lost its case in the lower courts, but in 1958 the Supreme Court accepted its appeal and, based on the court's ruling in *Roth v. United States* (1957), issued a *per curiam* decision (unsigned decision without any written dissent) in favor of ONE. In effect, the decision in *One, Inc. v. Olesen* said it was OK to send gay and lesbian periodicals through the mails, subject to the same restrictions as straight publications, as put forth in *Roth*, opening the floodgates for the subsequent rise of the LGBT press.

The obscenity standards would be further refined by the Supreme Court in *Miller v. California* (1973), which created a stricter test that must be met in order to find a publication obscene. However, as late as 1974, Canadian lesbians en route to the Lesbian Writers' Conference in Chicago had their publications confiscated at the border.

The 1960s and 1970s

I joined the movement and wrote for my first gay periodical in the late 1960s. The balance of this article is largely a subjective recollection of the Chicago papers I contributed to or am familiar with firsthand. A definitive history must be left to future scholars. Some generalizations apply, however.

Very few of the writers and production people in the early period covered by this article were journalists or had experience with publishing periodicals. A number were writers in other media. Almost all were activists. Many went on to make exceptional contributions to the movement or their chosen fields. All the early periodical ventures were undercapitalized; most were not run as businesses. Until the 1980s, most papers relied heavily on unpaid volunteers or offered low wages. All were subject to burnout, successive staff turnovers, and fiscal naïveté. Financing was always iffy—most papers accepted advertising, including classifieds; some had members or subscribers; and fundraisers or benefits to supplement the coffers were common. All but a significant handful succumbed within a year of birth.

Most of the early publications were "DRTs," that is, put together on someone's dining-room table. Some of the publications (especially lesbian) deliberately eschewed a professional-looking format, highlighting their disdain for the Establishment. Others, in those pre–personal-computer days, made herculean efforts to pass muster—*e.g.*, justifying right-hand margins manually in typed copy. Even with later typesetting equipment, the keylines and paste-ups for preparing camera-ready copy were done manually. And photographs had to be sent out to be screened to halftones before they could be used in layouts.

Most periodicals appeared monthly, and almost all had common content and circulation elements. Members or subscribers received copies by mail ("plain brown wrapper"), and there was some delivery in bulk to bars and other businesses. As monthlies, content was light on "news" and higher on commentary—all carried content taken from mainstream media. Announcements, coverage of local events (including sports reporting from the mid-1970s onward), a calendar, and a directory of services and bars were common, as were occasional book, theater and restaurant reviews.

A further observation is that the increase in the number and quality of publications in this period can be related directly to the technological innovations that took us from carbon paper to computers and from keyline to digitized layout. By the 1970s, campus organizations had access to photocopiers, and "instant printers" were to be found in every neighborhood. The city had a gay-friendly rotary press that produced our periodicals and a number of other underground tabloids.

Historian John D'Emilio [CGH: 2, 3] further notes a distinction between Chicago gay-male and lesbian publications, using the examples of *The Chicago Gay Crusader* (which he said "tended to report on news and events. It was about the activities of a movement") and *Lavender Woman* (which was "about culture, consciousness and ideas"). I don't wholly disagree; but to lesbians of the day who, as women, had been written out of history and literature, everything in their papers *was* news. The poster for the 3rd Annual Lesbian Writers' Conference proclaimed: "The men ask 'Where is your Shakespeare?' and the women reply, 'She was a lesbian and you burned her books.'" Reclaiming lesbian history and literature made for news; several women's papers were heavy on poetry contributions as well. *Lavender Woman* also viewed party politics with disdain, unworthy of coverage, a tool of the patriarchy. Notably for a 1970s underground periodical, it evinced but little interest in the anti-war movement except as it touched lesbians directly. Male papers, on the other hand, with men subject to the draft, covered the issue more intently.

But *Lavender Woman* explored and analyzed the burning alive of lovers Camilla Hall (Mizmoon) and Patricia Soltysik as they and others were surrounded by the FBI at their California "safe house" after the fallout from the Symbionese Liberation Army's kidnapping of Patty Hearst and her later participation in a bank robbery. The grand-jury network that sprang up across the country to help the FBI track Susan Saxe and Katherine Ann Power, fugitives from a fatal bank robbery, supposedly hiding in some fictitious lesbian underground, was also covered intently. Government "fishing expeditions" of that sort netted a number of gay and lesbian activists and landed more than a few in jail. Civil rights and racism were issues covered by both gay male and female publications, though racism with less impetus, in retrospect, than was really needed.

The Only Game in Town in the 1960s—Mattachine Midwest

Mattachine Midwest independently incorporated in 1965 and started its own newsletter. For most of the rest of the 1960s and well into the 1970s, the *Mattachine Midwest Newsletter* retained the same format: 5½ by 8½ inches, on colored stock, up to 24 pages saddle-stitched. (The first issues were 8½ by 11 inches, stapled.) Copy in my day was typed on an IBM typewriter with variable typing elements. Headlines and display were set in various point sizes of Letraset type (individual paper letters backed with double-sided tape set in a composing stick, similar to letterpress composition). Layout supplies were obtained through the auspices of the mother of former Chicagoan Craig Rodwell (founder of Oscar Wilde Memorial Bookshop in New York City in 1967).

The format was initially set up by MM member Ralph Mann, a professional at layout and design who later drowned in Mexico. When I started, issues were prepared in the tiny apartment of publications chairman Valerie Taylor (a writer well-known for her lesbian pulp novels, who made her living by writing for trade journals).

Photos had to be separately screened. The newsletter carried some advertising (camera-ready copy, often prepared by us). Printing and binding were done at an office-services firm downtown, and subscriptions were maintained and mailed by an Addressograph-plate method that required constant updating. Circulation fluctuated around 2,000. Bulk copies were delivered to local bars and organizations, and some out-of-town venues—with a copy going to the Chicago Police Department.

In addition to covering the doings of the organization—outreach programs, speaking engagements, fundraisers—the *Mattachine Midwest Newsletter* also had columns of gay-related news abstracted from the local and national mainstream media, and it reported on local police activities, bar raids, results from polling political candidates and, in the post-Stonewall period, the rise of approved campus gay and lesbian organizations at the dozen-or-so Chicago-area colleges and universities. Civil-rights attorney Pearl Hart wrote a piece, reprinted as a popular pamphlet, "Your Rights If Arrested."

All local mainstream media reported on Mattachine Midwest's theater-party benefit at the opening-night performance of Mart Crowley's *The Boys in the Band*, held at the Studebaker Theatre on December 2, 1969. Thereafter, MM was the "go-to" source for the Chicago mainstream press on gay issues. Many of the organization's officers and newsletter contributors used pseudonyms, which was common in those days of justifiable paranoia about the costs of coming out.

In his "President's Column," Jim Bradford (James B. Osgood) pushed radical issues and urged joint efforts with other liberation movements. In 1968, he discussed the summer's Chicago convention of the North American Conference of Homophile Organizations, or NACHO, as well as bar raids, arrests, and ongoing talks with the Police Department. His 1969–1970 editorials on the slayings of Black Panthers Fred Hampton and Mark Clark called for the prosecution of the police responsible. In a short July 1969 column, William B. Kelley mentioned the commotion at the Stonewall bar and the cutting back of bushes in park cruising areas of New York City. In the next issue he followed up with secondhand coverage of the ensuing demonstrations.

My first front-page byline was also in 1969: on the Hooker Report, the National Institute of Mental Health–authorized study that basically said we were like everyone else and homosexuality should be decriminalized. In 1970, I wrote a column suggesting that we proclaim a day when every gay person in the nation should "come out," effectively defeating discrimination by our relationships and numbers. As gay-liberation groups grew on an ever-widening number of campuses, each was reported on. Also in 1970, the *Mattachine Midwest Newsletter* ran its first full-page ad for *The Advocate*, which was shifting from a Los Angeles local publication to a newspaper aimed at a national audience. A stronger nationwide link was being forged.

Editor Arrested for 'Outing' Cop

The *MM Newsletter* often called attention to dangerous cruising areas, identifying several arresting officers by name and description. In 1970, Editor David Stienecker became possibly the first gay newsman to be arrested on a charge of criminal defamation, in connection with an article he wrote in late 1969. The piece "A Gay Deceiver? Or Is He?" alluded to the entrapment of men in Lincoln Park toilets by a particular young vice cop whom he identified later by name and photograph, suggesting the cop's zeal was more personally satisfying than a matter of diligence. Stienecker's decision to fight his arrest, with lesbian attorney Renee Hanover, made him a local icon for newly empowered post-Stonewall gays and other movement people. Charges were eventually dropped and, although Stienecker lost his daytime job, the ACLU felt he did not have sufficient grounds for a First Amendment case. [Kuda: 82–83]

In the early 1970s, under new leadership, the format of the *MM Newsletter* changed to 8 by 11 inches, saddle-stitched, in black ink on heavy white stock. The content became less strident and more socially oriented as other papers came onto the Chicago scene. By the late 1970s it had accumulated an unpaid $3,000 printing bill. Guy Warner, who founded the local PFLAG and later became Mattachine Midwest's sixth president, negotiated a settlement, and the newsletter continued to run erratically until 1985. [Poling: 118–120]

The Tabloid Years

Chicago Gay Liberation had formed on the campus of the University of Chicago, triggered by the response to an ad placed by student Henry Wiemhoff in the college paper, the *Chicago Maroon*, seeking gay roommates. Its members issued the ***Chicago Gay Liberation Newsletter*** at irregular intervals, printed offset in black ink, on 11-by-17-inch, white 60-pound stock, folded. Content included coverage of events, announcements, a directory, suggested reading, and both classified and display ads. Its "Stonewall Commemorative Edition" of June 18, 1970, ran a five-point Statement of Human Rights calling for the end of discrimination against homosexuals and other oppressed peoples. The issue carried a schedule of Gay Pride Week events, an article on the local chapter of the Daughters of Bilitis, and details of the appeal of a Texas sodomy case to the Supreme Court with a call for donations to aid in deferring the legal expenses.

In September 1970, CGL split. Many members formed the Chicago Gay Alliance, an organization with the intent of working for a gay-rights bill and to effect other legal changes within the existing political system. The ***Chicago Gay Alliance Newsletter*** was run monthly on an offset press in two formats. Eleven issues from November 1970 through December 1971 were distributed unstitched, on 11-by-14-inch, 20-pound white paper, folded.

In June 1971, Frank Robinson had published our first tabloid-size newspaper, ***Chicago Gay Pride*** (Frank was a novelist and sci-fi writer who was then writing *Playboy* magazine's adviser column). Again completely typewritten, with manually justified margins, copy was pasted up on layout boards with Rubylith film laid on where photos were to be keylined. The essentially camera-ready copy and photographs were then delivered to a printer (Frank remembered that the first printer he approached objected to the "dressed-up penis on the back-page ad" and refused to print). Other ads were more "respectable." A few thousand copies were gang-run by a local web press. The front page announced the opening of the first gay community center on Elm Street, in a building that was slated for eventual demolition but burned down after CGA vacated the premises. Among the articles included was an extensive gay bibliography. Distribution was through existing organizations and bars during Pride Week.

The *CGA Newsletter* would continue publishing in a different format as ***Chicago Gay Pride*** beginning with Volume 2, No. 1, in February 1972, appearing at irregular intervals, with a lot of advertising, until June 1973. The new format was 8½ by 14 inches, unstitched, on heavy folded white stock, offset-printed with black ink and a color cover, running an average of 20 pages. In the March 1972 issue the publications chair wrote that the *CGA Newsletter* (*Chicago Gay Pride*) "seems to be the principal publication of gay people in Chicago" and indicated that the small crew of "three people or less" needed help "soliciting advertising, typing copy, preparation of art work, and running our Multilith 1250 press." At that time CGA had a mailing list of about 1,300, and costs were around $300 an issue. In addition, it had problems related to miscalculating postage, which resulted in missed issues.

In the summer of 1972, I was one of a cadre recruited by Frank Robinson when he started a second tabloid, ***The Paper,*** to cover gay news, alternative theater and other cultural events neglected by the mainstream press. Again the format was 20 pages, three columns, hand-typed on an IBM Selectric (with the changeable elements that allowed two point sizes of several faces, including italics), with manually justified margins and heavy on photography and graphics. Coverage included interviews with prominent gay figures, theater reviews, and an extensive feature on the local drag scene. Proposed as a serious venture, *The Paper* had established a business structure and solicited substantial advertising in the hopes of becoming self-sustaining. As the second issue was in preparation, Frank sold his proposal for a novel to Hollywood, quit *Playboy* and left for the West Coast. [Baim: 93–94] Without his out-of-pocket support and editorial skills, the newspaper folded after the second issue. This and subsequent tabloids would be printed by Fred Eychaner's Newsweb Corp. press. Frank's novel would become a film (*The Towering Inferno*) and he would go on to write speeches for Harvey Milk.

The Chicago Gay Crusader

The Chicago Gay Crusader was founded by activists Michael Bergeron and William B. Kelley and ran as a monthly from May 1973, when *Chicago Gay Pride* ceased publication, through April 1976. It was a tabloid format, manually typed by Kelley, with photography largely by Bergeron, who also did layout on boards provided by their printer, Newsweb. The *Crusader* had male and female contributors and was initially directed at a mixed audience with heavy emphasis on rights issues. Kelley wrote many of the articles of substance (politics, police, etc.), while other activists volunteered columns on their special areas of interest or helped with distribution. No one was paid. Early on, generous photo coverage was also devoted to the local bar and entertainment venues, including shows featuring female impersonators.

Advertising and donations paid most of the bills, with an occasional fundraiser thrown in to balance the budget. The *Crusader* also organized fundraisers for other causes, including the aftermath of the fatal firebombing of the Upstairs Bar in New Orleans on June 24, 1973—during Pride Week. The paper's best-remembered headline was from the January 1974 issue: "20,000,000 GAY PEOPLE CURED!" The reference was to the American Psychiatric Association's decision to alter its diagnostic criteria, effectively taking homosexuality out of the illness category.

Kelley and Bergeron were immersed in the life of the community—Bergeron founded a handful of service organizations including Beckman House, an early social-service agency with an information hotline (929-HELP) and drop-in space that picked up the slack when CGA left its community center on Elm. He published an annual directory listing bars, organizations and services, called *The Chicago Gay Directory*. This project was funded by restaurateur Jack David of the Up North and circulated free in the community.

Kelley, who had a history of working as a volunteer with local and burgeoning national organizations, joined Renslow and Associates, Ltd., affording him the freedom to continue working for gay causes. Kelley had picketed Independence Hall in the 1960s with Barbara Gittings and Frank Kameny, was an officer in the pre-Stonewall NACHO, and was in the group of leaders called to the Carter White House meeting with Midge Costanza in 1977. Bergeron eventually went over to *GayLife* as editor after Renslow bought the paper.

The Lesbian Decade

During the 1970s and spilling over into the 1980s, the lesbian-run media grew exponentially. According to Bonnie Zimmerman (former member of the *Lavender Woman* collective, writer, author and academic who was editor of the encyclopedia *Lesbian Histories and Cultures*), more than 500 community newspapers and 100 women's bookstores were launched nationwide in the 1970s. Gay and lesbian historians still largely neglect the Midwest and concentrate on the bicoastal aspect of the "post-Stonewall" period. Rodger Streitmatter, in his books on the underground press, neglects *GayLife*, the *Gay Crusader*—and even the *Mattachine Midwest Newsletter* with its 20-year run—in his analysis of the rise of the gay press. His treatment of the lesbian press in Chicago is even worse. He does cover the several-year run of *Lavender Woman* but then cites *Killer Dyke*, a radical tabloid with a small circulation, as a "major influence."

Killer Dyke was a spur-of-the-moment pastiche put together in late 1971. Writers such as Martha Shelley and Judy Grahn had their work cut-and-pasted from other publications. Original writing by a few young gay men was also featured, including the first of a three-part interview with Ron Vernon, a founder of the short-lived Chicago Third World Gay Liberation. Unfortunately, *Killer Dyke* ran only a few issues. The other two parts of Vernon's piece, "Growing Up in Chicago Black & Gay," would not be published until three years later in *The Chicago Gay Crusader.* Printing of *Killer Dyke* was paid for from unspent funds allocated to a university publications budget line. Half a dozen Chicago lesbian papers had much longer runs and wider circulation, including *Blazing Star*, which ran almost a dozen years in various permutations.

Lavender Woman (1971–1976)

In 1967, after a rally of 5,000 people in Chicago's Civic Center Plaza during the founding meetings of the National Conference for New Politics, a group of women formed a radical feminist caucus in protest to the callous treatment by men at the conference. A new feminist group emerged that brought out a newsletter called the *Voice of the Women's Liberation Movement*. Later, the Women's Caucus (of Chicago Gay Liberation) was meeting independently of that mixed group for all the usual reasons. In 1971, women from a variety of groups formed another feminist collective and with "reasoned rage" put together a new newspaper. Two caucus members, Margaret Sloane and Susan Moore, were part of the new collective that produced *The Feminist Voice*. Margaret Sloane edited a dedicated page for lesbians headed "Lavender Woman" in the first issue of the *Voice*.

The caucus then decided to start its own newspaper, initially supported by member dues and later sustained additionally from subscriptions and the proceeds of a concert by Linda Shear's lesbian-separatist band Family of Woman. *Lavender Woman* was able to publish a multipage tabloid, with handwritten headlines and carrying no advertising (a political decision) except exchange ads from other women's publications. *LW* began in November 1971 and ran almost monthly through July 1976; distribution was by mail subscriptions, and copies were sold at local women's bars and meeting spaces. The paper's origin coincided with the rise of lesbian popular culture and women's music, presses, newspapers and magazines across the U.S. A few early issues were pulled together by a loose-knit collective under the leadership of Sloane (who was quickly recruited to work on the nascent national feminist magazine *Ms.* by Editor Gloria Steinem).

I went to a couple of *LW* meetings but was put off by the collective process in which an ever-changing group "ruled" on the body of work for each issue, sometimes overruling the previous group's decisions. It seemed to me that the collective was more interested in process than in getting out a newspaper. Content was initially egalitarian (including a poetry section edited for a while by Vernita Gray); copy was submitted using a variety of typewriters and laid out without retyping or editing. Newspaper layout sessions, and "bagging" the issue for mailing, took place by volunteers in private homes. The collective was predominately separatist-identified, white, college-educated, white-collar women. Issues of race and class were heatedly discussed in, and out of, print. In late 1974 the collective voted to begin accepting advertising, only from women-owned businesses, excluding bars. The history of the *Lavender Woman* collective and newspaper (which attained national stature, running more than five years)—with its confrontation of racism and its ideological conflicts—is detailed in a 1985 book, *Are We There Yet?*, by onetime member Michal Brody.

Among the splits that occurred from *LW*, two resulted in new papers. Betty Peters withdrew over differences with the collective and founded a back-to-the-land group, Amazon Nation, which got out **Cries from Cassandra**, a single-issue tabloid in June 1973.

In the meantime, the Women's Caucus of CGL renamed itself Chicago Lesbian Liberation and continued to contribute financially to the support of *Lavender Woman* until the collective voted to separate itself from the organization in 1974. As the two entities set out to divide resources from their common bank account, a scandal emerged involving embezzlement (eventually resolved by the intervention of attorney Renee Hanover). Essentially left without anything, the women of CLL felt they were entitled at least to some space in *LW* to cover their activities, as they were effectively losing their voice after sponsoring the paper for years.

As a result of arbitration, it was agreed that CLL could have one page in *LW* over which it would exert complete autonomy; in exchange, it would relinquish all claims to the name Lavender Woman. The **Chicago Lesbian Liberation Newsletter,** in a four-to-eight page saddle-stitched, 8½-by-14-inch folded format on magenta paper (printed at an "instant printer"), ran concurrently with *CLL*'s sheet in *LW* from October 1973 through July 1974.

When a cartoon submitted (which lambasted separatists as sexist, discriminating against their "fairy Mary" brothers in the movement) was deemed unacceptable by the collective, *LW* refused to honor the arbitration further, unilaterally pulling the CLL page. CLL, a more racially diverse, more blue-collar organization, declared the arbitration violated and void and reclaimed the name. In retaliation, CLL prepared its own newspaper titled *The Original Lavender Woman*, using the same printer in the same format and being distributed free (causing great confusion) at the same bars and organizations where *LW* was sold. However, *OLW* did carry advertising to cover costs—including ads from bars and a woman-owned funeral home. It ran for only two issues, an undated Volume 1, No. 1 (that came out in July), and No. 2 (October 1974) with a cover announcement on the opening of a new lesbian center on Wrightwood Avenue. *Lavender Woman* published its last issue in July 1976, having succumbed to the usual burnout, but only after having played a major role in the creation of a local and national lesbian community.

Blazing Star, an erratically appearing bimonthly, started in 1975 as an outgrowth of the lesbian contingent of the Chicago Women's Liberation Union and, later, the New American Movement (the organization also included heterosexuals). It was the first lesbian paper to have a definite political stance and a target audience. The paper was socialist-feminist, highlighting the anti-gay mobilization of the right. The subhead below the banner read: "Come Out Fighting."

Articles took positions on everything from Angola, the Alaskan pipeline and abortion to racism, sexism and women's rights. The anti–Anita Bryant campaign and other forces at work against the backlash in cities that had passed pro-gay laws received considerable coverage. Bryant was a frequent front-page subject; her Dade County "Save the Children" organization had set off a reaction from the gay community that resulted in a campaign to boycott Florida orange juice, which eventually resulted in getting Bryant dropped as the industry spokesperson. But by 1978 *Blazing Star* was also including articles on bars and bookstores as well as local and national political events, efforts to ratify the ERA (Equal Rights Amendment—how soon we forget!) and passage of gay-rights legislation.

Initially, the expense of printing *Blazing Star* was donated by a CWLU member who owned an offset press; the low overhead allowed the paper to be distributed free. [Wessel: 3] The format was originally 8½ by 11 inches, black ink on white, with a lavender colophon of the thistle-like flower. It switched to a newsprint tabloid in the late 1970s (after *LW* folded) before becoming a "semi-autonomous" two-page insert in *GayLife* in 1980. [Wessel: 5] Longtime editor and contributor Christine Riddiough, Elaine Wessel and newcomer Diana B. Harper (nom de plume of Jorjet Harper) continued in the new format. The insert of a "women's section" was a practice later repeated by *Sister Spirit* and still later by the "Entre Nous" section in the *Windy City Times*.

In 1976, following a weeklong midsummer Women in Print Conference in Nebraska that drew 138 representatives of periodicals, bookstores and women's presses, I edited and published the first seven numbers of the *Women in Print Newsletter*. Further issues of the *WIP Newsletter* were published by a Midwestern press collective that included Chicago printer/publisher Metis Press.

Another periodical, *women's news . . . For A Change*, was a free tabloid that was founded in 1977 by five lesbians but that adopted an inclusive stance. One of the founders was a women's music producer who wanted an outlet for publicizing her shows. She also brought in advertising revenue from the new women's record labels and retail outlets. Others had joined to provide outreach and links to services for the myriad women's organizations and events that were popping up almost daily. An extensive local calendar and resource lists were featured throughout the paper. The philosophy guiding inclusion was that lesbians were perceived first and foremost as women and that they encountered most of their discrimination as women. Lesbians faced the same economic disparity as their sisters, had the same problems trying to adopt as single parents, were equally the victims of molestation and rape, faced the same androcentric health-care system and were increasingly becoming minority entrepreneurs requiring outlets to reach their prospective customers. The paper folded in 1978.

Starting in late September 1979 and continuing into 1981, Rhonda Craven had been getting out a monthly, two-sided single sheet **Lesbian Community Center Newsletter** covering items of interest and events at the center, then located in Links Hall on Sheffield Avenue. Angela Van Patten, who had briefly been a part of *Blazing Star*, debuted **Journey-Womyn,** a multipage small-format paper, on November 1, 1979. Years later in conversation, Van Patten told me she started the paper because she was only recently out and it seemed like a good way to meet women. Her paper ran for six issues before merging with **The Catalyst: Chicago Womyn's Paper**, which was founded concurrently by a quasi-collective, again with a few of its members from *Blazing Star*, but in a tabloid format. It ran seven issues (January 15 to July 15, 1980). The combined venture, **Journey Womyn: The Catalyst,** continued in the larger format as a monthly until mid-1981.

Also in my collection are two copies of **Lunatic Fringe: A Newsletter for Separatist, Anarchist and Radical Feminist Lesbians of Chicago**, written and published by the pseudonymous Sydney Spinster. The first issue is dated No. 1, July 1980; the last reads "Late July 9981" (perhaps a misprint or a new separatist calendar). The paper ran 300 copies for nine issues, in two columns, typed, from four to eight pages in length, double-sided in black ink, corner-stapled on 8½-by-11-inch, 20-pound white or goldenrod stock. Spinster wrote: "I am very concerned that we hear from wimmin who don't live in the heart of things; aren't northsiders, or are uncomfortable or unable to take part in wimmin's organizations or activities … we should be proud of being the lunatic fringe! We are daring and visionary. Now we can speak to each other in our own voice." In the last issue, she indicated she was moving to Minneapolis but had hopes for the "new" publication: "Rhonda Craven's article on racism in the first issue was a good start."

That "new publication" was another tabloid, **Sister Source, a Midwest Newspaper**, which debuted in August 1981 (absorbing Craven's *LCC Newsletter*) with writers such as Janet Soule, Anne Driebelbis and Mary McCauley. It even featured cartoons by the nationally syndicated Nicole Hollander. Women from several sources came together to form a lesbian-feminist publishing collective. They planned to expand into a Midwest journal with women from Milwaukee, Cincinnati, Madison, St. Louis and Kansas City on board. An early article covered the Judy Chicago artwork, *The Dinner Party*. The last issue, dated October 15, 1982, announced that it was interrupting publication pending internal reorganization. It did not resume publication; I don't have circulation statistics.

Chicago *GayLife* (1975–1985)

Founded by Grant Ford and Abe Olivo in 1975, **GayLife** had as its first editor Valerie Bouchard, who had edited the McCormick Theological Seminary paper. It was professionally typeset (later by Vassar graduate Sarah Craig, who had her own typesetting business and was also a contributing writer) and distributed in Chicago and other Midwestern cities. *GayLife* would publish for 10 years. An editorial in the first issue announced the hopes that the paper would "unite the many gay factions in Chicago and promote dialog between gay people and the straight world." After it appeared, Michael Bergeron and Bill Kelley gave up the *Gay Crusader* following a run of 26 issues, to avoid redundancy and to be able to devote more time to their considerable activist ventures.

When *GayLife* began experiencing financial difficulties because of tax problems, entrepreneur Chuck Renslow first became a silent partner, then purchased the newspaper outright and took the title of publisher in 1981. Bergeron came on board as editor and, at his initiative, *GayLife* became the first gay newspaper to join the City Hall press corps (1980). Also in 1980, *Blazing Star* was added as a sort of "women's" supplement. Pockets of separatism continued in the lesbian community throughout the period of this essay—co-gender organizations and publications had uphill struggles for support. After Renslow took over, Kelley was a mainstay of the paper in various capacities including contributor, copy editor and adviser.

The editorial department and staff went through continual changes well into the early 1980s; by then their total number was reported to be around 30-plus (including sales reps, technical staff and the distribution team) and the paper had become a 24-page weekly with expanded photo coverage. Over time, editors included Steve Kulieke, Albert "Bill" Williams, Sarah Craig and Karlis Streips, a journalism graduate (possibly the paper's first). In 1980, Greg Sprague contributed a series of features on Chicago's gay history. In 1981, several women were added to the staff following a settlement resulting from a discrimination charge. Two full-time reporters (Chris Heim and Charlotte Versagi) and a graphic artist (Mary Kay Ryan) joined, while Sarah Craig continued on as a freelance writer. In 1982, I joined as staff writer for a year, then continued freelance.

Other innovations included use of news boxes for distribution (*The Advocate* began using them in San Francisco 10 years earlier, but had to sink them in cement to avoid vandalism; *The Chicago Gay Crusader* also had news boxes) and getting reporters accredited with the Police Department. In late 1982, a merger between *GayLife* and Wisconsin's *Escape* brought Erin Criss into the management staff; the reorganization resulted in letting several staff members go. Ryan and Heim (a senior staff reporter whose AIDS coverage had been nominated for an award by the nascent national Gay Press Association) disputed their dismissals and filed discrimination charges with the Illinois Department of Human Rights. A decision in favor of the two women resulted in a monetary settlement. Because of content and the types of advertising, *GayLife* was considered (especially in the lesbian community) as a male paper; but at this time (1983) it perceived itself as the *only* gay newspaper in Chicago and decried what it saw as a lack of support from the women's community.

In late 1984 a fresh journalism-school graduate joined the staff and, by June 1985, that graduate, Tracy Baim, began her short tenure as managing editor. In September 1985 she joined an exodus of staff to start Jeff McCourt's new venture, *Windy City Times*. The September 25, 1985, issue of *GayLife* announced the staff walkout and indicated that it had filed a $1.5 million lawsuit for damages against the new paper. A judge ruled that the document had technical difficulties and gave *GayLife* a month to file an amended complaint. Some former staffers kept the paper going for a few more months; it published a final issue in 1986. No further mention was made of the lawsuit.

Gay Chicago Magazine (1976–2011)

In 1976, **Gay Chicago News** was founded by Ralph Paul Gernhardt, who had previously had some success with a telephone newsline. In 1977, he was joined by a journalism grad, Dan Di Leo, who had considerable print publishing experience. They produced **Gay Chicago Magazine** with the subhead: Your Guide to Entertainment. *Gay Chicago* focused on bar news, theater, social events and other entertainment; ergo, it was of predominately male interest, though women's bar coverage was included.

Di Leo helped found the Gay (later, Gay and Lesbian) Press Association and was its national president in 1988. Several well-known activists such as columnist Jon-Henri Damski and political cartoonist Danny Sotomayor got their local "print" outreach start at *Gay Chicago*; others, such as Rick Karlin and Richard Cooke, would contribute to many print venues. While offering only news abstracts throughout its history, other later columns gave legal and financial information, offered book and theater reviews, and included a roving-reporter type of candid-photo questions and responses. A gay astrology chart and a heavy section of personals were popular additions.

Started in tabloid format as *Gay Chicago News*, it shrank to pocket size on newsprint as *Gay Chicago Magazine* in 1977, then grew to saddle-stitched 8-by-10-inch newsprint and some years later added a slick, full-color magazine cover with a rainbow-logo masthead. In later years, the weekly would run 75 to 100 pages and become the longest-running gay periodical in Chicago until it ceased publication in September 2011, shortly after again changing its format, this time to a tabloid.

The Rest of the Story

In addition to the newspapers cited above, there were dozens of other smaller magazines and newsletters issued in Chicago during this 20-year period (1965–1985)—I have more than 100 examples. Bookstores, bars, all kinds of organizations: social groups, political groups, religious groups, veterans—dozens of emerging professional organizations—each had its own method of print communication. They ranged from a slick little 1972 magazine (*Michael's Thing Chicago*) to a mere two-sided monthly flier that published for 31 years (Mountain Moving Coffeehouse, 1974–2005) to full-fledged multipage newsletters (*Kinheart Womyn's News*, which became the *Kinheart Quarterly* and then *The Kinheart Connection*, 1983–1991). Others served specialized audiences of only a few hundred (fliers for Miss Harriet's private traveling "house parties" of the 1980s). [Kuda: 9] Some downsized into oblivion after years of publication, such as the Rev. Grant Gallup's erudite and droll *Integer: Newsletter of Integrity/Chicago* (1977–1981). Robert Ford published **Thing**, a radical black gay arts magazine, until his death from AIDS complications in 1994.

Not only did all these organs of communication serve to unite various factions; they also helped build a community. The papers called people to create safe spaces, to demand decent service and dancing in bars and eliminate discriminatory carding, to demand an end to police harassment. They surveyed politicians, clergy, the medical/psychological establishment and academia on issues germane to the community and fostered dialogues on sexism and racism. In the days before the Internet, they summoned vast numbers of people to picket, boycott or to show up at legislative hearings or as support in court. They increased our visibility, and strengthened our numbers, as we demanded our equal rights. As of this writing, though most of these varied and vital voices have passed from the scene or slipped into cyberspace, print is still alive and well in Chicago. It "won't be over till the fat lady sings," and right now she's tied to a chair with a sock in her mouth.

"The revolution is not what we say when we speak together; the revolution is our speaking together." Beth Hodges

Selected Bibliography:
— Anderson, Margaret. *My Thirty Years' War: An Autobiography*. New York: Covici, Friede, 1930.
— Baim, Tracy. "The Revolution ... Will Be Reported On," in *Out and Proud in Chicago*. Chicago: Surrey Books, 2008: 92–97.
— Baim, Tracy, and Owen Keehnen. "Media and Community: GayLife Newspaper," in *Leatherman: The Legend of Chuck Renslow*. Chicago: Prairie Avenue Productions, 2011: 285–316.
— Brody, Michal. *Are We There Yet? A Continuing History of* Lavender Woman, *a Chicago Lesbian Newspaper, 1971–1976*. Iowa City: Aunt Lute Book Co., 1985.
— D'Emilio, John. "Writing for Freedom," October 22, 2008, <http://www.chicagogayhistory.org/articlearchives.html?AID=19646>.
— Enke, Anne. *Finding the Movement: Sexuality, Contested Space, and Feminist Activism*. Durham: Duke University Press, 2007.
— Foster, Jeannette H. *Sex Variant Women in Literature: A Historical and Quantitative Survey*. New York: Vantage, 1956 (reprinted: Diana Press 1975 and Naiad Press 1985).
— Frank, Laura. "We Are Nobody's Caucus: Separatism in Chicago's Gay Civil Rights Movement, 1960–1980" (unpublished senior honors thesis). Madison: University of Wisconsin, 2008, available online at <https://www.box.com/shared/9nysnvr3af>.
— Gallo, Marcia M. *Different Daughters: A History of the Daughters of Bilitis and the Rise of the Lesbian Rights Movement*. New York: Carroll & Graf, 2006.
— Harris, Neil, ed. The Chicagoan: *A Lost Magazine of the Jazz Age*. Chicago: University of Chicago Press, 2008.
— Heap, Chad C. *Homosexuality in the City: A Century of Research at the University of Chicago* (exhibition catalog). Chicago: University of Chicago Library, 2000.
— Heap, Chad. *Slumming: Sexual and Racial Encounters in American Nightlife, 1885–1940*. Chicago: University of Chicago Press, 2009.
— Hodges, Beth. *Print Is Our Medium: The Text of a Speech Delivered Before the 3rd Annual Lesbian Writers Conference, Chicago, September 17, 1976*. Chicago: Womanpress, 1977.
— Katz, Jonathan. *Gay/Lesbian Almanac: A New Documentary*. New York: Harper Colophon, 1983.
— Katz, Jonathan Ned. *Gay American History: Lesbians and Gay Men in the U.S.A., a Documentary History*. New York:

Thomas Y. Crowell, 1976.

— Kepner, Jim. *Rough News, Daring Views: 1950s' Pioneer Gay Press Journalism*. Binghamton, New York: Haworth Press, 1998.

— Kuda, Marie. "Hunting for History: The Lesbian in Chicago Periodicals," Chicago *Outlines*, July 1988: 41, 48.

— Kuda, Marie. "'Pacesetter' brings parties to black lesbians," *GayLife*, August 13, 1982: 9.

— Kuda, Marie J. "Chicago's Literary Renaissance," in *Out and Proud in Chicago*. Chicago: Surrey Books, 2008: 28.

— Kuda, Marie J. "Chicago's Stonewall: [The Trip and Stienecker Cases]," in *Out and Proud in Chicago*. Chicago: Surrey Books, 2008: 79–83.

— Peck, Abe. *Uncovering the Sixties: The Life and Times of the Underground Press*. New York: Citadel Press, 1991.

— Poling, John D. "Mattachine Midwest: The History of a Chicago Gay Rights Organization, 1965 to 1986" (master's thesis). Normal, Illinois: Illinois State University, 2002.

— Potter, Clare. *The Lesbian Periodicals Index*. Tallahassee: Naiad Press, 1986.

— Shand-Tucci, Douglass. *The Crimson Letter: Harvard, Homosexuality, and the Shaping of American Culture*. New York: St. Martin's Press, 2003.

— Sprague, Gregory A. "Chicago's Past: A Rich Gay History," *The Advocate*, August 18, 1983: 28–31, 58.

— Streitmatter, Rodger. *Unspeakable: The Rise of the Gay and Lesbian Press in America*. Boston: Faber and Faber, 1995.

— Streitmatter, Rodger. *Voices of Revolution: The Dissident Press in America*. New York: Columbia University Press, 2001.

— Vice Commission of Chicago, Inc. *The Social Evil in Chicago: A Study of Existing Conditions with Recommendations by the Vice Commission of Chicago*. Chicago: The Vice Commission of the City of Chicago, 4th ed. 1912 (1911) (1st ed. reprinted: Cornell University Library 1991).

— Weimann, Jeanne. "Chicago's Feminist Periodicals: Where Issues Burn Instead of Bras," in *women's news ... For a Change*, April 1977, 1:1, 2, 12.

— Wessel, Elaine. "The Decline and Fall of Feminist Publications in Chicago, 1971–1983" (unpublished paper for Journalism 377). Chicago: Roosevelt University, 1983.

Chicago's Gay and Lesbian Press: a personal note by Marie J. Kuda

Chicago's GLBT press paralleled the growth of local organizations, and this highly subjective overview begins with my association with the ***Mattachine Midwest Newsletter*** (1965–1985) in the late 1960s and writing for Frank Robinson's pioneer efforts ***Chicago Gay Pride*** (June 1971) and ***The Paper*** (July and September–October 1972). Over the ensuing years, I would contribute items to ***The Chicago Gay Crusader*** (May 1973–April 1976), ***Lavender Woman*** (1971–1976), ***The Original Lavender Woman*** (July–October 1974), ***women's news . . . For A Change*** (April–October 1977), Chicago ***GayLife*** (1975–1985), ***Blazing Star*** (1975 to early 1980s), ***Gay Chicago Magazine*** (1976–2011), **Chicago Outlines** (1998–2000) and ***Windy City Times*** (1985 to date). In some cases, I also performed layout, ad solicitation and composition, graphics, photography, editorial, billing and distribution functions. I also contributed gay-related articles to other Chicago non-gay media such as the ***Reader***. In the 1960s through the 1980s, I was peripherally involved with dozens of organizations, bars, bookstores, university groups, etc. that published a broadside, or newsletter, or newspaper, and I collected samples of each at meetings or conferences.

The M. Kuda Collection, Library and Special Collections, The Kinsey Institute for Research in Sex, Gender and Reproduction, Indiana University, Bloomington, holds copies of all the periodicals (1965–1985) mentioned in this article and the texts cited in the bibliography. Some of the "lesbian" periodicals are held by Northwestern University Library, Evanston, Illinois, www.library.northwestern.edu/print/libraries-collections. Many of the publications can also be found in the Robert Ridinger periodicals-on-microfilm collection at Northern Illinois University, De Kalb. The Margaret Anderson, Henry Blake Fuller and Mark Turbyfill papers are held by the Newberry Library, Chicago. Gregory A. Sprague, Pearl M. Hart and Robert Ford papers are in the Chicago History Museum. Valerie Taylor papers are held by Cornell University Library, Human Sexuality Collection, Ithaca, New York. Additional information on many of the individuals or organizations mentioned in the article can be found online at either www.glHallofFame.org or www.ChicagoGayHistory.org.

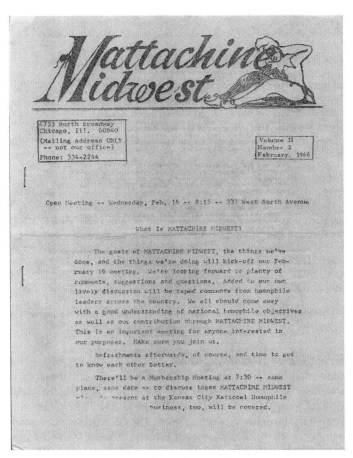

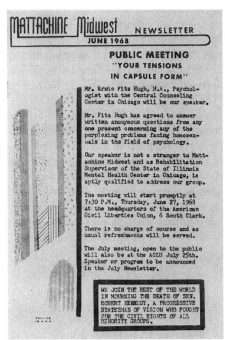

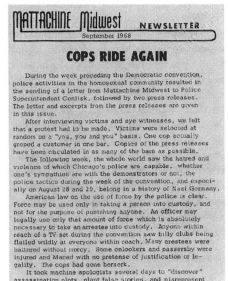

Mattachine Midwest Newsletter, February 1966. This has a faulty lower-left corner. The obscured material dealt with a Mattachine Midwest membership meeting that would be discussing ideas MM planned to present at the February 1966 meeting of the National Planning (later, North American) Conference of Homophile Organizations in Kansas City.
Courtesy of William B. Kelley

Mattachine Midwest Newsletter, June 1968 (left) and September 1968 (right).
Courtesy of the M. Kuda Archives

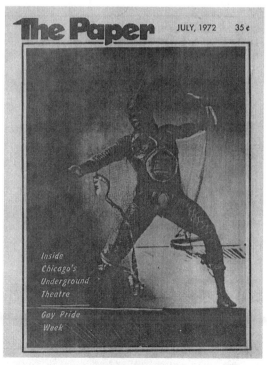

LEFT: *Chicago Gay Liberation Newsletter*, June 18, 1970.
RIGHT: February 18, 1972. Chicago Gay Alliance's overnight compilation of a gay-rights platform adopted by a 1972 national conference it hosted in Chicago. This compilation was to be ratified at the next day's session.

All images on this page courtesy of the M. Kuda Archives

LEFT: *Chicago Gay Pride*, 1971.
ABOVE: *The Paper*, July 1972.

The Chicago Gay Crusader's first issue, May 1973.

The Chicago Gay Crusader, February 1974.

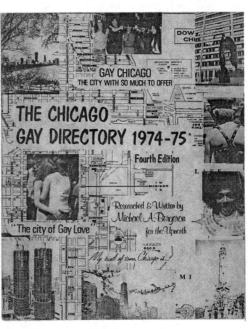

LEFT: *The Chicago Gay Crusader*'s 1975 post-Pride issue.
ABOVE: *The Chicago Gay Directory*, 1974–75.
All images on this page courtesy of the M. Kuda Archives

**A portion of the cover of *Killer Dyke*
newspaper, October 1971.**
All images on this page courtesy of the M. Kuda Archives

the family of woman

a benefit concert

STORY on PAGE 5

ABOVE: *Lavender Woman*, **September 1972.
BELOW: First issue of *The Original Lavender
Woman* in July 1974.**

C.L.L. NEWSLETTER
BY CHICAGO LESBIAN LIBERATION INC.

TOWARD SOLIDARITY

It has occurred to me that it would be actually beneficial to C. L. L., to itemize some of the particular jobs and responsibilities which must be filled before we can efficiently run our organization and regain our solidarity.

Hopefully, requesting volunteers for these jobs through this newsletter and letting people know what is going on, will enable us to establish the structure eventually which a lesbian feminist center can be based. We have funds; what is needed now is commitment and cooperation.

It has also occurred to me that we have to redefine some of our goals. Merely being lesbians seeking an alternative social outlet has not been enough to keep us together. I believe that we should become active feminists and gay liberationists. The oppression of gays and of women has been institutionalized in our society. It is presently glaringly reflected in job discrimination, in Chicago's "Woman's court", and in the attitudes of many people in the media, in the school systems, and in the legislature. It is time that we joined together among ourselves and other groups to fight and do away with institutionalized discrimination. I do not mean to impose a political viewpoint on anyone, also, I think the continuation of social activities and rap groups are important. It takes some time to get the sludge of institutionalized inferiority out of our systems, out of every nook and cranny of our minds. But once our pride and self respect has been rejuvenated, let's do something about the origin of the disease of intolerance.

People are invited to submit suggestions about projects they might like to see developed, i. e. a group to publicize the goings on at Womens Court; possibly a coordinated project around ERA; or a project to develop skills or review job problems experienced by lesbians and women in general, or whatever you would like to see done.

Also we would like to help lesbians in the northern suburbs or in the south side to get together. Several people have come to Mon. nite meetings wanting to know what is going on in these areas.

Social activities are still important to us. Since basketball has become popular lately, I was wondering if women would be interested in treking or co-ordinating groups in other sports such as tennis or skiing. Perhaps we could get a weekend skiing or tobaganing thing together. Any and all ideas about activities are welcome.

Here are some basic things that need to be done in order to spread information and to strengthen our organization. I do not mean that everything will be just fine if these things are accomplished, but we will be off to a good start.

1) Someone to volunteer to memo announcements for the Mon. nite meetings (a machine is available) 2) A few people to distribute this newsletter to bars, bookstores, etc. 3) Someone to locate various feminist films and secure one each month for Monday night. 4) About four more volunteers to shift a center from 7p. m.-11 p. m. one

(OVER)

**1973 issue of the *C.L.L. Newsletter* for
Chicago Lesbian Liberation.**

LEFT: *Blazing Star,* **June 1975.**
ABOVE: *Blazing Star,* **November 1977.**
All images on this page courtesy of the M. Kuda Archives

women's news … For A Change,
April 1977.

LEFT: *GayLife*'s first issue, June 20, 1975.
ABOVE: *GayLife,* June 24, 1977.
All images on this page courtesy of the M. Kuda Archives

LEFT: *GayLife,* July 19, 1984.
RIGHT: *GayLife,* September 13, 1984.

Gay Chicago News

A GERNHARDT PUBLICATION — October 7, 1977 — FREE CIRCULATION

This Week October 8-14

. . ends with "If you're gay, wear blue jean day." Friday, October 14th has been proclaimed "a day for uptight 'straights' to be scared back to wearing suits and dresses." Promoted by the NGTF, following the success the idea received last year on many campuses across the nation, including the University of Illinois, the day should prove interesting on a national scale. The gents seen right, although attired in faded levis, quite obviously would not find it necessary to wear jeans to pronounce that they are gay. Seen wearing the hat is Paul Nash, manager of the Log Jam. The display is o.k. because that's his lover, Brooks Going.

GC/Newsphoto by Jim Groonis

"Teachers beware: .. Courts don't care!"

The general consensus of opinion following the U.S. Supreme Court's opening day refusal to hear the case of James Gaylord, a fired openly gay

sition for a homosexual teacher is to remain in anonymity. However, Jane Clark, General Counsel for the Illinois Education Association told GC-

it does not imply acceptance of the lower appellate court's ruling.

James Gaylord, a 13 year high school teacher with an

Youth & sex abuse back in the news

The arrest of 33 year old David Buzzek, a Ravenswood YMCA desk clerk and North Side Boy Scout program commissioner, on charges stemming from photographic and sexual involvement with a 17 year old have once again headlined the implication of a child pornography ring.

Buzzek, who lived alone at 4429 N. Central Park, was arrested September 28th after police raided his apartment and found nude photos and films of adolescent boys, some involving sexual activity. According to daily newspaper reports, police moved in on Buzzek as the result of questioning a youth leaving his residence. The 17 year old ward of the state (DCFS) who lived at Buzzek's place of employment told the

police that he had been paid $30 to pose for nude pictures. Other reports indicated that the teenager also had sexual relations with Buzzek. Police indicated they had worked a month on the case following a report from Boy Scout officials involved in the production and distribution of pornographic material.

According to the *Chicago Sun-Times*, David J. Buerklin, director of Boy Scout Field Services in the The Chicago Area Council, said that they suspected Buzzek's involvement in "the gay-liberation parade." Buerklin added, "that started us off on the whole trail" which lead to another scout official

(cont. on page two)

News Front

Chuck Renslow, left, and Leonard Matlovich   Photo by Dan Di Leo

Gay Chicago
MAGAZINE
ISSUE NUMBER 22   OCTOBER 20, 1978

Your Guide to Entertainment Through October 29, 1978

ABOVE: *Gay Chicago News*, October 7, 1977.
LEFT: *Gay Chicago*, October 20, 1978.
All images on this page courtesy of the M. Kuda Archives

PART TWO:

The Journalists

"If you do not tell the truth about yourself you cannot tell it about other people."

— **Virginia Woolf**

6

Harry Hay

By Owen Keehnen

The occasion I had for interviewing Harry Hay was his 80th birthday on April 7, 1992. I had just read the wonderful biography of him, *The Trouble With Harry Hay*, by Stuart Timmons, from Alyson Publications. I was sort of intimidated to meet Hay. He was Mr. Gay Movement. The head honcho and ground zero of gay politics, so to speak.

Any fears I had were promptly dispelled upon our introduction. He was so warm and friendly and, for lack of a better word, so mod. I was almost immediately at ease with him. Hay was such a sweet and generous and humble man and one who had definitely lived an incredible life.

It's easy to forget that there was a time in the not-so-distant past when gays and lesbians had no political rights. Nada. But gay and lesbian activism didn't just happen one stifling June night in 1969 at the Stonewall Inn. The seeds of power and identity that erupted that evening had been firmly planted years before.

In 1950, Harry Hay established the Mattachine Society, which laid the foundations for activism some two decades before Stonewall. In addition to this achievement, Hay co-founded the Radical Faeries in 1979. He was the first elected chair of the Southern California Gay Liberation Front, and he worked fearlessly with the Citizens Committee to Outlaw Entrapment. He was also a staunch member of the Communist Party and a Hollywood actor during the 1930s.

Perhaps his greatest contribution was his tireless life as a gay theorist, scholar and historian. He was a born teacher and was always anxious to share his knowledge with listeners. Hay died 10 years after our interview—on October 24, 2002, at age 90.

Owen: When did you first become aware of the need for an organization like the Mattachine Society?

Harry: I first began to feel the need for a brotherhood of people like me, though I wasn't quite sure what that meant, when I was 14 in 1926. I'd known for quite some time that I was different from the others, but I didn't know how or why or what it all meant. Then I was 14, and suddenly I discovered what it all meant, and from there on out I always wanted to get a brotherhood of people like me together.

Owen: So your intent with the Mattachine Society was the formation of a brotherhood?

Harry: Yes, and in this brotherhood we were going to find out who we were. In those years, we weren't even in the *Encyclopædia Britannica*. We didn't know anything about ourselves. When we began the Mattachine Society, we were in the process of developing a positive gay identity. We wanted to see ourselves as good people. The first time we sat down to meet, we didn't even know what to ask each other.

Owen: What turned out to be the question everyone wanted to ask?

Harry: Everyone was just curious. You see, the Mattachine Society was really not the first of its kind, but, in the groups before, everyone would just drop out after five meetings or so. We needed a vehicle by which to get people to come together.

Owen: What was it?

Harry: We started to talk to each other, specifically about the Kinsey Report [on male sexuality], and we began to realize we had more in common with each other than we had with our families. It was exciting, and all of a sudden no one wanted to miss a meeting. We wanted to know each other's experience, and a brotherhood was beginning to develop. At that point, we weren't thinking politically; we were thinking about who we were and what we had in common.

Owen: What happened with the Mattachine Society?

Harry: In the Mattachine Society, we were doing what would later be termed "consciousness raising" or "peer counseling," only, in those years, we didn't have phrases like that or even concepts like that; but after the organization won a case on an entrapment charge, we were inundated with guys that were right of center—and we were all left of center. We were inundated with the first wave of assimilationists. They didn't believe in the brotherhood. What they wanted to do was get the law changed and then everyone could just settle down and be happy, but they didn't give a damn about the brotherhood.

Owen: In addition to your many achievements, weren't you the first person to put forth gays as a cultural minority as well?

Harry: Yes. My insistence on that was what finally got me pounded out of the Mattachine Society in 1953. The wonderful thing about that was, when Stonewall came about 16 years later, all the people assumed we'd thought of ourselves as a cultural minority since day one.

Owen: How did the concept of "cultural minority" come to you?

Harry: I was an educator and I loved theory, and one was the theory of a national minority that was a common language, a common territory and economy, and a common psychological makeup that manifests itself in a common community or culture. Anyway, we had them all except a common economy, which would have made us a nation, but, with three out of the four characteristics, from a left point of view we had a cultural minority. We needed to recognize we had these things in common and have them work for us and not against us.

Owen: You were an actor in the 1930s. What was gay Hollywood like in that decade?

Harry: Most places had one naked bulb, and you really couldn't see the people across the bar from you. In other words, it was a form of cruising indoors. Gay Hollywood was a series of very well-covered-up cliques. They were all over the city, but none of them ever knew each other. And you never brought anyone you cruised to your clique. He could be a front man for the cops.

Owen: How did you meet your mentor and onetime lover Will "Grandpa Walton" Geer?

Harry: When I met Will, he was the leading man in a show I was cast in, called *The Ticket of Leave Man*. Will was so wonderful, I used to sit in the wings every night and just moon over his performance. At that time he was one of those sort-of-ugly men who could be gorgeously sexy.

Owen: Wasn't Will Geer the person who introduced you to the Communist Party?

Harry: He was indeed. He wasn't terribly interested in theory. He didn't know a great deal about Marxism. He was very much caught up in the romanticism of the struggle but was never very strong on theory. I'm the opposite; I have to know everything I'm doing, or I have trouble with it. During this time, I tried to interest him in my theory of the brotherhood, but he just couldn't see it or understand why.

Owen: You were married to a woman with whom you had compatible ideological beliefs even though you were gay. Do you think compatible personalities can conquer sexual differences?

Harry: No. No, they can't. She knew about everything. I told her. You must understand, this was in the late 1930s, and in the 1930s we were just starting to get Jung and Freud in English. We didn't have anything written down on us. I was looking for someone who would fight with me and stand with me on the shared principles of the CIO and the Communist Party. So, I went to the first Jungian to open an office in Los Angeles, and he said to me, "Maybe you're not looking for a girlish boy; maybe you're looking for a boyish girl." Whenever someone asks a question in two parts, always answer the first part and never the second. I answered the second. I desperately, desperately needed to find a compatible, charming and magnificent companion—she was that. Only, after the second or third time we were together, I had to visualize a man.

Owen: Back in 1967 you said on television, "Gays should reject society's negative stereotypes and insist on defining themselves." Do you feel much progress has been made in that direction?

Harry: Yes, I do. I think the contributions especially on the stage with people like Harvey Fierstein and the marvelous gender-fuck of The Cockettes—there are so many wonderful people, and they all show we have an enormous amount to contribute. There was a marvelous story in the *Gay Community News* on the OutWrite speakers, and one of them was a fine lesbian sister by the name of Dorothy Allison who spoke of herself as an outlaw, and I thought, "Oh, goodness, I have to write her. I feel the same way."

Owen: What exactly is your definition of an outlaw?

Harry: Outside the system. When I was 8, I understood this for the first time. The guys all told me I threw a ball like a girl, so I asked the girls if I threw a ball like a girl, and they said, "No, you throw a ball like a sissy." The point is, as far as the boys were concerned, sissy and girl are the same thing, but as far as the girls are concerned the two are very different. If you had that experience and believed what the boys said, then you bought your first sexist remark. The girls would have told you the truth; you are neither masculine nor feminine. The neitherness is who we are, and the neitherness is our power, and out of the neitherness comes our contribution.

Owen: You've spent a great part of your life sifting through gay history. Why do you think gays and lesbians have been constantly oppressed throughout history?

Harry: We have to look at organized religion as a way to control populations. And we are the one people willing to go to the gallows to do the different thing that we do. So, consequently, we are a threat at all times to the established authority. We have been persecuted because, in effect, we gave them the middle finger. We are going to do what we want, even if we have to burn for it, and we have. This is another definition of the outlaw. …

Don't forget, we are the people that can have dreams for which we don't yet have words. Maybe my accomplishment has been to find some of those words.

[This interview is from the July 1992 edition of Outlines, *a Chicago gay newspaper that later merged with* Windy City Times. *It also appears in Owen Keehnen's 2011 book,* We're Here, We're Queer: The Gay '90s and Beyond.*]*

Harry Hay, circa 1980s in San Francisco.
Photo by Rink

Outlines **newspaper in Chicago ran this double feature on Harry Hay and on Phyllis Lyon and Del Martin, both interviews by Owen Keehnen, in July 1992.**

7

Del Martin and Phyllis Lyon

By Owen Keehnen

Del Martin and Phyllis Lyon embodied both a life of service and the concept of enduring love. They met in 1950 and started their relationship in 1952. In 1955, they were among eight San Francisco–based women who were looking for an alternative to the dangerous bar scene of entrapment and raids. They formed what began as a social club, creating the Daughters of Bilitis, the first known lesbian organization in the U.S. The name was from the poem "Song of Bilitis," by Pierre Louÿs, about a lesbian living on the isle of Lesbos with Sappho.

Though the group was originally intended to be social, the Daughters quickly became involved in the gay-and-lesbian-rights movement, focusing on education (both among lesbians and the general public), building self-esteem (since being gay or lesbian at the time was considered sick, demented and criminal), advocating legal rights, and publishing the monthly newsletter, *The Ladder*. Martin and Lyon were also the first out lesbian couple to join the National Organization for Women, and in 1967 Martin was the first open lesbian to be elected to a position within the organization. The couple remained extremely active in politics on both local and national levels—both of them even served on the White House Council on Aging in 1995.

In February 2004, they became the first couple officially married in the city they loved, San Francisco. Sadly, the validity of that marriage was overturned by the courts later that year. The couple were remarried in June 2008. Once again they were given the honor of having the first legally recognized same-sex wedding in San Francisco.

Two months later, on August 27, 2008, at age 87, Del Martin died from complications resulting from a bone fracture in her arm.

The occasion for this 1992 interview with the couple was the 20th-anniversary edition of their 1972 groundbreaking book, *Lesbian/Woman*, republished by Volcano Press. The book is an all-encompassing and thoughtful overview of lesbian life in the 20th century and was very illuminating for the time. The new edition was updated to show the influence of the gay and lesbian liberation and consciousness movement in the U.S.

Owen: What was your initial purpose with starting the Daughters of Bilitis?

Del: When we first started, it was a very secret lesbian social group. We had parties at each other's houses and discussion groups. We avoided the bars, which were frequently raided.

Phyllis: That was in 1955.

Owen: What were the bars like then?

Phyllis: Actually, they were all right, outside of the police problem. They were not usually in a better part of town. There was dancing but no touching.

Owen: Were you aware at the time you were a part of the gay and lesbian movement?

Del: There was no movement. Everyone was very much in the closet and had great difficulty meeting people. Actually, Phyllis and I had been very isolated until someone asked us if we wanted to get in on this private social club. We said yes.

Phyllis: When we did start the Daughters of Bilitis we didn't know there were any other organizations. We subsequently discovered the Mattachine Society had started, as well as ONE, Inc., in LA. At that point, that's all there was.

Owen: Can you describe the first meeting of the Daughters of Bilitis?

Phyllis: Those first meetings were just us getting together to discuss what we were going to do and how we were going to do it. By the fourth or fifth meeting, we realized we had to reach out and get other people.

Owen: Was everyone just mainly curious about meeting other lesbians?

Phyllis: Oh, sure. In 1955, there were no papers or anything.

Del: There were purges in the government and the services and police raids. It was a very scary time.

Phyllis: People were living in real fear.

Del: And if you were caught in a raid, your name and address would be in the paper.

Phyllis: Sometimes they would call your employer as well. So that was the social climate. In the first official meeting, other than the eight of us, we had three additional people.

Owen: So if that was the climate, did you have a pledge or oath of secrecy or a way to check out people?

Phyllis: No, we didn't. We were naïve. We didn't assume that there would be spies, not for a while.

Owen: I guess I'm just paranoid.

Phyllis: Well, later on we thought about it.

Del: In fact, later on we learned we had been infiltrated by the CIA and FBI.

Owen: So what were some things the Daughters of Bilitis did as a political as well as a social group?

Del: We were really pretty scared, which isn't surprising since we were faced with the fact that we were considered to be illegal, immoral and sick. Before you have a movement, you have to have some self-esteem, so we had to work on that and to allay fears. We had professional people come and talk to us about the law and things we needed to know. Mainly, though, we needed to gain self-esteem and self-acceptance.

Phyllis: Just the fact that we got started was a political act.

Owen: It must have taken an amazing amount of courage just to meet.

Del: We heard many tales, after we acquired an office, of people who came down to the office building who were afraid to come inside or stood across the street and took weeks or months or maybe never to get to the office.

Phyllis: A year after starting, we still didn't have many members and decided we had to do something, so we started what we thought to be a newsletter called *The Ladder*. Also, in October 1956, we started public discussions, and that was how we got people to come talk to us about our rights. They told us things like—that we didn't have to plead guilty to something just because we were gay. That's what was happening—people felt so guilty about being gay that they would plead guilty to whatever the police said. Also, what public meetings did was give lesbians the chance to come in as "the public" and see if they wanted anything more to do with us. So both those things, *The Ladder* and the public meetings, really helped the Daughters of Bilitis get out into the world, but in a still-secret way.

Owen: Something like *The Ladder*, too, could provide a voice and maybe a bit of identity.

Phyllis: Yes, exactly.

Owen: Was it monthly?

Phyllis: Yes, monthly.

Owen: How do you think World War II affected lesbian consciousness?

Phyllis: The opportunities increased; there were suddenly so many opportunities that weren't around before. For a lot of women, it was a means of getting away from their homes and the little towns they were in and see the world and meet more women. I don't know if it brought lesbian visibility up, outside of the fact that so many of them got thrown out of the service, sometimes without even knowing themselves [that they were lesbians] but because they "appeared to be." What it did was land a lot of lesbians in San Francisco and other large cities, where the beginning of, not really a community, but the beginning of lesbian and gay activity could occur.

Owen: Del, you proposed the NOW resolution for lesbians?

Del: I didn't propose it. What happened was, there had been a lot of internal warfare in New York NOW around the lesbian presence in the National Organization for Women. Aileen Hernandez succeeded Betty Friedan as national president of NOW. In 1971, when she [Hernandez] was president, the national convention had been held in LA. She allowed Phyllis and me to convene a lesbian workshop.

There had been resolutions that had come from Atlanta, Detroit and San Francisco. The LA chapter had written this beautiful position paper about why lesbians should be included as feminists and that our rights were of concern to women. We were having a workshop, and we kept having so many sign up that we kept postponing it until finally we had the main ballroom. Phyllis and I had to be referees in this big debate, and most of the people there were in favor of our cause. So, one woman stood up and said, "Let's make the LA paper our resolution," which we did.

Owen: *Lesbian/Woman* has come out in a 20th-anniversary edition from Volcano Press. What was your original intention in writing the book?

Phyllis: Originally, we wanted to write a book about lesbians. We hoped it would be a vehicle of education to non-lesbians as well, which it was to a certain degree.

Del: It was also a vehicle of education for lesbians all over the country and, in many instances, also helped their parents understand.

Phyllis: Interestingly, it was also of value to young gay men who were struggling with coming out.

Owen: Why was the time right to update it?

Del: It had been out of print for several years, and apparently there had been some requests to get it back in print.

Phyllis: From bookstores, too. That was the reason. We also felt in rereading it that although some of it was dated, many of the things that were happening to lesbians in 1972 were still happening to lesbians in 1992 in many areas of the country.

Del: In looking at the update, an interesting difference between them is, in the first part of the original every name we use is a pseudonym. In the second one, everyone uses their real name, so in many ways that shows how much has happened in the past 20 years.

Phyllis: When we wrote the original, we didn't even ask people if they wanted their real names used. We assumed they wouldn't want that done and used pseudonyms for everyone.

Del: I think the update shows the strides and advancements we've made in the past 20 years despite the religious crusades against us. People ought to be aware that although there is all this negativism, we have been steadily making advances.

Owen: It's amazing from a historical perspective.

Phyllis: I don't know of any parallel of there being so much change so rapidly. Moving from being so in the closet you were afraid to even tell yourself you were a lesbian to being elected to the New York Legislature.

Owen: How long have you two been together?

Del: 39 years.

Owen: What's your secret to your enduring relationship?

Phyllis: Everyone wants to know that! We've known each other so long—our ideas are similar, we like many of the same things, we come from the same background, but mostly because we are very much in love with each other.

Del: We were friends [first] before we moved in together. Phyllis was a "straight lesbian" for a while.

Phyllis [laughing]: I was a little slow. We're talking about the late 1940s, early 1950s. I knew nothing about it. In those times, we didn't talk about sex, period.

Del: Even if you knew the words and went to the library, all the literature was so negative. There was no way you could identify with the people they were describing.

Phyllis: When *Lesbian/Woman* came out, and this was as late as 1972, there were very few books dealing with lesbian or gay-male issues. Now you've got so much, of course.

Owen: What advice do you have for today's activist groups?

Del: There's a lot of talk about a need to unify, and I think we tend to do that when there's a crisis—but I think we have to be less critical of other groups that are using tactics that we might not personally use. No one group has the answer to all our needs. To bring about change, we need to use all perspectives.

Phyllis: We need to face problems from every direction possible.

Del: Then people can choose what works best for them.

Phyllis: I also think we need to keep going—keep moving forward in education, politically, legally and so on. We need to never forget that we need to keep educating the general public.

Del: Coming out is also important. Those who know gays or lesbians personally tend to support us. Those so adamantly opposed to us tend to be people who to their knowledge have not met any gay or lesbian people. You don't have to come out in a newspaper or on television—just come out to people. Another thing that is so wonderful that's happened in the past 20 years is that we've become an international movement, which is just amazing to us coming from the '50s. We really can't believe that all this is happening.

[This interview is from the July 1992 edition of Outlines *newspaper, a Chicago gay newspaper that later merged with* Windy City Times. *It also appears in Owen Keehnen's 2011 book,* We're Here, We're Queer: The Gay '90s and Beyond.*]*

Top: Phyllis Lyon and Del Martin in Chicago, 2007.
Photo by Tracy Baim

Del Martin and Phyllis Lyon in Chicago, 2005.
Photo by Mel Ferrand

8

Jack Nichols

By Owen Keehnen and Tracy Baim

Jack Nichols was among the most significant journalists of the gay liberation movement. His tireless work on behalf of the Mattachine Society of Washington, his efforts to bring the issue of gay rights to a national public consciousness, his work to unify community members and incite gay pride, his participation in the campaign to remove homosexuality from the list of psychiatric disorders, and merely living his life as an out gay man since the early 1960s have combined to make us better as a result of his efforts.

In the final years of his life, Nichols jumped fully into the Internet in his writing and editing for GayToday.com. Before he died of cancer at age 67 in 2005, Nichols released a sexy memoir, *The Tomcat Chronicles: Erotic Adventures From a Gay Liberation Pioneer*. Clearly this man was just as passionate and outspoken about sex as he was about his politics.

Jack Nichols, Gay Pioneer, by J. Louis Campbell III, is a 2007 book that wonderfully chronicles his life. Here is a brief summary of all that Nichols accomplished:

— In 1961, he co-founded the Mattachine Society of Washington with Frank Kameny (this group was independent of the national Mattachine Society). The group produced publications, first the *Gazette*, and later *The Homosexual Citizen*.

— In 1965, he co-founded the Mattachine Society of Florida.

— In April 1965, Nichols was an organizer of the first gay protest march in front of the White House. This was the first of a series of government protests of which he was part.

— From 1965 to 1969 he was in the Annual Reminder Day pickets held in front of Independence Hall in Philadelphia.

— He was among a few key individuals pushing for change in the categorizing of gays as mentally ill by the American Psychiatric Association.

— In 1967 he was among the first gay Americans to appear on national TV, on the sensational "The Homosexuals" episode of *CBS Reports*, a show hosted by Mike Wallace. While he used his pseudonym, Warren D. Adkins (because his dad was in the FBI and had threatened him), Nichols still was pictured—another gay man was shown in shadows behind a plant.

— In 1968, Nichols and his partner, Lige Clarke, started the "Homosexual Citizen" column for the straight *SCREW* sex magazine, beginning with its first issue of November 3. This was the first LGBT column in a non-LGBT publication. It ran until 1973. (Nichols was also editor of *SCREW*.)

— In April 1968, Nichols and Clarke started a "New York Notes" column for *The Advocate*.

— In 1969, Nichols and Clarke were not in town for the Stonewall rebellion, but they soon jumped on the story (for *SCREW* and then also for *The Advocate*).

— In 1969, the owners of *SCREW* put up the funds for Nichols and Clarke to start *GAY*. The new publication switched to weekly for a brief time, making it the first gay weekly in the U.S. *GAY* published columns by Dr. George Weinberg, who coined the word "homophobia." Lesbian pioneer Kay (Tobin) Lahusen was the paper's first news editor. *GAY* competed with *Gay Power*, produced by *Kiss*, a tabloid that competed with *SCREW*. *GAY* started as a biweekly on November 15, 1969 (the issue may have been dated December 1 according to WorldCat), and then went weekly from April 20 to September 28, 1970. Nichols and Clarke left after the July 1973 issue when their request for more money for the staff was denied. WorldCat shows the last issue was June 1974. *GAY* was not a free publication like some other gay papers; the first issue sold 20,000 copies and, two issues later, they were at 25,000.

— In 1997, Nichols began his last media adventure, moving him into the Internet revolution. He worked at GayToday.com from February 3, 1997, to September 30, 2004.

What follows are excerpts from a 2004 interview with Nichols by Owen Keehnen, taken from Keehnen's book, *We're Here, We're Queer*.

Owen: *The Tomcat Chronicles* is an erotic memoir of your life from 1960 to '64. Why did you choose to narrow your focus to these years?

Jack: I wrote *The Tomcat Chronicles* as a series in 1991 for *Contax*, Florida's statewide bar guide. The publisher, Bill Watson, also founded *TWN* (*The Weekly News*), the state's oldest gay newspaper. He asked me if I'd be willing to pen some erotic stories for *Contax*, assuring me I could use a pen name. But I told him I'd gladly use my own name and that I'd give him true accounts of my own experiences.

I asked him, "At what age would you like me to begin, when I was 11?" I could almost hear him cringe on the phone. So, instead, I decided to begin when I was 23, a period during which I'd initiated and participated in a very wild spree, hitchhiking with a handsome hillbilly across the eastern part of the USA. The wild spree began to subside in January 1963, and in mid-1964 I met another mountain man, Lige Clarke, the beautiful creature whose upside-down-backside-out yoga photo appears on the cover of the book. Lige, the movement pioneer who incarnated my fondest hopes and dreams, spent the next decade at my side until he was gunned down in automatic fire at a mysterious roadblock in February 1975 [in Mexico].

Owen: The tales in your book are very hot. Did you have any qualms about the degree of sexual explicitness?

Jack: I'm among those who see an America still suffering miserably from its anti-sexual Puritan heritage. In recalling my own sexual experiences, I had the advantage of writing about them in hindsight, showing how I developed my sexual viewpoints. Today I'm a staunch and unrelenting advocate of condoms. Qualms? Ha! In 1969, I was the very first managing editor of *SCREW*, the world's most outrageous, mostly straight, sexual tabloid, published by Al Goldstein. It was first on the newsstands to carry frontal nudes. In 1977 and '78, I was also editor of the then-oldest mass-circulation sex-therapy magazine, *Sexology*.

Owen: Did you worry sexcapades would detract from the gay political history you also discuss in the book?

Jack: Very few early movement strategists admitted that the word "sex" appears in the middle of the word "homosexual." I look to a future in which sex is appreciated as a positive rather than a negative aspect of our lives. Feelings of sexual shame and guilt do great damage. The introduction to *The Tomcat Chronicles* was written by the scholar-historian James T. Sears, who first suggested that they be turned into a book showing that not all activists favor a sexually sanitized movement.

Owen: Something that's striking about this memoir is how positive you were about being gay and gay sex at the time. What factors do you think helped you avoid so many of the prevailing stigmas and self-hatred of the time?

Jack: I was, no doubt, precocious. I came out at 13 and became a full-fledged self-accepting gay teen after reading the poet Walt Whitman at age 15 and works by Edward Carpenter, the grandfather of gay liberation, as well as Donald Webster Cory's groundbreaking book, *The Homosexual in America*. As early as 1955, I was sharing Cory's book with my gay friends who attended high school.

Owen: I liked how *The Tomcat Chronicles* almost made you a self-taught sex therapist for a lot of your tricks. Do you consider it as a sort of fieldwork for your more structured activism in the years following?

Jack: You got it: I'm self-taught. I graduated only from sixth grade. But by the time I was 20 I owned nearly a thousand works of philosophy. Walt Whitman became my literary mentor, and my movement work was simply a natural outcome of old Walt's activist advice. I've always thought that ideas by themselves are invisible unless we bring them into the arena of action.

Owen: How would you characterize the underground gay world in those pre-Stonewall years? It sounded much more extensive and connected than I imagined.

Jack: Well, there was no dancing, no hugging, no kisses allowed in the few [New York] city bars. There were, of course, two or three creaky old bathhouses like the Everard in Manhattan, and you've read in *The Tomcat Chronicles* about Miami's odd little backyard bar, Googies, where one day "the bushes" were eliminated by what locals called an act of God, a tornado. Cruising in city parks or around the Greyhound bus stations was endemic.

Most gay folks were very proper and extremely closeted, and everywhere there was a great deal of sexual shame and guilt. Cory's book introduced me to the fact that the worst effect for those treated as criminals and discriminated against was to make these people doubt themselves, sharing society's general contempt for others in their group.

Owen: In the early 1960s you also worked with the Mattachine Society, for gay civil rights and to have being gay removed from the list of psychological disorders … . What about the political climate of the era is wise for activists to keep in mind today?

Jack: Between 1960 and 1967, when Frank Kameny and I would discuss our activist strategies with most other gay males in Washington, D.C., they just shrugged, telling us we'd never succeed. Frank and I—and just a few other activists—were considered radicals by many of our conservative movement cohorts because we insisted on taking a strong stand against the mental-health professionals who'd labeled us sick. Those same movement conservatives also damned us for initiating the first picketing protest demonstrations at the White House. Today, I'd say, it is wise to remember that the conservatives we [will] have with us always.

Owen: And how did your activism continue in the following years?

Jack: When I moved in 1967 from Washington, D.C., to Manhattan, I was the sales manager for Underground Uplift Unlimited, the nation's largest producer of those counterculture slogan buttons that everybody was wearing in the '60s: buttons with sexual-freedom slogans such as "More Deviation, Less Population," or "Make Love, Not War." I think these buttons changed more minds than books did.

Then, in 1968, in its first issue, *SCREW* hosted a weekly column I co-wrote with Lige Clarke titled "Homosexual Citizen." It was the first time that a rampantly straight publication had published an uncensored gay column, and we kept it going for five years. At nearly the same time, Lige and I edited America's first gay weekly newspaper, *GAY*, which hosted all of the gay pioneers and crusaders of those times.

In 1972, Lige and I wrote *I Have More Fun With You Than Anybody*, published by St. Martin's Press, history's first nonfiction memoir by a male couple. It was humorous and philosophical and thus very well-received. Next, St. Martin's coaxed us to write the first nonfiction book of advice about male relationships, one in which we replied to actual letters from our readers. It was titled *Roommates Can't Always Be Lovers*. After Lige's murder, I wrote *Welcome to Fire Island*, which celebrates gay communities in the Pines and in Cherry Grove.

In 1975, my major work was published by Penguin Books—*Men's Liberation: A New Definition of Masculinity*. It examines the drawbacks of conventional male role-training—machismo—and it went into German and Greek and into several university textbooks. It's aimed at both straights and gays. I did quite a bit of men's-movement work throughout the 1970s.

In the 1980s I kept a weekly flow of columns going into gay papers in Miami and Atlanta, and between 1986 and 1991 I crusaded in Florida for Cure AIDS Now, an AIDS activist group that generated quite a bit of national publicity. I organized noisy protests against Jerry Falwell and Ronald Reagan. For the Reagan protest I dressed as Death, carrying a sign with an ostrich on it and reading: "Reagan Ignoramus = AIDS." In 1996 my book *The Gay Agenda: Talking Back to the Fundamentalists* was published by Prometheus Books. It beats up on religious fanaticism.

Owen: Do you consider your current work as editor of the Internet magazine GayToday. com an extension of your activism as well?

Jack: Oh, sure. And I'm thankful to the huge gay website, Badpuppy.com, for originating GayToday as a free news service for its readers and for others. The Badpuppy staff rediscovered me here in this little beach town where I live and where I'd never expected to be rediscovered. They literally knocked on my door, and thus I've been an editor again for almost eight years. The Badpuppy folks chose the newsmagazine's name, GayToday, and thus it seemed slightly mystical that after co-editing the original *GAY* 30 years ago, I'm now editing GayToday.

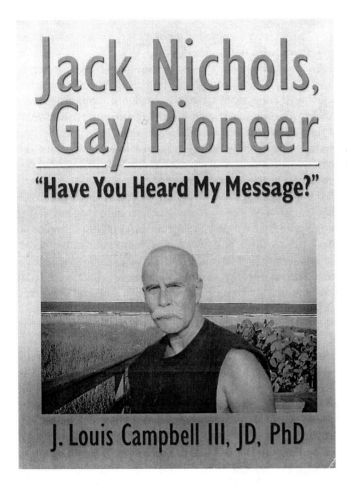

Jack Nichols, Gay Pioneer **came out in 2006 from Routledge.**

9

Activism, Journalism and the Changing of the Guard

By Allen Young

When I was 13 and a student in the eighth grade in 1954, my social-studies teacher, William Biel, started a unit called "Mass Media of Communication." Around the same time, I was teaching myself to type, and I undertook a class journal as my project for this unit. My goal was to write up the news about our class and our school each day.

This was my introduction to journalism, and I've been writing, mostly in a journalistic style, ever since. The next big step for me came about a year later, when a senior at my school, Fallsburg Central High, was looking for someone to succeed him as school sports writer for the *Evening News Weekly*, published in the nearby Sullivan County seat of Monticello, New York. Somehow, probably guided by faculty members, the senior found me and passed the baton.

Starting in the fall of my sophomore year, at age 15, and for the rest of my days at Fallsburg Central, I wrote for the *Evening News Weekly*, not only sports but also a school news column and occasionally even front-page news stories about scholastic or teenage life. I was thrilled to have a byline and to be paid five cents a column inch.

I can't really say who instructed me on journalistic style, but I do recall that one of the young editors of the *Evening News*, Alan Eisner, took time to improve my skills. He later went on to be a reporter and editor for *Newsday* on Long Island.

In many ways, I was self-taught. My parents, who wrote some personal letters and not much else, encouraged my interests and sometimes even criticized my writing. Perhaps I had natural writing ability the way some people have natural musical talent. I was an avid reader, though my parents did not subscribe to any daily newspaper except perhaps the *Daily Worker*, the Communist Party organ. The only publication I am certain I read with any regularity was a left-wing weekly, the *National Guardian*. My school bus driver used to let me read his newspaper: New York's *Daily News*, a right-leaning tabloid not well-regarded by either my parents or journalism professors. I did not become familiar with *The New York Times* until I was a college student.

In high school, I became sports editor of the school paper, *The Comet*, and our yearbook, *Focus*. But it was my involvement with the *Evening News Weekly* that made me a "real" journalist.

In my applications to college, I put much emphasis on my interest in journalism as a career, and when I arrived at Columbia College (the men's undergraduate division of Columbia University) in New York City in the fall of 1958, one of the first things I did was sign up for the staff of the *Columbia Daily Spectator*. My ambition was clear to me at the outset: to become the editor-in-chief of *Spectator*.

As a budding journalist in the late 1950s, I became familiar with the technology of the day. If I were to hear a recording today of the sound of a Linotype machine or a flatbed printing press such as the ones used in the production of the Monticello *Evening News* or *Spectator*, I would recognize those sounds immediately, though more than a half-century has passed. You'd be hard-pressed to find actual working machinery like this anywhere in the United States today, in the era of computerized typography and offset printing.

I was an eager-beaver reporter at *Spectator*, starting immediately in my freshman year, and I honed my journalistic skills under the guidance of the brilliant and energetic upperclassmen who ran *Spectator*. The daily newspapers of the Ivy League had a rich tradition of connections to the world of real journalism, and I found that exciting. Famed former *Spectator* editors included James Wechsler, the outspoken liberal editor of the *New York Post*; Reed Harris, who had been expelled from Columbia for his editorials and who later battled against Senator Joseph McCarthy (R-Wisconsin); Max Frankel, *New York Times* reporter; and Theodore Bernstein, assistant editor of *The New York Times* and author of an outstanding journalism textbook.

I loved being a reporter, and I covered many interesting stories for *Spectator*, including speeches by visiting personalities, sports events and internal Columbia University politics. When I was chosen as editor-in-chief at the end of my junior year, and my best friend and (secret) lover Eric Levine was named managing editor, we were both thrilled at this not-unexpected turn of events.

Being editor-in-chief of *Spectator* put me in a position to mix journalism and activism for the first time. A group of red-diaper babies (children of Communist parents) at Columbia, under the leadership of Eric Foner, started an organization called ACTION. Eric, who later became a nationally recognized historian and a chair professor at Columbia, was the son of Jack Foner, who had lost his job at City College of New York in the McCarthy era.

Spectator under my leadership supported ACTION by publicizing many of its activities on the front page; another editor-in-chief might have ignored this small organization. The most memorable of these activities was a civil-disobedience action against a scheduled air-raid drill. Supported by faculty members who signed a statement rejecting the practice of air-raid drills (which required everyone to go to marked fallout shelters on the campus or at least to remain indoors), ACTION urged students to gather outside in the center of the campus when the sirens sounded—defying the law and risking arrest.

The political argument was that such drills made survival in a nuclear war seem feasible, and thus promoted the idea that nuclear war was thinkable, rather than unthinkable. There were hundreds who joined the Columbia campus demonstration, which was one of several similar actions in major cities. This widespread refusal to cooperate with air-raid drills soon put an end to the practice.

I continued to link my political views to journalism, and an event in Latin America during my college years helped shape my career goals. On New Year's Day in 1959, the Cuban Revolution led by Fidel Castro succeeded in ousting the U.S.-backed dictator Fulgencio Batista. As the new Cuban regime took shape and presented itself as an independent, free-wheeling vehicle for social change, I decided to learn Spanish and shape myself into a foreign correspondent specializing in Latin American affairs.

In my first year of graduate school, at the Stanford University Institute of Hispanic American and Luso-Brazilian Studies, I worked on the monthly *Hispanic American Report* and obtained a master's degree. My writing on current events in Cuba and Colombia, based mostly on secondary sources such as newspaper clippings, was highly politicized, following the lead of the institute's director, Ronald Hilton, a Briton who was highly critical of U.S. foreign policy and sympathetic to Latin American leftists. I also learned Portuguese so that I could be effective in covering Latin America's largest nation, Brazil.

The following summer, I had my first full-time job as a professional journalist, working as a reporter for the Middletown, New York, *Times Herald–Record*, a newspaper that had made history by being the first American daily newspaper to be printed by the offset method. I covered many interesting stories, ranging from the status of onion farming in nearby Florida, New York, to the usual crimes and fires.

Two incidents from that summer stick with me: a homicide and an important historic event. In the first case, the torso of a dead body was found, and I was interviewing police outside the building where an autopsy was being performed. A state trooper told me that the smell was horrible but he also invited me to go inside to see for myself. I declined, feeling a mixture of pride in myself, for not being manipulated by the cop who probably wanted to see the local "Jimmy Olsen" throw up, and guilt, for not being a "go for everything" reporter.

The other memorable occasion was the March on Washington in August 1963, where Martin Luther King gave his "I have a dream" speech. I traveled with my then-girlfriend Susan Carey on a bus, with African-Americans (still called Negroes at the time) and some white sympathizers from Middletown, to the nation's capital. My article about the march, stressing the local angle, made the front page. If it hadn't been for my own political inclinations that led me to express an interest in going on the march, I'm sure the editors of the *Times Herald–Record* would have settled for wire-service coverage.

The next year, at the Columbia University Graduate School of Journalism, I honed my craft under the direction of the school's dedicated and excellent faculty, and I was influenced by the many fine young journalists who were my classmates. I also landed a coveted position at *The New York Times*, as stringer or campus correspondent from Columbia.

If you look up *The New York Times* issue reporting the assassination of John F. Kennedy, you will find a reference to bells tolling on the Columbia campus, a small incident taken from my memo to a reporter working on the story. In the same November 23, 1963, edition of the *Times*, there also is my full-length article based on an interview with Columbia's head of counseling, who was commenting on a Harvard-based controversy about premarital sex on college campuses. I remember arriving at the *Times* newsroom the day of the assassination and asking the assignment editor if he still wanted me to write up the campus sex story, and he replied, with some annoyance, that of course he wanted the story because Kennedy's death was not the only news of the day.

As one would expect at the nation's leading journalism school, objectivity was touted as an important value. Despite my left-wing views, this insistence on objectivity did not bother me, as I intuitively favored fairness in my writing. However, while I clearly was capable of writing a balanced news story, I also realized that there were ways I could slant the news to suit my own views and might choose to do so. I maintained my interest in Latin America and, as the school year ended in the spring of 1964, I applied for and received two scholarships that paved the way for me to spend the next three years as a freelance journalist in Latin America.

While in Brazil on a Fulbright scholarship (administered and funded under the U.S. State Department), and then in Chile on a scholarship from the Inter-American Press Association, I wrote dozens of newspaper articles on many topics. As a freelancer, I could pick and choose, though occasionally I received assignments. Most of my articles were published in *The New York Times* and *The Christian Science Monitor*. I also wrote for The Associated Press, *The Patriot Ledger* of Quincy, Massachusetts, and some small socialist periodicals. There were numerous articles published in *The New York Times* travel section, and mostly political and human-interest articles in the *Monitor*. For the last of three years in Latin America, I was an English teacher at the American School in Rio de Janeiro and also continued my freelancing. It also was in Brazil in 1964 that I finally accepted myself fully as a gay man, and stopped my efforts at being heterosexual.

Those years, 1964–67, involved major escalation of the U.S. intervention in Vietnam, and I was often outspoken among my Latin American friends about my opposition to the war and about my sympathy for the Cuban Revolution. But on other occasions, I did not reveal those views, as I felt discretion was the better part of valor.

So infatuated was I with Brazil and the gay men I was meeting that I considered becoming an expatriate. However, as I met and talked with professional journalists about my career goals, I concluded that my future as a foreign correspondent required me to return to the United States to get an actual job with a news organization and work my way up. So in the summer of 1967, I came back to the United States and began job-hunting in earnest. I set my sights high and applied to four newspapers: *The Christian Science Monitor*, *The New York Times*, the *Los Angeles Times* and *The*

Washington Post. I was interviewed at all four papers but was offered a job only at one: the *Post*.

The *Post*'s city editor, Stephen Isaacs, was about to hire me but told me that the final stamp of approval had to be given by the managing editor, Ben Bradlee, who later became nationally known when the *Post* excelled in covering the Watergate scandal. When Bradlee asked me about my interests, I hid my left-wing political background and inclinations but mentioned "civil rights," and he responded sharply with a question, "You aren't one of those activists, are you?" I lied, saying that of course I wasn't, and I got the job.

I moved into a rather sterile but comfortable studio apartment in the Adams-Morgan section of Washington, just the sort of place that a young bachelor might choose (though "bachelor" is not a word I've ever used for myself).

I was 26 years old and riding high, starting to work for one of the nation's most prestigious newspapers. My first assignment was the night police beat, with occasional opportunity to write obituaries and other local news. One news story was not assigned to me but was my initiative based on personal friendship with a Columbia classmate, Philip Stein. Phil and his wife, Phyllis, who lived in a nearby suburb, were pioneers offering instruction in the Lamaze method of natural childbirth, which, in 1967, was both offbeat and newsworthy.

At the *Post*, I knew I would have to work my way up through police beat, metropolitan news, perhaps some aspect of the federal government, and finally a chance to be sent abroad as a foreign correspondent. While I enjoyed the work, doubts quickly enveloped me. The Vietnam anti-war movement was growing. I wanted to be a part of it, yet knew that my job precluded that.

In October 1967, I got together with several of my old friends from New York City and attended a large anti-war demonstration at the Pentagon, but I had to leave early to go to work. As a reporter for the city desk, I wrote an article for the *Post* the next day about protesters who were arrested and jailed. I did not like the feeling of being an objective observer when I was not. Despite some anxiety about my job security, I attended the march; I knew that if Ben Bradlee had seen me marching I would have been fired.

At the police station each night, I suffered an experience I found humiliating and contradictory. The cops despised the *Post*, seeing it as left-wing. They called it the "L Street *Pravda*," a reference to the street where the *Post* was located and to the official organ of the Communist Party of the Soviet Union. Those cops couldn't have known it, but I was much more of a communist than anyone at the *Post*! I was hardly one to defend my employer, because to me the *Post* was not particularly left-wing or even liberal, given the mentality of Ben Bradlee and the fact that the *Post* was supporting Lyndon Johnson's Vietnam policies and belittling the anti-war movement.

When trained to do the night police beat, the overtly racist practice of the newspaper became clear to me. In the case of homicides, I was taught to treat deaths in white neighborhoods as more important than deaths in black neighborhoods. I was told to determine if the victim was black or white and to proceed accordingly. If a victim were white, I was to ask many more questions and obtain as much information as possible; if black, just the bare minimal information was adequate for the *Post*'s purposes.

Around the time of the October 1967 Pentagon march, I met the people at the *Washington Free Press*, one of the many so-called underground papers popping up all over America, and I wrote an article for the *Free Press* about my experience as a police reporter (using a pseudonym). I also met Ray Mungo and Marshall Bloom, who had founded Liberation News Service the previous summer. I decided that LNS was a good place for me to be, and I quit the *Post* to join Mungo and Bloom in their enterprise, which soon became known nationwide as a sort of radical hippie version of The Associated Press.

That was probably the biggest single decision of my life, not only as it related to my identity as a journalist, but because it represented a great step toward personal liberation. I knew this on a conscious level; I clearly remember remarking to myself at the time that as a gay man I could never be comfortable in a place such as the *Post*. Although LNS was also a repressive environment for a sexually active gay man such as myself—the unspoken assumption was universal heterosexuality—change was in the air even in those pre-Stonewall years. There was an "old boys" feeling in the *Washington Post* newsroom, and nothing like that in the LNS headquarters at 3 Thomas Circle. Furthermore, Bloom and Mungo were also closeted homosexuals. A frequent visitor to the LNS office in those days (1967–68) was *New Republic* writer Andrew Kopkind, also closeted at that point in his life. Who knew!?

Change Is in the Air

My three-years-plus-a-few-months with LNS, from 1967 to 1971, have always seemed to me the most intense period of my life. Those years incorporated both the anti-war movement during its strongest and most effective times and the first year of the post-Stonewall gay liberation movement.

I defined myself clearly as an activist-journalist during this time and could not have been more dedicated or hard-working. I helped to promote the anti-war movement through analytical articles about government policy and enthusiastic reports on the often-exciting anti-war demonstrations. Airlines were offering "youth fare" in those days, and there were many opportunities to travel for little money.

I attended meetings of Students for a Democratic Society and visited various campuses, including the University of California in Berkeley, the University of Wisconsin in Madison and the University of Michigan in Ann Arbor. Abbie Hoffman taught me a method of traveling free by forging a boarding pass, though this method worked only on Northwest Airlines. It scared me, but it worked the two or three times I used it.

Using my LNS affiliation, I finagled a free trip to Sofia, Bulgaria, in the summer of 1968 to attend the World Youth Festival, a Soviet-sponsored cultural and political gathering. My New Left fervor in Sofia left no time for cruising or making contact with other gays. Now, as a gay man familiar with the role of gay men in the arts, it seems shameful that I didn't make an effort to meet musicians, dancers and others during the festival. It was all politics for me!

During the time I was there, LNS (which had moved from Washington to New York City) went through a schism typical of many political organizations. Ray Mungo wrote a humorous but self-serving account of this in his popular book, *Famous Long Ago: My Life and Hard Times With Liberation News Service.* Mungo, his colleague Bloom and a few friends "moved" LNS to a farmhouse in Montague, Massachusetts, near Bloom's Amherst alma mater.

The rest of us stayed in the New York City basement near Columbia University and churned out the news for our own version of LNS, rejecting the rural lifestyle option as a form of escapism. (I could not possibly have predicted my own move to rural Massachusetts only a few years later, nor my agreement with these words near the end of Mungo's *Famous Long Ago*: "I wish everyone would pay as much attention to trees as I do ... .")

The writings of Herbert Marcuse, a college professor who became something of a "guru" to the New Left, influenced me politically during that period. His essay "Repressive Tolerance" in a book titled *A Critique of Pure Tolerance* (with Barrington Moore and Robert Paul Wolff), offered philosophical justification for the lack of free speech and free press in socialist countries and belittled the value of the First Amendment in the United States.

Marcuse argued that the majority of the population in the U.S. was politically repressed because workers failed to understand their plight under capitalism. He blamed this on mass media of communication, claiming that the corporate power behind these media outlets essentially prevented alternative viewpoints from breaking through. This argument was very convenient for New Leftists like myself who saw the "establishment media" as the enemy and who continued to defend socialist regimes in Vietnam and Cuba where the press was rigidly controlled and dissent was punished. My travels to Cuba in 1969 and 1971, both times the guest of the Cuban government, were the catalyst for my break with Marcuse's analysis and my renewed respect for the American Bill of Rights.

Although we churned out reams of news and analysis, life with LNS was much less "professional journalism" and much more a lifestyle featuring endless political discussions and communal living.

There wasn't much distinction between play and work, though for several months in 1969 and 1970, the LNS "collective" rented a farmhouse in Fleischmanns, New York, where we enjoyed the rural quiet, punctuated occasionally by our own foolish target practice with a .22 rifle that I owned. This had some fanciful connection to our revolutionary goals, but we were never serious about using guns for anything except target practice.

We had fabulous dinners and occasionally smoked pot and went to movies, and there was a fair amount of boyfriend/girlfriend stuff that did not include me and sometimes made me slightly uncomfortable, in part because I sensed that people saw me as "asexual." Actually, I went to downtown Manhattan on occasion to explore the gay cruising places, but I was in no position to develop a serious relationship. My identity as a gay man remained a secret part of my life until I became involved with the Gay Liberation Front starting in January 1970.

I wish Marshall Bloom, depressed and closeted, had stuck around long enough to benefit from gay liberation. Bloom committed suicide on November 1, 1969. I got the news from Jerry Rubin and Abbie Hoffman in U.S. District Judge Julius Hoffman's courtroom in Chicago, where I was covering the Chicago Seven trial for LNS. Jerry and Abbie, who were wearing black armbands, told me about Marshall's death. It took me a while to figure out that Marshall's repressed sexuality was likely a factor in his decision to take his own life, and later I wrote about Marshall for the Boston gay paper called *Fag Rag*.

Gay Liberation

The emergence of gay liberation took me to a new phase, personally and as a political journalist. I started attending meetings of GLF and, shortly thereafter, departed from LNS. I moved into a gay commune in a big downtown loft owned by textile designer and fellow gay liberationist Carl Miller—and I devoured the new gay periodicals, including *Come Out!* in New York City and *Gay Sunshine* in San Francisco. The writing consisted of a mixture of political diatribes and personal confessions, and not much journalism, but there was quite a bit of interesting and provocative writing.

I didn't really feel comfortable writing for *Come Out!* because I was so new to gay political life. I felt I needed to listen and learn. *Come Out!* didn't survive very long.

I found a home of sorts with *Gay Sunshine*, published in San Francisco but seeking a national audience. The paper's name was a play on words—"sunshine," bringing things out in the sunlight, and orange sunshine, a form of LSD. The post-Stonewall gay movement, for its first year at least, was a pretty drug-oriented crowd, primarily favoring psychedelics and marijuana.

I wrote frequently for *Gay Sunshine*. I liked the format. I interviewed Allen Ginsberg in 1972 for *Gay Sunshine*, and that was later published as a chapbook. *Gay Sunshine* went on to publish many interviews with gay cultural figures, and I added an interview with Elaine Noble.

I was also part of an important living arrangement mixed with politics called The 17th Street Collective, more than just a gay-male commune.

We started putting out our own newsletter called *Gay Flames,* with most of the work done by me and collective member Bob Bland. The paper had a small circulation and a small format. We used to print that, probably on an offset press, then fold and collate the copies and hand them out free. It was mostly distributed on the streets of Greenwich Village. We did a few issues, maybe 15. It was not on a regular schedule.

I put a lot of effort into that and, of course, I was meeting gay liberationists from all over the country. We were communicating, mostly by mail, a little by phone—there was no email in those days—and people came from all over, including Great Britain and Australia.

There were some gatherings where we met people from other places. I met people from Boston who had started *Fag Rag*. I wrote a number of articles for *Fag Rag*. One of the articles I was proudest of was about gentrification. I co-wrote an article about the death of J. Edgar Hoover, "Hoover Goes Underground." We assumed Hoover was homosexual, largely because we knew about his tight relationship with Clyde Tolson, so the article was about powerful homosexual men who are deeply closeted, perhaps sexually active, perhaps totally repressed, who did evil things.

I also started writing for *The Advocate*, a California-based but nationally circulated periodical in a newspaper format at the time, the *Gay Liberator* in Detroit, and the Boston-based *Gay Community News*.

There was also an opportunity to partner with a Boston gay organization that paid a clipping service to clip out any article with the word "homosexual" or "gay" in it. I shared the cost of that so I would get all those articles. That turned me on to some interesting stories that might otherwise have been lost. When Nobel Prize–winning author Pearl S. Buck (*The Good Earth*) died, she left her money to a gay man who was her very close friend and who was assisting her with the work of helping orphans in Asia. In her will, she left most of her money to this man, and her family contested it. I picked that story up for *The Advocate*.

For *The Advocate* I did the following, among others: I covered a gay wedding at a Boston Unitarian church in the 1970s. I covered the Massachusetts candidacy of Elaine Noble, who was the first openly gay or lesbian person to win a state legislative post in the U.S. I reviewed Martin Duberman's 1973 book *Black Mountain: An Exploration in Community*, which had some gay content. Duberman came out as gay in that book and has become one of the best-known and most prolific gay academics.

One of the things about the early gay press that bothered me at a certain point was the lack of pay. At first it was not a concern to me, because the papers were all-volunteer efforts and no one was making money. But as soon as papers started to accept more paid advertising and they became more businesslike, I started questioning the idea of writing for no pay. *The Advocate* had always paid me. *Philadelphia Gay News* paid me for a column I did for them. But *Gay Community News* refused to pay me. I had done a lot of writing for them without charge, and once they seemed to be more successful I thought they should be paying their writers. They had very strong left-wing views and were disdainful of capitalism, but they were selling ads, though not too many because they were hostile to the business community. Among the ads were those for gay churches with their paid ministers and gay psychologists who did not work for nothing. I felt it was a question of fairness for gay writers who serve the community with our profession. And at the time, I started to need more money to live on. I became angry about this and stopped writing for them.

Beyond Newspapers

In the early 1970s, I got together with fellow GLFer Karla Jay to produce an anthology that was titled *Out of the Closets: Voice of Gay Liberation* and was published by a small press, Douglas/ Links Books. It was also released as a mass-market paperback and was the first gay anthology seen by thousands of people. The introduction to the anthology contained an essay I originally wrote for *Ramparts*, perhaps the first article by a gay-liberation journalist to appear in a national magazine. *Ramparts* was launched in the Vietnam War era, not quite underground but not quite mainstream, either. The essay was both confessional and journalistic, reflecting the "personal is political" ideology that had emerged from the feminist movement.

While *Out of the Closets* had some of my own writing in it, the project utilized my editing skills more than my journalistic ones. The book was printed in several mass-market editions and was a pioneering work, influencing many gay men and lesbians to become engaged in the new movement or at least to change their outlook from one of shame to one of pride.

The book came about from a project I had started in New York. I started clipping gay articles when I was active in GLF and living at The 17th Street Collective and producing *Gay Flames*. I would put these articles, from all over the place, together in a packet called the *Gay Flames Packet*. They were copies I made of gay articles from smaller papers, put into a plastic envelope and sold for $2 or $3. New York's Oscar Wilde Memorial Bookshop, started by Craig Rodwell in 1967, sold the packets, and I sold some through mail order. Karla and I met and discussed these and other writings, and how they could work as a collection. She had some connections to the publishing industry, which was significant to finding a publisher. This became the first anthology of the new voices of post-Stonewall gay liberation.

Karla Jay and I produced two more anthologies, *After You're Out: Personal Experiences of Gay Men and Lesbians* and *Lavender Culture*. On my own, I sought out renowned poet Allen Ginsberg, perhaps the most famous openly gay figure in the world at the time, who agreed to be interviewed for a gay periodical. The result was the *Gay Sunshine* Interview, initially published in 1973 in *Gay Sunshine* in San Francisco, then reprinted in many periodicals and in a chapbook, and later translated for publication in Spain, France, Italy, the Czech Republic and Brazil.

In the mid-1970s, following the success of *The Hite Report*, Karla Jay and I were asked to produce a survey-based study of gay men and lesbians. The result was *The Gay Report*, published by Summit, a division of Simon & Schuster. This 800-page book provides the most insightful and complete picture of the social and sexual lives of gay men and lesbians in the years prior to the AIDS plague. However, it was not a commercial success, and we could not find anyone to publish a paperback edition.

None of these books was a big money-maker.

By then (the late 1970s), I had left New York City and was living in rural Massachusetts in an economically depressed and somewhat isolated region. I bought land there with four other gay men, all of us looking for a rural lifestyle and more self-sufficiency as part of a national back-to-the-land movement, at a time when most gay men were seeking life and freedom in big cities. I needed to find a way to make a living and ended up acquiring a job as a reporter for the *Athol Daily News*, circulation 5,500. The pay was minimal, but it was enough to live on and help me get my octagonal house completed. After living for six years with no electricity, I could afford to pay for installation of electric power, a drilled well, and more.

At the *Athol Daily News*, I found myself in a curious situation. I loved being back in the newsroom of a daily newspaper, and I certainly had the skills to do the job. I was surrounded, however, by people with no journalistic training, skills or ethics. Eventually, I became the assistant editor, while also continuing to do a lot of reporting and feature writing. I gradually backed away from my "activist" approach to journalism and covered the news using more standard journalist style, striving to be objective. I remained out of the closet and did not have any problems related to that, fortunately.

Cuba Libre

While living in the woods of rural Massachusetts and working at the *Athol Daily News*, my past did not elude me. The Mariel boatlift from Cuba to Florida in 1980 led me to write a book titled *Gays Under the Cuban Revolution*. Based in part on my own travels to Cuba, but also carefully researched, the book was lauded by many Cubans but not much appreciated by the left. Fidel Castro and Che Guevara were sacred cows to leftists, even gay leftists. This book explored my political evolution away from the dogmatic left while it detailed the oppression of gay men and lesbians in Cuba, blaming it primarily on Castro's essentially Stalinist ideology and form of government. The book was published in 1981 by Grey Fox Press, a small press in California that had published my Ginsberg interview, and also in Spanish by a Cuban-owned publishing company in Madrid, Spain. I was and still am especially proud of a jacket blurb for the book written by renowned lesbian writer Rita Mae Brown. She wrote, "*Gays Under the Cuban Revolution* will not please people who want their politics spoon fed. This book should be force fed to people who confuse government policy with government reality. Allen Young uses his typewriter like an uppercut. Be alert when you read this man."

While working at the *Athol Daily News*, I became intrigued with the idea of writing a regional guidebook, covering this unique area known as the North Quabbin Region. I opted for self-publication and produced *North of Quabbin: A Guide to Nine Massachusetts Towns* and published it under the name Millers River Publishing Co., my own creation. My book was well-received, selling more than

5,000 copies, and I followed this by contacting other local writers and publishing about a dozen books over the next few years. My "small press" perched on the border between "hobby" and "business," and I concluded it would be quite impractical for me to give up my newspaper job to become a full-time publisher.

Moving On

Looking back on the early years of gay media, perhaps one of the most significant differences I see is how much gay issues are now covered by straight media. Our issues were disappointingly ignored or misunderstood by the mainstream. There were almost no openly gay journalists in the straight media. Randy Shilts helped change this when he went to work for the *San Francisco Chronicle* in 1981. He became the first openly gay reporter covering the "gay beat" at a mainstream American newspaper. Later, *The New York Times* woke up and started doing a somewhat better job of covering gay issues, even getting to the point of publishing gay wedding details in the society pages.

I still see a need for the gay press. I think that openly gay journalists have insights and access to news and culture that other newspapers, owned and operated primarily by heterosexuals, don't have. I think a gay journalist working in a heterosexual environment is bound to feel restrained and limited—gay journalists don't always cover the gay news and may not want to cover it, unfortunately. Someone working for a gay newspaper is devoting himself or herself to gay community, news, culture and readers. That's really important, and I hope it continues.

Now, as a retired openly gay journalist in a rural community, I am writing a column for my former employer, the *Athol Daily News*. I write on many different topics and, in more than three years of doing this, I have written more than 150 columns. I have come out in print via my column as gay, Jewish and atheist.

When a local state senator came out as gay, I wrote my column about that. And when President Obama endorsed same-sex marriage in the summer of 2012, I not only wrote about it in my column; I also made sure that the editor had some nice photographs of happy local gay married couples! When I moved here 39 years ago, I had no idea how easy it would be to exist as openly gay in a traditional New England rural community, with a primarily working-class population. This is truly heartening, and thus it still pains me to see gay people struggling with their identities and harboring fear and shame.

The simple gay-liberation message, "Come out of the closet," remains as relevant today as it was in 1969 when the Stonewall rebellion happened, but at least that message is getting better coverage in the media than it did back then.

**Allen Young at a 1969
anti–Vietnam War
demonstration.**
Photo by David Fenton

**Allen Young,
circa 1990.**
Photo by Robert Giard

10

Martha Shelley

By Sarah Toce

Martha Shelley was in Greenwich Village the night of New York's Stonewall riots on June 28, 1969. The events would forever change the course of not only her life, but that of the entire lesbian, gay, bisexual and transgender community.

"It was a hot, clear night and I was taking two women from Boston on a tour of the Village and the lesbian bars. They had come to New York City to meet with Daughters of Bilitis members because they wanted to form a DOB chapter in Boston," Shelley said. "We passed by the Stonewall and noticed some young men throwing things at cops. The Boston women were taken aback. 'That's just a riot,' I told them. 'We have them in New York all the time.'"

Shelley added: "I wasn't trying to be cavalier—this was the height of the anti-war movement. Martin Luther King had been killed the year before, and Harlem (where I was working at the time) went up in flames. A few months later, there were riots in Chicago at the Democratic convention. I didn't go to that, but I was at a lot of anti-war demonstrations, and sometimes there was violence. So I assumed this was more anti-war stuff. I escorted the women back to the apartment where they were staying and went to my lover's house. I only found out that it was gays rioting about 48 hours later."

Members of DOB were encouraged to take new surnames in an effort to evade possible FBI surveillance. She would change her last name from Altman to Shelley at this time.

Immediately following Stonewall, Shelley became one of the founding members of the Gay Liberation Front. GLF was a direct response to the Christopher Street riots, would catapult the gay-rights movement into the mainstream, and would ignite a new generation of gay and lesbian political activists to take action against the perceived anti-gay government that held them captive—emotionally, physically, sexually and otherwise.

"As soon as I found out that gays were rioting against the police," Shelley remembered, "I called Joan Kent, who was running our local DOB chapter, and said, 'We need to have a protest march.' She said that if the Mattachine Society agreed, the two organizations could co-sponsor it. So I called Dick Leitsch, the head of New York Mattachine, and he said to come to a meeting at Town Hall and propose the march idea to the membership."

The response was overwhelming, according to Shelley. "Town Hall held 400 people, and it was jam-packed with 398 men, one female member of Mattachine, and me. When I proposed the march, Dick asked how many were in favor. Everyone's hand went up. So he said, 'Whoever wants to organize it, go to that corner after the meeting.' A few of us formed a march committee. We subsequently met at the Mattachine Society office to work out the details. It was another hot day. We were tremendously excited, and we were drinking beer. People say that I first suggested the name Gay Liberation Front, but I don't remember that. All I remember is pounding my hand on the table and shouting, 'That's it! That's it! We're the Gay Liberation Front!'"

Not everyone was immediately sold on the idea, however. "Dick got very upset," Shelley said, "because he thought we were forming another organization right there in his office and might take away membership from him. So we hastened to reassure him that this was just the name of our march committee, but we were lying through our teeth.

"Next, someone called a meeting at Alternate University, otherwise known as Alternate U (or alternate you). It was a warehouse-office kind of space where lefty anti-war people taught classes in Marxism, karate, printing, Spanish and so on. We leftists who were in the more traditional gay organizations like DOB and Mattachine met with gays who were in lefty organizations, and that fusion became the GLF.

"For me this was the place where everything I believed in came together—anti-war, economic justice, feminism, the cultural changes spearheaded by the hippie movement, and what I believe to be the basis for all our liberation struggles: the right to control your own body, because if you have control of your own body, the government doesn't have the right to draft you and ship you off to kill or be killed. You can smoke dope or not smoke it, sleep with your own or the opposite sex and so on. You can't be forced to bear a child against your will—a right we're still fighting about now."

The Gay Liberation Front formed *Come Out!* magazine during this time. The publication ran from 1969 to 1972 and carried with it a voice of passion and inclusion.

"Every leftist group at that time had a newspaper or magazine to express its ideas," Shelley said. "*Come Out!* was ours. We sold it on the streets of New York. Some newsstands carried it. And it went to other cities as well. It was the voice of people who'd been silenced; it reported on events in our community, events that never made it into *The New York Times*. You didn't need [to have] a degree in journalism from an Ivy League university in order to write for *Come Out!*, so the quality was uneven, to say the least, but the passion behind it was heartfelt.

"And, unlike *The New York Times*, we didn't have to worry about losing advertisers or losing access to the halls of power. On the other hand, we didn't always hold ourselves up to high standards in terms of rigorous inquiry, and I regret that."

Shelley's commitment to the feminist movement was growing and expanding as she gleaned more of an insight in regard to the economy and women in the workforce. Her loyalty toward equality for women was ever-present as she worked overtime to distribute *Come Out!* to the masses.

"I had two jobs on the paper, aside from writing for it," she said. "I worked part-time in a typesetting shop (that was before everyone had computers), and the owner was an old radical who [type]set stuff for the Black Panthers in her spare time. So, I could go in there after hours and set copy for *Come Out!* Then I'd turn the copy over to the layout people, and they'd lay out the paper and send it to the printer. When the paper came back, I'd grab a bunch of copies and go out onto the streets of Greenwich Village and hawk them.

"One cold day, after selling out the paper, I went into a coffee shop to warm up. A professor from New York University was there talking with a student. He was an economic determinist. I overheard him saying that the women's movement was succeeding not because of its ideas, but because the economy needed women in the workforce."

Although infuriated at first, Shelley later realized that the professor had a valid point. "That made me angry," she said. "I was one of the people generating feminist ideas, and those ideas were having a huge impact on women. But years later, I developed a broader perspective. Now I've come to believe that it is the interaction between economic, technological, cultural and ideological factors that gave rise to modern feminism.

"Some technological examples might be machinery that obviates the need for heavy manual labor, and reliable birth control. And once a woman is in the labor force, not dependent on a man for income or forced to bear more children than she can support, she can divorce Mr. Wrong or even live as a lesbian if she wants. She can do this as an ordinary, working-class person instead of having to be an heiress like Gertrude Stein."

The urgency to report the news regarding the feminist movement is still valid today—possibly more than ever, Shelley believes. "I think that urgency is even more valid, given the attacks on women and gays coming from the right wing," she said. "We have different organizations now and different means of communication, due to the Internet. We need to make use of every available avenue, because our adversaries aren't going to stop.

"It should be obvious by now that their economic aim is to suck up every cent from the 99 percent and to take back control of our reproductive organs. I think it was Rick Santorum who said that a pregnancy resulting from rape is a 'gift from God.' So, I suppose, the rapist is God's holy instrument. We made a few gains in the 1970s, but ever since then the right has been trying to roll us back to the 19th century."

In 1970, Shelley entered the radio field with Lesbian Nation on New York's radio station WBAI—a move that seemed natural to her since she was used to organizing marches and creating change from within the community. "I was a public speaker for DOB and the Gay Liberation Front, so I was comfortable being in front of a microphone. It was just a matter of learning the technology—how to use a tape recorder and how to edit tape," she said.

The inspired activist moved to Oakland, California, in 1974 and became involved with the Women's Press Collective. There she released *Crossing the DMZ* and other works. Her poetry also appeared in *Ms.* magazine.

Her advice to the up-and-coming generation of journalists is simple: Follow your heart, your gut, your passion.

"Many years ago, when I was really, really broke, a woman suggested that I get a job writing advertising copy in order to pay the bills," she said. "I looked at her as though she'd suggested I go to Times Square and sell pussy. Once you've sold the most precious part of yourself—your writing soul—you'll have a very hard time getting it back again. I think about the journalists who beat the drums for the Iraq War, the ones who were 'embedded' with the military and reported whatever they were told to say, and the ones who still faithfully regurgitate press releases from the government as though this was real news.

"I don't think too many young LGBT journalists are going to break into those circles, where they are getting paid handsomely to do public relations and propaganda for the 1 percent. So, we are free to say what we believe. The major pressures might be from within the community.

"A young journalist is going to be influenced, as I was, by the culture and ideology of the time. When I look back at my earlier writing on *Come Out!* I can see times when I went along with the crowd and censored myself. So it's important to look at your day's work and think about what you didn't say, as well as what you did say."

Although completely immersed in the journalism field, it was never a full-time venture for Shelley. "I never had a normal career. I've mostly had part-time jobs that allowed me to write and be a political activist," she said.

Her day job is medical-legal research. After hours, she works closely with Code Pink, a women's anti-war group. "I am also involved with an anti-foreclosure committee of We Are Oregon, an organization fighting for economic justice. My most recent book is *The Throne in the Heart of the Sea*, a historical novel with a major lesbian character. It's available through www.ebisupublications.com."

Martha Shelley in the early 1970s.
Photo by Steven Dansky

Martha Shelley in 2012.
Photo courtesy of Shelley

11

Perry Brass

By Sarah Toce

A finalist for multiple Lambda Literary Awards, author of 16 books, gay-rights activist and a Stonewall observer, Perry Brass has married civil rights with sexuality, religion and a sheer desire to speak the truth throughout his 45-year career in journalism. Brass stepped into the national gay civil-rights movement when he became the co-editor of *Come Out!*, published from 1969 to 1972 by New York's Gay Liberation Front.

"Working on *Come Out!* was one of the main reasons I joined the GLF," Brass said. "I had seen copies of the first and second issues of the paper; I joined during the third issue. At that point, there was no place to publish work that could be considered openly gay, with the exception of the *Mattachine Review* or *ONE* magazine, and both of these were pretty staid—although Allen Ginsberg published poetry in *ONE*. But there was no place with a radical political slant to publish what I wanted to say and had been writing and keeping to myself, which was that it was 'OK' to be openly, unashamedly queer and that what was being done to LGBT people was inhumane. We were not 'sick,' it was what was going on around us that was sick."

"There were a few artsy 'avant-garde' magazines which might publish you as a freak show, but nothing like *Come Out!*," he added. *"Come Out!* was published by a collective, which meant that all pieces had to be 'edited' by the whole collective, in that anyone could comment about it. However, a few people were more 'collective' than others, [and] their voices carried more weight. In the beginning, I had to tailor a lot of my thinking to a 'party line' that was not always my own. This, frankly, alienated other people as well, who dropped off the paper because they could not concur with it. However, by the fifth issue it was being published out of my apartment in Hell's Kitchen, so I was basically keeping the paper alive."

Being present during the Stonewall rebellion in the early morning hours of June 28, 1969, enthralled the 21-year-old Savannah, Georgia, native. "I was delighted with Stonewall, just ebullient," Brass said. "The idea that we had fought back against the cops enthused me—it put a lot of energy into me. The gay scene (hidden bars, constant fear) before Stonewall was appallingly depressing, although the fact that being queer was like being part of a very private club has always appealed to some people."

Not all of Brass' contemporaries agreed with his palpable enthusiasm. "Some of my friends were disgusted by Stonewall. They were still trying to be 'preppy' gay boys who could get along in the 'real world' of money and position," he said. "That attitude still clings to a lot of people, like Log Cabin Republicans. I am convinced the LCRs would have been completely against Stonewall and have sided with the police."

Brass spent the next three years working full-time as an activist, a revolutionary in the deepest sense of the word. "That changed my life; my professional life merely followed," he said. "One thing it did confirm to me was that your inner life, the life that longs to be free, to express your innermost feelings, is your real life. It is what sustains and feeds you. There is now a huge denial of this, in a blind, hopeless acceptance of the dumbest version of 'common sense,' which has led to a numbing cynicism, depression and the alienation endemic in American society."

He continued along those lines: "The GLF people and our radical family and friends were a throwback to Whitmanesque America, part of our real heritage as Americans and human beings. We have, though, seen some attempts to throw off this cynicism and alienation in the 'Occupy' movement, and the initial romanticism around Obama's first election. These situations become more symbolic than real; that is my sad reaction to them."

The amount of energy that went into distributing *Come Out!* was immeasurable, according to Brass. "I ate, slept, dreamed and worked on the paper," he said. "We realized while we were doing it that it was going to be a historical document, part of history being made and recorded. Also, a lot of the paper was 'bootlegged,' was produced 'under the counter' to keep costs down. We printed it at night with the help of people who worked in the peace movement, at printing shops that during the day produced advertising circulars on small, hand-run presses. We typeset it at a movement type house (no desktop publishing in those days) that typeset movement magazines on huge machines."

Fear of backlash regarding the gay news of the day was not a concept lost on Brass. "The backlash would not just come from the straight world, but the gay one, and our own world, that of radical queer politics as well," he said. "We dashed a lot of the political correctness of our period by publishing material that was critical of the Cuban revolution (then one of the darlings of a lot of American radicals); by publishing material that was openly sexual but not sexist (at the time, sex and politics were indeed strange bedfellows); by publishing material about gay youth—another hot-button topic, which it still is; by publishing work that criticized not just the mainstream world, but our own world— this is always very sensitive."

Some members of GLF would not speak to Brass because of the stigma associated with such topics. "I learned later that I had become stigmatized in gay literary circles for years as being part of the old 'liberation' generation, instead of the newer, more accommodationist one of the late 1970s and certainly the 1980s," Brass said. "This 'accommodationist generation' was championed by big-ticket New York publishing, which had felt that any kind of literary material about LGBT people had to be 'balanced.' In other words, it had to show how sick, perverted, disgusting, limiting and revolting we are—like queer Jim Crow on a literary level."

One notable story in Brass' memory of his reporting days at *Come Out!* included Cuban re-education camps. "Cubans were putting us [gay men] in 're-education' camps that were nothing more than prisons or concentration camps," he said. "I had learned about this firsthand from people who knew about it, and had read in *Granma*, the Cuban national political organ (their version of Russia's *Izvestia*), that gay men were no longer going to be 'allowed' to be part of the Cuban educational system. Since all of Cuban culture was organized as an educational effort (not a bad idea in itself if you want to have a national reason to support culture; we don't), this basically announced that the Cuban state had a stake in ostracizing gay men, driving them into the closet or out of Cuba. I exposed this, when most radical media in America would not go near it."

Come Out! published the first gay works by historically important writers Rita Mae Brown, Dennis Altman, Martha Shelley and Steven Dansky. The entire run of the paper is reproduced on the website www.OutHistory.Org, as well as in *The Come Out! Reader*, published by Christopher Street Press through Blurb. Brass said this "makes it the most important single historical document of this liberation era of the gay movement."

The collective's manifesto was, "Gay Liberation Front is a coalition of radical and revolutionary homosexual men and women committed to fight the oppression of the homosexual as a minority group, and to demand the right to the self-determination of our own bodies," according to OutHistory. org.

Brass ventured into books after his stint at *Come Out!*. He wrote *Albert: or, The Book of Man*; *The*

Lover of My Soul; *Angel Lust*; *The Substance of God*; and, most recently, *King of Angels,* with religion taking center stage in each of the plotlines. It was intentional. "Religion does have a real place in my work. There have always been gay men and women who were involved in religion. In many cultures they were protected as sacred 'divines,' or exponents," he said.

At the onset of the HIV/AIDS epidemic, in the winter of 1982, Brass' partner—a physician—lived in New York and witnessed "the beginnings of a set of problems that later became part of the AIDS diagnosis: for instance, young men coming down with diseases of an impaired immune system that would normally be seen in men twice their age." He was volunteering at the Gay Men's Health Project clinic (since renamed Callen-Lourde Community Health Center), the clinic that "with two of my friends, Marc Rabinowitz and Leonard Ebreo, I had helped start in New York's West Village [in 1971]," Brass said.

"The need was amazing," he added, "but it was also an indication of how fast gay liberation itself had come out of the closet—that people could openly accept the need. The first night we opened the clinic, using only fliers we had distributed on the streets of the West Village, when we thought no one would show up (maybe half a dozen guys), men lined up down the block. We saw about 50 men that night. My involvement with the clinic came about as part of my involvement with the movement, but a very particular involvement that melded politics with open feelings of compassion and intimacy. This is now almost completely gone. The LGBT movement has become so corporatized that these basic human feelings are missing—too missing."

While working with Gay Men's Health Project, Brass continued his career in journalism by joining forces with *Motive* magazine. "This [partnership] came about through my friendship with Roy Eddy, who was on the *Motive* editorial staff," Brass said. "Roy had lived in Nashville, where *Motive* was being published, and moved to New York after coming out, to work on *Come Out!,* which was fantastic. I was delighted to be able to contribute to *Motive* [because] it was very much a part of the ethos of this time of personal liberation becoming political liberation. It was published by the Methodist Church as their 'youth organ,' but the church did not see how radicalized youth were becoming. The church later, as I put it, cut off their organ, so that the Gay and Lesbian Liberation issue of *Motive* became its last issue."

The Male Muse, edited by Ian Young, was the first anthology of openly gay poetry published in English, and Brass' work was included in it.

"*The Male Muse* was published [in June 1973] by Crossing Press, which was started by a wonderful couple, Elaine and John Gill. John was gay, and Elaine was aware of it. So their publishing of *The Male Muse* made sense to everyone. It was a fantastic anthology; I am very proud that I was the second-youngest poet published in it. The anthology sold well and was in hundreds of libraries. It still has a life of its own, bought secondhand and read," he said. *The Male Muse* has been out of print for several decades.

Digging deeper into poetry, Brass became involved with the advent of *Mouth of the Dragon,* the first magazine published in America that was openly dedicated to gay male poetry. It was edited by Andrew Bifrost. "A new magazine that has taken on the mantle of *Mouth of the Dragon, Assaracus,* is being published out of Little Rock, Arkansas, by Bryan Borland, a marvelous young poet who has started Sibling Rivalry Press, his own press," Brass said.

In 1984, Brass' play dealing with the emerging issue of AIDS (*Night Chills*) won a Jane Chambers International Gay Playwriting Award. The Jane Chambers International Gay Playwriting Award was administered by Meridian Gay Theatre, headed by Terry Helbing, who was a great force in gay theater in the 1980s. The Jane Chambers competition was often reported on in the *New York Native* and lasted a few years. *Night Chills* was never published.

When asked if the award changed his career, Brass said, "Somewhat, in that the Jane Chambers Award was really recognized back when we had a flourishing national LGBT theater movement. I became more recognized as a playwright at a time when I was writing plays. I wrote plays for eight years and then, with my partner, started Belhue Press to put out my own books. I got a lot of support in the gay theater community and am grateful for that; but I was crazy about journalism and books, and that was going to be my main focus."

Having played an integral part in gay and lesbian media for nearly 45 years, Brass has seen trends come and go, watched fashions walk the runway right out of style and then back again, and witnessed firsthand the oppression and injustice of his brothers and sisters. So, what has changed in the media since he began his career as an inspired youngling?

"The media itself has become much more fragmented, as the audience has also; there is also the advent of social media, which I feel, sadly, really reduces a lot of the message we had in *Come Out!* of radical personal change (meaning going back to the 'roots,' to the structure) to a 'style' or 'fashion' message, or a message drained of personal activism," Brass said. "Although it is possible to go 'viral' and get a million people to sign a petition, say, for gay marriage, in the old days we could produce a demonstration in a week that would bring out more than a thousand people to the streets to reinforce a message. I keep wondering: With chronic unemployment, with 40 million people without health coverage, with epidemic homelessness especially among young people, with a war that doesn't stop and shouldn't have started, with the constant abridgment of human rights we have right here—where are the people on the streets? Where are they?"

Today Brass' journalism career is inspired by sharing the raw truth: "I have believed most of my life that people will easily believe the most complicated lie rather than the simplest truth. When I was a kid growing up in the South during the horrors of racial segregation and constant sexist violence, I realized early on that there are two 'realities': the 'reality' of things as people wanted them to be, and the actual existence of things as they really are. So that inspires me to present things as they are. And I am also inspired by the heroism of everyday life, and my friends who have acted heroically, something I think that we gay men do well when, in the most 'normal' of situations, we allow ourselves to act authentically, heroically."

Perry Brass in 1972.
Photo by J. LaRue

Come Out!, May 1970.

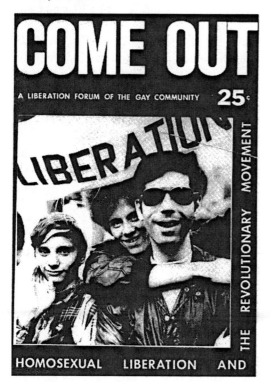

Come Out!, early 1970s.

Come Out!, winter 1972.

12

Jeanne Córdova

By Sarah Toce

Her breadth of work in journalism has been woven throughout our culture's modern history—staking claim at some of the most precarious moments in the gay civil-rights movement. For better, for worse, for richer, for poorer, she has been there and she has worn no veil. Jeanne Córdova most recently documented her years of journalism and activism in "a memoir of love and revolution," *When We Were Outlaws*, with a foreword by Lillian Faderman.

Córdova began her civil-rights journey by entering a convent.

"Entering the convent at age 18 was my first step toward becoming a lifelong social-justice activist. In high school, I made the pivotal decision to join the Immaculate Heart of Mary order instead of a cloistered Carmelite novitiate. I chose the IHMs because I saw that they were an out-in-the-field, liberal order. In the black ghetto was where I saw poverty, racial injustice and the refuse of capitalism. Here I was radicalized and knew I had to become a social worker.

"I chose the convent because I knew I wasn't interested in the world of men and women, marriage, children—'that' lifestyle. Being in the service of God within a community of women felt natural and right. I'm sure the fact that I fell in love with God at the age of 7 and made a vow to dedicate my life to him was much informed by my strong Catholic parents' teachings (one Irish woman and one Mexican dude), as well as my latent lesbianism."

It was a lesbianism that could never be wholly explored until her departure from the religious establishment and the patriarchal ties that bound.

"I left the convent because of my political radicalization and inability to justify the Roman Catholic Church's teachings and actions regarding social justice, and its ongoing battle with my IHM order to keep women in line under patriarchy. My newly realized lesbianism was actually secondary to falling out of love with the Catholic Church, which I had questioned all my life," she recalled.

In 1972, Córdova met a lover who was the daughter of someone involved with the Los Angeles chapter of the Socialist Workers Party. The inspired activist turned her attention to Vietnam War protests and began working more steadily for the rights of the lesbian, gay, bisexual and transgender community.

"As I marched and organized with tens of thousands on the streets of LA, I realized that one day the lesbian and gay struggle, as we called it then, had to grow into a mass movement also, in order to effect civil rights on a federal level. I wondered if we ever would or could become as big as this anti-war movement. It taught me that we needed allies, because we are only 10 percent of the population," Córdova said.

At the age of 22, when most young people are falling in love for the first time, Córdova was earning her master's in social work. From there she began organizing the lesbian community into action. One might wonder if she overlooked the potential of a very active love life.

"I did have a totally active love life, but it had to be sandwiched in between the cracks of my movement life, so between 10 p.m. at night and 8 a.m. the next morning. This mostly meant [my relationships occurred] in bed having sex."

Organizing the lesbians into a marching herd was also no easy task, according to Córdova.

"One of the hurdles was that most of the professional lesbians—the social workers, nurses, teachers, real estate agents, chiropractors, dentists, doctors, etc.—were afraid to come out and march or use their real names in print or sign any gay mailing lists. Another big hurdle was talking the dykes into organizing with the gay men; many separatists wanted nothing to do with men and thought of gay men no differently than straight men."

Rallying gay men into action was a separate challenge. "Grappling with the men's eternal sexism was another issue. We dykes had to simultaneously teach the men—every meeting was a 'teaching moment'—not to make sexist assumptions, like 'the girls' will march behind us or make the coffee.'"

"The largest hurdle was, of course, going on TV and radio," she added, "and finding ways to convince straight people that gays were not criminals who wanted to infect their children. Trying not to hate the straight world for what it did to gays psychologically—the suicides, alcoholism, drugs, and decades of therapy—was very hard for me, personally, having grown up a Catholic. I didn't meet any gay-neutral straights until my 40s."

Perhaps by sheer will, frustration, the desire to change the direction of the gay liberation movement, or everything all rolled into one, Córdova began a publication that would be groundbreaking for its time. In December 1971, the publication, *The Lesbian Tide*, was voluntarily severed from the Los Angeles chapter of the Daughters of Bilitis at the request of Córdova and Barbara McLean, who had been a leader of Chicago's DOB starting in 1966 until a job transfer took her to Southern California in 1969. The women wanted to change *The Lesbian Tide* from a newsletter to a national monthly lesbian feminist magazine. They succeeded—it was celebrated by the lesbian community at large but flew mostly under the radar as far as the straight world was concerned. After DOB's national publication *The Ladder* folded in 1972, *The Lesbian Tide* filled an important gap until it, too, folded, in 1980. (See Marcia Gallo's *Different Daughters: A History of the Daughters of Bilitis and the Rise of the Lesbian Rights Movement.*)

Speaking of the magazine, Córdova recalled, "[The lesbian community] was outrageously supportive. As I show in [my book] *Outlaws*, over the years about 150 different lesbians and transwomen came to work for free as writers, photographers, layout artists, distributors—everything. It would not have survived without their largely donated staff labor."

Many of *The Lesbian Tide*'s writers would go on to pen books. Among them were Sarah Schulman, Karla Jay, Sharon MacDonald, Achy Obejas, Nancy Toder and Shirl Buss.

"We were proud that we paid $10 per story and $5 per photo—but that was ridiculous. As lesbian historian Yolanda Retter, Ph.D., said, *The Lesbian Tide* became 'the national newspaper of record for the lesbian feminist decade.'"

After *The Lesbian Tide* folded, Córdova became human rights editor of a progressive newspaper, the *Los Angeles Free Press.*

"I was first hired as the *Freep*'s token 'Chicana, feminist, lesbian' columnist. My weekly essays became known as 'that dyke column' by the largely straight readership, but it got people listening to my voice as I covered the [1973] Battle of the Sexes, the famous tennis match between female (and closeted lesbian) tennis player Billie Jean King and male tennis star Bobby Riggs," said Córdova.

As her politics became better-known, she moved into the investigative-reporter role and began editing all the human-rights stories for the paper. "In this position I became an integral, full-time staff member and covered big stories of the day like the kidnapping and capture of Patty Hearst by the leftist urban guerrilla group, the Symbionese Liberation Army," she said. "*Outlaws* covers the in-depth stories of five or six of my most interesting adventures with Angela Davis, Nazi terrorists, and secret meetings with underground FBI fugitives. It was totally different than my role as publisher and news editor at *The Lesbian Tide*. 'The story' was center stage."

Male domination in media was ever-present at this time in her career, according to Córdova.

"The sexism, male rivalry and politics at the *Freep* was a brain twister from working with an all-lesbian staff who presumed we were all fighting for the same larger cause on *The Lesbian Tide*. I got a lot of professional training in having to write the same news story for two widely different audiences who looked at American life through widely different lenses. I did get my first book out of those columns (*Sexism: It's a Nasty Affair*) and a core plot line of my third book, *Outlaws*, from those years. I'm not sure I slept much during that decade of my life."

Córdova crossed over from being a radical activist to becoming the publisher of the first gay and lesbian telephone directory in the USA, called *Community Yellow Pages*. The move was both a personal and a professional one for the journalist.

"In 1980, after 10 years with *The Lesbian Tide*, my first spouse—the features editor—and I broke up, and fewer and fewer women seemed to be coming to help staff. Lesbian feminism was waning and being taken over by a new generation of lipstick lesbians in LA. I saw that the movement was morphing from its radical base into something more mainstream because the fundamentalist right was launching expensive ballot initiatives against us. It seemed to me it was time for middle-class, well-employed lesbians and gays to come out of the closet, meet each other and start supporting these expensive anti-gay battles," recalled Córdova.

"On a personal level, at age 33, I was exhausted and tired of being desperately poor ... but I wanted to stay in gay publishing. So, it occurred to me, 'What if I created a vehicle for professional gays to come out of the closet? What if I could prove that it wouldn't hurt their careers but instead could help them?'"

The *Community Yellow Pages* took shape, and a new movement was formed, but not without hard work.

"I started walking the streets of Hollywood talking to shop owners, selling them ads to be in a new telephone book that would be marketing only to gays and lesbians. Miraculously, the idea caught on," she said. "In 1982 we published a 99-page book that looked exactly like a straight telephone book. The next year the *Community Yellow Pages* (a nice closet-type name) doubled to 200 pages. Twenty years later, it was 400 pages and published 100,000 copies per year. Every lesbian, gay man and gay-friendly straight person in Southern California was using it!"

Concurrently, Córdova became part of the Stonewall Democratic Club that her mentor, Morris Kight, founded in 1975.

"Becoming its president from 1979 to '81, I founded a statewide campaign called 'Destination New York' that was part of a national gay and lesbian effort to seat a record number of queers (33 from California among 80 nationally) as official delegates to the 1980 Democratic National Kennedy/Carter Convention in New York," she said. "In between all this, Stonewall was strongly backing Jerry Brown's candidacy to become governor of California (yeah, now he's done it again!), and we met regularly with LA City Council people and other elected officials, pushing on them to enact more protections in housing and employment for queers."

When asked what advice, if any, she would give to a young journalist covering the marriage-equality movement today, Córdova responded: "In addition to reporting on new states and new news, I'd be interested in analyzing what effect the marriage-equality movement was having on the rest of the LBGTQ lifestyle and struggles—what is not being seen. I'd focus on what aspects of the queer-relationship lifestyle might help the heterosexual institution of marriage, which seems to be dying and becoming irrelevant to how modern society is re-creating itself. I'm also fascinated that marriage and AIDS have been the only two issues that have caught on with the straight world—why is that?

"The best part [about media now vs. 20 years ago] is that we get to know everything much more quickly and hear 20 dozen points of view on every news item. The worst part is that it's more complex for the individual to find the news she wants. You have to be Internet-savvy and know where to go. Also, we get the news faster now, but we only get the headlines and a short online paragraph. We get much less depth, analysis and truth."

Analysis and truth were two items marked off on her to-do list for her new memoir, *When We Were Outlaws*.

"After 40 years of being an activist, and 20 years of being a lesbian publisher, I was 50. I'd always promised myself that one day I'd return to the love of my life—writing. I sold the gay and lesbian *Community Yellow Pages*, sold my house, and for some nutty reason decided the best place to write this book was all alone in Mexico, my father's homeland," she said. "Yes, doing the roots thing seemed to fit well with doing the writer lifestyle. I'd always wanted to be a full-time writer. I figured I was old enough, and had enough stories to write another memoir, so out popped *When We Were Outlaws*, a memoir of love and revolution."

Pan to the present time eight years and four drafts later.

"I missed the queer community so much that I had to return to Los Angeles," she said. "I came home in 2007 and plunged back into finishing the book, finding a publisher, and [rejoining] lesbian activism. This time I became a cultural activist, organizing history, art and cultural events for my queer lesbian tribe in LA. Right now I am doing that while also writing a sequel to *Outlaws* which will focus on discovering the legacy of lesbian feminism and what practices and world views queer women today have inherited from this movement."

Raising the banner at the historic National Lesbian Conference at UCLA in 1973. The event drew 2,000 women from 45 states.
Photo by Dorthy Nielson in *The Lesbian Tide*. Courtesy of Jeanne Córdova

The Community Yellow Pages, 1982.

CLONING OF A NATION!

The Lesbian Tide, May–June 1973.

Jeanne Córdova in 2012.
Courtesy of Córdova

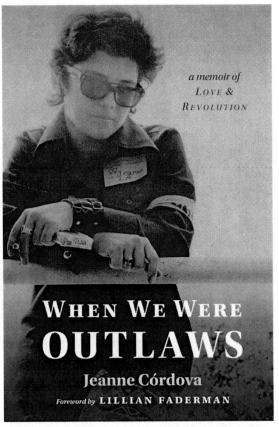

Córdova's book from Spinster's Ink in 2011.

13

Karla Jay

By Tracy Baim

Karla Jay is one of the pioneers in gay journalism. She has written for dozens of lesbian, gay and mainstream publications since the 1960s, and she is author, co-author or editor of several important books, including *Out of the Closets: Voices of Gay Liberation* with Allen Young, the first post-Stonewall anthology of LGBT writing, and *Tales of the Lavender Menace: A Memoir of Liberation*.

Her first writing as a lesbian was for an underground anti-war newspaper, *Rat Subterranean News*. Robin Morgan was the one who convinced Jay to write for *Rat*.

"That was the first time I wrote as a lesbian for a magazine," Jay said. "I had written earlier for a free publication called *UR: University Review*, which was distributed very widely across the U.S. on campuses, like *The Village Voice*, as a freebie. I had a lot of really interesting experiences writing for the *University Review*, but it wasn't as a gay journalist. I met very interesting people such as writer Anaïs Nin."

Jay was part of a women's takeover of *Rat* after the paper's male editors were accused of sexism. On January 24, 1970, women seized the *Rat* offices in Manhattan's East Village, successfully publishing it for its few last issues.

Jay also wrote for *Come Out!,* the short-lived newspaper of the equally short-lived post-Stonewall Gay Liberation Front organization. Since she had spent some time on the West Coast, Jay interacted with the gay pioneers working in California, and covered San Francisco and Los Angeles events for gay publications.

"There were a lot of early gay papers," Jay said. "These included Detroit's *Gay Liberator*, New York's *GAY* and *Come Out!,* and ones all over the country. In the beginning, gay publications were really so important in just existing, The news and what was placed around it—listings of events, demonstrations, dances or the existence of a gay bookstore, all of these things were so important to get out.

"People don't understand today, for example, that there had to be a lawsuit in New York to get the words 'gay' and 'lesbian' in the Yellow Pages and White Pages phone books. People don't even know what a phone book is. But to get those words listed was so important. A lot of people who couldn't find others like them, they would dial information and could not find that word anywhere, even in library card catalogs, etc.

"These gay papers were piles of information for them—to pick up these papers and just hold onto them and to know they weren't alone. Even if they weren't brave enough to go to a dance or demo, or even stand on the sidelines of a march, the papers were a lifesaver for so many people to know they weren't alone. It's important for people to understand the value of that, and how important it was for people who grew up thinking we were the only people like ourselves—alone in the world. That's one of the things the gay press did.

"You may find a copy of a gay paper on the street, in a garbage can, on a subway seat, a bus seat, and it would help save your life. Just being there was life-saving. That was true of *Out of the Closets* as a book, when it got into people's hands. I applaud the press today, and what it is doing."

Jay also wrote countless articles for *The Lesbian Tide, Majority Report, Gay Community News, off our backs, Lesbian Connection, The Advocate*, and *Philadelphia Gay News*. *The Lesbian Tide* was based on the West Coast, so Jay was its East Coast correspondent.

She estimates that she wrote for dozens of gay and lesbian papers over the course of her career, totaling thousands of articles. Jay's main emphasis was on cultural reporting, including music and literature. She also did investigative pieces and was unafraid to take on controversial topics in the LGBT community.

Her work also included writing for *The Village Voice, The New York Times Book Review* and *Ms.* magazine.

She was among the highest-profile openly lesbian journalists of her day, and one with a unique perspective because she wrote for so many mainstream as well as gay publications. While there was little pay in the gay media, and early papers were not very objective or professionally written or edited, she still looks back on those papers fondly.

"There was a big difference in those early days of gay press vs. mainstream," Jay said. "When you wrote for the mainstream press, there was an expectation that however badly you'd be paid, at least you would be paid. *The New York Times* did not pay well. I wrote for *Ms.* magazine, and they paid. The best I was paid was from *The Chronicle of Higher Education*. The pay scale was excellent, because they were a trade publication for a specific audience.

"On the other end of the spectrum was the gay press, which paid nothing, but the other side of it was that nobody really was making money. Only a few publications, like *Lambda Book Report, The Harvard Gay & Lesbian Review* and *The Advocate*, could pay $25 or a bit more. *The Advocate* paid. But these were small amounts of money, and those of us who were the early members of the LGBT press corps, we paved the way for people who are now making money as journalists. I'm very pleased that some of today's journalists can make a living, but the people of my generation had to make a living doing something else."

Jay said the 1970s gay press certainly had its divisions, especially between men and women. Most of the co-gender papers really were more male, which is why lesbian papers served such an important need. Jay continued to write for both LGBT and mainstream publications, including those against the war, to make sure a gay perspective was in the mainstream and underground media.

Because a lot of gay papers did not pay, Jay said that those people who dedicated their time to writing often had an ax to grind. "The coverage was often quite biased and not very objective," she said. "You got what you got, and it may or may not have been professional. The standards varied a lot. There was not a lot of fact-checking. When I wrote for *Village Voice* or *Ms.* magazine, the fact checkers would call me and go over pieces I wrote, whether gay or not, with a fine-tooth comb. But nobody ever challenged any of the facts I put forth in gay papers. They just published it as if it were true.

"I tried very hard to substantiate my stories. I covered culture. It disappointed me that a lot of people who were writing about trials, arrests and serious news were not being factual at all. A lot of 1970s queer journalism was very unreliable—often the letters to the editor were the most interesting, and entertaining, part. People would challenge the veracity of the articles quite loudly and offer alternative truths."

Jay was not a lesbian separatist, but she respected and worked well with those who did separate from men. She said because she is a pacifist, she does not see others as enemies. She preferred to build coalitions. "Lesbians are in reality too small a group to have an impact on the larger society by ourselves," she said. "I do have a lot of respect for lesbians who are separatists and who wanted to be rid of the patriarchy."

Jay worked with a gay man, Allen Young, on several important LGBT books. They corresponded mainly through the mail, given the high cost of long-distance calls in those days.

Jay had an especially strong connection with *Philadelphia Gay News*, where she was able to write on a wide range of topics. She interviewed Audre Lorde and Rita Mae Brown, among a series of cultural interviews. When she was on tour for her books, she would interview people across the country and was also able to write a number of travel pieces.

In the 1980s and 1990s, she continued to write for *The Advocate* and *The Village Voice*, where she did an exposé of the exploitative pricing of gay and lesbian tours.

In recent years, she has mainly focused on teaching and fiction writing and is a Distinguished Professor of English at Pace University. She is now legally blind, which has not stopped her, but which limits her reading choices to those available through audio.

She writes audio book reviews for Reviewingtheevidence.com and, until recently, reviewed audio books regularly for *Publishers Weekly*. She was on the board of the Lambda Literary Foundation and in 2009 won a local Jefferson Award for public service.

Jay, a strong advocate for the gay press some 42 years after she first wrote for it, said, "If we didn't have the queer media, we would be in big trouble. We definitely need LGBTQ media. We wouldn't see the full spectrum of who we are if we left it up to the mainstream media. We would think that everyone wants to get married, and serve in the military and have a family with two children and a dog and a white picket fence. For those of us who have different aspirations, those of us who want to change society, we would be completely left out of the picture without alternative media.

"Also, the books I most like to read, that are from our own presses, the alternative presses—Spinsters, Magnus, Bella, etc.—those are never going to be reviewed in *The New York Times Book Review*. Those are not their advertisers. If we put our fortunes in the hands of the mainstream media, we are really going to suffer. We have to have our cultural future in our own hands. That's where places like *The Gay & Lesbian Review Worldwide* (formerly *The Harvard Gay & Lesbian Review*), for example, come in. They are such an important and irreplaceable institution, just to name one publication.

"The LGBTQ press covers the diversity that the mainstream press really doesn't care about. Our queer press in the U.S. is going to talk about the plight of queer people in the Islamic world, China, South Asia. We're the only ones who are going to do that and have a global perspective. We are invaluable. We are the only ones who are going to care about us. You cannot expect the mainstream to care about our fate."

Karla Jay in Greece, 1978.
Courtesy of Jay

Karla Jay, circa 1971.
Courtesy of Jay

Karla Jay's 2000 autobiography from Basic Books.

Karla Jay in the 1980s.
Photo by Jill Posener, courtesy of Jay

14

Frank Robinson

By Tracy Baim

In June 1971, Frank M. Robinson started Chicago's first tabloid-size gay newspaper, *Chicago Gay Pride*. It continued as the organ of the Chicago Gay Alliance from February 1972 through June 1973, but Robinson did not stop there. In the summer of 1972 he started *The Paper*, which focused on entertainment and gay culture. It was a well-designed tabloid written for both men and women. Only two issues were published.

Both papers were very significant contributions to the early years of gay newspapers in Chicago, filled with facts, photos and openly gay and lesbian people writing about their lives.

Robinson is a Chicago legend. He served in the Navy in World War II and the Korean War, worked at *Science Digest*, wrote the advice column for *Playboy* magazine, and became a very prolific writer. He collaborated with the late Tom Scortia on a novel, *The Glass Inferno*, which became a film classic under a slightly different name: *The Towering Inferno*. He has numerous books to his name, but his critical role in early gay media has gone mostly unacknowledged.

After he moved to San Francisco in the mid-1970s, Robinson became a speechwriter for Harvey Milk, and wrote some of Milk's most important speeches, as documented in *The Mayor of Castro Street: The Life and Times of Harvey Milk*, by Randy Shilts. Because of his work with Milk, Robinson was given a role as an extra in the 2008 biographical film *Milk*.

In 2008, I interviewed Robinson in his San Francisco home.

"I'd been involved in both Chicago Gay Alliance and Chicago Gay Liberation," Robinson said. "The newspaper came out of that. I typed up the whole thing, by hand. I was doing that the same time I was doing *Playboy*. We also put out a newsletter—there were three people involved, both of whom died of AIDS. One was a poster boy for *Newsweek*; he was on the cover of *Newsweek*, and he originally put [*The Paper*] out. Then I had a guy named Henry [Wiemhoff], he took it over. Henry is kind of an icon in my own head. Henry was involved in a chapter of Chicago Gay Lib down at University of Chicago, and he and I got together, platonically."

Robinson was born and raised in Chicago, and went into the Navy toward the end of World War II. After a brief second tour, he majored in journalism at Northwestern University. He worked for various magazines, including *Rogue*, a porn magazine in New York, and later in the mid–1960s at the *Tattler* porn magazine in Los Angeles. He also freelanced for *Playboy*. "I'd written a couple science fiction stories for *Playboy*, they picked them up. I did an interview with Robert Heinlein," Robinson said. Then one day, his liaison at *Playboy* asked if he wanted to be the *Playboy* Advisor. He was perhaps among the first "queer eye for the straight guy" men.

"*Playboy* had had a roundtable discussion on homosexuality, and they had all of the usual suspects, some of the gay liberationists before Stonewall," Robinson said. "After Stonewall they wanted me to bring it up to date. There was a meeting at the University of Chicago; after Stonewall happened, the lid was off; this was the biggest mass movement since the anti-Vietnam protests, because Gay Liberation units showed up at practically every college campus in the country. At this time there was a Midwest meeting from all over. *Playboy* sent me down to cover it. I was undercover at *Playboy* at this time, but they sent me down to cover it. They probably knew me better than I knew myself. I went down there and I was blown away.

"This was the first time I met college kids who were gay. Nobody knew I was gay. At least I wasn't out [at *Playboy*]. I'm sure that they knew I was, but that's in retrospect. At the time, I joined Gay Lib while I was at *Playboy*. I went on the '100-man-march' down Michigan [Avenue]. There were about 100 of us. If you went down Michigan, you passed right by [the] *Playboy* building. I was marching along right by the side, pretending to be a reporter and all that. This one kid, he was carrying a sign about gay liberation, he turned around and it was like a message from God. He thrust the sign into my hands—'Here, you carry it for a while'—and I did. I went all the way down to City Hall; we had our little kiss-in. Chicago is very liberating. People staring at us curiously, but no catcalls, anything. This would have been [June 1970] after Stonewall, the lid came off. It had come partly off in San Francisco about several years before."

On New Year's Eve of 1964 in San Francisco, police harassed a dance sponsored by religious and gay groups. The incident sparked outrage and led to coverage in the mainstream media. Lawyers were even arrested. "How can you charge anybody with 'associating with a gay person'?" Robinson said. "But they did. The newspapers blew up and the city blew up, and that was the end of police harassment for the most part."

Robinson moved to San Francisco in the early 1970s to work on his fiction career.

During Robinson's time as a speechwriter for San Francisco activist and later Supervisor Harvey Milk, he came to know Milk well and was devastated by his 1978 assassination. "For at least five years after, I couldn't talk about it without breaking into tears," he said. "I had lost my Martin Luther King."

Robinson's book *The Glass Inferno* did have a gay character in it. The character was ultimately cut from the movie adaptation, *The Towering Inferno*, which was based on both *The Glass Inferno* by Robinson and Scortia and *The Tower* by Richard Martin Stern.

"The only thing I regretted, and nobody knows this, is one of the main characters is a gay man, in *The Glass Inferno*," Robinson said. "He was an interior decorator, the stereotype, but it was very heroic. Considering it was 1974, of course it got cut. Who in Hollywood at that time was going to play that role? Certainly neither [Steve McQueen] nor Paul Newman. We couldn't give any interviews, because this was going to be known as [the producer and co-director] Irwin Allen's *The Towering Inferno*. It was not going to be Robinson's *The Glass Inferno*. Twentieth Century Fox has been noble. [Almost every] single year since 1974, I get a check."

Despite his beginnings in early gay media, Robinson was never stereotyped as a gay writer. He was a writer who happened to be gay, writing best-selling fiction books. "However, I have to qualify this," he said. "Tom and I had a prominent gay character in *Glass Inferno*. *The Dark Beyond the Stars* has heavily gay overtones. There are gay characters in *The Reading*, which followed *The Dark*."

How did he make it big in the mainstream? "Primarily it's because of the type of writing that I do," he said. "Primarily, I've been a professional writer and editor all of my entire life, and I was editing for *Playboy*, I edited for *Science Digest*. My very first job as a kid was a copy boy for INS, International News Service. It was like UPI, AP, only it was owned by Hearst at the time. I mean when I was born, God obviously stamped my ass with 'you are a writer.'"

Frank Robinson in 2006 surrounded by his 1970s gay newspapers, at his San Francisco home.
Photo by Tracy Baim

15

Alan Bell

By Sarah Toce

In 1977, *Gaysweek* was a weekly gay and lesbian newspaper in New York City, at the time one of only a handful of weekly lesbian and gay papers in the world. There was a local weekly called *Michael's Thing*, but it was not a newspaper—more of a booklet of bar ads. *Gaysweek* was poised to fill the void in the Big Apple's gay community and serve as a connecting force pre-HIV/AIDS outbreak. At the helm of the revolutionary newspaper was Alan Bell, an inspired graphic designer and journalist.

"We started *Gaysweek* in 1977, and although there may have been some talk about illness, it wasn't part of the public consciousness; it wasn't part of the public discourse for the 103 issues that we did from 1977 to '79," Bell said. It was only months after they shut down *Gaysweek* that what later became known as AIDS started to be discussed by the scientific and gay communities. "One of the things that we continued to think about and mull over through the years is, 'How would things have gone differently if we had managed to hold on for six more months?' Because, of course, once HIV hit, then everybody and their brother was interested in what the lesbian and gay news had to say, and we were at the center." [The first official announcement of a medical scare came in 1981.]

In an interesting footnote to gay media history, *Gaysweek* won a contested U.S. Patent and Trademark Office application; *Newsweek* had opposed the name on trademark grounds.

Bell remembered his time with fondness. "We had a typesetting machine, which was about the size of a small desk—this was back in the days of *Gaysweek*—and it had a memory board inside of it, which was about 8½ by 11, and it was about a half-inch thick, and the memory board held 4K of memory. 4K! Not 4 gigs, 4 megs—4K! And we wanted a 16K board; that was the holy grail. The 16K board cost like $3,000 or something, but we really wanted the 16K board because it would allow us to have something like 40 fonts rather than four fonts. I go back to those days and I think about that, and I just laugh and laugh."

From *Gaysweek*, Bell moved on to *BLK*—an expansion from the newsletter that originated with Bell's work on Black Jack, a Los Angeles African-American gay men's safer-sex club he founded.

"I think that *BLK* came together because there were a number of forces happening at the time," he said. "There were people in the black gay community who thought that there needed to be a publication and, since I had done *Gaysweek*, that I was the one to do it. I was working in typesetting and printing at the time, and people had said, 'Yeah, you need to do it. You need to jump back into it. You need to do it.' And I had basically said, 'No. Been there, done that. I really don't need all that headache again.'"

Then something changed internally for Bell, and the little newsletter he was managing transitioned quite seamlessly into a much bigger project with full-on impact.

"What happens is, over the years you forget about the bad stuff, you forget about the problems, and you remember the good stuff," he said. "So I think over the 10 years between '79 and '88, I began to warm to the idea. I was doing Black Jack, and we were doing fliers, and then the fliers turned into bigger fliers, and then the fliers had notes on them, and then the fliers turned into one-page newsletters, and then the one-page newsletters turned into back and front, and at one point the newsletter, *Blackjack*, was eight pages.

"And so then it was just a hop, skip and a jump to deciding, 'Yeah, let's do a publication.' Because the thinking was that the newsletter, we're starting to put news and stuff in it, and it's really only going to a small group of people. So if we're going to do this, we might as well do it for people who aren't just members of Black Jack. And actually, I think those last few issues of the *Black Jack* newsletter were publicly distributed; we took them to bars."

The divine forces nudging Bell to turn *Black Jack* into *BLK* for the greater good of the community were avant-garde activists Phill Wilson, Morgan Pinney and Charles Stewart. "Charles and Phill are both African-American; Morgan was white. He's no longer with us. I remember a meeting at—I think it was Morgan's house, where we had a serious conversation about making *BLK* happen."

He added, "In both *Gaysweek* and *BLK*, one of the things that was important to me was to be comprehensive and evenhanded. I think that a lot of people who start publications have in mind a particular agenda that they want to push or to make sure it gets out in the world. They are really activist—they want to push a certain political agenda, or they are an artist and they want to make sure their art gets covered or something. Coming out of a journalism background, I really see the function of journalism as getting the information out there and then it's someone else's job to take that information and figure out what to do with it. If it turns out that we highlight the fact that lesbian teachers are being fired in Wisconsin, it's our job to bring that to the public's attention, and it's somebody else's job to then do something about that."

This was the reasoning behind the lack of editorial opinions in *Gaysweek*. "We didn't have an editorial page," Bell said. "I felt that it wasn't our job to do that. It was our job to get the information out, and we did not have an editorial page. Now with *BLK* that changed somewhat, and there was an editor's column. But the editor's column didn't function so much as the voice of the newspaper; it functioned in fact as the editor's voice."

With the Internet, social media and blogging now the prominent force for social justice within the gay-rights movement, withholding one's editorial opinion may not always necessarily resonate with the younger generation of journalists coming up behind Bell.

"It was different then, because we didn't have all these voices to balance out each other," he said. "So my feeling is that if we were going to include the entire community and be inclusive, that we needed to be quiet and let other people speak. So certainly, if people had points of view, both in *Gaysweek* and *BLK* we tried to get those points of view into the paper. But we got those points of view into the paper because we interviewed somebody, or because we did a news story, and that's how we got the various points of view in the paper, not because the newspaper or the publication took that point of view."

Being an LGBT newspaper in itself was already taking on a political position, according to Bell. "I should say here just to be clear, that I'm not so naïve to know that a newspaper can't be entirely neutral," he said. "I mean, the very fact that we were a lesbian/gay newspaper takes a certain political position. So it was advocacy journalism in a way, but it wasn't advocacy journalism with our opinions on our sleeve. If *BLK* were alive today and if *BLK* had a robust website, I would do my best to try to find a black gay Republican and make sure that black gay Republican did a blog on the website, I really would."

As in all things in life, there were moments when this approach wasn't successful. "Particularly in *Gaysweek*, I can remember that the women on the staff were not pleased and felt that the paper was way too male—and that it didn't reflect the lesbian and feminist point of view to the degree that it should," Bell said. "So we did have those—I think battle is too strong of a word, but they did jump on me to hold my feet to the fire."

Knowing what he knows now about the LGBT media specifically, might there be anything he'd go back in time and do again if given the chance?

"If I had a to-do-over again, yeah, I would try to hold on with *Gaysweek* longer. *Gaysweek* actually was not failing at the time. It was kind of moving sideways," he said. "What I kept hoping was that there would be a big explosion of interest or something—*The New York Times* would write an article about us, and then all of a sudden it would just blow up. And try as I might for that big breakthrough, it never happened. So, it's not like we couldn't pay the print bill or we were getting evicted; it's just that it became routine and regular, and you get up and you do this, and we were a weekly; there was a lot of work. This was before computers. I mean, this is back when there was typesetting and this was a 16-page paper every week. I think that if I had felt there was a light at the end of the tunnel, in terms of the publication being successful as a publication, then I would have been able to hold on for those six months.

"The perception at the time was that we were going to do the same thing forever and ever and ever and ever and were just going to barely make it. Yes, we'd pay the print bill, but we'd barely be able to pay the print bill and it would be like this forever and ever and ever. So, I think that may have been a failure of nerve or a failure to hold on for the long term."

As for *BLK*, Bell said: "I'd also grow the paper more slowly. We were so excited to move from an eight-page newsprint, reprinting content, to a 68-page color glossy with original well-researched stories, that we grew too fast, outpacing our ability to produce such a magazine given our limited resources. If I had it to do over again, I'd do a better job of keeping the lid on it."

BLK is alive and well, albeit in a very different format.

"*BLK* still exists, but it doesn't produce lesbian and gay newspapers. We are custom publishers and graphic designers, that's the way I can paint it. So, those production skills from putting out newspapers, we're now a hired hand. We do newsletters and publications for other companies. For instance, when you get on an airplane and you pick up the airline magazine from the seat pocket, *American Way* or whatever it is, that magazine is not produced by American Airlines. Because American Airlines, they don't know how to publish a magazine, they know how to fly airplanes, right? So, American Airlines hires 'XYZ' publishing company to produce a magazine for them, and American Airlines says, 'These are the parameters as to what we want in the magazine,' and obviously they have approval of what goes in, but aside from the general direction, the publishing company handles all of it. They write the stories, take the photos, and all the ads and all of that, and then produce this magazine for American Airlines. We do the same thing except for smaller companies and organizations."

That's half the business.

"The other half is just plain old graphic design. We're doing fliers and tickets and all the stuff a graphic design company would do," he said. "That's what *BLK* had morphed into, and that's what we're doing now. Personally, after all these years, I decided to go back to school, so I am working on finishing up my master's degree at Cal State University. Do not ask me what or why I need a master's degree, I don't—I don't think the boss is going to give me a raise if I wind up with a master's degree, but I really so enjoy the academic learning environment, and I enjoy writing, and I'm just having a ball being in the academic environment."

Bell also serves as the head of the Los Angeles InDesign Users Group. "InDesign is the software of choice now for doing publications, and so there is a group of people in Los Angeles who use that software who get together every two months, and I am head of that group, so that's kind of a fun thing, too. I keep busy."

Preserving his legacy for the future benefit of the LGBT community plays a very important role in Bell's day-to-day.

"I'm 67 now—I'm thinking about legacy matters," he said. "I tend to be a pack rat, but not to the degree that I need to be on TV. I do have everything related to *BLK* and everything related to *Gaysweek* that I managed to salvage. Old records and old check stuff, it's all here. And it's been on my mind like, 'What do I do with that? And where does it go?' People have made suggestions, because there's lesbian and gay archives, there's also reasons that maybe it should go to the Schomburg [Center for Research in Black Culture, in New York], which is not lesbian and gay, but it's black. And then there's Syracuse University, that has *Gaysweek*'s papers, and Syracuse University wants *BLK*'s stuff, just because they already have *Gaysweek* stuff. But then there's UCLA, and UCLA wants it because I went to UCLA as an undergraduate. So, it's nice to be wanted, and as I get older, I think these parts of conversations, and thinking about the legacy—those sorts of things are all on my mind. So, the relevance of all of that is that I'm glad to do this, because I'm thinking how things will be when I'm no longer here."

Gaysweek, December 5, 1977.

Alan Bell circa 1971 in New York City.
All images this chapter courtesy of Bell

Gaysweek, September 11, 1978.

Issues of *BLK*:
(clockwise from
left) August 1989,
April 1989, June
1990.

BLK's Issue No. 1, December 1988.

BLK,
January 1994.

BLK,
September 1992.

BLK, February 1994.

Black Jack Newsletter, December 1987.

BLACK JACK NEWSLETTER

December 1987   Black Jack, Box 83515, Los Angeles, CA 90083

CALENDAR OF EVENTS

Friday, December 4--Safe Sex Meeting--$6
Gold Members   Green Members
9 p.m.   9:30 p.m.
(Admission Pass enclosed)   Lucy's Drive-in
                                      3535 W. Imperial Hwy.
                                      (at Western Ave.)
                                      Los Angeles

Saturday, December 12--Non-Sexual Social Event--$18
Gold and Green Members
8 p.m.
Gary Jones and the Yuppets
4619 W. Washington Blvd.
Los Angeles

Saturday, December 19--Safe Sex Meeting--$6
Gold Members   Green Members
9 p.m.   9:30 p.m.
(Admission Pass enclosed)   Lucy's Drive-in
                                      3535 W. Imperial Hwy.
                                      (at Western Ave.)
                                      Los Angeles

Friday, January 8--Safe Sex Meeting--$6

Fri., Sat., Sun., Jan. 15, 16, 17--Trip to Lake Arrowhead

Saturday, January 23--Safe Sex Meeting--$6

THIS MONTH'S MEETINGS

Beginning in December, we will have two safe sex j/o meetings. This new
meeting will be held on the third Saturday. If there is enough interest,
we will continue to meet twice a month on the first Friday of the month
and the third Saturday.

The December meetings will be held in Los Angeles near Gardena. Our
accommodations consist of two big rooms, two televisions, two video
recorders, and a long bar. There will be door prize tapes at each meeting.

In addition to December's regular Black Jack safe sex j/o meeting, a
special non-sexual social event has been planned. All members and their

BLACK JACK NEWSLETTER

AUGUST 27, 1988

Calendar of Events

Friday, September 2, 1988, 9:30 p.m..........September Safe Sex Meeting
Saturday September 17 or 24, 1988..........Weekend Trip to Palm Springs
Friday, October 7, 1988, 9:30 p.m..........October Safe Sex Meeting

Black Jack Has Telephone

You can now reach Black Jack by telephone at 213-338-1516. The phone
is answered by machine practically all of the time with a long
announcement designed for prospective new members. But you can leave a
message after the beep, and someone will get back to you.

September Safe Sex Meeting

The September safe sex meeting will take place this Friday in
Hollywood. Gold Members: Your pass is enclosed. Green Members:
Assemble at Wendy's Restaurant, 7135 Sunset Blvd. (at La Brea) at 9:30
p.m. Be on time. If you show up at 9:35 p.m., we'll be gone.

Weekend Trip to Palm Springs

Because we can get a special deal during the month of September on a
suite of rooms at a luxurious resort in Palm Springs, the group is
discussing a weekend trip to that hot city either September 17 or 24.
If you think you'd like to go, call the office at 213-338-1516.
Otherwise, watch your mail for further information.

Government to Tax Penises

Until now, the only thing the United States government has not taxed
is your sex organ. This is due, in part, to the fact that 40 percent
of the time it is just hanging around unemployed, 20 percent of the
time it is pissed off, 30 percent of the time it is hard up, and the
other 10 percent of the time it is in the hole.

On top of this, it has two dependents and they are both nuts. However,
due to the new Federal budget and anticipated loss of revenue, it has
become necessary to place a tax on sex related appendages beginning on
October 1 of the current tax year.

Your amount of tax will be determined according to size. Please
confirm this information on page two (2), section seven (7), line
three (3) of your standard 1040 form.

9-12 inches .... Luxury Tax $30.00
7-9 inches ..... Pole Tax $25.00
4-7 inches ..... Privilege Tax $15.00
3-4 inches .....Nuisance Tax ..... $ 5.00

Anyone under 3 inches is eligible for a refund. Anyone over 12 inches
must file under Capital Gains, as it is assumed at that size that a

Black Jack Newsletter, August 1988.

BLACK JACK NEWSLETTER

JANUARY 1, 1989

Calendar of Events

Friday, January 6, 1989, 9:30 p.m. .... Safe Sex Meeting
Saturday and Sunday, January 21 and 22, 1989 ..... Trip to La Jolla and Safe Sex Meeting
February, 1989 (exact date to be determined later) .... Sports Outing to see Clippers Game
Friday, February 3, 1989, 9:30 p.m. .... Safe Sex Meeting
Sunday, February 20, 1989, 7 p.m. .... House Party
Friday, March 3, 1989, 9:30 p.m. .... Safe Sex Meeting
Tuesday, March 14, 1989 at 8 p.m. .... Theater Party to the Alvin Ailey Ballet
Saturday and Sunday, March 18 and 19, 1989 ..... Trip to Palm Desert and Safe Sex Meeting

Choose the Right Pass

Gold Members will find two passes along with this newsletter. Be sure to choose the correct one
for the meeting you wish to attend. If you do not have the correct pass, you will not be
admitted.

New Computerized Telephone System

Black Jack has a new computerized telephone system so you no longer have to listen to the long
introductory message for new members if you'd just like to leave a message. If you don't have a
touch tone telephone, just wait for the short outgoing message to finish, then leave a message. If
you have a touch tone telephone, you can likewise leave a message, but you can also access
other functions. The telephone number is still 213-338-1516.

January Safe Sex Meeting

The January safe sex meeting will be a jock strap meeting. Anyone
who shows up at the front door to the room in a jock strap (and
nothing else, except perhaps an overcoat), will be admitted FREE.
Anyone who brings a picture of a black man wearing a jock strap, OR
who himself is wearing a jock strap (and nothing else, except perhaps
socks and shoes) by 10 p.m., will get a dollar back on his admission.

The meeting will take place in the Hollywood-Laurel Canyon area. Our
two-bedroom suite includes a living room, dining room, kitchen and
two bathrooms.

In addition to our usual complement of videos and refreshments, we're
setting aside an area for members who wish to play whist and dominoes. One of the door prizes
will be a dinner for two at any of the Acapulco Mexican Restaurants.

Black Jack Newsletter, January 1989.

KUUMBA

A Poetry Journal for Black Lesbians and Gay Men   Fall 1991 $4.50

Kuumba, fall 1991.
**This was another
Bell publication.**

B–Men Issue No. 1, 1993,
also produced by Bell. It
changed to *B-Max* when
it became cosexual.

16

'Our Readers Are Our Writers' at *Gay Community News*

By Maida Tilchen

Thanks to the U.S. government, I spent the best years of my life working and writing for the lesbian/gay press. It started at my VISTA volunteer (domestic Peace Corps program) training in Chicago in 1973, where I was trained in Saul Alinsky tactics. An Alinsky community organizer gets people to participate together so they can visibly show their numbers to those in power in an effort to change an oppressive system. In my growing-up years as a loner, bookish and confused lesbian-to-be, I had never had any leadership role or training. Those three weeks of training taught me what felt like the secrets of those people who make things happen in the world, something I had never thought I would do.

I was a mediocre VISTA volunteer at my placement in Bicknell, a mined-out coal town in southwestern Indiana. My job was to educate and organize the Head Start mothers. Despite my social conscience, as a 24-year-old Long Island, middle-class, Reform Jew, I didn't have much ability to be an effective soldier in the War on Poverty.

Reading the anthology *Voices of Women's Liberation*, I identified with Susan B. Anthony, who in 1840 traveled by buggy in rural upstate New York, organizing women for the first women's rights convention. In my 1960 Chevy with U.S. government license plates, I was traveling my four rural counties trying to help impoverished women deal with Indiana's archaic and demeaning support systems. But the most inspiring sentence I read in that book was one from Black Liberation: "You don't get radicalized fighting other people's battles."

My battle, it turned out, was not poverty or even women's rights. My battle was lesbian and gay liberation, and I was radicalized in two ways. One was by reading, and the other was by doing.

Because of an unexpected and life-changing experience with a woman a few years earlier, I knew I was a lesbian. Because of a complete lack of information or contacts, I had done little other than agonize about it. I had joined VISTA in part to spend a year during which I could avoid it. At training, I had signed a statement that I was not homosexual and would be kicked out if I was. I had planned to use the time to help poor people instead of dealing with my own issues.

But in the decrepit farmhouse where I lived as a VISTA, I inherited from former volunteers a huge stack of anti-war, lefty magazines. There I read Allen Young's 1971 *Ramparts* article about how he came out in the Liberation News Service and the anti-war left. It was the first article of gay liberation I ever read, and it was life-changing. I had planned to spend my VISTA year in the closet, but Allen's writing caused me to open the door and go looking for the lesbians. I found them in Bloomington, 80 miles northeast, the home of Indiana University and the most active lesbian/gay community in the rural Midwest at that time.

After a year of weekends coming out in Bloomington, I moved there and soon became a "community organizer," unpaid by the U.S. government but well-trained by it. With my then-partner, also a former VISTA, we helped to organize conferences, lesbian educational programs, concerts, events, political actions, reading groups and more. We organized whatever we felt should happen, using our VISTA training and experience. No one told us what to do or not to do. We did it on free time from our paid jobs and graduate school.

In Bloomington, I quickly ran into conflict with the lesbian separatists, who then dominated the out lesbian community. As a Jew whose family had been torn apart by conflict over interfaith marriage, as a feminist and as an admirer of the "black and white together" phase of civil rights, separatism was not for me. This was a minority view and I often felt isolated within the lesbian community.

My escape was reading the two lesbian/gay periodicals that sincerely tried to be feminist and bring women and men together: *The Body Politic* from Toronto and *Gay Community News* from Boston. Both were intended for national audiences and both had a lefty political focus. These were my people.

I had no journalism training, but I began to write book and women's music reviews. They ran almost everything, and no one asked me for credentials. *GCN* listed me on the masthead as "foreign correspondent." A *Body Politic* artist did a lovely illustration for one of my articles.

In 1979, I got my first center spread in *GCN*, a detailed account of the National Women's Music Festival. Opening the paper to that center spread was one of the greatest thrills of my life. I was a real writer. As with being a lesbian activist/organizer, no one said what I could or could not do. Anyone could be a writer in the lesbian/gay press then.

At the 1979 March on Washington, I met the *GCN* staff for the first time, and the bylines I had read and the signatures on letters I had exchanged over the last four years turned into real people. Three months later I moved to Boston.

I planned to keep working in my professional field of educational technology and volunteer for *GCN*. I even had a lucrative job offer to design educational materials to help prevent cancer. But *GCN* board member Eric Rofes urged me to take an opening on the collective staff as promotions manager. Hmm: Prevent cancer for a five-digit salary and benefits, or work for *GCN* for $83 a week and have a job history that might end most future employment?

When I joined the *GCN* staff, I was given the recently vacated desk of David Brill, an investigative reporter who died mysteriously and was widely believed to have been murdered because of his stories. My predecessor as promotions manager, Mel Horne, was stabbed to death a few months later in an apparently homophobic attack. The windows of our downtown second-floor office had a bullet hole. Regularly, many phone callers cursed at or threatened us. I received a death-threat letter.

As promotions manager at a time when there were no mailing lists of potential subscribers—because few people wanted to be on such a list—I was challenged to somehow reach our customers. I spent a lot of time mailing packages of sample copies to bars, restaurants and lodgings listed in gay guides. We hoped they would not just throw them out when they saw our political headlines and lack of photos of naked men. I also did information tables at Pride and similar events. With a few other small businesses, I helped organize the first lesbian/gay business organization in Boston, which did cooperative advertising.

Although based in Boston, *GCN* was intended as a national newsweekly. It started as a newsletter in 1973 and was always a nonprofit owned by the community. Our motto was "our readers are our writers." *GCN* had an editorial commitment to feminism, anti-racism and all the usual lefty causes.

At 31 in 1980, I was the second-oldest of our paid staff members, although the dozens of loyal volunteers spanned a full range of ages. There was gender balance not by deliberate quotas but by choices of women to participate. Coming from the separatist wars in Bloomington, I felt at home and safe at *GCN*.

We were housed in a run-down building near Filene's, Boston Common, and the graveyard of many Revolutionary firebrands. Across the hall was Glad Day, a gay bookstore, and partitioned off behind a wall of stacks of old *GCN* issues was the office of *Fag Rag*. Our old wooden mailboxes were the physical home of many local lesbian/gay organizations, such as BAGLY for gay youth. We had a motley assortment of old typewriters and phones. Copy was run over to Cambridge for typesetting by a gay-owned firm. Layout was done by cutting and pasting typeset copy onto tabloid-size layout sheets. The walls were covered with front pages of back issues. An "Elaine Noble for Congress" straw hat was the most striking decoration, although most of the staff was so political with a small "p" (as in not involved in organized party politics) that when Ted Kennedy's office invited six of us to meet with him, many people scoffed. I went and was so thrilled I can't remember a word he said.

Volunteers did a great deal of the work, from writing to layout to office renovations. Our offices were the de facto lesbian/gay center for New England. People came to come out or to pick up, often by volunteering on the partylike Friday nights when papers were prepared for mailing in closety envelopes. When the phones rang, it might be a subscriber screaming about an unsealed envelope flap or a scared young voice asking, "How do you know if you are gay?" Sometimes it was someone about to commit suicide.

Lesbian/gay notables stopped by when in town, and I interviewed many of them, so I met most of the politicos, writers, historians, artists and musicians of the early-'80s lesbian/gay liberation scene. I was especially moved to meet Aaron Fricke, the first high-school student to break the prom barrier. Another very young writer was Bennett Klein, who as an attorney took a landmark HIV case to the U.S. Supreme Court. Urvashi Vaid came to see the offices and went on to join the *GCN* board. I even met Allen Young, whose *Ramparts* article had inspired me.

We also had regular visits from Dennis, a probably schizophrenic artist who would watercolor on our desks for hours; Joey, a young hustler who almost put into jail a few of our guys who were trying to help him get off the streets when the cops grabbed him; and Earl, the totally deaf foster child of a lesbian volunteer, who ran around the office screaming. It was a noisy, unpredictable, messy workplace, and I had the time of my life working there.

There were eight people on the actual paid staff. We officially got $83 a week, more or less, depending on what was in the checking account. Our only benefit was free use of the lesbian/gay Fenway Community Health Center, then housed in a tiny basement complex.

At weekly meetings, everyone on the staff had a voice in editorial and advertising content. One of the funniest discussions involved a pathetic, straight, traveling salesman who wanted us to run an ad for a "mammary mug," which was a ceramic coffee cup with boobs that one could drink out of. We all agreed it was sexist, but he was just so sad that we ran it anyway.

A less funny discussion almost destroyed the staff unity. One of our regular photographers submitted a photo essay on "the boys of Provincetown." In addition to the focus on almost-nude, conventionally beautiful bodies, something *GCN* avoided, some of the boys were underage. The dispute about feminism, aesthetics, artistic license and legalities did not split along gender lines, but it did have friends furious at friends. The resolution was that two opposing editorials ran, with photos of older "boys." For my view, I received a personal letter from a volunteer acquaintance calling me a Nazi.

Promotions manager was my paid job, but I spent most of my free time writing. I did book reviews and author and publisher interviews. I covered women's music extensively, including reviews, interviews and economic analysis. I wrote on Jewish and anti-nuclear issues. Once, my photo was on the cover and it was fun to see it sold on newsstands. It's hard to believe now that I wrote it all on a typewriter, often cutting and pasting scraps of paper to assemble the final article. (And on that salary I couldn't afford to buy a typewriter—a nice subscriber lent me hers.)

I am also a legacy for the lesbian press. One of my earliest cover stories for *GCN* was excerpts from letters between myself and my lesbian aunt, Helen D. Weinstock (1919–2005). She wrote me: "Glad to hear that you have seen *The Ladder*. We used to assemble, fold, and staple the sheets together. Of course I knew Phyllis Lyon and Del Martin." Helen, who took the name "Ilana Weinstock" when she moved to Israel in 1970, sent lesbian/gay news of Israel to *GCN*. (An expanded version of our letters was published in *Nice Jewish Girls: A Lesbian Anthology*, edited by Evelyn Torton Beck, from Persephone Press, Inc., of Watertown, Massachusetts, in 1982.)

Our readers, who were our writers, could write articles or letters. The letters page was the liveliest section of the paper. Meeting new people, I learned never to say I worked for *GCN*, because I would get screamed at for everything that had ever been in the paper. (But having an unusual first name, I usually couldn't hide well.) I learned that I could never predict what would upset a reader. I'm sure this piece will upset someone, probably a *GCN*-er who remembers something differently. Hey, that will be just like the good old days.

In those days, mass media used the term "lifestyle" as a euphemism for lesbian/gay lives. Working at *GCN* was truly a lifestyle for the staff and dedicated volunteers, because GCN was all we did. On a slow day, we would usually be griping about our lack of love lives, *and* about how ironic that was, since we were sure we were at the very center of lesbian/gay life.

Our readers were our community. Richard Goldstein, of *The Village Voice*, did a group interview and invited our writers to write for the *Voice*. I was excited about it until I tried to think what to write. All my ideas came down to explaining lesbian life and culture to straight people, but I had nothing to say to straight people. It made me realize I wasn't a journalist, I was an activist who used writing to organize my community and motivate them to make change.

GCN ran articles about and opinions from the fringes of the lesbian/gay movement, such as the Radical Faeries, the lesbians opposed to sexual fantasy, and the early bisexual-rights movement. *GCN* ran stories that you didn't see then in other lesbian/gay papers, and may not see now in the current lesbian/gay press, such as explanations of the legal inequalities faced by men charged with sex crimes against boys, and exposés of the fire hazards in lesbian/gay bars. *GCN* was always losing advertisers over such content, but some would come back because it was one of the few places where local lesbian/gay businesses could advertise in those days, long before the full-page AIDS-drug, liquor and auto ads that support many lesbian/gay periodicals today. When a privately owned and more politically conservative lesbian/gay paper called *Bay Windows* was started by a better-funded gay man, many advertisers permanently abandoned *GCN*.

The *GCN*, Glad Day and *Fag Rag* offices were destroyed by arson in July 1982. *GCN* didn't miss an issue, and community support kept it going for several more years, but my time on the staff came to an end. Somewhat burnt out, and realizing I had been in Boston for more than two years and didn't know anyone not at *GCN*, I resigned in 1982, although I continued to write for *GCN*.

In 1988, I volunteered to be a writing tutor at Cambridge Rindge and Latin, the public high school. Spread wide open on a classroom desk was the latest issue of *GCN*. Shocked, I looked around—did anyone else see this? Did they know there was a lesbian/gay paper right there in the classroom? But I was the only one who thought it was strange. Times had sure changed. In 1991, I was hired by a straight woman as a college writing tutor, mostly because I was a published writer. She thought it was great that my portfolio was of lesbian/gay articles. That led to a very successful and meaningful career for me at a college for nontraditional working adult students.

I am still writing about lesbians. I thank the U.S. government and the lesbian/gay press for giving me the confidence, politics and writing skills to write *Land Beyond Maps*, my award-winning historical novel about lesbians in New Mexico in the 1920s, published in 2009.

**Maida Tilchen and her aunt, Helen D. Weinstock, at the *Gay Community News*
offices in 1981.**
Photos by Susan Fleischmann

17

Victoria Brownworth

By Sarah Toce

Dubbed the "activist writer" by Lambda Literary, Victoria Brownworth has shed many a colorful skin throughout her 30-plus-year career in mainstream and alternative media.

"My career as a journalist was born out of my involvement as the star witness in the first big federal police-brutality trial in Philadelphia while I was a senior in college. My first published piece was in *The Philadelphia Inquirer*, about my experience. I had always been an activist—my parents were Socialists and civil-rights workers, so I grew up surrounded by serious activists who were changing the country. It was an easy direction to go in. I'm not sure I was wired any other way."

Perhaps the first order of business was learning how to keep her thoughts to herself and out of the fray when compiling a story—even though many of her heroes in the field did not necessarily perfect the notion themselves.

"One of the basic tenets of journalism is to keep yourself out of the story, but every important journalist I've ever been interested by has been very much in the story. I think of George Orwell, for example, or Edward R. Murrow, or Marie Colvin, who was killed recently in Syria. Passion infuses writing, so you are inevitably part of the story you are covering. I've never covered a story that didn't have a political element to it. Of course, now I write almost exclusively about politics, so the activism aspect is always right below the surface."

Taking her own advice was not always easy. "While I was spending a lot of time in London in the late 1980s, I was writing about apartheid and about female genital mutilation, because those were issues that were localized there," she said. "The apartheid protests were daily and, while I was living there, a scandal broke where it was discovered that girls were being mutilated by well-respected doctors at their parents' behest. How could I ignore that story?"

It was during this time that Brownworth became the first out lesbian columnist writing a column in a daily newspaper. Brownworth also made news as the first AIDS columnist for *SPIN* magazine. "The work I was doing on AIDS had gained a great deal of national attention," she said, "and the then-editor of the magazine had been my editor previously at *The Philadelphia Inquirer*. He asked me if I would be interested in doing an AIDS column for the magazine, and, of course, I said I would. I knew that the column would reach one of the most important demographics—people 35 and under."

The move was arguably a lateral one for Brownworth, but a welcome transition nonetheless—and it sparked a new conversation among a very different group of people.

"I was already one of the lead reporters on AIDS in the country at the point when I began doing the column for *SPIN*, so there was no resistance on my part," she said. "One of the issues, however, was that I needed to focus the column on heterosexuals, and that was a new direction—actually groundbreaking, considering the resistance to the concept of heterosexual transmission at that time."

Professionally, reporting on HIV/AIDS became Brownworth's calling card and proved fruitful for the most part. "It became a lead focus of my reporting for nearly a decade," she said. However, reporting on the epidemic that indiscriminately killed friends and family members was a challenge emotionally.

"It affected me personally because so many of the people I knew and had met died. As a young reporter—I was in my 20s and 30s when I was covering AIDS—it was so difficult to watch people just a little older than I was, or even my own age and younger, dying," she said. "Those of us who were immersed in that period of pandemic AIDS in America were obsessed with it. It was like living in a time of war. And I don't mean the attenuated kind of war like Iraq and Afghanistan, but I mean like London during the blitz in World War II."

The competition brewing between genders working side by side was fierce. "For almost the entire time I was working exclusively in newspapers, I felt that sexism was oppressive and overwhelming," Brownworth said. "I was the only woman writing about AIDS; I was the only woman in the newsroom in a lot of circumstances. I had an experience while working in Philadelphia, in fact, where another writer actually wrote a play and made me a character who was an evil diva writer. It was shocking, but none of my male colleagues thought so.

"I don't know that I ever pushed through the stereotyping. I was always perceived as this pretty, fluffy blonde. I wasn't a Marie Colvin, but I pushed through the adversity because the work I was doing was so important to me."

When a fellow reporter attempted to steal her work, Brownworth had other plans. "I was covering a big story in which the photographer, who was better-known than I was at the time, stole my story. Literally stole it," she said. "You couldn't do that now because of computer time-stamping and so forth, but we were still using typewriters and notebooks then. I had to actually call in an attorney at the last minute on a Friday afternoon—the story was scheduled to run that Sunday—to get my name on the piece. So, it was often very stressful. I'm glad it's easier for women now than it was then."

Slogging in the trenches has paid off immensely for Brownworth. "I think once you win enough awards, as I have, you have a name. I mean, I made a name for myself in two of the biggest cities in America—New York and Philadelphia—and I think that makes a difference. I think being able to do that has a high difficulty factor. I can call people and email people and pitch stories and not have to go through channels," she said.

Writer's block? No such thing, according to Brownworth. "Writer's block doesn't exist," she said. "It's a myth formulated and perpetuated by rich white male writers in the 1930s and '40s who spent a lot of time being drunk and not writing and then getting depressed about it. As I tell my writing students, if you think you have writer's block, you are suffering from one of two things: depression, in which case you need a therapist and/or an antidepressant, or laziness (which is far more likely), in which case you need to just sit your ass down and write.

"If you are a writer, there is always something to write about. It's just a matter of doing it. If you don't have a story to tell, you aren't a writer."

At age 33, Brownworth received a shocking blow when she was diagnosed with primary progressive multiple sclerosis. "I was devastated by that diagnosis, which I received in a week that I was being filmed by England's Channel 4 for a documentary based on a series of articles I had written about lesbians on death row," she said. "I had been covering a story about a year before, out in California, and gotten rather ill. I attributed it to the heat, but it was part of a five-year process of being diagnosed. This not knowing what was wrong with me was problematic while I was traveling for stories, working 18-, 20-hour days sometimes."

The diagnosis of MS led to the end of her investigative-reporting career. "I had to retool my writing career entirely," she said, "because I couldn't know from one day to the next how I would feel. For example, from 1995 to 1998, I was almost wholly in bed with a severe exacerbation. I did a lot of work over the phone, and at that time I was working as a columnist for the *Philadelphia Daily News* and also as a columnist and feature writer for *POZ*, the AIDS magazine. I also started writing books."

If she could name one thing that has changed the journalism field drastically since the 1980s, what would it be? "In a word: technology," she said. "I started out in journalism working on typewriters and having to physically get copy from one place to another. Then we got computers and everything changed. When we got email, it just streamlined everything. The Internet revolutionized reporting because the kind of irritating, searching-through-microfiche kind of research can now be done via computer, thanks to the great god Google."

Brownworth does keep a few issues close to her heart, like a quill pen on parchment paper.

"Issues of racism, sexism, classism and homophobia have always been important to me and always will be," Brownworth said. "Over the past couple of years, I have been very involved in writing about the civil liberties abuses of the Obama administration, which the ACLU itself cites as the worst in decades.

"Recently, I have done a lot of writing about the case of Private Bradley Manning, one of the six whistleblowers being prosecuted by the Obama administration under the 1917 Espionage Act. Manning is being held in indefinite detention, which Obama signed into law. Manning is a queer political prisoner of this administration, but we barely talk about him."

Brownworth also offered views regarding censorship from within her own community. "I have also been writing about the dramatic number of deportations under this administration—four times as many as under the Bush administration," she said. "But I have found for the first time that I am being censored—a lot of the queer press is very pro-Obama and doesn't want to look at the issues, because they believe he is their friend. But I would like to see what the response would have been if George Bush had said he was 'evolving' on civil rights. I have no time for bigoted straight people to catch up to our queer lives. That includes the president I voted into office."

Leaving neither side unscathed, Brownworth added: "Most recently, I've written about the contraception fight spurred by the Republicans, who on the one hand say that they want less government and then work at trying to control the lives of women every chance they get. These issues all involve self-determination, so they are of vital import to the LGBT community—and, of course, to all women."

The outspoken writer currently pens columns for political blogs and about television shows, works as an editor for various publications, and writes books, short stories and essays in anthologies and academic journals. Variety is the key to longevity, according to Brownworth.

"I've always had a wide range of interests, but had I not become ill, I would have continued to be an investigative reporter and possibly even a war reporter, I think," she said. "I was very drawn to reporting on conflicts. I've been forced to work within the confines of my illness and the limitations it has placed on me. I feel grateful that I have a myriad of interests and that I can write in and for different venues. I'm still a news junkie, and politics infuses everything I do, so I would say that the unifying element to all my writing is the importance of giving voice to the voiceless. The one format I haven't tackled is playwriting. I would still like to write a play. Something queer, naturally."

Today in her "spare" time, she runs a press called Tiny Satchel Press.

"Tiny Satchel Press is my new baby," she said. "I founded the press in 2010 to publish young-adult books for kids, who I felt from working as an acquisitions editor were not being represented. I've lived in a neighborhood that is almost wholly African-American and mostly poor for 20 years now, and I felt there weren't books for the kids in my neighborhood, the kids I was mentoring. And there aren't enough books for LGBT kids, either. Or kids who aren't middle-class. I wanted books for the kids who couldn't afford to go to Hogwarts with Harry Potter. I wanted the kind of books I wanted to read as a child—because we all need books that have us in them. We all need characters with whom we can identify."

The need for diversity even from within the ranks was important to Brownworth. "Tiny Satchel Press is focusing on books for LGBT kids and kids of color. So far, every book we have published has been nominated for at least one award, and one of our authors won the prestigious Moonbeam Award last year," she said. "I'm up for a Moonbeam myself this year [she won], as well as a Lambda Literary Award, which is very exciting. We have a new line of books coming out—a novella line—that I am really excited by. The stories are terrific. Our website is gorgeous. We do all our books in both print and e-book. We just published the first lesbian teen vampire novel. It's fantastic."

Speaking of e-books, does she read them? Not likely, she said: "I think e-books are classist. You can't pass an e-book to your other poor friends. You can't buy a used e-book. You can't walk around the used e-book store and look at the variety of e-books. So—print. Always print."

Victoria Brownworth, circa 1980s.
Photo by Tee Corinne

A Victoria Brownworth story in *Philadelphia Gay News*, bottom left, September 13, 1991.

18

Gay Press: High Expectations

By Lisa Keen

In the 2012 HBO docudrama *Game Change,* the character of Steve Schmidt, a senior adviser to Republican presidential nominee John McCain, makes a startling assessment of today's journalism:

"No news story lasts more than 48 hours anymore," he said. "News is no longer meant to be remembered. It's just entertainment."

That wasn't just a scripted line. Schmidt recalls saying that, "verbatim."

It's a stinging indictment of the news media. But it's also a stinging indictment of news consumers.

It says the average adult American no longer expects to receive significant reports of news that can be used to help him or her form an opinion or decide a course of action. Instead, he or she expects to receive information that is entertaining.

If this is true, then the average American is making important decisions, such as for whom to vote for president, based on an emotional reaction to some interesting pieces of information, rather than a studied decision based on useful, factual news.

There is no doubt that more and more "news organizations" cater to this phenomenon of entertaining information. The 24/7 news networks are largely a series of talking heads and video clips.

One might argue that it's useful to hear seasoned political observers offer an array of opinions on various candidates and political developments. One could also argue that their banter is ginned up to maximize its entertainment value and, in doing so, amounts to the equivalent of pink slime.

Video clips from an important event, such as police abuse of a citizen, are useful in helping establish facts beyond a subjective doubt and build pressure for appropriate action. Video clips of drunken and half-naked people being pulled out of their cars by police? Not so useful.

LGBT news media are under pressure, too, to generate a constant stream of content. And, as a result, many are as guilty as the mainstream of running infotainment as if it were news. On a recent day, for instance, a visitor to one gay news website would have seen the "top story" amounting to Ellen DeGeneres spoofing the movie *Titanic*. At another site, the top "news" was a report that the White House press secretary had no response to a question *about a question that was not asked* of the president by a gay couple who had planned to ask the question during the annual White House Easter-egg hunt.

So, how does the consumer hoping to avoid junk news know what to look for and where to look?

First, it's important to be able to recognize the difference between real news and junk news (aka infotainment). Real news coverage is a substantial *report* of an event, discovery or development with a significant *impact* that *merits attention* by a *large number of people*. For media directed toward LGBT people, the report should merit the attention of a large number of LGBT people. President Obama speaking to the annual Human Rights Campaign dinner is news: The most powerful leader in the world draws attention throughout the world wherever he speaks, and when he speaks to HRC, he speaks to and about LGBT people, and many people all over the world listen. His support, or silence, influences others.

A tweet is not news coverage. It is not a substantial report, though, at its best, it can be a reference ping to an unfolding news development.

A blog can deliver news, depending on the blog. As an article on the Poynter.org website put it a few years ago, "the news is what's important, not the medium." But blogs, aka Web logs, started out as a scroll of personal observations, or opinions, about whatever the blogger cared to write about.

There's room for confusion here, because nearly every major news organization now has multiple blogs on its news website, and many of these blogs are written by reporters. And there are blog websites that do not purport to be news organizations but that do, in fact, deliver news—Scotusblog.com, for instance.

Second, a reader should be able to distinguish quality reporting from just information delivery. Example: reporting poll results. How questions are worded—especially when they involve anything gay—is important.

Beginning in 2003, an ABC/*Washington Post* poll asked respondents, "Do you think it should be legal or illegal for homosexual couples to get married?" For years, a majority—about 58 percent—said "illegal." But as soon as the pollsters changed the wording and started asking "Do you think it should be legal or illegal for *gay and lesbian* couples to get married?" the majority started saying "legal." Many news reports fail to account for these hidden factors, either because they have such limited time or space to cover the poll or, worse, because they don't recognize them.

A quality news report will include the numbers and how they've changed, but it will also explain how other factors may be in play with the numbers, such as language, timing (polls taken just after a big news story can affect respondents' answers), and whether respondents are being reached on a land line or cellphone.

Third, it's important to see through a news organization's bias, which can go both ways on LGBT matters. For example, when the well-respected Williams Institute released a report in April 2011 estimating that 3.5 percent of the adult population identifies as LGBT, the Associated Press report focused on the percentage who identified as *homosexual*: 1.7 percent. This, noted AP, was "a much lower figure than the 3 percent to 5 percent that has been the conventional wisdom in the last two decades, based on other isolated studies and flaws noted in Kinsey's methodology." Buried deep in the story was the fact that another 1.8 percent identify as bisexual and that 8.2 percent had had a sexual partner of the same sex. The bias in that report made the LGBT community look much smaller than it really is.

Fourth, readers should make sure they are getting the kind of detail they need. Back in the early 1980s, many gay men died because of the spread of HIV, but many more *would* have died had it not been for the urgent reporting every week in gay newspapers distributed throughout the LGBT community.

Yes, some mainstream papers did run the occasional story about the mysterious "gay disease." But some of that reporting was the kind that alarmed the general public, leading many to believe it was dangerous to even go near a gay person.

And mainstream publications did not publish information to encourage gay men to use condoms, get tested or watch their T-cell counts, or to let them know where they could go to find specific, confidential help and counsel. The community relied on the gay press to do that back then, and there are many similar issues today. For instance, if a reader wants to find out if a proposed federal budget includes funding for the president's programs to prevent bullying, he or she is not likely to find that from a mainstream news organization.

Finally, readers may want to remember that news becomes history. When historians endeavor to analyze and record what has happened over time to a group, such as LGBT people, most of them do considerable research. That research includes interviews with key players, examination of original documents and reading of previous reports. Many of those previous reports are from newspapers and other media outlets.

To some extent, historians rely on news reports to identify who the key players are. That's one reason it is a bit unsettling to see many LGBT community papers today relying heavily on The Associated Press for their coverage of LGBT matters.

The other reason it's unsettling is that, if LGBT community papers become too reliant on stories produced by a mainstream news organization, they risk giving away the shop. Readers are overwhelmed today with the number of options they have for news and for information. Diluting the uniqueness of LGBT papers through the heavy use of copy that is already widely available in dominant mainstream news vehicles makes visiting an LGBT media outlet less compelling. And that silences our community's voices, to the world and to ourselves.

In the interest of full disclosure, this last criticism is self-serving. My news service produces news stories to sell to LGBT news organizations, and much of our potential business is raked away by The Associated Press, which, as a mammoth organization, can produce and sell its articles much more cheaply.

But what's also true is that it's a tough world in which to operate an LGBT news organization today. The community expects its newspapers to keep up with the warp-speed pace of news delivery, and there is no concomitant clamor for depth in coverage of LGBT news and no commitment to seeing that the community-owned news organizations have the funding necessary to tackle in-depth and independent coverage. Without the resources to tackle in-depth coverage, LGBT papers and readers are left with Schmidt's stark reality—that "no news story lasts more than 48 hours anymore. News is no longer meant to be remembered. It's just entertainment."

But it could be much more.

Lisa Keen.

19

Rex Wockner

By Sarah Toce

Rex Wockner's name has been linked to more than 325 gay and lesbian publications in the United States and internationally since 1985. He earned his degree in journalism from Drake University. Radio was his first port of call before landing a full-time gay media job at Chicago's *Outlines* (now *Windy City Times*) newspaper, then moving on to create a news service that syndicated stories and photos around the world.

So much has changed in journalism over the span of 27 years. The rotary telephone has been replaced with a cellphone you can fit in your coat pocket. The huge Apple Macintosh computer is extinct, and we now have an Apple iPad that does almost everything short of washing your clothes. Recorders now plug into ports on new tiny laptops that can stow away anywhere you could imagine, including the back pocket of the airplane seat in front of you. Pens now have the ability to record your every move. Big Brother sees everything you do. And the Internet has a mind all its own and even talks back to you through software programs. With all of this in mind, I decided to ask the media powerhouse how he stays intrigued with the field despite its many alterations.

"The gay civil-rights movement is in its final years now, and 'media'—in whatever old or new form—is how we stay informed," Wockner said. "I'm interested in information more than in any particular information-delivery vehicle. I stopped working as a reporter last year—because I needed a sabbatical, but also because that work seemed less relevant than previously. Information now spreads in a variety of formats before anyone has time to format the information into traditional news style.

"The Internet has given almost every person on earth the means to publish. Everyone now can be a reporter. Those who do a decent job will have followers, no matter what format their reporting takes. I don't see a downside to this. Good stuff will rise and bad stuff still will be ignored or rebuffed. The Internet also has removed from the 'gatekeeper' role the people who had enough money to be publishers (people with access to printing presses or with broadcasting licenses). They no longer determine what information is reported and what information isn't [reported]. I see no downside to this, either. More voices, more perspectives, more information—a more complete picture than we ever had before."

When asked if there were any modern media trends he wished would just "go away for good," Wockner answered the question with another question: "Besides those sensationalistic teasers for your local TV news that appear immediately before the resumption of the program you're watching?" Then, in all seriousness, he replied: "I'd like older media companies to focus on how people actually want to consume information today, and to figure out how to monetize providing that information. And I'd like many of the world's millions of citizen journalists to slow down just enough to do a bit of rudimentary fact-checking before they hit the button."

Wockner's been on a personal and professional voyage since he became aware of the gay-rights movement in 1979. He would take on a more committed role a few years later in 1984.

"I think I first got involved in 'the gay-rights movement' in 1984 in Champaign-Urbana by making contact with the Gay Illini group and making friends there who were activists," he said.

It was while he was advocating on HIV/AIDS issues that he had a chance meeting with Tracy Baim, who had founded *Outlines* newspaper in Chicago in 1987 (after co-founding *Windy City Times* in 1985). She traveled downstate from Chicago to cover an AIDS forum and met Wockner, a fellow Drake graduate. She discussed his freelancing for the paper, and he later became a full-time reporter. He stayed full-time for several years while also building a network of LGBT media around the world that published his syndicated reporting in their local markets. Thereafter, he left the *Outlines* staff and moved to California, while continuing to publish most of his syndicated work in *Outlines* (which later purchased and merged with *Windy City Times*).

"I first became aware of the gay-rights movement in 1979, when I subscribed to *The Village Voice* and started reading about it. The two biggest running stories of my gay-press career were ACT UP (the AIDS Coalition to Unleash Power) and Prop 8. Both 'stories' continued for years, were very interesting and frequently exciting, and changed the course of the movement nationally."

Gay-rights activists formed ACT UP in 1987 at the height of the HIV/AIDS epidemic with the tagline of "turn anger, fear and grief into action." The first sociopolitical event took place in March of that year on Wall Street in New York City. ACT UP addressed issues such as research, drug testing, prevention education, government intervention and measures to combat the disease in Africa.

Wockner's ACT UP coverage was not only a professional steppingstone but also personal: During that period of the HIV/AIDS crisis, he was losing many of his friends to the disease. "About half of my friends died before combo therapies mostly halted the decimation in about 1996," he said. "Careerwise, AIDS meant I had to be a medical reporter, a pharmaceutical reporter, and someone who found himself physically in the middle of sometimes-explosive civil-disobedience situations."

Wockner chased the story, and sometimes the story chased Wockner.

"I went places where big stories were happening, such as the first marriagelike civil unions (Denmark), the first same-sex marriages (the Netherlands), the first public gay events in the USSR, the international AIDS conferences and big international LGBT conferences, the gay marches on Washington, ACT UP mega-demos, the same-sex-marriage battle in Maine," he said.

The one thing that remained consistent, despite the inconsistencies in lawmaking and health care, was Wockner—and his camera. The papers would have a story and images to serve as illustration when Wockner was on the scene.

He is now waiting to see what the future holds for journalism.

"I granted myself a sabbatical last year while/until journalism remakes itself for the post-newspaper era," he said. "Any gaps that has created in gay journalism are indeed being filled by a variety of younger folks utilizing a variety of media models. Many of them, of course, are not reimbursed for their efforts. I still keep up daily with breaking gay news, in whatever format, and share links with my mailing list. I doubt there's a future for news reporting for weekly print media. At the same time, I don't think anyone has yet figured out the future of traditional newspaper-type journalism in the wake of the Internet era."

What three things would Wockner never admit to the press if pressured?

"On a few occasions, I became good friends with sources and probably wasn't able to be objective anymore. I suppose most journalists have faced this," he said. "Sometimes I didn't write stories because I didn't have the energy to deal with people who would go ballistic over them, [and lastly] I don't really have many secrets."

A 1991 Danny Sotomayor cartoon about Rex Wockner's attempts to cover the National Lesbian Conference.
Courtesy of Lori Cannon

Rex Wockner (center) on the job in 1988.
Photo by Cliff O'Neill

Rex Wockner (right) at the 1987 March on Washington.
Photo from *Outlines* newspaper

20

Robert Ford

By Owen Keehnen

While most of the people featured in this book had a connection to the regional gay newspaper movement in the U.S., Robert Ford's is a more unusual story. He was part of the burgeoning 'zine movement of the late 1980s and early 1990s. Those publications were usually radically different from traditional media. Thousands of individuals across the country, people of all sexual orientations and genders, produced their own media in the days just before the Internet was launched for all the world to use. Most gay newspapers have been dominated by Caucasian voices, and Robert Ford, a proudly out African-American gay man, was among a new generation of activists looking for a place for their own vision of queer identity.

Ford's legendary *Thing* 'zine, the "she knows who she is" magazine, began in late 1989 as a couple of hundred copies produced by three friends. Success came quickly. The third issue was sent to the printer for a run of 1,000. Sales continued to escalate; distribution climbed. The style and layout became graphically slicker, but the content remained hip, urban and sassy. The sixth issue had a print run of 2,000 and, just in the last couple of issues, *Thing* rose to a printing of 3,000 per issue.

Those numbers may be relatively small in the magazine world, but in the 'zine world they are gigantic. In early August 1993, Robert Ford, the publisher, editor, co–art director, and primary driving force behind *Thing*, announced that newly released issue No. 10 would be the final one. *Thing* had come to an end, but it rode the crest of 'zine popularity with a quality and style that helped set the pace as well as the standards of the underground 'zine movement. It was the format's greatest success story.

Thing helped define a huge and relatively unexplored part of the gay/lesbian/trans/queer movement: the 'zine explosion. It was big news when Robert Ford announced that *Thing* was ceasing publication. I remember biking to Robert's walk-up apartment the day we did this interview. In the hallway on the landing just outside his door were basically the *Thing* archives with not-so-neat stacks of all the back issues.

I am greatly relieved to know that every issue is in the archives at the Chicago History Museum. It was too important a cultural movement to be lost. Robert welcomed me that day with a weary smile. He was sick at the time, really sick, but despite his illness, he was as charming as ever as we discussed what led to his decision to end *Thing*, his thoughts on the 'zine movement, and what projects he had lined up for the future.

Just months after this 1993 interview was published, Robert Ford, 32, died of AIDS complications—and another incredible, powerful and vibrant voice of the queer movement was silenced. Before he died in 1994, he was inducted into the Chicago Gay and Lesbian Hall of Fame.

Owen: What considerations led to your decision to have issue No. 10 be the final *Thing*?

Robert: Lots of them. Financial decisions were important. *Thing* was always barely able to pay for itself, but it never was really self-sufficient as a publication. It would always reach a zero bank account between issues. *Thing* had reached an odd scale, too small to generate lots of funding and too large to run without a staff.

Owen: Was *Thing* the first 'zine you worked on?

Robert: I was always interested in publishing. A couple years before, I did a magazine called *Think Ink*. It was very black and not very gay, but it was pretty queer-friendly, though that wasn't a defining point for it. It lasted a couple of issues. It never made any money, but it was a learning process. It got me to dive in and get my hands dirty. I learned a lot about putting out a magazine. Then after *Think Ink*, I started seeing more 'zines cropping up: *My Comrade, Pansy Beat* and *Sin Brothers*. I also had a Macintosh [computer] and I think part of me was looking for something to do with it. I found something, all right.

Owen: What original vision did you have when you began publishing *Thing* in late 1989?

Robert: The original intent was to do a 'zine very clearly from a black underground focus. Trent Adkins, Lawrence Warren and I were the three founders of the original *Thing*. We were all fans of what was happening in the underground because there was so much in the way of a black sensibility there. We didn't want to fault the magazine media for not being that, but we saw the possibility for an alternative media. We knew for ourselves what a rich and important cultural thing gay black men have and share. We wanted to make a magazine that would be a way of documenting our existence and contribution to society. Our idea was not so much radicalize or subvert the idea of magazines as to make one from our own point of view. It wasn't about deconstructing what a magazine is; it was playing within its perimeters.

Owen: You did it well enough that *Thing* evolved into a national publication very quickly. How did that happen?

Robert: Our first issues were extremely 'zinelike. All the material was either written by the three founding members or lifted from various places. I guess about the time of issue No. 3, I began actively soliciting other writers and started being more of an editor. At that time, we went to a larger size and started having shorter features and arts-related news in the front, big features in the middle, and recurring columnists in the back. Around that time, the 'zine went national, so the focus had to be taken from the personal and the local and be more national as well.

Owen: The word 'zine is tossed around so much. What does that mean to you?

Robert: Any magazine not put out by a corporate entity. It's derived from the idea of fanzines. The individual is paying homage to their slavish obsessions, whatever they may be. A lot cropped up as fanzines around certain stars. *Thing* isn't really out of that tradition, but then, I look at all the underground personalities I was drawn to and see *Thing* was very much defining what was important for itself—someone can be famous because *Thing* thinks they're famous. It showed fame isn't necessarily something conferred by the masses.

Owen: How do you think 'zines have influenced mainstream publications?

Robert: I think the lines got blurred a lot. *QW* always seemed like a 'zine to me in its short existence, certainly much better-financed, slicker and glossier, but you still got the feeling it was a small, underpaid group who just really passionately believed in what they did. It didn't seem created by marketing gurus. It seemed created because the people themselves believed the editorial content was important. *Monk* is another example. It's printed on glossy paper with Absolut ads, but its whole reason for being is very 'zinelike.

Owen: Where do you see the world of 'zines headed?

Robert: I remember some people complaining at the last Spew ['zine convention] about how there was a lot of bad coming-out 'zines with ACT UP graphics and some campy gay graphics slapped together with nothing really to say. I think that's changing. Now that 'zines aren't as novel of a format, people aren't just doing them to rant. I think the ones coming out now are more thoughtful.

Owen: What's in store for you careerwise at this point?

Robert: One of the things that made me decide to fold *Thing* was that I was getting offered to do other kinds of projects and immediately turned them down because *Thing* had become my life's work. I decided to concentrate on different kinds of writing. I'm doing a weekly music piece for *Babble* [a now-defunct Chicago gay publication], and I'm also doing a bimonthly column for *Plus*, which I'm very excited about. [Before folding *Thing*] when I was approached to do an African-American AIDS column, I immediately said no, but I wanted to do that column. I had a lot to say about those issues.

Part of what impacted *Thing* folding was my personal health. I've gone through a series of opportunistic infections and I'm hanging in there on a day-to-day level. Going through a few OIs has really made me step back and take stock of things. *Thing* had reached a point where it was creating more stress in my life. I wanted a way to get the creative stuff out of me, but not so taxing on a day-to-day level.

Owen: What ideas do you have for your *Plus* column?

Robert: I would like to keep the structure loose so sometimes I can be more theoretical and other times I speak from a more personal point of view. Every column will focus on HIV; some will focus on HIV and race, some on HIV and my sexuality as an African-American gay man, some on both.

Owen: Your *Plus* column sounds like it has the potential for the kind of direct impact most writers dream about.

Robert: Well, part of the reason I started *Thing* was that I wanted to write but, as it went on, I realized the one thing I wasn't doing was writing like I wanted to.

Owen: What's going through your mind when you think about the final issue of *Thing* being on the newsstands?

Robert: I look back on it with a sense of closure and completion. I'm excited about my upcoming projects. *Thing* the quarterly has died, but sometime in the next month or so I'd like to regress a little bit and put out another real 'zine that has no issue date, no expectations, that promises no issues after that, that is just kind of out there in your face.

[This interview was conducted in 1993. It is reprinted here from Owen Keehnen's book, We're Here, We're Queer: The Gay '90s and Beyond.*]*

Robert Ford of *Thing* 'zine.

The cover and three inside pages of the fall 1992 *Thing* 'zine.

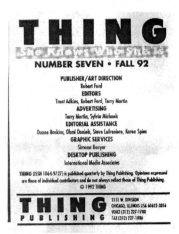

21

Headlines, Heroes and History

By Karen Ocamb

Almost two weeks after California Governor Pete Wilson vetoed the long-fought-for gay rights bill AB 101, I found myself sitting next to Jim Kepner on the 384-mile bus ride from Los Angeles to Sacramento for yet another outburst of outrage over the ease with which government sloughs off LGBT people as second-class citizens. It was National Coming Out Day, October 11, 1991, and I marveled at how this 68-year-old was determined to drag his already-frail, stooped body out to a wildly unpredictable protest march at the Capitol. But as one of the original citizen journalists of the LGBT movement, he felt the need to participate in history being made, which I needed to dutifully record.

Without fuss or fanfare, this modest gay man with twinkling eyes treated me to an LGBT "oral history" and a master class in advocacy journalism. My thinking shifted. I was rooted in mainstream professionalism—the high bar of "objective" reporting to which "advocacy" was anathema.

But suddenly "objectivity" itself was challenged. What if the truth lies not in the facts discerned by a mainstream reporter who parachutes into a scene and relies on statements by the loudest eyewitness, but rather in nuance and historical context unimagined, unobserved or unavailable to the outsider?

That's why there is such a need for LGBT, minority and "specialty" press to provide insight, balance and often accuracy to stories where chasing and grasping nuance is too often perceived as a chore or a luxury by mainstream reporters on deadline.

Los Angeles is one of the birthplaces of the LGBT press. "Lisa Ben"—a pen name for Edith Eyde—started *Vice Versa*, the first known lesbian publication, in Los Angeles in 1947. The newsletter/ magazine, laboriously typed in carbon copies, enabled lesbians to connect with each other at a time when homosexuality was a ruinous crime, an official psychological perversion and a religious abomination for which "cures" were imprisonment, lobotomies and castration for men.

A few years later came *ONE*, an outgrowth of the Los Angeles-based Mattachine Society through a new organization called ONE, Inc. Soon after, the Mattachine Society founded its own journal, the *Mattachine Review*.

Most of the *ONE* contributors were amateur journalists. Del Martin and Phyllis Lyon, founders of the Daughters of Bilitis and its publication *The Ladder*, however, were university-trained journalists. They created the DOB newsletter *The Ladder* and wrote three books, starting with the iconic *Lesbian/ Woman* in 1972.

The *PRIDE* (Personal Rights in Defense and Education) *Newsletter* was transformed into *The Los Angeles Advocate* (later *The Advocate* national magazine) after a 1967 police raid on the Black Cat bar in Los Angeles' Silver Lake neighborhood. It reported on who was beaten where, police raids and protests well before the Stonewall riots in New York in 1969.

The gay liberation movement sprang up at the same time as students, women, blacks and Chicanos were finding the power in their voices, too. They were more aggressive than the civil-rights and early counterculture movements that blossomed during the presidency of John F. Kennedy. The sexual-liberation movement picked up steam, too, with the publication of Betty Friedan's 1963 book *The Feminine Mystique* and the wide use of the birth-control pill.

But it was *ONE* magazine that pried open America's puritanical closet door. The FBI had been trying to shut *ONE* down for some time. Eventually, Kepner's March 1954 cover story "The Importance of Being Different" prompted Senate Foreign Relations Committee Chairman Alexander Wiley (R-Wisconsin) to write a protest letter to the U.S. postmaster general about the "so-called 'magazine' devoted to the advancement of sexual perversions," according to Jim Burroway of BoxTurtleBulletin.

The defiant editors subsequently asked their legal counsel to write up what the rules were for an October 1954 cover story, "You Can't Print It!" But in the same issue were a fictional love story with a happy ending, a poem about morals charges and two ads—all of which postal officials determined meant the magazine was "obscene." The LA post office seized the "You Can't Print It!" issue and charged *ONE* editors with sending an "obscene, lewd, and/or lascivious" publication through the mail in violation of the 1873 Comstock Act.

ONE sued, and its young attorney Eric Julber argued the case pro bono before the federal courts. He lost before the district and appeals courts. Then, to the surprise of many, the U.S. Supreme Court took the case and, in its first decision on homosexuality, issued a one-sentence ruling on January 13, 1958, that overturned the lower courts' rulings and expanded freedom of speech and freedom of the press. The ruling also enabled the five-year old *Playboy* magazine to be distributed through the mail, injecting even more excitement into the sexual-liberation movement.

A quarter-of-a-century later, the gay- and sexual-liberation movements were brought up short with the revelation that AIDS was sexually transmitted. To compensate, new sex-phone businesses emerged and became a solid financial advertising foundation for gay publications.

In 1987, all the pent-up grief and fear turned into a righteous and sexy outrage with the formation of ACT UP. The LGBT press covered the protests with excitement while most mainstream reporters followed the "facts" as presented by the Los Angeles Police Department or other government officials. Dave Johnson, a onetime reporter for the old *Los Angeles Free Press* and the executive director of Being Alive, started writing a regular column for a thin gay-activist weekly called *The News*, run by Sandy Dwyer. Johnson argued that it was the virus, not sex, that was bad. The mood in LA shifted again, as the long pall of depression started to lift—though gay publications such as *Frontiers*, *Update* in San Diego and the *Bay Area Reporter* in San Francisco still looked like the photo/print version of the NAMES Project AIDS Memorial Quilt because there were so many obituaries inside their pages.

So much death yielded heady risk-taking. I was freelancing for *The Advocate* under Editor-in-Chief Richard Rouillard and Editor Mark Thompson when Rouillard challenged everything, promoting Queer Nation, starting the Sissy Awards and, in 1991, publishing Michelangelo Signorile's outing of Assistant Defense Secretary Pete Williams at a time when the Pentagon was purging gays. Rouillard also changed *The Advocate*'s subhead to read, "The national gay and lesbian newsmagazine."

My journey in LGBT journalism started in the late 1980s. So many friends were outed by—and then died from—AIDS, I felt morally obligated to come out. But I didn't know how to be useful other than to write about what I saw. My first piece was an essay for *Frontiers* titled "Ten Days That Shook the FDA," about the August 1989 hunger strike in West Hollywood by ACT UP's Wayne Karr and Lou Lance, both of whom had AIDS. At the same time, Dave Johnson, then LA's first AIDS coordinator, was testifying before Congress, and Mark Kostopolous, Michael Callen and so many others were storming the Food and Drug Administration, demanding compassionate release of experimental AIDS drugs.

Two months later, in October 1989, 400 people surrounded the Federal Building in LA's Westwood neighborhood, demanding access to experimental drugs in the glacial FDA pipeline. About 80 people were arrested.

I wasn't trained as a science or medical writer, and I worried about getting the facts wrong. But I tried—learning about antioxidants and free radicals for a piece in Sean Strub's new *POZ* magazine in

1994, for instance. Fortuitously, *Frontiers* News Editor Aslan Brooke was a former Army nurse who understood the emerging A-to-Z vocabulary of the new HIV medications. Eventually, ACT UP/LA's Bruce Mirkin and I struck up a kind of unspoken deal: He covered mostly science and medicine, while I covered politics and events.

Mike Salinas, the news editor at the *Bay Area Reporter*, called me an "environmental" reporter because of my emerging "you-are-there" style. I started thinking of the homebound person with AIDS who would have loved to attend the event I was covering. I imagined a friend reading my story out loud so the sick person with AIDS, or PWA, could imagine being there.

At times, this was humorously challenging. I had to ask the guy from the Gap, sitting next to me, what was so fabulous about this new Isaac Mizrahi collection that looked to me as if the models (and Sandra Bernhard) were wearing shag-carpet jackets. But even more difficult was trying to capture the textures, back stories, subplots and nuances in a very limited space on the printed page. And herein, perhaps, lies a big difference between mainstream and minority reporting. The *Los Angeles Times*, for example, wrote about the 1995 L.A. Shanti "Tribute to Joe Layton" in the entertainment section as a "Pop Music Review: Midler, Others Pay Tribute to Joe Layton." Reporter Don Heckman actually reviewed the event.

Nowhere in the story did Heckman mention that Layton died of AIDS complications, as the *Times* had previously reported. In fact, AIDS was mentioned only once—in the context of the kinds of services L.A. Shanti provided. But for me, the whole event was about AIDS. The show was hosted by comedian Bruce Vilanch, who by this time joked that he had emceed so many AIDS benefits, he should have a card that read "AIDS-R-US." The *Times* reviewer only mentioned Carol Burnett—but gays and PWAs knew her as the actress and comedian who did the first TV public service announcement for the new American Foundation for AIDS Research in 1985, the year Rock Hudson died and Elizabeth Taylor, Dr. Michael Gottlieb and Dr. Mathilde Krim started amFAR.

Heckman ended his review in this way: "Closing her headliner segment of the show, [Bette] Midler's tribute of 'Happiness Is Just a Thing Called Joe' and 'Wind Beneath My Wings' was both tender and heartfelt, a fitting conclusion to a well-produced evening."

Twelve years later, I still remember that L.A. Shanti event: how a large black-and-white portrait of Joe Layton was unfurled—taking everyone's breath away and prompting Bette Midler to step backward slightly, momentarily overwhelmed. She recovered and explained who Layton was to her, sharing with people who she knew would understand. As her voice choked, she turned to the portrait of her friend and sang, "Did you ever know that you're my hero, and everything I would like to be? I can fly higher than an eagle, 'cause you are the wind beneath my wings."

There was not a dry eye in the Wiltern Theater as Midler concluded, the thunderous standing ovation an emotional outlet for all the love and grief stored up inside so many. I didn't feel worthy or skilled enough to capture that miraculous moment. But I knew I had to struggle through it. I cried as I typed, imagining the homebound PWA listening to my words.

It is a privilege to capture such moments, the gems of our LGBT history and the legacy upon which the next generation stands.

The irony is that, for all our maturation, we still ask questions similar to those Kepner asked in that March 1954 cover story for *ONE* magazine, written under the pen name Lyn Pedersen.

"Are homosexuals in any important way different from other people? If so, ought that difference be cultivated, or hidden under a bushel, or extirpated altogether?" Kepner wrote. Homosexuals are "natural rebels ... . Most become inured to breaking the rules. They must reject what they learned as children and still hear repeated about them. ... It should barely be necessary to state that I am interested in defending my right to be as different as I damn please. And I've picked up the notion that I can't protect my own rights without fighting for everyone else's."

Jim Kepner died on November 15, 1997. He was 74. By then, Kepner's massive collection of LGBT books, other publications and memorabilia had become the International Gay and Lesbian Archives, which merged with ONE Institute. His memorial in the Academy of Motion Picture Arts and Sciences auditorium was packed with LGBT pioneers.

I sat in the back, dutifully taking notes, wondering at the nuanced mystic bond, the history shared among these LGBT brothers and sisters over the dark years and the brighter years to come.

Jim Kepner, Harry Hay and Morris Kight. At this March 19, 1994, event for the Southern California Library for Social Studies and Research, Hay was being honored along with Paul Monette, Jackie Goldberg and Virginia Uribe.
Photo by Karen Ocamb

Karen Ocamb (center), David Mixner and Hillary Clinton in 1991 when she was on the campaign trail. Photo by Karen Ocamb

22

The Passing Parade:
Cultural Reporting in an Age of Heroes

By Jorjet Harper

There are several large plastic storage bins in my back room filled with stacks of clippings of articles I wrote for the Chicago gay and lesbian newspapers *GayLife*, *Windy City Times* and *Outlines* during the 1980s and early 1990s, and for other GLBT publications, including New York's *OutWeek* magazine, the *Bay Area Reporter* in San Francisco, *Frontiers* in Los Angeles, *Bay Windows* in Boston, the *Washington Blade*, the *Dallas Voice*, *TWN* in Miami, *Southern Voice* in Atlanta and the *Lambda Book Report*.

Looking through these articles and photos from decades ago is a weird experience for me. The stories themselves are from a bygone era—with names and faces, events and controversies that seem so distant now, in light of where we are today—and yet I can relive the emotional environment of that time as if I'd been there just yesterday.

It's difficult to convey how exciting—sometimes even thrilling—it was to work in gay and lesbian media at that time in U.S. history. To be in the midst of the gay and lesbian cultural renaissance (or more accurately, naissance, since nothing like it had ever happened before) that took place in the latter half of the 1980s, to think about it and to report on it, was nothing short of exhilarating. All those passionate discussions we had about the burning issues of the day, and marches, and demonstrations, and kiss-ins! At the same time, the appalling horror of AIDS—the plague that came out of nowhere and snuffed out so many gay lives—cast its shadow over everything and everyone I knew. The highs and lows we experienced were steep, to put it mildly, and sometimes followed so closely on one another that there was hardly room to take a breath in between.

The first newspaper I contributed to in Chicago, after moving here from New York in 1979, was a little feminist periodical called *Blazing Star*. *Blazing Star*—named, for some symbolic reason I no longer remember, after the liatris flower—was the project of a group of socialist-leaning lesbian feminists I met sometime in 1980 who were members of a Chicago chapter of a national socialist-feminist organization called the New American Movement (NAM). Judy MacLean, Hannah Frisch, Chris Riddiough and Elaine Wessel were the core members of the *Blazing Star* group. There were quite a few other, more occasional participants whose names I no longer recall, some of whom had nothing to do with NAM and simply wanted to work on a lesbian-feminist newspaper.

We met weekly at each others' apartments, discussed ideas for articles we thought would be good to have in the next issue, and parsed out who among us would write them or who we could tap in the women's community to write on a particular topic. During production time, at a storefront office location, we met with a lesbian (unfortunately, I don't recall her name, either) who never offered input on content but donated her time typesetting and laying out the pages for us.

The paper was all-women-written and all-women-produced, and it was one of a number of feisty little lesbian-feminist, we-are-women-hear-us-roar newspapers that appeared and disappeared in the feminist adrenalin surges of the 1970s and early 1980s. In general, these papers communicated news, ideas and literature of various political and social congruences, sometimes not overtly lesbian but usually with a core of lesbian-feminists to spur them on, and were part of the larger Women in Print movement that was politically robust at that time.

Times have definitely changed, but it should be said that when women got together without any participation by men, without being observed by men, it was often profoundly freeing and powerfully creative. Events that took place in "women-only space," produced by women, were, in my opinion, a vital component of the women's liberation movement. In those days, meetings of lesbians interested in print media could be by turns inspiring, enlightening, touching, heart-wrenching, stirring, amusing and goofy—and occasionally lunatic (not in the good sense of the word) when they became dominated by strident separatist ideologues.

As one example of many, I remember a Women in Print conference I attended in Madison, Wisconsin, where discussion went on in all seriousness for about an hour on the merits of including in the group's statement the "demand" that public libraries keep all lesbian books and periodicals under lock and key and allow only lesbians to view or borrow them. Questions of how this was to work in practice were fielded: How can librarians determine who is a lesbian? Should there be a separate card catalog as well for these women-only books? If the librarian is a man, can he look at the books? And even: But aren't we "allowing librarians too much power" if they are the gatekeepers of "our" books, unless the librarians are also lesbians? Etc., etc.

The first time I sat through a meeting where this kind of radical posturing was going on, I was astonished, looking around to see if the speakers were tripping; later on at these types of discussions I just gave up expecting any conversation to emerge that had practical consequences, and amused myself doodling in my notebook.

There were also discussions about the best way to spell "women" so as to eliminate the "men" from the latter half of the word—"wimmin," "womyn," "womon" and even something like "wombmoon" were proposed and used in various radical separatist contexts. It was silly, yes, but also an indication of how, in those heady days of second-wave feminism, everything, even orthography, was scrutinized for signs of sexism.

In contrast, the *Blazing Star* group was very sharp, witty and sincere about effecting social change, and I gravitated towards them. We distributed each issue of *Blazing Star* ourselves, of course, delivering bundles of papers to designated lesbian locations. I remember that once, in Hannah Frisch's car, we got a flat tire in the rain and had to pull up right outside a gay bar on Clark Street a few blocks north of Fullerton Parkway.

The car was so loaded down with newspapers that we had to take the heavy bundles out of the trunk in order to jack up the tire. Though *Blazing Star* was an all-women (code: lesbian) newspaper, some gay men in Chicago certainly knew of it. Rather than pile all the bundles on the street and ruin papers in the rain, we went into the gay bar to ask if we could stack them there for a bit. Initially, all the men inside (and it was only men) were very unfriendly and treated us like intruders—one loudly shouted "Fuck off!" at us—until they saw what newspaper we were delivering. Then they instantly became very nice to us, helping us lug the paper bundles inside, and in minutes three of them had even fixed the tire for us.

I mention this story to illustrate that while there was certainly a cultural energy barrier between many gay men and lesbians in the early 1980s, there was still a very real sense of community that was protective, and a recognition that we were all in it together.

During our weekly *Blazing Star* meetings, much time was spent discussing the intersections among lesbian liberation, feminism and socialist politics; the latest ideological crisis (there always was at least one) inside the lesbian community; and the gossip about which couples had broken up or gotten together. As a newcomer in Chicago, I often had no idea who was being gossiped about, but as a newcomer to the community, I found both the ideological discussions and the trash talk highly educational.

I was a feminist former hippie acid head, not really a revolutionary leftist politico, so I was much more interested in our discussions of gyn/ecology, compulsory heterosexuality and archeological evidence of ancient goddess worship than I was in talking about cultural hegemony, dialectical materialism or the differences between the Leninists and the Trotskyists—but I was willing to hear about Gramsci as long as we also got around to talking about Adrienne Rich.

Even with our enthusiasm, feminist zeal and the latest gossip, it was a shitload of work to put out each new issue all on a volunteer basis, and those who had been at it quite a bit longer than I had were in various stages of burnout or looking to do something different with their politics. Also, as I recall, NAM was becoming reluctant to foot the paper's printing costs. After not too many months, and many discussions that were both heartfelt and heated, the core group of women of *Blazing Star* decided to stop printing as an independent newspaper and become a section in the city's main gay newspaper, *GayLife*.

GayLife

Embedding *Blazing Star* in *GayLife* worked out pretty well for a time, but the *Blazing Star* group as a whole disintegrated. Judy MacLean moved to San Francisco (and went on to write for the *San Francisco Chronicle* and *The Advocate*, among other publications), and Chris Riddiough moved away (to Washington, D.C., and continued her feminist and socialist activism there). Attempts to recruit new group members failed. Several of the less-active volunteers, who didn't like the idea of working in any way with "the boys" and were therefore not happy with the "merger" decision, splintered off to create more new and, unfortunately, short-lived women's newspapers.

Soon after *Blazing Star* "merged" with *GayLife, GayLife* changed management from Grant Ford—the publisher who had invited *Blazing Star* into *GayLife* and who, the group felt, was sincere in his desire to boost lesbian readership of the paper—to Chuck Renslow, the colorful, notorious Chicago leatherman who didn't seem to care one way or another about whether lesbians read Chicago's gay newspaper.

As the *Blazing Star* section of *GayLife* imploded, I began to write articles directly for the editor of the paper, Steve Kulieke. He seemed content to let me write about whatever topics interested me—usually some aspect of the growing women's-music movement or the lesbian-feminist movement. For example, I reviewed the groundbreaking book *Lesbian Nuns* and did a feature article on Mary Daly, music reviews of Ferron and Margie Adam, and an interview with Holly Near (you can Google these people if you've never heard of them, of course). I covered women's-music festivals and interviewed local musicians in the Chicago gay and lesbian entertainment scene. I even did several cartoon strips for the paper.

The first time I wrote an article about a gay man rather than a lesbian, the editor (by then Steve Kulieke had left for San Francisco, too, and it was Bill Williams) decided that I was enough of an asset to be paid for my pieces. He offered me $15 an article. Which I took.

I had been writing reviews and interviews for *GayLife* on and off for three or four years when Tracy Baim, right out of journalism school, became editorial assistant in 1984. When she was promoted to managing editor in the summer of 1985, that shook things up a bit. I started doing more and more writing, and since I could type well, she showed me how to use the typesetter so I could also begin to help out with the typesetting and make more money. She also instituted a new women's section in the paper, *Sister Spirit*.

Let me explain a bit about production procedures back then. Imagine a newspaper office without a single computer. (I know—it's hard for me to imagine, too, and I was there.) Think *Mad Men*, except everybody is queer and in bluejeans, in a setting more darkly Dickensian than brightly lit Madison Avenue.

As a freelancer, I typed on my electric typewriter at home. When I was satisfied with my often copious rewrites and had a clean typed copy of my story, I took the bus to the *GayLife* office to drop it off with the editor. The office was located at 222 West Huron Street, behind the Merchandise Mart in the *Blazing Star* "merger" days, then it moved to the Andersonville neighborhood, just two doors north of Renslow's well-known bathhouse (lesbian sep "fundamentalists" thought of it more as a spunk-encrusted patriarchal den of iniquity) Man's Country on Clark Street.

The editor read the pieces of paper, maybe made some pencil marks on the sheets, and then put them in a bin with other stories. The typesetter retyped by hand every sheet of paper in the bin, on the keyboard of a typesetting machine. This machine was massive—perhaps the size of two refrigerators put together—and it arranged the words in neat columns with justified margins on photographic paper, developed the paper internally in a self-contained "darkroom," and dropped it out of a chute on the side of the machine, still wet with chemicals.

After the paper dried, the art director would take these sheets, cut them close-cropped around the text with scissors or a paper cutter, roll a special sticky wax onto the back, and position each one on a large layout sheet. The wax made each little piece of paper sticky but removable, so the arrangement could be changed like puzzle pieces until the designer or art director was happy with it. When ready, each of these layout pasteup sheets would have many such pieces of paper stuck to it, and this would become the original for that printed page when it was taken to the printer. Everything in the newspaper—columns, ads, page numbers, lines that separated the space visually—was laid out by hand.

The *GayLife* office was long and thin, dusty and funky, with this big old typesetting machine about halfway to the back. I remember that one afternoon, while I was typesetting, a group of employees, all men, had gathered around the small office television to watch a report about AIDS; the report claimed it was possible that one gay man in five was already infected. To be "infected" back then was a death sentence. There were five gay men watching the report, including Bob Bearden, *GayLife*'s sales manager. "My God," he said, "if that's true, one of us is going to die." They all just looked at each other. What could you say? It was incomprehensible.

I had attended my first AIDS funeral that May—Chicago entertainer Christopher Street, someone I had known from my open-mic guitar-playing days at His n' Hers bar. He had come down with a cold that turned into pneumonia, and he died three weeks later. That was typical then; almost as quickly as you heard someone had been diagnosed, he (or, much more rarely, she) was already dead. No cocktails, no nothing.

Gay papers and magazines were all speculating with increasing urgency as their obituary sections became noticeably longer, and the tabloids were shouting about the "gay plague." The general public was just beginning to realize the scope of the epidemic. Reports about AIDS at that time were confusing and often conflicting. Nobody really knew how contagious it was—only how lethal. Everyone was spooked. The mainstream media began reporting widely about AIDS only after actor Rock Hudson died in October 1985. Many straight people were doubly shocked, because they'd had no idea he was gay.

In early 1985, Bob Bearden's lover Jeff McCourt, whose nom de plume was Mimi O'Shea, became *GayLife*'s entertainment editor. We met one evening at the old Parkway diner at Clark and Fullerton to discuss future articles I might write.

Jeff had a closeted day job in downtown Chicago as an options trader; his style was the antithesis of Bob's. Bob was calm, soft-spoken and charming. Jeff was operatic and hyper—but he certainly had a lot of energy. At our meeting, he talked nonstop, hardly letting me get a word in edgewise. He had big ideas for how to improve the entertainment section, he said, and was writing articles in that week's paper not only as Mimi O'Shea but also as Hanz Gunther.

He said the Mimi O'Shea name started as "a kind of joke." He didn't tell me what the joke was, but I sat there trying to interject a sentence now and then about my concerns as a writer, and I managed to get in one or two remarks that seemed to register.

I mentioned that I wanted to review the recent biography of Alan Turing by Andrew Hodges.

Jeff had never heard of Turing, but was quite interested when I began telling him about Turing's vital importance to British intelligence in World War II and in the history of computer science, and how as a gay man he was later sentenced in court to a "rehabilitation therapy" of estrogen injections that probably led to his suicide. Jeff said by all means I should go ahead with the review. My Turing story ended up as the lead feature in the entertainment section of the Pride issue. Jeff was effusive in his praise. He said it was the best piece he'd ever seen in *GayLife* and it "saved" the entertainment section of the Pride Week issue.

After that, Jeff was receptive to all my ideas for biographical and cultural features. And as managing editor, Tracy was a little human dynamo, filled with seemingly boundless enthusiasm for the gay and lesbian movement and how she could contribute to it as a journalist. But *GayLife* was in bad shape financially. Paychecks began bouncing—more and more frequently—and there's nothing that lowers employee loyalty like having to hastily cash a paycheck for fear it will bounce. Sometime in the late summer, Jeff and Bob were in negotiations with Renslow to purchase *GayLife*. Then Jeff told me that after reviewing all the finances, he and Bob were thinking of simply starting an entirely new paper.

Bob, who was bringing money into the paper as sales manager only to see his own paychecks bounce, was ready to walk. Tracy—whose paychecks had also been bouncing—trusted and admired Bob, and if he went, so would she. And I trusted and admired Tracy, so if she was going to leave *GayLife* to help start a new paper, I was onboard with that. The art director, Drew Badanish, came in as the third investor (with Bob and Jeff) to start the new paper.

This was the first staff "mutiny" in the so-called Chicago Gay and Lesbian Press Wars. But it wouldn't be the last.

Jeff came up with the new paper's name: the *Windy City Times*. He told me he thought it would be best—easier to sell ads to non-gay businesses—if there was nothing "gay" in the title. I didn't like that—to me it sounded closeted. But I was just a freelancer and part-time typesetter, after all—and after a while I warmed to the name.

Windy City Times

I no longer have a copy of the first issue of *Windy City Times*, from September 25, 1985, but I recall the herculean efforts, the long hours, and cycles of excitement and exhaustion during those initial months, as the paper started to get off the ground.

I had a lot of new ideas for things to write for *Windy City Times* that had never occurred to me at *GayLife*. Being there at the beginning of the new enterprise, I felt more involved. All sorts of exciting topics in feminist, lesbian and women's writing in general began to emerge for me on this expanded writing horizon, and gay men's literature was, at the time, just at the beginning of an astonishing burst of creativity, one that was fascinating to follow.

At first, the office was in Jeff and Bob's big condo apartment on Melrose Street just off Lake Michigan. We had use of typesetting equipment in a Loop office building at Lake and Wabash right next to where the el tracks curved, but we could only use it on nights and weekends. This typesetting machine was quirky; it didn't run properly if the room temperature was higher than 60 degrees. Tracy, Toni Armstrong Jr.—who also typeset—and I spent many an evening in this uncomfortable cold, working from late evening until dawn.

It isn't easy to typeset with gloves on; my fingers were often numb by the time the pile of articles was all entered into the machine. I remember nights when Tracy and I took turns, one typesetting while the other tried to get an hour or two of sleep on the office rug. The huge empty office building was creepy enough, but braving the Loop streets to get to a 24-hour hamburger joint for your "lunch" at 4 in the morning meant you had to navigate your way through a seriously scary obstacle course, dodging hookers, pimps, drug addicts, bellicose drunks and gang kids on the prowl, with the frequent loud sounds of smashing glass in the alleyways to keep you frosty. (In the '80s, the Loop had not yet been transformed into the evening entertainment hub it is today, with its many office-to-residential building conversions, late-night dining establishments and high-end hotels.)

By that November, Jeff and Bob somehow managed to install a typesetting machine into the empty basement of their condo building. I don't know how they placated their neighbors, and there was a spot of trouble with a city inspector since it was a residential building. I was glad I didn't have to be in the Loop at midnight anymore, but if anything, it was colder than in the creepy office building, since the basement was unheated and had a broken window. In fact, the door that led to the street was broken off its hinges, and you had to lift the whole door to move it.

Imagine trying to type in an unheated basement when it's 8 degrees outside. The bulky typesetting machine surrounded you like the flat faces of giant ice cubes, freezing to the touch, and a penetrating cold kept leaching into the room. I brought a small space heater from home, and that helped a bit, but it couldn't really compete with the cold. Were we dedicated or just crazy?

Bob reinforced the windows with plastic and tried to arrange plastic draperies around the machine to keep the heat in for us—and not incidentally to keep dirt and debris from the basement ceiling from falling on the typesetting machine. In short, working conditions were less than ideal. But we were activists on a mission, so we pressed on. Everyone worked really hard, determined that the new paper should succeed.

By November, just about everybody got sick from spending extended periods of time in that unhealthful basement atmosphere. Bob, however, never got better. He became noticeably thinner and continued to be sick into December. I saw him now and then in his bathrobe upstairs in the office part of the condo, where at least it was warm. By late January, he was hospitalized, near death from AIDS, on a respirator. He got better, and worse, and better again. Bob managed to fight off the pneumocystis but then developed some other immunodeficiency-related problems, including a blood infection.

Understandably, Jeff was a basket case, and Tracy, who was a lot closer to Bob than I was, was devastated. But Jeff had to double up and do Bob's job as well as his own. For a while, Jeff alternated between stoically going out with his attaché case to sell ads, and lying in what appeared to be a semi-catatonic state on the living-room sofa of their condo, staring at the ceiling. We struggled on, very demoralized and sad, but gathering new recruits and supporters and advertisers.

We published issues that I thought were far better, more comprehensive, more wide-ranging and readable, more balanced in reporting, than *GayLife* had been. After a while, Jill Burgin assumed the sales rep responsibilities. Drew Badanish continued as art director for a few more months. Tracy was running the entertainment section as well as the news. Jon-Henri Damski divided his time between writing his whimsical, philosophical columns and visiting Bob in the hospital.

As it happened, the first actual *Windy City Times* AIDS death was not Bob Bearden's but that of our travel writer, Richard Cash, who was a longtime friend of Bob and Jon-Henri. He went into the hospital to get tests to see if he had AIDS and died there two weeks later. It was another serious shock to the barely 4-month-old newspaper.

That spring (rather miraculously, under the circumstances, and largely because of Tracy's efforts, in my opinion), *Windy City Times* was still going (*GayLife* had by then gone out of business) and the "office" finally moved into an actual office space—in the building behind the Rodde Center on Sheffield just north of Belmont. A new mood, more businesslike, set in. There was far more space, on two floors (having no basement with falling debris or broken windows was also a big plus), and the paper was finally functioning like an actual business, with more freelancers and staff coming on. I kept on writing and typesetting, but also became the books editor.

At this stage, I remember a lot of arguing and shouting. A lot. At the condo, I think people refrained from shouting since Bob was sick in the next room. There were no such restrictions now, and tempers were just as frazzled.

Every GLBT newspaper back then had to figure out how to balance the tension between business practices and advocacy. *Windy City Times* wasn't "just" another newspaper, but a political voice for gay and lesbian rights and for the community. Different people, both on the staff and in the community, had different ideas about what that political voice meant, and different levels of concern, and different opinions of what should be done, and how. We were all pretty much making it up as we went along.

But Jeff became more and more rigid, possessive and dictatorial, though he often clearly didn't know what he was talking about and had little patience for learning about the dynamics of community organizations. I remember one big staff meeting where we were all sitting with our chairs in a circle. Jeff, in a major freakout over some little photographic arrangement he didn't like, leaped into the middle of the circle, threw down several copies of the paper and vigorously stomped up and down on them, screaming all the while, like a child having a tantrum. Everyone, myself included, froze. But I thought to myself, OK, he's under a lot of pressure, but I can't put up with this abusive crap much longer.

At the time, Bob was still alive, home from the hospital but not capable of returning to work again or of doing much of anything. He mostly stayed in his bedroom at home. After a final, terrible bout of seizures, Bob died in January 1987; it was just a year and a half after that AIDS television report we watched at the *GayLife* office.

In the year of *Windy City Times'* founding, 12,000 people in the U.S., mostly gay men, were diagnosed with AIDS—and half of them were already dead. It was a chilling, alarming statistic then— two years before ACT UP was founded, two years before the first AIDS quilt panel was sewn. Today, while it's estimated that 14,000 people become infected every day, it's no longer the science-fiction-made-fact, apocalyptic crisis it was within the LGBT community when every week young, otherwise healthy gay men, whom you knew and liked, vanished off the face of the earth in the wake of a rampaging disease caused by an as-yet unknown organism.

After Bob's death, Jeff's behavior spun further out of control. He became even more erratic and irrational—insufferable, really. There were murmurs that he had become addicted to cocaine. I don't know if that was true but, judging by the way he was acting, it was certainly plausible.

By the summer of 1987, many of the staff of *Windy City Times*, including Tracy, myself, Jill Burgin and others, were poised to start a new paper yet again. There was a certain inevitability to this, since Jeff was no longer someone any of us wanted to work for, but we still wanted to do gay and lesbian journalism—and there was an attitude that, hey, we'd done it once, so we could do it again.

Outlines

Outlines, the newspaper that was founded by refugees from Jeff McCourt's *Windy City Times*, began publishing in June 1987. (In 2000, Tracy Baim and her company bought the name *Windy City Times* from McCourt, and the *Outlines* name was transformed back into *WCT*.) Tracy initially tried to buy the paper (with investors) through an anonymous offer but, when Jeff found out, he was outraged—even though he had considered selling it after Bob died. After driving his staff away with his crazy behavior, Jeff's animosity toward his new competition was sometimes cloak-and-dagger, sometimes Laurel & Hardy. I recall one organizational meeting of *Outlines* in which a columnist who had previously written for *WCT*, sitting on a sofa, bent over and a tiny tape recorder fell out of his pocket and bounced onto the rug—he was recording our meeting to take back to Jeff! I never found out if Jeff had sent him on this burlesque attempt at espionage, or if it was his own idea, but this same fellow was spotted more than once lurking in the street, looking up at the *Outlines* office windows late at night. Weird stuff like that went on during *Outlines'* beginning year or two.

The owners who invested in *Outlines* included Tracy, Nan Schaffer and Scott McCausland. Schaffer and McCausland were, luckily, very hands-off, allowing the paper to grow and giving Tracy the latitude she needed to make well-considered, independent editorial decisions.

I joined *Outlines* as its arts and entertainment editor. It was my first full-time job on a gay and lesbian paper—full-time meaning hovering around 80 hours a week. Some nights I'd have just enough time to go home and take a shower, nap for two hours with my girlfriend, and go back into the office. I was never so exhausted in my life. Yet I remember those intense years at *Outlines* now with great fondness.

Tracy had a vision of a truly balanced gay and lesbian newspaper—in the sense of providing equal coverage of men's and women's news. Previously, gay and lesbian papers were generally aimed at one group or the other: papers run by gay men that were exclusively gay or overwhelmingly gay with a smattering of lesbian news thrown in, like *GayLife*, and small all-volunteer newspapers like *Blazing Star* that were strictly for lesbians, or for feminists and produced by lesbians. The fact that our paper consciously strove for parity between men and women was something quite innovative. *Outlines* also featured stories by and about bisexuals and transgender people—though it would be years before the community "officially" recognized itself as LGBT. I am very glad to have witnessed that evolution.

When I think back to all the LGBT newspaper offices I spent any time in, the first *Outlines* office is the space I remember best, probably because it was filled with light. It was essentially one large open space, on the third floor of a loft building on Belmont Avenue at Lakewood, about six blocks west of the Belmont el stop and eight blocks west of what was then fast becoming "Boys Town" on North Halsted Street. A few people found it annoying that the space was so open, because almost everything in the office could be overheard by everyone else. But this stimulated really interesting off-the-cuff office conversations that sometimes led to new ideas, articles and opportunities.

The building housed a number of little corporations, arts groups and some light manufacturing. Right next door to our offices was, I remember, a business that manufactured action figures and other small toys. Its staff often kept their door open and, walking by, I could see people inside making little figurines from molds; the smell of hot resin and plastic often wafted into the corridor. For a while the Chicago-based progressive monthly newspaper *In These Times* (which coincidentally had some ties to NAM and former *Blazing Star* members) had offices on the floor below us, and the building was owned by that paper's publisher.

The loft building was run-down but exuded a bohemian charm I found very appealing—real exposed brick walls in places, big, tall windows that let in thick columns of sunlight during the day, and beautiful high ceilings. This charm could fade quickly when the heat didn't work or the bathroom pipes clogged, but it was a great space for a newspaper. Our office furniture was, well, let's say eclectic; each of us had gone to the used furniture warehouse on Western Avenue and picked out the desk and chair and lamp we preferred, so nothing matched and some pieces were quite scuffed, but we were all comfortable, having chosen to our own liking. The look of the place was unified visually by the original solid wood flooring and the equally old ornate ceiling tiles.

We had a lively pigeon hangout on the roof and, more often than not, during our frequent, animated office conversations about the current state of homos and homo sapiens, the wind outside would shift and we could hear a chorus of cooing and mating noises from the birds upstairs.

Rather than the standard behemoth typesetting machine, Tracy invested in multiple early Apple computers—which themselves would be considered antiques now, of course—that were a great advancement in sizing and arranging articles on a page. We learned to use Quark as the layout program, and now writers could "typeset" their words onscreen or, if they had a home computer, bring them in on a floppy disk so they could flow right into the layouts without the need to be retyped. This was a huge time saver. But every story that came into the office on paper from a freelancer still had to be hand-typed into the computer, because there was no such thing as email.

Plus, every phone call still came through a single land line that had an extension at each desk. How was that even possible? How did reporters ever find out about anything in a timely fashion, all of us clicking extension buttons and shuffling through paper Rolodexes to find phone numbers? And anyone who was out of the office and not at home was simply unreachable. I can't fathom how we managed anymore. Stone Age. Pre-Gutenbergian.

Of course, there were no digital cameras, either. Ages ago, I had taught adult-education courses in film-developing. I took up photography again while at *Windy City Times* and, by the time *Outlines* started, I'd built a darkroom in my apartment. I spent a portion of my working time painstakingly (compared to today) developing my film and that of other staff photographers who had no darkroom facilities, then making prints for the paper. (Once made, those prints would still have to be professionally transformed into halftones by an outside firm.)

Outlines staff members I recall most clearly, almost 30 years later, are Scott Galiher, Jill Burgin, Stephanie Bacon, Richard Small, Janet Provo, Bill Burks, Rex Wockner, Johanna Stoyva, Pat Bechdolt, Rhonda Craven, MJ Murphy and Rachel Pepper. Tracy Baim, freelancer Michèle Bonnarens and Angie Schmidt are still among my close friends today. There were many others—freelancers, activists from various organizations—who were in and out of the office frequently, and even more writers who sent in stories from California, Washington, D.C., and elsewhere.

You never knew when a well-known gay author or a nationally known activist might stop by, as they often did. It was fantastic to be able to call up Larry Kramer for information and to interview Audre Lorde or Lily Tomlin. It was a time of further discovery for me, too—freelancers would send in eye-opening interviews with Hollywood celebrities, stories on new filmmakers such as Gregg Araki, reviews of a groundbreaking new book by Vito Russo.

And every week, I found out more about authors and artists and historical figures who were gay or lesbian, as new books about them came out, and I'd turn what I'd learned into an article on Joe Orton, or Constantine Cavafy, or Margaret Anderson and Jane Heap. I did a lengthy series of articles on Sappho—the original Lesbian—and what was known about her, in articles that formed the basis for my later "Tenth Muse" columns in *HOT WIRE: The Journal of Women's Music and Culture*.

In my capacity as a writer, I continued to concentrate on cultural events but also did some news reporting. For instance, I did *Outlines'* ongoing updates of Karen Thompson's efforts on behalf of her lover, Sharon Kowalski, who had been severely disabled in a car crash in 1983. The legal battle went on for years, as Kowalski's homophobic father, who was her legal guardian, kept Kowalski isolated from Thompson in a nursing home with no rehabilitation and refused to accept that his daughter was a lesbian. The case inspired books, plays and a documentary film, and it brought attention to the need for durable powers of attorney for gay and lesbian couples. It was finally resolved in Thompson's favor in 1991 and became a landmark in establishing gays and lesbians as legal guardians of their partners.

I did movie reviews, interviews, opinion pieces, puff pieces, pieces about housewares and real estate and jewelry and wines, all sorts of things, basically whatever we needed written that I couldn't or didn't have time to assign to anyone else. To make the paper appear to have more writers than we did (à la Jeff McCourt at *GayLife*), I came up with several pseudonyms. I wrote Lyric Opera reviews under the regal name Johanna Buckingham (a composite of my two grandmothers' names); I did theater reviews under another name—Lisa something; and home lifestyle reviews as Randy Levertov.

A lot of us who worked at *Outlines* lived and breathed community current events, and the sense of community-building was palpable. When we weren't actually working on specific newspaper tasks, we'd sit around the office and discuss the waves and waves of controversies that were always swirling around and, in one way or another, making news. Some of these discussions resulted in opinion pieces.

I recall especially a "debate" in the form of two opinion pieces side by side, that began as an office conversation when Rex Wockner complained that he wasn't being allowed entry to cover a debate about racism in the women's community that was held at Mountain Moving Coffeehouse, a local all-women's venue. Rex argued he should have been admitted; I argued for the coffeehouse's right to keep men, including reporters, out if they wanted to.

I also did a lengthy interview with the newly selected International Ms Leather at the time S&M was just beginning to be discussed widely. I knew little about it, but that turned out to be an advantage since I asked basic questions, and the few leatherdykes I knew (and I didn't even know I knew any till they came out to me after the interview) were quite happy to see the topic featured in the newspaper. I also did long interviews with Mary Daly and Sonia Johnson. I could go on and on. I found almost all of this intellectually engaging, even when I didn't agree with others' opinions about some aspect of culture or politics or sexual psychology.

There was always more to do and a feeling of urgency about the time I had to do it in. On the nights when I wasn't working late at the office, I'd be going to gay and lesbian plays, readings, musical performances, dances—or going to a funeral. The reality of AIDS intensified my commitment to gay and lesbian rights, and I think this may have been the case for many LGBT people at that time.

The Wikipedia article on LGBT history dismisses the 1980s as "a dismal period for homosexuals."

"Dismal" is not how I'd describe it at all. Frightening, yes, and calamitous, with AIDS hanging over the heads of so many talented, earnest young men I knew, and with the obituary section of the paper ever-growing, week after week. But the '80s were also a time of enormous expansion in activism (most prominently, the rise of ACT UP), advances in gay rights, and the birth of cultural institutions.

Not dismal. Energizing. Often even amazing. The gay and lesbian movement was coalescing into some primordial landmass rising from the sea, right in front of my eyes. I had the freedom to let my mind roam wherever my curiosity about new gay and lesbian cultural territory would take me, and to write about it, and enlist other writers who wanted to write about it, too. Though the pay was meager, the hours were endless, and the deadlines were often stressful, I felt that those of us working at *Outlines* were involved in important, meaningful work that was effecting real social change.

Local gay cultural organizations—choruses, art groups, bands, drama and dance troupes—and professional organizations that had begun in the late '70s and early '80s had, by the mid-to-late '80s, sprung up in so many places that they were starting to have annual regional and national gatherings that we covered. And there were the many annual women's-music festivals back then. Out gays and lesbians were still nowhere to be seen on television (the first ongoing gay TV character I ever saw was played by Martin Mull on *Roseanne*, in the early 1990s, though there were apparently a few such roles on earlier shows). But there were enough independent films made about us by then to spark the growing number of gay and lesbian film festivals. As arts and entertainment editor, part of my job was to make sure these events were given ample coverage, and the films, presentations and concerts were reviewed with thoughtfulness and care—especially since we knew that some of these LGBT-themed offerings, no matter how excellent they might be, would not be covered anywhere in the mainstream media.

In the early years of my involvement in gay and lesbian journalism, I had assumed that most mainstream stories simply had no gay or lesbian "angle." By the late 1980s, as an editor at *Outlines*, I realized that there were very few stories that didn't have one—though you might have to look a little more closely to find it.

The mainstream press was still loath to report anything at all about gays and lesbians except AIDS-related news. This became glaringly obvious after the "Great March"—the October 11, 1987, National March on Washington for Lesbian and Gay Rights, in Washington, D.C. Those of us who worked in the gay and lesbian press scurried from event to event there, taking notes for articles, snapping photos, doing interviews and viewing the AIDS Quilt at its unveiling. Almost everyone from *Outlines* had made the trip to D.C., and the emotional impact of that trip served to further cement us together as a newspaper team. The number of marchers was estimated by activists during the day as half a million, and by the police at close to that number, but it was reported in *The New York Times* as 200,000. This blatant minimization of the crowd numbers underscored the ongoing vital need for our own media, since the mainstream was still bent on ignoring our issues and our impact.

The same muting of our visibility by the mainstream news was apparent at the Olivia Records 15th-anniversary concert at Carnegie Hall in 1988, with a gala reception afterward in the Waldorf-Astoria's Grand Ballroom. I was part of a large Chicago contingent at the event, and it was quite spectacular, with hordes of dykes in tuxedos strolling up Park Avenue from the concert hall to the Waldorf. Today, mainstream newspapers and magazines would be all over a story like that. But back then, according to Wikipedia, "the two [Olivia] concerts at Carnegie Hall in New York were the largest-grossing concerts at that venue in its history. Yet *The New York Times* barely mentioned the show." We did a full-page spread on it, of course, with lots of photos.

I have an especially vivid memory of one night at the office in early December 1987. James Baldwin, the most eminent black gay author of the 1950s and 1960s, had just died—only three days, in fact, after the sudden death of Chicago Mayor Harold Washington. It was snowing outside, beautiful fluffy flakes, and I was alone in the office all night writing my full-page tribute to Baldwin, which was due the next morning, and would be the opening feature of the arts and entertainment section in the next issue.

It was more than a bit eerie, alone in the cold winter quiet of this big space, with a desk phone ringing once in a while in the empty office (and the occasional unnerving sound of pigeons mating outside the window). But I remember what a deep sense of satisfaction I had, putting into words what Baldwin had meant to me growing up, and explaining the extent of Baldwin's importance as an out gay black intellectual to people who might not know, or be too young to remember, how groundbreaking his books had been during the 1960s.

I began freelancing for out-of-town publications, too, in the late 1980s. I wrote a number of stories for *Outweek*, the brash, no-apologies weekly LGBT magazine that started up in New York in 1989. I did a cover story for them that, I'm pleased to say, was the first story written by anyone in the history of the planet, apparently, on the subject of lesbians in the Girl Scouts. A picture of Patsy Lynch, one of *Outweek*'s own photographers, graced the cover of that issue—she had her hand up in the gesture of a pledge, and looked very somber in her actual old Girl Scout uniform. (That image was conceived to avoid potential lawsuits, as editor Andrew Miller had been advised by *Outweek*'s lawyers—since Patsy had been a real scout and was dressed in her own personal merit-badge sash, the publication couldn't be sued for "impersonating a Girl Scout"!) For that story, I spoke with dozens of former and current scout leaders and camp counselors; the ones still involved in scouting all requested anonymity. I also interviewed some very nervous spokespeople at Girl Scout headquarters in New York. The piece was later reprinted in Nancy Manahan's anthology about lesbian Girl Scouts, *On My Honor*.

Outweek was a fun mag to read as well as write for, with Mike Signorile's cogent rants about outing and Susie Day's clever, often-sly humor pieces. *Outweek* brought the issue of outing to the forefront of community debate and, in fact, did a very controversial, even notorious piece on outing that was simply a list of celebrity names, with the headline "Shhhh … ."

I started writing a humor column myself in 1991, called "Lesbomania," in a little weekly offshoot of *Outlines* called *Nightlines* (now *Nightspots*). Most of my humor writing was designed to show the irrationality and illogic of homophobia—an easy target, really, but it gave me great satisfaction to ridicule anti-gay bigots and pundits. I did gay spoofs and parodies of television shows and movies, too, and I also poked fun at some of the crazy things that went on inside the lesbian community. My guiding light was the principle, still valid today, that gays and lesbians have put up with enough homophobic shit, and now we deserve to have a good laugh. Among my shenanigans, I examined the "scientific evidence" that lesbonauts from outer space visited the Earth in prehistoric times. I "reported" on the "War Between the Butches and the Femmes." I revealed the secret lesbian codes embedded in great Renaissance art works. I outed (quite convincingly, I think) Santa Claus, Godzilla, the Abominable Snowman, and the Loch Ness Monster as lesbians, and wrote gay and lesbian versions of *The X-Files*, *West Side Story*, *Star Trek*, *Hansel and Gretel*, *Cinderella* and more. The column was syndicated in a number of LGBT papers around the country, and in 1994 and 1996 many of the pieces were gathered into two book collections, *Lesbomania* and *Tales From the Dyke Side*. I did theatrical readings from the books—with visual enhancement in the form of cartoons—at the Bailiwick theater in Chicago during Pride Week, at the Center in New York, and in a number of bookstores and other venues in the U.S. and Europe. I had a blast—and a good laugh, I hope, was had by all.

The Antithesis of Secrecy

As late as the mid-1980s, I could still encounter well-meaning straight people who, when I told them that I wrote for the gay and lesbian press, would react with perplexity and respond by asking me some variation of the question, "But what do gay people need a newspaper for?"

Despite the valiant activism of previous decades, and the Stonewall riots, and the Pride parades, the phrase "gay community" was an oxymoron to these people. The idea of a serious movement for gay rights that would combat our status as an oppressed—and still at that time often reviled—minority, that would benefit by sharing resources and information, had not yet occurred to them. I don't think they were being disingenuous in asking such a question, or homophobic in the modern sense; they just had never even thought about gay anything before, or perhaps thought all talk of sexuality was embarrassing.

But I think their question was based on a then still-lingering general assumption that gay sexuality was intrinsically clandestine. That the only thing gay men or lesbians would find of interest in their own publications was a classified section to find sexual partners, with perhaps a smattering of information about which bars in town catered to homosexuals—but then why would anyone want to print that, when it would only make it easier for the cops to find these places and raid them?

The idea that gay people would naturally and rightly prefer to be closeted, and moreover that the whole infrastructure of their social lives would be best kept secret, still had a certain currency among a few older gay men I knew, as well as among clueless straight people. In 1985, you could still smell that whiff of shame—and secrecy, so long providing a layer of protective invisibility for the gay "demimonde," can also generate a seductive sense of power.

LGBT newspapers, by documenting our lives and announcing our concerns—especially once the AIDS epidemic hit—forever obliterated the notion that secrecy is a preferred, sensible or even prudent strategy for gay people in this country, and at the same time, the visibility of gay media kayoed straight people who just didn't want to ever have to hear about or deal with the subject.

The emergence of matter-of-fact, widely circulated gay newspapers was in itself a form of coming out. (The first time someone got up the nerve to read a gay paper on a bus or train was a common, memorable, coming-out toe-in-the-water experience for a lot of people. The first time the person's face at a social event appeared in the gay newspaper was another—after all, not everyone in the photo was necessarily gay … .) And by supporting and encouraging individuals to come out, gay newspapers created the momentum for the paradigm shift that we see everywhere today.

Working for the LGBT press in Chicago was a rare opportunity to combine activism and culture, and to feel that I was contributing something tangible to the movement for LGBT rights. Plus, I was constantly learning new things and meeting fantastic, admirable people. I look back almost in awe on the hope and the triumphs of those times amid the poignancy of our tragic losses.

Decades ago, a friend of mine told me that her fundamentalist Christian sister had remonstrated with her about being a lesbian, saying, "Why can't you at least have the sense to lie about it?" Her immediate answer was, "Because that would make me a liar." Ironically, homophobes who persist in vilifying our sexuality as something "indecent" will never understand or acknowledge the basic sense of decency that has propelled much of the LGBT movement. I saw many instances of actual heroism in those days, of otherwise ordinary people who realized that coming out, however difficult for them, was an act of dignity, of personal integrity, of openness, of risking personal safety for the sake of honesty. And I saw many instances of bravery in the face of bureaucratic nonsense, ignorance, violence and hatred—and the struggle continues in many places today. The LGBT media solidified and amplified our collective courage. I feel privileged to have been among the people who documented those heroic times as they unfolded.

Blazing Star, a Chicago lesbian paper, merged with *GayLife*, a co-gender paper, in late 1979. In the January 4, 1980, issue of *GayLife*, the newspaper ran this photo of an event celebrating the merger and the first issue of *Blazing Star* inserted into *GayLife*. From left: Jorjet Harper (writing as Diana B. Harper then), Judy MacLean and Chris Riddiough.
Photo by Steve Kulieke

Jorjet Harper in 1986.
Photo by Kathleen O'Malley

Jorjet Harper and Kathleen O'Malley in the Chicago Pride parade circa 1989, riding in the *Outlines* newspaper contingent.

23

The Long Haul

By Tracy Baim

Working in the gay press should probably be measured in dog years. Right-wing threats, death and destruction, physical assaults, robberies, property destruction, and that's not to mention the internal struggles within our great rainbow community—it all makes those years seem so much longer.

But while hundreds of reporters have come and gone through the years of gay media in Chicago, I feel very fortunate to have done this since 1984, one month out of journalism school. I had been doing newspapers since I was 10 years old, shadowing my mother, Joy Darrow, when she was managing editor of the *Chicago Defender*, creating a family newsletter, and then working on grammar-school, high-school and college newspapers, as well as starting my own feminist newsletter in college.

Still, when I graduated with a journalism degree from Drake University in Des Moines, Iowa, in May 1984, I assumed I would never have a career in journalism. I didn't think I could be an out lesbian and a reporter, so I readied myself for a typesetting career supplemented by activism and journalism—just as in college. I packed up my 1966 Mustang with all my college memorabilia and headed home to Chicago.

Within a few weeks, my mom heard about a part-time job at *GayLife* newspaper. I worked doing typesetting and some writing for it while also freelancing for the *Chicago Tribune,* where my stepdad Steve Pratt was a reporter and editor of the City Trib section. And to pay the bills, I was typesetting at night for an advertising firm. Given the low wages and lousy hours, attrition was a fact of life in the gay press. I moved up from editorial assistant to editor of *GayLife* in 12 months—in time for the June 1985 Pride edition.

I was really lucky to graduate when I did. There were a few dozen Chicagoans who had done the heavy lifting of gay journalism in the 1960s and 1970s, into the early 1980s. They started newspapers, radio shows and newsletters. They fought harassment, struggled to pay the bills and somehow created a thriving media world by the time I started at *GayLife*. My role models included Marie J. Kuda and William B. Kelley, who had reported in the 1960s for the *Mattachine Midwest Newsletter*, and Toni Armstrong Jr. and Jorjet Harper, who were lesbian journalism pioneers.

By the summer of 1985, there were stirrings at *GayLife*. When a group left to start *Windy City Times*, I joined them as founding managing editor. I left again, 18 months later, to start *Outlines* newspaper, and then added subsequent sister publications over the years. I explain more about this history in the chapter on *Windy City Times*; what follows is a set of more-personal observations about my more than 28 years covering the LGBT community.

Bars, Bombs and Crises

Since there were so few pages in the gay newspapers, and of course no Internet, the power of the press in the 1980s was in choosing just what to cover. It was always a battle for space, and to this day there has never been an edition where we didn't have far too much to print. Making decisions on what to include, whom to cover and what photos to run was always difficult. A lot of what we were writing about was news briefs, AIDS developments and local organization events.

From the start, I was plunged deep into the gay and feminist communities. I covered Mountain Moving Coffeehouse for Womyn and Children, the Pride Parade, sports leagues, gay and lesbian business owners, gay bars and, most importantly, the growing AIDS crisis.

My first bylined cover story for *GayLife* was June 14, 1984, about a man arrested for placing 24 bombs in Chicago, claiming to be the "North American Central Gay Strike Force Against Public and Police Oppression." He was a lone wolf, likely not gay. But I have to say that I did not even remember that story until recent years when I started to work on gay history projects, including co-writing and editing *Out and Proud in Chicago: An Overview of the City's Gay Community* and launching www. chicagogayhistory.org. Having worked pretty much seven days a week—16-to-18-hour days—on LGBT news and issues for all these years, it's funny how little I remember of some of the actual stories. But the memories come flooding back when I page through those yellowing issues of the papers.

In that same *GayLife* issue, I also wrote about the closing of the Jane Addams feminist bookstore, after seven years in business. I took photos of the Pride Parade that month and covered the Proud to Run Race.

My first major interview was with ex-Mormon Sonia Johnson, running a third-party race for U.S. president. My interview ran July 12, 1984, and she attacked even Geraldine Ferraro, who was the Democratic vice-presidential pick that year. (Johnson later came out as a lesbian.)

One article I wrote in the June 20, 1985, issue of *GayLife* led to a series of articles (including some at subsequent papers) on the anti-gay terror striking the University of Chicago and Hyde Park community. A right-wing newspaper, the *Chicago Patriot*, had been published by students and included offensive remarks about AIDS, gays, investment in South Africa and more. Later, when I worked on related stories about events at the U of C, and actual anti-gay attacks, I received phone calls at home threatening my life if I continued to cover the stories.

Of course, I continued investigating the stories, but I was scared. In later years, we received threats, usually through the mail, including some suspicious powder soon after the September 11, 2001, terrorism attacks. We also were robbed of all our computers, suffered additional robberies and even had our windows shot at (when we were not there). Our news boxes were vandalized (dirty diapers being a favorite) and stolen. I was arrested covering an early-1990s Easter Sunday pro-choice demonstration at a right-wing church on the Northwest Side. The arrest and threats were never a deterrent—they usually were a motivator.

I also wrote a lot of editorials for *GayLife* and subsequent gay papers, but I was always most comfortable doing news articles and interviews. I did some fluff stories, business profiles, and lots of sports news since I played in the lesbian sports leagues, and I took thousands of photos a year. And because I am a pack rat for history, I have saved almost every press release and photo—including those by other photographers. To preserve that history, I am scanning those and donating the originals to the Chicago History Museum.

Once I made the move to *Windy City Times*, I felt freer to explore all parts of the LGBT community. I had never felt constrained by *GayLife* Publisher Chuck Renslow, but *Windy City Times* soon had a larger advertising base and therefore more space to cover the community. It was all about the space.

Even though I was managing editor, at a small paper that means doing everything, including typesetting and delivery. I found that such chores kept me more interested than just doing writing or editing all day. The cover of our first *Windy City Times*, on September 26, 1985, was my story about the new Committee on Gay and Lesbian Issues appointed by Mayor Harold Washington.

The years 1985–87 were among the most devastating and exciting in Chicago's gay community. AIDS was tightening its terrifying grip on our city, slightly delayed from the East and West coasts. We lost some of our own staff and one of our *WCT* founders, Bob Bearden, to AIDS. There was a large push for the city's gay-rights bill, gays were running for office, more gay businesses were opening, sports and culture groups were thriving, new nonprofits were starting, the 1987 March on Washington sparked a huge growth in local groups back in cities such as Chicago, and ACT UP formed to take a no-prisoners approach to fighting for access to a cure for AIDS.

During my 18 months as managing editor of *Windy City Times*, until May 1987, I was so excited and honored to cover this incredible growth in the community. The highlight was a huge downtown rally in July 1986, when all parts of the community came together to push for a city gay-rights bill vote. There was a buzz unlike any I had witnessed earlier. There were people of all races and genders, thousands strong in Daley Center Plaza. I snapped photos, took notes, and had tears in my eyes seeing such community unity. We ran the phone numbers of all 50 aldermen and encouraged readers to call their elected officials.

That unity has rarely shown itself, but when it does, I am a sucker for the emotions of the moment. Yet I am also realistic, and for the most part the community's divisions have been the hardest part to cover. The sexism, racism, ageism, classism and geographic divisions make this city a smoldering pot, not a melting pot. I was called a "cunt" and other names by men threatened by a woman publisher.

Of course, there are also the sinister elements, those who are just gays gone bad, who steal from nonprofits, abuse drugs and alcohol, destroy businesses and organizations, or even in some cases murder. I have covered my share of serial and spree killers within the gay community, those so distorted and so ashamed of their own true selves that they have to kill to cope, from John Wayne Gacy (who was arrested long before I started but who was put to death in 1994) to Larry Eyler (who was on the scene when I started at *GayLife*) and later Jeffrey Dahmer and Andrew Cunanan.

The high-profile cases of murders and suicide have been especially traumatic to write about. The 1998 killing of Matthew Shepard in Wyoming, the murders of numerous transgender, lesbian and gay Chicagoans, and now the spike in reported LGBT youth suicides are very difficult to report. *Windy City Times* did a series on youth suicide in 2010, and at that time I wrote about my own suicide attempt while in college. I have infrequently used personal difficulties to relate the stories of our movement, but it is not easy getting so personal with the political.

So it is not all parades and galas, bartenders and athletes, that keep this gay world spinning. As a journalist, you can get pretty disgusted and burned out with the difficult stories.

But then, what always kept me going was the true heroes of our community, those who were martyred for our movement in deaths due to AIDS, cancer, murder, car crashes or other tragedies, or those who have been able to soldier on, keeping committed to their activism for decades, despite the burnout, despite the bitter community infighting.

Notable Moments

There were many other notable moments over my 28 years:

— Meeting and interviewing Mayor Harold Washington in 1986 was a highlight for me as a 23-year-old journalist. He was a big teddy bear of a man, warm and fierce at the same time. Covering his re-election was exciting and rewarding. And I even had the guts to ask him about the rumors about his sexuality (he denied them).

— The push for the city's human-rights ordinance was at a fever pitch in the mid-1980s. The forced (and failed) vote under Washington led to heightened community activism, and eventual passage under Mayor Eugene Sawyer in 1988. The work of the Gang of Four and hundreds of other activists and politicians was fantastic to watch and cover. Reporting about the City Council for the final winning vote in 1988, under Mayor Sawyer, was phenomenal.

— In 1985, I drove to northern Minnesota to interview Karen Thompson in one of the more tragic stories of the 1980s gay movement. Her partner, Sharon Kowalski, was severely injured in a November 1983 car accident, and Sharon's family won court victories to keep Karen out of her life. This badly affected Sharon's recovery and future health. Interviewing Karen less than two years after the accident, and after Sharon had been moved to a nursing home, was difficult, but her story served as an example to gay couples across the country to get their legal paperwork in order. Sadly, these types of cases still happen.

— Attending and covering the 1987, 1993 and 2000 Marches on Washington were life-changing experiences, as was being at the 1994 Stonewall 25 March combined with the Gay Games in New York. Priceless. The 1987 march and related events were especially pivotal and inspiring, including taking photos of the NAMES Project AIDS Memorial Quilt, and Chicago attorney Renee Hanover and others being arrested at the U.S. Supreme Court protest.

— I witnessed the courage of black LGBT activists in pushing for inclusion in Chicago's Bud Billiken Parade. Janice Layne recommended applying to be in the parade, and when activists won (with the help of Lambda Legal) and subsequently marched in the event, I was happy to walk the route taking photos. This was a wonderful event to cover, and the acceptance from the onlookers brought tears to my eyes. I had watched the parade as a child, because my mom, Joy Darrow, covered the parade for the *Chicago Defender*.

— Starting *BLACKlines* and *En La Vida* newspapers brought emotional highlights for me, especially the first-anniversary party for *BLACKlines* at the DuSable Museum, with my mom mixing the punch. This was just shortly before she died, so it is an important memory for me. Since Joy, as a white woman, had been managing editor of the *Defender* for eight years, she was especially proud of me for launching *BLACKlines*. The economics couldn't support those papers after 10 years of publishing, but I was very happy to have been publisher of such important monthly media.

— Receiving the 2005 Community Media Workshop's Studs Terkel Award, presented by Terkel himself, was a career highlight. I am also thankful for the other journalism and community awards I have received, including induction into the Chicago Gay and Lesbian Hall of Fame at age 31.

— Being co–vice chair of the board of Gay Games VII in 2006 was a once-in-a-lifetime experience as an organizer, showcasing Chicago to the world—and breaking even, financially. I think we did our city proud, despite the odds (and people) against us. Doing outreach for the Games and speaking in more closeted towns, including Crystal Lake (where our rowing events were held), proved educational even to this jaded journalist.

— Founding the Chicago Area Gay and Lesbian Chamber of Commerce in 1995 was also an important accomplishment for me. I believe it was the first gay and lesbian business group to use the word "chamber" in its title, and now that has been replicated all over the country. Around that time I also received the *Crain's Chicago Business* 40 Under 40 Award, which made me feel accepted beyond the gay community.

— The chicagogayhistory.org website has been a labor of love for me, interviewing hundreds of current and former Chicagoans on gay issues. I want to do many more—only time and funding restrict all it can be.

— Producing the films *Hannah Free*, starring Sharon Gless and terrific Chicago actors, and *Scrooge & Marley* with a host of actors—well, those are experiences I can't even compare to anything else. And they are simply other ways to tell our community's stories—journalism on the big screen.

— Interviewing Barack Obama in 2004 for his U.S. Senate run, and doing a 2010 in-depth book on him, *Obama and the Gays: A Political Marriage*, are certainly high points of my journalism career. Going to the White House for his June 2012 Pride Month reception, and getting a hug and kiss from the president, was amazing. I have since done other books that touch on segments of Chicago gay history, including biographies of prominent gay and lesbian leaders (Chuck Renslow and Jim Flint, both published in 2011, with Vernita Gray currently in production).

Journalism Juggling 101

The funny thing for me all these years has been the multiple hats I have had to wear, just to keep doing what I love most: reporting. Some people have criticized the conflicts of interest I have to navigate in doing this, but it was the only path I knew to follow in order to keep doing the work. I decided to run my own paper at age 24 so that I could control my own destiny—as a writer. It took me a long time to claim the title of "publisher" at *Outlines*, even though that was what I was—and nobody else was doing that work. For decades, I have been lucky enough to have shareholders in the paper who have allowed me to make a lot of mistakes as I worked through sleepless nights on a very long learning curve.

So I do sales, writing, editing, photography, delivery, opinion columns for *The Huffington Post*, and whatever else it takes to keep *Windy City Times* visible and thriving.

And I don't take that surviving lightly. Having almost died a few times in my life, I have never taken my days for granted. I also came of age as a gay media reporter when the city had just a few dozen diagnosed cases of AIDS. This was like coming into a war zone, as people on our own staff, and all over the gay community, began to die very quickly, with no end in sight. I was covering the deaths of men (and some women) my age or just slightly older. Many of them never received coverage in the mainstream media, so it fell on the gay press to document their lives. Looking back over thousands of obituaries over the years, and hundreds of funerals I attended, it was the greatest honor to cover the war years, as a young person just getting to understand what her "community" was, making sure our community's heroes are not forgotten.

I remember their faces, their smiles, their anger and their tears. And that is what keeps me motivated.

1986 staff photo for *Windy City Times* newspaper, founded the previous year in Chicago. Front row, from left: Managing Editor Tracy Baim, Publisher Jeff McCourt (who died in 2007), Larry Shell, Benjamin Dreyer, William Burks. Back row, from left: M.J. Murphy, Chris Stryker, Hugh Johnson, Steve Alter, Shani (first name only), Jorjet Harper (hidden), Lawrence Bommer, Yvonne Zipter, Albert Williams (hidden), Chris Cothran (who died in 1996), Jill Burgin, Jon-Henri Damski (who died in 1997), and Mel Wilson.
Timed photo by M.J. Murphy for *Windy City Times*

Tracy Baim interviewing Mayor Harold Washington in 1987.
Photo by William Burks

Tracy Baim interviewing Mayor Richard M. Daley after his retirement announcement in 2010.
Photo by Hal Baim

Tracy Baim at Chicago Pride in the late 1980s, as publisher of *Outlines* newspaper.

Tracy Baim receiving the 2005 Studs Terkel Award from the Community Media Workshop— presented by Terkel himself.
Photo by Hal Baim

PART THREE:

Longtime Papers

"Your silence will not protect you."

— **Audre Lorde**

24

Bay Area Reporter

By Zak Szymanski, *B.A.R.*

"Gay bars—when they weren't being raided—were the one place where everyone could meet and be themselves," *Bay Area Reporter* founder Bob Ross said in an interview with the newspaper before his death in 2003.

The restaurant worker, Tavern Guild president, and bar culture insider disliked the "vicious gossip rags" about town, and so at a time when gay organizing seemed to have reached a critical moment, Ross decided to launch his own publication.

The first issue of the *B.A.R.*— initials that acknowledged gay culture as well as the initials of Ross and original business partner Paul Bentley—was dated April 1, 1971, but hit the streets on April 2, 1971, Ross' 37th birthday. Ross pasted up all the pages by hand, copied them, and delivered them to local bars from his 1969 Ford Mustang. Within a few years, the *B.A.R.* became known as the insider gay news source about town and, later, as one of the most respected LGBT voices in journalism nationwide.

Like most gay publications, the *B.A.R.* has an interest in covering certain topics that often are specific to the community: sex and sexuality, AIDS, sodomy laws, the military ban, marriage equality. Yet its increasingly high standards and universal appeal have been earned through its longstanding commitment to a sex-positive platform and its unique relationship to the diverse factions of the local community, providing open forums and firsthand accounts of San Francisco culture that captured gay history even before it had been made.

"It was wonderful. We used to get a lot of coverage," said Marlena, owner of San Francisco's famous Marlena's bar, the Hayes Valley establishment that still houses all the early memorabilia of the esteemed royal drag system known as the Imperial Court. "The *B.A.R.* and the Imperial Court worked hand in hand for years to support each other."

The front covers of many early 1970s newspapers were dedicated to the Imperial Court's Emperor and Empress candidates, contests and events.

In those days, said Marlena, it was a different, riskier drag culture in which people could not afford high-quality wigs and were easily clocked as (guessed to be) men in dresses: "You couldn't walk down the street in drag 40 years ago. Today, there's a freedom the queens of my youth didn't have."

There's less media attention on the Imperial Court these days, something Marlena attributes to the fact that gay people now have more options for community. Still, she said, the Imperial Court system remains strong, continuing to raise money for charity, providing entertainment for the larger gay community, and carving out new space for the transgender community as well.

"Every Emperor and Empress is well respected, and there's still a little bit of magic there," she said, pointing out that a little more newspaper coverage these days could go a long way. "We do need to figure out a way to penetrate the bigger community and let them know we are there with them, not just for them."

Politics was a relatively new area to the gay community, but as local power grew, the *B.A.R.* had its finger on the pulse of local events with an eye toward influencing the national climate. Nowhere was this more apparent than in the paper's coverage of Harvey Milk, the state's first openly gay elected official and longtime friend of Ross. Milk became the *B.A.R.*'s political columnist, but he stopped being a regular contributor once he started his runs for elected office (eventually winning a San Francisco supervisor post).

"The *B.A.R.* for quite some time was the only means of communication of any news whatsoever in the gay community. Bob took a liking to Harvey as the gay rebel, even though Bob himself could be a bit stuffy," said Jim Rivaldo, Milk's campaign manager. "Harvey respected the gay-bar scene more than the gay establishment that he so harshly criticized. [Harvey] was the sort of pushy, 'grab it, they'll never give it to you' advocate of gay rights rather than the 'nurture and educate our straight friends so they'll support us' faction. Harvey introduced in many ways a political consciousness in the main communication medium of our community. The *Chronicle* and *Examiner* never would have covered anything gay unless a gay person ran screaming in the street naked. But Harvey brought a political presence to the *B.A.R.*"

Milk's last column criticized the practices of the San Francisco Chamber of Commerce, which had refused to speak out against the homophobic Briggs Initiative in 1978. The Briggs Initiative sought to ban LGBT educators from teaching in California's public schools.

"In case the chamber hasn't noticed ... we are not going away, or back into our closets. ... In fact we are going to take an even stronger part in our government and its decisions. In fact we will become an even stronger political and economic force in the city, the state, and the nation," Milk wrote in the *B.A.R.*

The events that followed, of course, were tragic. Before the next issue of the *B.A.R.* hit the streets, Milk and Mayor George Moscone were gunned down in City Hall by former Supervisor Dan White, an ex-cop with conservative leanings who often clashed with the men.

Much of the *B.A.R.*'s next issue was dedicated to Milk's memory, though by the time it was printed, the shootings were old news, and Milk's ashes had already been scattered at sea.

"The mood was festive. Many had brought along food and drink, joints were passed around," the *B.A.R.* said of the event that laid Milk to rest.

Milk had already predicted his assassination as an openly gay political man, and in a tape-recorded political will he named several possible openly gay successors to his city supervisor seat. The *B.A.R.*'s Ross was among those named, but many of Milk's friends believed Ross to be too conservative for the job, and then-Mayor Dianne Feinstein instead chose Harry Britt, a decision that may have helped to define the gay political split for years to come.

"Bob's sense of politics was extremely personal. There were a number of instances where he— and by extension the newspaper—was all over the place as a result of Bob's personal clashes and positive experiences with various people, gay or otherwise," said Rivaldo. "But to his credit he pretty much relinquished day-to-day operations to his staff. He developed the paper into a powerful voice that was unambiguous and forceful about the gay stuff on the ballot and candidates' positions on gay issues. And today the quality of writing and level of sophistication and analysis of complex social issues is impressive. The *B.A.R.* goes into a lot of detail, even to the point that the big papers now quote the *B.A.R.*"

The Epidemic

No gay issue helped to shape the need for timely and accurate news as much as the first several years of the AIDS epidemic. The *B.A.R.* became a weekly publication in the 1980s, in part to fill the need for information on the disease that was devastating the community. (The *B.A.R.* itself lost more than 10 employees, according to Ross.)

Back then, full-page advertisements from the San Francisco AIDS Foundation warned *B.A.R.* readers that rimming and fisting were considered unsafe activities until more research was done on HIV transmission.

It was front-page news in 1986 that some Bay Area corporations had decided not to fire their employees with AIDS and would continue to provide them with health-care coverage.

"Our philosophy is to treat all employees with dignity and respect, and our policy about AIDS reflects that it's like any serious illness," a Levi's spokeswoman told the *B.A.R.*

But many companies did not operate the same way, and thus the gay community also found itself with an economic crisis on its hands.

"Our friends were getting sick and losing their jobs and getting thrown out of their places because they couldn't make rent, and we thought that shouldn't be happening," recalled Rick Booth, a co-founder of the AIDS Emergency Fund. "So that's how we got started—right here in my living room."

Ross and the *B.A.R.* faithfully supported AEF in its mission to make emergency grants to people in need. The paper publicized AEF events and made financial contributions as well.

"A lot has changed in terms of the laws and the treatments, but back then it was pretty grim," said Booth. "We constantly relied on the *B.A.R.*; we had to keep informed. And I think the paper also really enhanced the organization tremendously. That period brought out the best in an awful lot of people."

A powerful symbol of the personal toll of AIDS was evident in the November 16, 1989, issue when then–Art Director Richard Burt compiled the pictures and names of everyone who had died that year. The section ran for eight pages. To this day, people still occasionally call to inquire about it.

AIDS news in the *B.A.R.* has consistently made national headlines—from the famous "No Obits" cover of 1998 to the paper's coverage of some significant political protests and events.

"Castro Held Hostage," read a 1989 headline on a front-page story detailing the police occupation and excessive force used during a peaceful neighborhood AIDS protest organized by ACT UP. That event became known as the "Castro Sweep," and media attention shed light on the contentious relationship between gays and police, prompting calls for reform.

Community Voices

The *B.A.R.* has always been known for its unique feature stories that only a gay community newspaper would cover.

"Ammiano loses a parachute," read a 1978 headline about the openly gay teacher who was profiled in the *San Francisco Chronicle* for having an unconventional classroom. Turns out, the *Chronicle* piece mentioned that Tom Ammiano's classroom contained a silk parachute, which the San Francisco Fire Department deemed a fire hazard.

"In a visit to Buena Vista Elementary School, [fire inspectors] found Ammiano to be surprised but cooperative," said the *B.A.R.* "My kids don't smoke and I'm the only flaming thing in that room," Ammiano quipped.

If there's one feature of the *B.A.R.* that has always been lively, it's the letters section. Even in the early days it was not uncommon to feature pages and pages of community infighting.

Letters from the 1980s included a "Cover Up" letter to fat lesbians that sparked months of responses; a weeks-long debate about whether bodybuilding was a sport; and a handful of public admonitions against gays who were not considered representative of the community.

Though some may believe that ACT UP only recently became controversial in San Francisco, many community leaders wrote to the *B.A.R.* to protest the historic group's militant tactics and street blockades even way back when.

Racial tensions also were addressed in the letters pages, especially after some gay leaders blamed the 1989 defeat of a domestic-partners measure on communities of color because of neighborhood voting statistics. Others wrote in to point out that the *B.A.R.* had mistakenly identified the nonprofit organization Shanti as "no longer gay-identified" because of its new Executive Director Eric Rofes' decision to do more outreach to communities of color.

And, of course, local and personal concerns always were given ample space.

"Is anyone aware that the city is building a rail connection along the Embarcadero that will connect Fisherman's Wharf to Castro Street?" an alarmed man wrote in the 1980s. "Can you see it now? T-shirt shops and hot-dog stands serving a million tourists on Upper Market ... the death of our neighborhood focal point."

Another man ran an open letter to community members who perfumed their genitals. "When I want to suck cock," he wrote, "it is not the flavors of Chanel or Dior I crave!"

The *B.A.R.*'s mix of humor, analysis, community input and political advocacy tapped into local sentiment and helped to set the tone for the LGBT movement worldwide.

"It has become a valuable awareness tool. Plus, the second section is still entertainment, so it hasn't given up its role as the source of cultural information, fun, gossip and all that stuff," summarized Rivaldo. "We have a real precious thing in San Francisco that no one else in human history has. We were right here to really get the movement under way no matter how exotic and strange the world may have thought it was. There was an early legitimacy, and we have inspired people around the world to do it."

Looking Ahead

After marking 40 years in 2011, the *B.A.R.* continues to make changes. The paper unveiled its latest print redesign and has also recently updated its website, allowing people to offer their immediate comments on stories via Facebook.

Thomas E. Horn, who became the paper's publisher after Ross died in 2003, said in an email, "[W]e need to be on the cutting edge of new technology," including social media.

He added, "We also need to appeal to a younger demographic whose interests lie less in news and more in just 'what's happening.'" That sentiment led to BARtab, the monthly LGBT nightlife guide and website, which the paper launched in 2011.

Finally, he said, "If we produce a quality product that is relevant, the readers will come."

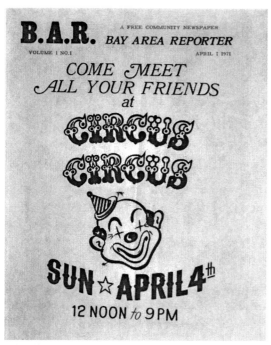

Bay Area Reporter's first issue, April 1, 1971.

Bay Area Reporter, March 15, 1972.

ABOVE: *Bay Area Reporter*, November 11, 1976.
RIGHT: *Bay Area Reporter*, August 5, 1982.

Bay Area Reporter, **November 16, 1989,
showing a string of AIDS-related deaths.**

Bay Area Reporter, **August 13, 1998.
The news was that this was the first
issue with no obituaries since the AIDS
epidemic exploded in San Francisco.**

Bay Area Reporter, December 18, 2003.

ABOVE: *Bay Area Reporter*,
December 18, 2003.

LEFT: *Bay Area Reporter*, June 19, 2008.

25

Bay Windows

By *Bay Windows* staff

When Sasha Alyson launched Boston's *Bay Windows* in 1983, he could not have dreamed the paper would eventually be at the center of the effort to bring marriage equality to Massachusetts and the rest of New England. According to Marc Solomon, former campaign director for MassEquality, "*Bay Windows* waved the flag, rallied the troops, held advocates and lawmakers accountable and exposed those working against equal rights."

Alyson did recognize that the Boston gay and lesbian community needed a new voice with a different perspective. The newspapers available were the *Gay Community News* and a "bar rag," *The Mirror*. Alyson, a reader and supporter of *GCN*, felt the community needed more local news, and more coverage of the illness recently named AIDS (formerly gay cancer or GRID). Alyson felt strongly that the community needed more political coverage and that elections should be covered.

The early years presented one main challenge: money. "A few years later, classified and phone-sex ads became a major source of income," Alyson told *Bay Windows*, "but in 1983 it was hard to find advertisers."

In 1985, Alyson sold *Bay Windows* to Jim Hoover. Alyson continued to publish LGBT-focused books through Alyson Publications (which he established in 1979) and launched Alyson Adventures, a travel company for LGBT clientele.

At the time, Hoover was publisher of *South End News*, serving the Boston neighborhood affectionately known as the "gay ghetto" (*South End News* remains *Bay Windows'* sister publication). Hoover professionalized the business side and brought on Editor Jeff Epperly, who raised the journalistic standards of the organization. Epperly's leadership on covering the AIDS epidemic and politics resulted in award-winning articles. His coverage of current presidential candidate Mitt Romney's early support of the gay community continues to haunt Romney. Hoover was a founding member and later became president of the now-defunct National Gay Newspaper Guild.

Hoover would tell of how advertisers often didn't want him to return phone messages because the call would have to go through the receptionist. "I spent most of my time whispering on the phone," he once told the staff. Businesses, both straight and gay, were afraid of being connected to a gay publication.

Advertising revenue boomed in the 1990s, thanks to a strong presence of local businesses, real estate offerings, personal ads, and national companies. Editorial content and news reporting continued to become more focused and hard-hitting.

In 2003, Jeff Coakley and Sue O'Connell purchased the paper from an ailing Hoover, who eventually died in 2009 after a battle with multiple myeloma.

Coakley and O'Connell increased advertising revenue, both in print and online, and made *Bay

Windows a major LGBT news source for the mainstream media. Susan Ryan-Vollmar joined as editor and further improved the breadth and depth of coverage. Just as Ryan-Vollmar took the helm, Pope John Paul II died. *Bay Windows'* April 7, 2005, issue, titled "The Holy Father's Homophobia," was "timely, informative and persuasive and exemplified the role of the GLBT press at its best: to provide a GLBT perspective that the mainstream media has missed," wrote reader Mark Merante. The issue went on to win honors from the New England Press Association.

As Massachusetts continued to become more accepting of its LGBT residents, the community moved to the suburbs (what Coakley called "gay sprawl"). *Bay Windows* followed, by adding major supermarket chains and news boxes to the distribution plan.

Bay Windows was at the eye of the storm during the legal effort and the lawmakers' debate to make same-sex marriage legal. Finally, in 2004, couples were able to marry. Media from around the world looked to the paper for insight and resources to inform their coverage of same-sex marriage.

Over the years, *Bay Windows* has evolved from its free-form, feature-heavy beginnings to the more hard-news–focused LGBT advocacy paper that played a pivotal role in bringing marriage equality to the state.

"The multiyear, multiplatform work done to deliver the first state into the world of marriage for same-sex couples has yet to be duplicated," MassEquality's Solomon told *Bay Windows*. "The courts, the lawmakers, the advocates and the community joined to deliver a perfect storm of powerful advocacy. *Bay Windows* newspaper was a key ingredient in this passionate mix. Without a strong media advocate, the battle might still be going on."

Taking advantage of emerging blog technology helped to keep the community informed. Solomon noted that "publishing special editions, live blogging from the legislature during crucial votes, all gave a voice to our efforts."

Here are some highlights from 29 years of *Bay Windows*, the paper of record for the LGBT community of New England.

Foreshadowing Marriage: Volume 1, Issue 1

In the March 1983 inaugural issue, Alyson penned a feature titled "How We Met: Local Couples Tell Their Stories." One of the featured couples was Ralph Hodgdon and the late Paul McMahon. The article showed side-by-side photos of the couple, one taken soon after their first meeting in New York's Central Park in 1955 (both men were decked out in stylish hats, with McMahon looking rather dapper in his bow tie), and another taken around the time of the issue's publication. Another 25 years later in 2008, Hodgdon and McMahon became local icons of the civil-marriage–rights movement, appearing at nearly every public rally and Statehouse debate on same-sex marriage with a sign announcing their decades-long commitment.

Happy Valentine's Day, Wear a Condom!

After more than 25 years of AIDS, most of the LGBT community became aware of the basics of safer sex. The same can't be said of the early days of the epidemic. The February 16, 1984, issue featured a full-page ad from the AIDS Action Committee giving the community a crash course on the subject. With skyrocketing infection rates and deaths, AAC didn't dance around the topic. The Valentine's Day ad assessed risks and safer-sex practices for anal sex, oral sex, mutual masturbation, watersports, rimming, fisting and other activities.

Reasons to Be Joyful

In July 1986, in the midst of the AIDS crisis, the late activist Eric Rofes wrote a column that listed 10 things he loved about being gay. And given that it was meant as a rallying cry during a deadly epidemic, the list was less "I double my wardrobe" and more heartfelt and inspirational. Take reason No. 3: "Knowing the miracle in each of our lives that somehow gave us the courage to do what we thought could never be done—to take that first step over the threshold of our first gay bar, to march in our first lesbian and gay pride parade, to tell our parents or our grandparents or our children, to kiss someone hard on the mouth and know what it meant to us."

Live! Nude! Lesbians!

The January 8, 1987, issue featured 12 women who filed a civil suit to get an injunction against enforcement of a Cape Cod area regulation banning nudity. The women claimed that the ban on nudity violated their First, Fourth, Fifth and Ninth Amendment rights. Accompanying the story was a photo of a group of butch, topless women being arrested on the beach by Provincetown police at a demonstration against the nudity ban. Not surprisingly, all the photographers visible in the background were men.

Wonder Boy

Michael Chabon is now known as the ridiculously gay-friendly Pulitzer Prize–winning novelist responsible for books that are heavy on gay content, such as 1995's *Wonder Boys* and 2000's *The Amazing Adventures of Kavalier and Clay*. The July 7, 1988, edition of *Bay Windows* introduced this relatively unknown 24-year-old who was releasing his first novel, *The Mysteries of Pittsburgh*. *Bay Windows* book critic Philip Gambone gave the book rave reviews and even gave Chabon bonus points for writing steamy sex scenes involving Art, the is-he-or-isn't-he-gay protagonist. Chabon may now be a well-known name, but *Bay Windows* was a fan from day one.

Lesbian Midwives Help People Out

In 1989, the fact that gay and lesbian people (there wasn't much coverage, if any, of the bi and trans populations) could hold ordinary jobs and lead ordinary lives was considered news. A February 16 cover story profiling lesbian midwives Anne Arkin and Valerie Hodenius exemplified the notion. While both women worked primarily with straight clients, they also discussed their experience working with lesbian parents-to-be. Arkin told a story showing how lesbians were turning traditional concepts of motherhood on their heads: "Arkin said that one lesbian she worked with in San Francisco told her that she had gotten pregnant 'the old-fashioned way'—with an artichoke-heart jar and a turkey baster. Another lesbian client, who consulted with Arkin soon after, also said she got pregnant 'the old-fashioned way.' 'Oh,' said Arkin, 'you mean the artichoke jar and a turkey baster.' 'No,' the woman said, 'intercourse.'"

Chronicling an Epidemic

As part of its ongoing coverage of HIV/AIDS, the paper published the column "AIDScope," which included the latest news on the epidemic and a chart from the Centers for Disease Control showing the numbers of AIDS cases counted in the U.S. since the beginning. In April 1990, the CDC found that more than half of the 124,000 AIDS cases in the U.S. were in gay men. Each issue of the paper also included a fair number of obituaries, nearly all of them concerning gay men who had succumbed to AIDS. The April 19, 1990, issue included five.

Lesbians and Breast Cancer

In 1991, the Human Rights Campaign Fund (now known as the Human Rights Campaign) honored Dr. Susan Love, the breast-cancer researcher and surgeon. At the time, there was much speculation in the lesbian community that lesbians were at a higher risk for breast cancer simply for being lesbians. Love dismissed the idea. If anything, she said in the December 26 issue, some lesbians may be at greater risk for getting sicker from the disease than heterosexual women because they do not get regular gynecological care. "What brings most women in to the gynecologist between ages 20 and 40 is birth control. If you're not doing that, then you're not sort of compelled to go to the gynecologist. You don't go as often, so you're less likely to get checked and you're less likely to get a mammogram. You may even be worried about homophobia in the medical system."

Promoting the Paper

An in-house, December 26, 1991, advertisement for *Bay Windows* asked, "Will the Real Gay Community Please Stand Up?" The ad read: "The truth of the matter is that there is no single gay community. We are young and old; rich and poor; white- and blue-collar; liberal and conservative; white, black, brown, and anything else you can think of. *Bay Windows* understands this diversity. That's why we don't toe any party lines, we don't take 'contributions,' and we don't allow our reporters to work with outside groups or organizations. *Bay Windows* isn't a hobby: it's a newspaper with full-time, paid reporters and editors who take their work seriously. And we take you just as seriously."

Colin Powell: Who Wants to Pee With a Gay in the Room?

During a House Budget Committee meeting, U.S. Representative Barney Frank grilled General Colin Powell, chairman of the Joint Chiefs of Staff, about why gay people were prevented from serving openly in the military. Powell's response, in the February 13, 1992, issue of *Bay Windows*, was essentially that straight people think gay people are icky. "It is just my judgment and the judgment of the chiefs that homosexual behavior is inconsistent with maintaining good order and discipline. What do I mean by that? I mean it is difficult in a military setting where there is no privacy, where you don't get choice of association, where you don't get choice of where you live, to introduce a group of individuals who are proud, brave, loyal, good Americans, but who favor a homosexual lifestyle, and put them in with heterosexuals who would prefer not to have somebody of the same sex find them sexually attractive, put them in close proximity, ask them to share the most private facilities together, the bedroom, the barracks, the latrines, the showers."

Youth Commission Formed

Massachusetts Governor William Weld, a Republican, reacting to the Legislature's failure to pass a bill forming a Commission on Gay and Lesbian Youth, created one via executive order. During a press conference announcing the move, Weld declared: "There's really no greater tragedy I can think of than the loss of a young life to suicide. The pressures on youth can be tremendous, and for homosexual ... teenagers, those pressures may be multiplied a number of times over." Weld's press secretary, Virginia Buckingham, later assured *Bay Windows* in the February 13, 1992, issue that the new commission would be charged with making "recommendations regarding funding" and that "their recommendations are going to be taken very seriously."

OutWrite Comes to Boston

After two years in San Francisco, the OutWrite conference moved to Boston in 1992. The March 5 issue highlighted coordinator Sue Hyde. The conference attendees included a *Who's Who* of the LGBT publishing world: Allan Gurganus, Dorothy Allison, Michael Bronski, Walta Borawski, Leslea Newman, Alison Bechdel, Eric Orner, Felice Picano, Phil Gambone, John Preston and Pat Califia.

The Gays March in South Boston

After Judge Hiller Zobel ruled that the St. Patrick's Day parade was a public event thanks to the $8,000 that the city of Boston contributed to the parade, 25 members of the Irish-American Gay, Lesbian, and Bisexual Pride Committee of Boston marched in the annual parade. *Bay Windows* covered the parade in the March 19, 1992, issue. Dozens of police officers protected the group, which the crowd pelted with "smoke bombs, firecrackers, condoms, latex gloves, beer cans, bottles and rocks." Mayor Ray Flynn issued a statement about the violence from Kennedy Airport in New York, after he returned from a trip to Ireland. "The Irish, who have seen hardships created by hatred and discrimination, are appalled by this sort of behavior in the U.S.," Flynn said. "Parade organizers in Cork [Ireland] have accepted gays in the parade there to show that the Irish tradition is one of inclusion."

Hitting the Pink Ceiling

Bay Windows interviewed Linda Villarosa in its April 23, 1992, issue. She had come out as a lesbian in an essay for *Essence* magazine. She speculated that her decision to come out ruined her chances to become editor-in-chief of the magazine. "It's all these subtle things, but I really think that has happened. If you ask people, they will deny, but I think that is clearly happening. In a way, that makes me mad, but in a way, I never wanted to be editor-in-chief. ... But I think that did happen, because I think they would be much too nervous to have a lesbian as the editor-in-chief."

Friend of Bill

In the January 28, 1993, issue, Worcester resident Michael Quercio told of meeting presidential candidate Bill Clinton during a campaign stop at a Boston fundraiser. During the dinner, Quercio told Clinton that he was HIV-positive. "My right hand was shaking his right hand and then, when I told him I was positive, he took his left hand and clasped both our hands that were already in a handshake. He held my hand—both my hands—throughout the whole two-minute conversation that we had. Never did his eyes move from my eyes. He was glued to the conversation." After his election, Clinton invited Quercio to a "Faces of Hope" luncheon attended by 52 others who had impressed Clinton during the campaign.

Hot New Talent

An advertisement in the February 4, 1993, issue for a show promoted by Revolutionary Acts titled "New Women's Voices" touted four new women musicians, including The Chenille Sisters, Kristina Olsen, Tish Hinojosa and … Ani DiFranco ("To-the-bone lyrics … a voice that can rock the boat one minute and the cradle the next").

Practicing for 2004?

George W. Bush, who was challenging Texas Governor Ann Richards for the Lone Star State's top political post, distanced his campaign from anti-gay comments made by a state senator who also chaired Bush's East Texas campaign operation. The senator, Bill Ratliff, complained that Richards had appointed openly gay people to government jobs. "I simply don't agree to appointing avowed homosexual activists … to positions of leadership," Ratliff said. "I think it elevates the lifestyle. It tends to elevate the lifestyle to the equivalent of the traditional family." Bush told The Associated Press, as published in the September 1, 1994, issue, that the appointment of gay people to state posts was "not an issue" for him and that Ratliff "is a fine state senator. He's still going to stay on my campaign. He is speaking for himself."

No Place Like Home

Just months after opening the Sidney Borum, Jr. Health Center on Boylston Street in Boston, the Justice Resource Institute announced plans to open a community center for gay and lesbian youth. Paul Ricciardi, coordinator of JRI's youth programming, told *Bay Windows* in the December 1, 1994, issue that he was unsure how many teens would take advantage of the center. "Currently other youth programs offered through JRI see upwards of 30 teens a week. A dance held [for gay teens] last month at the Arlington Street Church saw an attendance of 300 teens."

How Are Those Connections Working Out for You?

December 1, 1994: After the Republican sweep of Congress, national Log Cabin Republicans founder Rich Tafel told *Bay Windows* of the Newt Gingrich–led GOP: "If they're going to listen to anybody, they'll listen to me." Of Tafel, *Bay Windows* reported: "An ordained Baptist minister, he professes to have a network of gay Capitol Hill staff members—many of them deeply closeted—which he has developed throughout Congress. Tafel maintains that the partisan nature of his organization and his connections put him in the right place at the right time."

Famous Lesbian Comedian!

Sporting big hair, Suzanne Westenhoefer's smiling mug advertised a performance in the February 2, 1995, issue. She appeared at Boston's Berklee Performance Center (tickets just $15!). Her special hook? She's the "1st Out Lesbian to have HBO Special"!

Lesbian Avengers Take on Paul Cameron

Discredited researcher Paul Cameron presented a talk titled "Do Homosexual Teachers Pose a Risk to Pupils?" at the annual conference of the Eastern Psychological Association in Boston. Conference attendees challenged Cameron's findings. "Several audience members said the small number of homosexuals included in the study would invalidate any of its conclusions about gays," *Bay Windows* reported in the April 6, 1995, edition, noting that one straight man, to much laughter, told Cameron that his study seemed to conclude that men should not be in classrooms. Cameron was greeted at the conference by a protest from the Lesbian Avengers, who wielded signs reading "Fight the Religious Right in Science and the Classroom" and "Paul Cameron Is a Threat to Humanity."

Activist Donates Award to Gay Youth

David LaFontaine, founder of the Coalition for Lesbian and Gay Civil Rights and an original board member of the Governor's Commission on Gay and Lesbian Youth, announced he would donate the $25,000 grant he received from the Stonewall Awards to gay youth groups. *Bay Windows* reported in the July 3, 1996, issue: "When asked why he feels he received one of this year's Stonewall Awards, [LaFontaine] responded, '[The Commission] has done something that people thought was impossible: secure public funding for gay rights programs in the schools. This is what terrifies the radical right the most.'"

www

In 1998, *Bay Windows* launched www.baywindows.com, the first LGBT website in New England.

Slamming Fox News

In a steaming November 12, 1998, editorial, Editor Jeff Epperly laid into television station WFXT for its sweeps-week exposé on gay men having sex in public. "The lead-ins made it sound as if the men involved were having sex with 'crowds of people' including 'children' in full view. Yet all that WFXT could come up with was one poor 68-year-old man trudging around a Weston park. That elderly man stupidly came up to a WFXT employee (who was wearing a hidden camera) and began masturbating. … The 68-year-old was arrested and was then interrogated by [the reporter] as he was being hauled away. … Until Fox stops airing shows like 'World's Deadliest Police Chases' and 'Married With Children'—and their blood-drenched newscasts—nobody affiliated with that network has much ground to stand on when worrying about the well-being of children."

Rita Hester Murdered

On December 3, 1998, *Bay Windows* reported on the murder of Rita Hester, a trans woman who was well-known in Boston. In its reporting, though, *Bay Windows* made itself the target of ire from the trans community by describing Hester as "a gay man who lived as" a woman and putting quotes around the name Rita.

Trans Community Reacts to Hester Coverage

Two letters to the editor in the December 11, 1998, issue took *Bay Windows* to task for its characterization of Rita Hester as a "gay man." "Do you guys think we are all drag queens just because so many of us are stuck in your bars because it is one of the only safe places for us to be? Or just because we happen to have one thing and one thing only in common with you: our cocks?" asked one letter writer. Another noted the irony of *Bay Windows'* having reported that the *Boston Globe* and *Boston Herald* were criticized by trans activists for "referring to Rita as male. Yet you did no better, even with the clue. At the very least, you could have noted that you weren't sure how to talk about Rita, now that she is no longer here to speak for and name herself."

Protests Outside *Bay Windows*

Trans activists protested outside the offices of the *Boston Herald* and *Bay Windows* over both papers' continued refusal to refer to Rita Hester as a woman in their news coverage of her death. *Bay Windows* reported in the December 17, 1998, issue: "Calling their protest the 'Truth Rally,' participants carried signs that read 'Cover Our Lives, Not Just Our Deaths,' 'Burn the *Herald*' and 'Burn *Bay Windows*.' Led by police, protesters marched from the *Boston Herald* building two miles to the offices of *Bay Windows* in Boston's South End neighborhood. While walking, they shouted slurs such as '*Bay Windows*, get a clue; take time to enlarge your view.'" Jeff Epperly, who was editor at the time, today sees the trans community in a different light: "When transgender leaders became angry with me, instead of listening to them I dug in my heels. Thus started a long-standing feud that I truly regret. Or, said another way: No excuses. I'm sorry. I was wrong."

Activists Call for Grassroots Effort to Defeat Anti-Marriage Bill

Longtime gay activist David LaFontaine, a founding member of the Governor's Commission on Gay and Lesbian Youth, called for a grassroots campaign to educate lawmakers on the needs of same-sex couples in order to defeat a proposed anti-marriage bill. "I think that same-sex couples are relatively invisible in our society, and until we can make people realize just how many people's human lives are affected by DP and marriage issues, the [governor and lawmakers] won't understand the importance of the legislation," LaFontaine told *Bay Windows* in the February 11, 1999, issue. "There has to be a real grassroots effort in the same way we have made progress around youth issues through rallies and lobby days at the Statehouse. It's a terrible mistake to rely on a couple of visible gay activists, however skilled and well-placed they may be. If we can rally a couple thousand teenagers every year for a youth march and rally, then we should certainly be able to rally a couple thousand gay and lesbian adults on Beacon Hill."

He's a Survivor

Richard Hatch, winner of the inaugural *Survivor* TV series, gave *Bay Windows* a rare sit-down interview in the September 27, 2000, issue, after news of his lawsuit against his hometown of Middletown, Rhode Island, became public. Hatch alleged that town officials violated his rights by arresting him and charging him with abusing his son during an early-morning workout and then releasing confidential information about the case to the media. "I'm still in control of my life," Hatch said. "What's meaningful to me is still the same. This is just another blip on the radar, another experience."

And It Begins

Gay & Lesbian Advocates & Defenders announced on April 11, 2001, that it had filed suit against the Massachusetts Department of Public Health in Superior Court on behalf of seven same-sex Massachusetts couples. The couples had been denied marriage licenses. The suit was called *Goodridge v. Department of Public Health.*

LGBT Boston—Still Segregated

The February 28, 2002, issue of *Bay Windows* reported that African-American LGBT people felt isolated from the larger, whiter LGBT community. "But in a city that continues to struggle with racial issues in just about every walk of life—housing and education, most notably—adding gay to the mix isn't always easy, or beneficial. ... [One African-American activist] agrees that the Boston gay community is segregated, and goes a step further. 'I think the gay community is more racist than the mainstream community,' he says. 'I think it's more segregated, I think it's more intentionally segregated. In terms of being a member of the same-gender-loving community of African descent, I think that the mainstream gay community in some ways goes out of its way to not be involved with black issues. To not show you black faces. I think that they don't take the black community seriously."

Senate President Supports Civil Unions

Just two months before the Supreme Judicial Court issued its landmark 2003 ruling in the *Goodridge* marriage case, Senate President Robert Travaglini announced that he would support a civil-unions bill but that he wouldn't act on any legislation affecting same-sex couples until the court ruled. *Bay Windows* reported in the September 11, 2003, issue that "State Sen. Cheryl Jacques, D-Needham, a co-sponsor of civil union legislation, is encouraged by Travaglini's statement. 'I think what the Senate president has done in coming out in support of civil unions is very courageous,' said Jacques. 'I think it shows his heart is in the right place, that he supports equality for all families in Massachusetts, including gay families.'"

Couples Can Wed

On November 18, 2003, the Massachusetts Supreme Judicial Court ruled that same-sex couples should be allowed to wed. *Bay Windows* published a special edition (in advance of the weekly November 18 issue). Each side braced for battle.

Save the Date!

In the wake of the Massachusetts ruling, same-sex couples and the wedding industry moved into high gear to prepare for May 2004 weddings. A Chelmsford, Massachusetts, couple told *Bay Windows* in the December 4, 2003, issue that they had tentatively settled on a wedding date of May 22 but they had yet to wrestle with "decisions about florists, caterers, music, rings, invitations, cakes, outfits, and any number of the other components that go into planning a wedding." A public relations manager for Bloomingdale's told *Bay Windows* that the store was "planning an event to market their registry to same-sex couples." She said the store had designated a section of its registry website about four years earlier for same-sex couples planning commitment ceremonies. *Bay Windows* launched a weekly advertising section devoted to wedding planning.

At Last! May 17, 2004

Celebrations marked the first day as marriage equality began in Massachusetts. The city of Cambridge got a jump on the festivities by offering a May 16 late-night party at midnight, allowing couples to register for marriage licenses. Media from around the world focused on Cambridge. In Boston, on the morning of May 17, Mayor Tom Menino greeted couples applying for licenses. *Bay Windows* published "It Takes Two," its largest Gay & Lesbian Wedding Planning Guide.

The *Bay Windows* float in June's Gay Pride Parade featured a rolling billboard with a mock *Bay Windows* cover, featuring stories about how the world didn't end on May 18, 2004, the day after marriage equality took effect, as anti-gay activists had "predicted".

With Pride and Love

Massachusetts Governor Deval Patrick and his family sat down with Editor Laura Kiritsy for the June 12, 2008, edition of *Bay Windows*: "This is the first time that Katherine Patrick has spoken to the media about being an out lesbian and the support she has received from her parents, Gov. Deval Patrick and First Lady Diane Patrick." Talking about her reaction to her dad's standing up for LGBT rights, the 18-year-old Katherine Patrick said that "of course, he didn't know that I was gay then." With a laugh, she added: "So, for someone so publicly to fight for something that doesn't even affect him was just like, 'That's my dad,' you know? ... That's all I could think. I was very, very proud to be part of this family, and this state in general."

10 Stories of Care

Boston's venerable Fenway Community Health Center, established in 1971, dedicated its new headquarters and renamed itself Fenway Health. Stephen Boswell, the agency's president, told *Bay Windows* in the May 9, 2009, issue that, at 100,000 square feet, it was probably the largest building ever built for an LGBT-focused organization. Fenway cared for 15,000 patients and received 70,000 patient visits each year.

Another Step Forward

In the November 23, 2011, issue of *Bay Windows*, the cover photo showed Governor Deval Patrick signing the transgender equal-rights bill into law. Patrick was surrounded by activists and members of the transgender community. Gunner Scott, executive director of the Massachusetts Transgender Political Coalition, told *Bay Windows*, "We are so grateful for his leadership in getting this bill passed and for his unwavering commitment to ensuring that all residents of the commonwealth, including transgender people, are treated with dignity and respect under the laws of our state."

Bay Windows, November 20, 2003.

Bay Windows' first issue, March 1983.

Bay Windows, May 20, 2004.

Bay Windows, June 1, 2006.

Bay Windows, April 7, 2005.

Bay Windows, June 12, 2008.

26

Between The Lines

By Kate Opalewski, *Between The Lines*

Over the years, many of Michigan's LGBT publications have come and gone, but *Between The Lines* has sustained itself as the longest continuously published LGBT newspaper in the state.

The paper began in April 1993 as a monthly. The first publisher, Mark "MaxZine" Weinstein, produced a dozen issues and then turned publishing responsibilities over to Shannon Rhoades and Julie Enzer. They continued publishing the newspaper as a monthly for close to two years, and in December 1995 Susan Horowitz and Jan Stevenson, the current owners, purchased it. During the next three years, Horowitz and Stevenson took the publication from monthly to biweekly to weekly, adding a website, www.pridesource.com, in 1997. Horowitz and Stevenson have continued to publish *Between The Lines* for the past 17 years.

As the 20th anniversary of *Between The Lines* approaches in 2013, *BTL* has looked back on how the publication has played a pivotal role in improving the quality of life for the LGBT community and helping educate the public on the laws—just and unjust—under which citizens in Michigan live.

Weinstein, then 27 years old, launched the publication in Ann Arbor in March 1993. He saw the need for a more organized form of communication within the gay and lesbian community. The 1980s had been an emotionally devastating time because of the HIV/AIDS epidemic and the death of thousands of young gay men. It was the era of Ronald Reagan and George H.W. Bush, when gay and lesbian people devoted themselves to fighting repressive legislation.

"I had been living on the road and was so worn out from death and travel," recalled Weinstein. "I found myself back in Ann Arbor constantly reading sad letters." The devastating epidemic, coupled with the scarcity of gay and lesbian publications in Michigan, inspired Weinstein to create a newspaper. He joined forces with David Rosenberg, an activist for ACT UP (AIDS Coalition to Unleash Power), and contributors such as Shannon Rhoades and Tim Retzloff, now a Yale University LGBT Ph.D. historian, to create a monthly publication as a vehicle for information and activism.

Operated from his bedroom at HeiWa House, a progressive co-op on Hill Street in Ann Arbor, Weinstein established the paper's independence and willingness to cover controversial material. Weinstein and his editorial staff suffered a minor setback when News Printing Inc., of Northville, refused to print their first issue; however, Ypsilanti Press agreed to print the paper soon after. The premiere black-and-white issue consisted of only 12 pages, called attention to the radical right in Michigan and addressed News Printing Inc.'s refusal to do business with the gay and lesbian publication.

After the Ypsilanti Press agreed to print *Between The Lines*, Weinstein gathered several helping hands to distribute 10,000 copies to local LGBT bars, bookstores, coffeehouses and other places LGBT people frequented. Supporters of the paper volunteered to expand the distribution to Grand Rapids and Flint. This initial positive response allowed the paper to grow quickly, doubling in page length.

During the first few months of publication, Weinstein wrote a story called "Homophobia to the Max," about Maxie's Nightclub, that would greatly shape the relationship between the paper and gay bars. Maxie's was a straight-owned bar with one or two openly gay employees in the Detroit area that welcomed a gay night. The article addressed an extremely homophobic straight performer who was invited to Maxie's and publicly announced that gay people should be attacked or killed. Weinstein contacted the Triangle Foundation—now Equality Michigan—and spoke with then–Executive Director Jeffrey Montgomery about the establishment's contradictory message.

After the article was published, reactions were mixed. Many readers supported Weinstein's decision to report on the bar, but many gay-bar advertisers claimed they would never place ads in the publication again. "They claimed they would never advertise with me because it was considered wrong to criticize a gay bar," recalls Weinstein. "I thought it was ridiculous. It wasn't even a gay bar—they just had a gay night. But if you criticize one, you criticize them all."

Weinstein discovered that some bars were throwing out the newspapers soon after he dropped them off. A few months later, he pushed the envelope further and ran a story about the finding of a body behind a gay bar on Woodward Avenue in Detroit. Numerous readers called Weinstein, infuriated, claiming that he should not have reported the death. Advertisers felt the news was "not in the best interest of the community" and could hurt their image, as the incident may have been the result of a gay-bashing.

Overcoming violent attitudes and behaviors toward the LGBT community was one of many struggles that led to the March on Washington, the third and largest LGBT civil rights demonstration to that point, in April 1993. Around 800,000 marchers descended on the nation's capital. When Urvashi Vaid and the National Gay and Lesbian Task Force conceived the march along with many other leaders, the hope for a better future for LGBT people was widespread. There were promising medications on the horizon to treat HIV/AIDS, Bill Clinton had been elected president amid promises to be a major advocate for LGBT rights, and it appeared at the time that the ban on LGBT citizens' serving in the military would soon be over.

Another legacy of the 1993 March on Washington was the emergence of literally hundreds of new LGBT grassroots organizations and regional community centers nationwide. Back in Michigan, *Between The Lines* documented the LGBT community's building of important agencies across the state, including Affirmations Community Center in Ferndale, AIDS Partnership, Michigan Pride, the Triangle Foundation and the many LGBT workplace organizations that began in the 1990s.

By April 1994, Weinstein had become weary and frustrated with the business of publishing. As a result, he turned *Between The Lines* over to contributor Shannon Rhoades, who became editor and publisher of the monthly paper that month. During her tenure, she added a second print color to the covers, maintained a 24-page average per issue and established an editorial board to provide community input on content. She further strengthened the paper by incorporating under the name Diva & Empress Publications Inc. with then–co-owner Julie Enszer, chair of the editorial board.

Between The Lines continued to cover important stories, such as the September 1994 vote (63–36) by the U.S. Senate to cut off federal funds to any school district using educational materials that in any way "supported homosexuality." This occurred during a debate on reauthorization of the Elementary and Secondary Education Act that provided $12.5 billion in federal funds to the nation's public schools. Senator Joe Lieberman supported this amendment, which was offered by reactionary Republican Senator Jesse Helms.

In October 1994, 13 years into the AIDS epidemic, the Midwest AIDS Prevention Project issued a warning to the public that the HIV infection would "skyrocket if people aren't safer." Craig Covey was the director of MAPP and had a regular column in *Between The Lines* that covered the politics of AIDS. "People on staff either had the expertise or went to the people with the expertise for their information. The newspaper had an insider view that most mainstream reporters did not," said Tim Retzloff, former *Between The Lines* assistant editor. "As a result, the newspaper developed a good, solid reputation as a credible paper."

Because of her health issues, Rhoades was unable to plan for the longevity of the newspaper and sold it to Susan Horowitz and Jan Stevenson in December 1995.

Horowitz, a native of New York, is an ethnically Irish daughter of adoptive Jewish parents. She was a human-rights activist by high school and co-founded (with a credit card that had a $500 limit) the lesbian/feminist printing company Tower Press in 1975, at the age of 22, as a way to call attention to lesbian and gay issues while working as a commercial printer. She developed the *NYC Pride Guide* in 1982, a trail-blazing community magazine for LGBT people in New York, and published it annually for the next 19 years. In 1989 she helped to co-found The New Festival, an international film festival screening cutting-edge LGBT films, and was the festival's first executive director through 1993. She served on the board of directors of the National Gay and Lesbian Task Force in 1987 and then again in 1993, where she met Jan Stevenson.

Born in the suburbs of Cleveland, Ohio, Stevenson had a passion for music at a young age. She earned a master's degree in music at Yale in 1979. After playing bass for a number of chamber orchestras, she realized she didn't like the music business and returned to school to earn her master's degree in business administration. Afterward, she became a Detroit corporate banker. Though successful, Stevenson left her lucrative job to care for her parents in the late 1980s for three years until both died. Stevenson then volunteered for Affirmations Community Center in Ferndale and became its first executive director in 1993, building it into a half-million-dollar nonprofit in less than five years' time.

Prior to *Between The Lines'* genesis, Stevenson felt the gay and lesbian community had difficulties organizing and communicating. When the opportunity arose to purchase the newspaper as a project, Stevenson—now the CFO, sales manager and co-publisher—jumped at it.

"Covering the issues and the community activities is what drives me. I also really enjoy talking to our advertisers and helping them to understand the gay community as an attractive market for their products and services. Often (less so, as acceptance grows), I am the only LGBT person they have had an in-depth conversation with, and the chance to educate potential allies is both rewarding and inspiring," said Stevenson.

After Horowitz and Stevenson took over, *Between The Lines* remained a monthly for the next 15 editions. There had been 33 issues published up to that point. When the pair assumed control, they put out their first issue from their home in Farmington, Michigan, where pizza-fed volunteers would often work in the basement to get the issues completed. A lot of the layout was done manually, and physical art boards were either picked up or driven out to their printer in Mason, Michigan.

The publication broke many LGBT-themed stories before the state's daily newspapers covered them. "Today, the dailies are a bit more responsive; however, they will never aggregate all the stories on our lives in one place—help shape the impact and the context. That is our intention when we begin a new issue. What is happening on the ground? What are our nonprofits and volunteers up to? How we help educate and make important advocacy connections is part of our editorial planning," said Horowitz, the editor-in-chief and co-publisher.

Horowitz's publishing and Stevenson's activism backgrounds helped them gain immediate support. "Within a few months, we added the concept of special issues to the mix, the most important of which was our 1996 *Between The Lines* Voters Guide. It was the first one we did, and we continued to do it every two years since that time. We also began to mail that issue to more than 70,000 people. That guide averaged 32 pages, and it helped educate voters on the issues important to them when it comes to advancing full equality for LGBT Michigan citizens. We did this with the cooperation of other LGBT political groups around the state," said Horowitz.

In 1996, *Between The Lines* followed up on the issue of schoolteachers' being out in their classrooms, as Byron Center High School teacher Gerry Crane became a controversial figure. Word of a private commitment ceremony the previous year with his partner, Randy Block, had leaked to the public, and parents and leaders of Michigan's Byron Center community began to urge the school board to terminate Crane. After a board meeting where the members condemned homosexuality but said they lacked legal grounds for dismissing Crane, the tension in the community made it difficult for him to live and work there. He negotiated a settlement with the school system and resigned. *Between*

The Lines continued to cover the story until January 1997, when Crane suffered a heart attack from which he never recovered before dying at 32.

Between The Lines was gaining momentum by printing LGBT stories that were making national news, such as the murder of a gay man, Scott Amedure, by Jonathan T. Schmitz after the two men's appearance on *The Jenny Jones Show*. Almost 300 articles were written in the U.S. in January 1996 on the case.

The publication made national news itself in 1996 when Ford Motor Company's Vice Chairman and Chief Financial Officer Allan Gilmour publicly announced that he was gay in an exclusive *Between The Lines* interview just after he retired, making him the highest-ranking corporate leader in America to come out publicly. Gilmour had spent 35 years with Ford, and he rejoined the company in 2002 as vice chairman and CFO before permanently retiring from Ford in 2005. Now president of Detroit's Wayne State University, Gilmour has become a leader and major funder of Michigan's LGBT community.

In the late 1990s, the issue of domestic-partner benefits was in the forefront, and workplace organizing for LGBT employees was a central area of focus, especially at the Big Three auto companies. In May 2000, all three of the automakers simultaneously announced they intended to offer same-sex domestic-partner benefits.

"This was a huge gain to follow and report on, and it was due to the tireless work of the LGBT employee groups at these companies. In fact, there are six large companies in Michigan that get 100 percent ratings today from the Human Rights Campaign corporate rating system, and it impacts thousands of lives in this state and across the country and the world," said Horowitz.

Within a year and a half, *Between The Lines* had enough news to go biweekly and did so with its 58th edition in October 1997. At the time, 70 percent of *Between The Lines* advertisers were gay-owned or gay-related. By 2002, however, 70 percent of advertisers were straight-owned or not necessarily gay- and lesbian-related. "Today, I have fewer conversations with our clients about 'what gay people are like' and more about general economic conditions, changes in the media industry and new products in social media," said Stevenson. "Our largest advertising sectors in 2012 are banks and other financial institutions, car dealerships and professional home service providers, followed closely by concerts and entertainment, pet services and personal-service professionals."

Between The Lines launched its sister website, www.pridesource.com, in 1997, advancing each year with technology. "We have tried our best to keep up and utilize the technology available," said Horowitz. "The biggest change has been the reach our articles now have. We also benefit from being able to stay connected with readers 24/7 and updating stories between print editions. The website also has added value, and the space online, of course, is infinite. We are not impeded by the cost and limits of print in providing information, connections and resources to readers."

Between The Lines covers a state in which the government has been especially unwelcoming, with rare exceptions. "Michigan is a battleground state. This has focused us, and we have been able to bring core issues to the front lines for many folks in the state that otherwise might not have given us a thought," she said.

The publication reported on significant events such as Mayor Dennis Archer's participation in a fundraiser at Gigi's Bar and Lounge in October 1997; it was the first time a Detroit mayor had appeared at a gay bar. Archer was praised for being accessible to LGBT leaders, and he used the opportunity to meet with voters in favor of domestic-partnership ordinances.

In 1998, *Between The Lines* took second prize for the best publication in the national Vice Versa Awards for Excellence in the Gay and Lesbian Press, co-sponsored by the organizations Q Syndicate and Gay.net.

As an advocacy publication, emphasis on developments that had an impact on LGBT and allied citizens across Michigan became a major focus, as people such as U.S. Representative Barney Frank, an openly gay Democratic congressman from Massachusetts, founded the National Stonewall Democrats. *Between The Lines* documented the progress made by this grassroots network of LGBT activists within the Democratic Party. By 2003, the University of Michigan chapter became the first of its kind on a college campus. It has worked toward open housing, lifting the ban on gay men who wish to donate blood, and statewide anti-bullying campaigns.

In February 1999, *Between The Lines* received a vicious death threat delivered in a Michigan House of Representatives envelope. The letter warned of an impending firebomb and attacked recently proposed hate-crimes legislation that would have amended Michigan's Ethnic Intimidation Act. Had the legislation passed, it would have added sexual orientation to the categories covered in the state's hate-crime law. In reference to the Michigan Gay Pride March held every year in June, the letter stated, "I will be the one throwing bricks at you at the next Pride march."

Though no attacks took place, Horowitz said she and Stevenson established this as a hate crime and sent a copy of the letter to Representative Lynne Martinez, who introduced the hate-crimes bill in the state House of Representatives. "It may have been motivated by an editorial cartoon in the paper's February issue critical of the Family Research Council, a radical conservative lobbying group that had been waging an aggressive anti-LGBT battle. The letter appeared to be sent from a supporter of the FRC," said Horowitz, who initiated an FBI investigation along with investigations by local police and postal authorities.

The threat did not prevent *Between The Lines* from moving forward. In getting back to business, Horowitz said the staff realized they were rewriting stories to keep them current and decided to jump into the weekly schedule.

"The reality is that much of the cost in current equipment and labor was the same to run a weekly as it had been to run the biweekly," said Horowitz about making the change in March 1999 with the paper's 95th edition. "We also found that advertisers were willing to support our weekly effort with little resistance. There were a number of major advertisers that stuck with us through the transitions from monthly to biweekly to weekly. It had a major impact on visibility of our issues and the ability to educate folks."

Around this time, *Between The Lines* moved from Horowitz and Stevenson's Farmington home to an office building next door. The paper remained true to its activist roots, sending out around 70,000 voter guides and galvanizing readers around the 2000 campaign of Debbie Stabenow, one of the state's U.S. senators.

By 2002, *Between The Lines* became a 52-page weekly with 50,000 readers. The publication shared the spotlight with Michigan mainstream media during a televised town meeting hosted by ABC's Peter Jennings. This spoke volumes about how far the LGBT press had come. It was with this momentum that the publication became deeply involved in the 2004 nationwide anti-gay marriage battles.

"We provided resources, office space and support to the volunteers and staff for that campaign. I took four months off to work almost full-time on the campaign," said Horowitz. To the community's dismay, all 11 states with ballot propositions against same-sex marriage were lost to anti-marriage forces, and George W. Bush was re-elected president. That didn't stop Horowitz and Stevenson from being married in Canada in 2005.

"I know our passion for these issues is how we met, and it has helped me grow in ways I would have never have been able to without Jan's support and energy and balance," said Horowitz. "I admire and respect her and think she is one of the smartest people I have ever met. That drives how we work together most of the time. I know going through financial challenges would never have been possible if we were not going through it together. Some people might think it would break you up, and I suppose it could have, but it just provided an opportunity to accept and grow and support each other. It is a rare and beautiful truth, and I try not to take it for granted, though I often fail at that."

The strength of their relationship, personally and professionally, carried the pair through the next few years, as the country entered a recession in 2008 and the Detroit area suffered because it is so closely tied to the automotive industry.

"And, like every other business, we had to move very quickly to adjust—including losing staff, unfortunately. It was quite difficult to respond to the economic cliff in front of us. The hardest part was saying goodbye to some terrific people who had worked with us for quite some time," said Horowitz.

"It was not a clear path, and there has been tremendous adversity, but the team we have was determined to keep this paper going, and we have," she added. "It would not have been my choice to go through something as difficult and scary as these past few years, but it has made us stronger and more focused. We have a renewed sense of possibility now, too, with a staff of eight terrific and energized people along with a wonderful group of freelance writers in the state and nationally."

Today, readership has increased because of the website's growing success, even with printed pages trending down to an average of 44 from the 52-page average pre-recession.

"Some of the decrease in print pages is due to the rise in online readership, and some is due to the economic downturn," said Stevenson. "In 2007, our two largest advertiser segments were real estate and auto dealerships. Of course, both of those sectors were decimated in the recession, and our advertising revenues reflected problems in those industries from 2008 to 2010. Recently, we have seen a resurgence of both sectors, along with a rising tide of economic activity in Michigan, and we've seen lots of businesses come back into the paper and online."

Plus, added Horowitz, the Michigan business and nonprofit community really hunkered down and everyone worked with one another to find a way back from the abyss. "There is so much energy on the ground here in the state. People fought back against the threat of the automobile industry going bankrupt without federal help. They fought back to bring new ideas to the region too," Horowitz said.

"It's been amazing to witness this up close and see the resilience of the people here," she recalled. "At no time did it seem plausible that we would give up and close the paper. We knew it was needed to cover all the issues that our community faces. After the 2010 election, with the entire state government now controlled by Republicans, we are more determined than ever to continue publishing. This current body of legislators has aggressively attacked us. There has been a renewed assault on LGBT lives, and I am glad to add to the voices that say no to inequality. We are in a unique position to capture the voices of support and opposition, and I hope it helps energize and inform citizens here in the state."

In 2009, Q Syndicate, the nation's largest provider of professionally produced content to the LGBT press, was purchased by *Between The Lines'* parent company, Pride Source Media Group. *Between The Lines'* editorial staff works with some of the finest freelance writers in the country, creating unique and powerful content that is then published by hundreds of other publications in the U.S., Canada and the U.K. The acquisition of Q Syndicate has opened up opportunities for Chris Azzopardi, *Between The Lines'* entertainment writer, to interview some of the biggest stars in the entertainment industry, including Cher, Lady Gaga, Meryl Streep, Justin Timberlake, Jack Black, Natalie Portman, Julia Roberts, Clint Eastwood and Rufus Wainwright, to name a few. His stories appear in *Between The Lines* and in as many as 50 other regional LGBT newspapers that subscribe to Q Syndicate.

Now, in its Livonia office, *Between The Lines* continues to strive for acceptance and recognition. "It often strikes me how far behind our political leaders are to the general population, especially business people and entrepreneurs who see LGBT people as their employees, customers, vendors and professional associates," said Stevenson.

Asked how *Between The Lines* plans to move forward and hang on to its place as the oldest continuously published LGBT newspaper in Michigan, Horowitz responded: "We just get up and start each day anew. We have never missed a deadline and have no plans to. We have remained humble and nimble and—most of the time, I think—responsive to the needs of covering the community. It's not easy, but the rewards are what keep me going.

"Each year, Pride season is the most concentrated opportunity for feedback throughout the state. We take it seriously and we try and respond to requests—sometimes, demands—in a timely way. When people thank us for being there or recount how it changed their life, that is pretty big to take in. I know it is critical to have independent regional LGBT media, and I am grateful to be able to do this work."

Between The Lines' first issue,
March 15, 1993.

Between The Lines, February 9, 2012.

Between The Lines, April 12, 2012.

27

The *Dallas Voice*

By David Webb, for the *Dallas Voice*

When *Dallas Voice* Publisher Robert Moore recollects the birth of his 28-year-old LGBT magazine, he appears a bit amused by the memory. It's as if he still can't quite believe what has happened since the first issue hit the streets May 11, 1984, and the *Dallas Voice* began its steady rise to prominence as the LGBT publication of record in Texas.

"There was never a plan," Moore said. "I just went to work every day. I never thought I would launch my own business and be successful."

Moore, a native Texan who grew up in Dallas–Fort Worth, reflects on those early days as he sits at the conference table in his spacious, meticulously organized office atop an Oak Lawn building where the *Dallas Voice* occupies the third floor. A squad of 16 full-time employees, assisted by numerous freelancers and delivery drivers, contributes to the weekly production and delivery of the publication's print and online magazine. Over the years, the *Dallas Voice* has transformed after several makeovers from a basic front-page newspaper format into a brightly colored feature cover.

Signs of success stand out in the *Dallas Voice*'s tasteful, finely furnished offices. Awards for merit in journalism, business excellence and community service combine with hip art on the office walls, desks and bookcases to present an air of sophistication and achievement.

After almost three decades in business, the *Dallas Voice* still operates in Oak Lawn, which is known as the historical center of LGBT life in Dallas. It is one of the ritzier ZIP codes in the city, and the area commands some of the highest-priced commercial rents in Dallas. Moore's ability to preserve the publication's presence in Oak Lawn, rather than moving his headquarters to a less-expensive part of Dallas, reveals another sign of the *Dallas Voice*'s success.

At the beginning, Moore saw no such stability in store for the magazine when he and his two partners, Don Ritz, of Dallas, and William Marberry, of Houston, launched the publication. The three scrambled to scrape enough cash together to kick off a business enterprise that probably should have failed because of its undercapitalization, not to mention its status as a gay-owned business and the unknown variables that circumstance would involve.

"We each put in $250 to launch the *Dallas Voice*," said Moore, who graduated from Texas Tech University in 1977 with a communications degree. "We had the massive capital investment of $750, of which $500 went to pay the first month's office rent."

At the time they decided to launch the *Dallas Voice*, Moore and Ritz both worked for the *Dallas Gay News*. A Houston publisher, who also ran an LGBT newspaper in the Gulf Coast city, put the *Dallas Gay News* together from the ads, photographs and copy Moore and Ritz sent to him, then shipped the newspaper back to Dallas. Marberry previously had worked for the publisher of the *Dallas Gay News*, but he had already struck out on his own as the publisher of other alternative publications in Houston at the time the *Dallas Voice* partnership formed.

What the Houston-based publisher of the *Dallas Gay News* apparently failed to understand was that Dallas' LGBT residents loved all kinds of sports, including softball, rugby, golf, tennis, bowling, swimming and any other activity that appealed to the athletic-minded. Moore and Ritz knew that and tried to publish what other members of the community wanted to see in the newspaper, while their publisher tended to be more entertainment-oriented.

"We would spend all Sunday afternoon in 100-degree-plus heat taking photos, send them to Houston, he would send the paper back and there would be no softball news," Moore said. "We would say, 'Where is our softball news and the rest of the sports coverage?' He'd say, 'Nobody cares about sports news—this is a gay paper,' which was absolutely ridiculous."

Meanwhile, Marberry had become aware of the growing dissension between Moore and Ritz and the publisher of the *Dallas Gay News*, and he made the pair an intriguing business proposition. He would help them go into business in Dallas publishing their own LGBT newspaper.

Intuition might suggest that Moore and Ritz would have jumped at the opportunity to publish their own newspaper, but it turned out to be more of a tiptoe than a leap into entrepreneurship for them. The thought of launching a business scared Moore, who was in his mid-20s at the time. Like most people of that age Moore had accumulated little to no money or other assets to sustain him while he built a business.

"I was very reluctant to come in and start doing this because I was like, 'How am I going to do this? How am I going to make a living? How am I going to support myself?'" said Moore about his and Ritz's getting the call from Marberry and their subsequent discussion of the proposition.

As it turned out, although Moore had not acquired much money at that point in his life, he had made a very good friend in the form of a roommate. His friend and roommate, Tim Barnes, offered to help Moore go into business for himself.

"He said, 'I think you should do this, and I will help you,'" Moore said. "For the first six months we could take no money out of the company at all, and I had no money. Tim paid my rent, fed me, kept the electricity on and gave me money to put gas in my car so I could go to work every day. Tim had a little ledger with neat, tiny handwriting where he put down the bills and my share of them. After six months we were able to start paying ourselves a little money, and I began to start paying Tim back. It took me well over a year to pay him it all back. You can never repay that sort of debt to someone. It's not possible."

Once Moore, Ritz and Marberry finalized their agreement, came up with the *Dallas Voice* name and opened the doors of the business, the trio of partners divided responsibilities and set to work putting a new brand of gay journalism into motion in Texas. Unlike the "bar rags" of the day, it more closely resembled the model followed by traditional journalists, and the newspaper quickly attracted the attention of mainstream publications and, more importantly, the LGBT community.

"We did not intend to use this newspaper as our own personal soapbox," said Moore, who noted the new publishers wanted the newspaper to speak for the community and for the community to speak through it. "We believed it was important that the journalism we did was straightforward, and that it was not advocacy journalism."

Moore sold advertising and attended Dallas events as the promotional face of the publication, Ritz served as writer and editor and Marberry took care of the production of the newspaper from his Houston office. Within six weeks the *Dallas Gay News* folded, and all the freelancers joined Moore and Ritz at the *Dallas Voice*. Their only real competition in Dallas at that point was *This Week In Texas*, more commonly referred to as "*TWIT*," which was a statewide publication covering the bar scene and other adult venues in Austin, Dallas, Fort Worth, Houston and San Antonio. It included a smattering of news and was considered the "gay bible" of what to do for fun in Texas. There also was a small gay publication called the *Metro Times*, but the newspaper's publisher viewed it as a hobby rather than a business.

"We wanted the *Dallas Voice* to be a business and a successful enterprise," Moore said. "We wanted to be able to hire a staff."

The first issue of the *Dallas Voice* published Friday, May 11, 1984, after an announcement the previous week of its impending debut. The 24-page issue's front page featured the headline, "Dallas Gay Community Pulls Together for Election," and featured a picture of a board member of the Dallas Gay Alliance, posting precinct vote totals during a city election. The story analyzed the effectiveness of the gay community's "bloc voting" to help elect candidates.

In the first issue there was one mention of AIDS buried in a story. In retrospect, the reference to the epidemic appears to have been a harbinger of the biggest crisis the *Dallas Voice* owners and their future staff members would come to face in both their personal and professional lives.

The front page also featured a story about Pride III, a community organization promoting Dallas Gay Pride activities. In future years, the Pride issue would become the newspaper's largest annual issue.

In addition to entertainment news, editorial cartoons, news reports, personal-opinion lifestyle columns and sports coverage, the first issue included lots of photographs and ads. The terms "lesbian" and "transgender" were seldom used in the early days of gay journalism, but women and transgender people were featured in the *Dallas Voice* from its first issue forward.

Gay bar ads dominated the pages of the first issue, but apartment complexes and florists ran ads as well. The gay-owned retail store Crossroads Market ran an ad and so did a gay choir, the Turtle Creek Chorale.

"It was well-received," Moore said. "We were on the ground, and the face of gay publishing in Dallas. When we wanted to go out on our own, we already had the relationships. They liked us, trusted us and wanted us to succeed. They supported us."

The timing apparently could not have been better for the introduction of an LGBT-oriented publication to Dallas featuring news, opinion and entertainment. "We came along at the right time to be able to combine all three of those things and have it focus just on Dallas," Moore said.

Recollecting the financial hurdle the company initially had to clear, Moore attributes the main reason for the venture's working to Marberry's credit line with a printer in Galveston. With a couple of publications in Houston under his direction, Marberry was able to convince the Galveston printer to float the *Dallas Voice*'s publication, week by week, in those early days. With every production batch sent by bus to the printer, a check for the printing of the previous week's newspaper went along. Then the printer shipped the newspaper to Dallas by return bus for distribution.

After about a year of that arrangement, it became clear that every step of the newspaper's production needed to take place in Dallas, so Moore and Ritz bought Marberry out of the partnership. They established a production office in Dallas for the layout of the newspaper and contracted with a local printer to produce the newspaper.

Before buying Marberry out, Moore had finally begun to realize that the *Dallas Voice* would actually provide him with a living. His work weeks ran much longer than 40 hours, with a vacation nowhere in sight for years to come, but the publication was thriving.

"After we had been in business six months, I began to think, This is going to work," Moore said. "You get into a rhythm, you feel confident about the support you are going to get. You get the paper out every week, and you're able to sell the ads. People pay the bills, the freelancers turn in their stories, you get it out in print and then you do it another week. A rhythm sets in, and it becomes expected."

That was just the beginning, the realization that the business appeared to be capable of generating enough money to pay all the bills and pay the salaries of the owners and any employees they hired. Eventually the pages of the publication began to feature professional ads, such as one for a Highland Park dentist, in addition to the ads for the bars, bathhouses and boys—"the three B's"—that financed the launch of the *Dallas Voice*.

"I would say within three, four, certainly at the end of five years, I realized it was going to be a much bigger force in the city than I ever thought it was going to be," Moore said. "There's a difference between 'it's going to make it' and 'it's going to become really successful.' Businesses can struggle and waddle along without ever really taking off."

In 1989 the late Annette Strauss realized that the LGBT community and the *Dallas Voice* could help her become the city's first elected female mayor. Strauss and her handlers went to the gathering of the Oak Lawn Bowling Association at Bronco Bowl to ask for support. She sat in the car and waited to go in until it was ascertained no reporters and no cameras lurked inside waiting for her. She went inside, shook hands with 800 gay bowlers and left. Afterward, the *Dallas Voice* reported it happened, and Strauss ran a political ad in the newspaper a week before the election, which did not give opposing candidates an opportunity to respond critically to her appearance. She won the election.

By the time the *Dallas Voice* celebrated its 10th anniversary, Moore realized that the business had grown "phenomenally" and he felt "very fortunate." The *Dallas Voice* had a full-time editor, Dennis Vercher, who had joined the staff in 1985 as its first full-time employee two years after the newspaper's debut, and there were several other employees engaged in sales, production and the general operation of the newspaper. Ritz had relinquished the role of editor to concentrate on the newspaper's administrative and accounting functions.

Tammye Nash, who joined the *Dallas Voice* staff as a reporter under Vercher's supervision in 1988 and served in that position for 13 years, remembers that 32 pages was a big issue back in those early days of the newspaper's life. That would amount to fewer than half the number of pages in a large issue today.

"One of my first big stories was about the controversy over including 'lesbian' in things," Nash said. "Back then everyone used 'gay' as an all-inclusive word, but there was a group of activists who insisted that the community needed to be more obviously inclusive."

It's hard to imagine what might or might not have happened had HIV/AIDS never surfaced in the early 1980s, but the epidemic certainly proved to be a bigger story than Moore and Ritz or the publishers of any other LGBT publications across the country could possibly have imagined. Many gay Texans got their first shred of news about the upcoming epidemic from a short news piece in *TWIT* in the summer of 1981 about gay men in New York City and San Francisco suffering and dying from Kaposi's sarcoma and pneumocystis pneumonia.

Several years later—at the same time Moore and Ritz realized they were riding an unprecedented wave of success—the LGBT community they loved and served was facing its greatest challenge ever with the evolving health crisis. *Dallas Voice* readers looked to the newspaper for the latest news about what was happening in medical research, the legal ramifications of the epidemic and who was dying locally.

"AIDS was the biggest story by then," Moore said. "We went through this whole period where it was just one depressing story after another and running obituaries after obituaries after obituaries, not knowing who was going to be next. It was particularly bad early on when people were getting sick and dying and no one knew why. It's easier to deal with a tragedy if you know what is going on. You can get your mind around it mentally."

The epidemic took as devastating a toll on the newspaper's staff as it did on the community at large. To date, eight former staff members have died of complications from the virus.

HIV/AIDS dominated LGBT news for years, but publishers, editors and reporters who thought they had seen the climax of their professional lives with the identification of the virus, the introduction of widespread blood testing and the development of life-saving treatments were destined to see yet another phenomenon. A wave of LGBT activism followed that led to larger numbers of people than ever before, coming out and living openly. The LGBT community grew in both enthusiasm and numbers.

"I know the response to AIDS lifted us to many other issues because the community came to maturity, becoming able to feel its power and realize its goals," Moore said. "If we were going to fight to keep people alive, then we also wanted to fight to live with dignity, to work where we wanted, to live where we wanted and have the relationships we wanted. There's no question but that AIDS was a catalyst for many other issues that were not health-related, because we became organized like we never were before."

As the LGBT community's social and philanthropic organizations, businesses, churches and neighborhoods expanded, so did the *Dallas Voice*. At the same time, openly gay candidates began running for public office and winning, beginning with the election of a city councilman in 1993 and representing huge markers of success for the LGBT community.

"I would say it absolutely allowed our business to grow and our readership to grow, because people wanted to be involved," Moore said. "They wanted to become educated, and they wanted to know the facts. They wanted to know how the politicians and the public institutions were functioning, and they wanted to know how their own organizations were reacting. They wanted to be a part of a vibrant, thriving community, and we were the channel to get that information out to the community as a whole."

That developing thirst for involvement motivated Tammye Nash to seek employment at the *Dallas Voice*. She was working at a weekly newspaper in Daingerfield in East Texas when she heard about the ad the *Dallas Voice* had placed in its employment section seeking a reporter.

"I applied because I thought it would be nice to work with other people like me for a change," Nash said. "I wanted to be myself at work, and I thought it would be a great way to get to know more about the community and to get to know more people in the community."

Nash was another Texas native, and the longer she worked at the *Dallas Voice*, the more committed she became to helping advance the community's cause.

"I realized that working for the *Voice* gave me the chance to do something to help make the community better," Nash said. "By documenting the people and events in the LGBT community, by reporting on them, I was helping people become educated, informed and active. I believe that the LGBT media and the people who work for the LGBT media have played a huge role in the progress we have made in the past 20 to 30 years as a community. Working for the *Voice* allowed me to be a part of that."

An attraction to the idea of working in the LGBT media also lured Advertising Director Leo Cusimano and Classified Advertising Manager Greg Hoover to the *Dallas Voice* 19 and 16 years ago respectively—and has kept them there.

Cusimano, who grew up in New Orleans, began working for the *Dallas Voice* as a part-time graphic designer in 1993 after working for advertising agencies and for the art department of a mainstream Florida newspaper. He moved from that newspaper's art department in 1992 when *The Dallas Morning News* business section profiled Moore, Ritz and their success in attracting mainstream advertisers to the pages of a gay publication. The story prominently featured the advertising of one of the *Dallas Voice*'s biggest clients, Prestige Ford, and it sent a shock wave through the city's business community. Many business people suddenly saw an opportunity to reach a new customer base they had never before considered.

"When that happened the phones started ringing off the hooks, and Robert said, 'I need to expand our staff and hire another sales representative,'" said Cusimano, who apparently also saw an opportunity arising for him. "And I said, 'I can do that.'"

Cusimano realized 15 years ago that his work in advertising could play as big a role in advancing LGBT goals as the journalists working in the newsroom covering the volunteer work of LGBT activists. He called on the manager of a T.G.I. Friday's restaurant in an attempt to sell advertising and discovered someone who knew little about the LGBT community. The manager told Cusimano he was concerned that if he advertised in the *Dallas Voice* he would wind up with only drag queens in his restaurant, but he agreed to give it a six-week trial run. Six weeks later the manager couldn't wait to sign a long-term advertising agreement, saying, "You guys drink and have lots of money. You're well educated. There's never a problem with the bill. You tip well. More than anything, you've changed my mind about the gay and lesbian community." That also proved to be a turning point for Cusimano, who had always wanted to improve the lot of others at the same time he personally prospered.

"That's when I had to step back and look at what had happened," Cusimano said. "Yes, I made money for myself and my company, but more than anything else I changed somebody's impression of my community. That was gold to me. That's where my passion developed, and I realized this was more than a job for me. It was a career. At the same time, I can help change people's opinion about our community. That's why I have been here as long as I have."

Greg Hoover, an Oklahoma native, also had a background in graphic arts and yearned to work in the LGBT media. He applied for jobs at the newspaper three times before he finally got hired for the front desk position in 1996. After two months serving as the receptionist and answering the phones, Hoover was promoted to classified advertising. Six months later he was promoted to classified advertising manager, and he's been in that position ever since.

"It's been wonderful," Hoover said. "I can't imagine working for a better place. To watch the gay and lesbian community grow during that 16 years has been amazing. When I first started working here, people didn't use the words 'gay' and 'lesbian.' Nothing on television was gay and lesbian, and I rarely saw gay and lesbian movies anywhere. As time went by, I saw the world open up slowly but surely. Every day has been a step forward. Today, I'm just as proud to work here as when I first got my job here."

During Hoover's time, he has seen the size of the staff nearly triple, the technology transform from paste-up to computer-generated pages and the advertising categories change with the times. Before everyone acquired a computer at home, personal ads in the newspaper used to be a big percentage of the *Dallas Voice*'s classified advertising income. That disappeared with computer chat rooms and the development of other forms of social media, but the demand for classified advertising in the *Dallas Voice* never dissipated in the way it did at mainstream newspapers.

"Our customers have always been very loyal," Hoover said. "They want to advertise to people who understand the gay and lesbian community. They want to serve the gay and lesbian community. I have customers with me today who were here 16 years ago. Not a lot, you know people move on, but I do have some of those customers, which says a lot about the advertising in the *Dallas Voice*. They wouldn't continue to do it if they weren't getting the response they needed."

Moore acknowledges he is fortunate to have had stability in every department. Vercher served as editor for 20 years and, when he died of complications from HIV/AIDS, Nash took over as senior editor for five years. The current senior editor, John Wright, is only the fourth editor in the newspaper's 30-year history. The longevity in service by department heads likely has resulted from Moore's management philosophy.

"I want to treat people fairly," Moore said. "I feel like I allow people the freedom to do their work without interference or intense oversight. I'm no micromanager. I believe my role here is to help this staff be successful. I don't get involved in the issues of a department unless there is a moral, ethical or legal decision to be made. If you are working hard and are committed and you get your work done, then you are going to be successful here. And people like that."

Over the years, the newspaper gained respect because it developed as a solid source of news that could be trusted by the LGBT community and the city as a whole. The editorial policy of the newspaper has held gay organizations and businesses and their policies accountable, a practice that sometimes has put the *Dallas Voice*'s staff at odds with some LGBT leaders and their followers. Some have expressed surprise and dismay when the *Dallas Voice* staff reported all sides of an issue or refused to ignore a story. But that reputation has ensured that government officials and political, business, social and religious leaders throughout the city trust the *Dallas Voice* to be fair and accurate. Most political candidates and their consultants understand that the *Dallas Voice*'s advertising and editorial departments must be given the same attention as all of Dallas' other media outlets.

"There's something about becoming successful that allows you the freedom to do that," said Moore of the standards the publication has developed over the years. "You're not likely to want to slaughter sacred cows if you might not have any meat the next month."

For the first 14 years of the *Dallas Voice*'s operation, Moore had the assistance and counsel of his business partner Ritz, but that changed in 1998 when illness forced Ritz to resign his day-to-day duties. Ritz retained ownership in the company until Moore bought out his partner's interest from the estate after Ritz's death. All the decisions made from that point forward would be the responsibility of Moore alone.

"It was scary to a degree, but Don was an extremely good teacher," Moore said. "My partnership was absolutely the right mix of responsibilities and personalities and talents, and we set off each other's weaknesses very well."

The next decade managing the newspaper alone would at times be troubling ones for Moore. In 2001 he launched a statewide publication known as *Qtexas* with the intention of replicating the model of *TWIT*, which had just failed after a series of ownership changes. But Moore's *Qtexas* also failed. After shuttering *Qtexas* and to shrink the competition, Moore bought out *Texas Triangle*, which as a statewide publication combined news and entertainment. He rebranded it as *TXT*, but by the end of 2004 he realized it also was a failure and shut it down.

"I thought that I was smart enough to succeed in Texas where *TWIT* had failed," Moore said. "I was going to do a statewide entertainment guide and make it work, but I couldn't do it, either. The statewide model didn't work anymore. It was a difficult, humbling lesson."

More trouble arose with a steady and severe decline in the health of Dennis Vercher, who as the longtime editor of *Dallas Voice* knew all the community's secrets and its other history. Up until the time he grew frail, Vercher had a full comprehension of everything that had occurred while he was editor.

"He contributed hugely to the publication's success," Moore said. "He was competent, steadfast and wanted to work. He wanted to work every day. I can't tell you how many weeks of vacation Dennis took in 20 years, but it wasn't many. He wanted to come in and work while he was sick, even up to the bitter end. It created a dignity for him. He didn't want to give up."

After launching the newspaper under tough financial circumstances, Moore revisited hard times during state and national economic downturns in 1991, 2001 and 2008, with the latter proving to be the most severe. During the national recession of 2008, Moore took several drastic measures to keep the newspaper afloat as its size shrank considerably.

"It was a huge challenge to us, as it was to companies around the country," Moore said. "We made a lot of decisions to cut back."

The newspaper has continued to publish in Dallas without major competition, and it is the longest-running LGBT newspaper in Texas.

When the *Dallas Voice* first came onto the scene, mainstream newspapers barely touched issues related to LGBT people, and alternative publications such as the *Dallas Observer* had an unofficial quota on the number of "gay" stories they would publish. Those policies have changed considerably over the years, but Moore still does not see newspapers such as *The Dallas Morning News* or the *Dallas Observer* as threats to the survival of the *Dallas Voice*.

Mainstream newspapers and alternative newspapers with a primarily heterosexual audience can't provide the depth of coverage of LGBT issues that the *Dallas Voice* offers, Moore said. The gay newspaper covers all the general issues, such as political races involving gay-favored mayoral candidates, but moreover its coverage has a distinct, deep and detailed gay focus. The city's other newspapers can't compete, because the bulk of their general audience is not that interested in all the local news about what LGBT political, charitable, social and sports organizations are doing, Moore noted.

"They've done an extremely good job of covering gay marriage, presenting the legal argument and publishing nice photos of couples who have been together for 20 years," Moore said. "But they probably won't sit down with them and talk about when and where they met, about the trials and tribulations the couple has had with legal issues and their relations with in-laws."

The same applies to issues such as the repeal of "Don't Ask, Don't Tell" and the plight of transgender people, who struggle to gain acceptance in a society that has not moved as quickly and sympathetically on that issue as it has on some gay issues.

Many people wondered if the *Dallas Voice* would falter after Vercher's death, but it has continued publishing and serving the LGBT community without a lapse in quality or commitment. A measure of a newspaper's success often is provided by the impact of the stories it publishes. In recent years, the *Dallas Voice* investigation of a transgender bus driver's complaint led to the addition of gender identity to Dallas Area Rapid Transit's nondiscrimination policy. Another story about Omni Hotels' employment benefit policies and its contract to run the city of Dallas' convention hotel led to the offer of domestic-partnership benefits to hotel employees. And when the *Dallas Voice* wrote about

Parkland Hospital's long delay in seeing new patients in violation of federal law, the delay was quickly corrected.

The biggest challenge facing the *Dallas Voice* today appears to be the same one facing all publications—how to survive in an era when people increasingly are looking to the Internet for news and journalism-related entertainment. Moore has placed his faith in the current senior editor, John Wright, to move the *Dallas Voice* forward in the new technological age.

"I would say John and what he brings to the role can get us there," Moore said. "He is extremely engaged. He has a good pulse on where the business is going in digital media, the evolution of the distribution models and the connectivity of today to touch all of those bases. He has a vision for how he sees the publication evolving."

Wright's vision of the *Dallas Voice*'s future is simple enough in the distribution of the editorial content, but it becomes more complicated in terms of how the operation will produce revenue in the future.

"No one really knows where we are going to be 10 years from now," Wright said. "We're moving more and more toward online. My vision is to be as adaptable as possible in a sense that we're ready for whatever comes our way and to be able to quickly adjust."

Wright envisions the *Dallas Voice* as primarily a daily or even hourly newspaper online, with the website updated on a 24-hour, seven-day basis.

"The future is going to be challenging, but it's also exciting because we're really going to get to do stuff we've never been able to do before and get to reach more people than ever before through the Web," he said.

Editors and their staff usually don't concern themselves about revenue issues, because those are the domain of the publisher and the advertising department, but such issues are difficult to ignore today. Most of the revenue comes from print ads, but consumers quickly are moving toward more exclusive use of the online media.

There obviously will come a day when Moore or his successor will be forced to figure out how to maximize online revenue in order sustain the *Dallas Voice*'s operations.

After 30 years in the business, Moore said the future of the *Dallas Voice* without him at the helm is something he thinks about often these days. There could be a day coming when he sells the newspaper or signs it over to someone else's care through a management contract. Every major decision he makes now is made with the realization that it will affect the work of whoever follows behind him. After all, everyone retires at some point, but Moore is determined to ensure that the *Dallas Voice* outlives him.

Dallas Voice's first issue, May 11, 1984.

Dallas Voice, May 1, 1998.

Dallas Voice, May 2, 2003.

Dallas Voice, December 23, 1988.

Dallas Voice, October 31, 2008.

Dallas Voice, November 7, 2008.

Dallas Voice, February 11, 2011.

Dallas Voice,
November 18,
2011.

28

Frontiers Magazine

By Karen Ocamb

LGBT journalism has strong roots in Los Angeles. First, there was Lisa Ben's mimeographed *Vice Versa* in 1947. Then the thoughtful *ONE* magazine emerged from members of the Mattachine Society and ONE, Inc., in the early 1950s. *The Los Angeles Advocate* started as a newsletter from an activist group after the police raided the Silver Lake neighborhood's Black Cat Tavern in 1967 and protests ensued. LA's LGBT community counted on the paper to find out where to go for kiss-ins, protests and other demonstrations before and after the 1969 Stonewall riots.

In 1974, *The Los Angeles Advocate* was purchased by David Goodstein and moved to San Francisco, leaving a vacuum in news coverage for one of the most politically significant gay hotspots in the country, a vacuum that would not be filled till almost a decade later, though the politics of gay liberation continued unabated. Nationally recognized politico David Mixner, who was running Los Angeles Mayor Tom Bradley's re-election campaign, came out and joined the Municipal Elections Committee of Los Angeles, the nation's first gay political action committee. In 1977–78, Mixner, MECLA and grassroots activists from the Stonewall Democratic Club worked with Harvey Milk and activists in San Francisco to defeat the state's infamous anti-gay Briggs Initiative.

In 1979, President Jimmy Carter's mother, Lillian, was among those attending a "roast" of gay businessman Sheldon Andelson at a fundraiser for the Los Angeles Gay Community Services Center where Governor Jerry Brown gave the keynote address. That year, Brown also appointed MECLA member Stephen Lachs to the Los Angeles County Superior Court, making him the first openly gay judge in the country. And in 1980, Brown appointed Andelson to the University of California Board of Regents. Later, with help from straight politico Bob Shrum, Mixner invited Senator Ted Kennedy to speak at a MECLA dinner.

In 1981, *Los Angeles* magazine published an article trumpeting gays as the hot new marketing demographic. "[G]ay consumerism meant more than conspicuous consumption: It was also something of a political act," Lillian Faderman and Stuart Timmons wrote in the book *Gay L.A.*

But it was the lack of a print voice for the gay community that spurred Greg Carmack and Jerry Hyde to sit around a kitchen table in 1982 and envision *Frontiers* magazine. The first edition featured a two-color front cover with 35 pages of copy and ads. By 1983, that much-trumpeted gay consumerism had not found its mark in the magazine, and the new publishers were having financial problems. They approached Mark Hundahl, a straight businessman who had just become co-owner of the popular gay Probe disco, and asked for $5,000. Hundahl agreed—in exchange for two years' worth of advertising.

"Greg told me that he and Jerry started the magazine to be an advocacy magazine," Hundahl said. "They made *Frontiers* the voice of the Los Angeles gay community and had the foresight to become part of the strong advocacy movement across the United States. In L.A., lots of people wanted to read it. It struck a nerve at the right place and right time."

Gay businessman Bob Craig joined *Frontiers* in 1983 and tried to break Hundahl's contract, but was unable to do so. Two years later, Hundahl moved Probe's business to a new magazine called *Edge*, where he met David Stern, who would become his business partner.

Craig quickly became the sole owner and publisher of *Frontiers* and took the community-advocacy mission to heart—reprinting Larry Kramer's famous AIDS polemic "1,183 and Counting" on the cover of the March 30–April 13, 1983, issue. Bar owners threw the magazine out, saying it was bad for business. But by 1984, when it became starkly clear that the government was not rushing to stop or find a cure for AIDS, bar and disco club owners became havens for fundraisers for new community groups. In March, *Frontiers* featured Joan Rivers on the cover for an AIDS fundraiser at Studio One that raised $45,000 for AIDS Project Los Angeles, L.A. Shanti and Aid for AIDS.

Craig also used *Frontiers* to publicize and advance the movement to incorporate West Hollywood, the popular gay mecca between Hollywood and Beverly Hills. After the cityhood battle was won in 1984, Craig was elected chair of the West Hollywood Incorporation Committee and, according to the *Los Angeles Times*, coined the term that came to identify WeHo. "I would suggest that if you are gay, Camelot is on the horizon," Craig said just before Election Day. Reporters soon called West Hollywood the "gay Camelot" after voters elected a majority-gay City Council.

But with President Ronald Reagan's re-election in 1984 and the massive deaths from AIDS complications, the gay community faced harsh, hate-filled realities. In 1985, Craig helped to found and became treasurer of LIFE AIDS Lobby and used *Frontiers* as a vehicle to provide news about different pro- and anti-gay bills in the state Legislature. Craig "saw the importance of our visible presence in the political world," former lobby Executive Director Laurie McBride told the *Times*. "He championed the work at the state level because he saw that it was a critical area that was being neglected."

In 1986, a year after the death of Hollywood actor Rock Hudson, *Frontiers* helped fight the Lyndon LaRouche AIDS quarantine initiative. But Craig refused to cover the rowdy ACT UP/LA when it launched on December 7, 1987. That year, Craig started *Dispatch*, a biweekly arts and entertainment publication that eventually became the short-lived *Frontiers After Dark*. But the news desk was busy: On October 11, the ubiquitous Morris Kight, who co-founded the Los Angeles Gay Liberation Front, Christopher Street West Pride Parade, and the Gay Community Services Center, helped to lead the Second National March on Washington for Lesbian and Gay Rights, along with other Angeleno stars—Cesar Chavez and Whoopi Goldberg.

In 1988, members of ACT UP/LA held an editorial meeting with Craig, after which the magazine started covering the activist group. Indeed, Craig was one of 88 community leaders—including the Reverend Troy Perry, founder of the Metropolitan Community Churches—who were arrested on October 11 at the Federal Building in L.A.'s Westwood neighborhood on the same day more than 1,000 ACT UP protesters swarmed the U.S. Food and Drug Administration headquarters in Rockville, Maryland, demanding faster approval of experimental AIDS drugs. Later that day, political activist Jean O'Leary and psychologist Rob Eichberg launched National Coming Out Day, commemorating the 1987 March on Washington.

The following year, *Frontiers* shocked the LGBT community by placing a cop on the front cover. It was a milestone: That cop was Los Angeles Police Department Sergeant Mitch Grobeson, who had filed a discrimination suit against the department alleging anti-gay harassment, including being left without backup in a dangerous situation. The case was a glimpse into anti-gay workplace discrimination in a job most gays thought was off-limits. ACLU attorney Jon Davidson subsequently got Grobeson's case included in the Christopher Commission report after the Los Angeles riots of 1992. Additionally, as *Frontiers* contributing reporter, I challenged new LAPD Chief Willie Williams about gay cops during his first live televised news conference—and I have interviewed every police chief since.

The *Frontiers* staff faced another editorial dilemma in 1990 when the new group Queer Nation plastered West Hollywood with quirky posters outing major entertainment and political leaders such as mogul David Geffen and Los Angeles City Councilmember Joel Wachs. But it took Governor Pete Wilson's veto of the LIFE Lobby-sponsored gay-rights bill AB 101 to cause conservative Publisher

Bob Craig to change his party affiliation from Republican to Democrat and extensively cover the two-weeks-plus of demonstrations that resulted from the veto. In 1992, *Frontiers* featured presidential candidate Bill Clinton on the cover.

On April 25, 1993, *Frontiers* covered the next March on Washington, which featured gay service members who came out expecting President Clinton to lift the ban on open military service, as promised. When Clinton announced the Don't Ask, Don't Tell policy, *Frontiers* News Editor Aslan Brooke, a former Army nurse, was among those who couldn't contain her rage and joined the protesters in West Hollywood.

In 1997, Bob Craig, Mark Hundahl and David Stern created a sister publication, *IN LA* magazine. "*Frontiers* would be more like *Newsweek* while *IN* would be the gay *People*," said Stern.

But after Craig died of AIDS complications on April 28, 2000, everything changed. Craig had not left a will, so control fell to his sister, who listened to guidance from *Frontiers* staffer Hope Hendricks. Subsequently, longtime staffers and contributors were fired and, over the years, the magazine went through several editors and two more publishers as well as attempts to find a new identity and mission.

In 2007, Hundahl and Stern bought *Frontiers*—which had become more of a *People* magazine—and merged it with *IN*, which had become more like *Newsweek*. "I respected Bob's vision and his capabilities," Hundahl said—to which Stern added that *Frontiers* continues to strive to fulfill its original mission "to build and help unite the LGBT community."

In May 2012, *Frontiers* celebrated its 30th anniversary with acknowledgments from Los Angeles Mayor Antonio Villaraigosa, West Hollywood City Councilmember John Duran and Los Angeles Gay & Lesbian Center CEO Lorri Jean, and a community still thankful for a loud Los Angeles voice for LGBT advocacy.

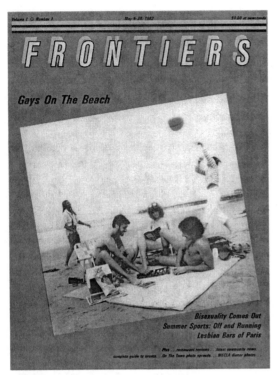

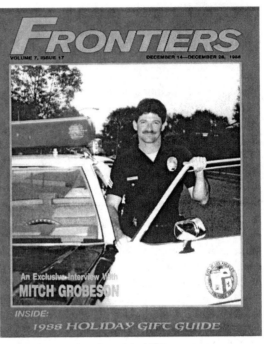

Frontiers, December 14, 1988.

Frontiers' first issue, May 6, 1992.

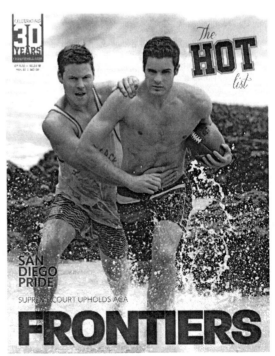

Frontiers, January 11, 2012.

Frontiers, July 11, 2012.

29

Gay City News

By Paul Schindler, *Gay City News* Founding Editor-in-Chief

By the customary standards for marking progress in any enterprise, 2012 is a significant year for *Gay City News*. It was 10 years ago this past May that its co-founders, Troy Masters, the associate publisher, and Paul Schindler, the editor-in-chief, teamed up with Publisher John Sutter to launch the newspaper as an affiliate of Sutter's Community Media group of publications that already included *The Villager* and *Downtown Express*, which serve the historically diverse neighborhoods of Lower Manhattan.

Rolled out a mere eight months after the 9/11 tragedy badly roiled the economy of the city's downtown districts, *Gay City News* was a rare entrepreneurial effort that embraced New York City's promise for continued vitality at a very uncertain moment in the nation's history. A decade later, that bet has proved smart—the newspaper has enjoyed its strongest financial performance in 2010, 2011 and 2012, and this year's June 20 LGBT Pride issue was the largest and most profitable in its history.

Ten years is a good run for any small business, but in launching *Gay City News*, Masters and Schindler were in fact continuing to carry a gay media torch they had picked up more than a decade before. In 1988, responding to the darkest days of New York's AIDS crisis, Masters left behind a career in mainstream publishing to join a group of activists in a startup gay magazine called *OutWeek*. In 1995, after more than a decade working in municipal government finance on Wall Street, Schindler joined him at *LGNY*—the immediate predecessor publication of *Gay City News*—which Masters published. Schindler eventually served as *LGNY*'s editor-in-chief for four years.

Masters and Schindler continue at the helm of *Gay City News* and maintain an editorial team composed primarily of committed and regular freelancers—among them Duncan Osborne, Andy Humm, Susie Day, New York Law School professor Arthur S. Leonard, Dr. Lawrence Mass and Brian McCormick—who have been fixtures in New York's LGBT press dating back to *OutWeek* and earlier.

Gay City News' continued success at a time when print media generally have sustained serious reversals is due, in significant respects, to its role in a niche market where there is no substitute for the voice of the community at a time of both political gains and persistent obstacles. To be sure, the New York media—including *The New York Times*, *The Village Voice*, and *The New York Observer*, to name just those that have proven most adept—pay keen attention to the community and add to wider public understanding of LGBT people's political challenges and cultural contributions.

But, at a time when LGBT issues have taken center stage in the national conversation, the political progress in New York has been extraordinary—though, of course, incomplete—and that is a complex and nuanced story. When *Gay City News* launched, New York did not yet have a statewide gay-rights law. The newspaper's first issue reported on the enactment of a transgender civil-rights law by the New York City Council, but the effort to broaden state law to include protections based on gender identity and expression remains stalled today.

New York Mayor Michael Bloomberg, recognized in 2012 as a national leader on marriage equality, would not even seriously entertain questions about the issue from LGBT journalists a decade ago. A divorced man, he would laugh off its importance by asking why anyone would want to get married. He first endorsed equal marriage rights in 2005, the same day he announced the city would appeal a Manhattan trial judge's ruling in favor of same-sex plaintiffs seeking the right to marry. New York's highest court overturned that victory the following summer, finding no right to marry for gay and lesbian couples under the state constitution.

Advocates bounced back from that disappointment with impressive alacrity. Less than a year later, with the support of the new Democratic governor, Eliot Spitzer, the state Assembly approved a marriage equality bill. It took another four years, one failed vote in the state Senate, and the determined personal commitment of another Democratic governor, Andrew Cuomo, to secure the law's enactment, making New York the sixth state to give its gay and lesbian couples full civil equality.

Even as the LGBT community has made dramatic gains—including the enactment of a state anti-bullying law that provides school students with protections based on categories including sexual orientation and gender identity and expression—troubling remnants of the bad old days persist. In 2008 and 2009, *Gay City News* broke a significant series of stories about the false arrests of gay men in adult video stores on trumped-up prostitution charges. The ensuing public attention led to acknowledgment by the Police Department, the mayor and the district attorney that serious mistakes had been made and resulted in dismissal of numerous pending criminal cases.

Earlier reporting of public sex arrests in a Hudson River park in New Jersey that overlooks Manhattan—as with the video-store busts, written by Duncan Osborne—led to calls in the state Legislature there for an investigation of the trial judge and to an appeals court's throwing out one conviction and raising questions about a persistent pattern of judicial misconduct.

Hate crimes and anti-LGBT murders have also been a critical part of *Gay City News'* reporting in the past decade—whether the horrific stabbing death of Sakia Gunn, an African-American teenage lesbian attacked in Newark in the early morning hours of Mother's Day in 2003, or the 2006 killing of Michael Sandy, an African-American gay man lured to a beach in Brooklyn through a gay chat site and chased onto a nearby parkway where he was hit by a car, later lingering in a coma for days prior to his death. These deaths and others—including the 2010 shooting of DeFarra Gaymon, an African-American bisexual businessman from Atlanta approached by a county sheriff's deputy in a Newark park— typically only received mainstream coverage, if at all, after significant reporting by *Gay City News*.

AIDS and housing homeless LGBT youth are also issues on which *Gay City News* has been the principal source of reporting in New York. As the mainstream press, rightly in some respects, has increasingly focused on the tragedy of untreated HIV disease in the developing world, *Gay City News* has consistently tracked the unflagging pace of new infections among gay and bisexual men, especially those who are young and those from communities of color. No other news source in the city has followed the slog that AIDS service providers face in maintaining public funding of prevention and treatment efforts in an era of significant budget cutbacks.

Similarly, though the mainstream press has highlighted some high-profile efforts to address the needs of the city's startlingly high population of homeless youth—up to 40 percent of them LGBT or questioning—*Gay City News* again is the paper of record on the ongoing battles at City Hall and in Albany for adequate funding.

These issues, coupled with the extraordinarily vibrant New York arts scene in which the LGBT community plays such an active and visible role, make for an ambitious agenda that defines *Gay City News'* mission.

Despite the newspaper's staying power and success over the past decade, however, there remains a persistent notion that New York has not been a friendly town for the LGBT press. It's undeniable, of course, that no publication here has sustained the sort of longevity enjoyed in some other leading American cities, the most outstanding example of which is the four-decade-plus run of the *Washington Blade*.

Still, the oft-repeated dismissal of New York's gay press scene ignores not only a rich history of vital publications that uniquely matched their times but, as importantly, the remarkable continuity among key players in LGBT media here over the past quarter-century.

In the immediate post-Stonewall years, a series of newsletters and newspapers, often affiliated with particular activist factions, sprang up, the best remembered of which is *Gaysweek*, a publication that came out between 1977 and 1979.

In 1980, Charles Ortleb, the publisher of *Theater Week* who had launched *Christopher Street* magazine in 1976, began the *New York Native*, a publication that lasted until 1997 and in its early years was influential and widely circulated. Ortleb had earned credibility in the gay community with *Christopher Street*, a literary magazine that included work by authors Edmund White, Andrew Holleran and Quentin Crisp as well as editor Michael Denneny.

Undoubtedly the most influential article ever published in the *Native* was Larry Kramer's 1983 jeremiad "1,112 and Counting," a frightening tally of the growing AIDS death toll that demanded action from both the government and gay men themselves. Less noted—but also of great significance—was a May 1981 article by Dr. Lawrence Mass, the first published report about the emergence of a rare deadly cancer that was killing gay men in New York and California. Mass' reporting came more than a month before the federal Centers for Disease Control and Prevention first acknowledged the crisis in its *Morbidity and Mortality Weekly Report*. *The New York Times*, in turn, brought the issue to national attention in an early-July story.

More than 30 years later, Mass remains active in the fight against AIDS as a physician engaged in bringing critical health issues to the attention of the LGBT community through the press. For *Gay City News*, he has written about numerous topics, including hepatitis C; the human papillomavirus, or HPV; and specific health risks facing the gay-male bear community.

Despite the *Native*'s prominence, Ortleb became increasingly fascinated by AIDS denial and conspiracy theories, in 1987 publishing an interview with Peter Duesberg, the key figure among those challenging the science of HIV as the cause of AIDS. By the time *OutWeek*, which ushered in a brash new editorial voice, emerged in New York in 1988, the *Native* was well along in its decline, shunned by most community leaders and activists because of its misguided AIDS reporting. When it was finally shuttered in 1997, *LGNY* slyly asked in a headline, "Was It Chronic Fatigue Syndrome?"

OutWeek, founded by Kendall Morrison, a phone-sex industry entrepreneur, captured the anger that had for several years animated ACT UP and would soon lead to a brief period of in-your-face activism defined by Queer Nation. Michelangelo Signorile's crusading efforts to spotlight the hypocrisy of powerful but closeted gay men who remained silent as other gay men died was the highest-profile work to come out of *OutWeek*—his columns had many in the community rushing to newsstands each week to get their hands on a copy of a publication that achieved nationwide attention with a circulation that numbered only in the low thousands. In 1990, shortly after Malcolm Forbes' death, Signorile reported in *OutWeek* on his secret homosexuality.

Even if Signorile's colorful reporting and urgent voice garnered the greatest attention for the newsmagazine, a new standard in political, health, crime and arts reporting for New York's queer community was achieved under the editorial leadership of Gabriel Rotello, a former party promoter who has gone on to be a respected author (1997's *Sexual Ecology*, which examined the ongoing problem of HIV transmission) and filmmaker (HBO's Emmy-nominated *The Strange History of Don't Ask, Don't Tell*). Rotello's stable of contributors included Duncan Osborne, Andy Humm, Ann Northrop, Arthur S. Leonard, Susie Day, Sarah Pettit and Andrew Miller. Osborne, Humm, Leonard, Day and Miller all remain active in New York's LGBT media as *Gay City News* contributors.

OutWeek proved to be something of a shooting star. In mid-1991, bickering among the magazine's investors resulted in an abrupt closure. Troy Masters, the advertising director, moved quickly to enroll investor William F. Chafin in launching a new publication, *QW*, the nation's first glossy gay and lesbian weekly magazine, which premiered in the fall of 1991. (*OutWeek* had a glossy cover, but was newsprint inside. The now-defunct *Genre* gay men's magazine also started that year, but was never weekly. *The Advocate* was a newsprint publication prior to becoming a glossy magazine, and now it is an insert in *Out*.)

Key *OutWeek* staff members and contributors followed Masters into the new *QW* publication. Seeking a departure from the angry editorial tone of *OutWeek*, Masters selected *Interview* magazine and *OutWeek* contributor Maer Roshan to be *QW*'s editor-in-chief. Roshan went on to be a deputy editor at *New York* magazine, editorial director of Tina Brown's *Talk* magazine, founder of *Radar*, and now *The Daily Beast*'s West Coast correspondent.

By the time *QW* came onto the scene, LGBT politics in New York was increasingly focused on working, to the extent possible, on the inside in regard to everything from AIDS to electoral strategies. In 1992, Democratic presidential contenders Bill Clinton and Jerry Brown both sat down with *QW*'s editorial board, demonstrating the newfound clout of the LGBT press and community. A March 1992 front-page story in *The New York Times* declared that the magazine was proof of the gay community's advance into the cultural mainstream.

Still, *QW* could at times exhibit the same edgy flair that won *OutWeek* its admirers. A cover story on the 1992 Republican convention pictured Pat Buchanan at the podium under the headline "The New Reich."

Unfortunately, the HIV epidemic's ongoing tragedy was soon felt directly at *QW*. In October 1992, Chafin succumbed to an AIDS-related brain tumor and Masters was forced to suspend publication.

Even with the death of a dear friend and the demise of two publications with which he had played key roles, Masters was not yet prepared to give up on his commitment to LGBT press visibility in New York. Throughout 1993, fully expecting other entrants to emerge—though none did—he planned for the launch of a newspaper-formatted product. With essentially no working capital, in March 1994 he started *LGNY*—short for Lesbian and Gay New York—a biweekly he initially published out of his East Village studio apartment.

Within two years, the newspaper had an address on Fifth Avenue, just east of Chelsea, which was by then the perceived center of gay life in the city. Recognizing that *The Village Voice*'s decision to distribute without charge signaled the end for newsstand sales of weekly publications in the New York market, Masters introduced the first stand-alone street boxes for an LGBT publication in the city's history.

By 1995, *LGNY* had also launched a website, well ahead of most newspapers, straight or gay, including *The New York Times*.

Paul Schindler joined *LGNY* in late 1995, first as a freelance contributor and later as news editor. In early 1997, he became editor-in-chief, a position he has held, at that newspaper and at *Gay City News*, ever since.

Although the advent of protease inhibitor treatments in 1995 and 1996 finally put New York on a course of declining annual AIDS deaths, the city's large population of HIV-positive gay men and the persistence of high new-infection rates made gay sexual culture an issue of contentious debate in the community in the mid- and late 1990s. The controversy, which often played out in heated public forums pitting self-described sex radicals against urgent advocates of individual responsibility, ran parallel to a city crackdown on sex and nightlife venues, led by Mayor Rudy Giuliani.

LGNY focused considerable reporting on the mayor's crusading efforts, but also engaged the debate over sexual culture. When a group of sex radicals formed Sex Panic, the newspaper devoted a special issue to dueling essays by gay activist Jim Eigo and Michael Warner, then a literature and American studies professor at Rutgers (together representing the liberationist perspective), and journalists Michelangelo Signorile and Gabriel Rotello (who were leading critics of public-sex venues for their lack of safe-sex norms).

A 2001 Signorile article, in which he was harshly critical of former *New Republic* editor Andrew Sullivan for advertising on a barebacking website even as he published a series of high-profile pieces about the "end" of AIDS, generated at least 350,000 hits at www.lgny.com and led to a firestorm of controversy that spilled over into Salon.com and the Poynter Institute's Media News.

The economic upheaval in New York later that year, when the attack on the World Trade Center turned many dozens of blocks of Lower Manhattan into a security zone, threatened to cripple *LGNY*. Throughout late 2001 and early 2002, Masters and Schindler investigated a number of opportunities for recapitalizing the newspaper or launching a new enterprise.

John Sutter's Community Media group of newspapers included neighborhood publications that dated as far back as the 1930s. They chronicled the valiant and successful efforts to preserve Greenwich Village and other historic neighborhoods from wholesale redevelopment, as well as the massive growth in Manhattan's Wall Street district with the construction of the World Trade Center and later the World Financial Center on Hudson River landfill. Sutter's publications were dedicated to preserving community journalism in a city dominated by media conglomerates, and Masters and Schindler soon came to agreement with him on a partnership for preserving New York's LGBT press with the launch of *Gay City News*.

Backed by the capital strength and advertising-sales depth of a multi-title newspaper group, *Gay City News* was able to retain freelance contributors and staff members seasoned over years at *OutWeek, QW* and *LGNY*. Dance critic Brian McCormick and gallery and film reviewer Aaron Krach, contributors for five years at *LGNY*, served as arts editors at *Gay City News*. Given New York's outsized arts scene, the newspaper often devotes close to half of its editorial hole to coverage of theater, film, dance, opera, popular music, galleries and books. The editors at *Gay City News* treat the arts the way many mainstream dailies around the nation approach sports.

Duncan Osborne, the newspaper's associate editor, has focused considerable attention on AIDS funding, HIV transmission, crime, and police harassment of the LGBT community. His reporting on the persistence of high infection rates among young gay and bisexual men and the city's chronically inadequate response has been the only serious coverage of that issue in the New York media.

Osborne's 2005 book *Suicide Tuesday* grew out of his reporting at *Gay City News* on the crystal meth crisis that shook New York's gay male community during the middle years of the past decade. The newspaper's comprehensive coverage of that issue—including the law-enforcement response at the local and federal levels—and its sponsorship of community forums aimed at increasing public awareness about this new epidemic's dangers earned *Gay City News* a community service award from the New York Press Association.

The coverage Osborne has given to arrests for public sex and at video stores in Manhattan turned those stories into controversies from the New Jersey Legislature and appeals courts to the 2009 city elections in New York. His reporting on the video-store false arrests forced every candidate for mayor, Manhattan district attorney, and City Council in the borough that year to address questions of ongoing police harassment of gay men.

Osborne's knowledge of the police and the courts has informed his reporting on a host of anti-gay murders, including the 2008 murder of an Ecuadorean immigrant in Queens who was mistaken for gay by his assailants as he walked home late on a December night, huddled with his brother for warmth. The murder case against those responsible for the 2006 killing of Michael Sandy, the gay man lured to the Brooklyn beach, included hate-crime enhancements, in response to which one defendant came out as bisexual in an unsuccessful attempt to beat the rap.

In 2003, reporting by Mick Meenan, then the newspaper's deputy editor, on the late-night stabbing of Sakia Gunn—the African-American teenager in Newark murdered after telling men cruising her and her friends from a car that they were lesbians—garnered national attention for the case. As hundreds of her high-school peers marched through Newark from her funeral to the burial site, many carried aloft the *Gay City News* cover that bore her picture. Meenan's reporting was judged the news story of the year by the New York Press Association.

New York Law School professor Arthur S. Leonard continues as the newspaper's legal correspondent, building on work he has produced for 32 years since founding *Lesbian/Gay Law Notes* in 1980.

The newspaper has also made a strong commitment to international reporting. Writing in *Gay*

City News, Doug Ireland, a veteran newsman who spent years during the Cold War as a European correspondent for a variety of leading U.S. publications, was the first journalist to report on the wave of targeted anti-gay murders that has swept Iraq since the 2003 U.S. invasion.

After those early reports, Michael Luongo made two trips to Iraq, in 2007 and 2009, spending more than a month there in total and writing a five-part series over several years that chronicled underground gay life, as well as the emergence of a slightly more visible community as violence there has subsided. Luongo's reporting was recognized by the New York City chapter of the Society of Professional Journalists for outstanding reporting by a newspaper under 100,000 in circulation.

Ireland's international reporting also included the earliest Western interviews with Nikolai Alexeyev, Moscow's leading LGBT rights advocate, and Victor Mukasa, a lesbian trans activist who has fought violent homophobia in Uganda. His reporting on anti-LGBT repression in Iran has been detailed and comprehensive, but also drew fire from Scott Long, then director of the LGBT desk at Human Rights Watch. An ongoing battle between Ireland and Long led *Gay City News* to devote a special issue, with half a dozen contributors, to examining the appropriate role for Western journalists and activists in highlighting and combating homophobia and anti-LGBT violence within Islamic and other developing nations.

The newspaper's international reporting is the best example of the way in which online visibility allows *Gay City News'* mission to be broadened. Increasingly, the demands of a 24-hour news cycle challenge the editors to rethink their approach to traditional beats at the newspaper. The ability to speak to a national and global audience is an unprecedented opportunity to link *Gay City News'* work to LGBT communities far beyond New York. Imagining what the digital future holds for journalism remains an ongoing conversation at *Gay City News*—both editorially and from a business perspective. The newspaper's success, to date, in improving its financial performance in the face of industry declines offers a sound basis for optimism.

Gay City News' first and foremost mission, however, is definitive coverage of the local scene in New York City and state. With every issue, the newspaper strives to keep its profile high among local decision-makers, elected officials and other media professionals. Since 2000, *LGNY* and then *Gay City News* have published exclusive, face-to-face interviews with then–first lady Hillary Rodham Clinton (a month before her election to the U.S. Senate), Senators Chuck Schumer and Kirsten Gillibrand, Mayor Michael Bloomberg, New Jersey Governor Jon Corzine, and New York Governors David Paterson and Andrew Cuomo.

Looking toward the future, in the June 2012 LGBT Pride issue, the newspaper did an in-depth interview profiling City Council Speaker Christine Quinn, an out lesbian widely considered a frontrunner for mayor in next year's election.

In 2009, *Gay City News* faced the task of reporting on the re-election effort of Mayor Bloomberg, who has established a positive reputation for his progressive views on gay rights. In a series of interviews, the newspaper pressed the incumbent on his AIDS record, the video-store arrests and the fact that, his support for marriage equality notwithstanding, he was the major financial patron for a group of Republican state senators virulently opposed to any gay-rights advances. Though the mayor enjoyed strong—but not universal—support in the LGBT community, the newspaper published a carefully argued endorsement of his Democratic challenger.

In 2011, after years of detailed reporting about the advocacy drive to enact gay marriage in New York, *Gay City News* saw Albany grow crowded with media from across the nation and even the world, fascinated by the prospect of a populous U.S. state moving proactively, without prodding from the courts, toward full equality. With the mainstream media increasingly focused on LGBT issues, the gay press faces a critical challenge staying on top of its game and ahead of the pack.

In the end, insight, know-how, contacts and hustle counted for a lot. From tapping the tight-knit circle of advocates working in close and largely confidential collaboration with Governor Cuomo, to analyzing just how bad the bite was from the ever-barking state Conservative Party on past gay-rights initiatives, *Gay City News* found all sorts of fresh and unique angles to inform its reporting. The toughest challenge proved to be the Pride issue print deadline, which came 48 hours before the final state Senate vote—no certain matter. When the victory was had, Cuomo gave his first interviews on the successful push to two journalists on the same day—Maureen Dowd at *The New York Times* and Paul Schindler at *Gay City News*.

[In August 2012, Community Media LLC, the parent company of *Gay City News*, was acquired by Jennifer Watkins Goodstein, who will replace *Gay City News* co-founder and Publisher John W. Sutter. Troy Masters remains co-founder and associate publisher, and Paul Schindler remains editor-in-chief and co-founder.]

The October 19, 2000, issue of *LGNY*, which was founded in 1995 and was *Gay City News'* predecessor publication.

***Gay City News*, May 10, 2002.**

***Gay City News*, May 16, 2003.**

Gay City News,
October 1, 2009.

Gay City News,
June 22, 2011.

Gay City News,
July 6, 2011.

Gay City News,
June 20, 2012.

30

GA Voice

By the GA Voice Staff

The late 1980s were pivotal years in gay and lesbian history with the creation of ACT UP, the second National March on Washington in 1987, the unveiling of the NAMES Project AIDS Quilt, the upholding of Georgia's sodomy law by the U.S. Supreme Court in *Bowers v. Hardwick* and the coming out of U.S. Representative Barney Frank (D-Massachusetts), among other milestones.

Atlanta, home of the civil-rights movement, also saw unprecedented activism during those years. Project Open Hand was launched to feed people with AIDS, Out on Film made its debut and the AIDS Research Consortium of Atlanta was formed. Waves of energy poured forth from the 1987 National March on Washington, galvanizing a struggling movement now faced with the soaring deaths of its people and a president who refused to say the word "AIDS."

The activism spawned by the march spilled into 1988, and that year the first issue of *Southern Voice* hit the streets. Its founder, Christina Cash, could not have predicted that *Southern Voice* would become the largest and most respected LGBT newspaper in the Southeast, or that it would die a very public death and be resurrected in 2010 as the *GA Voice*.

The history of *GA Voice*, the LGBT newspaper of record for Atlanta and the state of Georgia, cannot be told without including the history of *Southern Voice*. One would assume the story of *GA Voice*, launched in March 2010, would be short. Not so. Its history begins with, and its roots are inexplicably tied to, *Southern Voice*, which saw its premiere issue on March 1, 1988.

The short version goes something like this: *Southern Voice* launched in 1988 and quickly became the region's pre-eminent LGBT publication. Cash was approached by Window Media and sold to it in 1997. *Southern Voice* became the flagship of a chain of LGBT publications Window bought over the next few years. Flash-forward to November 16, 2009. Window declared bankruptcy and shuttered its remaining publications: the *Washington Blade, Southern Voice, Houston Voice, David, The South Florida Blade* and *411 Magazine*. A few months later, in March 2010, Cash and former *Southern Voice* Editor Laura Douglas-Brown launched *GA Voice*.

The longer version is a tale of both entrepreneurship and, most importantly, commitment to the local LGBT community.

"People think that the launching of *Southern Voice* in 1988 was an act of activism on my part," Cash reflects. "While that is partially true, *SoVo* was also an act of entrepreneurship and the realization of a dream I had for almost a decade of creating an alternative newspaper. In late 1987 there was a perfect storm of events, both personal and public, that led me to wake up one morning and say out loud, 'I am going to start a gay and lesbian newspaper.' I immediately began the process to make that happen, not having much of a clue where I needed to start. All I knew was that there was a need in Atlanta for it and I wanted to be the one to make it happen."

Cash started by reaching out to the editor of *Southline*, an Atlanta alternative weekly with a heavy focus on local news and politics. "I didn't know I needed to talk to the publisher," Cash said. "That's how little I knew about how a newspaper is structured."

Editor Paul Evans agreed to meet Cash for lunch and he brought along his food critic, Gary Kaupman. Kaupman, an out gay man, had plenty of ideas about what an LGBT newspaper should look like and offer its readers. He talked about former publications formed in the mid-1970s, such as *The Barb* and *Cruise*, that had survived for a while but were heavily dependent on bar advertising. Kaupman was also sure that there would be little financial support for a true newspaper in the community and that raising needed seed money would be next to impossible.

"Gary told me that I had no track record, no connections and no idea what I was trying to take on. He was right, but he was also excited by the prospect of having a true LGBT newspaper like the *Washington Blade*, so he suggested I begin as a nonprofit in order to at least get some grant money. He introduced me to local playwright Rebecca Ranson, the director of the Southeastern Arts, Media and Education Project (SAME). We talked and she agreed to take *Southern Voice* under SAME's umbrella. And so we began. I had a small amount of money to contribute and I threw it all in. I couldn't think of any better way to use it."

With a handful of volunteers, including one person committed to raise money from the community, Cash worked to design the newspaper, establish editorial guidelines and find distribution points. Most important, she says, was how to distinguish *Southern Voice* from other gay publications in the city that currently existed or might pop up in the future.

"I was riding MARTA [Metropolitan Atlanta Rapid Transit Authority] one day and I saw a young man reading a local newspaper. I decided then that I wanted a gay person riding MARTA to feel comfortable reading *Southern Voice*, free of any fear that he or she might be verbally or physically harassed. I also wanted that same person to be able to show 'their' newspaper to their parents. I wanted to be able to show it to my mother and I needed to be proud of it to do so. In order to do this, and to succeed, we needed to walk that very thin line between being an advocacy publication and also one with journalistic integrity," she said.

Making the Move

That MARTA ride led Cash to make several key decisions. One, the newspaper's primary focus would be local news and politics. Two, both men and women would be represented in its pages. Three, it would not be financed primarily by bar, alcohol and sex advertisers.

"All of those were risky moves," Cash said. "The only gay publications Atlanta had at that point, or ever had, revolved primarily around the bar scene, so they all carried male images, lots of sexually explicit advertising and bar events. It's as if nobody knew how to do it differently—or they were afraid to. My thought about it was that if I limited us to those types of ads and images, we would not be able to get the majority of advertisers out there—realtors, restaurants, car dealerships—who wanted to tap into the gay dollar. We needed that money to survive and to grow. I wasn't 100 percent sure people would want to read hard local news, even though we were in a huge wave of activism from the 1987 March on Washington and the *Bowers v. Hardwick* decision in 1986, which upheld Georgia's sodomy law. But I took a leap of faith, and. fortunately I was right," she said.

Southern Voice launched as a biweekly paper with 16 pages, a press run of 5,000 and a small handful of LGBT advertisers.

"We made just enough money on that first issue to pay the printer," Cash recalls. "The same was true for many of our early issues. Somehow, miraculously it seemed to me, the money showed up when we needed it—and always just enough to get by."

The newspaper established itself as a hard-news and political vehicle with its premiere issue. A large photo of a march in Atlanta to rally for the homeless graced the cover. A contingent of about 100 gays and lesbians carried signs demanding help for homeless people with AIDS and gay and lesbian youth. Inside, a slate of 1988 presidential nominee hopefuls clearly spelled out their positions on both general issues and those of particular interest to gay and lesbian readers.

"I was so proud of that issue," Cash reflected. "I would have that same feeling with the first issue of *GA Voice* many years later. To experience that twice is a blessing I could never anticipate."

In 1989, Cash established *Southern Voice* as a for-profit corporation and moved the newspaper into its own office.

"There were too many restraints as a nonprofit," Cash said. "We could not make political endorsements and I could not raise the kind of money we needed to get us to our next level through grants alone. We needed to be independent. I knew very little about business when I started the paper, but I had to learn very quickly in order for us to survive."

The paper continued to grow, and soon Cash was able to hire a circulation manager, more ad reps and a staff writer. The paper did without a fax machine until 1990. But circulation boomed and the newspaper received several awards from local groups. That year, too, Cash's then–life partner, Leigh VanderEls, joined the staff full time as publisher, and Cash assumed the role of editor.

"For the first time I did not have to juggle the business side and the content side," said Cash. "I could focus on improving our editorial product knowing that the sales staff and the business side were being handled well by someone I trusted."

In 1992, Cash raised a modest amount of money by selling shares in the corporation and obtaining a loan from a local bank so that *Southern Voice* could transition to a weekly publication.

"It was becoming very difficult to stay on top of all the local news that was happening as a biweekly," Cash said. "I also knew we could double our revenue without having to double our expenses by going weekly. The following year, 1993, we declared our first profit after being in business for five years."

A year later Cash and VanderEls bought an old warehouse near Emory University to house the growing newspaper and staff. They renovated about 3,000 square feet of the 16,000-square-foot building as offices and settled in.

"By that time we had a staff of 11 and numerous freelancers. Times were very, very good both for the community and for the newspaper. We had joined the National Gay Newspaper Guild and were carrying substantial national advertising in addition to a diverse base of local advertisers. Between ACT UP, Queer Nation and other street activists, we were stretched to cover everything—but we did. I was able to afford to hire an editor and was no longer tied to the business 24/7. I could actually have a life outside the office, since I was no longer tied to every deadline. The staff was amazing, talented, energetic and loyal. I look back at that time period as one of the happiest of my life even though we lost many friends to AIDS, especially from 1990 to 1995," she said.

In the midst of all that happiness, tragedy struck at *Southern Voice*. In April 1996, then-Editor Devon Clayton committed suicide. Cash and a staff writer found Clayton in his apartment, where he had hanged himself the night before.

"He had come to me a few days before and said he was depressed and having suicidal thoughts," Cash said. "I helped him find a therapist to talk to that day and he was admitted to a local psych hospital for evaluation. He called once while he was there and he sounded better. But then I did not hear anything for 48 hours. I called the hospital and they would not tell me anything because of confidentiality. I asked them to please just tell me if he was there or not. They told me he had been released the day before. I knew then that something was very wrong. Devon was responsible to a fault. It was not like him to not check in with me."

Cash found Clayton hanging in his kitchen an hour after that phone call. After reporting the suicide to the police, and being questioned for several hours, she had to return to the office to tell the staff.

"It's all a blur," Cash said. "All I remember doing is sitting on a sofa and staring or crying. My emotions kept jumping from grief to anger and back to grief again. I was in shock for many weeks."

Less than a month later, Cash said, the best thing that could have happened did. Her son, Chase, who is VanderEls' biological son, returned to live with them after spending the previous eight years with his father and stepmother as ordered by a Clayton County, Georgia, judge.

"The judge declared Leigh an unfit mother in 1987 because she was a lesbian," Cash recalled. "He gave no other reason. They gave Leigh less than an hour with Chase before he was whisked away. That fact is one of the biggest motivators for launching *Southern Voice*. It was something I could do to counter the injustice of that act. In fact, it was the only thing I could do."

The newly reunited family had settled into homework, baseball and teen angst when a few months later, in August, Cash and VanderEls were approached by an attorney who asked if they had any interest in selling the newspaper, something the couple had never considered.

"But with Chase at home, and two years of high school left, it sounded tempting to be able to devote more time to him and to our family. I had also just been diagnosed with post-polio syndrome, and my energy was at an all-time low. My doctors had told me I needed to rest more, and so we told the attorney we might have an interest and were open to hearing an offer," Cash said.

Nothing came of that first inquiry for months, and Cash continued with plans for growth, assuming the interested buyer had decided to pass. In early 1997 *Southern Voice* hired Cathy Woolard as publisher. Woolard, who had worked for both the National Gay and Lesbian Task Force and the Human Rights Campaign, was a longtime friend and a native of Atlanta. Cash and Woolard had worked closely together on the Atlanta Committee for the March on Washington in 1987.

"Within a month of Cathy relocating to Atlanta and starting her work with us, we heard from the attorney again. This time he had a hard figure to offer. We declined it and made a counteroffer," she said.

Again, months went by with no communication from the anonymous buyer or buyers.

"It was a difficult decision to keep the possible sale from the staff but we were not certain it would happen. We did not know if anything would come of it, and so we continued to make decisions for the company as if we were not going to sell," Cash recalled.

One of the forward-moving decisions was to hire a recent Emory University graduate, Laura Douglas-Brown, as an editorial intern. Douglas-Brown held a master's degree in English, but her passion was news and the LGBT community. Cash recognized her intelligence and potential immediately.

"She was the best journalist that ever walked through our doors," Cash said. "It only took a few minutes to realize what she could bring to the newspaper. Before she walked out the door, I was already envisioning her career with us."

Douglas-Brown joined the *Southern Voice* staff in January 1997. A month later, the Otherside Lounge, an Atlanta gay bar, was bombed. At the time, she had no idea the story would span most of the first decade of her career—Eric Robert Rudolph was sentenced in 2005 for bombing the gay bar, Centennial Olympic Park and two abortion clinics—but she knew she had found her calling.

"Working in the gay press was the perfect blend of my interest in writing and passion for LGBT civil rights," Douglas-Brown said. "We are journalists, not activists, but I strongly believe that the first step to encouraging people to speak up for their own equality is to educate them about where those rights stand now, and to introduce them to the individuals and organizations already fighting for change."

In early summer of 1997, Cash and VanderEls were told that their counteroffer was accepted and that the purchasers were a local attorney, Chris Crain; a longtime gay activist, William Waybourn; and a handful of undisclosed local investors.

"We knew next to nothing about Chris or William," Cash admitted. "We met a few times when they were doing due diligence prior to the close of the sale. They both seemed genuinely excited about the prospect of owning *Southern Voice* and reassured us that the business and editorial guidelines we had worked so hard to establish and maintain would remain."

On August 15, 1997, the sale closed and *Southern Voice* became the property of Window Media.

"The closing took 12 hours," Cash recalls. "Being attorneys, they asked for a lot, mostly in terms of protections that we simply could not provide, and we came very close to calling it off. I was prepared to walk away from the sale. I had very mixed feelings. The paper had been my life for 10 years and I had no idea how I would cope once I was no longer a part of it. At the same time, I was excited about being home for Chase and working to improve my health."

The first years under Window Media ownership proved exciting. The new owners brought new energy and new financial resources, with a strong professed commitment to covering local news. Douglas-Brown, hired as a staff writer shortly before the sale, delved deeply into local politics and city government. *Southern Voice* was named Best Gay Weekly in the Vice Versa Awards, a now-defunct journalism competition for the LGBT press, in 1997, 1998 and 1999, and staff writers also racked up multiple individual honors.

But Window Media's ultimate goal was to grow into a chain of newspapers that could share both financial and editorial resources. The company next bought the *Houston Voice*, followed by a gay paper in New Orleans. With the help of an investment fund called Avalon Equity, it finally acquired its biggest desires: the *Washington Blade*, as well as its companion newspaper, the *New York Blade*. Related companies also took on the national gay men's magazine *Genre*, as well as male-oriented nightlife magazines in several cities.

Mounting debt, the flailing economy and a top-heavy management structure that lost sight of the needs of the local communities finally brought down the Window-Avalon empire. Local journalists— including Douglas-Brown, who had been promoted to editor of *Southern Voice* in 2006—weathered bounced paychecks and erratic management decisions to try to keep covering their local communities, but they could not overcome the staggering financial crisis, which had mostly been hidden from them.

On the morning of November 16, 2009, more than 12 years after the sale to Window Media, Cash was looking at her Facebook page. A friend and former employee of *Southern Voice* had just posted that Window Media had declared bankruptcy and closed the doors of *Southern Voice* (and their other properties). There were posts and comments from dozens of people expressing shock, grief and fear that Atlanta would be left without an LGBT newspaper.

"I was stunned but I was not surprised when they folded," Cash said. "I knew they were in some serious trouble, and I had been contacted by an attorney with the Small Business Administration several years prior, looking for information on Window, Avalon Equity and David Unger. I was not much help to him. Once we closed the sale, I never heard a word from Crain. He never asked any questions, never sought advice—nothing. I never knew or had contact with Unger. I did hear from William a few times but that concerned late payments to us. That was the first hint I got that they were struggling, and that was in 2002. I was actually surprised they lasted as long as they did. I let the SBA attorney know I was interested in buying *Southern Voice* but I never heard anything back from him or anyone else about it."

The next few days were full of phone calls and email as Cash reached out to various people about the paper's demise.

"The first person I called was Laura," Cash said. "I knew she would need some support and encouragement. Laura had given her life to *SoVo* over the years. She had stuck with them through everything, and in 2006 they had the good sense to name her editor."

Douglas-Brown had become one of the leaders in Atlanta's LGBT community and was recognized numerous times for her skill as a journalist and for her service to the community. In 2008, she was awarded the National Lesbian & Gay Journalists Association's Sarah Pettit Memorial Award for Excellence in the LGBT Press, the highest honor given to a journalist working in gay media, based on her editorials and investigative reporting. That same year, Emory University honored her with its second annual Chesnut Award for Outstanding Service to the LGBT Community.

Cash and Douglas-Brown spoke on the phone while Douglas-Brown was still in the parking lot of the now-shuttered office.

"We talked briefly about the immediate situation. She was still at the *SoVo* office, locked out, and was comforting other staff members. We agreed to talk later that day," Cash remembered.

Douglas-Brown recalled the conversation as one of mourning that immediately turned to hope.

"I knew that what happened to Window Media happened for a lot of reasons, but not because Atlanta no longer needed an LGBT media outlet," Douglas-Brown said. "I was heartbroken for the community as much as for myself and the other employees."

Cash spent the rest of that day sorting through the implications of the closing of the newspaper. Now living in Dallas, she wondered how she could help or even if she should.

"It was a very emotional day," she recalls. "When I got really honest with myself, I knew that I had missed the newspaper. I tried other projects and dabbled in a lot of things over those 12 years. But it was never the same. I wanted back in."

Over the next few days, Cash and Douglas-Brown discussed the options. Both agreed that a city with the civil-rights history of Atlanta could not be left without a "voice" for its LGBT citizens.

Tentatively, fearful about whether a newspaper could sustain itself in the current economy, the two decided to take the plunge and try to launch a new publication.

"Two days after *Southern Voice* closed, Chris [Cash] gave an interview to a local online media outlet acknowledging what we were considering," Douglas-Brown said. "The outpouring of support was overwhelming, from people not only wanting a new media outlet but wanting us to do it. After that, it immediately became a question not of if, but how."

Within a few weeks, the two had reached out to the press, to former *SoVo* staff and to those people Cash believed would best support their efforts. Three weeks after Window shut down, Cash and Douglas-Brown held a community meeting to discuss their plans, ask for volunteers and choose a name for the new Atlanta LGBT newspaper.

"Both of us believed it was better to rename the newspaper. We knew we would have the opportunity to buy the *Southern Voice* name and remaining assets but we did not know if we would prevail if someone else bid on it as well. And we had to move quickly," Cash said. "We needed a name and so put out three for a vote. The people there that night overwhelmingly chose *GA Voice*."

The new name honored the media outlet's roots while also marking a break from the past.

"I thought it was important to include Georgia in the name because the LGBT community is growing far beyond Atlanta," Douglas-Brown said. "Through the years, I had also been asked a couple of times if *Southern Voice* was a Confederate publication, so we were glad to shed any possible connotation of that name."

Cash and Douglas-Brown knew that their first challenge was to gather the seed money necessary for pre-launch expenses. An attorney was needed to form the LLC, insurance had to be purchased, collateral materials created and an office space secured before launch. The seed money came from the two co-founders, donations from the public and a $12,000 grant from the Lloyd Russell Foundation.

Two of Douglas-Brown's former colleagues at *Southern Voice* were onboard from the first day. Ryan Watkins volunteered to create a website for the new effort to keep the community informed and provide an opportunity for donations, while Dyana Bagby continued to report LGBT news, even when the only place to post it was via Facebook.

As Douglas-Brown worked on ideas for the content of the new newspaper and website, Cash focused on the business side of the new effort.

"Once we had raised the seed money, I approached a good friend of mine, Tim Boyd, and asked if he would join us as an owner and manage the sales staff. He agreed and we were off and running," Cash said.

Early in the planning of *GA Voice*, Cash received a phone call from Todd Evans of Rivendell Media. The two had done business together when Cash owned *Southern Voice* and had a long history.

"Todd called to say he was excited about the new launch and he had plenty of ads to place with us once we were ready. I really appreciated that call, and knowing that Todd was already working for us gave me even more confidence going forward," she said.

With a free newspaper, totally dependent on advertising for revenue, Cash knew the quality of the local sales team would be paramount. Cash and Boyd launched a search for their key salesperson and found one in January 2010. Marshall Graham, who had worked for five years with the *Gay Community Yellow Pages* in Atlanta, agreed to come on board.

"Marshall was just what we needed," Cash said. "Her experience and sales ability have proven to be invaluable. I know we could not have made it this far without her."

Bo Shell, a graphic designer who had also worked with Douglas-Brown at Window Media, joined as art director, and the new team was complete.

"Words will never express how grateful I was to have Ryan, Dyana and Bo—all of whom are tremendously gifted and went through the brutal final days of Window Media—willing to make this leap with me," Douglas-Brown said. "Tim and Marshall brought critical business and sales experience, to add to Chris [Cash's] passion and years of success. In all, six of the seven of us had worked for *Southern Voice* in the past, and all seven had experience in LGBT publishing. 'Dream team' is a cliché, but here it was true."

"This is the most talented staff I have ever worked with," Cash agreed. "The level of commitment, loyalty and creativity impresses me every day. I don't see how we can fail with this staff. It's just not in the stars."

The first issue of *GA Voice* hit the streets on March 18, 2010, with the cover story on the ongoing battle between police and the owners and patrons of The Eagle, a well-established local bar that was raided in 2009. The headline "The Fight Continues" was appropriate both for the cover story and for the new publication's mission to continue covering the broader fight for LGBT civil rights.

The website appropriately launched a week before—*GA Voice* would be much more than a print publication. Entering the second decade of the 21st century, the staff knows that to retain readers and advertisers it must offer a multimedia package.

"Unlike former publications that were essentially newspapers that also had a website, *GA Voice* was conceived as a media outlet that publishes in two equally important ways—online daily, and every other Friday in print," Douglas-Brown said. "We constantly reach out to readers through social media and have become the most active outlet for conversations about our LGBT community."

The young media outlet's efforts, in print and online, have quickly been recognized and honored. In the National Newspaper Association's 2010 Better Newspaper Contest, *GA Voice* won second place in its size divisions for Best Website and second place for Best Investigative or In-Depth Story or Series. Douglas-Brown placed second for opinion writing and Dyana Bagby placed second for news reporting (small print division) in the Atlanta Press Club 2010 Awards of Excellence. Bagby was also named one of the Top 10 Atlanta Journalists on Twitter.

In 2011, the news outlet garnered four awards from the National Newspaper Association's Better Newspaper Contest: a first-place award for Best Humorous Column (Topher Payne), second place for Best Newspaper Website (Ryan Watkins, Web manager), second place for Best Sports Feature (Dyana Bagby) and third place for Best Original Editorial Cartoon (Mike Ritter).

GA Voice staff members have also been honored for LGBT community involvement. Douglas-Brown was nominated for Best Businesswoman in the 2010 and 2011 Atlanta Gay and Lesbian Chamber of Commerce Awards, while Associate Publisher Tim Boyd was nominated as Best Businessman in 2011. Douglas-Brown was also honored as an Atlanta Pride community grand marshal for 2010, as one of the 2010 Fenuxe 50 leaders in LGBT Atlanta, and as one of Emory University's 20 LGBT "Change Agents" in 2011.

Amidst the honors, *GA Voice* continues to grow.

"Although print still dominates in revenue, we have seen significant growth in our online sales," Cash said. "The website is updated frequently with breaking news and events and is not just a rehash of the print version. Our Facebook page is extremely popular, and the majority of the visits to our website come through Facebook."

"We have been in business for more than two years, and even though the economy continues to be challenging we continue to grow. Like with *Southern Voice*, it is a slow process until you reach this level of critical mass and then you grow almost exponentially. I feel we are reaching that point," she continued. "We launched *Destination: Gay Atlanta*, the official LGBT travel guide to Atlanta, in 2011 and it did extremely well. The 2012 edition of *DGA* was even more successful and plans are in the works to take our LGBT travel guide to other cities."

The Atlanta Convention and Visitors Bureau is *GA Voice*'s partner in the travel guide and has a dedicated website, www.gay-atlanta.com, for LGBT visitors. The digital version of *Destination: Gay Atlanta* is found there along with other content provided by *GA Voice*.

"Sitting on the steps of the locked *Southern Voice* office that cold November morning, I could not have imagined the success of *GA Voice*, but in retrospect it could not have happened any other way," Douglas-Brown said. "Like any young business, we face struggles, but I know that we will never lose sight of our mission and what is most important—providing a professional, experienced source of information and entertainment for Georgia's dynamic LGBT community. I am honored every day to be part of it."

Cash is equally optimistic about the company's future.

"There are different challenges with *GA Voice* than there were with *Southern Voice*," Cash said. "In the 1980s we were fighting for acceptance and scratching out advertising dollars from reluctant businesses that both feared and desired gay customers. Today, we are fighting the vestiges of the Great Recession and an industry that struggles to find its footing amidst advances in technology that have changed the face of publishing forever. I think I prefer the latter. It's an exciting time, and who knows what is around the corner for LGBT publishing. Somehow, I think it will be good for all of us."

(In October 2012, *GA Voice* launched *Atlanta Gay Weddings*, the city's first print guide to provide LGBT couples with inspiration for their big day. An annual publication, *AGW* is a guide with in-depth coverage of planning, gay-friendly wedding companies, gay-friendly honeymoon destinations, cakes, attire, legal concerns and more. *AGW* is published in partnership with *Equally Wed*, a national LGBT online wedding magazine.)

Southern Voice cover from June 20, 2008.

GA Voice's first issue, March 19, 2010.

GA Voice, June 25, 2010.

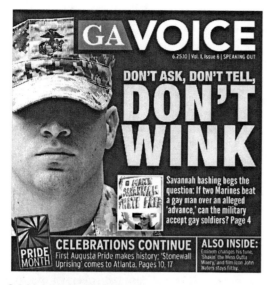

GA Voice, October 29, 2010.

Atlanta Gay Weddings, 2012–13.

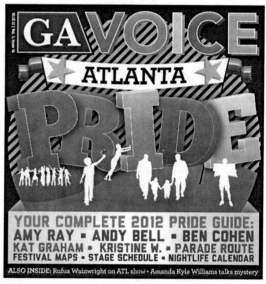

GA Voice, October 12, 2012.

Destination Gay Atlanta.

31

Philadelphia Gay News

By Jen Colletta for *Philadelphia Gay News*

On January 26, 1976, the inaugural edition of *Philadelphia Gay News* hit the streets of the City of Brotherly Love and Sisterly Affection. Though the publication launched with a bare-bones staff of volunteers, a negligible budget and no physical office, it grew to be one of the nation's most respected and award-winning LGBT media outlets.

PGN was born of a partnership between LGBT activist Mark Segal and media guru Jim Austin.

In 1975, Austin, then-publisher of *Pittsburgh Gay News*, launched a second venture, the *Ohio East Gay News*, and invited Segal on a four-city Ohio tour to promote the new publication. On the drive back to the Keystone State, the concept of a Philadelphia-based LGBT publication arose.

Throughout the 1970s, Philadelphia had seen a number of LGBT-focused publications, such as the *The Weekly Philadelphia Gayzette* and the *The Gay Alternative*, as well as a series of newsletters produced by other LGBT activist groups, but none were on a par with mainstream professional newspapers.

With the marriage of Austin's journalism know-how and Segal's activism background and city contacts, planning for the first edition of *PGN* began.

Getting the publication off the ground, however, was no easy feat.

Just weeks before the debut, Segal's LGBT activism led him to Philadelphia's City Hall—where he undertook a hunger strike, handcuffed to the city's Christmas tree, in a protest for LGBT rights. The several-day demonstration prevented Segal from going door to door for support of the inaugural launch, as he was the primary force generating ad sales.

With an initial budget of about $5,000 in borrowed funds, *PGN* was originally produced by a small group of volunteers who largely taught themselves the ins and outs of the printing business, a process Segal called "pure chaos."

The first issues were produced in the apartment of a local gay couple who, shortly before the first newspaper went to press, got into an intense argument.

"They had an all-out brawl, literally punching each other and rolling down the steps," Segal said. "I was just yelling, 'Don't get any blood on the flats!' So those first few papers were just a miracle."

PGN moved into an office within its first year in operation—a dilapidated building at 233 South 13th Street, in the heart of the city's Gayborhood, that the business leased from the city for just $1 a month.

The price break came with its own share of problems, however, as the space lacked adequate plumbing and electricity—it was powered through a generator, and staffers had to use glasses in the basement in place of a restroom.

Don Pignolet, office manager since the paper's inception, said building improvements were a group effort: His father came in to wire the building, and staffers pitched in to patch up a gaping hole in the office's floor.

The deteriorating ceiling became especially problematic on rainy days, when staff would have to rush to ensure tarps were in place to catch the torrents of water that came flooding into the building.

While the atmosphere was challenging to work in, former *PGN* reporter and editor Tommi Avicolli Mecca said it made him feel like a "true alternative journalist."

In the early days, *PGN* staffers typed stories on an IBM electric typewriter, and editors took pen to paper to correct mistakes.

The articles would then be processed through a typesetting machine and laid out on non-repro blue paper in a five-column format—a process that required physically cutting the stories with an X-Acto knife and securing them to the flats with wax applied to their reverse sides.

Headlines were created letter by letter with Prestype, and photos were processed onto a screen sheet that was then waxed onto the boards. Once the flats were complete, a staff member drove them to the printer.

For much of its first year in operation, *PGN* published monthly, which gave staffers more time to work on the tedious, labor-intensive layout process.

In its third month in operation, *PGN* installed vending boxes on street corners, in an effort, Segal said, to have the publication not "hide behind any closet doors."

The surrounding society, however, wasn't completely as prepared for the boldness of the *PGN* logo on city streets. In the early days of the paper, cars intentionally drove into the vending boxes, and small bombs and feces were placed inside.

"There's nothing I can think of that wasn't done to those boxes," Segal recalled. "But we made it a point that if a box was destroyed, we'd have another one waiting in the garage to be put back on the street the next day."

The publication initially was structured in two sections, the first of which appeared in both the Philadelphia and Ohio publications, and the second of which was Philadelphia-specific. Nine months after the launch, Segal bought out the chain from Austin and gradually began focusing the news on the Philadelphia area.

Around this time, the publication became bimonthly, and a weekly in 1982, with the shorter production schedule eventually necessitating the incorporation of new technologies.

PGN purchased its first IBM computer in the 1980s, but Segal said the staff was too wary of the new technology to use it initially. In 1988, *PGN* acquired a Lisa—one of the earliest Apple products—and gradually brought in a desktop computer for each of its employees, getting the devices onto a network and beginning the process of going digital. Segal said *PGN* was the first newspaper in the Delaware Valley to create its publication solely on a computer.

Since its inception, *PGN* has been committed to a code of professional journalism that has included meeting its publication deadline, which it has never missed in 36 years—despite technological gaffes and works of Mother Nature, such as a blizzard, during which Segal and staffers braved feet of snow to deliver the week's paper at boxes and businesses.

"Meeting deadline is a traditional thing for print media, and we weren't going to break that," he said. "We decided from day one that we were going to be a professional publication and everything that went along with that. The standards for us were higher than the [*Philadelphia*] *Inquirer* and [*Philadelphia*] *Daily News* because we had to prove ourselves more."

As the paper strove to maintain professional standards, it also developed its physical location. It moved from its 13th Street venue a few blocks to 1108 Spruce Street in 1983, a short-lived locale where staffers put the paper together in the dining room of the old Victorian mansion.

In 1984, *PGN* moved another few blocks and purchased its first building at 254 South 11th Street. When the paper arrived at 11th Street, the editorial and advertising staffs were able to be housed on separate floors—a technique that sought to encourage those departments to work separately and objectively.

By this time, *PGN* had developed its name among LGBT media circles and hosted one of the first-ever meetings of the Gay Press Association (later changed to the Gay and Lesbian Press Association) at its 11th Street location, where guests were greeted with a surprise visit from the city's mayor and members of a string band group from the Mummers—who host a local folk parade in which participants dress in elaborate costumes and perform on New Year's Day.

In 1996, Segal moved the office to 505 South Fourth Street, just north of South Street, from which *PGN* currently operates.

The growth of *PGN*'s business infrastructure would not have been possible without building its journalistic credibility, a slow and painstaking process.

PGN writer-at-large Timothy Cwiek, who began reporting for the paper in 1977, said that, in the beginning, reporters faced innumerable obstacles in their quest to produce comprehensive, well-rounded articles.

Since the paper launched long before the days of the Internet, reporters spent copious amounts of time in local libraries doing research and, once they collected their facts, interacting with potential sources was a persistent challenge, Cwiek said.

As representatives of a new publication—and one that focused on an oft-ridiculed community—*PGN* staffers looking for information for stories were hung up on, disrespected and discounted by sources.

Cwiek recalled speaking with a reporter at a local mainstream newspaper about the negative image of journalists in the city. Despite that impression, the reporter joked that she knew her sources would still read her stories, something Cwiek said often didn't hold true for his work.

"We were very marginalized in the beginning," he said.

While changing attitudes toward the LGBT community were likely integral in fueling public reception of *PGN*, the burgeoning AIDS epidemic of the 1980s also cast new light on the value of the publication.

PGN staffers had to learn the ropes of health reporting and sift through a glut of misinformation as the crisis spread throughout the gay community and other social sectors.

"We really came of age with the AIDS crisis: It matured us as a media outlet," Segal said.

At the time, many mainstream media outlets, both nationally and locally in Philadelphia, devoted scant attention to the epidemic, leaving the responsibility of disseminating information on the gay media's shoulders.

Former *PGN* reporter and current contributor Victoria Brownworth wrote for the publication in the beginning and through the height of the epidemic. Brownworth wrote the first stories in the nation on the drug AZT and about the disease's impact on women and children, issues scarcely addressed in mainstream or LGBT media at the time.

She gave readers an inside and poignant look at the scores of babies born with AIDS and abandoned by their mothers at the Bronx's Montefiore Hospital, and she sought to educate the public on how the disease was reaching far beyond the white, gay male population.

"At the time, women just weren't supposed to get AIDS. It was supposed to be a disease just affecting men," Brownworth said. "This was before anyone was talking about the bisexual conduit between straight women and gay men, when we didn't have the 'down-low' term yet or the 'MSM' label. None of that existed at that time, so writing about it was very controversial."

Brownworth's AIDS coverage for *PGN* also uncovered local irregularities, such as mismanagement in the AIDS Task Force and abuse at local housing units, where some AIDS patients were living among vermin. Once non-LGBT outlets began to notice the coverage LGBT outlets such as *PGN* gave to these issues, they began assigning beat reporters specifically to cover the HIV/AIDS crisis. While *PGN*'s coverage of the epidemic gained the publication ground with mainstream communities, it also shaped the way in which the LGBT community perceived the newspaper.

In the 1970s and early 1980s, there were deep divides in the community between the radical political activist and the "bar queen" segments of the population. *PGN* sought to walk the line between the two and tried out content that would appeal to varying types of readers.

Over the years, the paper experimented with a more magazine-style focus, offering such materials as poetry and extensive human-interest pieces. At other times, it geared its coverage to more hard news and fact-driven pieces about the LGBT-rights struggle.

PGN lost standing with some activists, Avicolli Mecca said, because it appeared too "conservative" and conformist. However, as AIDS began ravaging all parts of the community, *PGN* emerged as a strong leader that effectively unified and fought on behalf of community members of all political ideologies.

"We had been trying to straddle both worlds—with more featurey stuff and then also the political and activism coverage," he said. "But once AIDS set in, I think the *Gay News* by the early '80s emerged into a really solid radical publication because we were challenging the status quo. We were challenging the medical industry, the government and all these forces that were basically just letting gay men die."

PGN also worked to seek justice for innumerable LGBT victims of crimes.

Brownworth spent a considerable amount of time in rural Pennsylvania covering the 1988 shooting of two lesbian hikers, Claudia Brenner and Rebecca Wight, the latter of whom died at the couple's campsite. Brownworth said she broke the story and it later went national, drawing attention to anti-gay violence.

In Philadelphia, Avicolli Mecca followed a series of murders of African-American transgender women in an area of the city that was home to several queer and transgender bars. The cases were getting little attention from the Police Department, he said, until *PGN* began its coverage.

Around the same time, Avicolli Mecca delved into the murder of Anthony Milano, a gay artist who was brutally stabbed in a Philadelphia suburb in 1987. His two murderers were accused of killing Milano because of anti-gay animus. Growing up gay and Italian himself, Avicolli Mecca said he felt intrinsically tied to the victim by their similar upbringings—which made the story challenging to tell but kept him committed throughout.

"That story completely resonated with me. It was difficult to cover, but it was good for me to cover because it helped me as a writer," he said. "I literally threw myself into the story and put so much emotion into it. I would come home from the trial and just cry because it was so overwhelming to think of the hatred that was directed toward this kid."

Though *PGN*'s coverage of the Milano murder provided a fresh LGBT look at a case that made waves in mainstream media, more recently the paper has been one of only a few outlets that have followed the unsolved homicide case of Nizah Morris. The African-American transgender woman was killed in Philadelphia in 2002 after receiving a courtesy ride from police. Cwiek covered the story since its inception and has continued to press city officials on the management of the case.

While *PGN* has adhered to a tradition of aggressive advocacy journalism, the LGBT community itself has not been excused from being a target of the paper's scrutiny.

Brownworth spearheaded a series in 1983 exposing corruption at the Philadelphia LGBT agency Eromin Center, highlighting instances of abuse of public funding. One of the heads of the organization, which provided mental-health services to the community, offered to buy every copy of *PGN* before it hit the streets to prevent the story from getting out, an offer the publication declined.

After the stories ran, several Eromin employees were terminated and the agency was eventually shuttered. Though Brownworth was sued for libel and received death threats, she also was honored with several journalism awards—including a Pulitzer Prize nomination.

This was among the first times a queer paper investigated its own community. "Up to that point, we'd been the 'rah-rah' cheerleaders, talking about our own people in only positive ways, with the occasional pieces on the 'bad' straight community," Brownworth said. "But this series was very serious and led to the closing of the center, people losing their jobs and, while I'm sorry it ended up that way, the things people were doing were so terrible and doing so much damage to the community. I think that was a turning point for *PGN* and also for LGBT journalism in general." In more recent years, *PGN* covered instances of financial wrongdoing at several LGBT organizations and the arrest of a prominent gay businessman.

As *PGN* gained traction over the years, its political connectedness grew.

Segal noted that Philadelphia has a long history as a bastion of progressive politics, tracing its roots to Benjamin Franklin's "live and let live" convictions. However, the LGBT community—and the paper that represents it—wasn't always embraced by Philadelphia's elected officials.

Former Republican mayor Frank Rizzo (1972–80) was notorious for holding anti-gay positions but, after determined dogging by *PGN* reporters, Rizzo agreed to an interview in *PGN*, which Segal said turned many heads in the political community. The interview also opened communication between Rizzo and the community, and the politician eventually agreed to attend a community forum at the city's LGBT community center.

PGN's ability to showcase the size, breadth and strength of the LGBT community was instrumental in opening elected officials' eyes to the need to interact with the LGBT population—a relationship that *PGN* helped establish, Segal said.

"We wanted to show them that we are a very important voting bloc and that they needed to be paying attention to us," Segal said. "So we went after interviews with council people, mayors, governors, people that LGBT media were not used to talking to. We didn't give up on talking to them, because we knew how important it was to first show them that we existed and then the power our community had."

PGN harnessed that power to press elected officials on issues important to the LGBT community.

During his campaign for mayor in the early 1990s, Ed Rendell pledged to sign a proclamation granting city employees domestic-partner benefits; however, once elected, he saw pushback from the president of the City Council.

Through his political ties, Segal learned that some council members were resistant because Blue Cross Blue Shield, a major insurance carrier for the city, did not offer policies with such benefits. Segal urged local BCBS board members to bring the issue up for a vote, which they successfully did shortly thereafter, setting in motion the marketing of domestic-partner-inclusive insurance policies by BCBS affiliates across the nation.

PGN also printed a "ticking clock" on its front page, reminding Rendell of his promise to the community. The clock wasn't removed until the final order was signed.

As the publication's reputation among politicos grew, candidates from both major parties began approaching *PGN* to help them get their message out to the LGBT community. Now, *PGN* carries interviews with both Democratic and Republican candidates each election cycle. Many politicians also purchase ads in the paper.

The paper's political presence has also extended to the national scene, as *PGN* has interviewed numerous members of Congress, as well as former presidential candidate Hillary Clinton and, after some pressure, then-candidate for president Barack Obama.

PGN ran one of its most unusual—and controversial—front pages in its April 4, 2008, edition. Next to an interview with then-candidate Clinton, *PGN* featured a large blank space, signifying Obama's failure to grant an interview with *PGN* or any other local-level LGBT media outlet.

Obama did consent to an interview with *PGN* following his primary win—and later autographed the April 4 issue.

As *PGN* worked for its political coverage to be considered on a level playing field with mainstream outlets, it also fought for inclusion in the associations that represented those publications. The Pennsylvania Newspaper Association initially did not take well to the concept of a professional LGBT newspaper, rejecting *PGN*'s membership application for 15 consecutive years. After a coordinated effort by a number of mainstream publications across the state, PNA eventually admitted *PGN* in the mid-1990s. Segal later sat on the group's board of directors. Likewise, the Suburban Newspapers of America denied *PGN*'s membership request for many years but has since both accepted and recognized the paper and its work.

To date, *PGN* has received awards from the Pennsylvania Newspaper Association, the Society of Professional Journalists, the Suburban Newspaper Association (now the Local Media Association) and the National Newspaper Association, among several others.

Just as *PGN* felt entitled to the same access to journalistic circles as mainstream publications, it also approached advertising with a mind toward equality.

"We decided it was important that if companies wanted our money, they needed to start promoting themselves to the gay community," Segal said. "Gay people spend money everywhere, so we went after every account we could in the city of Philadelphia. If you were advertising in the *Inquirer* or *Philly* magazine, why not in the gay press as well? We were not asking, we were demanding."

Many LGBT publications rely primarily on LGBT advertisers, but *PGN* worked to expand its advertising base to include national accounts such as banks, alcohol companies and nonprofits. Nutritional retailer GNC was one of its earliest and most consistent national advertisers, Segal said.

Staying afloat in the challenging economy—especially with the gradual decline in print media—has been an obstacle that *PGN*, like most newspapers, has faced. In its early days, *PGN* relied on the income from its vending boxes, as the paper was sold for 50, and later 75, cents. Office manager Pignolet recalled staffers scouring for quarters from the boxes to pay the company's bills each month. The paper stopped charging in the early 1990s, as its advertising base solidified.

For the first several decades of publication, *PGN*'s classified advertising did a booming business, particularly the personals section. However, LGBT persons found new methods of meeting one another with the advent of the Internet and social-media outlets, and that section has since become near-extinct.

Being both proactive and prepared for such changes is something that has helped *PGN* to thrive, Segal said. The company launched its website in 1995 and has continued to refine it—and the new advertising possibilities it offers—on a regular basis.

"One of the reasons *PGN* is a living, breathing entity is because we were willing to change," Segal said. "We were willing to learn and grow and try new things as times change. In the recession, we had to look at who stopped advertising and who still needs to advertise. We've always watched our bottom line and made sure we know not just where our money is coming from today or tomorrow, but where it will be coming from next year."

When the recession hit in 2008, Segal said *PGN* did not lay off any employees—a testament to the company's adherence to a structured and smart business plan.

"All of our bills are paid, the taxes are up-to-date, everyone's being paid and we have health insurance for our employees," Segal said. "This is run as a business. We're a business with a strong passion for our community, but we always operate as a business."

Having a staff invested in the mission of the organization is equally important. *PGN*'s 14 staff members effectively work both independently and as a team to produce a quality paper each week, Segal said.

"You have to have a dedicated staff that you really care about. We have good people who have a passion for this work, and everyone knows their job," he said. "To realize we're on the cutting edge of the movement and we can help to make history and change in this society is one of the greatest gifts that I have as publisher. And to share that joy with the staff is the best part of my day."

Philadelphia Gay News' first issue, January 3, 1976.

Philadelphia Gay News,
January 19, 1984.

Philadelphia Gay News,
October 25, 1985.

Philadelphia Gay News, January 24, 1986.

Philadelphia Gay News, November 4, 1988.

Philadelphia Gay News, June 19, 1992.

Philadelphia Gay News, June 23, 2006.

32

Looking Back on 35 Years as a *Blade* Reporter

By Lou Chibbaro, Jr.

The *Washington Blade* and its online companion provide news and feature stories about the LGBT community to readers in the District of Columbia metropolitan area as well as to readers across the nation and throughout the world.

But in 1969, when a handful of D.C. activists founded a publication called *The Gay Blade*, the concept of the Internet would have seemed like science fiction.

"We used mimeograph machines," said Lilli Vincenz, a lesbian activist who was among a small group of lesbians and gay men who launched the *Blade*'s first edition in October 1969.

All were current or former members of the Mattachine Society of Washington, the city's first gay-rights group, which was principally founded by gay movement leader Frank Kameny.

Vincenz and former Mattachine Society member Nancy Tucker, who became the *Blade*'s first editor, recalled that the idea of starting a gay publication emerged in a meeting at Vincenz's home in Arlington, Virginia.

Vincenz said she and other people attending the meeting wanted to broaden the group's reach beyond its regular members and keep what was then a mostly closeted gay community informed of new developments that might have an impact on people's lives—socially as well as in the realm of current events.

Kameny said he welcomed the idea of creating a news publication, but reminded the committee members that Mattachine Society policies required that the group's board have authority to approve the publication's content.

"So they decided to do it on their own," Kameny said. "And that was fine with me."

The decision to create the *Blade* as an independent entity rather than make it an arm of the Mattachine Society of Washington set a precedent that the *Blade* has followed to this day.

Its successive editors and publishers have held that the newspaper could best serve the community as an independent watchdog of the LGBT movement while providing in-depth reporting on gay-related developments in government, politics and society.

"The *Blade*'s independence ensures our ability to cover the community and the larger movement in a critical and objective way," said *Blade* Editor Kevin Naff, who started as managing editor in 2002 and took over as editor in 2006.

The first monthly issue of *The Gay Blade* in October 1969 consisted of a single letter-size sheet and included 12 brief stories or announcements. One was about a Mattachine Society– sponsored blood drive. Another reported on an unidentified man's attempt to blackmail gays in the Dupont Circle area.

The *Blade*'s current publisher, Lynne Brown, arranged for a poster-size reproduction of that first issue to be displayed prominently in the lobby of the *Blade*'s offices.

The first issue was assembled in the basement of the home of two gay men in the city's Woodley Park section near Connecticut Avenue, N.W., according to Tucker and Kameny.

Tucker said that a few months later the "publishing" operation of the *Blade* moved into her apartment in Arlington. Over the next four years, the paper's headquarters followed her to another home in Arlington before moving into a basement apartment she rented in Kameny's house on Cathedral Avenue, N.W., in the Palisades area of Washington.

By 1973, with Tucker listed in the staff box as "Editor & Publisher," *The Gay Blade* had expanded to multiple pages and changed to a format of a letter-size page folded in half and produced through offset printing. A growing number of ads from gay bars and local gay-friendly businesses helped cover the cost of printing and distributing the paper to local gay establishments.

In what she viewed as a major technological breakthrough, Tucker said she obtained the latest version of an IBM electric typewriter (the Selectric) with interchangeable ball-shaped print heads containing different fonts, which enabled her to more easily type the pages before the paper was sent to the printer.

"I was doing all the writing and all the layout," said Tucker, who at the time worked as a writer and editorial assistant for trade associations, and later for the *Army Times* newspaper.

In the summer of 1973, Tucker determined that producing the *Blade* was becoming too much for one person to handle while maintaining a separate, full-time job. She put out an announcement in the paper calling for a series of meetings to recruit others to take on the duties of operating the *Blade*.

Beginning with its fourth-anniversary issue in October 1973, which bore a front-page headline "Changing of the Guard," a succession of rotating editors and volunteer writers produced the *Blade* through 1974. Later that year, Joseph Crislip, who used the pseudonym Chris Deforrest, emerged as the paper's editor.

During that period of transition, the *Blade* changed to a newsprint, tabloid format. In September 1975, the paper's name changed from *The Gay Blade* to *The Blade* after Crislip and its new crop of volunteers created a nonprofit corporation to serve as the paper's owner.

The following month, the paper published an article explaining that the name change came about after learning that another publication, one based in New York, already owned legal rights to the name *The Gay Blade*. Crislip also attempted to make clear that *The Blade* in D.C. was not seeking to become a "closeted" gay newspaper, even though social pressures at the time forced him and some writers to use pseudonyms.

Crislip, for example, worked for the Defense Department and felt it would harm his career if he were publicly associated with a gay newspaper.

From Volunteer to Mainstay

My 36-year association with the *Blade* began in July 1976 as a volunteer freelance writer.

I had worked full-time since 1974 as a reporter for a company that published newsletters on environmental, energy and science issues. Its offices were located in the National Press Building, which would decades later come to house the *Blade*.

Like Crislip, I decided that my own job could be jeopardized if I used my real name as a *Blade* reporter. So, in an effort to at least retain my ethnic heritage, I adopted the pen name Lou Romano. The need to do this became even more apparent a short time later, when I started a new job as a public information officer for a national trade association representing municipally owned electric utilities.

As someone who had come to the realization that I was gay just a few years earlier, I grew fascinated by the enormous potential in chronicling a fledgling gay-rights movement. I had an undergraduate degree in political science and was close to completing a graduate journalism program at American University. Up until early 1974, I had almost no contact with the gay community—in Washington or anywhere else.

This quickly changed as I began attending meetings of the Gay Activists Alliance of Washington and became a volunteer reporter and announcer for a local gay radio program called *Friends*, which, at the time, broadcast over Georgetown University's radio station. I looked for another outlet in gay journalism when the university closed the station, forcing *Friends* to temporarily end its weekly broadcasts.

By July 1976, the *Blade* was operating under Crislip's helm in a second-floor office at 1724 20th Street, N.W., near Dupont Circle. Deacon Maccubbin, founder of the city's gay bookstore Lambda Rising, had a lease on the entire building and sublet space to the *Blade*. He operated Lambda Rising and a "head shop" business he owned, called Earthworks, on the first floor.

With that as a backdrop, veteran D.C. gay activist Paul Kuntzler gave me a tip about a development that led to my first *Blade* story. He and a group of other gay Democratic activists hatched a plan to enter the name of a gay person in nomination for president of the United States at the Democratic National Convention set for later that summer in New York.

The objective, Kuntzler said, was to invoke an obscure convention rule that allowed someone's name to be placed in nomination for president after obtaining petition signatures from just 50 convention delegates. Kuntzler said the move would give convention visibility to the topic of gay rights following a decision by party leaders loyal to Jimmy Carter, who had captured the party's presidential nomination at that time, to refuse to include any mention of gays or gay rights in the 1976 Democratic Party platform.

Crislip, who immediately saw the story as a scoop for the *Blade*, placed it on the front page with the banner headline, "Gay to be Nominated at Dem. Convention."

Much to Kuntzler's disappointment, the plan was later vetoed in New York by the convention's only two openly gay delegates: Jean O'Leary, co-executive director of the National Gay and Lesbian Task Force, and Josephine "Jo" Daly, an official with the San Francisco Human Rights Commission. O'Leary and Daly said that Carter operatives asked them to withdraw the plan in order to ensure party unity and to avoid a potential controversy at the convention, with the promise that Carter and his administration would be sympathetic to gay rights.

Crislip's encouragement of that type of "inside politics" reporting was carried forward by Don Michaels, who succeeded Crislip as the *Blade*'s editor in October 1978. That was the same month I cast aside my Lou Romano identity and began writing as Lou Chibbaro Jr.

My decision to do so came one year after a deadly fire at the Cinema Follies, a gay adult movie theater in Southeast D.C., claimed the lives of nine men. Nearly all were closeted gays whose sexual orientation only became known to their families and co-workers when their bodies were identified after being removed from the charred rubble.

In thinking back on the stories I wrote about that fire and its aftermath, still in my role as a *Blade* freelancer, the theme of the "closet" seemed to loom as a forerunner to the tumultuous decade of the 1980s, when AIDS burst onto the scene and often resulted in the outing of closeted gay men.

Under Don Michaels' direction, I became part of a new team of *Blade* writers and assistant editors who scrambled to compete with the straight press, including *The Washington Post*, in covering one of the biggest "gay" sex scandals to hit the nation's capital in years.

Shortly before AIDS became one of the *Blade*'s leading stories of the '80s, a gay sex scandal broke out in Washington in the midst of the 1980 presidential election campaign.

Republican U.S. Representative Robert Bauman of Maryland, a staunch conservative known for berating Democrats on the House floor, was arrested for allegedly soliciting a 16-year-old male prostitute for sex at a D.C. gay bar that featured male strippers.

But what started out as a story about Bauman's political unraveling evolved over the next two years into a string of stories in mainstream media—mostly on TV—about widespread police and FBI investigations into various aspects of Washington's gay community. Most of these stories focused on allegations that appeared to become more sensational and fantastic with each passing week.

In a recurring pattern of law-enforcement–agency leaks to the straight press, news surfaced about alleged attempts by Soviet KGB agents to obtain client lists of gay-male escort services for the purpose of blackmailing high-level U.S. government officials and U.S. military members.

Local TV stations began to show silhouetted images of unnamed male prostitutes claiming to have served as paid FBI informants, hired to infiltrate gay bars to monitor alleged illegal activity such as prostitution rings, along with reports of supposed visits to gay bars by foreign intelligence agents.

While the Bauman caper began under the Carter administration, the full brunt of subsequent FBI and D.C. police investigations into gay bars and clubs emerged under the administration of President Ronald Reagan and its newly installed prosecutors at the U.S. attorney's offices in D.C. and Northern Virginia.

Was this a temporary blip triggered by a one-time investigation? Or were we headed back to the dark days of the 1950s, when police and federal investigators regularly monitored gay clubs and ensnared gay federal workers in anti-gay witch hunts? We doubted the latter was occurring, but after interviewing local gay activists, including veteran activist Frank Kameny, we decided to redouble efforts and gather more information.

In an effort to find out more about what was going on, the *Blade* joined forces in the spring of 1982 with *The Advocate* and the *New York Native*, New York City's main gay newspaper at the time, to undertake what appeared to be the first joint investigative reporting endeavor by the gay press.

Our work led to the publication of a *Blade* issue on August 6, 1982, that was dedicated almost entirely to the findings of the investigation. The main, front-page headline read, "Faceless accusers, reckless charges," followed by "Special Report: The Gay Community Under Attack."

The investigation found that many of the allegations reported in the mainstream media gave the false impression that gay clubs were targets of foreign spies and havens for prostitution. When questioned, law-enforcement officials, including a spokesperson for the FBI, insisted they were not targeting the gay community or gay bars. Their investigations, the officials said, were limited to specific allegations of illegal activity.

"Although the evidence is not conclusive, we at the *Blade* do not believe there is a witch hunt going on at this point," said a front-page editorial summarizing the findings.

"What we believe is at work is the convergence of a legitimate law enforcement investigation and the institutional homophobia that still pervades much of American society, including the federal government, law enforcement agencies, and the media."

At the time we launched our investigation, I had covered the gay-bar and police beat, along with the local and national political beat, for about four years.

However, when the Bauman case broke in the fall of 1980, my experience with the D.C. gay-bar scene had been limited to just a few of the larger dance clubs. I had little or no contact with the gay strip clubs located near a section of the downtown business district that, at the time, also served as the city's "red light" district for both gays and straights.

With the mainstream press publishing information leaked by law-enforcement agencies about Bauman's clandestine visits to gay hustler hangouts and strip clubs, we were initially shut out from those sources. And the FBI and the U.S. attorney's office, along with D.C. police, would only provide the *Blade* with their standard line of "no comment" on a pending case.

That meant our only way of obtaining more information on the case at that time was to go to the bars and clubs and retrace Bauman's steps, with the aim of talking to people who had contact with him.

My initial attempts at doing this proved more difficult than I expected. I first visited the Naples Café, a notorious gay hustler bar along the 1200 block of New York Avenue, N.W. The bar was located next to the old Trailways bus station and in the same building as the Terminal Inn, a seedy hotel that specialized in renting rooms by the hour.

I'll never forget the reaction I received when I walked through the front door of the Naples Café, notebook in hand, and began asking customers and a bartender about the Bauman case.

"I'm a reporter with *The Washington Blade*, the gay newspaper," I said. "I'm hoping to get some information about the Bauman case. Have you seen him here recently?" (In 1980, *The Blade* had changed to *The Washington Blade*.)

The first few men I approached responded with dead silence. They looked at me as if I were from another planet.

"I don't know anything about it," one man told me. Another man said, "That's not something people in here are interested in talking about."

I quickly got the message. This wasn't a subject that patrons of the bar were willing to discuss with a total stranger, even if he was a reporter with a gay paper. And I could understand their feelings, especially since the Bauman scandal was being reported widely in the mainstream press, and TV cameras were appearing outside some of the gay establishments Bauman reportedly had patronized.

The next day, I talked to Michaels and Steve Martz at the *Blade* to develop another plan of action to tackle this story. We would try calling everyone we knew in the gay community who patronized the clubs and bars. We would ask them to put us in touch with people they knew who, in turn, hung out or knew people who hung out at the bars Bauman patronized. And we would promise to keep people's names confidential to encourage them to talk to us.

This approach worked quite well. Within a short time, I had access to a growing network of people who knew all the ins and outs of the clubs in question. Some had seen Bauman at these clubs, although they didn't realize who he was until the scandal broke.

This network of sources would be especially helpful in our 1982 investigation into law-enforcement probes into some of those same gay establishments.

Bauman lost his re-election bid in November 1980, ending his political career. He later came out as gay and wrote a book about his personal struggle regarding his sexual orientation.

Unlike other politicians who have denied being gay or bisexual following a scandal or an outing, Bauman became involved in gay Republican circles and emerged as a gay-rights advocate. He currently lives in Fort Lauderdale.

Murder Mysteries

Flash-forward to 2009: President Barack Obama made history when he signed legislation authorizing the federal government to investigate and prosecute perpetrators of violent hate crimes that target victims because of their sexual orientation, gender, gender identity or disability.

The legislation bears the name of African-American victim James Byrd and white gay University of Wyoming student Matthew Shepard, whose 1998 murder became one of the nation's most widely reported hate crimes.

A 1994 *Washington Blade* investigation into the murders of 25 gay men in the D.C. metro area over a five-year period found, in retrospect, that many of the slayings had similarities to the Shepard case, although none were officially listed as hate crimes.

At the time of the *Blade* investigation, police had made arrests in only seven of the 25 cases. In subsequent editions of the *Blade*, no reports can be found to show that arrests were ever made in the other 18 cases.

As in the Shepard case, nearly all the 25 gay male victims studied in the *Blade* investigation were believed to have met their attackers at bars—usually gay bars. Investigators believe the killers in most of the D.C.-area cases tricked their victims into thinking they were interested in having a sexual encounter, with the intent of luring the victim to a place where they could rob or murder him.

There were no gay bars in Laramie, Wyoming, when Matthew Shepard was killed. Evidence that surfaced in the Shepard case shows that the two men charged with his murder—Aaron McKinney and Russell Henderson—befriended Shepard in a mainstream bar in Laramie and offered to drive him home.

McKinney's and Henderson's girlfriends later told police the two young men confided in them that they targeted Shepard for a robbery and plotted to give him the impression they were gay as a means of luring him out of the bar.

Instead of driving him home, they drove him to a remote field and tied him to a wooden rail fence, where McKinney struck him in the head multiple times with the barrel of a large pistol, inflicting devastating facial and brain injuries that led to Shepard's death.

While the Shepard murder took place in a remote field rather than in Shepard's Laramie apartment, the multiple head wounds he suffered were similar to those in 16 of the 25 gay murders reviewed in the *Blade* investigation. Police said the victims suffered multiple wounds in what they described as a pattern known as "overkill."

Some of the victims in the D.C. cases were struck in the head with heavy objects numerous times, as in Shepard's case, while others sustained several knife or gunshot wounds. Five of the 25 victims who were not subjected to multiple wounds died by strangulation, police reports showed.

Regardless of whether the victims were subjected to the "overkill" phenomenon, police records showed that all but one of the 25 cases involved discovery of the victim's body inside his home with no signs of a forced entry, leading investigators to conclude that the victims invited their killers inside.

The 25 cases reviewed by the *Blade* were typical of gay "pickup" murders that have occurred in the D.C. area and other parts of the country before and after the 1989–94 period reported in the May 20, 1994, edition of the *Blade* in an article titled "Murder Comes Knocking."

Coordinated by then–*Blade* Editor Lisa Keen, the paper's full news and features staff of 10 people spent more than a month working on the story. The project involved interviews with homicide investigators from D.C.'s Metropolitan Police Department as well as police departments in the surrounding Maryland and Virginia suburbs.

One of the surprising findings was that detectives from most of the jurisdictions in which we interviewed were unaware that gay-related murders very similar to the ones they were working on had occurred in a neighboring locality. Upon being told of the neighboring cases, the investigators said they would immediately contact their colleagues from the other jurisdictions to compare notes.

Virtually all the law-enforcement officials interviewed said they could find no evidence to suggest that a single serial killer was responsible for some or all of the murders. Instead, they said the available evidence suggested that individual perpetrators were responsible for the killings and that the cases were unrelated to one another.

Among other things, the law-enforcement officials said serial killers tend to use the same method or weapon to murder their victims and would not likely switch among knife, gun, blunt object and strangulation as a modus operandi.

Assuming that the law-enforcement assessment is correct, at least 18 murderers of gay men remained at large in the D.C. area for years after the 1989–94 murders occurred. Since as many as two dozen additional gay pickup murders, nearly all unsolved, took place in the years immediately before and after the period studied in the *Blade* investigation, far more than 18 perpetrators of gay-related murders would remain at large today.

Some outside experts interviewed for the *Blade*'s 1994 report, including an FBI specialist in serial murders, said at least some of the 25 cases could be linked to one perpetrator. An official with the FBI's National Center for the Analysis of Violent Crime said some serial killers use different weapons to carry out their murders.

A key question then and now is whether these murders should be considered anti-gay hate crimes. If so, the number of anti-gay hate crimes would swell to a level far greater than what official law-enforcement statistics currently show.

Sharon Stapel, executive director of the New York Anti-Violence Project, which monitors anti-LGBT hate crimes, and Chris Farris, co-chair of the D.C. group Gays and Lesbians Opposing Violence, each said the gay pickup murders have elements of hate violence.

The two said that although the perpetrators in many of these murders were targeting gay men in what police call a crime of opportunity, the underlying motive clearly was based on antipathy toward gays.

"We think they view gay men, at least in some instances, as an easy target because they perceive them as weak and vulnerable," Farris said.

Farris and Stapel said that while robbery may be one of the motives of a pickup murder, the recurring pattern of "overkill" leads them to believe that an element of hate is also present.

"We have seen that pattern for years," Stapel said. "The method of meeting has evolved from the bars to the Internet. But the motive seems to be the same."

"We think these should be considered hate crimes, even though it's unclear whether existing state hate-crimes laws could cover these cases," she said.

The *Blade*'s coverage of gay pickup murders in recent years shows that their numbers have dropped sharply since the early 2000s. Some activists, such as Farris, think the drop could be due to the Internet's role in facilitating sexual trysts, although that tactic comes with its own set of stranger-danger problems.

Bankruptcy and Rebirth

As a newspaper based in the nation's capital, the *Blade* has sought to cover the "gay angle" to national politics, including the White House and Congress, since I began writing for the paper in the mid-to-late 1970s. It was often a struggle, though, to gain access to government sources and White House spokespersons during the presidential years of Carter, Reagan and George Herbert Walker Bush.

Although other *Blade* reporters and I have had official press credentials to cover Congress since the late 1970s, White House access remained limited until the election of Bill Clinton. Clinton was the first major-party U.S. presidential candidate to aggressively court the gay vote, in his 1992 election campaign.

When Clinton entered the White House in January 1993, the *Blade*'s access to a presidential administration increased dramatically. For one thing, an unprecedented number of openly LGBT appointees to high-level positions in the administration, including positions at the White House, opened up a plethora of sources willing to talk to the *Blade*.

After years of trying to get my calls returned in previous administrations, I was taken aback when Clinton press secretary Mike McCurry told me at a White House reception for the press that the president saw one of my stories and liked it.

Clinton, like Obama as of this writing, never called on me or another *Blade* reporter to field a question at a White House news conference. But the Clinton administration clearly ushered in the full recognition of the *Blade* as a part of the White House press corps.

The administration of President George W. Bush had far fewer LGBT appointees. Yet the Bush White House during its first two years in 2001 and 2002 appeared interested in responding to my questions at White House press briefings by Bush's Press Secretary Ari Fleischer. And many Bush administration officials had cordial relations with the national gay GOP group Log Cabin Republicans.

All of that changed as the Bush White House geared up for Bush's 2004 re-election campaign, when White House political strategist Karl Rove and others distanced the president from his conciliatory statements about gays in the 2000 election campaign. I attended a Bush news conference at the White House in which he announced his strong support for a federal constitutional amendment to ban same-sex marriage.

From that point on, it became difficult if not impossible for me to reach White House press sources for comment. Scott McClellan, Fleischer's successor as Bush's press secretary, rarely if ever called on me to take my question at the White House press briefings.

The start of the Bush administration in 2001 also came at a time of big change for the *Blade*. Shortly after announcing plans to retire, *Blade* Publisher Don Michaels disclosed to the staff that year that he had arranged for the sale of the *Blade* to Window Media, a gay-owned company that was emerging as the nation's first LGBT newspaper chain.

In a staff meeting at the *Blade*'s offices on U Street, N.W., Window's co-owners William Waybourn and Chris Crain said their goal was to strengthen each of the papers they planned to acquire, including the *Blade*, by consolidating resources and utilizing reporters for papers in different cities to increase the ability to cover LGBT news for all the papers.

The management style of Waybourn and Crain was different from that of Michaels, but the

Blade appeared on the surface to continue the role for which it became known under Michaels—the newspaper of record for the LGBT community. However, behind the scenes and unknown to me and fellow reporters, Window and an investment company named Avalon Equity Fund, which acquired a controlling interest in Window, became saddled with enormous debt.

We learned of the seriousness of the debt problem in 2008, when news came that Avalon had defaulted on a series of loans from the U.S. Small Business Administration exceeding $38 million. The default prompted the SBA to obtain a court order placing Avalon into receivership, with the SBA acquiring control of its affairs. In an ironic twist, the development essentially placed the federal government in control of Window Media and all its newspapers, including the *Blade*. (Over time, the Window Media group of papers also included *Southern Voice, South Florida Blade, New York Blade, Houston Voice, David Atlanta, Eclipse, 411 Magazine* and *Genre*.)

Federal authorities did not seek to interfere with the *Blade*'s daily operation, but they informed then–*Blade* Publisher Lynne Brown, who worked for Window, that the SBA would seek to sell the *Blade* and other Window papers to offset some of Window's and Avalon's debt.

As most *Blade* readers know, it didn't work out that way. On November 16, 2009, Window Media's last two remaining corporate officers showed up in the morning at the *Blade*'s offices at the National Press Building to deliver news that would change our lives. Window had filed for Chapter 7 bankruptcy and was shutting down all its newspapers, including the *Blade*.

We had until 3 p.m. that day to clean out our desks and leave the premises, which would be shuttered until the bankruptcy court took further action. In a development hard to comprehend, the *Blade*'s long-standing role as the LGBT newspaper of the nation's capital was coming to an end just one month after its 40th anniversary.

I'll never forget how that fateful day marked both the end of the *Blade* and the beginning of a new, soon to be resurrected *Blade*. Under the direction of Publisher Brown and Editor Kevin Naff, the staff met in a coffee shop in the National Press Building the following day to map out plans for starting a new publication.

Since the *Blade*'s name was under the control of the bankruptcy court, we launched *DC Agenda*, which became known as the LGBT newspaper operated by the former *Blade* employees.

Meanwhile, in an unexpected turn of events, the dissolution of Window Media through its bankruptcy wiped out its enormous debt to creditors, clearing the way for Brown, Naff and Advertising Director Brian Pitts to form a new company that purchased the *Blade*'s name and remaining assets from the bankruptcy court debt-free.

In April 2010, the new company—Brown Naff Pitts Omnimedia Inc.—renamed the *DC Agenda* as the *Washington Blade*, ushering in a new phase of the *Blade*'s role as an LGBT community newspaper, national newspaper of record, and growing website with a renewed focus on social media and other means of digital transmission.

The *Blade* Through the Years

The *Washington Blade* began in 1969 as a one-page, monthly newsletter compiled by volunteers and based in an activist's apartment. It now has 20 full-time employees and is located in the National Press Building, just blocks from the White House.

1960s

October 1969: Nancy Tucker, Art Stone and a handful of activists publish the first issue of *The Gay Blade*. The newsletter, which is published monthly, consists of one side of a letter-size page, printed on a mimeograph machine in Tucker's apartment. The 500 copies are distributed to the city's gay bars.

1970s

July 1973: Its original editor, Nancy Tucker, leaves the *Blade*, calling for interested parties to take over the newsletter. That call is answered by Pat Price, who goes by the pseudonym Pat Kolar. It is also the first time in the *Blade*'s history that stories contain bylines, although nearly all of them are pseudonyms. • **July 1974:** After undergoing several size changes, *The Gay Blade* is printed on newsprint for the first time. It uses a format that is slightly larger than tabloid size, but by November 1974 the paper is reduced to the standard tabloid format that is still used today. • **November 1974:** *The Gay Blade* moves into its first offices, located on 20th Street, N.W., in Dupont Circle. • **November 1975:** *The Gay Blade* officially changes its name to *The Blade*, and the newspaper also becomes a nonprofit corporation under the name Blade Communications Inc. • **August 1976:** *The Blade* moves to a two-room suite on the 2400 block of Pennsylvania Avenue, N.W. • **October 1978:** Don Michaels becomes top editor and, essentially, publisher, a position he would retain until 2001. • **November 1978:** *The Blade* changes from being published monthly to biweekly, signifying the growth of D.C.'s gay readership.

1980s

February 1980: *The Blade* leaves its offices on Pennsylvania Avenue and moves to 930 F Street, N.W., above what would later become the 9:30 Club. • **October 1980:** *The Blade* reincorporates as a for-profit, employee-owned business and changes its name officially to *The Washington Blade*. • **January 1983:** *The Washington Blade* begins publishing weekly. • **November 1983:** Lisa Keen becomes top editor, a position she will retain until 2001. • **October 1984:** In celebration of its 15th anniversary, the *Blade* presents D.C.'s first gay film festival, staged at the Biograph Theatre in Georgetown. • **January 1987:** The *Blade* starts the year with a new office, located in the Victor Building at 724 Ninth Street, N.W.

1990s

September 1992: The *Blade* moves again, this time to 1408 U Street, N.W. • **April 1993:** To coincide with the 1993 March on Washington, the *Blade* publishes its largest issue to date, containing 216 pages. • **September 1995:** The *Blade* launches its website. • **October 1997:** *The Washington Blade* launches a sister paper in New York City, the *New York Blade News.*

2000s

May 2001: The *Blade* is purchased by Window Media, a gay-owned media company that also owns the *Southern Voice* newspaper in Atlanta. Chris Crain, a co-founder of Window Media, becomes the *Washington Blade*'s executive editor and William Waybourn its publisher. • **September 2006:** Crain leaves the *Blade*. He is succeeded by Kevin Naff, who will remain the paper's editor as of 2012. • **December 2007:** Lynne Brown is named publisher. • **February 2008:** The *Blade* relocates from U Street to the National Press Building at 14th and F streets, N.W. • **November 2009:** *Blade* parent company Window Media files for Chapter 7 bankruptcy liquidation; four days later the staff sticks together and launches a new publication called *DC Agenda*. The staff never misses a week of print publication despite the bankruptcy.

2010s

February 2010: *DC Agenda* Publisher Lynne Brown, Editor Kevin Naff and sales executive Brian Pitts purchase the *Blade*'s assets from the bankruptcy court and form a new company, Brown Naff Pitts Omnimedia Inc. • **April 2010:** Brown Naff Pitts Omnimedia re-launches the *Washington Blade* brand, which is later celebrated in a *Wall Street Journal* story. The paper opens new offices in D.C.'s thriving 14th Street Corridor. • **June 2011:** *Blade* reporter Lou Chibbaro Jr. is inducted into the Society of Professional Journalists–D.C. Chapter Hall of Fame, joining luminaries such as Bob Woodward; he is the only openly LGBT press journalist to be included in the Hall. • **May 2011:** The *Blade* hires its first-ever digital initiatives manager to focus on social-media outreach; by early 2012, the paper will have more than 10,000 Facebook fans and nearly as many Twitter followers. • **January 2012**: Brown Naff Pitts launches a new business venture, Azer Creative, a boutique advertising and marketing firm, and lands its first high-profile client, the official 2012 *Capital Pride Guide*.

The Gay Blade

October 1969   Vol. 1, No. 1
An Independent Publication Serving the Gay Community

BLOOD DRIVE LAUNCHED

The need for blood is crucial. Do help! Members and supporters of Mattachine are participating in a Red Cross blood donor program.

Give blood in the name of Mattachine (this is kept confidential). You will help the homophile movement and will make yourself, your immediate relatives and dependents (even if not related!) eligible for free blood for one year.

Join other gays in their first group donation. We'll meet in the main lobby of the Red Cross building at E St. between 20th and 21st NW between 5 and 6 pm on Mon., Oct. 13. Gay Is Good buttons will be given to all who participate.

The Homosexual Research Assn., Suite 5, 1350 N. Highland Ave., Los Angeles 90028 is advertising their porno at reduced rates. Don't buy! Models in movies and pictures are covered head to toe in black leotards.

Warning to Du Pont Circle people! Cars seen too frequently in the Circle area are having their license numbers taken down; their owners later are being harassed and blackmailed.

Is the gov't running a security check on you? Being blackmailed? Need draft counseling? Call Franklin Kameny, president of the Mattachine Society of Washington at 363-3881 for help on these and other legal complications of being gay.

New to DC bookstores will be The Same Sex, published by the United Church of Christ and containing literate articles by and about homosexuals. Should be available the third week in Oct.

Discussion group on "The Homosexual and the Media" will be held in late Oct. Call 931-1272 for details.

Seriously looking for a roommate? Want a gay landlord? Call Gay Blade editors to register with the Blade's roommate referral service. Don't bother if you want to talk dirty. We won't listen. 234-0064 after 5 p.m.

Off-Broadway: "And Puppy Dog's Tails" is an amusing evening. Only one lament: "There's nudity -- but no passion!"

To contact the Gay Blade, call 270-2018 or 931-1272, 6-9 pm.

GAY LIBERATION FRONT

After raids on the Stonewall bar and the usual police harassment, the NYC gay community has formed the Gay Liberation Front. First to feel its influence was the Village Voice. As the result of a picket, the Voice agreed to change its ad policy and allow the word "gay" to be used, thus permitting GLF and other homophile groups to advertise. "Come Out," GLF's house organ, will appear in early Oct.

HOMOPHILE MOVEMENT AND COLLEGES -- Franklin Kameny, DC Mattachine president, spoke at American U's Kay spiritual Center on Oct. 7 at the request of AU and Hillel. Topic was "The Homosexual Dilemma: What Every Heterosexual Should Know."

Also at AU: There's talk about having an all-college gay mixer dance in the DC area, similar to the one held last year at Columbia by its Student Homophile League.

SEE IF YOUR FAVORITE BAR CARRIES THE GAY BLADE. THE NEXT ISSUE WILL TELL YOU WHERE TO GET IT.

The Gay Blade's first issue, October 1969.

Washington Blade, December 24, 2010.

DC Agenda, March 26, 2010.

Washington Blade,
May 11, 2012.

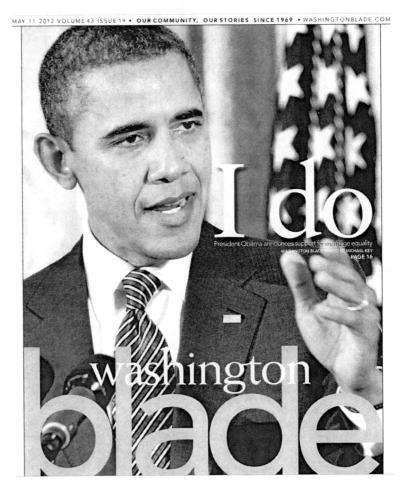

33

Windy City Times

By Tracy Baim

The internecine battles of the gay community are legendary. They are not limited to Chicago, or to any one segment of the community. And the gay media have certainly not been immune to these growing pains of the fledgling modern gay-rights movement.

Chicago's gay media have strong and deep roots. In Chicago, Henry Gerber started what is believed to be the first U.S. gay publication in the 1920s. *Friendship and Freedom* lasted just two issues, thanks to harassment by the postal service and police, but Gerber's work did not go unnoticed. And his courage still inspires Chicago journalists.

In the 1950s, Chuck Renslow and Dom Orejudos started the men's physique magazines *Triumph*, *Mars* and *Rawhide Male*. In the 1960s, the *Mattachine Midwest Newsletter* was a vital source for community news and information, including reports on police harassment, mainstream media bias—and the 1969 Stonewall protests in New York.

Soon more radical gay publications sprang up, including newsletters and tabloid newspapers. Most of the 1970s publications were all-volunteer, but by the end of the decade more business people got involved and tried to professionalize gay media with salaries and to pay for freelance stories, photography and delivery drivers. The local newspapers *Chicago Gay Crusader* and *GayLife* even added newspaper distribution boxes on the streets in the 1970s.

By 1984, *GayLife* and *Gay Chicago* were the two primary gay publications that survived the 1970s publishing startup frenzy. *Gay Chicago* was a magazine, focused mainly on what was happening in the bar and entertainment world. *GayLife* was a serious newspaper with coverage of news locally, nationally and internationally, plus entertainment, sports and features.

But by 1985, *GayLife* was being criticized as part of the old guard, and its publisher, Chuck Renslow, was especially under fire. Renslow was politically active and an owner of multiple businesses—the newspaper, bars and a bathhouse (at a time when AIDS was just beginning to strike hard in Chicago). He led the local Democratic gay organization and had run to become a convention delegate for U.S. Senator Edward M. Kennedy's presidential campaign in 1980. People were concerned that he had unfair influence over the community through the newspaper. I started working for Renslow in June 1984 and never saw a misuse of power, but in our community, perception becomes reality.

Sales manager Bob Bearden and his partner, Jeff McCourt, a part-time writer for the paper (under the pseudonym Mimi O'Shea), were making a move to buy *GayLife* that summer. But instead they went behind Renslow's back and decided to start their own paper, *Windy City Times*. Bearden, McCourt and Drew Badanish, from the art department, all lobbied me intensely to come with them. They each put in $10,000 to start *WCT*. I had been the managing editor of *GayLife* and would keep that post at the new paper. But I was just 22 years old. I didn't have the negative experience to lead me to a decision to abandon ship. After some soul-searching, and trusting in Bearden, I made the difficult decision to be part of the new company.

We launched *Windy City Times* on September 26, 1985. To say we started on a shoestring would be an understatement. While McCourt boasted of making a lot of money as a Chicago Board Options Exchange trader, the truth was that it was just bluster, at least by the time *WCT* started. And Renslow fought against *Windy City Times* for several months in the courts. I was forced to do a deposition and left the lawyer's office in tears. Nothing ever came of the lawsuit, but it was a drain on emotion, time and resources.

We worked out of Jeff and Bob's apartment on Melrose Street just west of Sheridan Road, a third-floor walk-up. There were images of naked guys in the bathroom—blatant sexual images I had to get used to at *GayLife* and at many subsequent gay newspaper offices. We originally did typesetting at a downtown firm, Tangible Type, owned by Chris Cothran and Sarah Craig. (Craig died in 1994; Cothran, in 1996. See Chapter 22.)

After McCourt's passing in 2007, *Chicago* magazine published an article about his death and noted: "Looked at today, the first issue [of *Windy City Times*] seems inadvertently portentous. The front page has three stories, one on Mayor Harold Washington assembling a 15-person committee on gay and lesbian issues—a first for Chicago—and two on a subject that would dominate gay life and politics for the next decade: the AIDS epidemic."

It was a struggle psychologically and emotionally, not to mention physically and financially. While *GayLife* staggered and then folded within a few months after our start, leaving us with no direct competition, it was still not easy trying to do a gay newspaper in 1985. Bob got sick within a few weeks, eventually learning it was AIDS. He became a hermit, and my girlfriend at the time, a nurse's assistant, helped him.

Jeff put pressure on Bob because the paper needed his talents—to sell ads. Bob just could not. He struggled out that Halloween, just four weeks after the paper launched, to take bar photos and work his accounts. But Bob could not deal with his diagnosis. His friends were dying, his partner was pressuring, and a newspaper was being run out of his home. We would be working late hours and hated to be in the way when Bob would shuffle out of his room to the kitchen—where we were pasting up the art boards.

In the spring of 1986 we moved to a separate office at 3225 North Sheffield Avenue, behind Gay Horizons (which now exists in another location as Center on Halsted), in the Rodde Center, the gay community center of that day. Our offices were next to the el train, so we paced our phone calls between those noisy neighbors. By the time Bob died in January 1987, the office dynamics had deteriorated.

Many people stepped up to help—freezing with the typesetting machines, writing articles and helping our reputation in the community. But I felt I was letting them down—Jeff and I were having power struggles. Jeff had no journalism background—he had only written gossip and entertainment prior to starting the paper—and I was very young.

Jeff had promised a hands-off approach to the news side, but he soon realized that was where his community power could come. He started writing editorials, including political ones. He and I came to a difficult decision in the 1987 aldermanic campaign when openly gay Dr. Ron Sable first challenged 44th Ward Alderman Bernie Hansen. Jeff wrote an editorial endorsing Hansen, and I did one for Sable. He started fuming about silly things like photo layouts, while people were not getting paid and didn't have insurance. I, for one, went a six-month stretch with no paycheck.

When an attacker came into the office with a bat one day, he asked for and went after Jeff directly, causing injury to one arm. No one else was hurt, but it was played by Jeff as a hate crime (he even testified in Springfield, Illinois, about the attack as part of a push for gay legislation). There were many ugly rumors, including some about drugs. The police calmed our staff down by hinting that it was not a general attack but probably drug-connected. The truth never came out, but it also made it difficult for all of us. When I left a few months later, one of Jeff's loyal allies even spread a rumor that I had hired a hit man to target Jeff!

With Bob gone, and with Drew Badanish bought out by Jeff, I had decided enough was enough. Not only was the office too stressful, but some of us now worried for our lives as well.

I started looking for investors to buy Jeff out. Jeff had indicated he was burned out and depressed, so it seemed like a good idea at the time. We made an offer through an attorney, but when Jeff found out I was behind the deal, he was furious. Sales Manager Jill Burgin had to step between us for fear something might happen. I wanted to walk out right then, because I was ready to start a new paper, and most of the dozen or so full-time staff were coming with me. But several of the staffers, including reporter Bill Burks, convinced me the right thing to do was stay and put out two more editions of the weekly *Windy City Times*. I agreed, as long as Jeff stayed away from me (we were on separate floors at this point).

After those two weeks, we moved full force into starting *Outlines*, in the *In These Times* office building at 1300 West Belmont Avenue.

As *Chicago* magazine noted in September 2007: "McCourt also enjoyed a good fight. When Tracy Baim left to found her own publication, *Outlines*, five months after Bob Bearden's death, she touched off what will probably go down in history as Chicago's last great newspaper war."

Even though I was the same gender as before, the fact that I was a woman with her name on "top" of the masthead made it easy for Jeff to really play the gender card. He successfully influenced advertisers away from *Outlines*, saying it was "just" a lesbian paper. He said I hated men, even though most of the people who left his employ to start *Outlines* were men. But just as with *GayLife*'s demise, perception is reality. *Outlines* always struggled with the gender issue and advertising. If getting ads in a gay paper was hard in the 1980s and 1990s, getting ads in a paper stereotyped as lesbian was even harder. But our reader statistics always showed a balance of around 60 percent male and 40 percent female. A typical gay newspaper at the time was 90 percent male.

Windy City Times and *Outlines* went head-to-head as weeklies for a few months, but by February 1988 I knew we could not keep up with the bills or get more investment money, so we went to a monthly newspaper format for the next nine years. The *Reader* declared Jeff the victor.

Jeff was really motivated. Albert Williams, who had worked at *GayLife*, was interim editor after I left. The paper was very active in pushing for the city gay-rights bill, taking a strong advocacy approach to the battle.

Jeff soon hired a young gun, Mark Schoofs, as editor, and he took the paper to another level. Mark (who won a Pulitzer Prize for AIDS reporting for *The Village Voice* after he left *WCT*) had a great team of both experienced and newer journalists putting out an award-winning weekly newspaper. Subsequent managing editors kept that pace going. Several times, *WCT* won a Peter Lisagor Award, a prominent Chicago journalism honor. The competition helped both papers, but being a weekly with a stronger economic base had many advantages.

WCT became one of the top gay newspapers in the country. Jeff was especially brilliant at getting mainstream businesses to advertise, which is what helped his paper grow in size. He was very much about size, and proudest of his ever-growing Pride editions of *WCT*. But Jeff also alienated a lot of people and was just as erratic and drug-influenced as he had been when I worked for him. Eventually, those internal demons would catch up to him, but for more than a decade he thrived—on the competition, the journalism and the business.

Jeff also got very involved politically, and *WCT* endorsed candidates at almost every level of office. While I was criticized for working on sports (I was co-vice chair of the Gay Games when they came to Chicago) and business (I founded the Chicago Area Gay and Lesbian Chamber of Commerce), Jeff had his hands in politics and entertainment. He tried to influence elections and lobbying efforts, he produced plays, and he was briefly president of a theater company. Jeff also was part of the National Gay Newspaper Guild to increase the clout of regional gay media. Those moves had their own conflicts of interest, but often publishers (of papers large and small) can't avoid all connections to the community.

Windy City Times also lobbied successfully along with 46th Ward Alderman Helen Shiller for increased AIDS funding under Mayor Richard M. Daley.

Jeff's Chicago Gay and Lesbian Hall of Fame biography states: "While maintaining *Windy City Times* as an independent voice, he embraced advocacy journalism and supported activism aimed at winning mainstream respect and political victories for Chicago's LGBT communities. During the 1986–88 stages of a long campaign to pass a Chicago human rights ordinance that would prohibit sexual-orientation discrimination, the newspaper's offices were known as 'Ordinance Central' because of McCourt's generosity in allowing activists to use space and equipment. The paper's editorials galvanized community and political support for the ordinance after initial defeats."

Mark Schoofs was quoted in *Chicago* magazine after Jeff died: "I wonder if Jeff was one of the last of the spectacularly self-destructive gay men. He was definitely a gay publishing visionary. The gay community was coming into its own in those years, and Jeff was one of the people who recognized that gays were part of mainstream America. He understood that gays were like Jews and blacks and Puerto Ricans and Irish people—another tile in the mosaic of America. He was incredibly flawed to the extent that he himself could not be part of that mainstream. But he was one of the people who made it happen."

Chicago also noted that *WCT* "benefited from the government deregulation of the telecommunications industry in the late 1980s, which, among other inadvertent side effects, spurred the development of the telephone sex industry—the ubiquitous 900 sex numbers of the era. The back pages of many lifestyle publications—including *Windy City Times*—were flooded with full-page come-hither ads for those services." Former *WCT* salesman Steve Alter told *Chicago*: "It was like money that dropped out of the sky. Suddenly what was a $300,000- or $400,000-a-year paper became an $800,000-a-year paper." With the money came a high-flying lifestyle.

Jeff's *WCT* featured award-winning columnists, including Jon-Henri Damski and Achy Obejas, who provided in-depth analysis of politics and the community. (Obejas shared in a Pulitzer Prize after leaving *WCT*.) ACT UP's Danny Sotomayor had been fired by *Gay Chicago*, and soon his controversial editorial cartoons were in *WCT*. But Jeff fired both Jon-Henri and Danny, and both immediately migrated to *Outlines/Nightlines* before they passed away (Danny in 1992 and Jon-Henri in 1997). Jeff suffered many similar losses of talented people; he attracted some of the best but, after a few years, most moved on. This was not a problem *WCT* alone faced; most gay media have a high turnover because journalists are now finally welcomed more into mainstream careers that can offer higher wages and often more respect—thanks in large part to the work of the National Lesbian & Gay Journalists Association.

"If McCourt had no problem attracting top talent, however, retaining it was another story," *Chicago* magazine's 2007 story noted. "Four years seems to have been the limit for most people. Some left for better jobs, but most simply were burned out from dealing with a person who—for all of his intelligence and drive—seemed at times completely oblivious of the impact of his actions on people." And the abuse of drugs only got worse. Steve Alter related Jeff's arrest for cocaine possession, which included a brief stint in Cook County Jail, in a post on the *Reader* website after Jeff died.

Louis Weisberg was editor of *Windy City Times* for five years until he was among those who left to start another competing paper in 1999. He told *Chicago* magazine: "We'd have editorial meetings where Jeff would be sitting there with white powder around his nose, drinking booze out of a bottle with Ryan Idol asleep on the couch. At some point we just knew this wasn't going to work—that this was no way to run a business." Jeff had a relationship with the porn star that was complicated and at times disturbing to Jeff's friends and employees. (Idol's real name was Marc Anthony Donais. In 2012 he was sentenced to 12 years in prison for attempted murder of his ex-girlfriend in 2009.)

Meanwhile, I was always trying something new to keep *Outlines* alive. I never did drugs or drank alcohol, but I was certainly a workaholic. We had started a weekly bar rag called *Nightlines* in 1990, which kept us covering news alongside bar photos (it became *Nightspots* in the early 2000s). Rex Wockner was our full-time reporter for several years; he helped to keep *Outlines* and *Nightlines* on the local journalism map—and he eventually became the most widely syndicated gay media reporter in the world. We had an amazing team of dedicated employees and freelancers, and we, too, won awards for our journalism and work in the community.

We also started *BLACKlines* and *En La Vida,* monthly newspapers for the African-American and Latino LGBT communities; both began in 1995, and they ran about 10 years each. Our website for *Outlines* started in 1996. (Jeff never owned the domain name WindyCityTimes. com, and later we had to fight in an international tribunal to get it back from one of Jeff's former employees.) We were trying to fill different media needs and niches, staying afloat with the generous support of community investors including Nan Schaffer and Scott McCausland. They were our angels in those early years, and Nan and so many others have remained supportive, even as we added Windy City Radio after buying the old LesBiGay Radio.

Windy City Times was a formidable opponent, and the staff kept it going despite both internal and external obstacles. This is why it was a truly unique set of circumstances that led *Outlines*, the much smaller company, to purchase *Windy City Times* in 2000—a David and Goliath story.

Newspaper War, Part 2

By 1997, *Outlines* seemed strong enough to make the change back to a weekly newspaper, so we took the plunge, something which, in retrospect, probably strengthened us for the battles ahead.

In the summer of 1999, Jeff McCourt suffered another walkout, as reported earlier in this chapter, but this time the way it happened (with no notice) somehow hit him so hard that he rebounded all the way back to me—he called me for the first time in 13 years, and we commiserated about the way they left him. I sympathized with him, but never underestimated the road ahead. Jeff was not giving up yet.

The exodus had been planned for a long time. Before they started their *Chicago Free Press*, some of the new venture's investors even met with me at *Outlines*—I, of course, didn't know they were starting a paper, and that they had just been fishing for business information from me, claiming to be interested in buying ads. The *WCT* staff took their last paychecks and left right before finishing the second-most-important edition of the paper (coinciding with Northalsted Market Days). Some staff remained, but the company was in deep trouble.

Jeff was left far more vulnerable after this staff defection than when I left, for a few reasons. First, when I had started *Outlines*, I did not have the type of deep pockets supporting us as the new *CFP* had. I was able to get friends and community members to buy shares in my company, and they trusted me to run it. (Some people believe I am an heiress to a nonexistent Clarence Darrow fortune, which is not true; my mom was a distant relative to Darrow, and my parents were very middle-class. All I received from them in starting *Outlines* was a $1,000 check from my stepdad, Steve Pratt, and my mother's help in typing articles—plus their fantastic emotional and moral support, which I believe is priceless and the most valuable thing they could have given me.)

Second, our original goal had been to buy *Windy City Times*, so starting a new paper was not ideal in 1987. By 1999, when *CFP* started, the gay market was larger and more appealing to mainstream investors and advertisers, which helped *CFP*. Third, Jeff himself was not nearly as strong as he had been in 1987, so he had a difficult time battling the new opponent. Fourth, it couldn't have been easy for him to have suffered a second and more debilitating staff walkout.

Fifth, the employees left Jeff right in the middle of a deadline, which meant Jeff could not recover quickly; when we left for *Outlines*, we gave Jeff two weeks' notice and did put out two more painful issues. Sixth, the top people leaving *WCT* for *CFP* were mostly men, and I have to say that this was an advantage in the marketplace. When I left, it was also mostly male staff who came with me (because the staff was mostly male), which meant, of course, that it was mostly men who founded *Outlines*. But with me "on top" and a few other strong women in positions of authority, we were stereotyped from the start by Jeff. *CFP* did not have that strike against them. Seventh, I was only 24 when I left to start *Outlines* and did not have as much experience; most of those who left to start *CFP* were much older and had been around the business far longer.

And finally, while Jeff did continue to publish for another year, he spent huge financial and emotional capital fighting the former staff that had gone to *CFP*. Jeff never sued me or *Outlines*, so his energy and money were not diverted into to such a fight earlier.

Dan Page, former production manager and art director of *Windy City Times*, wrote a scathing rebuke of those who walked out to form *CFP*, in a posting on the *Reader*'s blog after Jeff died in 2007. Dan had worked during the buildup to the walkout and had been privy to some of the plans, but he was not among the defectors. "The timing of the mutiny was planned to CRIPPLE Jeff (in every sense)," Page wrote. "They had hoped to buy the publication at firesale prices, and, if not, to destroy it. ... Jeff was out of town the weekend of the mutiny because two staffers, a couple, who were among the *Free Press* founders, had encouraged him to go to his Michigan summer house. ..."

In fact, Jeff learned about the defection from a reporter: Mike Miner at the *Reader* called him to ask about the mass resignations. "The reason I found myself breaking the bad news to McCourt is that he wasn't supposed to know it yet," Miner wrote in the *Reader* of August 5, 1999.

So, departing staff and freelancers (including Louis Weisberg, Lisa Neff, Jason Smith, Paul Varnell, Lawrence Bommer, Dave Ouano and Jennifer Vanasco) started *Chicago Free Press* and battled McCourt's *Windy City Times* for a year—both in the courts and for advertisers. *Outlines* just chugged along for that year, trying to dodge the bullets and stay away from a circulation and advertising-rate war. But because *Outlines* had gone back to a weekly schedule, it really helped us compete. It also positioned us well for what happened next.

While *WCT* staffers—including Dan Page, Karen Hawkins, Neda Ulaby, Aaron Anderson, Mark Bazant, Tony Peregrin, Gary Barlow and others—worked hard to keep the paper going, the fight drained Jeff so that even when the court case ended, and even though he reportedly won, he had lost the final battle. He was forced to close the paper in August 2000 (the last issue was in July), and I called him immediately to buy it. He agreed, and after a few weeks of negotiations, *Outlines'* parent company, Lambda Publications, purchased just the name of the paper and changed the corporation name to Windy City Media Group. There were no other assets, not even any archives, just a lot of bad will among advertisers, some staff and parts of the community.

We purchased it for around $400,000—the value of the paper's one year of national advertising, the only number that could be proved. He almost changed his mind about the sale—but his lawyers knew better (no one else expressed serious interest, and certainly not for that price), and they walked him through the sale until the final signature was completed. I was able to get new investors, but the rest of the money came from putting my home on the line for a loan from the bank.

Many people said I was crazy, but I do believe had we not purchased the brand of *Windy City Times*, *Outlines* was going to be killed by the competition at *Chicago Free Press*, which had deep pockets and a laser focus on market dominance. As part of the purchase, we also eventually got *WCT*'s seat on the National Gay Newspaper Guild, something that was highly coveted since only one paper per market was allowed membership.

Jeff and I met at my bank on the sale day. He and I sat outside of South Shore Bank, reminiscing about the old days. How hard it was—how it actually never got much easier. About people we had lost, about Bob, about their old three-story walkup apartment on Melrose. It was surreal, acting like old friends, when we had fought tooth-and-nail for 13 years. But sometimes that phrase "the enemy of my enemy is my friend" comes true—Jeff had been so wounded that he actually turned back to me as an ally. Jeff was chain-smoking and looked very frail. He had the shakes and looked far older than he should have. I honestly don't know how he survived another seven years after that day, dying in 2007 at age 51.

The buyout of the *Windy City Times* name was important for *Outlines*, because it gave us a mainstream recognition to face the continual media wars in Chicago. Some in the community did not support us, because they viewed it as helping Jeff get out of debt. But I tried to see the value to the community, and to our business, and in the end it was the right decision.

We merged the two weeklies into one *Windy City Times* in September 2000, and I felt as if I had got my baby back after it had been in foster care.

As for Jeff, his last years were lonely and painful. Mike Miner, in his *Reader* obituary May 7, 2007, wrote: "McCourt had one friend at the end, possibly the only one who knew about his death when it happened. Gregory Munson says he was hired seven years ago by McCourt's sister, Diane, his legal guardian, to be his 'chaperone.' At the time Munson was working for an agency, Always Caring. 'He had gotten mugged when he was staying in the Talbot Hotel,' Munson told me. 'To my understanding, they found him in an alley unconscious and he went into Northwestern Hospital in a coma.' When McCourt was transferred to a nursing home, Munson went to work for him. 'I was originally with him five days a week,' he says. 'As time went by, it dwindled down to two hours once a month. [His sister] said he was broke. He disputed that but he was afraid to go to court to fight. He just hated that he couldn't have more control over his own life.'"

Jeff's brother Dan McCourt said that at the end Jeff had nothing left; and it's true that Jeff got very little from the sale of his paper. He had almost $400,000 in debts (the IRS, his printer and his lawyers), so the sale cleared his name but left him little remaining.

Of course, the battles were not over. *CFP* continued to go after the new *WCT*, and a new rivalry was begun. *CFP* did change ownership in the mid-2000s, and eventually it was closed in May 2010. Meanwhile, *Gay Chicago*, which had been Chicago's oldest surviving gay publication, itself went through internal struggles and closed in September 2011.

The Next Generation

Once the two papers merged, *Windy City Times* continued covering LGBT news, politics, entertainment and more. *Outlines* had a strong team to move to *WCT* and retained some of the *WCT* staffers who had remained, in particular Karen Hawkins as news reporter, Marco Fernandez as sales representative, and Tony Peregrin, Jonathan Abarbanel, Mary Shen Barnidge and other well-known freelancers.

Politics continued to be a strong coverage area, with so many local, county, state and national elections happening almost every year. *Outlines* had had a policy of not endorsing candidates, so now the new *Windy City Times* also stayed away from such endorsements. Instead, the paper gave surveys to candidates in all races and rated them based on their responses. In the 2008 race for president, this proved important, because a 1996 *Outlines* survey for the state Senate, completed at that time by candidate Barack Obama, had shown he was fully supportive of same-sex marriage well before his later races for federal office.

AIDS also continued to be an important story for *WCT* and the community. In 2011, which marked the 30th anniversary of the epidemic's first diagnosed cases, *WCT* started a 13-month series on its impact. The series won a Peter Lisagor Award. It was also a finalist for a national Gay and Lesbian Alliance Against Defamation award, losing to *The Boston Globe*.

Other stories important during that time included the growth in the transgender-rights movement, the alarming increase in reported LGBT youth suicides, the fight to repeal the military's Don't Ask, Don't Tell gay ban, and the ongoing battle for the equal right to marriage.

But sometimes even simple business profiles can have a profound impact. A few years ago, when Chicago's Women & Children First bookstore was struggling, its owners allowed *Windy City Times* to tell their story in a front-page article. The store has been a key player in the Chicago LGBT community since 1979, and we knew our readers would want to know if it was at risk of closing. As soon as the article came out, thousands of dollars in donations poured in, and numerous other media picked up the story. The store is still in business in 2012. *WCT* has also done stories about family members and partners looking for donations to help cover funeral costs for loved ones, and the community steps up each time to help out.

With a team of staff and freelancers, *WCT* covers local, national and international stories that affect the community. Sometimes this is the coming out of the latest celebrity; other times, a violent anti-gay attack. What's important is to keep a balance of news, entertainment and features, representing the full lives of *WCT*'s readership.

Looking Back, Looking Forward

Jeff McCourt died of AIDS complications at age 51 in 2007. Soon after, I nominated him for the Chicago Gay and Lesbian Hall of Fame—he was inducted later that year. Few people are neutral on Jeff's legacy. Even those who left his employ have mixed feelings, about his mood swings, his drug use, his highs and his lows, his manic behavior and passionate loyalty—and his fierce competitiveness.

The bitterness caused by these wrenching gay newspaper schisms still has fallout today, but most of it is very much insider baseball, only relevant to a few folks who care about the why and how of the gay newspaper world.

Of course, if I were to do it over again, I would change many things. I am glad I helped start *Windy City Times*, but I would have gotten more of the deal in writing. Mostly, I would have tried to be a better boss. When I would go sometimes three or four days with no sleep, never going home, I had difficulty trying to run a business and be an editor and reporter all at the same time. Taking photos at a sports league in the morning, at a leather bar at midnight, going back to the office to write an editorial, and then trying to balance the books for payroll—that was just plain difficult. But in truth, I had much help in keeping it all afloat.

There have been many key players at *Windy City Times* and *Outlines* over the years. I hesitate to even start listing them all. And because I separated from *WCT* for 13 years, I did not work closely with many of the key middle-years employees. There were hundreds of people, including delivery drivers, photographers, salespeople, reporters, business staff, editors, interns, and the supportive investors and advisers.

There have also been some key people present from the very first issue of *WCT*, still helping today in some fashion. They include Toni Armstrong Jr., Jorjet Harper and Yvonne Zipter. Many started in the late 1980s and lasted for years, including Rex Wockner, Jonathan Abarbanel and longtime writer Marie J. Kuda. And there were hundreds more, including my partner of 18 years, Jean Albright. Plus key assistant publishers along the way: Pat Bechdolt in the early years, Terri Klinsky these past 17 years. Kirk Williamson as our art director, Andrew Davis as our managing editor and Amy Matheny as our top sales representative have each been with us more than a decade. And there are dozens more who continue to play important roles as we publish a daily online website and two print publications: *Windy City Times* weekly and *Nightspots* biweekly. Our newest reporter, Kate Sosin, is a huge asset, exploring new and vital connections to the community.

There is one iconic picture from the early *Windy City Times* era that features some of the first players at *WCT*, some who soon left to start *Outlines*, and some who stayed on for many years with Jeff. Pictured in that photo, with Jeff and me, were Larry Shell, Ben Dreyer, Bill Burks, M.J. Murphy, Chris Stryker, Hugh Johnson, Steve Alter, Shani, Jorjet Harper, Larry Bommer, Yvonne Zipter, Albert Williams, Chris Cothran, Jill Burgin, Jon-Henri Damski and Mel Wilson. It captures a brief moment in time, and brings back all the good and bad memories that were the glue holding *WCT* together in those formative 1980s.

We have also had to say goodbye to far too many young colleagues, most because of AIDS, some because of cancer and other tragedies: Jeff McCourt, Bob Bearden, Richard Cash, Bob Kraus, Mike Simanowicz, John Schmid, Jon-Henri Damski, Danny Sotomayor, Paul Adams, Joseph Beam, Tony Hassan, Marvin Patterson, Alfredo Gonzalez, Fernando Flores, Sarah Craig, GayBoy Ric, Chris Cothran, Kathleen O'Malley, John Pennycuff, our attorney Mary York, my mom and stepdad, and unfortunately the list goes on.

Next Up

There is a delicate tightrope we continue to walk, as a community-based paper that covers the good, the bad and the mixed of the LGBT movement. That means scandals at health clinics, drug arrests of leaders, domestic violence and financial mismanagement—at the same time promoting benefits and events, activists and organizations.

Windy City Times is also going through transitions similar to those of other gay and mainstream media companies. With more than 30,000 articles and 100,000-plus photos archived online, the website is a key growth area for the company. In 2010 an iPhone application was launched, followed by an iPad edition in 2011. And, of course, we participate in social media, content sharing and other opportunities to build audience.

We were never intimidated by "giving it away" for free online, since our papers were always free. The dilemma is on the revenue side—who pays for all that free content. Our solution is not to charge for online content—very few papers will survive on that model. Rather, we have to find other unique revenue streams, and that includes successful community-based events.

While online expansion is important, the primary strength of the company is still in its weekly print edition and its companion 22-year-old bar guide, *Nightspots*.

As part of an effort to streamline costs, the company went to a "virtual" office in 2008, just two months before the U.S. economy collapsed. This planned move made sense for a company that has most of its reporters and sales representatives in the field every day. It was an efficiency move that has actually strengthened the company to its best position in many years.

Given the closing of so many gay print publications over the past decade, *Windy City Times* is fortunate to still be able to serve the Chicago-area LGBT community. We benefited from an odd mix of luck, good timing, amazing support and wonderful staff. It was a unique blend, but it has worked very well.

Windy City Times' **first issue, September 26, 1985.**

**Windy City Times,
February 20, 1996.**

RIGHT: *Outlines'* **first issue,
June 4, 1987.**

BELOW: *Outlines* **returned to weekly,
September 3, 1997.**

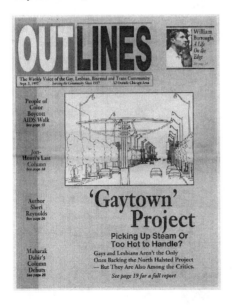

Nightlines, February 16, 1994.

BLACKlines' first issue, February 1996.

BLACKlines, July 1999.

Nightspots, February 15, 2012.

En La Vida's first issue, July 1996.

Clout! Business Report, March 1997. Published by **Outlines**, it lasted a few years.

Windy City Times, February 1, 2012.

Windy City Times, February 15, 2012.

Windy City Times, September 12, 2012.

PART FOUR:

Advertising the News

"News is something someone wants suppressed.
Everything else is just advertising."

— British press magnate Lord Northcliffe

34

Advertising: The Business of Newspapers

By Chuck Colbert

Over the last three decades, Rivendell Media, the nation's leading LGBT media-placement firm, has left its mark, connecting major national advertisers and local gay press. Equally important, Rivendell had a hand in helping LGBT media to organize and become professional journalistic outlets as well as profitable business enterprises.

Rivendell Media was founded in 1979. And yet, Joe DiSabato, its founder and first president, actually started the company years earlier as an entertainment-marketing firm by the name Rivendell Music Marketing. The name Rivendell—land of music—derives from J.R.R. Tolkien's *The Hobbit*.

DiSabato worked for a variety of record labels as a promoter. Among the tours he promoted were those of Elton John and Jefferson Airplane. Working in the field of marketing, DiSabato, a gay man, noticed the budding gay press. He was among the first to realize its potential for advertisers, and in launching his company he labeled the gay marketplace "the most potentially profitable untapped market in this country."

DiSabato's important influence was recognized by the mainstream during the 1990s, in an article on the gay press, when *The Wall Street Journal* covered DiSabato's work in the gay market.

As DiSabato started a process of defining the gay market from an advertiser's perspective, he established agreements with the various LGBT publications. Since Rivendell already had name recognition and had achieved a level of success in the music industry, DiSabato made only a slight change in the firm's name, from Rivendell Music Marketing to Rivendell Marketing.

In tapping into the company's music contacts, DiSabato changed Rivendell's focus forever with its first gay-press media campaign for RCA Records.

The year 1981 brought a first-ever major hard-spirits campaign, with Absolut Vodka leading the way. Absolut is still a client, having placed an ad campaign celebrating 30 years of reaching out to the gay community.

It was under the leadership of Michel Roux, then–president and chief executive officer of Carillon Importers, that Absolut targeted the gay market because of its trend-setting, early-adapter characteristics.

As Todd Evans, who now heads Rivendell Media, told *The New York Times* in 2012, "Absolut set the bar for virtually every company speaking to the LGBT consumer."

Absolut's 1981 ad placements ran with the tag line "Absolut Perfection." A halo hovered over the bottle.

Absolut was only the beginning. By the 1990s, just 19 of the Fortune 500 brands advertised their brands in U.S. gay media. By 2006, that number had risen to 175.

Today, Rivendell Media is a leading authority on the gay and lesbian press in the United States. As a media-placement firm, the company represents local LGBT publications across the country.

Rivendell also has helped to define further the gay market, giving advertisers the metrics they need to make more informed business decisions.

While Rivendell still places ad campaigns for the music industry, the client base has expanded to include a diverse group of advertising categories. They include alcohol and tobacco, airlines and travel, automobiles, beverages, cigarettes and anti-smoking, condoms and lubricants, electronics, entertainment, financial and insurance products, food, restaurants, nutritional products, online services, fitness and personal hygiene, pet products, pharmaceuticals, and phone and cable.

The firm places advertisements in the gay press for every major advertising agency in the U.S. and Canada.

Rivendell has a regular and active client base of nearly 1,200 companies. The firm represents more than 150 local, regional and national publications to advertising agencies.

But three decades ago, bringing the reach of gay media to Madison Avenue was a pioneering endeavor.

"Rivendell was the first to 'professionalize' the idea of gay media going after the ad market for numerous publications," said Mark Segal, publisher and founder of *Philadelphia Gay News*. "No one ever thought of that before."

Undoubtedly, DiSabato's trailblazing nudged the organization, growth and professional development of the LGBT press.

In 1984, Rivendell pulled together the National Gay Newspaper Guild (NGNG), a now-defunct group of the nation's most widely read regional gay publications. The first publications included *Bay Area Reporter* (San Francisco), *Bay Windows* (Boston), *Dallas Voice, Frontiers* (Los Angeles), *Houston Voice, New York Native, Philadelphia Gay News, Washington Blade, The Weekly News* (Miami) and *Windy City Times* (Chicago).

Other publications that joined the guild were *Southern Voice* (Atlanta), *Between The Lines* (Michigan), *Gay & Lesbian Times* (San Diego), and *New York Blade* (replacing the *New York Native*).

The Gay Press Association

Three years prior to NGNG, DiSabato was the driving force behind formation of the Gay Press Association. Rodger Streitmatter's important 1995 book, *Unspeakable: The Rise of the Gay and Lesbian Press in America*, took note of the organization's formation.

"We can no longer afford to be a lot of disconnected publications," DiSabato said then, adding, "We need a way of communicating better, especially given the current political climate." DiSabato was referring to Jerry Falwell and the Moral Majority's efforts to stymie gay-rights progress.

Both *The Advocate* and *The New York Times* covered the new group, noting that the "homosexual press" had increased circulation and garnered "the beginnings of respect from the rest of the journalistic world."

"The biggest step toward organizing" gay publications, wrote Streitmatter, occurred when DiSabato called a three-day series of workshops, in which 80 staff members from gay and lesbian publications participated to discuss advertising, distribution and editorial content. DiSabato was elected president of the Gay Press Association at its 1981 Dallas convention.

The Gay Press Association held its first meeting in New York on January 9–11, 1980. William B. Kelley reported on the convention for Chicago's *GayLife* in an article also picked up in other papers, including *Arizona Gay News*. There were about 80 representatives from almost 50 gay publications. DiSabato organized the convention. New York Mayor Ed Koch proclaimed the week Gay Press Week. During the convention, attendees voted against adding the word "lesbian" to the group's name, and no lesbian publications were represented at the meeting, though they were reportedly invited. There were also no African-American journalists at the initial meeting.

In May 1981 in Dallas, GPA elected the following officers: DiSabato as president, Mark Segal of

Philadelphia Gay News as vice president, Phil Nash of Denver's *Out Front* as secretary, and freelance writer Morgan Pinney as treasurer. More than 60 editors, publishers and others from gay media attended the Dallas event, according to *Arizona Gay News*.

"It was a magical moment in the history of the gay press," DiSabato told Streitmatter during a telephone interview. "Community strength is built on effective communications. We could see that a modern, professional, financially viable gay press could be the glue that would pull the whole country together. We felt a real high."

DiSabato had big ideas, one of which was a national wire service among members of the association to speed up communications and content sharing.

But some association members feared a computerized wire service would be a budget buster, and others questioned DiSabato's motives.

"People were leery about just what Joe had in mind to go across that computer network he wanted so bad," the late journalist and author Randy Shilts told Streitmatter in a telephone interview. For a time, Shilts wrote for *The Advocate*.

"He [DiSabato] was in the advertising business, not the news business. They noted that hidden in the middle of the various goals of the association was the statement: 'To promote a healthy business environment.' Some of us who were aware of the perennial conflict between church and state [advertising and news] weren't so sure Joe's priority was news," said Shilts.

The Advocate refused to join the Gay Press Association, dealing the new group "a major setback," Streitmatter wrote. Making matters worse, *Advocate* Publisher David B. Goodstein took out a full-page ad in *The New York Times* encouraging ad placements in his publication. Goodstein played up the idea of high disposable income among gay men.

The association lasted a few years, but it eventually fizzled in the late 1980s. Meanwhile, NGNG was gaining strength—though, unlike the GPA's inclusion of newspaper staffers as members, it was a limited-membership group of proprietors (and only one paper was allowed per region).

What is so important about organizing LGBT media? Doing so gave them economic clout, enabling placement of national advertising in regional publications.

"There was no way publications like ours could have ever gotten the attention of the New York City–based national advertising center," explained Jan Stevenson, publisher of *Between The Lines*. "Only Rivendell could do that, collectively representing significant numbers of LGBT publications," she said.

"If you want depth of numbers, more depth in the market across the country," said *Windy City Times* Publisher Tracy Baim, "then you have to get it from the regional gay media, including their companion websites."

As *Philadelphia Gay News* Publisher Mark Segal explains, local advertising is the "bread and butter" of LGBT niche publications. National ads are the "cream." And they are "sure nice to have," as most publishers readily acknowledge.

The number of LGBT media outlets in the U.S. has varied over time from a handful to more than 200, according to estimates. By 2009, however, the number dropped below 200.

Still, LGBT niche media reach an estimated 3 million readers. That long and deep reach into the gay market is no small accomplishment when compared with the much smaller readership of national LGBT publications, which is estimated at most to be several hundred thousand.

Historical Context

There were just a few gay publications from the middle 1950s through the late 1960s. The Stonewall rebellion, a spontaneous uprising at a New York City gay bar on June 28, 1969, by patrons against police, accelerated the growth of the modern LGBT civil-rights and liberation movement, and its media.

By the mid-1970s, "there was a feeling that anything could be done," said *PGN*'s Segal. Yet, "many of us believed we needed to have our own community newspapers, forums where we could discuss important issues and get out information. Newsletters from the various organizations that only went to their memberships weren't enough. We needed to reach the entire community, not just the activists, but those people who went to bars and those who were closeted. We wanted our own media. So, in the 1970s, that's when local gay media was founded."

Another reason for gay media was that the mainstream media didn't cover the community. "If they did, it was something horrible," Segal said. Coverage was either pejorative or focused on pathology.

Also keep in mind, said Thomas Horn, publisher of the *Bay Area Reporter*, "there was nothing, no community organizing tool, no communications device." In San Francisco, he explained, "there were various segments of the gay community that were quite large at this point. We had the Imperial Court community and drag queens on one side, the political gays on the other, and the leather community, various communities that had no way to get in touch with each other."

Even before Stonewall, Horn said, "gays were finding themselves in tense situations with local authorities," including police.

The late Bob Ross, *BAR*'s founder, "felt we needed a way to get the word out, to find out what was happening and to let people know what was happening," Horn explained. "Bob could do that through the paper. It was a way to organize and to mobilize the community."

The 1973 founding of the now-defunct *Gay Community News*, which is believed to be the first LGBT weekly newspaper in the country, had a similar effect in Boston.

"[*GCN*] was the end of the information desert, one of the seminal events in our community," said longtime Boston-area community leader Barbara Hoffman. "You can't imagine what it was like to live in the desert with no books, newspapers, magazines, movies, TV and no way to communicate to any numbers of us. Along came *GCN*, and we stopped being invisible. Suddenly, there was information and a way to connect. It was a monumental breakthrough."

Founders of early gay publications approached the enterprise from three primary perspectives—activism, business and journalism. Often, activists wrote about events that they themselves had organized.

"There is tremendous first-person, frontline reporting on the movement. The journalism was usually excellent," said *Windy City Times* Publisher Baim, citing the now-defunct *Chicago Gay Crusader*. Some of the city's early publications, she added, "are treasure troves of information."

The editorial mix differed by locality across the country. Political and gossip columnists as well as letters sections provided robust content, along with hard-news reporting and the coverage of nightlife and entertainment.

But early on, the business side was often a struggle, because advertisers other than bars, bathhouses and escort services were often reluctant to buy display ads.

Classified ads far outpaced display advertising—and they were moneymakers.

Prior to the launch of Craigslist, Manhunt, and Grindr, pages and pages of classifieds in gay media enabled people to connect. "When there was a mechanism to target the gay community through classifieds, that's what made *BAR* take off in terms of revenue," said Horn, the San Francisco paper's publisher.

The community was faced with Anita Bryant's anti-gay campaign in 1977. "Anita Bryant woke up larger portions of the gay community, helping to increase press runs," explained Don Michaels, former publisher of the *Washington Blade*. "Then came AIDS in 1981—a huge boost to the gay press as people turned to it to follow AIDS coverage because the mainstream [media] was kind of slow to get off the ground."

Michaels went on to say that many people initially feared that advertisers would run the other way. The reverse happened. Pharmaceutical ads—and million-dollar revenues—flooded LGBT media. During the early years, alcohol and beer, HIV/AIDS pharmaceutical advertising and phone-sex revenues accounted for the bulk of Rivendell's business.

As late as 1994, phone-sex ads were million-dollar accounts for Rivendell, according to Todd Evans, chief executive officer and president. From the mid-1990s to the present, national advertising increasingly diversified—for example, automotive, entertainment, financial services, travel and tourism categories—as Fortune 500 companies eyed the potentially lucrative gay market.

This new dimension necessitated a more professional sales and editorial endeavor. Robert Moore, publisher of the *Dallas Voice*, recalled his experience from 25 years ago as ad director. "I was very green, a good student, but I needed a good teacher," he said.

"The value with Rivendell is they taught me what was valuable information, what I needed to give to people and how to take a product and turn it into something that would get noticed," Moore said. Rivendell's methodology also applied to the local market. "Many of the issues are the same as national. You still have to know how to talk to people in an intelligent manner."

On the editorial side, "Rivendell made the gay press a more professional business," said Cathy Renna, managing partner of Renna Communications, a public-interest communications firm. The dynamic changed, she went on to explain, from "I'm at a gay paper because I am not really a journalist," doing "advocacy," and "can't get a job in the mainstream," to "I'm now a real journalist," able to work in the mainstream or gay media or both.

Rivendell's success also boosted workplace equality. "You can only run a paper on love, passion and politics for so long," said Bob Witeck, chief executive officer of Witeck Communications, a strategic public-relations and marketing firm. "You have to have a grounding and support of an advertising base" insofar as "commerce has been a big driver for LGBT civil rights. As business gets to know us, employees and their partners have driven the movement toward equality."

Changing Hands

Rivendell founder Joe DiSabato died unexpectedly from an asthma attack on August 20, 1991. He was on the way to a business meeting. His longtime partner in life and business, Michael Gravois, took over the company. Todd Evans purchased Rivendell Marketing on June 1, 1994, and again changed the name: to Rivendell Media, so as to further define the company's focus on media sales. From 1995 to 2001, the company doubled its business each year. In 2009, Rivendell opened an online division.

"It [DiSabato's death] was a real shock," lamented Publisher Susan Horowitz of *Between The Lines*. "Joe never lived long enough to see the outcome" of his pioneering entrepreneurship. Horowitz and DiSabato were close friends.

The 10 publishers and media observers interviewed for this chapter all agreed that Evans as the current proprietor inspired Rivendell's professional maturity.

"Joe wanted to go gangbusters and at times clashed with gay papers like ours that wanted to maintain an arm's-length relationship with advertisers," explained former *Washington Blade* Publisher Don Michaels. For example, "Joe pushed us big on running complimentary articles done by freelancers on a new book so that he could go back to publishers and say, 'Look, the *Blade* ran a flattering article.' We didn't do that.

"Todd Evans came along and gave a more balanced perspective in dealing with gay papers. He is basically a professional guy and respected our territory. He took Rivendell to a whole new level."

Evans continued the development of the first LGBT market surveys, which provided empirical data to advertisers about LGBT consumerism and spending habits, thereby increasing mainstream advertising interest in the LGBT press. Building upon DiSabato's organization of the National Gay Newspaper Guild, Rivendell compiled market demographics from readership surveys that members of the guild could share. "It was one of the first times I ever heard of the concept of the gay market," said Horowitz.

Nonetheless, reaching into the "gay market" has its "bicoastal" limitations. New York's Madison Avenue "just doesn't understand the Midwest," said Ted Fleischaker, publisher of Indianapolis-based *The Word*.

Another challenge is invisibility of the gay market and the invisibility within it—lesbian, bisexual and transgender people. For the most part, demographic studies so far have focused primarily on wealthy gay white men, the DINKS phenomenon of "double income with no kids." Still, there has been progress in looking at the lesbian market.

For all the pressing challenges facing LGBT media in the current economic downturn, DiSabato's vision and Rivendell Media live on. As Baim put it, "As Rivendell goes, so goes gay media. Their success is our success. When they experience weaker periods, it affects gay media significantly."

Added Rivendell's Evans, "We really are all in this together."

The National Gay Newspaper Guild members voted to close down during the post-2008 economic downtown, in part because several of its member papers, owned by Window Media, went into bankruptcy. It made more sense to close NGNG and wait to assess the status of gay media in those important media markets.

Eventually, Evans felt the air had cleared and it was time for a new association, this one broader in focus, and with a more open policy for membership. There are founding newspapers in this National Gay Media Association today, but other regional newspapers, magazines and even websites will eventually be welcome.

The list of NGMA newspapers includes some of those that were part of NGNG. The founders are *Bay Area Reporter, Bay Windows, Between The Lines, Dallas Voice, Gay City News* (New York City), *GA Voice* (Atlanta), *Washington Blade* and *Windy City Times.*

Portions of this essay first appeared in Press Pass Q, *a trade journal for gay media.*

The Village Voice on Joe DiSabato and Rivendell, November 12, 1979.

The following are examples provided by Rivendell Media of advertising in gay publications starting in the late 1970s and through primarily the 1990s. Rivendell Media places advertising in LGBT newspapers and magazines across the U.S.

The 1970s

American Gigolo movie

Ad ad for the book
Homosexuality in Perspective

Jerry Brown for President

Barney's NYC

Donna Summer ad

Patti LaBelle ad

An ad for Elton John

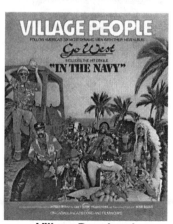

Village People ad

The 1970s (continued)

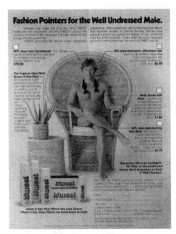

K'West lotion

Yves Saint Laurent

The 1980s

Absolut

An *All that Jazz* movie ad

Boodles British gin

The Mayor of Castro Street book on sale

Bette Midler's *Divine Madness*

John Anderson for President

The 1980s (continued)

Jägermeister

**Hanns Ebensten
Travel, Inc.**

International Male

Finlandia

***Kramer vs. Kramer* movie**

Pride Institute

Rémy Martin

**Kahlúa and Sabroso coffee
liqueurs**

Stroh's

The 1980s (continued)

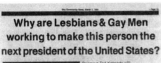

Why are Lesbians & Gay Men working to make this person the next president of the United States?

TUACA.
ITS TASTE HAS COME.

Senator Edward Kennedy for President

Tuaca Liqueur

***Midnight Blue* TV show on Channel J in New York City**

The 1990s

Sexually Transmitted Diseases...
Foiled Again!

LifeStyles CONDOMS

If you or a friend has AIDS...

MAC is no friend of yours.

Whatever you do, don't shake the magazine.

RÉMY MARTIN

LifeStyles Condoms

SmithKlineBeecham and Adria/Pharmacia, Mycobutin drug

Rémy Martin

The 2000s

THE FIGHT AGAINST AIDS
need not be a financial one

Access program, a viatical settlement company

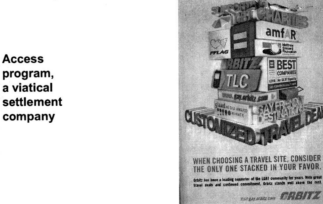

WHEN CHOOSING A TRAVEL SITE, CONSIDER THE ONLY ONE STACKED IN YOUR FAVOR.

ORBITZ

Orbitz

Joe DiSabato of Rivendell Marketing posing with 1980s-era gay newspapers.

The Gay Press Association held its first meeting in New York on January 9–11, 1980. William B. Kelley reported on the convention for Chicago's *GayLife* in an article also picked up in other papers, including here in the *Arizona Gay News*.

ARIZONA GAy NEWS

Volume 8 · Serving Arizona and the Southwest · Issue 4

Phoenix march plans move ahead

Mass. high court defines "lewd"

Gay press association formed

Separate Gay packets at Harvard

CONTINUED ON PAGE FOUR

35

The Currency of the Gay Movement

By Tracy Baim

"We Are a Movement, Not a Market!"

That cry of protest was especially common during the 1990s, at local and national gay marches and parades, culminating in complaints of corporate influence at the LGBT Millennium March on Washington in April 2000. But these issues are just as relevant today—the Occupy movement, which started in 2011 to criticize the greed of Wall Street and the wealthiest 1 percent of Americans, filtered over into some Pride parades in 2012.

Pride parades across the country are now filled with floats from companies with little depth of connection to the gay community. Some put together a float once a year and do nothing else to help their LGBT employees or consumers. Others do provide a wide range of support internally and externally for the gay movement.

In San Francisco, OccuPride briefly blocked the 2012 parade. The few dozen peaceful protesters slowed down the event, and their chants included "Community, Not Commodity" and "We're Here, We're Queer, We're Not Going Shopping." There were also some anti-corporate signs in Chicago's Pride parade.

How do we know the difference between those who just want us for the green we bring to the cash register and those who celebrate our complete rainbow lives?

Thankfully, there are tools to measure these companies, at least some of the larger ones in the Fortune 500, and especially those with consumer brand names. How well do companies actually walk the walk when it comes to gays?

Should it matter? There are some people who would like to ban all corporate involvement in the gay community. But given that gays control a lot of spending, pay a lot of taxes, and work at these companies, it would seem fair to seek to use that power to make corporations more accountable to those they employ and serve.

Some of this corporate activism has had a trickle-down effect on local gay newspapers, but a surprising number of companies that claim to be gay-friendly actually do very little consumer marketing to that niche. They give sponsorship or philanthropic (tax-deductible) dollars to relatively safe gay organizations, buy a couple of ads and call it a day. But in this chapter, I argue that a more aggressive approach to gay consumer marketing is needed by those companies that claim the mantle of supporting equality and diversity. Yes, it will help strengthen gay newspapers, but it is also a wise business decision.

In the Streets and the Office Suites

There is a decades-long tradition of fighting against both corporate and media homophobia (plus transphobia and AIDS-phobia). What used to be a protest against the hate has morphed into an effort to push for the love—and money—of corporate America. (Chapter 1 deals more with media bias and protests.)

In 1987 in Chicago, the effort to use the combined buying power of the gay community was in its infancy. Bar owners Marge Summit and Frank Kellas created the Gay Dollars Campaign, where individuals and businesses stamped their paper money with a "Gay $" stamp. The campaign was a response to a grocery store in a heavily gay neighborhood that warned its employees about the potential for catching AIDS from casual contact with gay customers. The campaign took off in Chicago and nationally, as an early consumer protest against corporate homophobia and AIDS-phobia.

There had been an earlier effort to mark bills as "Gay Money," in New York City, as reported by *off our backs* in February 1979. And in 1995, Martina Navratilova became the spokeswoman for the Rainbow Card gay credit card's sponsor, the nonprofit Rainbow Endowment (in 2005, Navratilova sued to stop the organization from using her name and likeness in ads, but her association with it remained until the card was discontinued in 2011 by Bank of America). Human Rights Campaign and other gay groups also offer affinity credit cards.

The Chicago-based Coalition Against Media/Marketing Prejudice announced in January 1988 that it was taking on the Stroh Brewery Company for remarks made in *The Wall Street Journal* by the ad agency handling Stroh's beer. Michael Lesser of the agency, Lowe Marschalk, had said: "I'm surprised beer companies [such as Anheuser-Busch] would think seriously of advertising in gay media. Beer imagery is so delicate that getting associated with homosexuals could be detrimental."

CAMMP's Art Johnston, co-owner of Chicago's Sidetrack bar, wrote a letter to the company in February 1988 asking for an apology and a marketing push to the gay community. As a result, Stroh took action, and no boycott was necessary.

CAMMP's next action soon followed: a protest against the Kellogg Company in Battle Creek, Michigan, for its TV commercial promoting Nut & Honey cereal, which featured an Old West trail cook threatened with being shot when the men for whom he cooks mistakenly believe he has called one of them "honey." Kellogg did not respond as quickly as the Stroh company, and Chicago activists spent over a year calling for action.

Kellogg cut off communication with CAMMP after asserting that the ad did not promote violence. CAMMP's Rick Garcia disrupted a 1988 shareholders meeting where shareholders voted 88 percent to 5 percent against pulling their company out of South Africa because of its apartheid laws. "Of course this company doesn't want to pull out of South Africa," Garcia told *Outlines* newspaper in May 1988. "It fits perfectly with their attitude toward CAMMP."

At the April 28, 1989, Kellogg shareholders meeting, Joseph Norton, 70, stood up, said he was a relative of the original Kellogg family, came out as a gay man and criticized the anti-gay ad. CEO Bill LaMothe said the company did not believe in violence and did not agree with the interpretation of the ad. However, the company unveiled a new ad that was more benign. Still, the pressure continued.

The highly visible work of CAMMP undoubtedly had an impact beyond just those two campaigns—it likely prevented other anti-gay messages in marketing. Now, more companies than ever are creating gay-specific images for marketing to the community. Today, there are far fewer examples of ads that are intentionally homophobic or transphobic. (See *Out and Proud in Chicago: An Overview of the City's Gay Community* for more details on the Gay $ and CAMMP campaigns.)

Gay newspapers provided a link between the protesters and the readers, making sure the falling trees in the forest were heard. The non-gay media rarely covered these pickets and boycotts.

Ultimately, the push for corporate and media accountability benefited gay publications. They were the primary go-to space for readers who cared about these issues. They also infrequently received advertising buys from companies who were slowly becoming less afraid to market to the gay community.

$700 Billion and Counting

The LGBT market in the U.S. is believed to control more than $700 billion in annual spending, and that's not including spending by our allies. As Prime Access, a New York–based marketing firm, states: "The multicultural marketplace isn't new, but it continues to change. Over the past decade, the Hispanic population has grown 58 percent. African-Americans and Hispanics account for 28 percent of all Americans. Gay consumers number 15 million and counting, spending $743 billion annually."

This definable "market" sprang from almost nothing just a few decades ago to where it stands today, with hundreds of LGBT media outlets and mainstream media going after gay dollars, and corporate brands competing in the marketplace.

Where did it all begin?

Early gay journals and periodicals had very few advertisements—and none from mainstream brand names. A few brave service providers (especially counselors) and local retail stores and salons placed ads, and mail-order catalog ads were popular, as were ads for gay bars owned by mostly straight businessmen (many of them from the Mafia).

Over the years, the community has grown and the media market has also grown and split into ever-narrower niche groups. There are publications for lesbians, for people with HIV/AIDS, for leathermen and -women, for gay bears (big, hairy men), for those who love sports and for many more categories and subcategories. The strongest publications are those serving a general LGBT community, either as national features magazines or as regional newspapers. Outside of the broadcast media, readership growth seems largest in national and regional gay websites, but, as of 2012, the bulk of the advertising money, for now, is mainly rooted in the printed page. Because of the Internet and the parallel economic downturn, the entire publication industry is in flux, and that is certainly true for gay media.

One of the companies that does business with gay publications is the advertising-rep firm Rivendell Media, profiled in the previous chapter. Todd Evans, who runs Rivendell, said that when the agency started in 1979, it represented 25 publications. Not all gay media worked with them, but many of the bigger regional papers did. By 1994, that number was more than 150, and in 2000 it was around 200 in the U.S. and Canada. There were hundreds more gay periodicals (more than 800 by the 1990s), but many of these were newsletters or organizational publications.

An important early survey of the gay market contributed in part to the growth of marketing efforts aimed at the community. Chicago-based Overlooked Opinions was a company that lasted only a few years, but nevertheless had a big impact in the marketing community. In 1992, it released its estimate of the value of the gay market: $514 billion. Later surveys continued to reinforce the economic clout of the gay community. As with any economic survey, though, it had its drawbacks, and some people began to stereotype the community as all wealthy, male, white and privileged—which is not only false but was used against the gay movement by right-wingers who said we didn't need any "special" rights, because we were already well off.

Despite the strength of the "gay dollar," as of this book's printing, Rivendell Media's core of papers is down to under 150. "The shakeout from 2000 to 2009 was really just a matter of who had good business practices and who did not," Evans said. "Who was smart both about the gay cause and the business, and who was just one or the other." Evans said that digital advertising is starting to grow more. He also said that while 2012 looks to be improving, the main difference now is that companies that advertise in the gay press do not plan as far ahead for advertising, because they want to adjust to the economic climate quickly.

Another person who has his finger on the pulse of how the gay media work is Rex Wockner. He was the most widely syndicated reporter in gay media ever. Wockner said that at his peak in 2001 and 2002 he may have syndicated to 100 newspapers simultaneously. Now, only a tiny number of papers are still around and can afford syndicated material.

Journalist Paul Harris saw that the gay media market was even strong enough to support a regular guidebook on the topic. In *The Harris Guide* (formerly the *Queer Press Guide*), he offered a comprehensive resource of LGBT media. The last edition appears to have come out in 2003. Hundreds of papers were listed, and reading through the index is almost like going through a cemetery, seeing all the papers that have now gone out of business. Harris died in early 2012. (There were other guides to gay and lesbian media, including *Our Own Voices: A Directory of Gay and Lesbian Periodicals, 1890s-2000s,* by Alan V. Miller. See resources in the back of this book for more recommended reading.)

Advertising: Don't Touch That

"You canNOT do a magazine like *The Advocate* for advertisers," wrote former *Advocate* Editor-in-Chief Judy Wieder on November 4, 2009, in the online Huffington Post. "They're not thrilled about newsmagazines. ... Go count the ad pages in *Time* or *Newsweek*. If those magazines depended on ads to survive, they wouldn't. It's their large circulation, their readership combined with their website visitors that carry the brands forward. We do it for the users, the readers. They will pay for it (online or in print) if you make it absolutely essential and as exclusive as possible."

Wieder was right that news stories were not attractive to advertisers. Gay newspapers also faced this dilemma—news was not always what the advertiser ordered. Advertisers frowned upon being placed next to ACT UP protest photos, or articles critical of the government, or those about hate crimes or suicide. Sex ads were also a turnoff, even though many non-gay alternative papers also ran highly sexual images.

Early gay journals such as *The Ladder, ONE, Mattachine Review, Drum* and others relied on subscribers just as *The Advocate, Curve, Girlfriends, Genre* and *Instinct* later did, but regional tabloid newspapers did not. As with many non-gay alternative tabloids, gay newspapers of the 1970s usually had a free-circulation model. These post-Stonewall papers were given away free at delivery locations and had a small number of paid subscribers. This is still true today.

LGBT media started to really shift by the 2000s, when the Internet began to have more of an impact. Media that adapted to the Internet early have survived better than those that came late to the table. But many of the gay-newspaper failures of the 2000s were more about business decisions and the faltering economy, not the competition online.

The business of successful newspapers includes being able to adjust to wide swings in the advertising base. In the early 1990s, most gay newspapers were filled with phone-sex ads. Some papers had not planned for the downturn when those ads dried up with the onset of Internet competition. During various recessions, when real estate, auto and other types of advertising crashed, again, some papers were better prepared. Pharmaceutical advertising has been a roller coaster over the years, requiring planning to be able to adjust to huge changes in revenues.

In some cases, the uneven playing field of national advertising is the reason papers in bigger markets have succeeded while others in smaller markets have foundered. A good example is Rivendell Media's getting a buy from a major corporate advertising client for papers in New York, Boston, Chicago, San Francisco and a few other top cities, while papers in San Diego, Iowa or North Carolina are left out because the advertisers aren't seeking those markets or demographics.

All of this is to say that gay newspapers are just like any other business and, specifically, like other newspapers. Some have been able to adapt to changes, and others have failed. Sometimes this is within their control, and sometimes it is not. And in some cases, bad decisions have meant the downfall of gay-press leaders. (In other cases, personal drug and/or alcohol abuse have brought down some publishers.)

The Advertisers

As noted above, in the 1960s, *The Ladder* carried few ads, and those they did have were mainly from other gay organizations. Some of the early men's publications had small-business, bar and mail-order ads. People did pay to have the periodicals mailed to their homes, and some publications were subsidized by membership dues from the organizations that published them.

In the 1970s, gay bars and bathhouses were important advertisers in *The Advocate* and many gay newspapers. Special events and entertainment venues started to advertise as well. Some gay papers were fortunate to get mainstream beer-company ads starting in the 1970s, including Old Style beer in Chicago.

Absolut vodka and Rémy Martin's Fine Champagne cognac were among the first national brands placing campaigns in gay media, starting in the early 1980s.

Marshall Field's even placed advertising in *Windy City Times* in 1987, thanks to a gay man who was well-positioned in the department store company's management.

By the 1990s, as the community's visibility and clout grew, in part because of the AIDS epidemic, some shifts took place in the types of advertising. There were the traditional bars and gay businesses, and finally more entertainment venues and professional services.

In addition to the growth of phone-sex advertising, there was a disturbing growth in viatical-insurance advertising (a viatical settlement allows you to invest in someone else's life insurance policy), taking advantage of gay men living with AIDS, gambling against their deaths.

There were also some financial mistakes that occurred in the gay niche, including problems caused by businesses defaulting on payments. One firm founded in 1991, New York–based Mulryan/Nash, placed advertising campaigns for clients in gay media, including campaigns for Agouron Pharmaceuticals and for Subaru of America. The firm went out of business in December 1999, almost on the eve of the new millennium. Dozens of publications were left with tens of thousands of dollars in uncollected revenues.

But on the good side, there was also an increase in travel-related advertising to the gay niche. Key West was an early leader in doing marketing across the U.S. for travelers to that South Florida destination. Virgin America was among the first airlines placing gay advertising, and it was joined by American, United, Orbitz, Expedia, Southwest and other airlines and travel agencies. Even Amtrak eventually started doing gay outreach in the 2000s. And in 2012, Amtrak created advertising that featured gay and lesbian families. The images were used in an online ad for *Instinct* gay magazine.

Miller and Budweiser beer brands increased their gay advertising in the 1990s, especially around sports teams and tournaments. Benson & Hedges cigarettes also placed gay media ads.

Benetton, the clothing company that enjoys controversy, sparked debate related to its 1991 use of a Therese Frare photo of David Kirby, surrounded by his family in his last hours of life. He was frail with AIDS complications, and Benetton used the image to illustrate the impact of AIDS. The company subsequently placed ads in national gay media, showing its support of diversity. Benetton even ran one with a large pink condom that ACT UP displayed to call attention to safer sex.

More fashion companies also started their outreach in the 1990s, especially in the four-color glossy national gay magazines such as *Out, The Advocate, 10 Percent, Genre* and *Instinct.* Kenneth Cole, Diesel, Banana Republic, Calvin Klein, Movado and Tommy Hilfiger companies created campaigns in the magazines, but not much of the advertising reached regional newspapers.

Other 1990s-era early adopters of advertising in gay media included IBM, Apple (which does very little gay marketing today) and American Express. The automaker Saab started its gay media ads in 1994 in *Out* magazine.

Another carmaker, Subaru, placed national gay ads starting in the mid-1990s. And in Chicago, it took an innovative community-based approach to advertising, thanks to Marv Pollack, an openly gay marketing professional. When I published *Outlines* newspaper, before merging it with *Windy City Times*, I worked with Pollack on a local campaign to do a giveback of funds to Howard Brown Health Center and later the Lesbian Community Cancer Project for each Subaru purchased as a response to advertising in gay newspapers.

Pollack pushed very hard to make the campaign work as a test case for Subaru nationally, and it was wildly successful. Subaru spent several years deep in the LGBT market, especially focused on lesbian car buyers. It even hired lesbian spokeswomen for TV ads, including Martina Navratilova.

The company had noticeable traction from its giveback efforts, and other car companies took note and mimicked the concept.

Other brand names in 1990s glossy magazines included Swatch, Sony Electronics, Xerox, Smirnoff, Tanqueray, Evian and a host of other beverage, entertainment and travel brands. Some, like Subaru, used gays in their campaigns. MAC Cosmetics hired RuPaul in the mid-1990s, making him the first "drag queen" supermodel.

But it wasn't until the 2000s that the real variety and depth of advertising started to expand beyond a few national glossy magazines and more heavily into the regional print media and the program guides for gay events. Even today, however, the four-color glossies, those few that are left, tend to be the only place for some brand names marketing to the gay community. In the past decade, newspapers have had access to lower-cost four-color processing on newsprint, so, even though most gay newspapers were black-and-white with a little color 20 years ago, these days almost all gay newspapers have extensive four-color options for advertisers.

Writing in *Advertising Age* on June 8, 2011, Andy Bagnall of Prime Access noted the state of gay marketing: "Many marketers are aware of the significant sales opportunity of the $743 billion lesbian, gay, bisexual, and transgendered market. LGBTs over-index in many categories (travel, spirits, automotive, among others) or have unique, often underserved needs (financial services and health care, for example) that make them a prime prospect for brand growth."

There are many reasons why the gay market is now more attractive to corporations. Here are a few:

— The professionalism of LGBT media, including expanded demographic surveys and better design. Also, there are more niche publications, professional business associations and gay chambers of commerce.

— The rise of the LGBT movement itself, and thus the mainstreaming of our issues.

— The growth of LGBT employee support groups at major corporations, making the companies more accountable to their employees and their clients. The Human Rights Campaign and Out & Equal groups began to assess and rank companies, while Commercial Closet ranks ads, and more companies try to be open to diversity.

This progress, in turn, helped push advertisers to go beyond the simple campaigns and to create more LGBT-specific marketing. Some of the early LGBT marketing efforts suffered from a few weaknesses:

— Companies often used the same ads in mainstream and LGBT media.

— When doing gay ads, some companies just relied on a "young, white, male, bare-chest" approach.

— The ads that were gay were so generic as not to represent any real reason for people to "act."

Now, campaigns are usually more sophisticated and targeted:

— They frequently are designed specifically for the LGBT market, are more diverse, and offer a good value.

—The best marketers, such as Orbitz, use their gay creative ideas in ads they run in mainstream media.

— While some ads are "gay-vague" and take a gay eye to understand them, sometimes that clever approach can work to break through the blur of advertising.

All is not progressive in marketing. Some ads are defensive or offensive, including some that run during the Super Bowl. There is still unfortunately a need to make sure companies are held accountable for their branding and advertising.

The Commercial Closet is an organization started by Michael Wilke (and now run by GLAAD, the Gay & Lesbian Alliance Against Defamation) that monitors general advertising and advertising that targets the LGBT consumer. The group is not as strong and visible as it once was under Wilke, but it still provides an important monitoring tool for advertising images in print and broadcast media from around the world. Some of the ads they consider are strongly pro-LGBT, but others are very offensive and rely on stereotypes for humor.

Here is what the CommercialCloset.org website says about its advertising library:

"Our collection focuses on mainstream corporate advertising and its incredible power to affect how the Gay/Lesbian/Bisexual/Transgender community is perceived. We collect worldwide corporate ads with direct references to GLBT people or a GLBT theme, including political ads and those from government and health agencies, nonprofits, gay and anti-gay organizations.

"Some references may not actually involve a gay person, just the idea of homosexuality or transgender. This may include cross-gender dressing, 'inappropriate' gender behavior, references to male-male rape, gay sexual practice, and some same-gender physical contact/interaction.

"Cultural perspectives on what constitutes homosexuality versus friendship vary greatly; our bias is through an American 'lens.' At our discretion, we collect some 'gay-vague' material—where sexuality is unclear and may allow for gay interpretations.

"The project also comprehensively tracks (but does not rate) print and Internet ads in gay media. Also, there are a handful of parody commercials from shows like *Saturday Night Live* and *MADtv.* We welcome old advertising and unaired 'spec' ads."

The website also states: "Our ratings are NOT intended to assess the likability or entertainment value of ads, nor are they supposed to inspire or reflect 'offense' by or for the entire GLBT community. [They] are intended as an attempt to assess what the imagery/narrative conveys about gayness and transgender—both perceived by audiences and intended by the advertiser."

The Commercial Closet monitoring website's list of advertising agencies placing lots of gay ads puts DDB Needham in first place, with 85 ads, including 43 for mainstream viewers, 37 for gay audiences, and five for dual audiences. Other top agencies making the most GLBT-themed commercials include TBWA Worldwide (52), Leo Burnett (46), Y&R (42), BBDO (40), Lowe and Partners (37), McCann Erickson (32), JWT (32), Saatchi & Saatchi (28), Publicis (22) and Euro RSCG (20).

Interestingly, some of the good ads see very little airtime or visibility. They almost seem designed to win awards, not help businesses actually reach the LGBT market.

Adweek's David Griner looked at "The 50 Gayest Ads Ever" on June 29, 2011. He asked: "Why is it still so shocking to see gay people in mainstream ads? At a time when every other demographic is practically shoehorned into marketing for the sake of diversity, gays and lesbians are still all but invisible in the TV advertising landscape. But while you might not have seen many yourself, gay-themed TV ads are definitely out there."

The top-10 ads he listed were from Miller Genuine Draft, Solo (Norwegian orange juice), Silverjet, Greater Philadelphia Tourism Marketing Group, Volkswagen, MTV, Sony, Kronenbourg 1664, Dolce & Gabbana and Johnnie Walker. Many of these were run only outside the U.S., including one in France for McDonald's that took 11th place.

Kenneth Cole Productions, Inc., the shoe and apparel company, has been a pioneer in supporting gay rights, and in 2011 it put its money behind a billboard in New York: "Gay People Getting Married? (Next they'll be allowed to vote and pay taxes.) — Kenneth Cole." Several corporations placed similar ads backing gay marriage in that state—including Macy's, which has been out front in support of same-sex marriage across the country.

Marriage is good for business, so those early states such as Massachusetts, Iowa, New York and California (which allowed same-sex marriage briefly) have benefited from the boom in nuptials.

The city of New York issued this statement on July 24, 2012: "Mayor Michael R. Bloomberg, City Council Speaker Christine C. Quinn, NYC & Company CEO George Fertitta and New York City Clerk Michael McSweeney today announced that one year after the enactment of the Marriage Equality Act, same-sex marriages in New York City have generated an estimated $259 million in economic impact and $16 million in City revenues. At least 8,200 same-sex marriage licenses were issued in the first year, accounting for more than 10 percent of the 75,000 marriage licenses issued in New York City since July 24 last year.

"The economic impact survey was conducted by NYC & Company and the city clerk's office and found same-sex marriages generated significant additional revenue for New York City's tourism industry with more than half of same-sex couples holding wedding celebrations in venues across the five boroughs. More than 200,000 guests traveled from outside of the city to same-sex marriage events, and more than 235,000 hotel room nights were booked at an average daily room rate of $275."

Another strong gay-owned brand that does good inside and outside the gay community is Mitchell Gold + Bob Williams, founded in 1989, a nationwide retailer and manufacturer of home furnishing products. They give back extensively to the causes they believe in, especially gay rights.

When columnist Dan Savage and his husband, Terry Miller, started the It Gets Better campaign in 2010 in response to several high-profile suicides of LGBT youth, he probably didn't see how massive the effort would be, not just for individual gays but also for corporations and organizations. Major companies, including Google, American Airlines, Best Buy and Facebook, created It Gets Better videos featuring their employees. President Barack Obama, Secretary of State Hillary Clinton and other politicians also submitted videos. It was a feel-good/do-good project that created little backlash for these major brands.

In 2012, Office Depot even teamed with Lady Gaga for her anti-bullying, gay-positive Born This Way campaign.

Backlash

Going gay does not come without landmines. But they seem less devastating than ever before.

When California (via the anti–gay-marriage Proposition 8), Tennessee and North Carolina passed anti-gay laws, a few courageous corporations with headquarters or stores there also took a stand. And some corporate leaders on the Boy Scouts of America board are trying to work from the inside to change that entity's ban on gays. So there are mixed results on corporate responsibility and outcomes—but certainly more positive moves.

Early support for gays was evidenced in response to a devastating 1992 gay loss in Colorado. That state's voters passed a law barring any municipality within its borders from passing pro-gay laws. A campaign to boycott Colorado cost the state tens of millions in lost convention business, plus countless tourism dollars. In 1996, the U.S. Supreme Court eventually overturned the law, but before that, there was a massive nationwide boycott against the state, and major events and conventions canceled their plans.

The victories sometimes come with setbacks. In North Carolina in 2012, one gay-owned company, Replacements Ltd. (which sells old and new dinnerware), faced a major backlash against owner Bob Page's support of gay marriage. "Hostile letters and emails poured into the company from customers canceling their business and demanding to be removed from its email list," reported *The New York Times* on May 25, 2012.

The *Times* added: "Most companies have traditionally tried to avoid taking positions on political and social issues. But corporate involvement in campaigns to support gay marriage has mirrored the shift in the nation's attitudes, from nonexistent 10 years ago to some involvement by major companies in 2008, when Apple, American Apparel, Google and Levi Strauss publicly opposed California's Proposition 8 to ban gay marriage (it passed). Last year, corporate support in New York was deemed critical to the Legislature's passage of a law allowing gay marriage. This year, major corporations based in Washington State, led by Amazon, Starbucks and Microsoft, have publicly opposed an effort to repeal the state's law permitting gay marriage, scheduled to take effect on June 7." Similar corporate support came in 2012 to fight a marriage ban in Minnesota.

In the early 1990s, Levi Strauss & Co. removed the Boy Scouts of America from its corporate giving list after the group banned gay men as employees. The Levi's company said the resulting call for a boycott had no impact on its bottom line.

In 2011, J.Crew faced controversy for the inclusion in its catalog of a story about the company's Creative Director Jenna Lyons and her family, which mentioned that she painted her 5-year-old son's toenails pink because it is his favorite color. The LGBT community welcomed it, while conservatives attacked it widely.

Riki Wilchins, executive director of the TrueChild organization, wrote on April 27, 2011: "What these reactionary commentators are doing is mining a much richer and deeper field of 'gender panic,' a pervasive sense of discomfort or social dislocation closely linked to the increasing visibility of young people—straight, gay, or transgender —who simply don't fit all the rules of the Gender Binary."

A fun corporate ad campaign made it all the way to bus-stop signage in San Francisco. Allstate Insurance featured a transgender model: "I dress in drag. But I don't race my engine." The ad was for the company's safe-driver discount program.

Off Target

Other companies have faced criticism from the LGBT community for their politics, even when they do have strong diversity policies and high rankings from Human Rights Campaign and other groups. This includes Target, which gave funds in 2010 to Minnesota Forward, a group that funded anti-gay candidates while Target was marketing to the LGBT community. The political donation was possible because of the 2010 U.S. Supreme Court decision in *Citizens United v. Federal Election Commission,* ruling that corporations are like people, so they can donate to political campaigns. This opened up a huge funding stream but also created a dangerous cliff for companies to jump off when it comes to offending people.

Even after activists called for a boycott and protests, Target refused to meet with gay groups. Some LGBTs are still boycotting the company. Meanwhile, in 2012, the company started more gay outreach by selling T-shirts to benefit a group working to defeat a gay marriage ban in Minnesota, where Target is based.

While Target did not issue a statement on its position regarding the proposed 2012 Minnesota gay-marriage ban (which voters ultimately rejected), it did release artwork for an advertisement featuring a white gay-male couple, forehead to forehead and holding hands—promoting the company's wedding-gift registry with the tag line "Be Yourself, Together."

USA Today ran this Associated Press item on June 1, 2012: "The T-shirt promotion will raise up to $120,000 for the Family Equality Council, a Washington-based group that is part of a Minnesota coalition pushing to defeat the constitutional amendment. The $12.99 shirts will be sold on Target's website through June, or while supplies last. They come in four designs, emblazoned with words such as 'harmony' and 'pride.' Singer Gwen Stefani designed one shirt featuring a rainbow and a cloud that says, 'LOVE IS LOVE.' …

"Target's move comes two years after it endured a backlash from gay rights supporters for giving $150,000 to a campaign group backing the conservative Republican candidate for Minnesota governor, Tom Emmer, who narrowly lost to Democrat Mark Dayton in a race that went to an automatic recount."

Windy City Times reported on July 25, 2012, that Target also began selling gay greeting cards in stores across the country. The cards, by Carlton Cards, a division of American Greetings, are for anniversaries and same-sex weddings.

"Target supports inclusivity and diversity in every aspect of our business," Target spokeswoman Molly Snyder told *WCT*. "We are pleased to be able to bring our guests a broad array of unique and differentiated products they want and need. In our greeting card department, Target offers cards that appeal to a variety of audiences for a range of special occasions including cards for the LGBT community, cards in Spanish, and cards that recognize ethnic and religious holidays such as Hanukkah, Kwanzaa and Hispanic celebrations."

Double Stuf and Double Latte

One company stood firmly by its LGBT employees and consumers when it faced a boycott threat from conservatives. Kraft Foods gave a grant to Gay Games VII in Chicago, and the company, along with Walgreens and more than 100 other Gay Games sponsors, was harassed for its support of the event. (I was co-vice chair of the Gay Games VII board and fundraising chairperson.)

Following are excerpts from a message to all employees from Marc Firestone, executive vice president of Kraft Foods in 2005:

"The true test of any commitment is how you respond when challenged. In recent days, [Kraft] has received many e-mails, the majority of them generated through the American Family Association, which objects to our sponsorship. While Kraft certainly doesn't go looking for controversy, we have long been dedicated to support the concept and the reality of diversity. It's the right thing to do and it's good for our business and our work environment. Diversity makes us a stronger company and connects us with the diversity that exists among the consumers who buy our products.

"It can be difficult when we are criticized. It's easy to say you support a concept or a principle when nobody objects. The real test of commitment is how one reacts when there are those who disagree. I hope you share my view that our company has taken the right stand on diversity, including its contribution to the 2006 Gay Games in Chicago."

The Gay Games ultimately had more than 400 sponsors and an economic impact of more than $50 million on the Chicago-area economy. Not one sponsor backed out, and the Gay Games in Chicago were the first to break even financially in more than 20 years of the events' history.

Kraft did not stop there. In 2012, it faced both strong support and some backlash for a rather benign support of gay pride—placing an image of a rainbow-color–filled Oreo cookie on its Facebook page. Oreo has many varieties, from traditional to Double Stuf.

As *The Washington Post*'s Dan Zak wrote on June 27, 2012: "The rainbow-colored Oreo graphic unveiled for LGBT Pride Month proves at least one thing: Gays are just as susceptible to clever marketing as straights. At long last! Equality under commercialization."

"We are excited to illustrate what is making history today in a fun and playful way," said Basil T. Maglaris, associate director of corporate affairs for Kraft. "Kraft Foods has a proud history of celebrating diversity and inclusiveness. We feel the Oreo ad is a fun reflection of our values. There has been a lot of buzz about the image, and it shows how relevant Oreo is to people even after 100 years."

Amazon.com founder Jeff Bezos and his wife, MacKenzie, at the request of longtime employee Jennifer Cast, stepped into the marriage fray big-time in 2012. They donated $2.5 million to help pass a same-sex-marriage referendum in their home state of Washington (the referendum did pass). Cast is a lesbian mom and heads the fundraising for the marriage referendum.

The New York Times reported on July 27: "Mr. Bezos, who founded Amazon.com in 1994 in Seattle and remains its president, now tops a growing list of heterosexual business executives who are replacing wealthy gay people as some of the biggest donors to the movement behind same-sex marriage and equality for gay men and lesbians. Bill Gates and Steven A. Ballmer of Microsoft each gave $100,000 to the referendum campaign, according to its officials. But with the seven-figure gift, Mr. Bezos—a famously private executive who runs a $48 billion-a-year retail empire—has now set the bar even higher."

Interestingly, Kraft and Amazon, despite these bold gay moves, have not done any significant consumer marketing to the gay niche, including through advertising in gay–owned publications.

Andy Bagnall of the Prime Access marketing agency noted: "First and foremost, there has never been a successful boycott due to supporting or marketing to gay consumers. A well-known conservative organization boycotted family-focused Disney for years because of Disney's outreach to gay customers. All the while, Disney experienced rapid growth and profit. The boycotters eventually gave up and proclaimed 'victory.' What kind of victory I'm not sure ... .

"Where there have been mishaps is in how marketers respond to threats of boycotts. A misstep here can turn off both gay customers and fair-minded straight customers (who comprise the clear majority). Years ago, Kraft supported the Gay Games in Chicago ... [They made a] clear, simple statement that resonated with gay consumers and Middle America.

"An example of how not to handle a threat of a boycott is a well-known automaker [Ford], which provided a series of clumsy, contradictory responses when it was targeted by the American Family Association in 2005. Such responses don't appease groups like the AFA and they only serve to anger everyone else.

"Best to follow Kraft's lead, or that of Home Depot. The latter has been under an AFA boycott for some time, and someone in support of the boycott called the company and its shareholders out on its support of the gay community. The response from Chairman-CEO Frank Blake: 'I appreciate your feedback and I hope all of our shareholders understand that we're a company that respects the diversity of our associates and our customers and the communities where we do business. In fact, the values wheel that I showed just a minute ago—one of our core values is respect for all people.'"

Bagnall notes that marketers faced similar unsuccessful threats when they first started to do marketing to African-Americans decades ago: "To the clients that ventured into the market early came substantial reward."

The anti-gay National Organization for Marriage is among the most recent in a long line of groups trying to force corporate America back into the closet. Several boycotts threatened in 2012 against pro-gay corporations ended up backfiring. NOM opted to boycott Starbucks for the company's support of the freedom to marry. The organization stated: "We are urging customers across the globe to 'Dump Starbucks' because it has taken a corporate-wide position that the definition of marriage between one man and one woman should be eliminated and that same-sex marriage should become equally 'normal.' As such, Starbucks has deeply offended at least half its U.S. customers, and the vast majority of its international customers." ThinkProgress called the NOM campaign a "dismal failure." As of July, the gay supporters on "SumOfUs" had 651,166 people signed up while "Dump Starbucks" had just 45,975 backers. Both of these were online campaigns.

Next, NOM praised Chick-fil-A owners' position against gay marriage.

I'll Have Chicken With That Homophobia

In a July 2012 interview with the *Biblical Recorder*, a North Carolina Baptist news journal, President and Chief Operating Officer Dan Cathy of the 1,614-store, $4 billion-a-year Chick-fil-A fast-food chain said about the company's support of the "traditional family": "Well, guilty as charged ... . We are very much supportive of the family—the biblical definition of the family unit. We are a family-owned business, a family-led business, and we are married to our first wives. We give God thanks for that."

Gay and mainstream media both picked up the story quickly.

The company issued a statement through Facebook trying to backtrack: "The Chick-fil-A culture and service tradition in our restaurants is to treat every person with honor, dignity and respect—regardless of their belief, race, creed, sexual orientation or gender. We will continue this tradition in the over 1,600 Restaurants run by independent Owner/Operators. Going forward, our intent is to leave the policy debate over same-sex marriage to the government and political arena."

This statement, however, only served to fuel the controversy. As Forbes.com wrote: "Translation:

'We'd like to close our eyes now, count to ten, and you should forget all about our fervently avowed political views—which we won't be changing—and go back to eating our chicken a lot.' Which didn't work."

While conservatives embraced the company, others, including some politicians, expressed their distaste for the brand. Boston Mayor Thomas Menino told the *Boston Herald*: "Chick-fil-A doesn't belong in Boston. You can't have a business in the city of Boston that discriminates against a population. We're an open city, we're a city that's at the forefront of inclusion." Chicago Alderman Proco Joe Moreno announced his intention to deny the chain a business license in his ward, but he and other politicians soon backed off similar threats when it was clear there was no legal basis for the denial. Moreno, however, has continued attempts to find ways to block the chain from his ward.

Even the makers of The Muppets rebelled, posting this statement on Facebook: "The Jim Henson Company has celebrated and embraced diversity and inclusiveness for over fifty years and we have notified Chick-fil-A that we do not wish to partner with them on any future endeavors. Lisa Henson, our CEO, is personally a strong supporter of gay marriage and has directed us to donate the payment we received from Chick-fil-A to GLAAD." Thousands of people liked and shared the statement, posted July 20, 2012.

The brand saw a bump in support from conservatives, who promoted a one-day lovefest for Chick-fil-A that turned out hundreds of thousands of people across the country. But YouGov's BrandIndex, a daily measure of brand perception among the public, reported July 27, 2012, about the controversy's negative impact on Chick-fil-A's brand.

"In the Midwest, Chick-Fil-A's perception jumped up for a week and has tapered off to where it was before the interview [with COO Dan Cathy] was published," BrandIndex wrote. "As the controversy has snowballed, the company's overall consumer brand health with fast food eaters has dropped to its lowest levels since at least mid-August 2010. It is also the first time Chick-Fil-A has sunk below the fast food consumer perception average of the top QSR restaurant chains. ...

"YouGov BrandIndex respondents in the South took Chick-Fil-A from an Index score of 80 on July 16th to its current 44. Chick-Fil-A's biggest drop took place in the Northeast, where it went from 76 to 35, a difference of 41 points. Fast food eaters in the Midwest was the only part of the country which drove Chick-Fil-A's perception higher, moving from a 45 score on July 16th to a 70 two days later, staying elevated, and then dropping back to where it was before the interview was published."

Though Chick-fil-A tried to have its homophobic cake and eat it, too, most corporate entities are moving in a pro-gay direction, having seen that conservative boycotts of their competitors and peers have never been successful. General Mills, Esurance, Google, Facebook, Office Depot, Whirlpool and dozens of other major brands have done gay outreach of some kind (in some cases supporting gay-rights laws or same-sex marriage), with no discernible negative effect on their bottom lines.

Marriott International is perhaps a lesson on how a conservative owner can separate his religious beliefs from his company, in this case a hotel chain that does not want to alienate the gays. "God and Gay Marriage: What Chick-fil-A Could Learn From Marriott," by Diane Brady, was published in *Bloomberg Businessweek* on July 26, 2012.

The reporter spoke to Bill Marriott, a Mormon, about the corporation. "The Marriott International (MAR) chairman has never tried to hide his deep faith, often referring to God in his writing and interviews," Brady wrote. "In Marriott's personal life, marriage is something reserved for a man and a woman. But he has long been reluctant to impose that view on the company his father founded. Not only could that crimp the company's $12 billion in sales, it might demoralize employees working in more than 3,700 Marriott properties worldwide. With Mitt Romney's presidential run and same-sex marriage in the headlines, we spoke about his stance as Mormon leaders were being held up for scrutiny again."

Marriott told Brady: "We have to take care of our people, regardless of their sexual orientation or anything else. We are an American church. We have all the American values: the values of hard work, the values of integrity, the values of fairness and respect." Brady wrote: "As a result, when his church actively campaigned against same-sex marriage in California, neither Marriott nor the hotel chain donated any money to the cause. Instead, he stepped into the drama by publicly reinforcing his company's commitment to gay rights through domestic partners benefits and services aimed at gay couples."

More LGBT Branding

In a historically ironic twist in 2012, JCPenney hired lesbian entertainer Ellen DeGeneres as spokeswoman (and used a gay couple in its catalog), taking heat from the right wing. When DeGeneres's sitcom *Ellen* dealt with coming out in 1997, JCPenney was among several high-profile companies to pull their advertising from the show. DeGeneres has had the last laugh, and paycheck. She is also a CoverGirl spokeswoman and did spokesmodel work for American Express. Other companies that pulled from the *Ellen* show included Chrysler and Wendy's, the fast-food chain. Wendy's faced a nationwide boycott from LGBTs, and the company was especially hurt in heavily gay areas. One store in Chicago's largely lesbian Andersonville area went out of business.

When the Oreo controversy broke in June 2012, The Huffington Post website ran a list of "25 LGBT Products & Companies Targeted By Boycotters." Joining Oreo on the list: Betty Crocker, Levi's, Cheerios, American Apparel, Walt Disney, Starbucks, Wheaties, Tide, Microsoft, Home Depot, Pampers, Pepsi, Safeway, Crest, Old Navy, the Girl Scouts, Macy's, Target, JCPenney, Pillsbury, Walgreens, Ford, Gap and Green Giant.

Diversity loves company.

But some people still do not like diversity.

In the summer of 2012, the Waha Bar & Grill in Waha, Idaho, confirmed it no longer carried MillerCoors and PepsiCo products because those companies supported the National Gay & Lesbian Chamber of Commerce, according to Ontopmag.com. MillerCoors said NGLCC "is one of the many organizations we are proud to support."

Among the chamber's other corporate supporters are IBM, Wells Fargo, JPMorgan Chase & Co., Motorola, Intel, Wyndham Worldwide, American Express, American Airlines, Ernst & Young, Aetna, Accenture, Jewel-Osco, Comcast, Johnson & Johnson, Kellogg's (ironic, given the earlier cereal controversy), Office Depot and dozens more.

The 2012 GLAAD Amplifier Awards included some of the innovative LGBT advertising of the previous 12 months. Among the nominees: JCPenney for its Father's Day ad featuring two gay dads with their children; Johnson & Johnson's anti-bullying campaign "Care with Pride"; Lexus for its celebration of the 45th Anniversary of *The Advocate*; Amtrak's "Ride With Pride" campaign; American Apparel for its LGBT Pride campaign featuring transgender model Isis King; and the You Can Play Project for its partnership with professional hockey players to help put an end to homophobia in sports. See www.glaad.org for details. The complete list of 2012 nominees follows:

Advertising - The Hot Spot (Mainstream Market)
"Care with Pride" (Johnson & Johnson)
"First Pals" (JCPenney)
"Make a Difference. Save a Life." (Desert AIDS Project)
"Never Hide" (Ray-Ban)
"Testing Makes Us STRONGER" (Centers for Disease Control and Prevention)

Advertising - The Hot Spot (LGBT Market)
"Lexus Celebrates *The Advocate*'s 45th Anniversary" (Lexus)
"Mom, Dad, I'm Electric." (General Motors)
"Orbitz Price Assurance" (Orbitz)
"Outrageous Through the Ages" (Absolut Vodka/*RuPaul's Drag Race*)
"Red Ribbon Runway" (Gilead Sciences/*RuPaul's Drag Race*)
"Ride With Pride" (Amtrak)

Digital - Out and Interactive
"*Advocate* Money Minute Presented by Wells Fargo" (Wells Fargo)
"Be You, With Us" (Marriott)
"Equality Is _____ " (Allstate Insurance Co.)
Oreo Pride Cookie (Kraft Foods)
"SAGECAP" (Services & Advocacy for GLBT Elders)

Public Relations - Out and Proud
"The Faceoff" (You Can Play Project)
"Land of Dreams" (Brand USA)
LGBT Pride 2012 (American Apparel)
"Project Honesty" (KY Brand)
"Weigh It Forward" (*Philadelphia Gay News*)

Very few of these companies with LGBT-inclusive chamber-of-commerce memberships and advertising do any significant advertising in regional or even national gay media. Among those that do are Absolut, Gilead, Orbitz, Expedia, Travelocity, American Airlines, MillerCoors, IBM, Jewel-Osco on a limited regional basis, and Wells Fargo in California.

Selling Out?

Support by financial institutions and banks that were blamed for the recent banking and mortgage crisis has caused some concern by gay activists, who feel many of the community's national groups have sold out to corporations that may support gays but have overall policies that harm some American people. Some of these banks try to reach gay consumers and gay-owned companies through advertising in local and national gay publications, but banks as a category are pretty weakly represented in gay-media advertising.

This debate flared up in 2011 when GLAAD's President Jarrett Barrios was forced to step down after he sent a letter in support of an AT&T legislative issue that had nothing directly to do with the gay community.

As the *Washington Blade* reported on June 23, 2011: "After a tumultuous two weeks for the Gay and Lesbian Alliance Against Defamation, which included the resignation of the organization's President, Jarrett Barrios, and seven members of the Board of Directors, Troup Coronado, a former AT&T executive at the center of the controversy resigned from the Board of Directors yesterday of his own accord, according to a statement from GLAAD. While GLAAD stood at the center of the scandal, the spotlight is [beginning] to shift to other organizations tied to Coronado through his work as a Board member or supporter, or his work as a liaison to LGBT organizations.

"Most of the organizations under scrutiny have endorsed the AT&T/T-Mobile merger, or had sent letters to the FCC [Federal Communications Commission], last year, supporting—inadvertently in some cases—the telecom giant's position against net-neutrality, a concept of continuing 'free and open' access to the entire internet regardless of internet provider.

"In almost every case, the organizations have retracted their statements against net-neutrality which included suggested language provided, in most cases, by AT&T .... GLAAD had also retracted their statements ... as did the National Gay and Lesbian Task Force, after the true meaning of some of the suggested language was called to their attention."

HRC and most other national and some local groups have this same problem, with many of these same corporations sponsoring their operations.

Out & Equal Workplace Advocates creates a forum for executives and their companies to work on LGBT issues in the workplace and to improve their image in the community. The group hosts conferences and summits, and it provides online tools for companies looking for more information on corporate equality. Out & Equal has a registry of employee resource groups and hosts both U.S. and global workplace summits.

The group's 2012 Global LGBT Workplace Summit in London was sponsored by IBM, Accenture, British Airways, Citi, Eli Lilly & Co., The Walt Disney Company, Deutsche Bank, Ernst & Young, Microsoft, Hewlett-Packard, *The Advocate*, *Gay Star News* and Carnival Corporation. More than 2,600 people attended the 2011 U.S. summit in Dallas, with sponsors including Dell, Hewlett-Packard, IBM, Northrop Grumman, American Airlines, Deloitte, Ernst & Young, JCPenney, Paul Hastings, Target, Xerox, Accenture, Citi, Corning, Genentech, Intuit, Marsh & McLennan Companies, Texas Instruments, Wells Fargo, Aetna, Alcoa, Anheuser-Busch, AT&T, Bank of America, DuPont, Goldman Sachs, Lockheed Martin, Mass Mutual, Microsoft, Morgan Stanley, PepsiCo, Pfizer, Toyota, The Walt Disney Company, MillerCoors and JPMorgan Chase. There are dozens of other major brands listed by Out & Equal as sponsors of its various events.

In an interesting development, a very activist, in-your-face group called GetEqual, which mounted two years of spirited protests against President Barack Obama and others who it felt were standing in the way of gay progress, received a significant portion of its initial financing from Jonathan Lewis, grandson of a co-founder of The Progressive Corporation insurance companies. According to the *Bay Area Reporter*, sources said he contributed more than $400,000 of the organization's $500,000 budget in 2010. A gay group protesting the president that is funded by a major corporate scion? That's a fascinating turn of events.

Capitalism: A Gay Love Story

John D'Emilio explains how capitalism played a role in the homosexual movement in his 1983 groundbreaking book *Sexual Politics, Sexual Communities*. One of the ways that it affected sexuality was by separating it from procreation, because of scientific advancements in birth control. In an essay for the book *Powers of Desire: The Politics of Sexuality*, D'Emilio argues that the emergence of gays is associated with capitalism: "It has been the historical development of capitalism—more specifically, its free labor system—that has allowed large numbers of men and women in the late twentieth century to call themselves gay, to see themselves as part of a community of similar men and women, and to organize politically on the basis of that identity."

Another excellent book on capitalism is *Selling Out: The Gay and Lesbian Movement Goes to Market*, by Alexandra Chasin. It was published in 2000, so it covers earlier movement issues regarding the conflicting interests of activists, newspapers and corporations. She explains how personal liberty became entwined with economic freedom over the course of early U.S. history.

Chasin writes that "capitalism has, as it has had for centuries in the West, liberal and liberalizing effects. In other words, capitalism enables a political struggle for rights. … . [C]onsumption becomes a form of political participation, perhaps supplanting other, more direct, models of participation. What are the consequences of defining an individual act of private consumption as a mode of political participation? … I argue that identity-based marketing and consumption are intimately related to identity politics, and that, working together, they are inimical to [thus they obstruct] progressive political change."

Chasin further explores the connection between advertising and gay newspapers, saying the gay press "has conveyed values through its editorial content." She argues that since much of the gay press is white-male-owned and male-dominated, this in turn has affected the view of who is and is not included in the gay "nation." She contends that advertising in the gay niche is similar to historic ways that advertising has helped assimilate immigrants in the U.S. culture: "[T]his body of advertising frequently promises that consumption is a route to political enfranchisement as well as social acceptance … ."

In her book, Chasin looks in detail at how the gay community was sold starting in the 1970s as a valuable market for advertisers. This trend picked up the most steam in the 1990s, as more demographic surveys focused on the wealthier, whiter parts of the community. The publisher of the gay porn magazine *Blue Boy* even took out an advertisement in *Advertising Age* way back in 1976, touting the value of his gay male demographic. *The New York Times* wrote about the ad in its July 17, 1976, edition, noting that *The Advocate* paid "little attention to national advertising because an outside expert examined the market and delivered a negative appraisal."

Chasin also reports on various gay boycotts over the years, starting with the first known gay boycott, in 1967, by San Francisco's Glide Methodist Church and its related organizations. Glide told its members to refuse to buy goods and services from companies that discriminated against gay people, as reported in *The Advocate* of November 3, 1967. Other boycotts occurred over the years, but Chasin said the national boycott against the Florida Citrus Commission, after Anita Bryant's successful Save Our Children campaign overturned the Dade County, Florida, gay-rights law, was the first nationwide, effective gay boycott. Chasin notes that the boycott was not unanimously supported within the gay community. She argues that "at the same time that the gay movement became national, it revealed itself as split along several different axes—race, gender, class, and agenda."

Another book that looks at these issues is *Stagestruck: Theater, AIDS, and the Marketing of Gay America,* by Sarah Schulman. Against the landscape of her battle with the creators of the acclaimed stage musical *Rent* for its similarity to her novel *People in Trouble,* Schulman looks at how the mainstream acceptance of only a narrow band of gay arts and culture undermines the actual experiences of many LGBTs.

Landmines and Brand-mines

The tricky navigation of corporate relationships will continue to cause trouble in the gay community. There are some gay activists concerned about sponsorship and advertising by companies that have bad records on union and labor negotiations. International Mr. Leather in Chicago has been protested because its annual events in recent years have sometimes been at the Hyatt Regency Chicago hotel, which is in the midst of a major labor strike. NAMES Project AIDS Memorial Quilt founder Cleve Jones is among those traveling across the country working on hotel union issues—and he is unafraid of confronting gay leaders who cross the picket lines. The union movement was among the first mainstream entities that embraced LGBTs in their ranks, so this presents a dilemma for the community.

Jones, the National Gay and Lesbian Task Force, a spokesperson from the National Stonewall Democrats, Pride at Work (a gay labor group), the National Organization for Women, the AFL-CIO, the National Football League Players Association and others joined forces in 2012 to announce a global boycott of the Hyatt hotels as a "response to the hotel company's extensive abuse of their workers and low wages."

As *Windy City Times* reported on July 23, 2012, "UNITE HERE has been leading the boycott against Chicago Hyatt hotels since August 2010, when the union and hotel chain came to a standstill in contract negotiations. Union leaders say the global launch of the boycott is the largest escalation against Hyatt since that time."

Another long debate raged in the gay community about the Coors Brewing Company. Beginning in 1977, Coors was the subject of a boycott for decades, and even the openly gay San Francisco Supervisor Harvey Milk supported the boycott. In Chicago, the gay bar owners almost all stood by the boycott, which was in part based on the right-wing connections and contributions of some of the company's owners. The June 6, 1985, issue of *GayLife* carried a front-page story, "Most bars boycotting Coors beer," a newspaper survey of 55 area bars by Paul Cotton.

But one bar manager, Michael Shimandle of Bulldog Road, said poor sales contributed to his decision to pull Coors, not just the boycott. He told *GayLife*: "I'm sure that if you checked out other corporations doing business in the gay community you could find just as much homophobia. I'm sure

Old Man Jack Daniels hates faggots as much as Old Man Coors."

In 1998, the Gay & Lesbian Alliance Against Defamation accepted $110,000 from Coors, causing anger in some segments of the community. Up until the 2007 launch of a joint venture between Molson Coors Brewing Company and the pro-gay SABMiller company, many Chicago gay bars still refused to carry Coors products, and some groups refused sponsorship money from the company. But once the business name changed to MillerCoors, almost all boycott efforts seemed to fall away.

As a publisher, I accepted a few ads from Coors even though, as a board member of Gay Games VII, I lobbied against accepting the company's sponsorship. I felt that it had the right to state its case in our paper but that sponsoring the Gay Games was allowing it to get visibility at a major international event while many in the gay community were boycotting its products. But we also covered the controversy in *Windy City Times*, and the anti-Coors bars placed advertising in our paper against the company. Coors was not happy and pulled future ads from our paper, but we felt it was our obligation to cover the story.

Another company that has faced a longtime gay boycott is Cracker Barrel Old Country Store, Inc. According to Wikipedia: "In early 1991, an intra-company memo called for employees to be dismissed if they did not display 'normal heterosexual values.' According to news reports, at least 11 employees were fired under the policy on a store-by-store basis from locations in Georgia and other states. After demonstrations by gay rights groups the company ended its policy in March 1991 and stated it would not discriminate based on sexual orientation. The company's founder, Dan Evins, subsequently described the policy as a mistake. From 1992 onward, the New York City Employees Retirement System, then a major shareholder, put forward proposals to add sexual orientation to the company's non-discrimination policy. An early proposal in 1993 was defeated, with 77 percent against and only 14 percent in support, along with 9 percent abstaining. It was not until 2002 that the proposals were successful; 58 percent of company shareholders voted in favor of the addition."

Despite this forced change, most LGBTs who remember the pickets and boycotts against Cracker Barrel still won't cross the threshold of its restaurants. The company also has faced lawsuits and federal investigations about alleged racism at its locations. Cracker Barrel founder Danny Evins died in January 2012.

Of course, some companies, such as Chick-fil-A, don't care about a backlash when they appear to be anti-gay. A few companies—and owners of companies—that gave funds to support the anti–gay-marriage Prop 8 measure in California were criticized and boycotted. Websites cropped up listing the donors to Prop 8. The Manchester Grand Hyatt San Diego hotel, which was owned by Doug Manchester, was one of the big targets of gay activists. Manchester now owns the former *San Diego Union-Tribune*, which he renamed *U-T San Diego* after its 2011 purchase.

The Pink Panthers Web blog lists dozens of companies and their history of anti-gay behavior. They include ExxonMobil, which eliminated Mobil Corporation's domestic-partner benefits and its prohibition on sexual-orientation discrimination when Mobil merged with Exxon Corporation in 1999. Pink Panthers also lists Wal-Mart, The Salvation Army, Domino's Pizza, Insure.com, Meijer Inc., Urban Outfitters and Dish Network.

One other development due to the growth of the Internet is that in some ways it is actually more difficult to monitor online which companies market to LGBTs. When the gay press was all "paper," right-wing groups monitored the pages for advertising and then targeted advertisers for protest letters and boycotts. With the Internet, many gay websites run advertising pulled from multiple sources, and it's not always clear what ads were specifically placed on gay websites versus those placed across multiple media channels without regard to which websites are for gays. (This system has also resulted in some embarrassing ad placements of right-wing politicians on gay sites.) There is more protective cover on the massive Internet, even while information is more accessible than ever before.

Handling Controversy

Even the most gay-inclusive brands have made missteps on the road to the rainbow. To avoid this, some of them work on the front end by hiring LGBT companies specializing in advertising placement, such as Rivendell Media; Community Marketing, Inc.; Prime Access; Gay Ad Network; SPI Marketing; Out Now Consulting; or Pink Banana Media. There are also communications specialists such as Cathy Renna of Renna Communications and Bob Witeck of Witeck-Combs Communications.

Both Renna and Witeck are respected members of the gay community, and their years of support of LGBT and AIDS nonprofits and activists have given them credibility with the media. Their clients do make mistakes, but having gay media professionals helps these clients navigate from the mistakes to making changes and making good.

Witeck also partners with Harris Interactive to conduct the Harris Interactive GLBT Specialty Panel, providing insight into LGBT attitudes, behaviors and buying patterns. Especially important is its polling of opinions on relevant issues: "Using a unique GLBT panel with thousands of double opt-in participants and growing, Witeck-Combs Communications and Harris Interactive make it possible to quickly, accurately and cost effectively ask the GLBT individuals and households their opinions about public issues, consumer behaviors or their acceptance of leading brands in the market. Our approach enables us to tap opinions and gather data from gays, lesbians and bisexuals in a safe, confidential manner that respects their privacy and speaks sensitively to their needs, concerns and preferences."

One interesting and controversial trend in marketing to the gay community has been called "pinkwashing." It isn't meant in a positive way. Pinkwashing involves a brand's allegedly promoting itself as gay-friendly, in order to attract gay dollars, but covering up other potentially controversial aspects of the brand—for example, banks that are foreclosing on millions of homeowners, yet giving money to sponsor gay events.

Lesbian author Sarah Schulman wrote this in an op-ed for *The New York Times* on November 22, 2011: "Last year, the Israeli news site Ynet reported that the Tel Aviv tourism board had begun a campaign of around $90 million to brand the city as 'an international gay vacation destination.' … The growing global gay movement against the Israeli occupation has named these tactics 'pinkwashing': a deliberate strategy to conceal the continuing violations of Palestinians' human rights behind an image of modernity signified by Israeli gay life. Aeyal Gross, a professor of law at Tel Aviv University, argues that 'gay rights have essentially become a public-relations tool,' even though 'conservative and especially religious politicians remain fiercely homophobic.'"

Another controversial group criticized by gays over the years is The Salvation Army. Though religious in nature, it has been targeted because of alleged discriminatory treatment of staff and clients, and its annual Christmas drives for donations (the famous Salvation Army red kettles and bell ringers) have been boycotted. While the organization used to ignore the adverse publicity, in recent years it has tried to claim it did not discriminate—partly because the boycott has been especially effective in large U.S. cities. The gay media have covered this debate for more than three decades.

Show Me the Money

If companies want to truly benefit financially from their minor diversity efforts (such as sending a letter protesting an anti-gay bill), they should build on them to create long-term brand loyalty in the gay community. Without solid marketing efforts, their work will continue to have no measurable positive economic impact, and other leading brands may overtake them in the diversity race.

It frustrates me how easy it is for corporations to get 100 percent on the Human Rights Campaign's Corporate Equality Index. HRC, to its credit, does keep adding to the degree of difficulty, including requirements of transgender health benefits and more. In 2012, despite tougher guidelines, 190 participants earned 100 percent from HRC.

As the 2012 report stated: "In the first year of the CEI a decade ago, 13 businesses achieved the top score of 100 percent.

"In its debut year in which 319 participants were rated, the CEI noted that most of the largest U.S. employers fell within the middle of the ratings bell curve: workplace protections on the basis of sexual orientation, domestic partner health care benefits and some internal inclusion practices were becoming more common but transgender inclusion lagged.

"Serving as a road map for businesses trying to earn a perfect rating, the CEI report enumerated the best practices for ideal employers among the LGBT community. Now in its 10th year, the CEI has moved the needle of change for previously average-rated employers, with a majority of the 636 participating employers this year ranking above 80 percent.

"The CEI paved the way for early industry leaders in LGBT workplace inclusion to inspire rapid change among competitors."

But I think some of the categories could be strengthened, or even made stand-alone. For example, "public commitment" is worth 15 points and asks the companies if they have conducted ongoing LGBT-specific engagement that extends across the firm, including at least three of the following:

— LGBT employee recruitment efforts

— Supplier diversity program with demonstrated effort to include certified LGBT suppliers

— Marketing or advertising to LGBT consumers (e.g., advertising with LGBT content, advertising in LGBT media or sponsoring LGBT organizations and events)

— Philanthropic support of at least one LGBT organization or event (e.g., financial, in-kind or pro bono support)

— Public support for LGBT equality under the law through local, state or federal legislation or initiatives.

Well, that's a pretty diverse list to pick from, and they are all very different from one another. This category is also ripe for manipulating, or taking the easy road with very little effort.

It should not be enough to stick one ad in a national gay magazine, or an ad on a gay TV show, or have a float in a Pride parade, or write one letter to a politician. Rather, this category should be divided up, and companies should be held to certain standards. One suggestion would be to compute the dollars spent on the marketing, philanthropic and supplier-diversity areas as a percentage of what the companies spend in these areas overall. The index could start with 1 percent and move up to 3 to 5 percent of money spent, which is on the very low end of statistics of the LGBT population in the U.S.

On the marketing side, these dollars will pay off, as many surveys have shown high early-adopter and loyalty levels of the LGBT consumer base. Such expenditures would also have a tremendous impact in the philanthropic and supplier-diversity areas.

As publisher of *Outlines* (now *Windy City Times*) newspaper, I decided to wear my business hat more completely in 1995 when I founded the Chicago Area Gay and Lesbian Chamber of Commerce. I saw a need to help LGBT-owned small businesses, but soon we realized that non-gay small businesses and corporations wanted to join. We did not allow them to serve on the board or control the chamber (subsequent leadership changed this policy), and we created a questionnaire asking them a wide range of questions about their LGBT employment policies, outreach efforts and more in order to qualify for membership. (This was a few years before HRC started such ratings.) It was a form of advocacy on my part, no doubt, but I also saw the way it could benefit LGBTs at those companies and in the community at large. Even though I am a publisher, at my core I don't want our community exploited or taken advantage of by companies that just want us for our money, without doing the hard work of being equal-opportunity enterprises.

Deciding to Jump In

Sophisticated corporations know better than to jump quickly into any market. Here are a few suggestions for those considering the gay market:

— Make sure your company is ready for this. Your own house should be in order with the proper employment policies.

— Don't just dip your toe into this market. Don't expect people to respond to one ad placed one time. Treat it as a long-term investment.

— Make sure you have consistent images and messages that reflect your brand. Also, make sure to represent various segments of the LGBT community, depending on your own target demographics. For example, if your company is about families or finance, make sure to have LGBT families and couples in various combinations.

— Don't speak down to the community. Show diversity; don't just say you are diverse.

— Become a strong partner with the LGBT community through nonprofit alliances, and boast about that in your ads.

— Use your LGBT employees and consumers in marketing research and decisions. One bad step can take years to overcome. But also do not assume your gay employees have all the answers.

— The campaign should have depth nationally and regionally, across different media channels: print and online and, if appropriate, broadcast TV and radio. One ad in the national LGBT press will not be enough to start the campaign. New statistics from the U.S. census and other research show just how diverse the LGBT community is, and marketers can use this information to fine-tune campaigns across the country.

— Align yourself with similar companies for your marketing push, working through chambers of commerce or tourism groups to increase clout and buying power.

— For tourism destinations, use low-cost opportunities for visibility. These include journalism trips for LGBT media, giving away prizes in contests, and bartering for cross-promotions.

— There are unique ways to reach the community through specialized media, such as B-to-B, travel, ethnic, gender-specific, the arts, and even leather, bear and other lifestyle media.

— Use events as a way to market to the community, through festivals, Pride, conferences, sports events, benefits, AIDS walks, and so on. There are thousands of events to choose from, so pick those that most match your brand.

— Use openly LGBT activists and celebrities of all kinds in your campaigns.

— And finally, the community will not simply jump because someone says "jump." The product you are selling still has to have some resonance and interest for the buyer. It is no different from the mainstream media decisions your company makes. Don't hold the gay community to a higher standard.

While the LGBT community in the U.S. represents more than $700 billion in annual spending, it is not single-minded. Homosexual does not mean homogeneous. The community can be brand-loyal, but it can also be finicky. There are many nuances to consider when trying to understand this community, but for those companies willing to do the work, the payoff can be very great.

As Community Marketing, Inc., states, there is no "LGBT market," but rather a whole series of markets within, "just as there is no singular 'Asian market.' The LGBT communities represent a broad and dynamic variety of interests, sensitivities, preferences and priorities. Those, plus variations in geographical location, age, income, relationship status, gender, sexual identity and more, make it even more important to discover which opportunities within [the LGBT community] will help you achieve your goals. Fine-tuning your approaches based on highly refined and well-targeted matches within [the LGBT community] will make your outreach initiatives more efficient and cost-effective, and will significantly improve your marketing ROI [return on investment]."

A useful way to think about this is to realize that there is also no "straight" market. Certain advertisers want to reach those who read *Vanity Fair*, while others want readers of *The Economist* or

Time, Essence or *Scientific American*. Some place ads during *American Idol*, others during *Nightline*.

For the past several years, Community Marketing, Inc., has published an annual community survey that has grown to have more than 45,000 respondents. Thomas Roth, president of CMI, said organizations cannot continue to "market to gay men and lesbians in the same manner." CMI held a conference in 2011 where it summarized some of its recent findings:

— 74 percent of CMI's survey respondents prefer the term(s) "gay and lesbian/lesbian and gay."

— 19 percent favor the title(s) "queer" or "alternative."

— Most ads lack representation of ethnic minorities, people 55 or over, and single gays and lesbians.

— The majority of advertisers use stock photography not authentic to the community.

Boldly Go …

There is one stellar example of a campaign that had measurable impact for a tourism entity. The Philadelphia LGBT tourism efforts are among the best-studied in the marketplace. Philadelphia broke into the top 10 U.S. destinations visited by gay and lesbian travelers in 2010—seven years after the launch of the Greater Philadelphia Tourism Marketing Corporation's groundbreaking "Philadelphia—Get Your History Straight and Your Nightlife Gay" campaign. The campaign ran in both mainstream and gay print publications, and even on TV. It also generated a lot of free media coverage.

According to CMI's 2010 LGBT Tourism Study, Philadelphia tied for the No. 9 spot on the list of most-visited destinations and tied for the No. 2 spot on the list of the destinations most effectively promoting to LGBT travelers. Before Philadelphia's gay-tourism marketing campaign started, the region was not even in the top 20.

Here's what the city of Philadelphia found:

— Despite the recession, Philadelphia's gay and lesbian travelers are spending more money (57 percent) on their trips than the region's general-market visitors.

— Both lesbians and gay men aged 18 to 35 rank Philadelphia a top-10 leisure destination.

— Many gay and lesbian visitors show equal or greater interest in non-gay vacation activities as compared to gay vacation activities.

— 90 percent report they have been to the city before, and 84 percent plan to return within the next year.

— People remember the "Philadelphia—Get Your History Straight and Your Nightlife Gay" campaign. Forty-three percent of respondents recognized at least one of the ads.

— People responding to the survey who were familiar with the campaign spent 36 percent more during their Philadelphia trip, $1,013 compared to $743.

According to CMI, every dollar that the tourism corporation spends on "Philadelphia—Get Your History Straight and Your Nightlife Gay" generates $153 in visitor spending.

This is a return on investment of 153 to 1.

By the Numbers

Given how important advertising is to the bottom line of almost every gay publication in the U.S., what are the trends? The 1990s were the peak years for most gay media, and those that survived did so because they adapted to changes. The 2000s were still strong, until the 2008–10 downturn in advertising placement across all print media.

As the economy has edged up, advertising sales have rebounded in some categories. But it is unlikely that most print media will replicate the boom years, especially in the classified sales category. Just as worrisome is the move of longtime print advertisers to online—where they spend less money per ad. While gay newspapers have websites, the advertising dollars can't support the same infrastructure (especially staffing) as print, at least not yet.

Increased costs of printing a newspaper, based especially on rises in the cost of newsprint and gasoline, are an added burden for print-based media. Some also acquired large debt during the good years. This puts print at a disadvantage when competing against newer and less cost-intensive online ventures.

Another interesting competitor in the gay category is the relatively new existence of TV gay-ad placements. Logo TV is a gay consumer network (with a lot of non-gay content), owned by Viacom, and it captures a good chunk of gay-marketing dollars each year. Bravo, owned by NBCUniversal, boosted its relationship with gays when it launched *Queer Eye for the Straight Guy* in 2003, and it is seen as a very gay channel. Even the traditional TV networks have gay-inclusive shows such as *Modern Family* and *Glee*.

The networks have come a long way since the controversy that arose when Ellen DeGeneres's character Ellen (and the comic herself) came out in 1997. Her talk show is now a huge success, and she has been joined on the daytime circuit by Anderson Cooper, who has also joined her on this side of the closet.

This means gay newspapers are not competing just with gay magazines and websites—they are also up against major corporate broadcast channels. These may help to expand the marketing money aimed at gays, but they also suck up most of the oxygen in the room.

There are a few bright spots. Studies reported in *Editor & Publisher* and other media show that readers still value news from reliable brand-name newspaper providers, and that print provides advertisers with a more proven response.

Smaller newspapers also have an advantage—and all U.S. gay newspapers are considered in that niche. They can respond more quickly to changes and adjust costs to keep in line with revenues.

The advertising-based revenue model will likely continue for most gay media. Online paywalls are risky and, while they succeed at larger companies, smaller newspapers will have a difficult time monetizing viewers online. There are some foundations giving grants to newspapers for special projects, but that foundation money will also be small and a tiny percentage of newspaper revenues. For now, the solution has to be a combination of continuing to hustle for print advertising and keeping on top of new technology and social media as a way to maximize revenues.

One interesting marker of success for the gay community is the fact that a few efforts have been made by non-gay publishers to reach the gay niche. This tradition goes back to the late 1960s, to the time of *Screw*, which owned *GAY*, but it is still rare. *Time* magazine in 1994 put tens of thousands of dollars into creating a prototype gay magazine called *Tribe*. After the American Family Association made protest noises, *Time* pulled out. In 2011, the *Chicago Tribune* explored (but decided against) a similar effort. Its companion free daily, *RedEye*, had a special pullout Pride section in 2012. Both the *Tribune* and the *Chicago Sun-Times* have had gay supplements in their papers as have many other mainstream and nongay alternative papers, including *The Village Voice*. And the *Desert Sun*, a Gannett paper, launched *Desert Outlook* in 2012, a bimonthly (six times a year) gay magazine. This likely makes them the first daily mainstream newspaper to launch an ongoing gay publication.

The Balance Between Church and State

The phrase "church and state" at a newspaper means the dividing line between the advertising-and-business side of a company and the editorial team. But there was never a true separation between these sides of a news company. Whether it was the business interests of publishers William Randolph Hearst or Colonel Robert R. McCormick, or nowadays Rupert Murdoch or Warren Buffett, there has always been a conflict to navigate. The best a journalist or editor could hope for was being left alone most of the time to pursue most of the stories. Throughout the last three centuries, there are examples of courageous newspaper people fighting against corruption in government, business and beyond.

In the gay community, most early periodicals were started by activists, not businesspeople or journalists. Some activists trained themselves to become better journalists, and by the 1970s, gay newspapers and magazines began to attract graduates of journalism schools or those with mainstream media experience. Even into the 1980s and 1990s, some chose to use pseudonyms for their gay-press work, so as not to hurt their career potential.

Businesspeople also started to see the value in gay media. David Goodstein was an investment banker who in 1974 purchased what was then a regional newspaper called *The Los Angeles Advocate* and transformed it into a national publication, *The Advocate*. Other businesspeople started their own publications in the 1970s, and some are still a going concern. Others were started by young men and women who became businesspeople simply because that was the only way to continue to publish. They learned on the job and eventually became successful in their craft.

So how is the separation of church and state in gay media? It is porous, no doubt. I have seen this in action from both sides of the fence, since I am a publisher who was trained as a journalist. When I started working at *GayLife* in 1984, there was discussion about how AIDS coverage was so negative and could hurt bar and bathhouse business, but there was never any censorship. (The newspaper's owner, Chuck Renslow, operated a bar and bathhouse, and, of course, many of the advertisers were other bars and bathhouses.) At *Windy City Times*, owner Jeff McCourt heavily pressured politicians and theater companies, along with mainstream retailers, to advertise. It strengthened his company, but did it also influence endorsements and coverage?

Rodger Streitmatter, in his book *Unspeakable: The Rise of the Gay and Lesbian Press in America*, said 1970s gay media often blurred the line between advertising and editorial. "*The Advocate* was a master of the technique," Streitmatter wrote, "willingly accommodating the desires of the burgeoning gay business community through uncompromisingly positive features about the bar and bath culture." But the author later adds: "As in previous generations of the gay press, what initially appears to be blatant pandering to advertisers can be defended. Creating their own businesses continued to be one of the prime ways gay people were advancing toward liberation."

In my own experience as publisher, it is a tricky thing to navigate a community you are so close to. If an executive from the *Chicago Tribune* serves on the board of a dance company, is the *Tribune* influenced in its reporting? We try to state conflicts that are relevant, such as my founding of the gay chamber of commerce, starting a gay marketing company, serving on the Gay Games board, or producing a movie.

Some gay newspaper publishers donate to political candidates, and others have started nonprofit organizations. There are gay reporters who have helped teach police courses or have spoken at conferences on mainstream media coverage.

Journalists accept free tickets to theatrical shows in exchange for reviewing, or free tourism trips to write about a city (a practice not confined to journalists at gay publications). I have even heard of one who had plastic surgery donated by an advertiser, and he subsequently wrote about the experience. I know some publishers who barter for bar tabs or restaurant certificates. There are probably thousands of examples of decisions that walk the tightrope between what is good to do and what is not. For each publisher, editor and reporter, making these decisions with the readers' interests in mind is a critically important job.

Another difficult issue for gay publishers and reporters is how to cover controversy within the community. That includes controversy at nonprofits and businesses that advertise. Small businesses, including bars, can be the bread-and-butter ad base for local gay newspapers. I know as a publisher that these are always the toughest stories to do—investigations of wrongdoing, theft, mismanagement or bad business practices usually result in threats to pull advertising. At *Windy City* Times, we have lost much business over the years following controversial stories. In 2011, Howard Brown Health Center stopped stocking our papers on its premises because of our coverage of its management problems. So the threat is real: Our company has had delivery locations denied and advertising contracts canceled. But our primary goal has to be to serve our readers first, not the advertisers; otherwise, the readers will eventually go elsewhere for the news.

This chapter began by quoting a slogan that we are a movement, not a market. Realistically, gay periodicals are in the same boat as mainstream ones. They rely primarily on advertising revenue to survive. Balancing the goals of the corporations and the needs of readers is never easy.

Few people want to be seen as belonging to a "market". But by using the clout of the gay dollar, the movement has actually changed the market. And this has, in turn, translated into significant changes within corporate and small-business America, in ways that have helped tens of millions of employees and consumers.

The following are advertisements scanned from the gay-newspaper and national-magazine archives of *Windy City Times*, starting in the late 1970s and through primarily the 1990s.

The 1970s

The 1980s

The Coors boycott was covered in this issue of *GayLife*, June 6, 1985

Marshall Field's

The 1990s

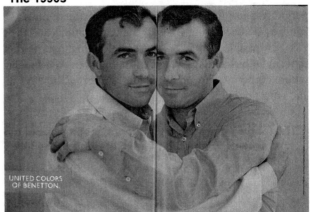

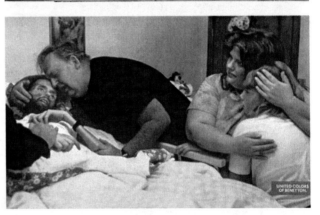

RIGHT and ABOVE: Benetton sparked debate related to its 1991 use of a Therese Frare photo of David Kirby, surrounded by his family in his last hours of life. He was frail with AIDS complications, and Benetton used the image to illustrate the impact of AIDS. Benetton even ran one ad with a large pink condom that ACT UP displayed to call attention to safer sex.

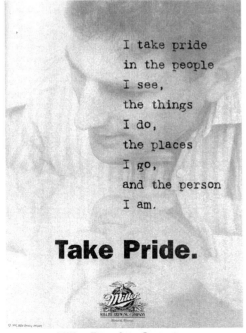

I take pride
in the people
I see,
the things
I do,
the places
I go,
and the person
I am.

Take Pride.

Miller Brewing Company

The Advocate Classifieds

Apple

The 1990s (continued)

Evian

Benson & Hedges 100's

Key West Business Guild

Bud Light

1990s–2000s

Calvin Klein

Berlin tourism

Armani Exchange (A/X)

Diesel

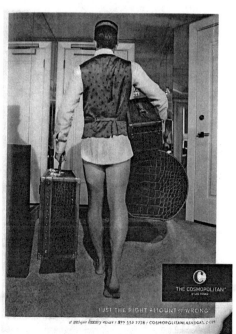

The Cosmopolitan Hotel (Las Vegas)

1990s–2000s (continued)

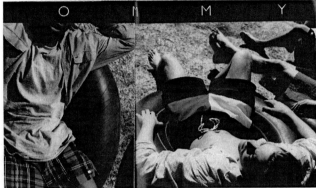

Tommy Hilfiger (right) and Movado watches (below)

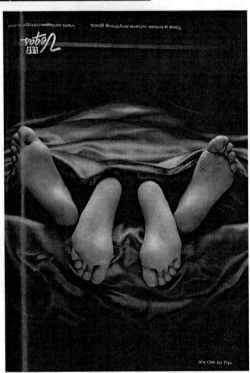

Las Vegas tourism (above) and Omega watches (left)

More 2000s

Expedia

Miami tourism

Kenneth Cole

Stockholm Gay & Lesbian Network.

2000s (continued)

Philadelphia Tourism (left and above)

San Francisco Tourism

Subaru

2006 (IBM)

2008 (American Airlines)

2008 (Ameriprise Financial)

2008 (Avis)

2008 (Cadillac)

2008 (Gillette)

2008 (Travelocity)

2008 (Macy's)

2010 (Paris Las Vegas hotel)

2010 (Orbitz)

2010 (Reyataz by Bristol-Myers Squibb)

2010 (SunChips by Frito-Lay)

2010 (Macy's)

2011 (Bridgestone Tires)

2011 (Chicago Cubs)

2011 (Kaletra by Abbott Laboratories)

2011 (Gilead Sciences, Inc.)

2011 (Kenneth Cole)

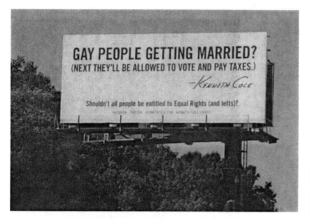

2011 (Live Nation)

2011
(Logo TV for *RuPaul's Drag Race*)

2012 (Allstate)

2012

2012

INSTINCT WOULD LIKE TO THANK ABSOLUT FOR 30 YEARS OF SUPPORT—FROM ITS
COMING OUT TO THE LGBT COMMUNITY IN 1981 TO ITS UNWAVERING LOYALTY TODAY.

ABSOLUT HAS ALWAYS BEEN THERE...

1980's

ABSOLUT COMMITMENT

ABSOLUT OUTRAGEOUS
Cocktails Perfected

CELEBRATING 30 YEARS OF GOING OUT AND COMING OUT

In 2012, Absolut marked its 30th anniversary of
advertising and marketing in the gay community.

ALWAYS *First*

ALWAYS *Loyal*

ALWAYS *Ours*

SINCE 1981

30 YEARS AND COUNTING

HERE'S TO 30 MORE YEARS

2012 (Allstate)

equality is _____.

What does equality look like to you?
Show it. Tell it. Share it.

allstate.com/equalityis

Allstate
You're in good hands.

2012 (Desert AIDS Project)

2012 (American Airlines)

2012 (American Airlines at Chicago Pride)

2012 (Amtrak)

2012 (Amtrak)

2012

We Didn't Invent Christian Hate Organizations
We Just Support Them.

Chick-fil-A's corporate positions on gay issues sparked a national debate, a boycott, and some very clever online responses.

2012

Not surprised fundies were outraged by this....

they didn't like the blacks and whites touching either.

JUNE 25 | PRIDE

2012 (Johnson & Johnson)

Stand up to make schools safe. For all.

Oreo cookies came out for Pride 2012.

2012 (JCPenney)

2012 (Lexus for *The Advocate*)

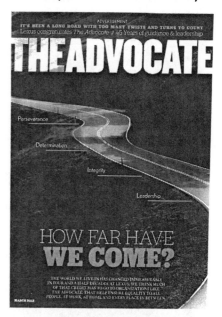

2012 (Walmart)

2012 (Broadway in Chicago ad for *Les Misérables*)

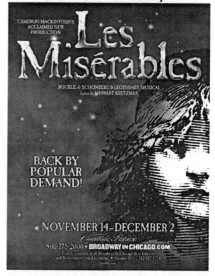

2012 (Mitchell Gold + Bob Williams)

2012 (Ray-Ban)

2012 (Ketel One Vodka)

2012 (Chevy Volt)

2012 (Miller Lite)

2012 (Target)

PART FIVE:
The Ongoing Role of Ever-Changing Media

"Our liberty depends on the freedom of the press, and that cannot be limited without being lost."

— **Thomas Jefferson**

36

Newspapers: Research Values

By Chuck Colbert

It should come as no surprise that academics in the fields of journalism and communication find LGBT media's history to be a rich resource for scholarship.

Three examples illustrate the point: Larry Gross' 2001 book *Up From Invisibility: Lesbians, Gay Men, and the Media in America*; Rodger Streitmatter's 1995 book *Unspeakable: The Rise of the Gay and Lesbian Press in America*; and Katherine Sender's 2004 book *Business, Not Politics: The Making of the Gay Market*.

As their works demonstrate, LGBT media have been indispensable in sustaining a community, building a movement and creating a gay marketplace.

Gross is a professor at the Annenberg School for Communication and Journalism at the University of Southern California. Streitmatter is a journalism professor at Washington, D.C.–based American University's School of Communication. Sender is a professor in the Department of Film, Television and Media Studies at the University of Auckland, New Zealand.

And yet, it's not just college professors teaching in media-related fields who find LGBT publications fundamental to their research and writing.

As Matthew Bajko, assistant editor at San Francisco's *Bay Area Reporter*, first noted in an April 7, 2011, article, historians, artists, authors, documentary film producers and directors all have turned to gay media outlets as sources for various projects.

"Historically, [gay] media has been essential to scholarship in the area of LGBT-related topics," Gross said during a telephone interview. "In the early days, a lot of the work that might have been published in more traditional academic venues could only be published in LGBT media."

Topics of interest to researchers run the gamut, everything from the rise of the homophile movement and subsequent emergence of gay-rights politics and sexual-liberation advocacy, to police harassment of gay men and the beginnings of the HIV/AIDS epidemic.

Early on, local gay media provided information about bars and the locations of events such as protests and rallies.

At the same time, LGBT newspapers covered police entrapment and arrests of gays—and gay men fighting back, suicides, murders, lawsuits and emerging health issues such as sexually transmitted diseases.

And just as publications are tapped for source material, so are gay journalists.

"Anything with numbers attached to it attracts researchers and academics," said Lisa Keen of Keen News Service, which provides LGBT-related content to gay media nationwide.

"I think the most calls I get are from people—not just academics—scrutinizing the data showing that about one in four or one in three gays votes Republican," Keen said. "When I've done stories about the 'best state legally for gays,' I've gotten a few inquiries seeking to know the specifics of my criteria and how I weighted each.

"The only other thing I recall getting a lot of researcher attention on was way back in the 1980s when I did a series of interviews from diagnosis to death with one of Washington, D.C.'s first people with AIDS. A number of academic publications reprinted it, including a journal for nurses," added Keen, who is a former *Washington Blade* editor.

At New York City–based *Gay City News*, Associate Editor Duncan Osborne said he has been a source "at most once or twice, if memory serves, for professors or Ph.D. candidates doing reports." One topic was "public sex stuff," he said.

Meanwhile, "*Gay City News* was used extensively in an Amnesty International report and a 2008 UNHCR [United Nations High Commissioner for Refugees] report," Osborne said. "Our stuff occasionally pops up in HIV/AIDS reports."

Tracy Baim, executive editor and publisher of Chicago's *Windy City Times*, and Kevin Naff, editor of the *Washington Blade*, say they routinely field inquiries from researchers.

"I get a lot of requests for news clips and photos," said Naff. "In certain cases and for some stories we're the only place, or one of the only places, where information exists on a given topic," he said.

In Chicago, Baim said that she, too, "receive[s] calls and emails from traditional academics, graduate students and postgraduate folks all the time, asking for specific articles on a specific date or generally on themes."

Writing their dissertations, students "might need a photo from a certain era," said Baim. "Sometimes I am interviewed for my individual take on things that I have covered over the years. But what is even more exciting is, over the last five to 10 years, I have also had calls from high-school and even grammar-school students doing projects related to the gay community and also on AIDS issues. One grammar-school student interviewed me at length a few years ago for a Chicago gay-history project on how the city's gay-rights ordinance got passed."

Baim said that while the vast majority of calls are history-related, others concern AIDS/HIV and health care. Here again, those inquiries are usually rooted in a historical context of how the community responded to the AIDS crisis—or the politics of the health-care response.

What accounts for so much LGBT history and politics in Chicago?

Baim points to the large number of colleges and universities in the metropolitan area and the Midwest. "A lot of LGBT people would be attracted here from small towns because they are more than likely to have a more welcoming environment," she said.

Also, Baim said, "Some great people, like [historian] John D'Emilio, have made their home here. George Chauncey also passed through as well," she added. "So they can't help but have an influence on their students."

The *Blade*'s location in the nation's capital, of course, gives the publication front-row seats to cover national LGBT politics and history. In the District of Columbia, local news is national, and national news is local. In that regard, the *Blade* can lay claim to being a sort of national LGBT publication of record.

Overall, gay media are a treasure trove of information, fleshing out specifics of LGBT life not found in mainstream media, including a measure of the gay community's texture and temperament.

As the *Blade*'s Naff explained, "Part of our mission is to scrutinize the movement," which sometimes entails taking leaders to task.

Playing a watchdog role, "the *Blade* at times has criticized gay movement leaders," said Naff, adding that it has asked questions "about sources of funding, is the money being spent appropriately, the salaries that people make, what are the strategies, and are they working."

Historian David Carter, at work on a biography of the late veteran gay-rights activist Frank Kameny, has turned to the *Blade* for its coverage of him over the years, Naff said.

What's more, consider two current hot topics of gays in the military and same-sex marriage. Here again, LGBT media detail a broader range and provide deeper coverage of community politics than can be found elsewhere.

While mainstream outlets often frame the same-sex-marriage debate as a clash between the religious right and the liberals, "the complexities come out in LGBT media," said USC's Gross.

"It's more complicated than marriage equality," he said. "It's a battle over who gets to decide what happens and whose strategy is going to win."

The LGBT community's philosophical thinking about marriage is also more nuanced. "Some are [putting forth] the old anti-assimilation argument, liberationists' arguments" against marriage for gays, said Gross. "Others think about [same-sex marriage] in class terms."

Yes, marriage is a basic civil-rights question, Gross said. Yet, "there are people arguing, 'That's not what we should be trying to accomplish.'"

The same goes for gays in the military, said Gross, about which some say, "Why are we fighting to join the military?"

Of course, history and politics are more often than not primary interests for researchers.

Take, for example, openly gay Timothy Stewart-Winter, an assistant professor of history at Rutgers University in Newark, N.J. He is writing a book about the rise of LGBT politics in Chicago, with a focus on how gay people got a voice in City Hall.

Local gay press "provided me a snapshot of how LGBT people were interacting in the public sphere, what they were saying to each other, what rights they were demanding, and what their worries and complaints were at different moments," he said.

"In a lot of ways, LGBT history since the early days of the homophile movement, which is where I am beginning, is the history of queer media," Stewart-Winter said. "You can track our political empowerment by looking at the publications that have come and gone and stayed around."

Over time, the gay community "used LGBT media as a place to hash out disagreements" and "what it is we are pursuing," said Stewart-Winter. "The LGBT press told me that we have grown exponentially not just in influence, but also in having the kinds of institutions who help people," specifically, people just coming out.

Sure enough, empowering more gay people leveraged the LGBT community's influence, with gay media functioning as a fulcrum.

For instance, during the 1980s the Chicago City Council voted three times on a gay-rights ordinance. The first two times it failed. After it failed, "*Windy City Times* printed a list of all 50 aldermen, their wards, and how they voted," explained Stewart-Winter.

Additionally, the newspaper published aldermen's phone numbers and encouraged its readers "to let your voices be heard in a very direct way," he noted. "Gay media also reported on voter registration projects, which were the kinds of things that politicians look at when making assessments," Stewart-Winter said. Accordingly, gay media certainly facilitated the Chicago gay community's gaining electoral clout. After all, "local politics runs on people being motivated to vote," he said.

In the future, expect more reliance on LGBT publications for scholarly pursuits, given the Internet's capacity to expand access to gay media archives as more outlets digitize entire collections.

Stewart-Winter mentioned one valuable online resource, LGBT Life, from EBSCO Publishing (www.ebscohost.com/academic/lgbt-life), which bills itself as "the definitive index to the world's literature regarding [LGBT] issues," boasting a database index and abstracts "from more than 200 LGBT-specific core periodicals," among other offerings.

LGBT Life's database provides access to articles from regional and national outlets, including *The Advocate*, *Lesbian News*, the *Washington Blade*, the *Bay Area Reporter*, and *Windy City Times*, as well as historically significant publications such as *ONE*, *The Ladder*, *Mattachine Review*, *Christopher Street*, and *The Body Politic*. LGBT Life covers academic disciplines as varied as psychology, religion, sociology, history and politics.

Another invaluable online resource is www.outweek.net, an Internet archive of all 105 issues of *OutWeek* magazine, published in New York City from June 1989 until July 1991.

A seminal lesbian and gay publication during a peak era of AIDS activism, *OutWeek*, founded by Kendall Morrison with Gabriel Rotello, redefined the role of the gay press not only in reporting news but also in creating it.

Increasingly, researchers are using the LGBT blogosphere.

News aggregators, blog sites and Internet pioneers—including Michael Rogers, John Aravosis of Ameriblog, Bil Browning at Bilerico, Andy Towle at Towleroad, Joe Jervis of Joe.My.God., Pam Spaulding of Pam's House Blend, and veteran journalist and blogger Rex Wockner—are essential for anyone interested in "paying attention" to the LGBT community. "They are enormously valuable in keeping abreast of what's happening," said Gross.

Nikki Usher, an assistant professor in the School of Media and Public Affairs at George Washington University, relies primarily on the Internet. In her research, when "specifically working on a piece about the LGBT community, I turn to blogs and websites and the like for my work," said Usher, "though I wish everyone had as great a digital platform as the *Blade* and *Windy City Times*."

Some of this material originally appeared in Press Pass Q.

37

Researching Mainstream vs. Gay Media

By St. Sukie de la Croix

History is made by those who were there at the time, and written by those who were not. If you were there, and you write about it, it's called autobiography, with all the testy foibles, memory lapses and biases that go with it. Autobiography is a good place to rewrite the past and settle old scores, light on truth, heavy on gossip, as it should be—a chance to bitch-slap your enemies, especially those cold in their grave and unable to claw their dry, skeletal remains out of the earth to defend themselves against the slander of an old queen. See *Memoirs* by Tennessee Williams.

Which is how I, a British gay man who knew nothing of the Windy City until I moved here in 1991, came to write *Chicago Whispers: A History of LGBT Chicago Before Stonewall.* It all started in a 1998 issue of *Outlines* (later, *Windy City Times*) when I began "Chicago Whispers," a 1,000-words-a-week column of lighthearted oral-history interviews. The first week began thus:

The first gay bar I went into ...

"I was 21 and had just decided that I was gay. I'd just finished Catholic College and decided it was time now, and I got into a cab and asked the driver to take me to a gay bar. That was in 1955. He said, 'I only know one.' And I said, 'I only need one.' He took me to a bar on the North Side called The Volleyball, which most of the old-timers will remember. I got out, I went in, I looked around, and I thought, 'Oh, my God!' Now I know they were drag queens, and pimps, and everything ... and I thought, 'If that's gay, then I'm not gay.' It looked like these people had no self-respect. I got into a cab and went home. It kept me straight for 10 years." — Arlene Halko.

"It was the Glory Hole. Early 1980s, 1983 or thereabouts. It was a long, narrow bar with round tables. I remember some very old clientele. I would imagine it was probably a hustler bar. Dimly lit. It was right by Carol's Speakeasy on Wells, next to the Bijou. It was a neighborhood bar that had cheesy little Go-Go boys on top of unstable tables ... a couple of times I was there, they almost fell off. There were a few bookstores nearby that were really active ... can't remember the names ... I think a couple of them are still there." — Don Creech.

"The first bar I was in was Nutbush City Limits. I was living in Oak Park at the time. One wonderful thing about suburban bars is that you don't have leather bars, and you don't have drag queen bars ... everybody's all together ... old, young ... this was about 1985 ... I wasn't really out at the time. I was going to a conservative Christian School, so I kept things very discreet, very anonymous, very one night, so that I didn't have to worry about it interfering with the rest of my life." — Rich Jentzen.

The column continued for six years with hundreds of LGBTs contributing, the most extensive gay oral-history project the city of Chicago had seen. It also resulted in my participation in seminars, speaking engagements, a 10-part series for the *Chicago Tribune*, and a Chicago Lesbian and Gay Bus Tour for the city government's Chicago Neighborhood Tours. I may not have known much about Chicago when I arrived, but within 10 years I was standing in front of students at the Adler School of Professional Psychology and corporate businesses such as Chubb Insurance, regaling them with tales of LGBT Chicago. The next step was to write a book.

My research would take me to university, law and medical libraries in Chicago, Madison and other cities. It would take me to museums where I leafed through dusty tomes and old documents, but mostly I sat for hours scanning newspapers that were on microfilm, or carefully turning the crispy, yellowing pages of hard copies. There were two types:

Mainstream papers: How they saw us

Gay papers: How we see ourselves

Before gay papers and publications in Chicago, the *Chicago Daily Tribune* and other publications wrote about homosexuals as if they were penning an anthropological study of some sinister, amoral tribe that had wandered out of the jungle, or an alien species landed here from Planet Homo. We were fifth-columnists on a secret mission to destroy the sexual status quo. In the *Chicago Daily Tribune* of May 28, 1948, a headline read: "Hold Professor Headed Orgies With Own Sex."

Columbia, Mo., May 27 (Special): The University of Missouri was rocked with scandal today by the arrest of a veteran journalism professor who allegedly was a leader of a ring of university students and townsmen who held "mad homosexual parties" in this college town.

E.K. Johnston, the arrested 50-year-old journalism professor, whose career stretched back to 1922 when he taught business administration at the University of Wisconsin (and included a 1929 stint at Northwestern University teaching advertising), gave himself up to Prosecutor Howard B. Lang and was charged with sodomy. He and two others who played a lesser role were jailed; the next day, he was released on bond and was suspended from his job.

On January 17, 1949, another *Chicago Daily Tribune* headline read: "Capt. Harrison Jails 24 in War on Degenerates":

In a drive against degenerates infesting vice and clip joints, Capt. Thomas Harrison of the E. Chicago av. station early yesterday arrested 15 men and nine women in taverns on the west side of N. Clark st., between Chicago av., and the river.

Accompanied by six detectives and a patrol wagon, Harrison questioned hundreds of patrons in taverns, sent degenerates to the police station for investigation, and broke up couples who had newly met.

Later the article read:

Harrison, who last week arrested 93 men in a raid on the Windup lounge, 669 N. Clark st. [sic; it was State Street], a hangout for perverts, condemned degenerates for the recruiting of adolescents.

Dr. Harry R. Hoffman, Illinois state alienist, agreed, and added that homosexuals should be incarcerated in institutions "for the protection of society."...

Capt. Harrison said that Chicago probably has at least 18,000 sexually maladjusted men, all potentially dangerous.

Boys as young as 12 have been approached, Capt. Harrison said, and unless they have been forewarned by parents, friends, or church leaders, might easily fall victim.

Many homosexuals, Capt. Harrison said, maintain luxurious apartments where they entertain young, unsuspecting "recruits" with food, music, liquor, and obscene literature.

"That's the beginning of the downfall of many boys and young men," Capt. Harrison said. "All families with boys should warn them early to beware of strange men at all times."

As gay-rights organizations began to emerge in the 1950s, it became clear that homosexual publications were needed to counteract the distorted view of homosexuals in the mainstream press.

In Chicago, there were a few early attempts at homosexual publications prior to 1960, but the first regular source of gay information was the monthly *Mattachine Midwest Newsletter*, first published in

July 1965, though it became irregular in the late 1960s because of a changeover in leadership and style of the group.

While researching *Chicago Whispers: A History of LGBT Chicago Before Stonewall* and its sequel, *Chicago After Stonewall: The Making of a Gay Community,* I leaned heavily on the gay press for research, and on the mainstream press to put LGBTs into the context of society at large. While the *Mattachine Midwest Newsletter* seemed radical at times, and at other times conservative, depending on the leadership, gay papers in the 1970s, such as *The Paper, The Chicago Gay Crusader* and *Lavender Woman,* mirrored left-leaning underground papers such as the *Chicago Seed,* using the same vernacular of the period.

Whereas the *Mattachine Midwest Newsletter* largely catered to a relatively small group of people, scattered and often closeted (though it was also distributed in some gay bars), post-Stonewall gay papers were aimed at a larger community, painting a fuller picture of the burgeoning "gay scene." As I've said, there were sporadic publications before, but for the researcher of out gay life in Chicago, the one defining month that opened a stream of continuous documentation began when Michael Bergeron published issue No. 1 of *The Chicago Gay Crusader* in May 1973. Prior to that, the early 1970s are a fallow period for historians and student researchers of Chicago gay history, with occasional articles in student newspapers such as the *Chicago Maroon* or the *Roosevelt Torch,* and in the alternative the *Seed* and the *Reader.*

May 1973 also saw the publication of Volume 2, No. 3, of *Lavender Woman,* giving male researchers an insight into the mysteries of lesbian separatism. The only lesbian publication in Chicago in the 1960s was the Daughters of Bilitis newsletter, the organ of an on-again, off-again organization whose activities were little documented; I have the minutes of a 1962 meeting, a handful of letters, an interview with a former president, but I've never seen a copy of the newsletter. In the early 1970s, lesbians came flying out of the closet on the coattails of the women's liberation movement.

In the May 1973 *Lavender Woman,* the cover showed a drawing of a woman leaping over a map of the USA and the words "Keep on Truckin' Mama." The paper was a far cry from the closeted gab-and-java meetings of the Daughters of Bilitis in the 1960s and contained articles on a broad range of subjects: Chicago lesbian counseling, the Artemis Players theater group production of the play *Trevor,* and lesbian mothers. Upcoming events included protests at Cook County Jail and a kiss-in at the Civic Center.

This was also a new age of out lesbian celebrities. Long before Ellen DeGeneres and U.S. Representative Tammy Baldwin (D-Wisconsin), there was Del Martin, co-author with Phyllis Lyon of the book *Lesbian/Woman,* who on April 9, 1973, spoke to more than 100 women at a meeting of Chicago Lesbian Liberation. "The Sisterhood not only feels good but is growing," Martin wrote in one fan's book. Then, on May 29, 1973, *Village Voice* writer Jill Johnston rolled into town to great fanfare, including an article in the July 6, 1973, issue of the *Reader.* These were the role models of the new Lesbian Nation.

The May 1973 issue of *The Chicago Gay Crusader* had a column by Margaret Wilson called "Lesbian Lore." Apart from that, the paper was mostly of male or both-gender interest, containing items on:

Politics: "Six confrontations. When will [Illinois Governor Dan] Walker get the message?"

Law: "GAY LAW STUDENTS MEET."

The arts: "ONE OF CHICAGO proudly presents an all gay production of 'Next Week, East Lynne' a hilarious old melodrama."

Social news: "June 22—FRIDAY 8:30--? GAY PRIDE DANCE—1720 N. Cleveland; $2/advance, $2.50/door."

Religious news: "CHICAGO PRESBYTERIANS DENY GAY MINISTER."

Gay groups: "Gay Speakers Bureau."

Gay bars: "Up North restaurant and bar Zodiac birthday party once a month."

Gossip: "ROBBIE CAYWOOD and RAMONA MERRILL moved to New Jersey ... to work a bit, and also relax and paint. They'll be missed, but we hope to see them back for Gay Pride."

After the publication of the May 1973 *Chicago Gay Crusader*, the torch was handed to *GayLife*, *Gay Chicago*, *Windy City Times*, *Outlines*, *BLACKlines*, *En La Vida*, *Chicago Free Press*, *Babble*, *GRAB*, *Nightspots* and other publications that came and went. Now we have the Internet. But that's another story.

© 2012 St. Sukie de la Croix

CAPT. HARRISON JAILS 24 IN WAR ON DEGENERATES

In a drive against degenerates infesting vice and clip joints, Capt. Thomas Harrison of the E. Chicago av. station early yesterday arrested 15 men and nine women in taverns on the west side of N. Clark st., between Chicago av., and the river.

Accompanied by six detectives and a patrol wagon, Harrison questioned hundreds of patrons in taverns, sent degenerates to the police station for investigation, and broke up couples who had newly met.

After being processed thru the police bureau of identification, all 29 were charged with disorderly conduct. Most were freed on bond. The women will appear in Women's court today; and the men will appear in E. Chicago av. police court.

Ten With Police Records

Ten of the men have minor police records, and one, James Bums, 34, of 619 Madison st., has a record showing more than 50 arrests, half of them in Chicago. He once served a prison term in Arizona for burglary, the records showed.

Harrison, who last week arrested 93 men in a raid on the Windup lounge, 669 N. Clark st., a hangout for perverts, condemned degenerates for the recruiting of adolescents.

Dr. Harry R. Hoffman, Illinois state alienist, agreed, and added that homosexuals should be incarcerated in institutions "for the protection of society."

18,000 In Chicago

Capt. Harrison said that Chicago probably has at least 18,000 sexually maladjusted men, all potentially dangerous.

Boys as young as 12 have been approached, Capt. Harrison said, and unless they have been forewarned by parents, friends, or church leaders, might easily fall victim.

Many homosexuals, Capt. Harrison said, maintain luxurious apartments where they entertain young, unsuspecting "recruits" with food, music, liquor, and obscene literature.

"That's the beginning of the downfall of many boys and young men," Capt. Harrison said. "All families with boys should warn them early to beware of strange men at all times."

Unofficial information received by Harrison indicated, he said, that most of Chicago's degenerates are members of a national organization run by a man named Brown living in or near Miami.

Dr. Hoffman said that for years he has campaigned against the problem. In his opinion, he said, the degenerates "are born and not made."

"Cure is secondary," Dr. Hoffman said. "They should be taken out of society as the first step."

Article on gay bar raid in the *Chicago Daily Tribune*, January 17, 1949.

38

Do We Still Need Gay News Media?

By Yasmin Nair

As I write this, there are two seemingly contradictory events unfolding. *The Chicagoan*, a 21st-century reprise of a long-defunct 1920s magazine, has debuted its first issue, at a whopping $20. And the *Chicago Reader* has been sold to the mainstream *Chicago Sun-Times*.

We are constantly reminded that things are bleak for media in general, even as we see occasional glimmers of hope. Those of us who work in LGBTQ media ("gay media" from here on) know that matters are even bleaker. For decades, gay media have functioned on a combination of volunteerism and a deeply felt sense that conventional media will not and cannot report effectively, if at all, on community matters. Depending on your generational memory, we can recall the times when mainstream newspapers outed gay men picked up during bar stings or refused to report on AIDS and perpetuated the most damaging stereotypes about HIV-positive people.

As recently as a decade ago, it seemed that "new media" in the form of blogging and the average person's ability to photograph, upload and document in the blink of an eye onto platforms that cost little or nothing to produce would change and rejuvenate media forever. Remember the "citizen journalist"? Media figures such as Thomas Friedman cooed breathlessly about how these dudes—and they were almost always dudes—with their mobile devices and willingness to go anywhere and do anything to document events happening around them would change the face of media and even, perhaps, the world.

Today, Friedman is safely ensconced (at least for now) in a newspaper that continues to pay him and others such as Maureen Dowd reportedly astronomical salaries while jettisoning long-term staff members and cutting the pension plans of foreign-citizen employees overseas.

In the meantime, in a parallel world, once-esteemed national gay publications face charges of not paying freelancers, another magazine is outsourcing its content to a non-news company, and prominent gay newspapers either pay nothing at all or so little that writers are usually drawn from the ranks of people with day jobs where they earn their living, or from those seeking bylines for portfolios, or, presumably, from those in possession of independent wealth. The number of gay newspapers has declined. In Chicago alone, the *Windy City Times*, where I write, is now the only print gay newspaper, after the demise of *Chicago Free Press* and *Gay Chicago*.

The gay blogosphere, once seen as the dawn of a revolution, is teetering on the edge of a precipice. To give only a few examples: The Bilerico Project, where I am a regular contributor, now has only one paid staff member, co-founder Bil Browning. Pam Spaulding's Pam's House Blend is now part of Firedog Lake, an online liberal site. The online gay news site 365.com has gone under. Queerty, so popular for its snark, shut down in the spring of 2011 and then re-emerged. Elsewhere, dozens of well-meaning sites by self-identified LGBTQ people feature posts that begin with apologies: "So, I know I haven't posted in months … ."

There is a tendency in some parts to bemoan the "loss" of such gay media and to wonder about how a community might sustain its journalism and news coverage. My own response is that while there needs to be a healthy combination of independent blogging and conventional journalism, the current crisis might be a time for us to say: Good riddance. Now, let's rebuild "gay media" from the ground up.

Let us begin by being honest: Much of what passes for gay media these days is of abysmal quality and probably deserves to die. There are several recurring problems with gay online media: a lack of accountability, an inability to engage in the simplest of questioning in the unrelenting quest for eyeballs and to drive traffic, and a general lack of journalistic integrity. But print media in general suffer from a similar lack of quality. Scour the headlines of any gay paper and, except for a few regional differences and some exceptions, they have a tendency to look exactly like each other. If you were to read a month's worth of gay newspaper reporting, these are the story patterns that would emerge:

— Gay marriage. Pass it now.

— Hate crime. A gay man was attacked outside his home.

— DADT and the military.

— *X* celebrity has come out as gay/lesbian/bisexual.

— Gay marriage.

— Gossip. Guess who's gay?

— Look at all these photos from all the parties over the weekend.

— Oh, that man who was attacked wasn't gay, after all. Never mind.

— Gay writer writes book about gay issues.

— Gay writer writes book.

— Gay marriage.

I mock with love. The gay press is a complex amalgam: part *Social Register*, part record of events, and a chronicler of lives and work that might otherwise be ignored. Even in an age of *Glee*, it can still be difficult for gay authors to find coverage elsewhere, either because their content is deemed too specific or because of old-fashioned homophobia. Chronicling our nightlife and our events is a crucial way to record how we exist in our day-to-day—or night-to-night—lives. As for coverage on celebrities: I frequently type the words "awful celebrity plastic surgery" into my search engine, so I would argue that there is a place for lots of scandal.

We still need gay media because the days when gays don't face homophobia are far from here yet. We need gay media because without them, our collective history would be reduced to bemused reporting by straight people who are clueless about our multiple and oftentimes conflicting realities (for evidence, see anything on gay issues by *The New York Times*, which seems to think the queer world only comprises white, wealthy men). We need a gay press for the same reason we need queer health-care resources: a place where our bodies and lives will not be shamed or forced to invent stories to explain away our syndromes and our scars.

Gay media's biggest reason for existence—the need to record our history along with the oppression we face—is also their biggest weakness. Over the years, gay media in general and gay news media in particular have become calcified into nothing more than a constant advocacy for "rights" (poorly defined) combined with a deep sense of perpetual victimhood.

That sense of constantly being under threat is not entirely unjustified. Queers still lack basic protections in the workplace (and openly "swishy" or gender-variant people are not likely to be hired at all), they are still harassed for being openly gay, and the most vulnerable among us, such as sex workers and trans people, especially those who can't or choose not to pass as gender-normative, are constantly under threat.

If LGBTQ people are engaged in sex work or street economies, they are doubly threatened: not just by random acts of violence but also by a system of police brutality that willfully targets them as deviants without rights. The irony is that people are coming out at younger ages, but this means that out trans, gay and queer youth are consequently more likely to be pushed out of their homes, more likely to be pushed into often-dangerous street work, more likely to be given fewer resources and more likely to be targeted as a vulnerable population.

Yet, when it comes to reporting or even recording such stories and experiences, gay media usually resort to tired and hackneyed pathologies; stories about youth, in particular, render them hapless creatures in need of rescue. Most dangerously, gay media suffer from the delusion that they can sacrifice the principles of journalistic integrity for the cause of community gay-rights advocacy.

The problem is that both "gay rights" and "the community" are largely fragmented and even illusory concepts. In an era when sexual identity is utterly diffuse and diverse, and when queers range across the political spectrum, from conservative to anarchist, what can we define as "the community"? Gay media suffer from their persistent adherence to the fiction of community at the expense of good journalism.

In September 2011, Nikki Usher blogged on The Neiman Journalism Lab that gay niche sites such as Bilerico and Queerty were foundering because they were not able to turn a profit. Picking up on her piece, the blogger David Badash wrote the ominously titled "Gay News Sites: Will Your Favorite Still Be There Next Year?" He emphasized, "An important point LGBT readers must remember: LGBT news sites and blogs often work as advocates for their community as well, something CNN, *The New York Times*, and other traditional news organizations do not. The loss of LGBT media is not only the loss of a news outlet, but the loss of a soldier in the battle for equality."

This idea that gay media are in the business of advocacy has been internalized by some working in and for them. The straight media indulgently view them as an "advocacy" wing, so much so that, picking up on my reporting about Chicago's Howard Brown Health Center, *The New York Times* described the *Windy City Times* as "a gay advocacy newspaper … ."

The problem with defining gay news sites as the definitive place for gay journalism, as David Badash did in his piece (which did not look at sites operated by gay newspapers), is that they have no system of accountability in place and they cannot act as any kind of reliable archive of queer history. We could argue that, perhaps, the fleeting nature of such sites is part of their allure and their nature. But their sensationalism and lack of integrity then become "industry standards," and readers lose sight of what distinguishes a carefully written story from a sloppy one. The other and larger problem is that such cut-and-paste journalism has long-term ramifications.

None of this is to state that there is no place for online-only news sites. But if bloggers cannot pay—money, that is—to recruit or train their writers to do the kind of journalism that takes time and effort and follow-up, they ought not to run stories pretending to be news coverage. These are aggregators, not journalists. It's dangerous to mistake one category for the other.

Contrary to Nikki Usher's point about profits, the problem for gay media is not that they cannot garner enough advertising dollars; the problem is that they rest upon the idea that their readers are too focused on identity to care about quality. Over and over again, gay media figures and bloggers make their case for support from the public, making doomsday threats about their imminent demise. At some point, when the dust from the battle for media relevancy has settled, we will see that the question uppermost in most readers' minds was: So what?

So what if gay media fail? So what, for that matter, if media in general fail?

The large pink elephant in the room has been sitting in our midst for all these debates, patiently waiting for us to acknowledge it: content.

In all of the talk about the end of journalism as we know it, media commentators rarely, if ever, discuss the one fact that should be staring them in the face: the lack of quality content that would actually make readers want to read or follow media in any form. Instead, commentators and those in charge of boosting revenue at various media outlets keep inventing a dizzying array of terms with which to cloud the problem. "Media platforms" is the new buzz phrase. As conventional wisdom would have it, the trick is to make sure that a publication is visible in a broad array of ways by which readers generally access their news and their consciousness of the world: Foursquare, Facebook, Twitter, email, YouTube, and others that have yet to be invented.

I think this is an entirely reasonable strategy, on the face of it. People's consciousness about the world they live in is constantly being modulated and defined by a multiplicity of "platforms," and it makes perfect sense to capitalize on this. I'm also glad to see that more news agencies are actually paying people to make sure their profile is being lifted across different kinds of media, as opposed to simply hiring their tech-whiz nephews for pittances and pizza. But I also see them missing the larger point of this new strategy: What are all these platforms supposed to lead to?

Going to a newspaper website these days is a bit like being the new kid thrust into a raucous party thrown by the most popular girl in school: You're there and kinda, sorta glad you were invited, but who the hell are all these people? On one side are the really cool kids twittering around, each one more inane than the next. One world-famous columnist just had a peanut-butter-and-jelly sandwich, and yet another announces her judgment of a movie, even though she's still watching it.

Somewhere, in the parents' bedroom, if you can get in, couples are making videos of making out, while there, in a corner, sits the resident film critic, desperately trying to seem relevant with a winding appraisal of neo-noir in the 1970s. Suddenly, you feel the tug on your jacket, by people imploring you to sit down, take it easy and comment on everything and anything you see going by. Speak up often enough, and you'll be rewarded with the Web equivalent of Jell-O shots: a chance to be called "Grand Commenter" or some such title.

If media in general are to embrace the diversity of media platforms, they ought to do so with caution and with an eye to making sure that all of this fluttering actually leads somewhere, and that it does not erode the quality of work produced by their writers. Instead of mindlessly following the logic of multimedia platforms for their own sake, media outlets ought to invest in those producing the content that will, ultimately, lead the eyeballs to their sites and generate revenue.

Years after the announcement that citizen journalists and bloggers would change the face of journalism, we are paying the price for the fiction that a bunch of free-wheeling people roaming around with little more than ill-informed opinions, the ability to point and shoot, and a knack for regurgitating news releases could actually sustain viable forms of media. Journalism is not a hobby and it ought not to be a labor of love, but a vocation.

What then, of gay media? Can they survive and, if so, in what form?

I submit that gay media can not only survive by making necessary changes but actually lead the way for conventional media outlets.

For starters, let's start paying the people who produce content and who keep our sites and papers afloat, and let's pay them well.

The era of demanding that everyone, from Web designers to accountants to everyone in between, should work for free or a pittance needs to end. Over and over, I have heard and read stories of and from people who recount the days they worked in cold and drafty or hot and humid conditions to put together gay papers with their own two hands, and how everyone chipped in and how much fun it was and how rewarding. To them, I write: That's wonderful, thank you for all your hard work and for making this possible. Now, can we move into this century and understand that the next step is to believe that people should be paid for their labor?

If we ourselves don't believe that the work we produce is worth it, how can we expect readers to feel the same way?

Let's begin crafting and paying for stories that take more time and effort but that explore this multiple-faceted "community" in all its complexity.

I firmly believe that there is a place for such in the gay press. Imagine, for instance, a story about gay bars and coffee shops that isn't just the usual one about evil straight people purging gays from their neighborhoods. In my own neighborhood, I've witnessed the dramas of openings and closings. The incidents and narratives are complex, involving gay gentrifiers who don't want unsavory gay establishments that might bring down their property values, and straight and poor people looking to frequent cheap gay bars. In other words, stripped of the usual clichés through which we tell our tales of cities and the "gay experience," what emerges is a complex account of capitalism and gay identity, to borrow from John D'Emilio, of a changing urban landscape told through the lives of gay people in one of the most neoliberal cities in the world.

What if the gay press became the go-to place for the straight world, an arena where it could understand, for a change, that "straight" is also a sexual orientation?

Imagine stories about sex laws that actually consider why women's rights are in fact deeply connected to queer issues. Proposed legislation that would penalize the carrying of condoms as a sign of prostitution is a problem for queers as well, and yet, so far, gay media pay little attention to this aspect of the story. Reproductive rights are an issue for the gay community, and not just because women can provide babies for gay men and lesbians to adopt, but because limits on abortion and related rights are the gateway to limiting sexual freedoms for all, including those already perceived as "deviants."

None of this kind of recharging means that we have to give up the elements that make gay media so very, very wonderfully gay and queer. While I never cared for Queerty and have frequently been its target, I do think there's a much-needed place for that kind of snark if we are to resist taking ourselves too seriously. I also think that gossip columns, if they are well-written and funny, are essential. Celebrities are a part of our cultural landscape, and we could cover them in interesting ways that go beyond the usual "So, tell me how wonderful you are" interviews that we tend to churn out (the straight press is as guilty of this).

We absolutely need to cover the work of queer writers, but in features and interviews that go beyond simply asking them to tell us about their childhoods and their favorite authors and simply praising them for just being queer.

And while not all gay media outlets have the resources to hire trained and capable foreign journalists, we could do a much better job of covering international queer affairs. For the most part, gay media's "international" coverage relies on gay white men who barely travel abroad or speak any languages other than English, cutting and pasting from foreign newspapers or email sent by their friends in other countries. Surely, we can do better. Let's not work from the tired assumption that "gay" or "queer" or "transgender" means the same thing across borders but, instead, recognize the complexity of queerness across the world.

In other words, gay media need to engage in a lot more self-respect and a lot less reliance on their status as an advocate for a community that no longer exists as such. If we don't make changes, and soon, we risk becoming irrelevant. At this point, we are far from a world that does not need gay media, and while straight media outlets are gradually writing more "gay" stories, they are still infrequent and, often, just wrong in their perception of the queer world as a homogeneous whole.

As LGBTQ consumers who are also often producers of gay media, we have to confront the limits of the demands we have placed on those who write and record on our behalf. If we continue in our misplaced belief that gay media are nothing more than advocacy, we ought to shut down and simply post news releases on every page. But, given the right amount of will—and a concerted push for resources—we can turn gay media into a publishing entity that not only is deeply relevant but becomes a guidepost for conventional media. Otherwise, we perish while we publish, if we publish at all.

39

The Future of Queer Newspapers

By Tracy Baim

Assessing the state of the LGBT print media universe is like pinning Jell-O to a wall. Whether discussing local or national publications, the situation is changing at such an accelerated pace that no one can predict the future of these media outlets. People are trying to calculate it, but no one has the answers. Because of the dual spears of the economic downturn and the ascent of the Internet, this inability to forecast is true of both gay and mainstream print-based companies.

In order to assess the future, this book set out to provide an overview of the past and current status of regional print publications, with a special focus on weekly and biweekly newspapers. Because boundaries between the different forms of print are permeable, we can't isolate them easily— especially since even the most successful brand names in gay media have changed over the years. One publication may have started as a monthly newsletter and then changed to a weekly newspaper and then switched to a monthly magazine. One may have started life as a small digest-size guide and become a monthly full-size feature magazine. Some started as local periodicals and became national.

Another factor making it difficult to predict the future is that the true state of the gay media has always been difficult to assess. Lists of the number of gay papers, compiled over the years, have varied widely in their totals and methods of counting. Often, organizational newsletters or quarterly journals were counted the same as weekly city newspapers or national glossy magazines. Sometimes lesbian-feminist papers were included, sometimes not.

But based on interviews, previous research and books done on the gay media, it appears that the following is a likely scenario of the state of U.S. gay media since the first newsletter published by Henry Gerber in the 1920s.

In the 1950s there were three main gay or lesbian publications. They were small-format journals associated with organizations. There were also men's physique magazines, perhaps a few dozen or more, that had a "wink-wink" understanding that their core following was among gay men.

By the early-to-mid-1960s, possibly a dozen or so additional publications launched that had a significant distribution (at least a few hundred copies) and an ongoing publishing schedule. These were primarily in bigger cities, and many were sent in the mail and passed among friends across the country. As the alternative press grew, so did the gay press, in part because of lower-cost access to printing technologies. Publications also started to become larger-format.

In 1969, things were shaken up after June's Stonewall rebellion in New York. Publications, some of them lasting just a few issues, began to proliferate. Still, there were probably fewer than two dozen ongoing gay publishing concerns with any significant distribution that year.

In the early 1970s, the true growth spurt began for gay, lesbian and lesbian-feminist media. *Our Own Voices: A Directory of Lesbian and Gay Periodicals*, compiled in 1991 by Alan V. Miller for the Canadian Gay Archives, listed about 150 gay publications of some kind for that era. *Our Own Voices* had started as a continuation of a 1981 project, *Lesbian Periodical Holdings in the Canadian Gay Archives*, which contained 15 pages listing periodicals actually housed in those archives. By the 1991 publication of *Our Own Voices*, more than 7,200 titles from around the world were included. It compared that total to the 309 titles in Vern L. Bullough's 1976 *Annotated Bibliography of Homosexuality* and to the 1,900 listed in H. Robert Malinowsky's 1987 *International Directory of Gay and Lesbian Periodicals*. *Our Own Voices* is unique because it included periodicals from more than 30 countries from 1890 to the end of 1990. (The research for *Our Own Voices* lives online now; see www.clga.ca.)

These numbers are a bit tricky because it can be like comparing apples to oranges to bananas and asparagus. *Our Own Voices* said it adopted the broadest use of the word "periodical": "It includes all serials published on a regular basis or irregular basis, as well as annuals. All post-1970 works directed at a diverse lesbian or gay audience are included; a few foreign feminist titles may have slipped into the work as well. ... Materials are aimed at special religious groups, professional or racial groups, and some groups with specialized sexual interests. The broadest definition of 'gay' or 'lesbian'—or 'homosexual'—has also been used. .... Titles on transsexuals, transvestites, and bisexuals are included. All community AIDS titles are listed ... ."

The continued growth of the LGBT movement in the 1980s, and the parallel devastation of AIDS, brought a new anger and energy, plus new resources, into the gay press movement. Lesbian-feminist publications continued to launch and grow, but many did not make it into the 1990s. Meanwhile, some of the community's strongest gay media efforts became more co-gender and flourished. There were early indications that mainstream advertisers might finally be interested in the "gay market," but gay media in the 1980s existed in more of a "for us, by us" decade. Some estimates show that hundreds of gay publications operated during the decade, but the few dozen strongest were still the weekly publications in bigger cities and *The Advocate*, which changed from a newspaper to a glossy magazine.

By the early 1990s, those counting were saying there were more than 1,000 LGBT media of some kind printing in the U.S., from newsletters to newspapers and magazines. That was the decade when corporate America truly woke up to the value of gay dollars, and as a result many more publications were launched or increased their frequencies and page counts. They added color, and glossy magazines thrived. One company, Window Media, started to buy up regional gay newspapers.

In the first decade of the 21st century, there were signs that the gay media growth of the 1990s was not sustainable. The national glossies started to crumble, many closed and most of those that survived were sold. Window Media collapsed under massive debt by the end of the decade. The mainstream media started to cover the community more, and corporations were reaching gays through general marketing. The amount of advertising money targeting gays did not seem to keep pace with the number of media being published, and there were dozens of closures of regional and national publications.

In his book *The Harris Guide 2003* (formerly *The Queer Press Guide*), journalist Paul Harris (who died in January 2012) documented more than 70 national publications—he included some journals— and 160 regional publications in that year.

Today, the volume of regional and national gay media is perhaps down to its lowest point since the mid-1970s. And it is still difficult to get exact numbers. Papers that folded in recent years are now being resurrected. In the final weeks leading up to this book's final deadline, at least three papers ceased publishing in print form. Ones that were weekly went biweekly or monthly. *Instinct* announced it was going from 10 times a year to six times in 2013.

Here is the approximate state of LGBT U.S. print media as of October 2012:

Newspapers (39):
— 12 weekly newspapers
— 13 biweekly newspapers
— 13 monthly newspapers
— 1 bimonthly newspaper

On the regional magazine, digest and glossy 'zine front (64):
— 8 weekly
— 14 biweekly
— 33 monthly or 10-times-a-year
— 7 bimonthly
— 2 quarterly
National magazines:
— 22

This amounts to 103 regional and 22 national documented LGBT-related media, not counting newsletters, professional journals, and more niche-oriented publications. (See the Appendix beginning on page 448.)

So there clearly has been a drop in the overall number of print publications serving the LGBT market in the U.S. (besides the fact that some are now published less frequently).

The frequency of a newspaper also matters in these days of the Internet, when daily online breaking news makes it difficult to remain relevant even as a weekly newspaper. To stay unique, papers must provide content in their online editions that does not cannibalize their print editions. If a paper has 52 issues a year, it carries higher costs but also can provide more opportunities to cover the community in print form. The biweeklies have a greater challenge, and the monthly newspapers have perhaps the most difficult time remaining unique and relevant for their audiences—and thus valuable to their advertisers. In September 2012, one longtime monthly tabloid newspaper, *Pittsburgh's Out*, founded in 1973, announced it was closing its monthly print paper and going to an online-only publication. Several other papers closed or went online-only in 2012.

Magazines have different obstacles. The weekly and biweekly bar guides are competing with social-media sites where people post their own bar photos, and with the websites for bars that list their own events. Those guides must continue to reinvent their content in print form to get people to see how the guides are germane to their lives. The monthly magazines need to focus on more long-form and investigative journalism that is unavailable online or in the gay newspapers, so as to give their subscribers (and advertisers) something to value. Those magazines that publish six times a year have even higher hurdles.

Broadcast programming is also suffering. In The Life Media, which launched in 1992 to produce high-quality LGBT *In The Life* television shows airing on the Public Broadcasting Service, announced in 2012 that it was discontinuing the production of broadcast content and focusing mainly on programs for the Internet.

High Cost of Business

The print media that have survived are in a very tenuous position. Here's why:

Weekly and biweekly newspapers have a high cost of doing business, with rising print and distribution costs. In general, they have the highest overhead in the regional press and therefore rely the most on advertising. But they are also probably the strongest to weather the storms, because they have professional editorial and sales staffs, paid to do their jobs.

The less-frequent newspapers have fewer staff members, and in some cases they are run by volunteers or even as a project of nonprofit organizations. This makes them easy to cut when the funds dry up. Monthly and bimonthly newspapers are perhaps at most risk of closing, or of having to reinvent themselves as magazines or as online-only endeavors.

In some ways this is an all-or-nothing proposition for newspapers. As they have to cut frequencies and print runs to match their advertising base, there will be a diminishing return that at some point will be too low to sustain. This is true for all print publications, not just newspapers. But the regional publications, which are mostly free-circulation, rely most heavily on the advertisers to cover their expenses.

The bar guides have the most direct competition from online resources, so that many of them are much at risk of changes in decision-making by the businesses that make up their core of advertising.

The more editorially focused magazines have a chance to continue to get their share of national corporate advertising, especially because they offer a four-color glossy format that many advertisers crave. Newsprint is not as attractive to some advertisers, although with changes in technology and cheaper access to color ink, many regional newspapers are providing lower-cost alternatives to the expensive national magazine buys. The regional newspapers also can provide much larger audiences than the national magazines can offer within key cities.

Given that the gay market overall is estimated to control more than $700 billion in spending, there actually are relatively few points of access to that community through print publications. The overall circulation of all these regional and national magazines is in the low millions. The quality of the publications varies widely, but it does help advertisers that Rivendell Media coordinates the placement of major national campaigns. Without Rivendell, it would be difficult for most businesses to try to access the gay market through print publications.

In the past, much of the competition for gay publications came from within the gay community. That is now only part of the story; most cities have far fewer gay publications—and many have none. Now the competition comes from the more progressive mainstream publications, online-only gay publications, social media, radio and broadcast television.

When I started working on this book in 2011, I expected to confirm that there were far fewer gay publications serving the local and national markets today than in the past. But I have to say that the status of the gay press is actually worse than I originally thought. That's because it's clear that many of the remaining papers are undercapitalized and understaffed. If they aren't losing money, they are lucky to be breaking even, based on a review of their advertising and page counts. There are of course the exceptions, the strong media companies weathering these changes very successfully, especially in large cities. Several of those papers are profiled in depth in this book, and they are part of the new National Gay Media Association, which is seeking to strengthen all gay media.

What about the holy grail of the Internet? Won't that save media? Even those publications with the best of websites will tell you the money still comes from print. At *Windy City Times*, we have seen 25 to 30 percent growth year-over-year in unique visitors to our website—but because of the costs of maintaining and hosting the site, it loses money, even with strong advertising from local and national sources. On a weekly basis, we have more than twice as many people viewing our content online than in print. But the advertising base online simply can't sustain the staff that the print publication can, and perhaps it never will meet *Windy City Times'* current staff expense levels.

Cutting Costs

One of the ways *Windy City Times* survived the 2008–09 economic downturn was to go to a virtual office. We cut our expenses by 30 percent in six months, in a planned move that just happened to occur right before the stock market crashed. We were lucky, not prescient. We simply saw no value in maintaining an office when most of our sales and editorial staffs worked outside the office or from home. Other news companies are starting to implement this option, or considering it seriously as a way to cut costs.

Other ideas to cut costs include working together with other local papers to seek shared hosting of regional websites with local public universities, or even private universities, to bring down the expense of online storage space. Sharing delivery with other mainstream papers is an option some papers are exploring. Some mainstream print companies that own their own printing presses are courting gay papers to use their presses. And sharing content across print media is also a way to save resources. *QNotes* in North Carolina offered its reporting team to help papers cover the Democratic National Convention in 2012, a great savings for those wanting to provide that coverage.

New Gadgets, New Revenues

Keeping up with new technologies is also important for all media, but it should be done with an eye on two things: strengthening the brand in the market, and potential revenue through either readers or advertisers. Right now, there is not a lot of money for gay media coming from phone applications and iPad Newsstand. They help position the name, but they carry an expense in time and money. Few regional papers have figured out a way to monetize such efforts, but it is still important to participate in them or papers will lose ground for their brand names.

Charging money for online content has been successful for only a few large names in media, including *The New York Times*. For smaller papers, this is a risky proposition, because adding a paywall sometimes will cut off search engines and a large volume of viewers. At *Windy City Times*, we do not have plans to create a paywall, because search engines and the numbers of people coming to our site are valuable. That said, we are always thinking of new ways to brand our content—for example, through books in print and online. So we will monetize content in other ways.

One way we have added to our revenue stream is through events. In the early 2000s we launched three successful events that we still run annually: Windy City Gay Idol, *Windy City Times* 30 Under 30 Awards and a Theater Series. These bring in revenue through sponsorships and ticket sales. They are an important part of our company, but have to be done right or they cost valuable staff time and advertising space without bringing in enough revenue to justify the effort that goes into producing them.

We have also toyed with "memberships" in the *Windy City Times* that would come with merchandise, access to early ticket sales, contests for prizes, and VIP access to some community events, theater, concerts and the like. We want to do educational programming and could offer this as a membership benefit. Our main issue is making sure we could properly administer such a membership plan, given the high cost of acquisition and maintenance.

One new revenue stream available to for-profit publications is foundation grant money for special projects. In 2011, we received a grant from the Chicago Community Trust, administered through Community Media Workshop, for a special series on AIDS @ 30. For that small grant, we were able to produce more than 200 articles over 13 months, winning awards and serving our community much better than would have been possible without that infusion of grant money.

My dream would be for foundations to really step up and enhance the regional gay newspapers with money and energy. Imagine if there were a multimillion-dollar effort to fund experienced investigative reporters in all 50 states, using shared resources for all gay media. In many states, without on-the-ground journalists covering gay issues, the gay message is not able to bubble to the surface amid all the noise from the anti-gay agenda. It would not even take a lot to sustain an ongoing gay media journalism project, one focused on public investigations, politics, human rights, AIDS, healthcare, and discrimination across the U.S.

I get excited imagining a time when the major foundations look at community media as an ally in covering LGBT and AIDS issues in depth, helping to uncover donors to anti-gay ballot measures, police harassment, transgender bias in housing, and potentially thousands of other stories that go unreported because of a lack of resources. We in gay media want to do more. Advertising can only sustain so much, and most gay media are freely distributed both online and in print. So foundations have a chance to really make a difference here.

Another similar approach might occur in support from "angel" investors in gay media, similar to what is happening in non-gay media. Billionaire Warren Buffett is stepping in to save local newspapers that he still sees as economically viable and important in their communities. There are gay millionaires and billionaires out there who could play a role in helping sustain gay media for generations to come.

Having angel investors or donors can, however, come with strings attached. By being independent, gay media remain freer, but are also more at risk. They are competing against the bigger media companies for readers and advertising dollars, but they are also more nimble to adjust to changes in the marketplace. Another idea, to merge and consolidate gay papers, has been tried before—it resulted in bankruptcy. Thus consolidation might not be the answer, but perhaps some other sustainable investment prototype is.

I believe the business model of gay media is still important, but a hybrid model of advertising, investor and foundation support could provide a new way to continue the movement forward on LGBT rights and progress on AIDS issues.

Advertising: Accounting and Accountability

Finally, I think one of the most important changes that can happen to shore up gay media is a change in attitude from companies that have LGBT customers, which is just about any consumer-based company in the U.S., from small to large.

There is the need, as I state in Chapter 35, for businesses to increase their advertising buys to be on par with the percentage of LGBTs in the population. I think this would be a smart economic move for companies not just in the LGBT space, but also for African-American, Latino, Asian and other niche media. For too long, brands have wasted their money throwing dollars at general consumer marketing and really undervaluing the proven loyalty of niche marketing. This is squandered money—it's time for these companies to get far more sophisticated in reaching this multidimensional quilt we call the United States. Diversity marketing has economic rewards for the companies, and intangible rewards for the communities they serve.

Such a change in advertising, of course, would benefit not just print media but also online and broadcast media. It's up to print media to make the case that they provide a unique value for building brand loyalty.

Which brings me to the reality of Internet vs. print media. They are simply different ways to achieve the same end: communication about LGBT issues. Most print media do have an online presence, and the quality varies greatly. That varied appearance is also true of online-only LGBT websites. Some have fantastic coverage of the community, and some are straight-owned companies with a gay channel that exploits the community while giving little back.

The range of online sites is even wider than that of print. There are straight-run websites, such as Gay Voices on The Huffington Post, AfterEllen and AfterElton, which have staff and update frequently. FiredogLake.com has gay blogs on its site, including the popular Pam's House Blend. There are websites, blogs and podcasts that are primarily by a small number of people, such as Joe.My.God, Americablog, Towleroad, Box Turtle Bulletin, Back2Stonewall, Petrelis Files, Wicked Gay Blog, Rod 2.0, and ones by Dan Savage, Wayne Besen and Andrew Sullivan. There are others that have several contributors, such as GoPride, GayToday, Bilerico, Queerty, The New Civil Rights Movement, The Seattle Lesbian and The L Stop. There are also gays in mainstream online media, including Chris Geidner of BuzzFeed. In the broadcast arena, Sirius Satellite Radio has its gay channel OutQ, Feast of Fun is a podcast, Ann Northrop and Andy Humm host Gay USA on New York cable (and podcast) and there are other terrestrial and online radio shows and podcasts, plus Logo and Here! TV networks.

I write a periodic blog on The Huffington Post to stay connected with a larger and partly mainstream audience, but my goal always involves cross-promoting *Windy City Times*. We allow The Huffington Post, ChicagoPride and others to aggregate our content because it's good for business.

This online universe is ever-expanding and difficult to track. But it is reaching the masses in ways print can't, because of the sheer expense of producing content in print form. So the solution to survival is harnessing the power of the Web in order to shore up the companies that also produce print publications—because my belief is that we need both.

If you take all the websites just mentioned and look at who is getting paid to do the work, you will see very few full-time paid news reporters and editors covering gay issues online or in the mainstream media (let's eliminate the celebrity and gossip categories that often pay the online bills by generating traffic). If the bulk of the reporting and editing work is being done by volunteers, there will inevitably be high turnover and therefore a lack of continuity, and historical perspective, in covering our movement. Most of the full-time news reporters and editors covering LGBT issues are working in traditional LGBT print media. And gay media continue to lose valuable talent as newspaper closings mean not just the loss of full-time reporters and editors, but also of syndicated freelance writers who in some cases have decades of experience covering the community.

The changes in the gay press parallel those in the mainstream media, albeit on a much smaller scale. The Newspaper Association of America reported that there was a $798 million loss in print advertising for the first half of 2012 compared to 2011. "That is only slightly offset by a $32 million gain in digital. The ratio of losses to gains is 25 to 1," according to Rick Edmonds of the Project for Excellence in Journalism, writing for Poynter.org.

As MediaPost.com reported in September 2012: "According to the U.S. Department of Labor's Bureau of Labor Statistics, total employment in the newspaper publishing industry has plunged from 414,000 in 2001 to 246,020 in 2011, equaling a 40.6% drop in 10 years. The 2011 figure is down 5% from 258,950 in 2010 and 20.4% from 309,000 in 2009. ... Separate figures from the American Society of Newspaper Editors indicate that total newsroom employment has shrunk from 56,400 in 2001 to 40,566 in 2012, for a 28.1% decline in a little over a decade. The 2012 figure is down 2.5% from 41,609 in 2011. ... The New York Times Company had 7,273 employees at the end of 2011, down 40% from 12,050 at the end of 2001."

As one letter-writer noted on the website, this is the "mass media" without the "mass."

Why Print?

Do we need print media? I am in the business of print and have been producing print publications since my first family newsletter, at age 10, for 125 people. It was all the news I could fit to print, and I was hooked forevermore by the value of communicating information.

But do I need to communicate through the printed page? The answer is complicated. I know our company is strong because we have a print component that is complemented by a comprehensive website. I know the website does not carry its own weight, and if we were to go online only, the business would be more like a hobby—a labor of love. I know that the print advertisers see a more loyal and beneficial relationship with our print readers, uncluttered by the myriad marketing messages online. I know that for the near future, print is actually far more democratizing of information than the Internet, which is still not available to all people in the same way that free print publications are.

I also know that the Internet is where the growth is, where the future is, and that those publishers who can figure out a way to combine print and online in a profitable formula will be the strongest ones serving their communities.

Another issue of historic significance is the archiving of our LGBT history. Old print editions of gay papers provide invaluable research material for historians and others looking for queer history. The problem with online-only efforts is that because they are often very personality-driven or done by a small team, once they go away, so do their archives. There have been dozens of examples of LGBT websites or blogs that simply disappear once their producers close down. Even most of those still in operation do little to create an easy way for their archives to be used, and some simply don't save old articles or columns. Those materials are thus lost to history—our archives, libraries and museums have not caught up with this new technology in a way that makes this work more permanent and saves it for the future.

Independent Voices

Readers and advertisers will certainly drive the future of print and online journalism. But there will always be a need for independent journalism, in whatever form it takes. With fewer independent voices in the increasingly corporate media landscape, we risk losing our ability to speak to one another, to be there for one another when the media forsake us, when politicians vilify us, when we are attacked with words or stones, when we want to have the depth of knowledge about our community that simply can't be found elsewhere.

In his book *Fighting for Air: The Battle to Control America's Media*, Eric Klinenberg speaks about the incredible consolidation of media in recent years. This has left little room for independent voices, and it's only getting worse. As the late media expert Daniel Schorr said, "Eric Klinenberg has given us a chilling report on how American news media, increasingly concentrated, have made a mockery of the commitment to operate in 'the public interest, convenience, and necessity.'"

Klinenberg says some alternative media may ultimately find their voice on the Internet only. The Internet can be a great equalizer, but unfortunately those who own access to technology channels, and those with the most money, will still dominate the debate.

The domination of the marketplace doesn't stop at ownership. It also includes lobbying for Internet preference. As reported in *SF Public Press* on November 10, 2010: "The ongoing, often arcane, battle over whether telecommunications companies may slow certain online services and charge fees to speed up others has morphed into a civil rights controversy. ... At stake: whether to preserve 'network neutrality'—the longstanding principle that all consumers can access whatever websites or applications they want on the Internet, at the same speed and without limitations imposed by Internet service providers." Or, as Wikipedia defines it: "Network neutrality (also net neutrality, Internet neutrality) is a principle that advocates no restrictions by Internet service providers or governments on consumers' access to networks that participate in the Internet. Specifically, network neutrality would prevent restrictions on content, sites, platforms, types of equipment that may be attached, and modes of communication. Network owners can't interfere with content, applications, services, and devices of users' choice and remains open to all users and uses." Corporations will have the money for lobbyists and could eventually wear down their opponents, creating a system loaded against smaller websites.

This control of the message is filtering across all forms of media, even those associated with educational institutions.

In 2012, the national Courage in Student Journalism Award went to the staff of *The Red Pen*, an independent newspaper at duPont Manual High School in Louisville, Kentucky, and to James Yoakley, former yearbook and newspaper advisor at Lenoir City High School in Tennessee. Yoakley has since been reassigned to teach seventh-grade English at Lenoir City Middle School.

The awards are given annually to student journalists and school officials who have demonstrated exceptional fortitude in defending freedom of the press, according to a news release from the award co-sponsors: the Student Press Law Center, the National Scholastic Press Association, and the Center for Scholastic Journalism at Kent State University.

Yoakley was named the non-student winner of the "Courage" award for his outspoken defense of press freedom in the face of two nationally publicized censorship incidents, award presenters stated. "First, administrators refused to allow the editor-in-chief of the newspaper to publish an opinion column about how atheists felt ostracized at the school. Then, the school board and superintendent publicly vilified students for publishing a first-person yearbook story, in which a student told his story about coming out as gay to his parents."

The Red Pen was launched by student staffers at duPont Manual's official student publication, *The Redeye*, "who became frustrated with edicts from their principal to refrain from mentioning topics that might cause controversy, including homosexuality. The students—Zoe Schaver, Patrick Hartel, Emily McConville, Kelsey McKim, Dakota Sherek and Virginia Johnson—used their own off-campus time to build a website, www.theredpen.org, and raised the money to distribute a print version," according to the award news release.

In the first issue of *The Red Pen*, in May 2012, Schaver wrote a letter to readers: "Rights are important. They make human existence worth it, and they make the operation of human society possible. Duties, of course, are important as well—the obligation to tell the truth, for one.

"And that's what all six of us seek to do as journalism students. It's our big, unrealistic dream. Last semester, we were fed up with the roadblocks we faced on our regular publications. For bureaucratic, safety, and other reasons, we got stopped from attacking the stories we most wanted to pursue. It wasn't any specific person's fault, but rather the trend toward suppressing controversy that exists across America and across the world. We knew through experience that this trend was nearly impossible to fight on school grounds, where rules, and, to some degree, conformity—at least on the administrative level—are highly valued. So we decided we needed *The Red Pen.* ..."

The wonderfully executed first issue of this alternative high school publication is available online at www.theredpen.org.

The Need for Amplification

Gay publications use their voices to amplify the issues and debates inside and outside our community. Now, they have to continue to make their case to advertisers who are looking for ways to amplify their own messages to the gay community. This creates an important (and sometimes awkward) symbiotic relationship between those seeing gays as consumers and the movement that needs media to investigate and cover the good and bad, the significant and fun within our communities.

The challenge is not that much different from the one that faced our early gay media pioneers from the 1920s to the 1950s. Sure, the mainstream "gets us" more than ever, but it really can dedicate only a limited amount of space to our issues. Its reporters often "parachute in" to cover complex community issues, and they often are tone-deaf to the nuances of our history and movement. Gay media are mostly gay most of the time, and the aggregate volume of content is vastly more than the mainstream would ever bother to cover. We cover not just the next gay celebrity coming out, but the wide array of stories that actually affect the community every day—not just Chick-fil-A protests that attract the TV cameras, but a wide range of other stories.

And even though the mainstream media are far more inclusive of gay voices and points of view than in earlier generations (as documented in Chapter 1), they still have a long way to go. There are still many cases where they feel the need to quote the "other side" on a topic such as gay marriage, because society as a whole is not fully accepting yet. But it is comparable to their asking the KKK for comment every time they do a story on interracial marriage. Sometimes, the two sides to a story are not equal, which is the point of view of the gay press and one that gives us our unique voice in covering LGBT issues. We start from a point of "Gay Is Good," as Frank Kameny said nearly 50 years ago. Everything else flows from this basic understanding, but that is not true for many mainstream media outlets with their non-gay lens.

David M. Halperin, a professor of English at the University of Michigan at Ann Arbor, wrote about the differentness of gay culture in an essay published September 3, 2012 in *The Chronicle of Higher Education*. The piece was adapted from his 2012 book, *How to Be Gay*, published by Harvard University Press. He wrote:

"We will be queer forever.

"What makes gay people different from others is not just that we are discriminated against, mistreated, regarded as sick or perverted. That alone is not what shapes gay culture. (That indeed could end.) It's that we live in a world in which heterosexuality is the norm. Heterosexual culture remains our first culture, and in order to survive and to flourish in its midst, gay people must engage in an appropriation of it that is also a resistance to it.

"So long as queer kids continue to be born into heterosexual families and into a society that is normatively, notionally heterosexual, they will have to devise their own nonstandard relation to heterosexual culture. Gay subjectivity will always be shaped by the primeval need on the part of gay subjects to queer heteronormative culture.

"That is not going to change. Not for a very long time. And we'd better hope it doesn't.

"Where would we be, after all, without the insights, the impertinence, the unfazed critical intelligence provided by gay subculture? And where would we be without its awareness of so much about the way we live our lives that is particular to specific social forms? Without that alienated perspective, those social forms would pass for obvious, or natural—which is to say, they would remain invisible. And so the shape of our existence would escape us."

John Teets was a mainstream writer and editor in Chicago during the 1970s and 1980s and is now an openly gay man reflecting on the role of gay media today. He says the closing of gay media outlets "breaks my heart ... more in fact than when mainstream papers succumb to the changing economics and technology of the business. Gay media bring awareness, sensitivities and insights to events and issues that simply go over the heads of almost all mass media. AIDS and equality, for example, simply wouldn't be the issues they are today without early, persistent and good coverage by the LGBT press (and blogs, in our brave new world). Our continuing (though now less pervasive) status as 'outsiders' lets us see things in a light that the straight world just doesn't appreciate.

"LGBT media reinforce our marvelous sense of community and political strength, and give the power of the printed word on paper to ideas and aspirations, as well as the monstrosity of violence and persecution."

I couldn't agree more. But to sustain these gay media, especially in their printed form, it's going to take innovation, a departure from past business practices, a shift to bold new ideas, and perhaps a hybrid model where both the community and foundations find a way to bridge the financial gaps in order to survive, thrive, and better cover this diverse community.

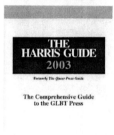
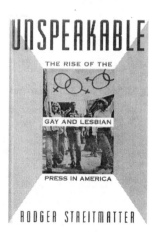
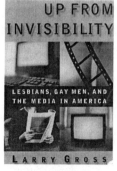

A few of the books that have addressed gays in the media, all referenced in this book's bibliography.

Local Gay and Lesbian Publications - U.S. Only

Provided with input from Rivendell, in confirmation with papers that responded to a survey for this book. There were frequently conflicting dates on websites and in media kits and email from papers themselves. This could be because of founding vs. first-published dates, changes in ownership, etc.

Newspapers—Weekly*

PUBLICATION	AREA	STATE	FREQ.	FORMAT	START	WEBSITE	EDITOR EMAIL
Bay Area Reporter	San Francisco	CA	Weekly	Tabloid	1971	www. ebar.com	c.laird@ebar.com
Bay Windows	Boston	MA	Weekly	Tabloid	1982	www.baywindows.com	soconnell@baywindows.com
Between The Lines	Detroit	MI	Weekly	Tabloid	1993	www.pridesource.com	editor@pridesource.com
Dallas Voice	Dallas	TX	Weekly	Tabloid	1984	www.dallasvoice.com	wright@dallasvoice.com
Florida Agenda	Miami/Ft. Lauderdale	FL	Weekly	Tabloid	2000	www.floridaagenda.com	editor@guymag.net
Philadelphia Gay News	Philadelphia	PA	Weekly	Tabloid	1976	www.epgn.com	sarah@epgn.com
San Diego LGBT Weekly	San Diego	CA	Weekly	Tabloid	2010	www. lgbtweekly.com	steve@lgbtweekly.com
Seattle Gay News	Seattle	WA	Weekly	Tabloid	1974	www.sgn.org	sgn2@sgn.org
South Florida Gay News	Miami/Ft. Lauderdale	FL	Weekly	Tabloid	2010	www.sfgn.com	jason.parsley@sfgn.com
Washington Blade	Washington	DC	Weekly	Tabloid	1969	www.washingtonblade.com	knaff@washblade.com
Windy City Times	Chicago	IL	Weekly	Tabloid	1985	www.windycitymediagroup.com	editor@windycitymediagroup.com
Wire Magazine	So. Florida	FL	Weekly	Tabloid	1985	www.wiremag.com	cubby@wireweekly.com

Newspapers—Biweekly (or Twice Monthly)

PUBLICATION	AREA	STATE	FREQ.	FORMAT	START	WEBSITE	EDITOR EMAIL
Ambush	New Orleans	LA	Biweekly	Tabloid	1982	www. ambushmag.com	ripna@ambushmag.com
Baltimore OUTloud	Baltimore	MD	Biweekly	Tabloid	2004	www.baltimoreoutloud.com	editor@baltimoreoutloud.com
Bay Times - San Francisco	San Francisco	CA	Biweekly	Tabloid	1978	www.sfbaytimes.com	editor@sfbaytimes.com
GA Voice	Atlanta	GA	Biweekly	Tabloid	2010	www.thegavoice.com	editor@thegavoice.com
Gay City News	New York	NY	Biweekly	Tabloid	2002	www.gaycitynews.com	editor@gaycitynews.com
Gay People's Chronicle	Cleveland	OH	Biweekly	Tabloid	1984	www.gaypeopleschronicle.com	editor@chronohio.com
Gay San Diego	San Diego	CA	Biweekly	Tabloid	2010	www.gay-sd.com	editor@gay-sd.com
Montrose Star	Houston	TX	Biweekly	Tabloid	2010	www.montrose-star.com/	brandy@glyp.com
Out Front	Denver	CO	Biweekly	Tabloid	1976	www.outfrontonline.com	holly@outfrontonline.com
Outword	Sacramento/No. CA	CA	2/month	Tabloid	1995	www.outwordmagazine.com	editor@outwordmagazine.com
Q Notes	Charlotte	NC	Biweekly	Tabloid	1986	www.goqnotes.com	editor@goqnotes.com
Watermark	Orlando	FL	Biweekly	Tabloid	1994	www.watermarkonline.com	steveb@watermarkonline.com
Wisconsin Gazette	Milwaukee	WI	Biweekly	Tabloid	2009	www.wisconsingazette.com	lweisberg@wisconsingazette.com

Newspapers—Monthly (or Close to Monthly)

PUBLICATION	AREA	STATE	FREQ.	FORMAT	START	WEBSITE	EMAIL
ACCESSline	Statewide	IA	Monthly	Tabloid	1986	www. accesslineiowa.com	editor@accesslineiowa.com
CommUNITY	Albany	NY	10/year	Tabloid	1972	www.cdglcc.org	aholbritter@capitalpridecenter.org
The Community Letter	Louisville	KY	Monthly	Tabloid	1990	www.www.thecommunityletter.com	editor@win.net
Conexión G	San Juan	PR	Monthly	Tabloid	2007	www.conexiong.com	conexiongpr@gmail.com
The Empty Closet	Rochester	NY	Monthly	Tabloid	1971	www.gayalliance.org	EmptyCloset@gagv.us
Gay Life	Baltimore	MD	Monthly	Tabloid	1977	www.baltimoregaylife.com	editor@baltimoregaylife.com
The Gayly Oklahoman	Oklahoma City	OK	Monthly	Tabloid	1983	www.gayly.com	editor@gayly.com
The Leather Journal	Los Angeles	CA	Monthly	Tabloid	1987	www.theleatherjournal.com	tljandcuir@aol.com
Out & About	Nashville	TN	Monthly	Tabloid	2002	www.outandaboutnewspaper.com	editor@outandaboutnewspaper.com
Outlook Columbus	Columbus	OH	Monthly	Tabloid	1996	www.outlookcolumbus.com	hayes@outlookmedia.com
PQ Monthly	Portland	OR	Monthly	Tabloid	2012	www.pqmonthly.com	info@pqmonthly.com
The Rainbow Times	Boston	MA	Monthly	Tabloid	2006	www.therainbowtimesmass.com	editor@therainbowtimesmass.com
The Word	Indianapolis	IN	Monthly	Tabloid	1991	www.thegayword.com	ted@midwestword.com

Newspapers—Bimonthly or 6 Times a Year

PUBLICATION	AREA	STATE	FREQ.	FORMAT	START	WEBSITE	EDITOR EMAIL
Central Voice	Harrisburg	PA	6/year	Tabloid	2003	www.thecentralvoice.ning.com	stevek@pressandjournal.com

Other Periodicals—Magazine, Digest or 'Zine Format—Weekly

PUBLICATION	AREA	STATE	FREQ.	FORMAT	START	WEBSITE	EDITOR EMAIL
David Atlanta	Atlanta	GA	Weekly	Digest	1998	www. davidatlanta.com	max@davidatlanta.com
Desert Daily Guide	Palm Springs	CA	Weekly	'Zine	1995	www.desertdailyguide.com	editor@DesertDailyGuide.com
Get Out!	New York	NY	Weekly	Digest	2009	www.getoutmag.com	mike@goothmag.com
Hotspots	Miami/Ft. Lauderdale	FL	Weekly	Digest	1985	www.hotspotsmagazine.com	scott@hotspotsmagazine.com
Guy Magazine	Miami/Ft. Lauderdale	FL	Weekly	Digest	2001	www.guymag.net	editor@guymag.net
Metro Weekly	Washington	DC	Weekly	Magazine	1994	www. metroweekly.com	editor@metroweekly.com
Next	New York	NY	Weekly	Digest	1993	www.nextmagazine.com	benjamin@nextmagazine.net
This Week in Texas (TWIT)	Statewide (Texas)	TX	Weekly	Digest	1975**	www.twitmagazine.com	allen@twitmagazine.com

Other Periodicals—Magazine, Digest or 'Zine Format—Biweekly or Twice Monthly

PUBLICATION	AREA	STATE	FREQ.	FORMAT	START	WEBSITE	EDITOR EMAIL
Boi Chicago	Chicago	IL	Biweekly	Digest	2000	www.boimagazine.com	boieditorial@aol.com
Echo Magazine	Phoenix	AZ	Biweekly	Magazine	1989	www.echomag.com	editor@echomag.com
Erie Gay News	Erie	PA	Monthly	'Zine	1993	www.eriegaynews.com	info@eriegaynews.com
Fenuxe	Atlanta	GA	Biweekly	Digest	2010	www.fenuxe.com	tyler@fenuxe.com
Frontiers IN LA	Los Angeles	CA	Biweekly	Magazine	1982	www.frontiersweb.com	editor@frontiersla.com
Gloss	San Francisco	CA	Biweekly	Digest	2004	www.glossmagazine.net	PaulEPratt3@yahoo.com
GRAB Magazine	Chicago	IL	Biweekly	Magazine	2009	www.GrabChicago.com	grabstacy@gmail.com
Lavender Magazine	Minneapolis/St. Paul	MN	Biweekly	Magazine	1995	www.lavendermagazine.com	andy@lavendermagazine.com
Metra	Detroit	MI	2/month	Digest	1979	www.metramagazine.com	metramag@aol.com
Nightspots	Chicago	IL	Biweekly	Digest	1990	www.windycitymediagroup.com	editor@windycitymediagroup.com
Odyssey Magazine	Los Angeles	CA	Biweekly	Digest	1991	www.odysseymagazine.net	cheyne@odysseymagazine.net
Odyssey Magazine	New York	NY	Biweekly	Digest	2009	www.odysseymagazine.net	cheyne@odysseymagazine.net
Out Post	Ann Arbor	MI	Biweekly	Digest	1990	www.facebook.com/opmag	OPost@aol.com
Outlines	Cleveland	OH	Biweekly	Digest	1997	www.outlinesmagazine.com	info@outlinesmagazine.com

Other Periodicals—Magazine, Digest or 'Zine Format—Monthly or Similar

PUBLICATION	AREA	STATE	FREQ.	FORMAT	START	WEBSITE	EDITOR EMAIL
Adelante Magazine	Los Angeles	CA	Monthly	Magazine	1998	www.adelantemagazine.com	ptorres@adelantemagazine.com
BAR TAB	San Francisco	CA	Monthly	Digest	2010	www.bartabsf.com	news@ebar.com
Blade California	Orange Co./Long Beach	CA	Monthly	Magazine	1991	www.jremedia.com/bladeca	blade.russell@gmail.com
Camp	Kansas City	MO	Monthly	Magazine	2004	www.campkc.com	cirqlate@gmail.com
Cue Columbus	Columbus	OH	Monthly	Magazine	2011	www.cuecolumbus.com	jessica@cuemagazines.com
Cue Pittsburgh	Pittsburgh	PA	Monthly	Magazine	2009	www.cuepittsburgh.com	jessica@cuemagazines.com
Desert Outlook	Palm Springs	CA	Monthly	Magazine	2012	www.mydesert.com	will.dean@thedesertsun.com
FLAME Magazine	Royal Oak/Detroit	MI	Monthly	Magazine	2012	www.Flame-Mag.com	tony@flame-mag.com
The Fight	Los Angeles	CA	Monthly	Magazine	2011	www.thefightmag.com	editor@thefightmag.com
Gay Parent NY	New York	US	Annual	Magazine	1998	www.gayparentmag.com	angie@gayparentmag.com
The Gay Rag	Key West	FL	Monthly	Digest	2006	www.keywestgayrag.com	info@keywestgayrag.com
Genre Latino	Miami/Ft. Lauderdale	FL	Monthly	Digest	2006	www.genrelatino.com	josue@GenreLatino.com
GET RI Magazine	Statewide	RI	Monthly	Magazine	2006	www.get-ri.com	getmag@cox.net
Girl STIR Magazine	Ft. Lauderdale (lesbian)	FL	Monthly	'Zine	2005	www.thegirlmagazine.com	editor@thegirlmagazine.com
ION AZ	Phoenix	AZ	Monthly	Digest	2001	www.ionaz.com	ionazeditor@me.com
Just Out	Portland	OR	Monthly	Magazine	1983**	www.justout.com	editor@justout.com
Lesbian News	Los Angeles (lesbian)	CA	Monthly	Magazine	1974	www.lesbiannews.com	ellalnmag@gmail.com
Letters From CAMP Rehoboth	Rehoboth Beach	DE	15/year	Magazine	1991	www.camprehoboth.com	steve@camprehoboth.com
Liberty Press	Wichita	KS	Monthly	Magazine	1994	www.libertypress.net	libertypress@cox.net
Metroline	New England	CT	Monthly	Magazine	1972	www.metroline-online.com	Editor@metroline-online.com
Odyssey Magazine Hawaii	Honolulu	HI	Monthly	Digest	1991	www.odysseyhawaii.com	odysseyhi@aol.com
Options	Providence	RI	10/year	Magazine	1982	www.optionsri.org	editor@optionsri.org
OutSmart	Houston	TX	Monthly	Magazine	1994	www. outsmartmagazine.com	greg@outsmartmagazine.com
Phoenix Rising Magazine	Fort Wayne	IN	Monthly	Magazine	2007	www.fwphoenixrisingmagazine.com	rob.grayless@ fwphoenixrisingmagazine.com
Q Salt Lake	Salt Lake City	UT	Monthly	Magazine	2004	www. gaysaltlake.com	editor@qsaltlake.com
Q Vegas	Las Vegas	NV	Monthly	Magazine	1978	www.qvegas.com	noah@qvegas.com
Quest	Milwaukee	WI	Monthly	Magazine	1993	www.quest-online.com	editor@quest-online.com
Rage	San Diego	CA	Monthly	Magazine	2007	www.ragemonthly.com	editor@ragemonthly.com
Rage - OCLA	Orange/LA counties	CA	Monthly	Magazine	2009	www.Ragemonthly.com	editor@ragemonthly.com
SCENE: Twin Cities LGBTQA Guide	Minneapolis/St. Paul	MN	Monthly	Digest	2005	www.myscenecity.com	contact@myscenecity.com
She Magazine	Statewide (lesbian)	FL	Monthly	Magazine	1999	www.shemag.com	info@shemag.com
Vanguard	Los Angeles	CA	Monthly	Newsletter	1997	www.lagaycenter.org	sstjohn@lagaycenter.org
Vital VOICE	St. Louis	MO	Monthly	Magazine	2000	www.thevitalvoice.com	dsly@thevitalvoice.com

Other Periodicals—Magazine or Digest Format—Bimonthly or 6 Times a Year

PUBLICATION	AREA	STATE	FREQ.	FORMAT	START	WEBSITE	EDITOR EMAIL
Boston Spirit	Boston	MA	6/year	Magazine	2005	www.bostonspiritmagazine.com	editor@bostonspiritmagazine.com
Our Lives	Madison	WI	6/year	Magazine	2007	www.ourlivesmadison.com	pfarabaugh@ourlivesmadison.com
GO Magazine	New York	NY	6/year	Magazine	2002	www.gomag.com	editor@gomag.com
Metrosource LA	Los Angeles	CA	6/year	Magazine	2004	www.metrosource.com	info@metrosource.com
Metrosource NY	New York	NY	6/year	Magazine	1990	www.metrosource.com	info@metrosource.com
L Style G Style	Austin	TX	6/year	Magazine	2007	www.lstylegstyle.com	alisa@lstylegstyle.com
Out in Jersey	Trenton	NJ	6/year	Magazine	1996	www.outinjersey.net	peterfrycki@outinjersey.net

Other Periodicals—Magazine, Digest or 'Zine Format—Quarterly

PUBLICATION	AREA	STATE	FREQ.	FORMAT	START	WEBSITE	EDITOR EMAIL
G Philly	Philadelphia	PA	Quarterly	'Zine	2011	www.g-philly.com	jshockley@phillymag.com
The Mirror	Miami/Ft. Lauderdale	FL	Quarterly	Magazine	2011	www.sfgn.com	norm.kent@sfgn.com

(In 2012, The Mirror announced it was going national)

National Gay and Lesbian Publications—U.S. Only

PUBLICATION	FREQ.	FORMAT	START	WEBSITE	EDITOR EMAIL
The Advocate	10/year	Magazine	1967	www.advocate.com	editor@advocate.com
B Magazine	Quarterly	Magazine	2012	www.bmag.us	peteriancummings@bmag.us
Bear Magazine	Quarterly	Magazine	1987	www.bearmagazine.com	steven.wolfe@bearomnimedia.com
Bleu (African-American)	6/year	Magazine	2006	www.thebleumag.com	devon@bleulife.com
Compete (sports)	Monthly	Magazine	2007***	www.competenetwork.com	editor@mediaoutloud.com
Connxtions /Regional (travel)	Quarterly	Magazine	2010	www.connextionsmagazine.com	shelly@connextionsmagazine.com
Curve (lesbian)	10/year	Magazine	1990	www.curvemag.com	editor@curvemag.com
Cybersocket	Monthly	'Zine	1997	www.cybersocket.com	editor@cybersocket.com
The Gay & Lesbian Review Worldwide	6/year	Magazine	1994	www.GLReview.com	editor@glreview.com
Gay Parent	6/year	Magazine	1998	www.gayparentmag.com	angie@gayparentmag.com
Instinct	10/year****	Magazine	1997	www.instinctmag.com	editor@instinctmag.com
Lesbian Connection	6/year	Magazine	1974	www.lconline.org	elsiepub@aol.com
MetroSource (National)	6/year	Magazine	1996	www.metrosource.com	info@metrosource.com
Next Door (art)	6/year	Magazine	2009	www.nextdoormagazine.com	indigo@nextdoormagazine.com
Noize	Quarterly	Digest	1994	www.noizemag.com	sweinstein@noizemag.com
Out Aloha /Regional (travel)	Yearly	Magazine	2012	www.outaloha.com	info@outaloha.com
Out City /Regional (travel)	2/year	Magazine	2012	www.outcity.com	info@outcity.com
OUT Magazine	10/year	Magazine	1992	www.out.com	ahicklin@out.com
Passport	8/year	Magazine	2000	www.passportmagazine.com	editor@passportmagazine.net
Pink	Quarterly	Digest	1990	www.pinkmag.com	editor@pinkmag.com
Swerv (African-American)	Quarterly	Magazine	2009	www.swervmag.com	jamilfletcher@swervmag.com
Trikone (South Asian)	2/year	Magazine	1986	www.trikone.org	editor@trikone.org

"Digest" refers to a small rectangular publication, "magazine" refers to a larger rectangular publication usually about 8½ by 11 inches in size, and "tabloid" refers to a larger newspaper-type publication. A "'zine" is a small publication that is usually square in shape or nearly square.

Compiled for this book by Tracy Baim in cooperation with Todd Evans and Alex Flanagan of Rivendell Media.
* Even though some call themselves magazines, Rivendell categorizes them as newspapers.
** Relaunched in 2012.
*** Founded in 2006; first issue printed in 2007.
**** Changing to six times a year in 2013.

Due to frequent changes on LGBT media, this list will have updates. If you want a more current list, email editor@windycitymediagroup.com and we will send a new one if it is available.

Bibliography

Books That Are Primarily Directories or Bibliographies

— *An Annotated Bibliography of Homosexuality*, by Vern L. Bullough, Barrett W. Elcano, W. Dorr Legg and James Kepner, Garland Publishing (1976). Lists 308 titles.

— *The Harris Guide: The Directory of the World's GLBT Press, Now Including Both Print and Broadcasting Media* (formerly *The Queer Press Guide*), by Paul Harris, Upstart Press (2003). Lists LGBT media from the U.S. and around the world.

— *Homosexuality: A Selective Bibliography of Over 3,000 Items*, by William Parker, The Scarecrow Press (1971).

— *Homosexuals Today: A Handbook of Organizations & Publications*, by Marvin Cutler, Publications Division of ONE, Inc. (1956). Marvin Cutler, like William Lambert, was another name of W. Dorr Legg (born William Dorr Lambert Legg).

— *International Directory of Gay and Lesbian Periodicals*, by H. Robert Malinowsky, Oryx Press (1987).

— *The Lesbian Periodicals Index*, by Clare Potter, Naiad Press (1986).

— *Lesbian Sources: A Bibliography of Periodical Articles, 1970–1990*, by Linda Garber, Garland Publishing (1993).

— *Our Own Voices: A Directory of Gay and Lesbian Periodicals, 1890s-2000s*, by Alan V. Miller (first published by the Canadian Gay Archives in 1991 with 7,200 titles, now available online at http://www.clga.ca/).

— *Out of the Closets: Voices of Gay Liberation*, by Karla Jay and Allen Young, Douglas Book Corp. (1972). Lists just more than a dozen publications. A 20th-anniversary edition with foreword by John D'Emilio was published in 1992 by New York University Press.

— *Words to the Wise: A Writer's Guide to Feminist and Lesbian Periodicals & Publishers*, by Andrea Clardy, Firebrand Books (1993). Earlier editions were also published.

The Most Relevant Other Books on This Topic

— *Are We There Yet? A Continuing History of* Lavender Woman, *a Chicago Lesbian Newspaper, 1971–1976*, by Michal Brody, Aunt Lute Book Co. (1985).

— *Business, Not Politics: The Making of the Gay Market*, by Katherine Sender, Columbia University Press (2005).

— *The Columbia Reader on Lesbians and Gay Men in Media, Society, and Politics*, by Larry Gross and James D. Woods (editors), Columbia University Press (1999).

— *Fighting for Air: The Battle to Control America's Media*, by Eric Klinenberg, Metropolitan Books (2007).

— *From "Perverts" to "Fab Five": The Media's Changing Depiction of Gay Men and Lesbians*, by Rodger Streitmatter, Routledge (2008).

— *Gay Roots: Twenty Years of* Gay Sunshine: *An Anthology of Gay History, Sex, Politics, and Culture*, by Winston Leyland, Gay Sunshine Press (1991–93). Two volumes.

— *Jack Nichols, Gay Pioneer: "Have You Heard My Message?"* by J. Louis Campbell III, Harrington Park Press (2007).

— *Long Road to Freedom: The* Advocate *History of the Gay and Lesbian Movement*, Mark Thompson (editor), St. Martin's Press (1994).

— *Making Gay History: The Half-Century Fight for Lesbian and Gay Equal Rights*, by Eric Marcus, Harper Perennial (2002). Revised paperback edition; first published as *Making History: The Struggle for Gay and Lesbian Equal Rights, 1945–1990: An Oral History*, HarperCollins (1992).

— The New York Times *on Gay and Lesbian Issues*, by Susan Burgess, CQ Press/Sage (2011).

— *News and Sexuality: Media Portraits of Diversity*, by Laura Castañeda and Shannon B. Campbell (editors), Sage Publications (2006).

— *Queer Airwaves: The Story of Gay and Lesbian Broadcasting*, by Phylis Johnson and Michael C. Keith, M.E. Sharpe (2001).

— *Queer in America: Sex, the Media, and the Closets of Power*, by Michelangelo Signorile, University of Wisconsin Press (2003). Third edition; first published in 1993.

— *Rough News, Daring Views: 1950s' Pioneer Gay Press Journalism*, by Jim Kepner, Harrington Park Press (1998).

— *Selling Out: The Gay and Lesbian Movement Goes to Market*, by Alexandra Chasin, Palgrave Macmillan (2001).

— *Sexual Politics, Sexual Communities: The Making of a Homosexual Minority in the United States, 1940–1970*, by John D'Emilio, University of Chicago Press (1998). Second edition; first published in 1983.

— *Smoking Typewriters: The Sixties Underground Press and the Rise of Alternative Media in America*, by John McMillian, Oxford University Press (2011).

— *Stagestruck: Theater, AIDS, and the Marketing of Gay America*, by Sarah Schulman, Duke University Press (1998).

— *Straight News: Gays, Lesbians, and the News Media*, by Edward Alwood, Columbia University Press (1996).

— *Tales of the Lavender Menace: A Memoir of Liberation*, by Karla Jay, BasicBooks (2000).

— *Talk Back! The Gay Person's Guide to Media Action*, by Lesbian and Gay Media Advocates, Alyson Publications (1982).

— *Uncovering the Sixties: The Life and Times of the Underground Press*, by Abe Peck, Pantheon Books (1985).

— *Unspeakable: The Rise of the Gay and Lesbian Press in America*, by Rodger Streitmatter, Faber and Faber (1995).

— *Up From Invisibility: Lesbians, Gay Men, and the Media in America*, by Larry P. Gross, Columbia University Press (2001).

— *Voices of Revolution: The Dissident Press in America*, by Rodger Streitmatter, Columbia University Press (2001).

Additional Books

— *About Time: Exploring the Gay Past*, by Martin Duberman, Meridian (1991). Revised edition; first published in 1986. Revised edition also appeared in 1994.

— *After the Ball: How America Will Conquer Its Fear and Hatred of Gays in the '90s*, by Marshall Kirk and Hunter Madsen, Plume (1990).

— *And the Band Played On: Politics, People, and the AIDS Epidemic*, by Randy Shilts, St. Martin's Press (1987). A 20th-anniversary edition was published in 2007 by St. Martin's Griffin and, in paperback, by Penguin.

— *An Army of Ex-Lovers: My Life at the* Gay Community News, by Ann Hoffman, University of Massachusetts Press (2007).

— *Art and Sex in Greenwich Village: Gay Literary Life After Stonewall*, by Felice Picano, Carroll & Graf (2007).

— *Becoming Visible: An Illustrated History of Lesbian and Gay Life in Twentieth-Century America*, by Molly McGarry and Fred Wasserman, Penguin Studio (1998).

— *Before Stonewall: Activists for Gay and Lesbian Rights in Historical Context*, by Vern L. Bullough (editor), Judith M. Saunders and Sharon Valente (associate editors) and C. Todd White (assistant editor), Harrington Park Press (2002).

— *Behind the Mask of the Mattachine: The Hal Call Chronicles and the Early Movement for Homosexual Emancipation*, by James T. Sears, Harrington Park Press (2006).

— *Boots of Leather, Slippers of Gold: The History of a Lesbian Community*, by Elizabeth Lapovsky Kennedy and Madeline D. Davis, Penguin (1994). First published by Routledge (1993).

— *The Boys of Boise: Furor, Vice, and Folly in an American City*, by John Gerassi, foreword by Peter Boag, new preface by author, University of Washington Press (2001). First published by Macmillan (1966).

— *A Brighter Shade of Pink: Magnus Hirschfeld, the Third Sex, and the Sexual Freedom Movement in Germany*, by Elena Mancini, Ph.D. thesis, Rutgers University Graduate School (2007).

— *Chicago Whispers: A History of LGBT Chicago Before Stonewall*, by St. Sukie de la Croix, foreword by John D'Emilio, University of Wisconsin Press (2012).

— *Christine Jorgensen: A Personal Autobiography*, by Christine Jorgensen, introduction by Susan Stryker, Cleis Press (2000). First published by Paul S. Eriksson (1967).

— *Coming Out Under Fire: The History of Gay Men and Women in World War Two*, by Allan Bérubé, Plume (1991). First published by Free Press (1990); 20th-anniversary edition published by University of North Carolina Press with new foreword by John D'Emilio and Estelle B. Freedman (2010).

— *Completely Queer: The Gay and Lesbian Encyclopedia*, by Steve Hogan and Lee Hudson, Henry Holt & Co. (1998).

— *Courting Justice: Gay Men and Lesbians v. the Supreme Court*, by Joyce Murdoch and Deb Price, Basic Books (2001).

— *Creating a Place for Ourselves: Lesbian, Gay, and Bisexual Community Histories*, by Brett Beemyn (editor), Routledge (1997).

— *Dancing the Gay Lib Blues: A Year in the Homosexual Liberation Movement*, by Arthur Bell, Simon & Schuster (1971).

— *Different Daughters: A History of the Daughters of Bilitis and the Rise of the Lesbian Rights Movement*, by Marcia M. Gallo, Seal Press (paperback, 2007). First published by Carroll & Graf (2006).

— *Encyclopedia of Homosexuality*, by Wayne R. Dynes (editor) and Warren Johannson and William A. Percy (associate editors), with the assistance of Stephen Donaldson, Garland Publishing (1990). Two volumes.

— *Encyclopedia of Lesbian and Gay Histories and Cultures*, Vol. 1 on lesbians edited by Bonnie Zimmerman, Vol. 2 on gay men edited by George E. Haggerty, Garland Publishing (2000).

— *Famous Long Ago: My Life and Hard Times With Liberation News Service*, by Raymond Mungo, Beacon Press (1970). Republished since, most recently by University of Massachusetts Press with new introduction by John McMillian and new epilogue by author (2012).

— *Forging Gay Identities: Organizing Sexuality in San Francisco, 1950–1994*, by Elizabeth A. Armstrong, University of Chicago Press (2002).

— *Gay American History: Lesbians and Gay Men in the U.S.A: A Documentary History*, by Jonathan Ned Katz, Meridian Books (1992). Revised edition; first published under name Jonathan Katz and with second subtitle *A Documentary* by Thomas Y. Crowell Co. (1976).

— *Gay and Lesbian Literature Since World War II: History and Memory*, by Sonya L. Jones (editor), Harrington Park Press (1998). Also published 1998 by Haworth Press as Volume 34, Nos. 3/4, of *Journal of Homosexuality*.

— *Gay by the Bay: A History of Queer Culture in the San Francisco Bay Area*, by Susan Stryker and Jim Van Buskirk, foreword by Armistead Maupin, Chronicle Books (1996).

— *The Gay Crusaders*, by Kay Tobin and Randy Wicker, Paperback Library (1972). Reprinted by Arno Press (1975); Kay Tobin was pen name of Kay Tobin Lahusen.

—*Gay, Lesbian, Bisexual, and Transgender Events, 1848–2006*, by editorial board including Lillian Faderman, Salem Press (2007). Two volumes.

— *Gay L.A.: A History of Sexual Outlaws, Power Politics, and Lipstick Lesbians*, by Lillian Faderman and Stuart Timmons, Basic Books (2006). Republished by University of California Press (2009).

— *The Gay Metropolis: The Landmark History of Gay Life in America*, by Charles Kaiser, Grove Press (paperback, 2007). First published by Houghton Mifflin as *The Gay Metropolis, 1940–1996* (1997).

— *Gay New York: Gender, Urban Culture, and the Makings of the Gay Male World, 1890–1940*, by George Chauncey, BasicBooks (paperback, 2003). First published 1994.

— *The Gay Report: Lesbians and Gay Men Speak Out About Sexual Experiences and Lifestyles*, by Karla Jay and Allen Young, Summit Books (1979).

— *Gay San Francisco: Eyewitness* Drummer*: A Memoir of the Sex, Art, Salon, Pop Culture War, and Gay History of* Drummer *Magazine, the Titanic 1970s to 1999*, by Jack Fritscher, collected and edited by Mark Hemry, Palm Drive Publishing (2008).

— *Gay Voices of the Harlem Renaissance*, by A.B. Christa Schwarz, Indiana University Press (2003).

— *Gender and Sexuality in 1968: Transformative Politics in the Cultural Imagination*, by Lessie Jo Frazier and Deborah Cohen (editors), Palgrave Macmillan (2009).

— *Hard to Imagine: Gay Male Eroticism in Photography and Film From Their Beginnings to Stonewall*, by Thomas Waugh, Columbia University Press (1996).

— *Hidden From History: Reclaiming the Gay and Lesbian Past*, by Martin Bauml Duberman, Martha Vicinus and George Chauncey, Jr. (editors), Meridian Books (1990). First published by New American Library (1989).

— *Homo Economics: Capitalism, Community, and Lesbian and Gay Life*, by Amy Gluckman and Betsy Reed (editors), Routledge (1997).

— *The Homosexual Handbook*, by Angelo D'Arcangelo, Ophelia Press (1969). Also published under other imprints in 1968–71.

— *Homosexuality: A History*, by Vern L. Bullough, New American Library (1979).

— *Homosexuality: A History*, by Colin Spencer, Fourth Estate (1995). Reissued in U.S. as *Homosexuality in History*, Harcourt Brace (1995).

— *Homosexuality and Male Bonding in Pre-Nazi Germany: The Youth Movement, the Gay Movement, and Male Bonding Before Hitler's Rise: Original Transcripts From* Der Eigene, *the First Gay Journal in the World*, by Harry Oosterhuis (editor), translations by Hubert Kennedy, Haworth Press (1991). Also published as Volume 22, Nos. 1/2, of *Journal of Homosexuality*.

— *The Ideal Gay Man: The Story of* Der Kreis, by Hubert Kennedy, Routledge (2000). Also published as Volume 38, Nos. 1/2, of *Journal of Homosexuality.*

— *Improper Bostonians: Lesbian and Gay History From the Puritans to Playland,* compiled by The History Project, foreword by Barney Frank, Beacon Press (paperback, 1999). First published 1998.

— *Infectious Ideas: U.S. Political Responses to the AIDS Crisis,* by Jennifer Brier, University of North Carolina Press (2011). First published 2009.

— *James Baldwin,* by Randall Kenan, with additional text by Amy Sickels, Chelsea House (2005). First published 1994.

— *Jim Flint: The Boy From Peoria,* by Tracy Baim and Owen Keehnen, Prairie Avenue Productions (2011).

— *The Lavender Scare: The Cold War Persecution of Gays and Lesbians in the Federal Government,* by David K. Johnson, University of Chicago Press (2004).

— *Leading the Parade: Conversations with America's Most Influential Lesbians and Gay Men,* by Paul D. Cain foreword by Jack Nichols, Scarecrow Press (paperback, 2007). First published 2002.

— *Leatherman: The Legend of Chuck Renslow,* by Tracy Baim and Owen Keehnen, Prairie Avenue Productions (2011).

— *The Lesbian Almanac,* compiled by the National Museum & Archive of Lesbian and Gay History, Berkley Books (1996).

— *Lesbian Culture, An Anthology: The Lives, Work, Ideas, Art and Visions of Lesbians Past and Present,* edited by Julia Penelope and Susan J. Wolfe, Crossing Press (1993).

— *Lesbian/Woman,* by Del Martin and Phyllis Lyon, Volcano Press (1991).

— *Lost Prophet: The Life and Times of Bayard Rustin,* by John D'Emilio, University of Chicago Press (2004). First published by Free Press (2003).

— *The Mayor of Castro Street: The Life & Times of Harvey Milk,* by Randy Shilts, St. Martin's Griffin (paperback, 2008). First published by St. Martin's Press in hardback (1982) and paperback (1988).

— *Media Q: Media/Queered: Visibility and Its Discontents,* by Kevin G. Barnhurst (editor), Peter Lang (2007).

— *Men and Women: The World Journey of a Sexologist,* by Magnus Hirschfeld, English version by O.P. Green, G.P. Putnam's Sons (1935). Republished by AMS Press (1974); also published as *Women East and West: Impressions of a Sex Expert,* W. Heinemann (Medical Books) (1935), and in other editions; originally published in Brugg, Switzerland, as *Die Weltreise eines Sexualforschers: Mit 47 Abbildungen,* Bözberg-Verlag (1933).

— *Moving Politics: Emotion and ACT UP's Fight Against AIDS,* by Deborah B. Gould, University of Chicago Press (2009).

— *Moving the Mountain: The Women's Movement in America Since 1960,* by Flora Davis, University of Illinois Press (paperback, 1999). First published by Simon & Schuster (1991).

— *My Desire for History: Essays in Gay, Community, and Labor History,* by Allan Bérubé, edited with an introduction by John D'Emilio and Estelle B. Freedman, University of North Carolina Press, 2011.

— *Obama and the Gays: A Political Marriage,* by Tracy Baim, Prairie Avenue Productions (2010).

— *Odd Girls and Twilight Lovers: A History of Lesbian Life in Twentieth-Century America,* by Lillian Faderman, Penguin (paperback, 1992). First published by Columbia University Press (1991) and republished (2011).

— *The Other Side of Silence: Men's Lives and Gay Identities: A Twentieth Century History,* by John Loughery, Henry Holt & Co. (paperback, 1999). First published 1998.

— *On Being Different: What It Means to Be a Homosexual,* by Merle Miller, Random House (1971). Republished by Penguin (2012), with foreword by Dan Savage, afterword by Charles Kaiser, and fragments of a foreword by Franklin E. Kameny; originally published in *The New York Times Magazine* (January 17, 1971).

— *Out and Proud in Chicago: An Overview of the City's Gay Community,* by Tracy Baim (editor), Agate/Surrey Books (2008).

— *Out for Good: The Struggle to Build a Gay Rights Movement in America,* by Dudley Clendinen and Adam Nagourney, Simon & Schuster (paperback, 2001). First published 1999.

— *Out in All Directions: A Treasury of Gay and Lesbian America,* by Lynn Witt, Sherry Thomas and Eric Marcus (editors), Warner Books (paperback, 1997). First published, with subtitle *The Almanac of Gay and Lesbian America* and with Don Romesburg as assistant editor, 1995.

— *Out of the Closets: The Sociology of Homosexual Liberation,* by Laud Humphreys, Prentice-Hall (1972).

— *Out of the Past: Gay and Lesbian History From 1869 to the Present,* by Neil Miller, Alyson Publications (2006). Revised edition; first published by Vintage Books (1995).

— *Outing: Shattering the Conspiracy of Silence,* by Warren Johansson and William A. Percy, Haworth Press (1994) and Harrington Park Press (paperback, 1994).

— *Pre-Gay L.A.: A Social History of the Movement for Homosexual Rights,* by C. Todd White, University of Illinois Press (2009).

— *Powers of Desire: The Politics of Sexuality,* by Ann Snitow, Christine Stansell and Sharan Thompson (editors), Monthly Review Press (1983).

— *Profiles in Gay & Lesbian Courage,* by the Reverend Troy Perry and Thomas L.P. Swicegood, St. Martin's Press (1991, paperback 1992).

— *Propaganda and Aesthetics: The Literary Politics of Afro-American Magazines in the Twentieth Century,* by Abby Arthur Johnson and Ronald Maberry Johnson, University of Massachusetts Press (1979). Republished in paperback with *African-American* in subtitle (1991).

— *Queer Commodities: Contemporary US Fiction, Consumer Capitalism, and Gay and Lesbian Subcultures,* by Guy Davidson, Palgrave Macmillan (2012).

— *A Queer History of the United States,* by Michael Bronski, Beacon Press (paperback, 2012). Originally published 2011.

— *Queers in History: The Comprehensive Encyclopedia of Historical Gays, Lesbians, Bisexuals, and Transgenders,* by Keith Stern, BenBella Books (2009). Previously published with subtitle *Hundreds of Prominent People Who Were Gay, Lesbian, Bisexual, or Transgender,* Quistory Publishers (2007).

— *Radically Gay: Gay Liberation in the Words of Its Founder,* by Harry Hay, edited by Will Roscoe, Beacon Press (1996). Republished 2001.

— *Rita Will: Memoir of a Literary Rabble-Rouser,* by Rita Mae Brown, Bantam Books (1997, paperback 1999).

— *Secret Historian: The Life and Times of Samuel Steward, Professor, Tattoo Artist, and Sexual Renegade,* by Justin Spring, Farrar, Straus and Giroux (2010, paperback 2011).

— *Sex Variant Woman: The Life of Jeannette Howard Foster,* by Joanne Passet, Da Capo Press (2008).

— *Slumming: Sexual and Racial Encounters in American Nightlife, 1885–1940,* by Chad Heap, University of Chicago Press (2009, paperback 2010).

— *Stonewall*, by Martin Duberman, Dutton (1993). Republished in paperback, Plume (1994), and fictionalized as the motion picture *Stonewall*, Strand Releasing (1995).

— *Tearoom Trade: Impersonal Sex in Public Places*, by Laud Humphreys, Aldine (1975). Enlarged edition with a retrospect on ethical issues; republished by Aldine (1979) and AldineTransaction (2005); originally published 1970.

— *To Be Young, Gifted, and Black: Lorraine Hansberry in Her Own Words*, adapted by Robert Nemiroff, art by Hansberry, introduction by James Baldwin, new preface by Jewell Handy Gresham Nemiroff, Vintage Books (1995). The 1968–69 off-Broadway play, first published in book form by Prentice-Hall (1969) and in paperback by New American Library (1970).

— *To Believe in Women: What Lesbians Have Done for America—A History*, by Lillian Faderman, Houghton Mifflin (paperback, 2000). First published 1999.

— *The Trouble with Harry Hay: Founder of the Modern Gay Movement*, by Stuart Timmons, Alyson Publications (1990, paperback 1991).

— *Virtual Equality: The Mainstreaming of Gay and Lesbian Liberation*, by Urvashi Vaid, Anchor Books (paperback, 1996). First published by Anchor Books (1995) and adapted by author to videotape presentation, Center for Instructional Design, Loyola University of Chicago (1997).

— *"We Can Always Call Them Bulgarians": The Emergence of Lesbians and Gay Men on the American Stage*, by Kaier Curtin, Alyson Publications (1987).

— *We're Here, We're Queer*, by Owen Keehnen, Prairie Avenue Productions (2011).

— *Who's Who in Gay and Lesbian History: From Antiquity to World War II*, by Robert Aldrich and Garry Wotherspoon (editors), Routledge (2002). Second edition; first published 2001.

— *Women Building Chicago 1790–1990: A Biographical Dictionary*, by Rima Lunin Schultz and Adele Hast (editors), Indiana University Press (2001).

Websites

— Tyler Alpern's website, comments by Brad Confer: http://www.tyleralpern.com
— Canadian Lesbian and Gay Archives: http://www.clga.ca
— Chicago Gay History Project: http://www.ChicagoGayHistory.org
— GLBTQ: http://www.glbtq.com
— GLINN gay media database online: http://www.gaydata.com
— OutHistory.org: http://www.outhistory.org
In addition, dozens of major universities have collections that include LGBT periodicals.

Biographies of Writers and Editors

Following are biographies of some of the essayists in the book. Not included are those who wrote essays for the papers they work for, or personal essays about their own work.

Tracy Baim is publisher and executive editor at Windy City Media Group, which produces *Windy City Times*, *Nightspots*, and other gay media in Chicago. She co-founded *Windy City Times* in 1985 and *Outlines* newspaper in 1987. She has won numerous gay community and journalism honors, including the Community Media Workshop's Studs Terkel Award in 2005. Baim started in Chicago gay journalism in 1984 at *GayLife* newspaper, one month after graduating with a news-editorial degree from Drake University. She is the author of *Obama and the Gays: A Political Marriage* (2010, Prairie Avenue Productions). She is also the co-author and editor of *Out and Proud in Chicago: An Overview of the City's Gay Community* (2008, Agate), the first comprehensive book on Chicago's gay history (see www.ChicagoGayHistory.org), and author of *Where the World Meets*, a book about Gay Games VII in Chicago (2007, www.Lulu.com). Her most recent books include a novel, *The Half Life of Sgt. Jen Hunter* (2010, Prairie Avenue Productions), and the biographies *Leatherman: The Legend of Chuck Renslow* and *Jim Flint: The Boy From Peoria* (both 2011, written with Owen Keehnen, and published by Prairie Avenue Productions). She was inducted into the Chicago Gay and Lesbian Hall of Fame in 1994 and was named a *Crain's Chicago Business* 40 Under 40 leader in 1995. Baim has been executive producer of two films: *Hannah Free* (2008, Ripe Fruit Films) and *Scrooge & Marley* (2012, Sam I Am Films, LLC).

Lou Chibbaro Jr. has reported on the LGBT civil-rights movement and the LGBT community for more than 30 years, beginning as a freelance writer and later as a staff reporter and currently as senior news reporter for the *Washington Blade*. He has chronicled LGBT-related developments as they have touched on a wide range of social, religious and governmental institutions, including the White House, Congress, the U.S. Supreme Court, the military, local and national law enforcement agencies and the Catholic Church. Chibbaro has reported on LGBT issues and LGBT participation in every U.S. presidential election since 1976 and has attended nearly all Democratic and several Republican presidential nominating conventions as a credentialed reporter since 1984. He has reported on the AIDS epidemic since it first surfaced in the early 1980s. In June 2011, Chibbaro became the first reporter from the LGBT press to be inducted into the Society of Professional Journalists D.C. Professional Chapter Hall of Fame. The office of the U.S. attorney for the District of Columbia recognized Chibbaro's local crime-beat reporting by presenting him with its 1998 Justice for Victims of Crime Award, citing his "outstanding service to crime victims and their families" through his news reporting. Since 2009, he has served as a Washington stringer filing radio news reports on LGBT stories he covers for the *Blade* to the SiriusXM radio network's OutQ News service.

Chuck Colbert, a freelance journalist based in Cambridge, Massachusetts, has been reporting for gay and mainstream audiences since 1991. He is a former New England chapter president of the National Lesbian & Gay Journalists

Association and served on the organization's national board of directors. A former senior correspondent and columnist for Boston's now-defunct *In Newsweekly*, he has been a frequent contributor to the *National Catholic Reporter*, where he covered the Boston archdiocese's clerical sex abuse scandal. He also contributes to Press Pass Q, the online trade publication for gay media professionals.

A pioneer in LGBT studies, **John D'Emilio** has written several books, including *Sexual Politics, Sexual Communities*; *Intimate Matters: A History of Sexuality in America*; and *Lost Prophet*, a biography of Bayard Rustin. The founding director of the Policy Institute of the National Gay and Lesbian Task Force, he currently teaches at the University of Illinois at Chicago.

St. Sukie de la Croix is an internationally published journalist, columnist, fiction author, playwright and photographer. In Chicago, he has written for *Outlines, Windy City Times, Nightlines, Nightspots, Chicago Free Press, Gay Chicago* and www.chicagopride.com. As a historian, de la Croix has published dozens of articles about Chicago's gay history and wrote *Chicago Whispers: A History of LGBT Chicago Before Stonewall* (2012, University of Wisconsin Press).

Writer and historian **Owen Keehnen**'s fiction, essays, erotica, reviews and interviews have appeared in hundreds of magazines and anthologies worldwide. He is the co-author (along with Tracy Baim) of *Leatherman: The Legend of Chuck Renslow* and *Jim Flint: The Boy From Peoria*. Keehnen is a founding board member of The Legacy Project and serves as secretary for that organization's LGBT history-education-arts program (www.legacyprojectchicago. org). He has written columns in such magazines as *Penthouse Forum* and *Men's Style* and was author of the Starz books, a four-volume series of interviews with gay porn stars.

Lisa Keen began reporting for the gay press in 1979. One of her first big assignments was to help cover the 1980 Democratic National Convention for the *Washington Blade*. As top editor of the *Blade* for 20 years, she covered the White House, Congress, presidential elections and the Supreme Court. In 1995, she won the American Bar Association's Silver Gavel Award for her coverage of anti-gay ballot initiatives and the court challenges to overturn them. She heads up her own news service, producing national news for client newspapers around the country. The author of two books, she is working on a third, about marriage-equality lawsuits in federal courts.

Marie J. Kuda is a Chicago-born activist, amateur archivist and freelance writer. She has written and lectured on gay/ lesbian cultural history for 45 years. Since 1990, her archives and her reference-book and newspaper articles have been mined for use by students and historians in everything from biographies to video histories—including this book.

Yasmin Nair is a writer, academic and activist who lives in Chicago's Uptown neighborhood. She is a co-founder and member of Against Equality, a queer radical editorial and activist collective, and is the policy director of Gender JUST, a grassroots organizing group. Her work can be found at www.yasminnair.net.

Margaret Rubick was awarded a master's degree in health advocacy from Sarah Lawrence College in 2010. She investigates and writes on topics related to health advocacy, including ethics, health-care law and illness narratives. An article on changes to the *Diagnostic and Statistical Manual of Mental Disorders* was published in the March–April 2012 edition of *The Gay & Lesbian Review Worldwide*.

Sarah Toce is a nationally syndicated journalist and editor. Her high-profile features have become the center of numerous publications throughout the U.S. Recently, she was among the reporting team for the *Windy City Times*' AIDS @ 30 series, which won the prestigious Peter Lisagor Award from the Chicago Headline Club and was nominated for a national Gay and Lesbian Alliance Against Defamation Award. She is editor-in-chief of The Seattle Lesbian online news magazine and managing editor of The Contributor online magazine. She is a graduate of the New York Conservatory for Dramatic Arts and a member of the Online News Association and the National Lesbian and Gay Journalists Association.

C. Todd White received his Ph.D. in social anthropology in 2005 from the University of Southern California, where he studied the origins of the Los Angeles–based homophile movement. His resulting book, *Pre-Gay L.A.: A Social History of the Movement for Homosexual Rights*, was published in 2009 by the University of Illinois Press. White currently serves as a visiting assistant professor of anthropology at Indiana University of Pennsylvania.

Editor Biographies

William B. Kelley has been a gay-rights activist since 1965, when he joined Chicago's newly formed Mattachine Midwest, and has helped to create or lead numerous organizations locally and nationally. He was a board member of the National Gay (now Gay and Lesbian) Task Force and was a founding board member and a co-chairperson of the National Lesbian and Gay Law (now LGBT Bar) Association. He is now a lawyer and, for its first 10 years, chaired the Cook County Commission on Human Rights after helping to lobby for its establishment. His career has included writing for and editing gay and non-gay periodicals and books.

Jorjet Harper is a writer, editor, photographer and artist. She is the author of *Lesbomania: Humor, Commentary, and New Evidence That We Are Everywhere* (1994) and *Tales From the Dyke Side* (1996), both published by New Victoria Press. Harper was inducted into the Chicago Gay and Lesbian Hall of Fame in 1998. She was a contributor to, and co-editor of, *Out and Proud in Chicago* (2008) and has edited numerous other books. Her grandmother, Minnie Buckingham Harper, was the first African-American woman to become a legislator in the United States. Harper is currently working on a memoir of her years as a hippie in New York City and San Francisco during the '60s, and on a series of large-scale oil paintings.

Index

This is an index to the main text and the Biographies of Writers and Editors section. Also see listing of U.S. Local Gay and Lesbian Publications on pages 448–449. For the book's general Bibliography, see pages 450–453. Also see endnotes for Chapters 3, 4 and 5 on pages 148, 161–162 and 176–177 respectively.

CPSIA information can be obtained at www.ICGtesting.com
Printed in the USA
LVOW05s1441251113

362759LV00006B/151/P